Fodor's

BELIZE

3rd Edition

by Lan Sluder

**Where to Stay and Eat
for All Budgets**

**Must-See Sights
and Local Secrets**

Ratings You Can Trust

Fodor's Travel Publications   New York, Toronto, London, Sydney, Auckland
www.fodors.com

FODOR'S BELIZE

Editors: Stephanie Butler, Kelly Kealy, Laura M. Kidder, Adam Taplin
Author: Lan Sluder

Editorial Production: Evangelos Vasilakis
Maps & Illustrations: David Lindroth, Inc., Ed Jacobus, *cartographers*; William Wu, *information graphics*; Rebecca Baer and Bob Blake, *map editors*
Design: Fabrizio LaRocca, *creative director*; Guido Caroti, Siobhan O'Hare, *art directors*; Tina Malaney, Chie Ushio, Ann McBride, *designers*; Melanie Marin, *senior picture editor;* Moon Sun Kim, *cover designer*
Cover Photo: Mark Lewis/Alamy
Production/Manufacturing: Angela L. McLean

Third Edition

ISBN 978-1-4000-1941-0

ISSN 1559-081X

SPECIAL SALES

This book is available at special discounts for bulk purchases for sales promotions or premiums. Special editions, including personalized covers, excerpts of existing books, and corporate imprints, can be created in large quantities for special needs. For more information, write to Special Markets/Premium Sales, 1745 Broadway, MD 6-2, New York, New York 10019, or e-mail specialmarkets@randomhouse.com.

AN IMPORTANT TIP & AN INVITATION

Although all prices, opening times, and other details in this book are based on information supplied to us at press time, changes occur all the time in the travel world, and Fodor's cannot accept responsibility for facts that become outdated or for inadvertent errors or omissions. So **always confirm information when it matters,** especially if you're making a detour to visit a specific place. Your experiences—positive and negative—matter to us. If we have missed or misstated something, **please write to us.** We follow up on all suggestions. Contact the Belize editor at editors@fodors.com or c/o Fodor's at 1745 Broadway, New York, NY 10019.

PRINTED IN THE UNITED STATES OF AMERICA

10 9 8 7 6 5 4 3 2 1

Be a Fodor's Correspondent

Your opinion matters. It matters to us. It matters to your fellow Fodor's travelers, too. And we'd like to hear it. In fact, we need to hear it.

When you share your experiences and opinions, you become an active member of the Fodor's community. That means we'll not only use your feedback to make our books better, but we'll publish your names and comments whenever possible. Throughout our guides, look for "Word of Mouth," excerpts of your unvarnished feedback.

Here's how you can help improve Fodor's for all of us.

Tell us when we're right. We rely on local writers to give you an insider's perspective. But our writers and staff editors—who are the best in the business—depend on you. Your positive feedback is a vote to renew our recommendations for the next edition.

Tell us when we're wrong. We're proud that we update most of our guides every year. But we're not perfect. Things change. Hotels cut services. Museums change hours. Charming cafés lose charm. If our writer didn't quite capture the essence of a place, tell us how you'd do it differently. If any of our descriptions are inaccurate or inadequate, we'll incorporate your changes in the next edition and will correct factual errors at fodors.com immediately.

Tell us what to include. You probably have had fantastic travel experiences that aren't yet in Fodor's. Why not share them with a community of like-minded travelers? Maybe you chanced upon a beach or bistro or B&B that you don't want to keep to yourself. Tell us why we should include it. And share your discoveries and experiences with everyone directly at fodors.com. Your input may lead us to add a new listing or highlight a place we cover with a "Highly Recommended" star or with our highest rating, "Fodor's Choice."

Give us your opinion instantly at our feedback center at www.fodors.com/feedback. You may also e-mail editors@fodors.com with the subject line "Belize Editor." Or send your nominations, comments, and complaints by mail to Belize Editor, Fodor's, 1745 Broadway, New York, NY 10019.

You and travelers like you are the heart of the Fodor's community. Make our community richer by sharing your experiences. Be a Fodor's correspondent.

Happy traveling!

Tim Jarrell, Publisher

CONTENTS

ABOUT THIS BOOK

Our Ratings

Sometimes you find terrific travel experiences and sometimes they just find you. But usually the burden is on you to select the right combination of experiences. That's where our ratings come in.

As travelers we've all discovered a place so wonderful that its worthiness is obvious. And sometimes that place is so unique that superlatives don't do it justice: you just have to be there to know. These sights, properties, and experiences get our highest rating, **Fodor's Choice,** indicated by orange stars throughout this book. Black stars highlight sights and properties we deem **Highly Recommended**, places that our writers, editors, and readers praise again and again for consistency and excellence.

By default, there's another category: any place we include in this book is by definition worth your time, unless we say otherwise. And we will.

Disagree with any of our choices? Care to nominate a place or suggest that we rate one more highly? Visit our feedback center at www.fodors.com/feedback.

Budget Well

Hotel and restaurant price categories from ¢ to $$$$ are defined in the opening pages of each chapter. For attractions, we always give standard adult admission fees; reductions are usually available for children, students, and senior citizens. Want to pay with plastic? **AE, D, DC, MC, V** following restaurant and hotel listings indicate whether American Express, Discover, Diners Club, MasterCard, and Visa are accepted.

Restaurants

Unless we state otherwise, restaurants are open for lunch and dinner daily. We mention dress only when there's a specific requirement and reservations only when they're essential or not accepted—it's always best to book ahead.

Hotels

Hotels have private bath, phone, TV, and air-conditioning and operate on the European Plan, meaning without meals, unless we specify that they use the Continental Plan (CP, with a Continental breakfast), Breakfast Plan (BP, with a full breakfast), or Modified American Plan (MAP, with breakfast and dinner), or are all-inclusive (including all meals and most activi-

ties). We always list facilities but not whether you'll be charged an extra fee to use them, so when pricing accommodations, find out what's included.

Many Listings

★	Fodor's Choice
★	Highly recommended
✉	Physical address
✛	Directions
📪	Mailing address
☎	Telephone
📠	Fax
🌐	On the Web
✆	E-mail
🎫	Admission fee
☉	Open/closed times
Ⓜ	Metro stations
💳	Credit cards

Hotels & Restaurants

🏨	Hotel
⇋	Number of rooms
⚲	Facilities
⍾	Meal plans
✕	Restaurant
⌂	Reservations
⤬	Smoking
🍸	BYOB
✕🏨	Hotel with restaurant that warrants a visit

Outdoors

⛷	Golf
⛺	Camping

Other

☺	Family-friendly
⇨	See also
✉	Branch address
☞	Take note

WHAT'S WHERE

BELIZE CITY 	Belize City is probably the first place you'll see in Belize, and often it doesn't make a good impression. The predominantly Creole city, with a population of less than 80,000, is hardly more than an overgrown town. But first impressions aren't everything. Under Belize City's ramshackle commercial center and not-so-pretty skin is an interesting old character. This is the business, media, financial, transportation, cultural, social, and—despite the capital being almost 50 mi away—political hub of Belize. Things are happening here—parties, live music, good conversation, and good food. Areas of the city, such as the waterfront along the harbor, have been spruced up and actually look inviting. Charming old colonial buildings dot the Fort George area. Houses are being painted, signage is being improved, and streets are being cleaned. Tourist police are running off hustlers. Cruise ships have brought a new bustle to downtown. It's not New York, but Belize City has a raffish charm that grows on you the more time you spend here.
THE CAYES & ATOLLS 	Though Belize has hundreds of islands in the Caribbean, only a handful are set up for visitors with hotels, restaurants, and tours, and the majority are in this area. The two largest and most populated cayes (pronounced *keys*) are Ambergris (*Am-bur-griss*) Caye, with around 8,000 people, and Caye Caulker, population 1,000. They're just a few hundred feet inside the Belize Barrier Reef. The Caribbean ambience and signature Belizean accent of Ambergris Caye make it the country's most popular place to visit. Though it's pretty touristy for Belize, it's nowhere close to the craziness of other Caribbean beach towns like Cancún and Playa del Carmen. The tallest buildings are only three stories, many of the streets are sand, and golf carts are the most common kind of transportation. Why go to Ambergris? You can dive, snorkel, swim, and fish to your heart's content, or stroll the streets of San Pedro, Ambergris Caye's only town. San Pedro, immortalized in Madonna's "La Isla Bonita," has tons of restaurants and is the only place in the country with decent nightlife options. North Ambergris, finally connected to town by a new bridge over the river channel, is beginning to flourish as an area for upscale beach resorts and vacation homes.
	Caye Caulker is Ambergris Caye's sister island—smaller, less developed, and a cheaper date. Caulker (whose name comes from *hicaco,* the Spanish word for coco plum) has

WHAT'S WHERE

the kind of laid-back, sandy-street, low-key island charm that travelers pay thousands to experience. Here, you can have it for peanuts.

Farther offshore, three South Pacific–style atolls—Lighthouse, Glover's, and Turneffe—have pristine waters and fabulous diving but little else, save a few dive and fishing lodges. Also off the coast are many small, remote cayes. Two, Tobacco and South Water, each have a handful of small hotels, and several others have a single lodge or hotel.

NORTHERN BELIZE

Northern Belize is the "Sugar Coast" of Belize, land of sugarcane and sweet places to visit. Corozal Town, up against the Mexican border, is one of the undiscovered jewels of Belize. There's not a lot to do, but it's a great place to do it. Go ahead: slow down, relax, and enjoy life. The weather's gorgeous (there's less rain here than anywhere else in Belize) and the fishing's excellent. Orange Walk Town doesn't have many attractions, but it's a gateway to the big, wild tracts of land in the northwest. Northern Belize is home to several top-notch jungle lodges and a half dozen notable Mayan sites, including Lamanai, with its stunning setting on the New River Lagoon, the largest body of fresh water in Belize. Sarteneja, in the northeast, is a sleepy fishing village on the sea, with only two tiny hotels. It's just waiting to be discovered by travelers who like to wander off the beaten path.

THE CAYO

The Cayo, in western Belize, has a lot going for it: wide-open spaces, few bugs, and friendly people. The major towns are San Ignacio–Santa Elena (population about 16,000), about 10 mi from the Guatemala border, and Belmopan City (population about 9,000), the sleepy little capital of Belize. The town of Benque Viejo del Carmen sits at the edge of Guatemala, a little more than an hour-and-a-half drive from the marvelous ruins of Tikal. About 20 years ago, the first small jungle lodges in the Cayo began operation around San Ignacio. Now, there's a flourishing mix of hotels, cottages, and jungle lodges in all price ranges near San Ignacio, on both the Macal and Mopan rivers, and in the Mountain Pine Ridge, a pine forest area that looks more like the southern Appalachians than the tropics. The area's loaded with natural attractions and packed with potential for outdoor activities—caving, canoeing, hiking, horseback riding, and mountain biking, to name a few. Several of the country's most accessible Mayan ruins are here, including Caracol, the premiere Mayan site in

WHAT'S WHERE

Belize, and Actun Tunichil Muknal, the Mayan cave that many call the highlight of their trip. Belmopan, between Belize City and San Ignacio, is the downsized capital of Belize, but there's not much to see or do within the town. The Belize Zoo is nearby, as are several excellent jungle lodges. Along the scenic Hummingbird Highway south of Belmopan are barely explored caves, rivers, and national park areas.

THE SOUTHERN COAST

Want beaches? The best on the mainland are in Placencia, an appealing seaside alternative to the bustle of Ambergris Caye. The peninsula has some 16 mi of beachfront along the Caribbean, a back-side lagoon where manatees are frequently seen, and a few dozen hotels and restaurants. In recent years, several of Belize's most deluxe resorts have opened on the peninsula. A real estate boom is underway. More than 1,000 condos are planned, but when you drive down the peninsula on the muddy unpaved road, you wouldn't know it. Between Dangriga and Placencia is Hopkins, which has new small seaside hotels and clusters of condos. Although the sand flies can eat you alive here (bring bug spray), you can get in some excellent fishing and beach time, take a day trip to the nearby Cockscomb Wildlife Sanctuary jaguar reserve, boat out to the reef, or enjoy some good snorkeling and diving.

TOLEDO & THE DEEP SOUTH

Rainy and lush, beautiful and remote, Punta Gorda in far southern Belize is the jumping-off point for the unspoiled Mayan villages of Toledo District and for onward travel to Guatemala and Honduras. Over the next few years, as the final few miles of the paving of the Southern Highway to Punta Gorda is completed and the road is extended into Guatemala, this area is expected to take off, so now's the time to see it. PG, as it's known, is Toledo's main city, but it's small—fewer than 5,000 people live here, mostly Garífuna, local Maya, and immigrants from Guatemala. Mayan villages, hardly changed for centuries, are dotted around PG. Ancient Mayan ruins here have architectural and construction styles quite different from Mayan settlements in other parts of Central America. Lovely cayes, the southern end of the Barrier Reef, and near-pristine waters offer terrific fishing, diving, and snorkeling.

WHEN TO GO

Belize is a year-round destination, but some times to visit are preferable to others. Belize, like much of Central America and the Caribbean, has two basic seasons: the rainy season and the dry season. The rainy season is June through October, extending in some areas through November or even December. The dry season runs from December through May. However, by "dry season" Belizeans usually mean the months in late winter and spring, February through May, when temperatures inland may reach 100°F. April is usually the hottest month of the year.

If you want to escape crowds and high prices and don't mind getting a little wet, visit in the rainy season. Though some restaurants may close and hotels may offer limited facilities, reservations are easy to get, even at top establishments, and you'll have the Mayan ruins and beaches to yourself. The busiest time in Belize is the Christmas–New Year's period, followed by Easter, but most hotels count the high season as mid-November through April.

The dry season can be a less attractive time for inland trips, with dusty roads and wilting vegetation, but this is a good time to visit the coast and cayes, with their cooling winds from the sea.

Climate

Belize is a small country, but there's considerable variation in weather from north to south, and also from the cayes to the mainland. Rainfall, for example, varies dramatically depending on where you are: the Deep South gets as much as 160 to 200 inches of rain each year, but the rest of the country gets a lot less, as little as 50 inches in Corozal. The cayes generally get less rain than does the mainland.

Belize's Caribbean coast often gets sweltering, humid weather with soaring temperatures, especially in summer, while the Mountain Pine Ridge, with elevations up to almost 3,700 feet, is cooler and less humid. In the Pine Ridge, on some nights in November to February, a fire in the fireplace can feel good. Overall, however, Belize's subtropical temperatures generally hover between 21°C and 29°C (70°F and 85°F), much like the weather in south Florida.

The western Caribbean's hurricane season is from June through November. September and October are the two prime months for tropical storms and hurricanes in Belize. Over the past century, about 85% of storms to hit Belize arrived in those two months; hurricanes, however, are relatively rare.

The chart shows average daily maximum and minimum temperatures for Belmopan City, Belize.

QUINTESSENTIAL BELIZE

If you want to get a sense of life in Belize, start by familiarizing yourself with some of its simple pleasures. There are a few highlights that will send you home saying, "Ah mi gat wahn gud guf taim" (I had a good time).

Belikin Beer

No matter where you are in Belize—whether you're seated at a seaside restaurant or perched on a bar stool in San Pedro—ask for a beer, and you'll be presented with a small dark bottle with an illustration of a Mayan temple on the front (in case you were wondering, that's the Temple of the Masonry Altars at Altun Ha). This is Belikin, Belize's national drink. You may find, like we did, how deliciously addictive this hoppy, malty lager is.

You'll soon notice the way it's served in bars and restaurants: the bartender folds a little white napkin and wraps it around the top of the bottle. No glass—you drink the beer straight from the bottle. If you like a darker beer, try the Belikin Stout.

The Jewel

Belizeans frequently talk about "the Jewel." They say, "Get yourself a piece of the Jewel." Or, "When are you coming back to the Jewel?" By Jewel, they simply mean Belize. And, of course, Belize is a jewel. It's a place of incredible natural beauty, of mint-green seas and emerald-green forests, of the longest barrier reef in the Western or Northern hemisphere, with more kinds of birds, butterflies, flowers, and trees than in all of the United States and Canada combined. Massive ceiba trees and graceful cohune palms stand guard in rain forests where jaguars still roam free and toucans and parrots fly overhead. Rivers, bays, and lagoons are rich with hundreds of different kinds of fish. And Belizeans them-

selves are jewels. The country is a gumbo of cultures—African, Hispanic, Mayan, Asian, European, and Caribbean—all getting along better than anyone would expect. Belize? It's a Jewel.

Bird-Watching

Once you see toucans at Tikal or the hard-to-find motmot in the Cayo, you, too, might get caught up in the excitement of searching for some of Belize's 600 species of birds. Many Belizeans know all their local birds (although the names they have for them may differ from those in your birding guide) and where the best places are to find them. Crooked Tree, Chan Chich at Gallon Jug, the New River and New River Lagoon near Lamanai, and much of the Toledo District in the Deep South are wonderful areas for bird-watching; keep your eyes peeled to the treetops and don't forget your binoculars.

Archaeological Treasures

Though the ancient Mayan empire—which once occupied much of present-day Guatemala and extended into Belize, Mexico, Honduras, and El Salvador—began to collapse around AD 900, it still left one of the richest cultural and archaeological legacies in the world. Only a fraction of the thousands of Mayan ruins have been excavated from the jungle that over the centuries has swallowed the splendid temples and sprawling cities. Evidence of the Maya is everywhere in Belize, from the lagoon-side temples of Lamanai to the caves of Actun Tunichil Muknal. All together, Belize has about a thousand Mayan sites, most small and unexcavated, with likely hundreds or even thousands still to be discovered.

IF YOU LIKE

Luxury Resorts

Deluxe duvets. 1,200-thread-count sheets. Your own villa on a private island or a jungle hideaway with fine wines and gourmet dinners. You may be traipsing around Mayan ruins or diving the Blue Hole during the day, but at night you can look forward to pampering at Belize's luxury jungle lodges and beach resorts.

- **Azul Resort, North Ambergris Caye.** It's all top of the line at this hip and exclusive beach resort. Kick back with a frozen mojito at the Rojo Lounge.

- **Blancaneaux Lodge, Mountain Pine Ridge.** Francis Ford Coppola's riverside jungle lodge hints of Beverly Hills.

- **Caye Chapel Island Resort, Caye Chapel.** Super-size beach villas sit next to a challenging seaside 18-hole golf course on a private island.

- **Cayo Espanto, near Ambergris Caye.** Really want to splurge? A stay on this small, private island will cost you, but you'll have your own butler, chef, and gorgeous views of the sea.

- **Inn at Robert's Grove, Placencia.** Imported steaks, a wine cellar, tennis, and hot tubs on the roof—who needs Hilton Head?

- **The Lodge at Chaa Creek, Cayo.** Soak up the carefully tended landscaping, deluxe garden suites, spa, Cuban cigars, and expensive cognac.

- **Turtle Inn, Placencia.** Francis Ford Coppola hand-picked the Balinese furniture and art in these thatch cabanas, but that's not even the best part. Just wait until you see the garden showers.

Fishing

Some of the world's most exciting sport-fishing lies off Belize's coast and cayes. Go for the "grand slam" of tarpon, bonefish, permit, and snook on the shallow flats between the mainland and the reef. Sailfish, wahoo, marlin, and barracuda abound farther out to sea. Several specialty resorts and fishing camps, such as Turneffe Flats and El Pescador, cater to the angler, but most hotels can help you organize excellent fishing trips.

- **Turneffe Atoll.** Bonefish, tarpon, permit, snappers, jacks, barracuda, wahoo, dorado, and billfish all ply the waters.

- **Glover's Atoll.** Shallow tidal flats around the atoll make for plenty of bonefish; there's also permit, jack, and barracuda.

- **Placencia.** If you don't want to pay the big bucks that the resorts charge farther north, head here. Budget hotels start around BZ$50 a night. Permit's the number-one catch inside the reef, or cast a line in the lagoon or the deep sea beyond the reef.

- **Punta Gorda.** If you're serious about fishing, this is where you need to be. There's world-famous permit fishing, and the Port Honduras Marine Reserve has at least 100 species of fish.

- **Ambergris Caye.** There's surprisingly good saltwater fishing on the northern cayes—look for bonefish, permit, and tarpon.

- **Chetumal Bay.** Your chances of coming home with something are best at this large fishery in northern Belize.

Caving

One of the most exciting ways to tour Belize is to head underground—there are hundreds of caves all over the country. You can canoe down subterranean rivers in some, ducking under low-hanging rock stalactites while keeping your eyes trained for Mayan artifacts. The easiest caves to visit are in the Cayo; you don't need a guide to visit open caverns such as Rio Frio and St. Herman's. Before you head out to cave, make sure to find out if it's open to the public, if you need a guide, and, if the cave has a river, if the water level is low enough for visitors.

- **Actun Tunichil Muknal.** Go here for amazing limestone formations, many undisturbed Mayan artifacts, and calcified human remains. It's the top caving experience in Belize.

- **Barton Creek Cave.** Canoe about a mile on an underground river through Barton Cave, which has some Mayan artifacts and skeletal remains.

- **Caves Branch Caves.** The Caves Branch River cave system has become a popular place for cave tubing.

- **Che Chem Ha.** This cave, once used by the Maya for grain storage and ceremonial rituals, is on private land about 25 minutes from San Ignacio in the Vaca Plateau.

- **Rio Frio Cave.** Though it's more a natural tunnel than a cave, it's still worth a visit for its large entryway and path above the Cold River.

Scuba Diving & Snorkeling

Don your scuba or snorkeling gear and soak up the cast of aquatic characters offshore and around the Barrier Reef. One moment you may come upon an enormous spotted eagle ray; the next you may find the feisty little damselfish, a bolt of blue no bigger than your little finger. Bloated blowfish hover in their holes; barracuda patrol the depths; and queen angelfish shimmy through the water with puckered lips and haughty self-assurance. Graceful sea fans and great chunks of staghorn coral add to the exhilarating underwater experience.

- **Blue Hole.** The underwater sinkhole, one of the most famous dives in Belize, forms a perfectly round, deep blue circle.

- **Glover's Reef.** This is probably the least visited yet arguably most pristine dive and snorkel area in Belize. You can see nurse sharks, and manta rays, and go wreck diving.

- **Hol Chan Marine Reserve.** Snorkel with nurse sharks and stingrays at Shark-Ray Alley and keep your eyes peeled for moray eels in the reserve.

- **Sapodilla Cayes.** Fringe reefs and patch reefs in shallow water around the cayes support tropical fish like spadefish and parrot fish.

- **South Water Caye.** If you want to shore snorkel, come here. The beach is sandy, and the island is one of Belize's most beautiful.

- **Turneffe Islands.** Mangroves line a shallow lagoon, creating a rich nursery for sea life where snorkelers and divers alike can see reef sharks, dolphins, eagle rays, moray eels, and turtles.

GREAT ITINERARIES

RUINS, RAIN FORESTS & REEF

Sample the best of all that Belize offers—ruins, rain forests, and reef—in only seven or eight days. If you have only five days, shave off some time in the Cayo and head to Actun Tunichil Muknal on Day 2 instead of Day 3.

Day 1: Arrival

Fly into the international airport near **Belize City** and immediately head out to the **Cayo** in Western Belize, about two hours by road from the airport. Stay at one of the superb jungle lodges, such as the Lodge at Chaa Creek or duPlooy's, or, for less money, Black Rock or Crystal Paradise.

Logistics: The best way to see the mainland is by rental car. Pick up a car at one of seven car rental agencies in kiosks just across the main parking lot at the international airport. If you'd rather not drive, you can arrange a shuttle van, take a bus, or ask your hotel in the Cayo to pick you up. Buses don't come to the international airport—if you're taking one, you have to take a taxi into town (BZ$50). There's currently no scheduled air service to the Cayo. (⇨ Essentials.)

Day 2: Exploring the Cayo

On your first full day in Belize, get out and explore San Ignacio and the beautiful hill country around the Cayo. Among the top attractions are the small but interesting Mayan ruins at Xunantunich, Green Hills Butterfly Farm, the Rainforest Medicine Trail at Chaa Creek, and the Belize Botanical Gardens at duPlooy's. Save a little time for walking around and shopping in San Ignacio. After a full day of exploring, have cocktails and a good dinner at your lodge.

Logistics: You can do all four attractions and San Ignacio in one day, if you have a rental car and if you don't dawdle. Sans car, you can hire a taxi for the day, or opt for your hotel's tours.

Day 3: Actun Tunichil Muknal (ATM)

Prepare to be wowed by the ultimate cave experience. Go into the mysterious and beautiful Mayan underworld and see untouched artifacts dating back thousands of years.

Logistics: You must have a guide for ATM, so book your trip the day before with an authorized tour guide. It's an all-day event, and you'll get wet—bring a change of clothes and wear walking or tennis shoes, not sandals. If you're badly out of shape or have mobility issues, this isn't a tour for you.

Day 4: Tikal

Tikal, very simply, is the most awe-inspiring Mayan site in all of Central America, rivaling the pyramids of Egypt and the ruins of Angor Wat in Cambodia. It's well worth at least two days and nights, preferably staying in one of the three lodges at the park, but even on a day tour, you'll get a sense of the majesty of this Classic-period city.

Logistics: Although you can go on your own, the easiest and most stress-free way to see Tikal is on a tour from San Ignacio—you'll leave around 6:30 AM and return in the late afternoon; lunch is usually included.

Day 5: Caracol & the Mountain Pine Ridge

You can't pass up a trip to Caracol, the most important Mayan site in Belize. The trip there is part of the fun—you bump along winding roads through the Moun-

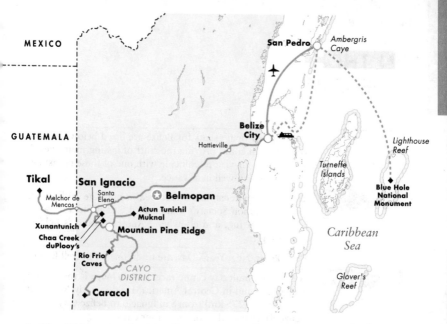

tain Pine Ridge, past the Macal River, and through broadleaf jungle. If you've seen enough Mayan ruins, skip Caracol and spend the day exploring the Mountain Pine Ridge—there's the Rio Frio cave and numerous waterfalls. A bonus: the higher elevation here means it's cooler and less humid than other parts of Belize. If you don't mind packing and unpacking again, for your last night in Cayo consider switching to one of the four lodges in the Pine Ridge. Our favorites are Blancaneaux and Hidden Valley Inn.

Logistics: From Blancaneaux or Hidden Valley, it's around a two-hour drive to Caracol, and about an hour longer from most lodges around San Ignacio. The road can be near-impassable after heavy rains, so check locally for the latest conditions.

Day 6: San Pedro
Return to Belize City by car, bus, or shuttle van. Then fly or take a water taxi to San Pedro (Ambergris Caye) for fabulous eating (our favorites are Rojo Lounge at Azul Resort, Rendezvous, and Casa Picasso) and water activities (like snorkeling Shark-Ray Alley).

Alternative: San Pedro's a bustling town, so if you want a more laid-back experience on the coast, stay on Caye Caulker instead. You still have access to the same snorkel and dive sites.

Day 7: Blue Hole
Take a day trip to dive or snorkel the Blue Hole at Lighthouse Reef atoll. Dive boats also stop at Half Moon Caye for other dives (or snorkeling) besides the Blue Hole.

Logistics: A trip to the Blue Hole involves a full day on the water, so bring seasick medicine and plenty of sunscreen. Dive boats to Lighthouse leave early, usually before 7 AM.

Day 8: Departure
Return to Belize City by plane or water taxi for your international flight.

Logistics: Plan on arriving at least two hours ahead of your international flight. Luggage is hand-inspected by security and there's often a long line at check-in.

ON THE CALENDAR

		The top seasonal events for Belize are listed below, and any one of them could provide the stuff of lasting memories. If you want your visit to coincide with one of these occasions, be sure to plan well in advance.
WINTER	Dec.	**Christmas Bird Count,** late December, usually the 30th, is the Belize Audubon Society's annual Bird Count, held in Belize City, Gallon Jug, and elsewhere. Another count is held in the spring.
	Jan.	**Horse Races,** New Year's Day, are traditional at Burrell Boom.
SPRING	Mar.	A grueling, multiday canoe race, **La Ruta Maya** is the longest race of its kind in Central America. Held in early March, it runs 170 mi (279 km) from San Ignacio to Belize City on the Belize River over the course of four days.
		Baron Bliss Day, celebrated on the second Monday in March, is when Belize City locals give three cheers for Baron Henry Edward Ernest Victor Bliss, a wealthy English sportsman who offered Belize an immense estate in return for a holiday devoted to sailing and fishing.
		San Pedro is one of the few places in Belize where **Carnaval** gets any attention. It's not Rio or New Orleans, but the town puts on parades, music, and street dancing performances during the week before Lent. On Fat Tuesday, it's paint day, and anyone on the streets might be splashed by a mixture of water and paint.
	Apr.	Bring a picnic lunch to Sarteneja on **Easter Sunday** for the sailboat regatta and races, when the usually sleepy fishing villages come alive with visitors and boaters. San Ignacio also has a two-day Easter Fair, with music, games, and sports.
	May	In Belize, Crooked Tree celebrates the local cash crop with the annual **Cashew Festival.** Held the first weekend of the month, the festival includes sale of jams, jellies, juices, preserves, and other delicacies produced here.
		On May 24 the country celebrates **Commonwealth Day,** which commemorates the birthday of Queen Elizabeth II, with a bicycle race from Belize City to San Ignacio.

SUMMER	
June	The **Día de San Pedro**, a three-day festival honoring St. Peter, is celebrated June 27–29 in San Pedro. The early morning boat parade, usually on the 29th, is the highlight.
	Lobster Festivals are held in Caye Caulker and Placencia to celebrate the beginning of the lobster-fishing season (June 15). The dates of the festivals vary from year to year.
Aug.	The Mopan Maya village of San Antonio in Toledo observes the **Día de San Luis Rey** in August (early September some years) with religious ceremonies and the Deer Dance. A similar festival including the Deer Dance is celebrated in San Pedro Columbia, a Ketchi village, on Easter.
	The **San Pedro Costa Maya Festival,** held in mid-August, is a four-day multicultural bash, with musical concerts, a beauty pageant, and other events, that takes place on Ambergris Caye.

FALL	
Sept.	The **Battle of St. George's Caye** celebrates the David-and-Goliath defeat of the Spanish navy by a motley crew of British settlers, buccaneers, and liberated slaves. This week of merrymaking in Belize begins September 10.
	Guatemalans around Tikal and nationwide celebrate their **Independence Day** on September 15 with traditional music, dances, and costumes.
	September 21 is **National Independence Day** in Belize, honoring the country's independence from Great Britain in 1981.
Oct.	Thousands of dollars in prizes are awarded at the **Belikin Spectacular: Blue Water Fishing Tournament**, in San Pedro, for the largest marlin, sailfish, wahoo, barracuda, tuna, and other fish caught on Pan-American Day in mid-October.
Nov.	**All Saints' Day**, also known as Day of the Dead, is celebrated November 1 in Guatemala, but much less so in Belize. Some Maya villages in Toledo observe All Saints' Day and also, on November 2, All Souls' Day.
	Garífuna Settlement Day, November 19, marks the arrival of Black Carib settlers, known as Garífunas, from the West Indies in 1823. Processions and traditional dancing are held throughout Belize, especially in Dangriga and increasingly in Punta Gorda and also in Hopkins and elsewhere.

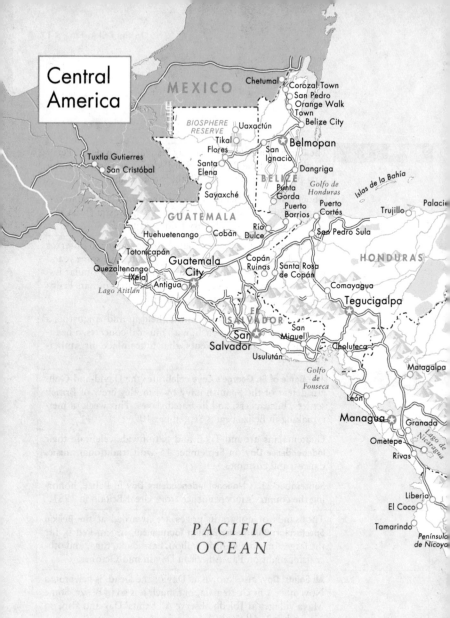

Central America

MEXICO

Chetumal
Corozal Town
San Pedro
Orange Walk Town
Belize City

BIOSPHERE RESERVE

Uaxactún

Tuxtla Gutierres
San Cristóbal

Tikal
Flores
San Ignacio
Belmopan

Santa Elena
Dangriga

BELIZE

Sayaxché
Punta Gorda

Golfo de Honduras

Islas de la Bahía

GUATEMALA

Cobán
Puerto Barrios
Puerto Cortés
Trujillo
Palaci

Huehuetenango
Río Dulce
San Pedro Sula

Totonicapán

Copán Ruinas

HONDURAS

Quezaltenango (Xela)
Guatemala City
Santa Rosa de Copán

Lago Atitlán
Antigua
Comayagua

Tegucigalpa

EL SALVADOR
San Miguel

San Salvador
Choluteca

Usulután
Matagalpa

Golfo de Fonseca

León

PACIFIC OCEAN

Managua
Granada

Ometepe
Lago de Nicaragua

Rivas

Liberia
El Coco

Tamarindo
Península de Nicoya

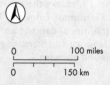

0   100 miles

0   150 km

JAMAICA

CARIBBEAN
SEA

NICARAGUA

Puerto
Lempira
Mosquitia

La Rosita
Puerto
Cabezas

Laguna de
Perlis

Isla de
San Andrés

Rama
Bluefields

Islas del
Maíz (Corn
Islands)

Bahía
Punta Gorda

COSTA
RICA

Tortuguero

Turrialba
Puerto Limón

San
José
Cartago

Quepos

Bocas
del Toro

El Porvenir

San Blas
Islands

Panama
Canal

Ciudad de
Panama

Puerto
Obaldia

Golfo
de
Nicoya

Bahía de
Coronado

Boquete

Golfo de los
Mosquitos

PANAMA

Bahía de
Panamá

La Palma
Sirena
Matapalo

David

Santiago

Chitré

Isla del
Rey

Yaviza

Península
de Osa

Golfo de
Chiriquí

Las Tablas

Golfo de
Panamá

Isla de
Coiba

COLOMBIA

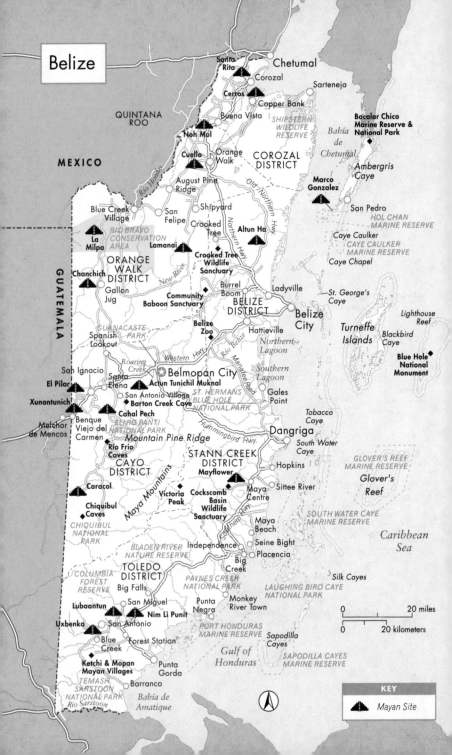

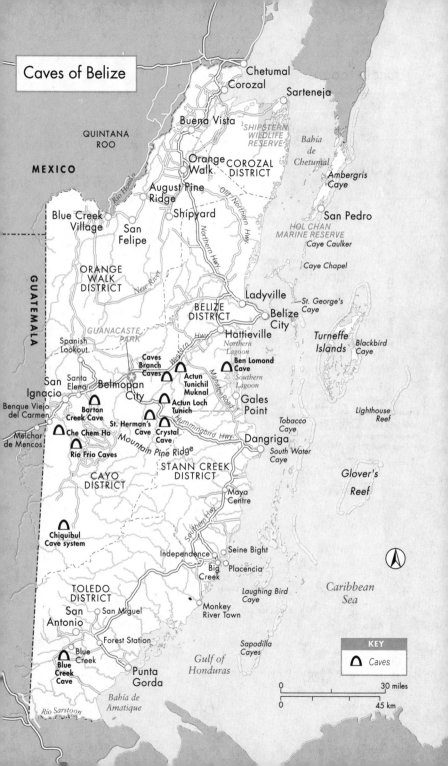

Caves of Belize

MEXICO

QUINTANA ROO

Chetumal
Corozal
Sarteneja

Buena Vista

Bahía de Chetumal

Orange Walk

COROZAL DISTRICT

August Pine Ridge

Shipyard

SHIPSTERN WILDLIFE RESERVE

Ambergris Caye

Blue Creek Village

San Felipe

San Pedro

HOL CHAN MARINE RESERVE

Caye Caulker

GUATEMALA

ORANGE WALK DISTRICT

Rio Hondo

Northern Hwy.

New River

Old Northern Hwy.

Caye Chapel

St. George's Caye

Ladyville

Belize City

BELIZE DISTRICT

GUANACASTE PARK

Spanish Lookout

Hattieville

Western Hwy.

Northern Lagoon

Turneffe Islands

Blackbird Caye

Santa Elena

San Ignacio

Belmopan City

Caves Branch Caves

Ben Lomond Cave

Southern Lagoon

Benque Viejo del Carmen

Barton Creek Cave

Actun Tunichil Muknal

Actun Loch Tunich

Gales Point

Lighthouse Reef

Melchor de Mencos

Che Chem Ha

St. Herman's Cave

Crystal Cave

Manatee Road

Dangriga

Tobacco Caye

Río Frio Caves

Mountain Pine Ridge

Hummingbird Hwy.

South Water Caye

Glover's Reef

CAYO DISTRICT

STANN CREEK DISTRICT

Maya Centre

Chiquibul Cave system

Southern Hwy.

Independence

Seine Bight

Caribbean Sea

Big Creek

Placencia

TOLEDO DISTRICT

San Antonio

San Miguel

Forest Station

Monkey River Town

Laughing Bird Caye

Blue Creek

Blue Creek Cave

Punta Gorda

Sapodilla Cayes

Gulf of Honduras

Bahía de Amatique

Río Sarstoon

KEY
⌂ *Caves*

0   30 miles
0   45 km

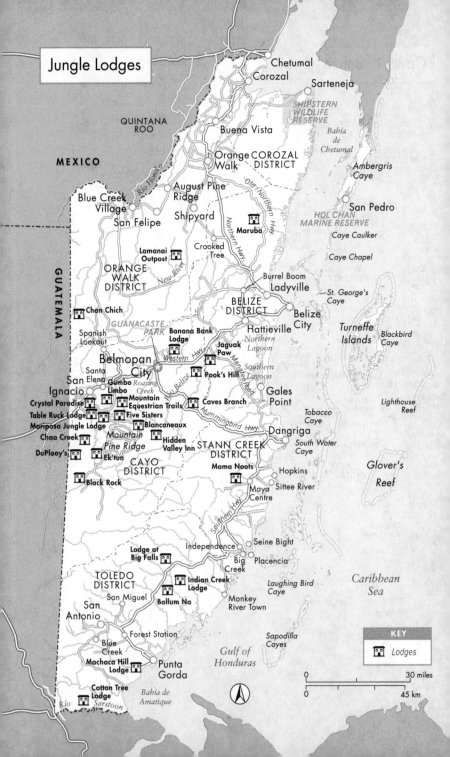

Jungle Lodges

MEXICO

QUINTANA ROO

Chetumal
Corozal
Sarteneja

SHIPSTERN WILDLIFE RESERVE

Bahía de Chetumal

Buena Vista

Orange Walk

COROZAL DISTRICT

Ambergris Caye

Blue Creek Village

August Pine Ridge

Shipyard

San Felipe

Rio Hondo

Old Northern Hwy.

Northern Hwy.

San Pedro

HOL CHAN MARINE RESERVE

Caye Caulker

Maruba

Caye Chapel

GUATEMALA

Lamanai Outpost

Crooked Tree

ORANGE WALK DISTRICT

New River

Burrel Boom
Ladyville

St. George's Caye

Chan Chich

GUANACASTE PARK

Spanish Lookout

Banana Bank Lodge

Belmopan City

Santa Elena

San Ignacio

Gumbo Limbo

Crystal Paradise

Table Rock Lodge

Mariposa Jungle Lodge

Chaa Creek

DuPlooy's

Mountain Equestrian Trails

Five Sisters

Blancaneaux

Mountain Pine Ridge

Ek'tun

Hidden Valley Inn

CAYO DISTRICT

Black Rock

Roaring Creek

Western Hwy.

Rio Belize

Jaguak Paw

Pook's Hill

Caves Branch

Hummingbird Hwy.

BELIZE DISTRICT

Hattieville

Belize City

Northern Lagoon

Southern Lagoon

Manatee Road

Gales Point

Turneffe Islands

Blackbird Caye

Lighthouse Reef

Dangriga

Tobacco Caye

South Water Caye

STANN CREEK DISTRICT

Mama Noots

Hopkins

Sittee River

Maya Centre

Glover's Reef

Southern Hwy.

Independence

Seine Bight

Placencia

Big Creek

Lodge at Big Falls

Indian Creek Lodge

Ballum Na

TOLEDO DISTRICT

San Miguel

Monkey River Town

Laughing Bird Caye

Caribbean Sea

San Antonio

Forest Station

Blue Creek

Machaca Hill Lodge

Punta Gorda

Cotton Tree Lodge

Rio Sarstoon

Bahía de Amatique

Gulf of Honduras

Sapodilla Cayes

KEY

Lodges

0   30 miles

0   45 km

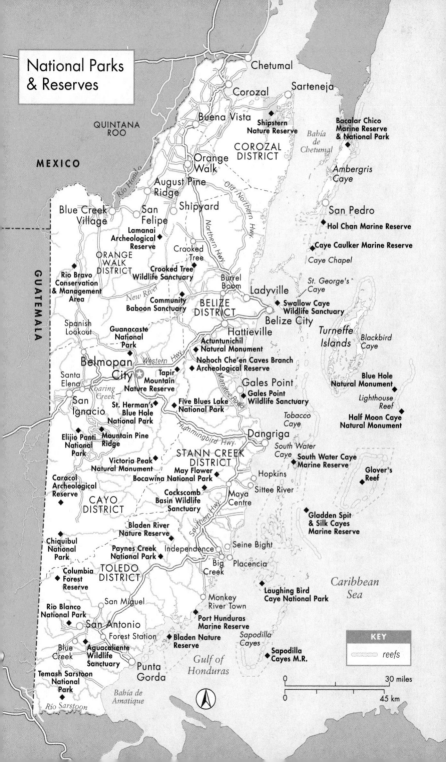

National Parks & Reserves

QUINTANA ROO

MEXICO

GUATEMALA

Chetumal

Corozal

Sarteneja

Buena Vista

Shipstern Nature Reserve

Bacalar Chico Marine Reserve & National Park

Bahía de Chetumal

COROZAL DISTRICT

Orange Walk

Ambergris Caye

August Pine Ridge

San Felipe

Shipyard

Blue Creek Village

Lamanai Archeological Reserve

San Pedro

Hol Chan Marine Reserve

Crooked Tree

Northern Hwy.

Old Northern Hwy.

Río Hondo

Caye Caulker Marine Reserve

Caye Chapel

ORANGE WALK DISTRICT

Crooked Tree Wildlife Sanctuary

Rio Bravo Conservation & Management Area

Burrel Boom

Ladyville

St. George's Caye

New River

Community Baboon Sanctuary

BELIZE DISTRICT

Swallow Caye Wildlife Sanctuary

Spanish Lookout

Belize City

Turneffe Islands

Blackbird Caye

Guanacaste National Park

Hattieville

Actuntunichil Natural Monument

Nohoch Che'en Caves Branch Archeological Reserve

Blue Hole Natural Monument

Belmopan City

Western Hwy.

Tapir Mountain Nature Reserve

Gales Point

Gales Point Wildlife Sanctuary

Lighthouse Reef

Santa Elena

Roaring Creek

Five Blues Lake National Park

Tobacco Caye

Half Moon Caye Natural Monument

San Ignacio

St. Herman's Blue Hole National Park

Manatee Road

Dangriga

South Water Caye

South Water Caye Marine Reserve

Elijio Panti National Park

Mountain Pine Ridge

Hummingbird Hwy.

STANN CREEK DISTRICT

Glover's Reef

Victoria Peak Natural Monument

May Flower Bocawina National Park

Hopkins

Caracol Archeological Reserve

Cockscomb Basin Wildlife Sanctuary

Sittee River

CAYO DISTRICT

Maya Centre

Gladden Spit & Silk Cayes Marine Reserve

Bladen River Nature Reserve

Southern Hwy.

Chiquibul National Park

Paynes Creek National Park

Independence

Seine Bight

Columbia Forest Reserve

TOLEDO DISTRICT

Big Creek

Placencia

Caribbean Sea

Rio Blanco National Park

San Miguel

Monkey River Town

Laughing Bird Caye National Park

San Antonio

Forest Station

Port Hunduras Marine Reserve

Sapodilla Cayes

Blue Creek

Aguacaliente Wildlife Sanctuary

Bladen Nature Reserve

Sapodilla Cayes M.R.

Temash Sarstoon National Park

Punta Gorda

Gulf of Honduras

Bahía de Amatique

Río Sarstoon

KEY

reefs

0   30 miles

0   45 km

Belize City

WORD OF MOUTH

"Early Monday morning we finally walked around Belize City. Their zoo is nice. Very small, but nice."
—gnrbernstein

"They basically carved trails out of a jungly area [at the zoo] for visitors and put fencing up. In other words, you're walking around on jungle paths and the animals are in natural environments. There are lots of informative, creative, hand-painted signs, and all of the animals are indigenous species: tapirs, several kinds of monkeys, jaguars, and other cats, toucans, etc. Highly recommended."
—hopefulist

By Lan Sluder

BELIZE CITY IS MORE OF a town than a city—few of the ramshackle buildings here are taller than a palm tree, and a short distance beyond the city center, streets give way to two-lane country roads where animals outnumber people. Any dining room downtown could leave the impression that everybody knows everybody else in this town, and certainly among the elite who can afford to dine out, that's probably true.

Although on paper Belize City looks like an ideal base for exploring the central part of the country—it's two hours or less by car to San Ignacio, Corozal Town, Dangriga, and even less to Altun Ha, Belmopan, and the Belize Zoo—most old Belize hands will advise you to get out of Belize City as quickly as you can. They point to the high crime rate, similar to or higher than the rate in an inner-city area of a large U.S. city, and to the relative lack of attractions in Belize City.

That's true enough, and certainly any visitor to Belize City should take the usual precautions for travel in an impoverished urban area, but Belize City does have an energy and excitement to it. There are good restaurants, the most varied shopping in Belize, a vibrant arts community, and, outside some of the rougher parts of town, nice residential areas and a number of pleasant hotels and B&Bs. There's also an easygoing sociability in Belize City. People meet on the street, talk, joke, laugh, and argue.

Numbers in the margin correspond to points of interest on the Belize City map.

ORIENTATION & PLANNING

GETTING ORIENTED

If you're prepared to go beyond a cursory excursion, Belize City will repay your curiosity. Belizeans are natural city dwellers, and there's an infectious sociability on streets like Albert and Queen, the main shopping strips. The finest British colonial houses—graceful white buildings with wraparound verandas, painted shutters, and fussy Victorian woodwork—are on the North Shore, that is, the Fort George area, near the Radisson Fort George, the most pleasant part of the city in which to stroll.

Fort George. The "colonial" section of Belize City is notable for its grand old 19th- and early-20th-century homes and buildings.

Marine Parade Harbor Front. Along the water near the Princess Hotel & Casino and BTL Park, there is more open, public space than there are buildings, making this a pleasant escape from the bustle of the city center.

The Commercial District. On the South Side, mainly on Albert and Regent streets, this is the commercial center of the city.

King's Park. Upscale residences line Princess Margaret Drive, about 2 mi (3 km) north of the city center.

TOP REASONS TO GO

BELIZE CITY IS THE KEY TO UNDERSTANDING BELIZE

If you haven't spent time in Belize City, you won't understand Belize. Belize City is the commercial, social, sports, and cultural hub of the country. It's even the political hub, despite the fact that the capital, Belmopan, is an hour west. The current prime minister, Dean Barrow, a lawyer who came to power in February 2008, former prime ministers including Said Musa, many of the other ministers, and nearly all of the country's movers and shakers live in or near Belize City.

GREAT PHOTO OPS

Belize City is highly photogenic, full of interesting faces, streets full of color, and charming old colonial houses. In short, Belize City has character.

COLONIAL ARCHITECTURE

Belize City rewards the intrepid traveler with a surprising number of interesting sights and memorable places, among them the everyday colonial-era buildings in the Fort George and Southern Foreshore sections, where people still live and work. For the most part, buildings are wood, with tin or zinc roofs. Many are in need of a bit of repair, but they still ooze Caribbean port-of-call atmosphere.

BECAUSE YOU HAVE TO

As a visitor to Belize, you'll almost certainly have to spend a little time in Belize City, whether you like it or not. The international airport is in Ladyville, at the northern edge of the city. Belize City is the transportation hub of the country, and most flights, buses, and car rentals originate here. If you're arriving late or leaving early, you'll have to overnight in or near the city. Make the best of it. Take care, but explore and enjoy the city.

The Northern Suburbs. Located along the Northern Highway between the city center and the international airport, this is the fastest-growing part of the metropolitan area, with middle-class residential sections such as Buttonwood Bay and Belama, some of the city's stores and supermarkets, and several hotels and B&Bs.

The Western Suburbs. Several new tourist attractions have popped up here, such as the Old Belize Museum. This multiuse commercial and residential area along the Western Highway, beginning at "Boot Hill" on Cemetery Road at the intersection of Central American Boulevard, is also on the way to the Belize Zoo, Belmopan, and the Cayo.

EXPLORING BELIZE CITY

Belize City is defined by the water around it. The main part of the city is at the end of a small peninsula, jutting out into the Caribbean Sea. Haulover Creek, an extension of the Belize River, running roughly west to east, divides the city into the North Side and the South Side. The North Side is, to generalize, more affluent than the South Side. The venerable Swing Bridge connects the two sides, although in modern times other bridges over Haulover Creek, especially the Belcan Bridge northwest of the city center, carry more traffic. At the mouth of the river, just beyond Swing Bridge, is the Belize Harbor (or Harbour as it's written locally, in the English style).

The only routes into the city are the Northern Highway from the north, and the Western Highway from the west. Coming from the north, follow the Northern Highway through several roundabouts (traffic circles) to Freetown Road and Barracks Road to reach the center. Alternatively, you can swing west on Princess Margaret Drive to Barracks Road, along the seafront. From the west, the Western Highway becomes Cemetery Road, which leads you to the center via the South Side and Orange Street. The city center itself is a confusing warren of narrow streets, many of them one way.

If you're staying in either the northern or western sprawling suburbs, a car is handy. There's no point-to-point bus system in the city, although buses (except the few express buses) going north or west will drop you almost anywhere. It's not customary to tip taxi drivers, unless they help you with luggage or perform other services. Most drivers are friendly and are happy to point out interesting sites to visitors.

Belize City earned a reputation for street crime in the early 1990s, but the government has made progress in cleaning up the problem. Crimes against tourists in Belize City are now relatively rare, and statistically as a visitor you may be safer in Belize City than in some other areas, such as the Cayo. Still, the crime rate in Belize City is comparable to that of a distressed inner-city area in the United States. In early 2008, Belize's crime problem spilled into the tourist zone when gang members fired shots into a bar across the street from the Princess Hotel and Casino. With incidences like this becoming increasingly frequent, it is more difficult for us to recommend that you spend time in Belize City, at least not in the downtown area after dark. Take the same precautions you'd take in any city—don't wear expensive jewelry or watches, avoid handling money in public, and leave valuables in a safe. Ignore offers to buy drugs. On buses and in crowded areas hold purses and backpacks close to your body. Check with the staff at your hotel before venturing into any unfamiliar areas, particularly at night. After dark, you should take a taxi rather than walk even a few blocks. Avoid leaving your rental car on the street overnight.

FORT GEORGE

This is the most pleasant and appealing section of the city, much of it cooled by prevailing breezes from the sea. It has stately colonial buildings that escaped the hurricanes of 1931 and 1961, several embassies (though the U.S. embassy was transplanted to Belmopan in late 2006), upmarket restaurants such as Harbour View that attract the city's elite, and the city's better hotels including the Radisson Fort George and the Great House, plus the Fort George lighthouse, a small park, and the Tourism Village.

WHAT TO SEE

① **Fort George Lighthouse and Bliss Memorial.** Towering over the entrance to Belize Harbor, the lighthouse stands guard on the tip of Fort George Point. It was designed and funded by the country's greatest benefactor, Baron Bliss. The English nobleman never actually set foot on the Belizean mainland, but in his will he bequeathed most of his fortune to the people of Belize, and the date of his death, March 9, is celebrated as a national holiday. He is buried here, in a small, low mausoleum perched on the seawall, up a short run of limestone stairs. The lighthouse is for photo ops only—you can't enter it. ⊠*Marine Parade.*

Image Factory. This commercial gallery selling art prints, books, and gifts doubles as a serious art gallery, exhibiting Belize's top avant-garde artists. Exhibit openings are usually on Friday. ⊠*91 N. Front St.* ☎*223/4093* ✉*Donations accepted* ⊙*Weekdays 9–5.*

④ **Marine Terminal.** You can catch a boat to Ambergris Caye, Caye Caulker, St. George's Caye, and Caye Chapel from this white clapboard building, which was a firehouse in the 1920s. While waiting for a water taxi, you can wander around the **Marine Museum,** where downstairs there are displays on marine life, and upstairs are models of boats that have sailed these waters and tools used by shipwrights. ⊠*10 N. Front St., at Queen St.* ☎*223/1969* ✉*BZ$4* ⊙ *8–5.*

③ **Museum of Belize.** This small but interesting museum was a Belize City jail from the 1850s to 1993. Displays on Belize history and culture include ancient Mayan artifacts, eclectic memorabilia, colorful Belize postage stamps, and an actual jail cell. Exhibitions change frequently. ⊠*Gabourel La.* ☎*223/4524* ✉*BZ$10* ⊙*Weekdays 9–5.*

⑤ **Swing Bridge.** As you might have guessed, the bridge spanning Haulover Creek actually swings. Weekdays around 5:30 AM and 5:30 PM, though some days it doesn't happen at all, four men hand-winch the bridge a quarter-revolution so waiting boats can continue upstream (when it was the only bridge in town, this snarled traffic for blocks). The bridge, made in England, opened in 1923; it was renovated and upgraded in 1999. It's the only one of its kind left. Before the Swing Bridge arrived, cattle were "hauled over" the creek in a barge. ⊠*Haulover Creek where Queen and Albert sts. meet.*

② **Tourism Village.** In the former Customs House, the Tourism Village (also called the Tourist Village) is predominantly geared to cruise ship passengers. In fact, Belizeans are often discouraged from going into the

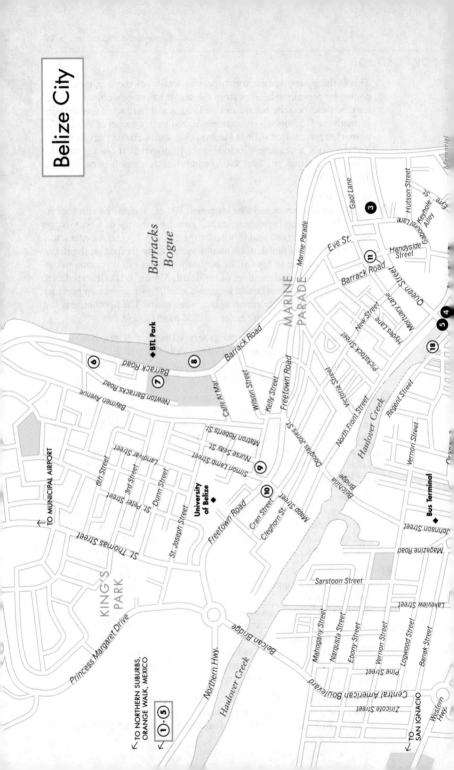

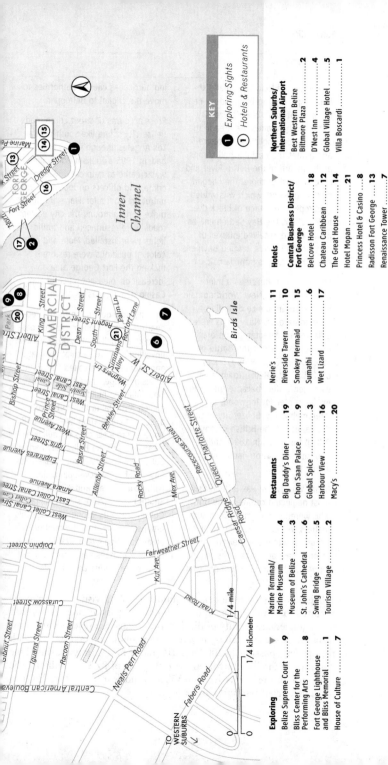

1

KEY

◉ Exploring Sights

① Hotels & Restaurants

Exploring

Belize Supreme Court	9
Bliss Center for the Performing Arts	8
Fort George Lighthouse and Bliss Memorial	1
House of Culture	7
Marine Terminal/ Marine Museum	4
Museum of Belize	3
St. John's Cathedral	6
Swing Bridge	5
Tourism Village	2

Restaurants

Big Daddy's Diner	19
Chon Saan Palace	9
Global Spice	3
Harbour View	16
Macy's	20
Nerie's	11
Riverside Tavern	10
Smokey Mermaid	15
Sumathi	6
Wet Lizard	17

Hotels

Central Business District/ Fort George

Belcove Hotel	18
Chateau Caribbean	12
The Great House	14
Hotel Mopan	21
Princess Hotel & Casino	8
Radisson Fort George	13
Renaissance Tower	7

Northern Suburbs/ International Airport

Best Western Belize Biltmore Plaza	2
D'Nest Inn	4
Global Village Hotel	5
Villa Boscardi	1

HISTORY

The Maya had long had small fishing camps—but no large cities—near the present-day site of Belize City, but they abandoned the area in the 1600s. A few English adventurers and pirates then established camps at the mouth of the Belize River and on cayes just offshore. They began cutting logwood, which was valued in Europe as a source of black dyes. In the 1700s the Bay Settlement, as it was called, received influxes of new British settlers, termed Baymen, and African slaves from Jamaica.

Spain claimed Belize as a minor backwater of its New World domain, but Spain's influence dwindled after some of its Navy ships were defeated by a ragtag group of Baymen in 1798 at the Battle of St. George's Caye, 9 mi (15 km) off Belize City. Belize Town, as it was then called, became the main export center for logwood, and, later, mahogany. Belize City became the capital of the British colony of British Honduras in 1892, and by 1904 its population had grown to about 10,000.

Belize was one of Pax Britannia's most neglected colonies. The British, who were usually generous in such matters, left little of either great beauty or interest in their former colony's capital. Belize City's rough reputation began after two devastating hurricanes caused authorities to move the capital to Belmopan.

Press accounts of street crime made Belize City sound like south-central Los Angeles, though it was never as bad. In 1995 a Tourism Police unit was created to help cut down on crime, and officers on foot or bicycle patrol are now a familiar sight. To make getting around the city easier, roads were resurfaced and traffic lights were installed. More and more colonial buildings were restored, making the Fort George area an increasingly pleasant place to stay. Casino gaming was legalized.

The city now gets more than three-quarters of a million cruise ship passengers annually. Late 2001 saw the unveiling of a cruise ship terminal and shopping area called Fort Point Tourism Village, and Carnival Cruise Lines plans to build a new US$50 million terminal in the Port Loyola area, with completion likely in 2008. Another proposal calls for building a causeway in the Belize City harbor out to Drowned Caye and Stake Bank Caye, and there developing, along with luxury hotels and a marina, another large cruise ship terminal. Conservationists strongly oppose this proposal, saying that it would disturb areas now home to a sizable population of manatees and would otherwise injure marine and bird life.

Village, or may even be denied admittance. As a visitor, you may be required to show your passport and obtain a pass to enter. Inside and in the immediate vicinity of the Tourism Village are several gift shops, restaurants, a car rental agency, tour companies, and taxi stands. With the opening, possibly in 2009 or 2010, of the new Carnival Cruise Line Terminal in the Port Loyola area (to the tune of BZ$100 million), the long-term future of this Tourism Village is unclear. ⊠ *Fort St.* ☺ *Open on days when cruise ships are in port.*

SOUTH SIDE COMMERCIAL DISTRICT

This area, along Albert and Regent streets, two parallel streets running north–south from Haulover Creek, is the commercial heart of the city. It has many small stores, banks, and budget hotels, along with several places of interest, including St. John's Cathedral and the House of Culture. A third parallel street, the Southern Foreshore, hugs the waterfront along the south side.

WHAT TO SEE

❽ Bliss Center for the Performing Arts. This building, overlooking the harbor from the Southern Foreshore, houses the Institute of Creative Arts and hosts cultural and arts events throughout the year. Renovated and expanded in 2004, the Bliss Center's 600-seat theater is headquarters for the Belize International Film Festival in February. A drama series, children's festivals, dance, art displays, and other cultural and musical performances take place at various times. ⊠ *2 Southern Foreshore, between Church and Bishop Sts.* ☎ 227/2110.

❼ House of Culture. Formerly called Government House, the city's finest colonial structure is said to have been designed by the illustrious British architect Sir Christopher Wren. Built in 1814, it was once the residence of the governor-general, the queen's representative in Belize. Following Hurricane Hattie in 1961, the governor and the rest of the government moved to Belmopan, and the house became a venue for social functions and a guesthouse for visiting VIPs. (Queen Elizabeth stayed here in 1985, Prince Philip in 1988.) Now it's open to the public. You can peruse its archival records, art, silver, glassware, and furniture collections, or mingle with the tropical birds that frequent the gardens. ⊠ *Regent St. at Southern Foreshore* ☎ 227/3050 🔁 BZ$10 ⊙ *Weekdays 9–4.*

❻ St. John's Cathedral. On Albert Street's south end is the oldest Anglican church in Central America and the only one outside England where kings were crowned. From 1815 to 1845, four kings of the Mosquito Coast (a British protectorate along the coast of Honduras and Nicaragua) were crowned here. ⊠ *Albert St.* ☎ 227/2137 ⊙ *Daily 6–6.*

❾ Belize Supreme Court. Not the oldest building in the city but one of the most striking, the Belize Supreme Court building is patterned after its wooden predecessor, which had burned in 1918. An 1820 court building had also burned down. The current building, painted white, has filigreed iron stair and balcony rails between two arms of the structure, and above the balcony a four-sided clock. This being Belize, the clock-faces all seem to show different times. ⊠ *Regent St.* ☎ 227/4387.

MARINE PARADE HARBOR FRONT

This rather nebulously defined area, which stretches from the Fort George section of Marine Parade to Barracks Road and then to the beginning of Princess Margaret Drive, could eventually be Belize City's equivalent of Havana's Malecón. Only a few years ago, it was an unsightly conglomeration of old buildings and vacant lots. With cleaning up and some gentrification, the area now has several good restaurants, condominiums, a hotel-casino, and a popular park.

WHAT TO SEE

Princess Casino. Belize City's only casino is usually bustling with local residents out trying their luck. It also attracts cruise ship passengers. The gaming complex has two movie theaters (the only movie theaters in Belize) and Belize's largest hotel. ⊠ *Barrack Rd., Kings Park* ☎ *223/2670* ⊕ *www.princessbelize.com.*

BTL Park. Belize Telecommunications Ltd., the telephone company, though often maligned by Belizeans, did a fine job when they adopted this park along Barracks Road and redeveloped it as a recreational area. It attracts local families for picnics, musical concerts, and other events, and it's often jumping even late in the evening. ⊠ *Newtown Barracks.*

WESTERN SUBURBS

For visitors, this part of the metropolitan area mostly is just a place to pass through on the way to the Cayo. However, local entrepreneurs have opened several businesses targeted to cruise ship passengers.

WHAT TO SEE

☯ **Gran's Farm.** A Belize City dentist opened this activity area that combines guided hikes along trails and walks in botanical gardens and orchards, canoe rentals on Hector Creek, and swimming. The botanical garden has some 600 species of plants and trees, including 60 types of fruit trees. Gran's Farm also has a restaurant, gift shop, and swimming pool. ⊠ *Mile 14½, Western Hwy.* ☎ *222/4219* 💲 *BZ$12–BZ$30, depending on which tours and activities you choose* ☉ *Tues.–Sun. 9–5.*

☯ **Old Belize Museum.** Many of the visitors here are tour groups from cruise ships, but you also can visit the museum on your own. In a large warehouse-style building, exhibits are devoted to the Maya, Garífuna, and Creoles in Belize City and the rain forest and displays on logging, chicle harvesting, and sugar production. Also at the site of the museum are a marina; a restaurant, Sibun Bite Bar & Grill, where you can get a decent hamburger; a gift shop; and Cucumber Beach, a small man-made beach that's the only one near Belize City. Newly opened in 2008are a zip line, 750,000-gallon saltwater swimming pool with an artificial reef, and a water slide. ⊠ *Mile 5, Western Hwy.* ☎ *222/4219* 💲 *BZ$30* ☉ *Sun. and Mon. 10–4, Tues.–Sat. 8–4.*

WHERE TO EAT

Though most restaurants here cater to locals, their number and quality rival those of tourist magnet San Pedro in Ambergris Caye. The city has inexpensive dives serving "dollar chicken" (fried chicken, a local favorite, though it no longer costs just a dollar), Chinese joints of 1950s vintage specializing in chow mein, and lunch spots for downtown office workers seeking Creole dishes such as cow-foot soup and rice and beans. Belize City also has upmarket restaurants serving the city's afflu-

CLOSE UP

Made in Belize

1

For such a little country, some of Belize's products pack a punch. Below is a list of possible souvenirs.

HOT SAUCE

One of Belize's best-known products comes from a little plant near Dangriga. This spicy sauce was originally created by Marie Sharp in her kitchen in the early 1980s. It comes in a variety of heat levels, from the moderate Mild Habanero to the fiery No Wimps Allowed, and, finally, Beware. **Marie Sharp's** (⊠ *3 Pier Rd., Dangriga* ☎ *522/2370 or 520/2087.*) also makes less dangerous products, such as jams, jellies, and other spices and sauces. Call ahead to set up an informal tour of the plant.

RUM

A favorite of rum connoisseurs, One Barrel, from **Travellers Ltd.** (⊡ *Box 623, Belize City* ☎ *223/2855*), has won international tasting awards in the gold rum category; Duurley's, another Travellers product, is also delicious. The company is run by the Perdomo family of Belize City. For distillery tours, contact Travellers Liquors Ltd.A good mixing white rum, and the one you'll see in most bars, is called Caribbean Rum. It is made by family-owned **Cuellos** (⊠ *2 Miles, Yo Creek Rd., Orange Walk Town* ☎ *322/2141*) distillery, which offers occasional distillery tours. Most rum is between BZ$14 and BZ$20 a bottle.

HARDWOOD FURNITURE

If the cost of shipping doesn't break your budget, the low-slung folding "clam chairs" are a favorite and made from the region's tropical hardwood. **New Hope Woodworking, Ltd.** (⊠ *Buena Vista St., San Ignacio, Cayo* ☎ *824/2188*) makes portable, small

wooden boxes. **New River Enterprises** (⊠ *14 Westby St., Orange Walk Town* ☎ *322/2225*) makes solid mahogany and other hardwood doors, some around BZ$2,400 plus shipping. They also make patio furniture. **Hummingbird Rattan** (⊠ *54 Hummingbird Hwy., Belmopan City* ☎ *822/3164*) and (⊠ *Coconut Dr., San Pedro* ☎ *226/2960*) uses bamboo, wicker, and rattan, sometimes mixed with mahogany, for indoor and outdoor furniture.

COFFEE

Gallon Jug Estates in Orange Walk District is the only commercial coffee producer in Belize (and it is small, with only about 100 acres of coffee plantings). Made with only arabica beans, Gallon Jug coffees are shade-grown and don't use pesticides, herbicides, or fungicides. Whole bean and ground coffee, packed in colorful gold and green, can be bought all over Belize.

BEER

With a nationwide monopoly on beer, the **Belize Brewing Co. Ltd.** is one of the country's most profitable businesses. The beer is perfect for sipping on the beach and there are four types to choose from: a lager, with 4% alcohol; Belikin Premium, also a lager, with 5% alcohol; Lighthouse, a pale lager, with 4.2% alcohol; and Belikin Stout, a dark beer with 6% alcohol. If none of these are to your liking, a few other foreign brands, such as Bud, Red Stripe, and Heineken, are available at a much inflated cost. Some cruise ship and Belize City tours include a stop at the Bowen brewery, and a half-hour tasting of the beers. For information, contact ⊠ *1 King St., Belize City* ☎ *227/2602.*

ent elite. Only a couple of these are "dressy" (by Belize standards, this means a nice collared shirt for men and perhaps a long tropical dress for women) and reservations are rarely necessary.

A few restaurants around the Tourism Village target cruise ship passengers, typically for lunch and drinks, but the one thing you won't find here are chain restaurants. In fact, there's only one fast-food chain restaurant anywhere in Belize, a Subway deli on Freetown Road.

WHAT IT COSTS IN BELIZE DOLLARS					
	¢	$	$$	$$$	$$$$
AT DINNER	under BZ$8	BZ$8–BZ$15	BZ$15–BZ$25	BZ$25–BZ$50	over BZ$50

Prices are per person for a main course at dinner, including tax and service.

$$$-$$$$ ✕ **Harbour View.** For the most romantic setting in the city, ask for a table
★   on the wraparound balcony overlooking the harbor. The friendly staff and consistently excellent food also make the Harbour View a favorite of Belize's power brokers. The seafood is especially good; try the snapper with mango chutney, cooked in a banana leaf. Pork dishes, especially Pork Picasso with a hot pepper relish, also are delicious. ⊠ *Fort St., near Tourism Village* ☎ *223/6420* ▤ *AE, D, MC, V.* ☉ *Closed for lunch on weekends .*

$$-$$$ ✕ **Riverside Tavern.** Owned and managed by Belikin beer baron Sir Barry
Fodor'sChoice   Bowen's family, Riverside Tavern opened in 2006 and immediately
★   became one of the city's most popular restaurants. The huge signature hamburgers are arguably the best in Belize. (The 6-ounce burger is BZ$16.) The Riverside has added new steak and prime rib dishes, from cattle from Bowen's farm at Gallon Jug. Sit inside in air-conditioned comfort, at tables set around a huge bar, or on the outside covered patio overlooking Haulover Creek. This is one of the few restaurants in Belize with a dress code; shorts aren't allowed at night. The fenced, guarded parking lot right in front of the restaurant makes it easy and safe to park for free. ⊠ *2 Mapp St., off Freetown Rd.* ☎ *223/5640* ▤ *AE, MC, V.*

$$-$$$ ✕ **Smokey Mermaid.** On the ground floor of the Great House hotel, a small shopping gallery leads to the Smokey Mermaid, where amiable servers deliver Caribbean-influenced seafood dishes, inventive pastas, and savory barbecues. (It's not smoky in here, by the way.) The large dining courtyard has a fountain, shaded by breadfruit and sapodilla trees and big turquoise umbrellas. The freshly grilled fish is excellent and comes from a 19th-century bricked grill. There's often a live band playing Belize-style reggae. During lunchtime on days when cruise ships are in port, the restaurant is packed with day-trippers attracted by coupons touting free drinks with meals. ⊠ *13 Cork St.* ☎ *223/3400* ▤ *AE, MC, V.*

$$-$$$ ✕ **Sumathi.** Formerly the Sea Rock, Sumathi serves tasty Northern Indian food, so don't let the ugly concrete facade turn you away. The restaurant uses an authentic tandoori oven—a large clay oven with intense heat—that cooks meat and seafood quickly, leaving it crispy

on the outside and juicy inside. Try the tandoori chicken, with cumin, ginger, and minty yogurt, served with *naan* (Indian flatbread). There are many vegetarian options, too. Service is attentive, and portions are generous. ⊠ *190 Newtown Barracks, near Princess Hotel & Casino* ☎ *223/1172* ▤ *MC, V.*

$-$$$ ✕ **Chon Saan Palace.** A local favorite for more than 30 years, Chon Saan
★   Palace is the best Chinese restaurant in Belize City, which is otherwise full of bad Chinese eateries. It has some 200 dishes on the menu, most Cantonese-style, such as sweet-and-sour pork. We like the Chinese-style crab legs. There's a live seafood tank with lobster and the catch of the day, kept alive until you're ready to eat it. On Sunday, the restaurant switches gears a bit and makes sushi. ⊠ *1 Nurse Seay St., at 1 Kelly St.* ☎ *223/3008* ▤ *MC, V.*

$-$$ ✕ **Global Spice.** It's unusual to include an airport restaurant in any listing of best restaurants, but Global Spice, near the "waving gallery" on the second floor of the main terminal, will leave you with a nice taste of Belize. In 2005 chef Jason de Ocampo won second place in the annual "Taste of Belize" cooking contest, which focuses on Belizean national and regional cooking. This is a good place to get that farewell plate of rice and beans. ⊠ *Philip S. W. Goldson International Airport, 2nd level of main terminal* ☎ *225/3339* ▤ *MC, V.*

$-$$ ✕ **Macy's.** Stewed iguana, known locally as bamboo chicken, is available on request here, but you can also try armadillo or brocket deer. Macy, the Jamaican-born proprietor of this five-table spot, says iguana is tough to prepare—it has to be scalded, then washed in lime juice and vinegar—but it's delicious to eat. Fish or chicken with rice and beans and other more traditional dishes also are served. On display is a letter from the bishop of Belize congratulating the staff on its catering feats and a photo of Harrison Ford, who commandeered the table by the door during the making of *The Mosquito Coast.* ⊠ *18 Bishop St.* ☎ *207/3419* ▤ *No credit cards.*

$-$$ ✕ **Wet Lizard.** Right next to the Tourism Village, overlooking the boardwalk where cruise ship tenders drop off passengers, there's no question of the target market of the Wet Lizard. Even so, it's become a popular bar and a place to grab a sandwich or hamburger, even for those not on a cruise ship. An expansion added a gift shop, snack bar, and tour operation. ⊠ *1 Fort St.* ☎ *223/2664* ▤ *MC, V.* ☺ *Weekdays 9–4*

¢-$$ ✕ **Big Daddy's Diner.** With a central location in the Commercial Center, just south of Swing Bridge, Big Daddy's is a popular lunch spot for downtown workers. The large portions served cafeteria-style come cheap, and the clean, sunny surroundings including ceiling fans and views of Haulover Creek out the big windows are extras that don't cost a thing. Come for breakfast and get a plate of fry jacks—fried bread, a bit like New Orleans beignets without the powdered sugar—eggs, and delicious Belizean bacon for around BZ$8. ⊠ *Commercial Center, 2nd fl., near Swing Bridge* ☎ *227/0932* ▤ *MC, V.*

¢-$$ ✕ **Nerie's.** Always packed with locals, Nerie's is the vox populi of dining in Belize City. The many traditional dishes on the menu include fry jacks for breakfast and cow-foot soup and *garífuna sere* (fish soup with coconut milk) for lunch. Stew chicken with rice, beans, and a soft drink

"Roots" Belizean

If you spend time talking with Belizeans, sooner or later conversation will turn to "roots." It's not a vegetable, but a term referring to people born in Belize who share a certain set of values. Usually, but not always, it connotes ordinary folk, not wealthy Belizeans. These are Belizeans who ride the bus instead of driving a new Ford Explorer.

"Being roots Belizean is a way of life, a mindset, and a unique set of values," says Wendy Auxillou, a second-generation Belizean who lives on Caye Caulker. Roots Belizeans enjoy the simple pleasures of life: talking with friends they run into on the streets of Belize City; skipping work or school to swim in the sea, river, or lagoon; sitting on a veranda on a hot afternoon; fishing in an old wooden skiff; raising chickens in the backyard for Sunday dinner. More recently, it's going to a local restaurant or bar for karaoke, as Belizeans have developed a genuine affection for the pastime.

Roots is about community involvement. Children are often looked after by aunts and grannies, as well as neighbors. Misbehaving children might find themselves answering to a slew of adults in addition to their parents.

It's going to the market and eating boiled corn, *dukunu* (boiled cornbread), *garnaches* (crispy tortillas topped with beans and rice), and Belizean-style hot dogs, which are wrapped in bacon and grilled with onions. It's buying bananas 10 for a Belizean dollar. It's enjoying the smell and taste of all the local fruits, like tambran, grocea, a dozen different kinds of mangoes, sapodilla, mamie, jicama, watermelon, pineapple, guava, and papaya. It's about going to restaurants with local flavor, like Caladium in Belmopan, Nerie's in Belize City, and Clarissa Falls near the Cayo.

"It's about eating johnnycakes or plucking chickens with your neighbor, just because," says one Belizean.

Some claim that the original and perhaps only roots Belizeans are Creoles, descendents of the rough-and-ready Baymen and freed African slaves. Others argue that anybody can be a roots Belizean, that there are roots Mestizos, roots Maya, even roots Mennonites.

—Lan Sluder

will set you back only BZ$10. ⊠ *Queen and Daly Sts.* ☏ *223/4028* ⊠ *124 Freetown Rd.* ☏ *224/5199* ▭ *No credit cards.*

WHERE TO STAY

Belize City has the country's largest hotels, though size is all relative in Belize. The Radisson, Princess, and Biltmore Plaza each have more than 75 rooms and strive, not always successfully, for an international standard. The city also has its share of small inns and B&Bs with character, such as the Great House, D'Nest Inn, and Villa Boscardi. Although easy on the pocketbook, the city's many budget and moderately priced hotels frequently have thin, inexpensive mattresses and scratchy sheets, and amenities such as room phones may be scarce. In Belize City, safety is an issue, especially at the cheaper hotels, so be sure to check that doors and windows securely lock and that the entrance is well lighted.

Several of the city's best hotels are in the Fort George area, but there are also good choices in the northern suburbs between downtown and the international airport. The Commercial District on the South Side (south of Swing Bridge) has the largest number of budget hotels.

WHAT IT COSTS IN BELIZE DOLLARS					
	¢	$	$$	$$$	$$$$
FOR TWO PEOPLE	under BZ$100	BZ$100–BZ$200	BZ$200–BZ$300	BZ$300–BZ$500	over BZ$500

Prices are for two people in a standard double room in high season, including tax.

$$$ **The Great House.** Among Fort George's loveliest sights is the colonial
★ facade of this large wooden house, across the street from the Radisson. Owner Steve Maestre converted his 1927 home into an outstanding inn. The large rooms have polished antique pine floors, with modern conveniences such as wireless Internet and dedicated fax lines. Tiers of wraparound veranda allow you to relax while taking in the sea breeze. On the ground floor there's a tiny gallery of shops and a good restaurant, the Smokey Mermaid. **Pros:** Lovely old inn, good location in the Fort George area. **Cons:** Rooms are all upstairs on second and third floors. ⊠ *13 Cork St.* ☎ *223/3400* ⊕ *www.greathousebelize.com* ➪ *16 rooms* ⚲ *In-room: safe, refrigerator, Wi-Fi. In-hotel: restaurant, no elevator, laundry service, public Wi-Fi* ⊟ *AE, DC, MC, V.*

$$$ **Renaissance Tower.** An alternative to staying in a hotel is this new condominium tower, with some units available on a nightly basis. All apartments are nicely furnished, with two bedrooms and fully equipped kitchens. Most have either verandas or balconies with sea views, and some have whirlpool tubs. You're a short walk from several restaurants and the Princess Hotel & Casino. Secure, free parking is available for guests. **Pros:** Spacious, 1,064 square foot suites with kitchens at rates comparable to better hotels. **Cons:** Lacks hotel amenities such as restaurant and pool. ⊠ *8 Newtown Barracks* ☎ *223/2614* ⊕ *www.renaissancetower.bz* ➪ *27 2-bedroom suites* ⚲ *In-room: kitchen, Wi-Fi. In-hotel: bar, public Internet.* ⊟ *AE, MC, V.*

$$-$$$ **Best Western Belize Biltmore Plaza.** This suburban motel mainly gets guests who don't want to stay in the downtown area. Management has made improvements to its pool, grounds, and rooms. Still, it is far from luxurious. "Deluxe" and "premier" rooms, with new carpets and mattresses, are worth the extra cost. The Victorian Room (BZ$14–BZ$40) serves entrées like stew chicken and grilled steak. If staying here, you'll probably dine in the restaurant, as there's little else within walking distance. There is a guarded and fenced parking

> **WORD OF MOUTH**
>
> I quite like the Biltmore, moderately priced hotel with a pool, rooms with a/c, cable TV, restaurant, bar, gift shop. Lively happy hour with music on Fridays.
>
> —KatieValk

lot. **Pros:** Comfortable, secure, motel-like suburban setting. **Cons:** Not much atmosphere. ⊠*Mile 3½, Northern Hwy.* ☎*223/2302* ⊕*www.belizebiltmore.com* ⟲*75 rooms* ⌂*In-room: safe (some), Wi-Fi (some). In-hotel: restaurant, room service, bars, pool, gym, no elevator, laundry service, public Internet, public Wi-Fi, no-smoking rooms* ⊟*AE, MC, V.*

$$-$$$ **Radisson Fort George.** Porters in white pith helmets perpetuate a sense of British colonialism at Belize City's best-known large hotel. Lush red and ocher fabrics, faux-leopard carpets, and reproduction rattan and hardwood antiques attempt to re-create the British raj of the 1880s, albeit showing some wear and tear. There are panoramic views of the sea through tinted glass from rooms in the six-story tower, while those in the villa wing across the road overlook the river and one of the hotel's two pools (however, a few rooms in this wing don't have any windows). Dining options include the expensive St. George's Dining Room, the Stonegrill where food is grilled at tables on heated volcanic stones, or the coffee shop, Le Petit Café. The Baymen's Tavern is one of the city's upscale watering holes. **Pros:** Belize City's best international-style hotel choice, waterfront location in Fort George area. **Cons:** Dated furnishings in some rooms, staff not always as friendly as you'd like. ⊠*2 Marine Parade* ☎*227/7400, 888/201–1718 in U.S.* ⊕*www.radissonbelize.com* ⟲*102 rooms* ⌂*In-room: safe (some). In-hotel: 2 restaurants, room service, bars, pools, gym, diving, laundry service, public Internet, executive floor, no-smoking rooms, airport shuttle* ⊟*AE, MC, V.*

$$ **Princess Hotel & Casino.** Big-time gambling arrived in Belize City when the casino opened at this sprawling hotel, the largest in Belize, in 2000. Though it's not the MGM Grand, the casino has tables for blackjack, poker, craps, roulette, and more than 400 slot and video game machines Belize's only movie theaters and bowling alley are also here, and the hotel has several popular bars and nightclubs, including Next and Club Level. Alas, the rooms and service aren't as exciting as the gaming. Even the most expensive rooms sorely need upgrading, and new carpets, linens, and a good spring cleaning are in order. Guests have complained about unpleasant odors in the hotel. The big money is in the casino, so guest service in the hotel is often notably lacking. Gamble here if you like, but don't stay here. **Pros:** Waterfront location, popular venue for meetings, Belize City's only casino. **Cons:** Rooms and hotel service are disappointing at best. ⊠*Kings Park* ☎*223/2670* ⊕*www.princessbelize.com* ⟲*175 rooms, 5 suites* ⌂*In-room: ethernet (some). In-hotel: restaurant, room service, bars, pool, gym, diving, laundry facilities, laundry service, no-smoking rooms, public Internet* ⊟*AE, MC, V* ⦿*BP.*

$ **Chateau Caribbean.** The breezy seaside location of this hotel is its strongest point. Behind the charming colonial-style exterior—it was formerly a hospital—some of the rooms badly need upgrading and refurbishing. Some scenes in the 1980 movie, *The Dogs of War*, were filmed here, and not too much has changed in the intervening years. As this is Belize, don't expect everything to work perfectly—your room's louvered windows might not close, defeating the air-conditioning. The second-floor restaurant has ocean views, and a menu with an unusual combination of Chinese and Caribbean dishes: you can have grilled snapper with rice and beans while your dining companion tries the sweet-and-sour pork. Menu prices are reasonable. **Pros:** Waterfront location, colonial atmosphere in public areas. **Cons:** Shabby rooms. ⊠*6 Marine Parade* ☎*223/0800* ⊕*www.chateaucaribbean.com* ↩*20 rooms* ♿*In-hotel: restaurant, room service, bar, no elevator, laundry service* ▤*AE, MC, V.*

$ · **D'Nest Inn.** In Belama Phase 2, a safe, middle-class suburb between
Fodor'sChoice · the international airport and downtown, D'Nest Inn is run by a charm-
★ · ing couple, Gaby and Oty Ake. Gaby is a retired Belize City banker, and Oty is originally from Chetumal, Mexico. The four guest rooms are furnished with antiques such as a hand-carved, four-poster bed. With a private entrance and your own key, you can come and go as you like. The two-story house is on a canal a few feet from the Belize River. Gardens around the house are filled with hibiscus, frangipani, roses, and other blossoming plants. This is our favorite place to stay in Belize City. **Pros:** Delightful B&B, charming and helpful hosts, delicious breakfasts included. **Cons:** Only a few restaurant choices nearby. ⊠*475 Cedar St.* ↔*From Northern Hwy., turn west on Chetumal St., turn right at police station, go 1 short block and turn left, then turn right on Cedar St.* ☎*223/5416* ⊕*www.dnestinn.com* ↩*4 rooms* ♿*In-room: refrigerator, Wi-Fi. In-hotel: no elevator, public Wi-Fi, no-smoking rooms* ▤*MC, V* ⦿*BP.*

$ · **Global Village Hotel.** This Chinese-owned hotel has little atmosphere, but it's sparkling clean, with modern furniture and fixtures, and a good value at BZ$100 for a double. Near the turnoff to the international airport, the hotel has free transportation to and from the airport and a fenced parking lot with 24-hour security. **Pros:** Clean, no-frills motel, airport pick-up and drop-off, secure parking. **Cons:** No atmosphere, mainly for an overnight en route to other locations. ⊠*Mile 8½, Northern Hwy.* ☎*225/2555* ⊕*www.globalhotel-bz.com* ↔*South of the turnoff to the international airport* ↩*40 rooms* ♿*In-hotel: restaurant, bar, no elevator, public Internet, airport shuttle* ▤*MC, V* ⦿*CP.*

$ · **Villa Boscardi.** If you're edgy about downtown Belize City, this B&B in the northern suburbs might be your cup of herbal tea. You'll stay in the quiet Buttonwood Bay residential area only a block from the sea. Its rooms are bright, sunny, and stylish, with hints of both Europe and Belize in their decor. An evening shuttle to downtown restaurants can be arranged for BZ$10; airport pick-up for up to three people is BZ$40, slightly cheaper than a regular taxi. **Pros:** Cheerful B&B in safe area, airport pick-up. **Cons:** Only a few restaurants nearby. ⊠*6043 Manatee Dr., turn toward sea off Northern Hwy. at Golding Ave., then left on 2nd lane to 5th house on right* ☎*223/1691* ⊕*www.villaboscardi.com* ↩*6 rooms* ♿*In-room: refrigerator (some). In-hotel: public Internet, no elevator, no-smoking rooms, airport shuttle* ▤*AE, MC, V* ⦿*BP.*

Belcove Hotel. Right in the middle of things, the Belcove is a popular budget hotel just south of Swing Bridge, literally at the edge of Haulover Creek. You can sit on one of the balconies of this three-story wood hotel, painted sunflower yellow, and watch the boats on the river. Some of the rooms are barely larger than the beds in them, but they're clean, and the staff is helpful and friendly. Airport pick-up is BZ$40. **Pros:** Good value, friendly staff, central downtown location. **Cons:** Funky atmosphere, be very careful after dark. ⊠*9 Regent St., just south of Swing Bridge* ☎*227/3054* ⊕*www.belcove.com* ⇖*12 rooms, 4 with shared baths* ⌂*In-room: no a/c (some), no phone. In-hotel: no elevator, airport shuttle* ⊟*MC, V.*

¢-$ ☷**Hotel Mopan.** Established in 1973 by Jean Shaw, a pioneer in Belize tourism, the Hotel Mopan is well known for attracting interesting, well-traveled guests, including archaeologists, adventurers, and birders. The hotel is now run by Shaw's children, who have upgraded and renovated it while keeping the rates affordable. There's an Internet room, guest quarters are bright and clean, and the staff is always helpful. **Pros:** Interesting clientele, clean and well-run. **Cons:** Not a safe area to walk in after dark. ⊠*55 Regent St., at south end of Regent* ☎*227/7351* ⊕*www.hotelmopan.com* ⇖*12 rooms* ⌂*In-room: no a/c (some), no phone. In-hotel: public Internet, public Wi-Fi, no elevator* ⊟*MC, V.*

NIGHTLIFE & THE ARTS

Travelers who like to use their vacations to catch up on their nightlife rather than sleep will find Belize City's scene limited at best. Although locals love to party, safety concerns keep visitors away from most nightspots except hotel bars, such as the bar at the Radisson Fort George or the Calypso Bar at the Princess Hotel & Casino. After dark, take a taxi, or, if driving, park in a fenced and secured lot, such as at the Princess.

Karaoke is a craze among many Belizeans. A hugely popular, locally produced karaoke television show, *Karaoke TV,* has been running on Tuesday nights on Channel 5 in Belize City since 2001. Most of the hotel bars have karaoke nights once or twice a week. Even in Belize, you'll hear tried-and-true karaoke favorites such as "Crazy" by Patsy Kline and lots of Elvis and vintage Sonny and Cher, and you'll also hear songs like "Bidi Bidi Bam Bam" by Selena and "Greatest Love of All" by Whitney Houston. Singers may go from country to Motown and hip-hop to funk and R&B to reggae, ska, and Latin soca. One KTV champion, Angelo Fabrio, a teenager from Corozal, specializes in Ricky Martin and Elvis impersonations. Belizean taste in music is nothing if not eclectic. At live music shows and clubs in Belize City, you can hear an equally diverse mix of music, although rap in all its variations is as popular in Belize City as in Los Angeles.

One uniquely Belizean style of music is punta rock. It's based on the traditional punta rhythms of the Garífuna, using drums, turtle shells, and rattles. In the late 1970s, Pen Cayetano, a Garífuna artist in Dangriga, began writing punta songs, updating the music with an electric guitar, keyboard, and other electronic instruments. (Cayetano now lives in Germany, although he visits Belize regularly.) Punta rock, earthy and sexy, swept Belize and later became popular in other Central American countries, a result of the export of the music by Andy Palacio, "the ambassador of punta rock," who died unexpectedly at the peak of his career in early 2008, and other punta rock stars. There's no one venue for punta, but Club Calypso at the Princess Hotel & Casino often has punta bands on weekends. *(See Bars below.)*

BARS

The bars at the upmarket hotels, particularly those at the **Princess Hotel & Casino** and at the **Radisson Fort George,** are fairly popular—and safe—places to congregate for drinks. The Riverside Tavern is a popular place to have drinks, either indoors in air-conditioned comfort or on the outside patio next to the water. If you have a layover at the international airport, you might have a beer at the nearby Manatee Lookout.

Baymen's Tavern (⊠ *Radisson Fort George Hotel, 2 Marine Parade* ☎ *223/3333*) is a spot at which to sip a rum and tonic, with live entertainment on weekends, usually a singer or a small band. There's also a more casual section of the bar, on an open-air deck, with views of a garden and the sea.

Club Next (⊠ *Marine Parade* ☎ *223/7162*) at the Princess Hotel & Casino, is a hot venue for live music, especially on weekends. Admission to live concerts usually costs BZ$25 to $BZ50.

Run by a Belizean who returned home after living in Canada, **Manatee Lookout** (⊠ *Northern Hwy., on Belize River ½ mi [1 km] south of the international airport access road* ☎ *205/2391*), a short cab ride (around BZ$8) from the airport, is a place to grab a beer and chicken wings if your flight is delayed. The bar has big windows and an open-air deck overlooking the Belize River, and you might in fact see a manatee. British commandos from the nearby army base at Price Barracks in Ladyville sometimes invade this bar in force, scouting rum and cokes.

At the **Riverside Tavern** (⊠ *2 Mapp St., off Freetown Rd.* ☎ *223/5640*) you can have drinks on the covered patio overlooking Haulover Creek or inside at the bar. Park your car safely in a fenced, guarded lot next to the tavern.

CASINOS

The only serious gambling in town is at the **Princess Hotel & Casino** (⊠ *Kings Park* ☎ *223/2670* ☉ *Noon–4* AM), which has live tables for blackjack, roulette, and poker, along with about 400 slots. Dancers from Eastern Europe and Russia put on shows, and there are free drinks and a buffet for players. It's open 365 days a year. You'll have to show your passport and register (no charge) at the reception counter before you can go in.

THEATERS

The main venue for theater, dance, music, and the arts in Belize City is **Bliss Center for the Performing Arts** (⊠ *2 Southern Foreshore, between Church and Bishop Sts.* ☎ *227/2110*), which seats 600. As a small, provincial city, Belize City rarely attracts international headliners. It's rare to have more than one or two shows a week at the center, and most of these are local performances—a children's dance group or a young singer's debut concert. You might see a karaoke show or a performance by a Garífuna dance or music group. Concert organizers try to bring in performing talent from around the country, and on a Saturday night you could hear a Mayan singer from Toledo or a marimba band from Benque Viejo del Carmen. Most shows are in English, with Creole often mixed in. Ticket prices vary but typically range from BZ$10 to BZ$40.

SPORTS & THE OUTDOORS

Belize City is a jumping-off spot for trips to the cayes and to inland and coastal areas, but the city itself offers little in the way of sports and outdoor activities. There are no golf courses, public tennis courts (there are courts at the private Pickwick Club), or other sports facilities of note around Belize City, other than a sports stadium named after the now-disgraced Olympic track star, Marion Jones, a Belizean-American. Unless you're on a cruise ship or otherwise have only a short time in Belize, you'll be better off going elsewhere for your sporting activities— to the cayes and Southern Coast for snorkeling, diving, and fishing, and inland to the Cayo, northern Belize, or Toledo for caving, cave tubing, hiking, horseback riding, canoeing, and other activities. ⇨*Chapters on Northern Belize, The Cayo, Southern Coast, The Deep South, and The Cayes and Atolls, and also the Beyond Belize City section below.*

DIVING & WATER SPORTS

Belize Dive Connection (⊠*71 N. Front St.* ☎*223/4526* ⊕*www.belize-diving.com*) runs trips from the Radisson Fort George dock. Dive trips to the Belize Barrier Reef, about 30–45 minutes away, cost around BZ$160–BZ$210 per person. Those to Turneffe Atoll cost BZ$300–BZ$340 per person and involve an hour to 90 minutes of travel time one way. Snorkel trips are BZ$110–BZ$200 per person.

Sea Sports Belize (⊠*83 N. Front St.* ☎*223/5505* ⊕*www.seasportsbe-lize.com*) will take you on a 30- to 45-minute trip to Goff's Caye or St. George's Caye for snorkeling (BZ$176) or to Turneffe Atoll for diving (from BZ$286).

FISHING

If you're a serious angler, you'll likely end up in Placencia, Punta Gorda, or even San Pedro, but you can arrange fishing charters from Belize City. Both the **Radisson Fort George** and the **Princess Hotel & Casino** have marinas, and local fishing guide services and lodges operate near the city.

Action Belize (⊠*Mile 3½, Northern Hwy.* ☎*223/2987 or 888/383–6319 in the U.S.* ⊕*www.actionbelize.com*) has 23-, 25-, and 27-foot boats and fishing guides that will take you out on the Belize River to try your luck with snook, cubera, and tarpon for BZ$240–BZ$800 per person for a full day, depending on the number of anglers.

Belize River Lodge (✉ *Box 459, Belize City, Ladyville* ☎ *225/2002* ⊕ *www.belizeriverlodge.com*) is the oldest continuously operating fishing lodge in Belize. Six-night fishing cruises on a 52-foot Chris Craft, with lodging, meals, guides, and transfers, start at about BZ$6,060 per person, based on four people.

Sea Sports Belize (✉ *83 N. Front St.* ☎ *223/5505* ⊕ *www.seasportsbelize.com*) has five- to six-hour deep-sea fishing trips for BZ$1,430 for up to four people, and reef fishing for BZ$1,120. Flats and river fishing expeditions for up to three people cost around BZ$825 for three to five hours of fishing.

GOLF

There are no golf courses in Belize City, but there's a spectacular one at Caye Chapel, about a half hour away by water taxi, or 10 minutes by plane.

Caye Chapel Island Resort (✉ *Caye Chapel* ☎ *226/8250 or 800/901–8938* ⊕ *www.cayechapel.com*) has an 18-hole, par 72, 7,000-yard course, beautifully laid out along the sea. At this exclusive and remote course, you don't have to worry about tee times or round limits. Unpredictable trade winds and crocodiles in the water hazards make play challenging. A day package at the island costs BZ$400 per person for all the golf you can play (8 AM–4 PM), golf cart and club rental, use of the beach and swimming pool, and round-trip air from Belize City. Members of your party who are not golfers pay BZ$200 including round-trip air from Belize City. Advance reservations required.

SHOPPING

Belize City has the most varied shopping in the country, but that's not saying too much. Rather than catering to leisure shoppers, most stores in Belize City cater to the local market and those from other parts of the country who need to stock up on supplies at lumberyards, home-building stores, appliance outlets, and supermarkets. Gift shops and handicraft shops are concentrated in the downtown area in and near the Tourism Village.

About a dozen ships per week call on Belize City, and each time the Tourism Village shops open their doors. Wednesday is usually the biggest day of the week for cruise ships in Belize City, often with three to five in port, and Saturday is another popular day. Rarely is there a ship in port on Sunday. The Web site Cruise Calendar (⊕ *www.cruisecal.com*) lists the days cruise ships visit ports, including Belize City.

Most stores in the downtown area are open Monday–Saturday from around 8 AM to 6 PM. On Sunday, nearly all stores downtown are dark, although some stores in the suburbs are open Sunday afternoon.

In a misguided effort at civic redevelopment, the city did away with the old markets at Swing Bridge in the 1990s, replacing them with a modern, two-story Commercial Center just south of Swing Bridge, with stalls and shops selling food and household items. Although clean, the Commercial Center doesn't have the atmosphere, or the customer base, of the old markets.

SHOPPING CENTERS & MALLS

To stock up on picnic supplies, head to the newly expanded **Brodie's** on the **Northern Highway, which is a mini-department store as well as a grocery store** (⊠ *Mile 2½, Northern Hwy.* ☎ *223/5587* ⊠ *16 Regent St.* ☎ *227/7070*).

Commercial Center (⊠ *South of Swing Bridge* ⏱ *7:30 AM–5 PM*), in a modern concrete building, is a rather drab market. The first floor has fruit and vegetable and other food stalls, and the second level houses **Big Daddy's Diner** *(see above)* and a few small shops, including several small gift and handicraft shops.

Fort Point Tourism Village (⊠ *Fort George cruise ship docks, east of Swing Bridge* ☎ *223/7008* ⏱ *When cruise ships are in port*) is packed with day-trippers when cruise ships are in port and is nearly deserted, or closed, at other times. It has around 30 gift shops, clean restrooms, a cybercafé, a car rental kiosk, restaurants, and other services. Vendors also set up booths on streets near the Tourism Village.

Save-U Supermarket (⊠ *Sancas Plaza at Northern Hwy. and Central American Blvd.* ☎ *223/1291*) is a good place for groceries, liquor, and sundries.

SPECIALTY SHOPS

One of Belize's premier art galleries, **Image Factory** (⊠ *91 N. Front St.* ☎ *223/4151*), is run by a nonprofit foundation. Its exhibitions change monthly, and its store sells works by more than 20 Belizean artists.

National Handicraft Center (⊠ *2 South Park St., in Fort George section* ☎ *223/3636*) has Belizean souvenir items, including hand-carved figurines, handmade furniture, pottery, and woven baskets. The prices are about as good as you'll find anywhere in Belize, and the sales clerks are friendly. It faces the small Memorial Park, which commemorates the Battle of St. George's Caye and is just a short stroll from the harbor front, the Tourism Village, and many of the hotels in the Fort George area, including the Radisson, Chateau Caribbean, and Great House.

BEYOND BELIZE CITY

If you're like most visitors to Belize, you'll spend at most only a night or two, if that, in Belize City before moving on. If you're heading west to the Cayo, plan to make a stop at the wonderful Belize Zoo, about 30 mi (49 km) west of Belize City. Going north or west, you can visit the Community Baboon Sanctuary, as there is road access to Bermudian Landing, where the sanctuary is located, via either the Northern Highway or the Western Highway. For other areas of interest, including Crooked Tree Wildlife Sanctuary and the Altun Ha Mayan site, within an hour or two of Belize City, see the Northern Belize chapter.

BELIZE ZOO

FodorsChoice ★

Turn a sharp corner on the jungle trail, and suddenly you're face-to-face with a black jaguar, the largest cat in the Western Hemisphere. The big cat growls a deep rumbling threat. You jump back, thankful that a strong but inconspicuous fence separates you and the jaguar.

One of the smallest, but arguably one of the best, zoos in the world, the Belize Zoo packs a lot into 29 acres. Containing more than 125 native species, the zoo has self-guided tours through several Belizean ecosystems—rain forest, lagoons, and riverine forest. Along with the rare black jaguar and the spotted jaguar, you'll see the country's four other wild cats: the puma, margay, ocelot, and jaguarundi. Perhaps the zoo's most famous resident is April, a Baird's tapir that is more than a quarter century old. This relative of the horse and rhino is known to locals as the mountain cow, and is also Belize's national animal. At the zoo you can also see jabiru storks, a harpy eagle, scarlet macaws, crocodiles, and many snakes, including the fer-de-lance. New at the zoo are bird-watching tours, ranging from day and overnight trips to week-long birding safaris.

The zoo owes its existence to the dedication and drive of one gutsy woman, Sharon Matola. An American who came to Belize as part of a film crew, Matola stayed on to care for some of the semi-tame animals used in the production. She opened the zoo in 1983 and in 1991 it moved to its present location. She's also an active environmentalist. "The Zoo Lady" and her crusade against the Chalillo Dam is the subject of the 2008 book The Last Flight of the Scarlet Macaw: One Woman's Fight To Save the World's Most Beautiful Bird by Outside magazine writer Bruce Barcott.

Besides touring the zoo, you can also hike or canoe through the nearby 84-acre Tropical Education Center. The center is involved in a green iguana breeding project. Dormitory accommodations, with outdoor toilets, are available at the center for BZ$60 per person; spiffier cabins go for BZ$132—BZ$143 double, including breakfast, dinner, and taxes. Cameron Diaz and the late Steve Erwin have stayed here. Overnighters can take a nocturnal zoo tour for BZ$30. For Tropical Education Center accommodations, call in advance, and be aware that the lodging area is a long hike from the zoo. ⊠ *Western Hwy., 30 mi (49 km) west of Belize City* ☎220/8004 ⊕*www.belizezoo.org* ✉*BZ$16 adults, BZ$8 children* ⊙*Daily 8–5.*

COMMUNITY BABOON SANCTUARY

☺ One of Belize's most fascinating wildlife conservation projects is the Community Baboon Sanctuary, which is actually a haven for black howler monkeys. Spanning a 20-mi (32-km) stretch of the Belize River, the reserve was established in 1985 by a group of local farmers. The howler monkey—an agile bundle of black fur with a deafening roar—was then zealously hunted throughout Central America and was facing extinction. Today the sanctuary is home to nearly 1,000 black howler monkeys, as well as numerous species of birds and mammals. Thanks to ongoing conservation efforts, you can see the howler monkeys in a number of other areas, including at Lamanai in northern Belize, along the Macal, Mopan, and Belize rivers in western Belize, and near Monkey River in southern Belize. Exploring the Community Baboon Sanctuary is easy, thanks to about 3 mi (5 km) of trails that start near a small museum and visitor center.

There are two routes leading to the sanctuary. If you are going north on the Northern Highway, turn west at Mile 13 onto the Burrell Boom Road. Go 3 mi (5 km) and turn right just beyond the new bridge over the Belize River. Signs to Bermudian Landing mark the turn. Stay on this road approximately 12 mi (20 km) to Bermudian Landing. If going west on the Western Highway, turn north on the Burrell Boom Road at a roundabout at Mile 15½ of the Western Highway, and go 9 mi (14 km) to the new bridge over the Belize River. Just before the bridge, turn left. Signs to Bermudian Landing mark the turn. Stay on this road approximately 12 mi (20 km) to Bermudian Landing.

You can also use the Burrell Boom Road as a short cut between the Northern and Western highways, avoiding Belize City. When taking this shortcut, you stay on the Burrell Boom Road rather than turning toward Bermudian Landing. When on the Burrell Boom Road, you may want to stop at the **Central Prison Gift Shop** at the Central Prison, on the road to Burrell Boom about 3 mi (5 km) from the Western Highway. Prisoners at the "Hattieville Ramada" make small craft items and sell them at the gift shop. ✉*Community Baboon Sanctuary, 31 mi (50 km) northwest of Belize City* ☎220/2181 ✉*BZ$10* ⊙*Daily 8–5.*

MONKEY BAY WILDLIFE SANCTUARY

☺ ⚠ Monkey Bay is a privately owned wildlife reserve on 1,070 acres near the Belize Zoo, established by Matt and Marga Miller in the 1980s. Here, you can canoe on the Sibun River, hike a 16 mi (31 km) nature trail along Indian Creek (only partly within Monkey Bay lands), or go bird-watching—some 250 bird species have been identified in the area. It has a natural history library with some 500 books and other reference materials, which visitors can use. The sanctuary also has educational and internship programs. In 2004 the reserve started a green iguana breeding and hatching project, to release young iguanas into the wild. Overnight accommodations are available, including tent camping (BZ$12 per person), a bunkhouse (BZ$22 a person), and rooms (BZ$35 per person) in the field research station, all with shared baths. Meals are also available at times, if an educational group is in residence. Otherwise you'll have to make your own meals. Homestays also can be arranged in nearby villages. Monkey Bay also has a rustic cabin in the Mountain Pine Ridge and is developing a hostel on Caye Caulker. Most of the reserve's facilities demonstrate high ecological awareness. For example, the bathrooms collect methane gas for cooking. Most programs are geared for overnight or multinight visits, but you can come on a day visit. Call in advance to see what activities or facilities may be available when you want to come. ⊠ *Mile 31, Western Hwy., 31½ mi (51 km) northwest of Belize City* ⬧ *Monkey Bay Wildlife Sanctuary, Box 187, Belmopan* ☏ *820/3032* ⊕ *www.monkeybaybelize.org.*

WHERE TO STAY & EAT

Just west of the Belize Zoo, the Western Highway is home to three similar restaurants in the same area: Cheers, JB's, and Amigos. Locals disagree as to which is the best, but, truth be told, they all have cold beer, unremarkable burgers, fries, and other snacks, along with beans and rice, and all have open-air seating, with decor heavy on T-shirts and other relics put up by tourists and British army troops. Cheers also has three cabins for overnight rental.

$$ ▦ **Black Orchid Resort.** Thank goodness, the owner changed the name of this small hotel from Belize R Us to Black Orchid Resort. By any name, it brings a bit of refinement to howler-monkey watching. The resort perches at the edge of the Belize River, and you can launch a canoe, kayak, or powerboat from the hotel's dock, or just laze about the riverside swimming pool and thatch palapa. The air-conditioned rooms are large, with custom-made mahogany furnishings. A three-bedroom, two-bath house (BZ$545 nightly for up to six people) is a good choice for families; a guesthouse with shared bath (BZ$87 double) is for those on a budget. The on-site restaurant serves good Belizean food (dinner BZ$36). **Pros:** Most upscale lodging near Baboon Sanctuary, lovely riverside setting. **Cons:** Not directly in the Baboon Sanctuary. ⊠ *Burrell Boom Village, 12 mi (20 km) from Baboon Sanctuary* ☏ *225/9029* ⊕ *www.blackorchidresort.com* ⬧ *4 rooms in hotel, 1 3-bedroom house, 2 rooms in guesthouse with shared bath* ⟁ *In-room: kitchen (some). In-hotel: restaurant, bar, pool, water sports, no elevator, public Wi-Fi, airport shuttle* ▤ *AE, D, MC, V.*

$$ ▦ **Orchid Garden Eco-Village.** A friendly and hardworking couple from Taiwan runs this little hotel and budding eco-complex on the Western Highway. It's convenient to most of the attractions near Belize City while being away from the city's sketchier vibes. Besides 18 simple but clean rooms, Orchid Garden has several gardens and mini-museums, including a mushroom house, an ecology display, and a collection of Belizean nature paintings and old Belize bottles. An overnight package includes room, two meals, and admission to the hotel's several museums, for BZ$280 double. Transfers from the international airport are BZ$80 for two. Longer packages include tours, transfers, and meals. **Pros:** Centrally located, clean rooms, and tasty meals. **Cons:** Not in a particularly scenic part of Belize. ⊠ *Mile 14½, Western Hwy.* 🕾 *225/6991* ⊕ *www.trybelize.com* ⊐ *18 rooms* 🕭 *In-room: no phone, no TV. In-hotel: restaurant, bar, no elevator, public Wi-Fi, airport shuttle* ⊟ *MC, V.* ⫟◎⫞ *MAP*

BELIZE CITY ESSENTIALS

TRANSPORTATION

For more information, see Essentials at the back of the book.

BY AIR

TO & FROM BELIZE CITY   Philip S. W. Goldson International Airport (BZE) is near Ladyville, 9 mi (14 km) north of the city. The international airport is served by American, Continental, Delta, TACA, and US Airways. Atlantic Air has service three days a week to San Pedro Sula, Honduras, from Belize City, and Maya Island Air has daily service to and from San Pedro Sula via Savannah (near Independence, across the lagoon from Placencia). Twice-daily flights between Belize International and Flores, Guatemala, on both Maya Island Air and Tropic Air were discontinued in late 2007 because Belize did not meet certain safety oversight standards of the International Civil Aviation Organization (ICAO), a United Nations affiliate, and the U.S. Federal Aviation Administration (FAA); attempts are being made to rectify this and restart service. There is no service to Mexico. Nonstop service from Europe has long been anticipated, but as of this writing nothing has been confirmed.

In addition to international flights, a domestic terminal at the International Airport has flights on Maya Island Air and Tropic Air to Ambergris Caye and Caye Caulker and the coastal towns of Dangriga, Placencia, and Punta Gorda. A Maya Island flight also stops at Savannah airstrip at Independence. The Belize City Municipal Airport, on the seafront about 1 mi (2 km) north of the city center, has domestic flights only; Maya Island Air and Tropic Air serve the same domestic destinations from here as from the international airport. However, fares from the municipal airport are about 10%–45% cheaper, depending on the destination, than similar flights departing from the international airport.

Taxis to town from the international airport cost BZ$50. Some hotels in and near Belize City also offer transfers from the airport, usually for around the same price as taxi fare. A few provide it for a little less than a cab. If you're renting a car, just walk out the main terminal across the small parking lot to the line of rental car offices.

BY BUS

TO & FROM BELIZE CITY   Belize City is the hub of the country's fairly extensive bus network, so there's service to most regions and to the Guatemalan and Mexican borders. Novelo's and its subsidiaries, Northern Transport and Southern Transport, formerly were the dominant carriers in the country, but Novelo's, following a series of financial problems, shut down operations in late 2005. Smaller carriers, of which there are nearly 100 around the country, scrambled to replace service. The country was divided into three zones—northern, western, and southern bus routes—with Belize City as the hub. The Novelo's terminal on West Collet Canal in Belize City reopened for use by other bus companies, and now most bus lines use this terminal. Bus terminals in Belmopan and Corozal also reopened. However, in some other destinations, the Novelo's terminals did not reopen, and bus companies have established small offices. The former owners of Novelo's have emerged as the operators of a new bus company, National Transport, which now covers many of the same routes as the old Novelo's line. In addition, a number of other regional companies, including Tillett's, James Bus Line, and Belize Bus, a drivers' co-op, also provide service on the Northern, Western, and Southern highways. The upshot is that on most routes there is again frequent service, although it is offered by many different bus lines, with schedules that change frequently.

For those going to Flores, Guatemala, or Chetumal, Mexico, two Guatemalan bus lines, Linea Dorada and San Juan, have daily service from the Marine Terminal near the Swing Bridge.

Information **Belize City Main Bus Terminal** (⊠ *W. Collet Canal, Belize City*).

WITHIN BELIZE
CITY
There's no point-to-point bus service within Belize City, but local non-express buses will stop and drop off most anywhere on the standard route. For example, if you're going from West Collet Canal downtown to Brodie's supermarket on the Northern Highway just north of downtown, you can be dropped off at or near Brodie's.

BY CAR
For car rental information see Car Rental in Essentials at the back of the book.

TO & FROM
BELIZE CITY
There are only two highways to Belize City: the Northern Highway, which stretches to the Mexican border, 102 mi (165 km) away, and the Western Highway, which runs 81 mi (131 km) to Guatemala. Both are paved and in good condition. Signs guide you to nearby destinations such as the Belize Zoo.

IN BELIZE
WITH A CAR
Finding your way around the city itself can be confusing. The downtown area's narrow one-way streets, sometimes without identifying signs, often end abruptly due to construction work or an inconveniently located river. However, as part of its effort to become more user-friendly for cruise ship passengers, who now number about a million a year, Belize City has added green directional signs in the downtown area. Big directional signs also are now posted, identifying key turns on the Northern and Western highways. With rare exceptions—the Princess Hotel & Casino is one—hotels in and near the city center offer mostly on-street parking, and you run the risk of a break-in if you leave the car overnight. Hotels in the suburbs north and west of

the city usually have fenced or otherwise secured parking. Give your nerves a break and explore the city by taxi or on foot in safer sections like the Fort George area.

BY TAXI

Cabs cost BZ$7—BZ$10 for one person between any two points in the city, plus BZ$1 for each additional person. Outside the city, and from downtown to the suburbs, you're charged by the distance you travel. Traveling between the international airport and any point in the city (including the businesses and hotels along the Northern Highway) is BZ$50. There are no meters, so be sure to agree on a price before you leave. Authorized taxis have green license plates. You can find taxis at Market Square or by Swing Bridge, or larger hotels will call them for you. For pick-up, call Cinderella Plaza taxi stand if you are in the downtown area or Belcan taxi stand if you are on the north end of the city.

Contacts **Belcan Taxi Stand** (☎ *223/2916*). **Cinderella Plaza Taxi Stand** (☎ *223/0371*).

CONTACTS & RESOURCES

BANKS & EXCHANGE SERVICES

U.S. dollars are accepted everywhere in Belize, but if you need to exchange another currency, you can do so at one of the five banks in Belize City: Alliance Bank, Atlantic Bank, Belize Bank, First Caribbean International Bank (formerly Barclays), and ScotiaBank. Most banks have their main offices on Albert Street in downtown Belize City, with smaller branches scattered around the city. Expect to be charged a 1%–2% fee if you exchange U.S. dollars. Fees for other currencies vary, but in general it's somewhat expensive to exchange currency other than U.S. dollars, even Canadian dollars, euros, and U.K. pounds. If you must convert currency, try the Belize Bank office at the international airport, or the main offices of banks in Belize City. Guatemalan and Mexican currencies can be easily exchanged at border areas.

The biggest employer in Belize—the Belize government—pays most employees on the 14th or 15th of the month, and on those days in particular banks in Belize are jammed, with customer lines often snaking around the outside of the building. Banks are also usually busy on Fridays.

Most banks in Belize City have ATMs, and, except for ATMs of Alliance Bank, all now accept cards issued outside Belize. If your ATM card has a Visa or MasterCard symbol, it will work in at least some Belize ATMs, and you can generally withdraw up to BZ$500 (US$250) a day. You get your cash in Belize dollars. With about 15 locations around the country, Belize Bank accepts foreign ATM cards on the CIRRUS, PLUS, and Visa Electron networks. Atlantic Bank ATMs accept foreign ATM cards with the Visa Electron symbol. First Caribbean branches in Belize City, Dangriga, and Belmopan, and all ScotiaBank ATMs, also work with non-Belize ATM cards. You should have a four-digit PIN. Try not

1

to depend on ATMs for all your cash, as ATM systems may be down, or the ATMs may be out of cash. Most banks offer cash advances on credit cards issued by Visa and MasterCard for a fee ranging from BZ$10 to BZ$30.

Banks **Alliance Bank** (⊠*Princess Margaret Dr.* ☎*223/5698*). **Atlantic Bank** (⊠*Freetown Rd.* ☎*223/4123*). **Belize Bank** (⊠*60 Market Sq.* ☎*227/7132*). **First Caribbean International Bank** (⊠*21 Albert St.* ☎*227/7211*). **ScotiaBank** (⊠*Albert St.* ☎*227/7027*).

EMERGENCIES

Karl Heusner Memorial, a public hospital that is merging with the private hospital Universal Health Services, and Belize Medical Associates, a private facility, both have 24-hour emergency rooms. Brodie's Pharmacy, at Market Square and on the Northern Highway, is open daily (hours vary). Belize Medical Associates Pharmacy has a pharmacist on call 24 hours. Your hotel, the U.S. Embassy or other embassies, and the hospitals can refer you to a dentist.

Hospitals **Belize Medical Associates** (⊠*5791 St. Thomas St.* ☎*223/0303*). **Karl Heusner Memorial Hospital** (⊠*Princess Margaret Dr.* ☎*223/1548*).

Pharmacies **Belize Medical Associates Pharmacy** (⊠*5791 St. Thomas St.* ☎*223/0302*). **Brodie's Pharmacy** (⊠*Regent St. at Market Sq.* ⊠*Mile 2½, Northern Hwy.*).

INTERNET, MAIL & SHIPPING

Most midlevel and upscale hotels in Belize City, and some budget spots, have Internet access, either wireless as at D'Nest Inn and the Great House, or in an Internet room as at the Radisson Fort George and Hotel Mopan. Cybercafés are now common in Belize City, as elsewhere in Belize. The problem is that these lightly capitalized businesses frequently are here today and gone tomorrow. Mail Boxes Etc. has good DSL connections, as does Angelus Press. Click & Sip is inside the Tourism Village. Your best bet is just to scout the area where you're staying for an open Internet café. Rates vary, but typically you'll pay around BZ$5 for a half hour, BZ$8–BZ$10 for an hour. The main post office, on Front Street near the Swing Bridge, is open weekdays 8–5. To ship packages, Mail Boxes Etc. can box and wrap packages and deliver them to the post office. Mail service from Belize City to the United States and other countries is generally fast and reliable (airmail to the United States usually takes about five days). For faster, though expensive, service use DHL and FedEx; both have offices in Belize City.

Internet Cafés **Angelus Press** (⊠*10 Queen St.* ☎*223/5777*).**Click & Sip Internet Café** (⊠*Fort St. in Tourism Village* ☎*223/1305*). **Mail Boxes Etc.** (⊠*166 N. Front St.,,* ☎*227/6046*.

Overnight Services **DHL** (⊠*38 New Rd.* ☎*223/4350*). **Federal Express** (⊠*32 Albert St.* ☎*227/3507*).

Post Office **Main Post Office** (⊠*N. Front St.* ☎*227/2201*). **Mail Boxes Etc.** (⊠*166 N. Front St.,,* ☎*227/6046*.

TOURS

Although Belize City is centrally located for day trips to the northern cayes and to inland areas in the middle of the country, few travelers use it as a base. The reasons include the city's reputation for street crime and hassle, and, more recently, the influx of cruise ships bringing crowds of day-trippers who crowd the area around the Tourism Village and monopolize cave tubing and snorkeling trips and tours to Mayan ruins. Except for attractions within an hour or so of the city, such as the Belize Zoo and Baboon Sanctuary, it generally makes sense to move on from Belize City.

Even so, if you're staying in Belize City you can take day trips to Altun Ha, Crooked Tree Wildlife Sanctuary, and Lamanai. You can also do day trips to nearby islands, including St. George's, Chapel, Caulker, and Ambergris cayes, either on your own or with a local tour operator. Your hotel can also arrange day trips.

S&L Travel and Tours is an established local tour operator that offers trips to Lamanai, Xunantunich, and Altun Ha Mayan sites; Belize Zoo; the Mountain Pine Ridge; and the Sibun River for cave tubing. Belize Trips' Katie Valk, a transplanted New Yorker, can organize a custom trip to almost any place in the country and also to Tikal in Guatemala. With her hotel connections she can even get you a room when everything seems booked. She's also a warden for the U.S. Embassy.

Several other Belize City–based tour companies are listed below. Keep in mind that most Belize City tour operators focus more on the booming cruise ship market, which brings customers by the thousands, than on individual travelers. Some of these cruise ship tour operators, while generally reputable, have no office and operate with a Web site and a cell phone, meeting customers at the Tourism Village. Katie Valk at Belize Trips is an exception, as she focuses on individual and small group travel.

Contacts **Katie Valk, Belize Trips** (⬡ *Box 1108, Belize City* ☎ *223/0376* ⊕ *www. belize-trips.com).* **Cave-Tubing in Belize** (☎ *605/1573* ⊕ *www.cave-tubing.com).* **Discovery Expeditions** (✉ *5916 Manatee Dr., Buttonwood Bay* ☎ *223/0748* ⊕ *www.discoverybelize.com).* **Gray Line** (✉ *71 N. Front St., Belize City* ☎ *223/6025* ⊕ *www.graylinebelize.com).* **Maya Travel Services** (✉ *42 Cleghorn St., Belize City* ☎ *223/1623* ⊕ *www.mayatravelservices.com).* **S&L Travel and Tours** (✉ *91 N. Front St.* ☎ *227/7593* ⊕ *www.sltravelbelize.com).*

VISITOR INFORMATION

The Belize Tourism Board, in new quarters at the New Horizons Building at Mile 3½, Northern Highway, is open Monday–Thursday 8–5, Friday 8–4:30.

Contacts **Belize Tourism Board** (✉ *Lower Flat, New Horizon Investment Bldg., Mile 3½, Northern Hwy., Box 325, Belize City* ☎ *223/1913 or 800/624–0686* ⊕ *www.travelbelize.org).*

The Cayes & Atolls

WORD OF MOUTH

"We just returned from a 10-day trip to Belize and we stayed in Ambergris Caye. Just about any place you go around there has fabulous snorkeling. You can book your trips when you get there, so don't fret. It is all very laid back. Try to get on with a smaller organization or individual so you don't end up on a boat with 10 other people who have never snorkeled before in their lives."

—JanieC

By Lan Sluder   **IMAGINE HEADING BACK TO SHORE** after a day of snorkeling, the white prow of your boat pointing up toward the billowing clouds, the sky's base darkening to deep lilac, spray from the green water pouring over you like warm rain. To the left, San Pedro's pastel buildings huddle among the palm trees like a detail from a Paul Klee canvas. To the right, the surf breaks in a white seam along the reef.

You can experience such adventures off the coast of Belize, where more than 400 cayes (pronounced "keys," as in the Florida Keys) dot the Caribbean Sea like punctuation marks in a long, liquid sentence. Most cayes lie inside the Barrier Reef, which allowed them to develop undisturbed by tides and winds that would otherwise have swept them away. The vast majority are uninhabited but for pelicans, brown- and red-footed boobies, and some creatures curiously named wish-willies (a kind of iguana). Island names are evocative and often humorous: there are Wee Wee Caye, Laughing Bird Caye, and—why ask why?—Bread and Butter Caye. Names can suggest the company you should expect: Mosquito Caye, Sandfly Caye, and Crawl Caye, which is supposedly infested with boa constrictors. Several, like Cockney Range or Baker's Rendezvous, simply express the whimsy or nostalgia of early British settlers.

Farther out to sea, between 30 mi and 60 mi (48 km and 96 km) off the coast, are the atolls, which are impossibly beautiful when viewed from the air. At their center the water is mint green: the white sandy bottom reflects the light upward and is flecked with patches of mangrove and rust-color sediment. Around the atoll's fringe the surf breaks in a white circle before the color changes abruptly to ultramarine as the water plunges to 3,000 feet.

ORIENTATION & PLANNING

ORIENTATION

Island hopping between Ambergris Caye, Caye Caulker, and Belize City is simple, though getting to other cayes can be more complicated. Caye Caulker Water Taxi Association water taxis—fast, open boats that hold 30 to 50 passengers—regularly connect Ambergris Caye and Caye Caulker, and on trips to and from Belize City, also stop on demand at Caye Chapel and St. George's Caye. Other than that, you're generally left to your own devices to find transportation between islands. You can charter a small boat with driver—typically BZ$400 and up a day—or negotiate a one-way or round-trip price. Remember that distances between islands in Belize often are substantial. For example, it's more than 50 mi (82 km) from San Pedro, Ambergris Caye, to the southern tip of Turneffe Atoll. Even at a rapid 20 mph clip, that's 2½ hours one way. You'll have little luck renting a powerboat on your own, as boat owners are reluctant to risk their crafts in the hands of someone without local knowledge of Belize's tricky waters. Plus, new laws require that even if you own your own boat, you need to obtain a Belize captain's license before you can take it out in Belize waters.

TOP REASONS TO GO

SCUBA DIVING

Dive destinations are often divided into reefs and atolls. Most reef diving is done on Belize's northern section, particularly off Ambergris Caye, but head to the atolls for some of the world's greatest diving opportunities. One caveat: the atolls and remote cayes, usually with just one or two small lodges, are far removed from the usual resort amenities such as shops and restaurants.

NO SHOES, NO SHIRT, NO PROBLEM

Unlike some parts of the mainland, the cayes are all about relaxing. "Go Slow" street signs dot the sandy roads, and you spend a lot of time lazing in hammocks or sipping beer in a beachside palapa alongside vacationing Belizeans.

SNORKELING

You don't have to don scuba gear to enjoy the colorful fish and psychedelic vistas under the surface of the sea. Some of the best snorkeling in the Caribbean is off the coast of Belize. This is one of the few places in the world where you can swim with (harmless) sharks and stingrays. Jump in a boat for a short ride out to the reef or to patch coral—it all makes the experience that much more exciting.

GOOD EATS

Because they attract so many free-spending tourists, Ambergris Caye and Caye Caulker have more restaurants than anywhere else in Belize, and some of the best, too. If you love to eat—especially fresh seafood—go to the islands.

BEACHES

While not your typical wide, sandy spreads, they're still classic postcard material, with windswept cocopalms facing expanses of turquoise, green, and purple waters. Some of the best beaches are on small, remote cayes, like South Water. In any case, you'll usually have a front-row seat, because most beach hotels in all price ranges are actually right on the beach.

If you're diving or snorkeling, a speedboat will take you to your destination. Power generally comes from two hefty outboards mounted on the back, and with the throttle open it's an exhilarating ride. Sit in the middle if you don't want to get splashed.

Once on the islands, you'll generally get around by golf cart, bike, or on foot. Ambergris Caye is the only island where you'll see cars and trucks, but you can only rent a golf cart or a bike on this or any other island. Around San Pedro, taxis are usually minivans, though some hotels will transport you in a jumbo golf cart. When you're going to remote areas of North Ambergris, the resort at which you're staying will often provide transportation via water taxi or a boat. On Caye Caulker, the only taxis are golf carts.

PLANNING

WHEN TO GO

Island weather tends to be a little different from that on the mainland. Although weather varies depending on the island's location (those in the far south get more rain than those in the north), the cayes are generally drier than the mainland. Storm squalls come up suddenly, but just as quickly they're gone, leaving sunny skies behind. Keep in mind that if you see rain in the forecast for Belize City, this doesn't necessarily mean it'll be wet in San Pedro.

HEALTH & SAFETY

Visiting Ambergris Caye is like a vacation in Florida—you'll face few health concerns worse than sunburn. San Pedro's water, from a treated municipal water supply, is safe to drink. More remote resorts on the north end of the island have reverse osmosis systems. On Caye Caulker, the water, usually from brackish shallow wells, often smells of sulfur. To be safe, drink only bottled water. On other remote cayes, the water usually comes from cisterns. Stick to the bottled stuff, unless you're assured the water is potable. At times, the sand flies on Caye Caulker and some remote cayes can be irksome—apply baby oil or another oily lotion liberally to your feet and ankles to keep them at bay. Insect repellent with at least 30% DEET helps ward off mosquitoes.

In terms of crime risk, the cayes are among the safest areas of Belize. However, petty thefts—and sometimes worse—do happen. With almost 20,000 people living on Ambergris Caye now, including many itinerant construction workers, the island has the same crime problems, including rapes and murders, as any area of similar population. There are drugs, including crack cocaine, on both Caye Caulker and Ambergris Caye. Ignore any offers to buy drugs.

RESTAURANTS & CUISINE

Ambergris Caye has the biggest selection of restaurants of any destination in Belize, and among them are some of the country's best. They range from simple beach barbecue joints to upscale, sophisticated eateries, where, especially if you eat lobster, you can easily spend BZ$100 a person, or more, including a drink or two. You have a wide choice of kinds of food on Ambergris, too: seafood, of course, but also steak, pizza, sushi, tapas, Chinese, Thai, Mexican, and French.

Caye Caulker has several small bistros where fish arrives at your table fresh from the ocean, and sometimes you find yourself eating with your feet in the sand. On other islands, you're usually limited to eating at your dive lodge or resort.

Many restaurants have sea views. Some are in thatch palapas, and others are in concrete or wood buildings that have windows open to catch the breeze. On Caulker and Ambergris cayes you won't have a problem finding places serving late-night snacks or breakfast in the morning, including the traditional Belizean breakfast of fruit, fry jacks, eggs (from brown eggs only), and delicious Belizean bacon or sausage, washed down with good Guatemalan coffee and fresh-squeezed OJ. On remote cayes and the atolls, you'll probably be at the mercy of your hotel's meal schedule, with specified hours for each meal.

ABOUT THE HOTELS

The more budget-oriented cayes, such as Tobacco and Caulker, have mostly small hotels and simple cabins, usually built of wood and typically without any amenities beyond a fan or two. Caye Caulker, for example, currently has only two hotels with swimming pools. At the other end, notably on Ambergris Caye, are deluxe condotels (condo developments where individual owners rent their units on a daily basis through a management company) and an increasing number of vacation villas, usually rented by the week. Some of these are extremely upscale, with 5,000-plus square feet of luxury and the latest toys, whirlpools, plasma TVs, DVD players, and custom kitchens. Nearly all the hotels on Ambergris Caye have air-conditioning, and a majority also have swimming pools. Air-conditioning is also available at nearly all the remote caye lodges, except at the very low end.

Regardless of which caye you're staying on, lodgings have several things in common: they're small (often just five or six rooms), low-rise, and almost always on the water.

One lodging category, sadly, is becoming an endangered species: the thatch cabaña or thatch hut. Why are there so few of these traditional island lodgings still around? They're easy targets for tropical storms and hurricanes; the thatch is expensive to maintain; and they're havens for creepie crawlies.

Off-season (typically just after Easter to around Thanksgiving), most island hotels, except some budget hotels, reduce rates by around 30% to 40%.

WHAT IT COSTS IN BELIZE DOLLARS				
¢	$	$$	$$$	$$$$
RESTAU-RANTS	under BZ$8	BZ$8–BZ$15	BZ$15–BZ$25	BZ$25–BZ$50	over BZ$50
HOTELS	under BZ$100	BZ$100–BZ$200	BZ$200–BZ$300	BZ$300–BZ$500	over BZ$500

Restaurant prices are per person for a main course at dinner. Hotel prices are for two people in a standard double room, including tax and service.

ABOUT THE WATER ACTIVITIES

The cayes are all about diving, snorkeling, fishing, sea kayaking, windsurfing, sailing, and even parasailing. Diving and snorkeling are excellent on the Barrier Reef and truly world-class around the atolls. There's great fishing, whether for bonefish, tarpon, or permit on the flats, or snapper, grouper or barracuda near the reef, or sailfish, marlin, tuna, and other big fish in the blue water outside the reef. Caye Caulker is known for its excellent windsurfing, especially in spring, and the Belize cayes are famous for kayaking. Boating and sailing are good in the protected waters inside the reef. Beach swimming, however, is only fair in many areas because of the shallow waters, mucky bottoms, and large

GREAT ITINERARIES

It's difficult to recommend itineraries on the cayes, because what you do and where you go depends greatly on the island where you're staying. If you're on a remote caye or atoll, your activities and itineraries are defined partly by your interests (whether it's diving, fishing, or just lazing in a hammock), and by the lodge's daily schedule (or lack of one). Your basic itinerary might go a little like this: dive, eat, sleep, and dive.

On the other hand, if you're on Ambergris Caye or Caye Caulker, you can set your itinerary around a wide choice of daily island activities, day trips to the mainland, snorkeling or diving on the Barrier Reef, and day trips to the atolls.

IF YOU HAVE 5 DAYS ON AMBERGRIS CAYE OR CAYE CAULKER

Spend your first full day getting to know the island. On Ambergris Caye, rent a golf cart or bike and explore the north and south ends of the caye. Have a beach picnic or enjoy one of the many good restaurants. If you're on Caulker, which is much smaller, you can explore on foot, or, if you prefer, on a bike or in a golf cart. On your second day on either caye, take a boat trip to Hol Chan Marine Reserve and Shark-Ray Alley for snorkeling, and spend the rest of the day on the beach or just hanging out in San Pedro town or Caulker village. On your third day, take a full-day dive or snorkel trip to Lighthouse Reef, with stops at the Blue Hole and Half Moon Caye. If you're not planning to spend a few days on the mainland this trip, take a tour to the Lamanai Mayan ruins, which includes an exciting boat ride up

the New River, on your fourth day; or, for some pampering, take one of the combined day trips to Maruba Spa and the Altun Ha Mayan site. If you do plan a mainland stay, then use Day 4 to try windsurfing on Caye Caulker, parasailing on Ambergris Caye, golfing on Caye Chapel, bonefishing in the flats, or sea or lagoon kayaking. On your final day, take a relaxing daylong catamaran snorkeling trip with a beach barbecue.

IF YOU HAVE 5 DAYS ON A REMOTE CAYE OR ATOLL

On arrival, take off your shoes, take a deep breath, grab a cold drink, and relax. This is what the islands are all about, with the cooling trade winds in your hair and no decisions to make except whether you want the grilled fish or the lobster for dinner. If you're on a dive package, you typically do two to three dives a day, weather permitting. On a fishing package, you'll be out on the flats or the reef all day every day. If you're not tied to a package, get up early and watch the sun rise on your first full day. Then spend the day exploring the island: go swimming, spend some time beachcombing, or snorkel off the shore. On your second day, take a dive or snorkel trip to the nearest atoll. On the third day, hire a guide and try your hand at fishing for bonefish or permit on the flats. On your fourth day, take a catamaran sail along the Barrier Reef, with stops for snorkeling and a barbecue on a deserted beach. On your final day, go kayaking around the island and relax on the beach.

amounts of sea grass near shore. Still, most resorts have a swimming area off a pier or on a part of a sandy beach where they've cleared the sea grass. The Caribbean here is usually crystal clear and around 80°F.

THE CAYES

ST. GEORGE'S CAYE

9 mi (15 km) northeast of Belize City.

Just a stone's throw from Belize City, this small caye is steeped in history. The state of Belize had its origins here, as St. George's Caye held the original British settlement's first capital. In 1798 the island was the site of a decisive battle with the Spanish. Islanders had only one sloop, while the Spanish had 31 ships. Their knowledge of the sea, however, helped them to defeat the invaders in two hours.

Getting to St. George's Caye couldn't be easier, as the boat trip from Belize City takes little more than 20 minutes. Affluent Belize City residents weekend in their private cottages here. Although St. George's Caye has great places to dive, many serious scuba enthusiasts choose to head out to the more pristine atolls.

WHERE TO STAY

$$$$ St. George's Caye Resort. In colonial days this long-established resort was a British favorite because of its proximity to Belize City. Today some divers favor the Canadian-owned resort for its casual style and good diving program. You have a choice of rooms in the main building (starting at BZ$860 double, in-season, including meals, water sports but not diving, and airport transfers) or thatch cottages partly over the water. A three-bedroom villa (BZ$7,085 per night for up to six persons) can accommodate families. Electricity comes from the lodge's own windmills, and the shower water is heated by the sun. The restaurant serves homemade bread and soups and grilled snapper or grouper, and coffee is delivered to your door in the morning. **Pros:** Comfortable, historical setting, good diving. **Cons:** Don't expect anything but water sports. ⊠*St. George's Caye* ☎*800/813–8498* ⊕*www.gooddiving.com* ⌨*8 rooms, 6 cabañas, 1 3-bedroom villa* ⚫*In-room: no phone, no TV. In-hotel: restaurant, bar, beachfront, diving, water sports, public Internet, no elevator, airport shuttle (boat)* ▭*AE, MC, V* ⦿*AI.*

AMBERGRIS CAYE & SAN PEDRO

35 mi (56 km) northeast of Belize City.

At 25 mi (40 km) long and 4½ mi (7 km) wide, Ambergris is the queen of the cayes. On early maps it was often referred to as Costa de Ambar, or the Amber Coast, a name supposedly derived from the blackish substance secreted by sperm whales—ambergris—that washes up on the beaches. Here the reef is just a few hundred yards from shore, making access to dive sites extremely easy: the journey by boat takes as little as

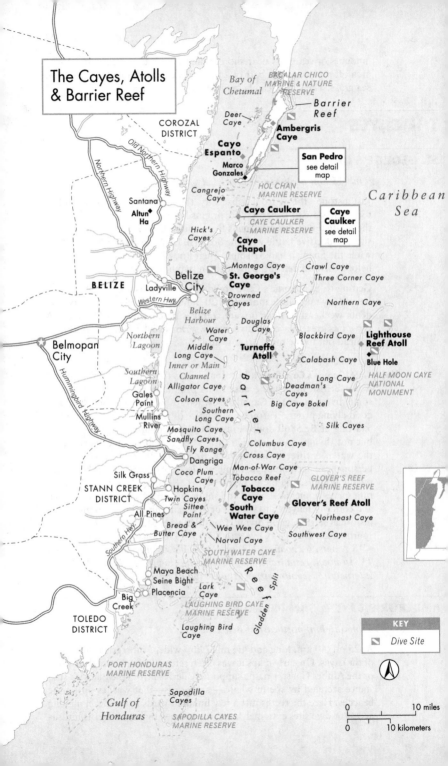

The Cayes, Atolls & Barrier Reef

Bay of Chetumal

BACALAR CHICO
MARINE & NATURE
RESERVE

Barrier Reef

COROZAL DISTRICT

Deer Caye

Ambergris Caye

Cayo Espanto

Marco Gonzales

San Pedro
see detail map

HOL CHAN
MARINE RESERVE

Cangrejo Caye

Caribbean Sea

Santana

Altun Ha

Hick's Cayes

Caye Caulker

CAYE CAULKER
MARINE RESERVE

Caye Caulker
see detail map

Caye Chapel

Montego Caye

St. George's Caye

Crawl Caye

Three Corner Caye

Belize City

Ladyville

Drowned Cayes

Northern Caye

Western Hwy.

BELIZE

Belize Harbour

Douglas Caye

Blackbird Caye

Lighthouse Reef Atoll

Northern Lagoon

Belmopan City

Water Caye

Turneffe Atoll

Blue Hole

Middle Long Caye

Calabash Caye

HALF MOON CAYE
NATIONAL MONUMENT

Inner or Main Channel

Southern Lagoon

Alligator Caye

Long Caye

Colson Cayes

Deadman's Cayes

Gales Point

Southern Long Caye

Big Caye Bokel

Silk Cayes

Mullins River

Mosquito Caye

Sandfly Cayes

Fly Range

Columbus Caye

Dangriga

Cross Caye

Coco Plum Caye

Man-of-War Caye

Tobacco Reef

GLOVER'S REEF
MARINE RESERVE

Silk Grass

STANN CREEK DISTRICT

Hopkins

Twin Cayes

Tobacco Caye

Sittee Point

South Water Caye

Glover's Reef Atoll

All Pines

Bread & Butter Caye

Wee Wee Caye

Northeast Caye

Norval Caye

Southwest Caye

SOUTH WATER CAYE
MARINE RESERVE

Maya Beach

Seine Bight

Lark Caye

Placencia

Big Creek

LAUGHING BIRD CAYE
MARINE RESERVE

Gladden Split

TOLEDO DISTRICT

Laughing Bird Caye

Reef

Barrier

PORT HONDURAS
MARINE RESERVE

Sapodilla Cayes

Gulf of Honduras

SAPODILLA CAYES
MARINE RESERVE

Northern Highway

Old Northern Highway

Hummingbird Highway

Southern Hwy.

KEY

⬊ *Dive Site*

0		10 miles
0		10 kilometers

HISTORY

Because of their strategic locations on trade routes between the Yucatán in the north and Honduras in the south, the Northern Cayes, especially Ambergris Caye and Caye Caulker, were long occupied by the Maya. Then, as now, the reef and its abundance of fish provided a valuable source of seafood.

The origin of Belize's atolls remains a mystery, but evidence suggests they grew from the bottom up, as vast pagodas of coral accumulated over millions of years. The Maya were perhaps the first humans to discover the atolls, but by the time the first Spanish explorers arrived in 1508, the Mayan civilization had already mysteriously collapsed and few remained on the islands.

In the 17th century, English pirates used the atolls as a hideout, plotting their attacks on unwary ships. The most famous battle in Belize history happened on September 10, 1798, when a ragtag band of buccaneers defeated a Spanish armada at the Battle of St. George's Caye.

The economy on the islands has ebbed and flowed, as pirates were replaced by wealthy plantation owners, who were eventually usurped by lobster fisherman. The atolls' first hotel opened in 1965 and soon began attracting divers from around the world. Today, tourism is by far the top industry.

10 minutes. Coast and coral are farther apart as you head south, which means a greater dependence on weather. Because Ambergris Caye was the first to cater to those hoping to witness Belize's undersea world, it's generally superior in the number of dive shops, experience of dive masters, and range of equipment and facilities it offers. San Pedro even has Belize's only hyperbaric chamber and an on-site doctor to tend to divers with the bends. Most dive shops are attached to hotels, where the quality of dive masters, equipment, and facilities can vary considerably.

WATER ACTIVITIES & TOURS

SCUBA DIVING & SNORKELING

Dives off Ambergris are usually single tank at depths of 50 feet–80 feet, allowing about 35 minutes of bottom time. Most companies offer two single-tank dives per day, one in the morning and one in the afternoon. Snorkeling generally costs BZ$60–BZ$80 per person for two or three hours or BZ$100–BZ$200 for a day trip, including lunch. In addition, if you go to Hol Chan Marine Reserve there's a BZ$20 park fee, but this fee is often included in the quoted rate. Diving trips run BZ$80–BZ$90 for a single-tank dive, BZ$130–BZ$150 for a double-tank dive, BZ$90–BZ$110 for a one-tank night dive, and BZ$400–BZ$500 for day trips with three dives to Turneffe Atoll or Lighthouse Reef. A snorkel trip to the Blue Hole is around BZ$370. In most but not all cases, these prices include the 10% GST that replaced the sales tax in mid-2006.

Fodor'sChoice ★ The reef's focal point for diving and snorkeling near Ambergris Caye is the **Hol Chan Marine Reserve** (Maya for "little channel"), 4 mi (6 km) from San Pedro at the southern tip of Ambergris. It's a 20-minute boat ride from the island. Hol Chan is a break in the reef about 100 feet wide and 20 feet–35 feet deep, through which tremendous volumes of water pass with the tides.

The 3-square-mi (8-square-km) park has a miniature Blue Hole, a 12-foot-deep cave whose entrance often attracts the fairy basslet, an iridescent purple-and-yellow fish frequently seen here. The reserve is also home to a large moray eel population.

Varying in depth from 50 feet to 100 feet, Hol Chan's canyons lie between buttresses of coral running perpendicular to the reef, separated by white, sandy channels. You may find tunnel-like passageways from one canyon to the next, and not knowing what's in the next "valley" as you come over the hill can be pretty exciting.

Because fishing is off-limits here, divers can see abundant marine life, including spotted eagle rays. There are throngs of squirrelfish, butterfly fish, parrot fish, and queen angelfish, as well as Nassau groupers, barracuda, and large shoals of yellowtail snappers. Altogether, more than 160 species of fish have been identified in the marine reserve, along with 40 species of coral, and 5 kinds of sponges. Hawksbill, loggerhead, and green turtles have also been found here, along with spotted and common dolphins and West Indian manatees.

Shark-Ray Alley is a sandbar within Hol Chan where you can snorkel alongside nurse sharks and stingrays (which gather here to be fed) and even larger numbers of day-trippers from San Pedro and from cruise ships. Sliding into the water is a small feat of personal bravery—the sight of sharks and rays brushing past is spectacular yet daunting. A night dive here is a special treat: bioluminescence causes the water to light up, and many nocturnal animals emerge, such as octopus and spider crab. Because of the strong current you'll need above-average swimming skills, especially at night. ⊠ *Southern tip of Ambergris Caye* ⌨ *BZ$20 marine reserve fee.*

The **Belize Barrier Reef,** the longest barrier reef in either the Western or Northern hemispheres, is off the eastern shore of Ambergris Caye. From the island, you see the coral reef as an almost unbroken chain of white surf. Inside the reef, the water is clear and shallow, and the reef itself is a beautiful living wall formed by billions of small coral polyps. Just outside the reef, the seabed drops sharply, and from a distance the water looks dark blue or purple. ⊠ *½ mi (1 km) east of Ambergris Caye.*

Development on Ambergris continues relentlessly, but the far north of the island remains pristine, or close to it. At the top of the caye, butting up against Mexico, **Bacalar Chico Marine & Nature Reserve** spans 41 square mi (105 square km) of land, reef, and sea. Here you may cross paths with whitetail deer, ocelots, saltwater crocodiles, and, according to some reports, pumas and jaguars. There are excellent diving, snorkeling, and fishing opportunities, especially off Rocky Point, and a small visitor center to get you oriented. You'll need a boat and a guide to take you here. An all-day snorkel trip to Bacalar Chico costs around BZ$170. ⊠*North end of Ambergris Caye* ☞*BZ$10.*

Amigos del Mar (⊠*Off Barrier Reef Dr. near Mayan Princess Hotel* ☏*226/2706* ⊕*amigosdive.com*) is perhaps the island's most consistently recommended dive operation. It offers a range of local dives as well as trips to Turneffe Atoll and Lighthouse Reef in a fast 48-foot dive boat. **Bottom Time Dive Spot** (⊠*Barrier Reef Dr. at Holiday Hotel, San Pedro* ☏*226/2634* ⊕*www.sanpedroholiday.com/dive.html*) offers a range of local dive and snorkel trips.

Ecologic Divers (⊠*Beachfront, on pier at north end of San Pedro* ☏*226/4118* ⊕*www.ecologicdivers.com*) is a new addition to the dive scene on the island, but already the shop has won a good reputation for safety and service. Operated by Elmer "Patojo" Paz, who has nearly 20 years of diving experience, **Patojo's Scuba Center** (⊠*At Tides Hotel at the north end of San Pedro* ☏*226/3202* ⊕*www.ambergriscaye.com/ tides/dive.html*) is a small dive shop with a good reputation. **ProTech Dive Centre** (⊠*Spindrift Hotel* ☏*226/3008* ⊕*www.protechdive.com*) has three dive boats, the largest a 38-foot diesel-powered boat with rear ladder, and first-class dive equipment.

Many dive shops and resorts have diving courses. A half-day basic familiarization course or "resort course" costs around BZ$300–BZ$325. A four-day PADI open-water certification course costs BZ$800–BZ$1,000. One popular variant is a referral course, where the academic and pool training is done at home, but not the required dives. The cost for two days is about BZ$600. Prices for dive courses vary a little from island to island, generally being a little less expensive on Caye Caulker. However, even prices on Ambergris Caye, which tends to have higher costs for most activities, are a little lower than on the mainland.

If you're staying on Ambergris Caye, Glover's Reef is out of the question for a day trip by boat. Even with perfect weather—which it often isn't in winter—a trip to Lighthouse Reef takes between two and three hours. Turneffe is more accessible, though it's still a long and costly day trip, and you're unlikely to reach the atoll's southern tip, which has the best diving.

If you want to hit the best dive spots in Belize and dive a lot—five or six dives a day—live-aboard dive boats may be your best bet. Live-aboards concentrate on dives around Belize's three atolls—Lighthouse, Turneffe, and Glover's—with most dives at Lighthouse and Turneffe. The boats depart from Belize City.

Expect to pay about BZ$3,000–BZ$5,800 for six days of diving. That price includes all dives, meals, airport transfers, and stateroom accommodations on the dive boat. It usually doesn't include airfare to Belize, overnight stays at a hotel before or after the dive trip, tips, alcoholic beverages, equipment rentals, Nitrox, marine park fees, port charges, and incidentals.

HOW TO CHOOSE A DIVE MASTER

Most dive masters in Belize are former anglers who began diving on the side and ended up doing it full time. The best have an intimate knowledge of the reef and a superb eye for coral and marine life.

When choosing a dive master or dive shop, first check the Web. Participants on forums and newsgroups such as ⊕ www.ambergriscaye.com and ⊕ www.gocayecaulker.com field many questions on diving and dive shops in Belize. On islands where there are multiple dive shops, spend some time talking to dive masters to see which ones make you feel most comfortable. Find out about their backgrounds and experience, as well as the actual crew that would be going out with you. Are they dive masters, instructors, or just crew? Get a sense of how the dive master feels about reef and sea life conservation.

Besides questions about costs and equipment, ask:

■ How many people, maximum, go out on your dive trips?

■ Is there a minimum number of divers before you'll make the trip?

■ What's the ratio of divers to dive staff?

■ What dive sites are your favorites, and why?

■ What kind of boat do you have, and how long does it take to get where we're going?

■ Who is actually in the water with the divers?

■ What kind of safety and communications equipment is on the boat?

■ What's the procedure for cancellation in case of bad weather?

■ How do you decide if you're going out or not?

■ If you're not comfortable with the answers, or if the dive shop just doesn't pass your sniff test, move on.

The itinerary of the *Belize Aggressor III* (☎ 985/305–2628 or 800/348–2628 ⊕ www.aggressor.com) has passengers embarking in Belize City, at the Radisson Fort George, on a Saturday and spending time until the next Friday at Turneffe and Lighthouse atolls, with as many as five or six dives each day. This orderly operation is run by a khaki-clad crew of five, who can accommodate up to 18 passengers. It uses a 110-foot luxury cruiser, refitted in 2007, powered by twin 500-horsepower engines and equipped with ultramodern communication systems. There's a hot tub and sundeck. Staterooms are spacious double-berth cabins brightened with sky-blue fabrics, lightwood trim, and multiple windows instead of small portholes. All have private baths, TVs, and DVDs, plus individual climate controls.

Peter Hughes Diving (☎ 305/669–9391 or 800/932–6237 ⊕ www.peterhughes.com) runs trips on the 138-foot *Sun Dancer II*, which can hold up to 20 passengers in 10 staterooms. It departs from the Radisson Fort George Hotel dock in Belize City on Saturday afternoon and moors at either Turneffe or Lighthouse Atoll. For the next six days, divers explore these two atolls, diving as many as five times a day. The ship moves two or three times a day.

SAILING

Belize will probably never rival the British Virgin Islands for sailing. The shallow water kicks up a lot of chop, and hidden coral heads and tidal currents are dangerous for even those familiar with the area. When you charter a boat you have to stay inside the Barrier Reef, but there's a lot of beautiful territory to explore.

LESSONS &
EQUIPMENT

TMM Belize (✉*Coconut Dr., San Pedro* ☎*226/3026 or 800/633–0155* ⊕*www.sailtmm.com*), which has a small fleet of catamarans (35–45 feet), has weeklong bareboat and captained charters out of San Pedro. It has another base in Placencia. Rates vary, depending on boat type and time of year, but range from BZ$5,200 to more than BZ$16,000 a week, not including provisions, cruising fee (BZ$30 per person), and incidentals. Skippers and cooks are each an additional BZ$200 per day. Split among three to eight people, the prices are competitive with hotel rates.

Discover Cruises (✉*San Pedro* ☎*226/2965* ⊕*www.traveltourbelize. com*) has trips on a catamaran, with snorkeling and a stop either at Caye Caulker or a small island for a beach barbecue. The boat leaves at 9 AM and returns at 4 PM. Cost is BZ$150–BZ$170. Private and group charters are also available.

El Gato (✉*San Pedro* ☎*226/2264* ⊕*www.ambergriscaye.com/elgato*) has day cruises to Caye Caulker, with two stops for snorkeling, for BZ$100.

Winnie Estelle (✉*San Pedro* ☎*226/2394* ⊕*www.ambergriscaye.com/ winnieestelle/*) is a 66-foot Chesapeake Bay trawler built in 1920 and restored during the 1980s. It is a large vessel, able to carry up to 40 passengers, making charter day trips to Caye Caulker and to snorkeling areas (BZ$1,320 for up to 12 people, additional persons BZ$110 per person). Longer trips also are available.

FISHING

Although southern Belize, especially Placencia, is the main sportfishing center in Belize, Ambergris Caye also has good opportunities for flats, reef, and deep-sea fishing. Expect to pay about BZ$450–BZ$600 for one or two people for a day of flats fishing for bonefish, permit, or tarpon, including a guide and a boat. Reef fishing for snapper, grouper, barracuda, and other reef fish costs around BZ$450–BZ$500 a day, including a guide and a powerboat. Deep-sea fishing outside the reef for billfish, sailfish, wahoo, and tuna runs around BZ$1,200–BZ$1,400 a day, depending on the number in your party and the size of the boat. **El Pescador** (☎*226/2398 or 800/242–2017* ⊕*www.elpescador.com*) is an upscale fishing lodge on North Ambergris. It offers fishing packages including room, meals, boat, and guide, starting at BZ$2,600 per person, double occupancy, for three nights.

For fishing that's easier on the pocketbook, you can fish for snapper, barracuda, and other fish from piers and docks on the island. No license is required. Buy bait, hooks, and tackle at small fishing tackle shacks on the beachfront in San Pedro. You can also wade out in the flats near shore on North Ambergris, just north of the river channel, and try your luck with bonefish. Keep an eye out for the occasional crocodile, and you'll have to dodge construction work on new condos going up in this area. You'll catch more with a guide and boat, but fishing on your own is inexpensive fun.

FISHING
GUIDES
George Bradley (⊠ *Back St., San Pedro* ☎226/2179 ✐*roxsam@btl. net*) specializes in fly-fishing for bonefish. **Pete Graniel** (⊠ *San Pedro* ☎226/2584) has a 30-foot boat that's good for trolling. **Fishing San Pedro** (⊠ *CocoNet Internet Café, San Pedro* ☎607/9967 ⊕*www.fishingsanpedro.com*) is a fishing-guide service run by Steve DeMaio that works with about a half-dozen guides on the island.

PARASAILING

Parasailing is terrific around Ambergris Caye. As you soar over the vodka-clear waters, suspended from a parachute and pulled by a speedboat, you can see rays, sharks, and other sea life.

Fido's Parasail Fun Sports (⊠ *Beachfront at Fido's on Barrier Reef Dr., San Pedro* ☎226/3513) has parasailing setups for one, two, or three persons. Singles pay BZ$140, doubles BZ$240, and triples BZ$330.

WINDSURFING & KITESURFING

Caye Caulker is better known as a windsurfing destination, perhaps because it attracts a younger crowd than Ambergris Caye, but the winds are equally good and consistent off Ambergris Caye. February through July sees the windiest conditions, with winds 12 to 20 knots most days. Kitesurfing, combining a windsurfing-type board pulled by a large kite, is also available on Ambergris Caye.

Sailsports Belize (⊠ *San Pedro* ☎226/4488 ⊕*www.sailsportsbelize. com*) offers windsurfing instruction at BZ$90 an hour, with equipment rental at BZ$42–BZ$54 an hour, BZ$144–BZ$164 a day, or BZ$460–BZ$550 a week. Five hours of intensive kitesurfing instruction cost BZ$660, and your initial kite-board rental, with an instructor on hand to assist, is BZ$132 for two hours. After that, kitesurfing equipment rentals are BZ$60 for a half day and BZ$90 for a full day. All rates include tax.

JET SKIS

Karibbean Water Sports (⊠ *South Beach Marina, San Pedro* ☎226/3205 ⊕*http://www.karibbeanwatersports.com*) has Yamaha Wave Runners for rent for BZ$220 an hour.

EXPLORING AMBERGRIS CAYE & SAN PEDRO

A few years ago, when you flew into the caye's main town, San Pedro, your plane's wingtips would have nearly brushed the laundry hanging in people's backyards. And once you landed, you could walk from one end of town to the other in 10 minutes. Today you need a bike just to get from one end of the airstrip to the other. Every year there are more cars, more souvenir shops, and more tourists. Ambergris will never be like Cancún, but it's the most developed—some would say overdeveloped—of the cayes. Although hard-packed sand streets are giving way to the concrete cobblestones of Barrier Reef and Coconut drives, which were paved in 2007, the most common forms of transportation remain golf cart, bike, and foot.

At its core, the town remains mostly unchanged: a couple of rows of brightly painted wooden houses flanked by the ocean on one side and the lagoon on the other. Old men lean over their balconies in the evenings to watch the world go by, and many people stroll down the roads barefoot. Stores and restaurants still have names like Lily's, Celi's, or Lee's. With an island population of nearly 20,000, San Pedro remains a small, friendly, and prosperous town. It has one of the country's highest literacy rates and an admirable level of awareness about the reef's fragility.

WHERE TO STAY & EAT

One of your biggest decisions in Ambergris Caye will be choosing a place to stay. There are three basic options: in or near the town of San Pedro, in the South Beach or South End area beyond town, or on North Ambergris, beyond the river channel. Access to restaurants, bars, and other activities is easiest in and around San Pedro. Accommodations in town are generally simple and reasonably priced (BZ$30–BZ$300), but rooms on the main streets can be noisy, not so much from cars as from late-night revelers.

For silence and sand, head out of town for resort-style accommodations. To get more privacy, consider the South End. Though it, too, is developing rapidly, it's still less hectic than in town, and it's only a golf cart or taxi ride away.

If you really want to get away, choose the more remote North Ambergris, which is reached mainly by water taxi. A new bridge across the river channel, which opened in early 2006, is already bringing more development to the north. The idea is that only golf carts, bikes, and pedestrians are permitted to cross the toll bridge (though some worry that eventually cars and trucks will also be allowed to use it).

With the exception of a few budget places, nearly all of the resorts on the island are on the sea. Most are small, under 20 or 30 rooms, and nearly all are four stories or less in height. Many are managed by the owners. The newer resorts and hotels are on North Ambergris Caye, of which the farthest-north resort, Tranquility Bay, is about 12 mi (20 km) north of San Pedro, or on the South End, where the most distant resorts are around 3 mi (5 km) south of town.

During the off-season (May–November), lodging properties often have walk-in rates that are up to a third less than advertised rates. But you'll usually have to ask for them, as otherwise you'll pay the regular rate.

CONDOTELS Besides full-service hotels and resorts, the island has condotels, which are individually owned condos managed by an on-site management company. The condo units usually are offered on a nightly basis, like a hotel, and in most cases the properties have full kitchens and most of the amenities of a regular hotel, except perhaps a restaurant.

VACATION HOMES Ambergris Caye has dozens of homes that can be rented on a weekly basis. These range from simple two-bedroom cottages that go for BZ$1,000–BZ$2,000 a week to luxurious four- or five-bedroom villas, which might rent for BZ$5,000–BZ$10,000 or more weekly. In most cases credit cards are not accepted. **Caye Management** (☏226/3077 ⊕ *www.cayemanagement.com*) is the island's oldest and largest rental management company.

Fairly new to the island are clusters of upscale homes or villas that are offered for weekly, and sometimes nightly, rental. These luxury homes, often with 4,000–5,000 square feet of space or more, typically have a shared pool and other resortlike amenities. Although they usually have no restaurant, they may offer food service prepared by a chef and delivered to the guests in the homes.

TIME-SHARES Time-shares have been on the island for years. Captain Morgan's is one of the most aggressive of the time-shares, with sales hustlers in golf carts prowling the beaches seeking would-be buyers. New to the island are upscale "fractional ownership" or "residential club" resorts, which sell longer-term memberships and rights to use the property, typically for two, four, or six months a year. One of these, Sueño del Mar, opened on North Ambergris in 2006.

RESTAURANTS Ambergris Caye has the largest and most diverse selection of restaurants in the country. Here you can buy cheap tacos or grilled chicken from a street vendor, eat barbecued fish on the beach, or, at the other end, dine on ceviche, lobster, and steak at upscale eateries. Even the most upmarket spots have a casual atmosphere, some with sand floors and screenless windows open to catch the breezes from the sea.

The largest concentration of restaurants is in town, but many, including some of the best on the island, are opening on the South End and on North Ambergris.

SAN PEDRO TOWN

$$-$$$$ ✕ **Elvi's Kitchen.** Initially, Elvi Staines sold burgers from the window of her house in 1974. Soon she added a few tables on the sand under a flamboyant tree. A quarter century later the sandy floor is still here, and the tree remains (though now lifeless and cut back to fit inside the roof), but everything else is changed. Enter through massive mahogany doors and you'll be tended to by a staff of a couple dozen. The burgers are still good, but for dinner Elvi's now specializes in upmarket dishes such as shrimp in watermelon sauce (BZ$36) or crab claws with garlic

Restaurants ▼

Blue Water Grill	4
Caliente	6
Cocina Caramba	2
DandE's Frozen Custard	1
Elvi's Kitchen	3
Estel's Dine By the Sea	7
Fido's Courtyard	8
Wild Mango's	5

Hotels ▼

Caye Casa	1
Cayo Espanto	8
Mayan Princess	4
The Phoenix	3
Ruby's	6
San Pedro Holiday Hotel	5
SunBreeze Hotel	7
The Tides Beach Resort	2

butter (BZ$75). For dessert, don't pass on the coconut pie. ⊠*Pescador Dr. near Ambergris St.* ☎226/2176 ⊟*AE, MC, V* ☉*Closed Sun.*

$$-$$$ ✕**Blue Water Grill.** Close to the beach and perpetually busy, this restau-
★   rant's seats are on a raised, covered deck with views of the Barrier Reef a few hundred yards away. The emphasis here is on seafood, and it's consistently well prepared, but there are wood-fired pizza and pastas, and Tuesday and Thursday are sushi nights. Owners Kelly McDermott and Chris Aycock run a tight ship, and by island standards the service is top-notch. The crispy coconut shrimp appetizers are our favorites. ⊠*Beachfront at SunBreeze Beach Hotel* ☎226/3347 ⊟*AE, MC, V.*

$$-$$$ ✕**Caliente.** Come here for a seat where you can catch sea breezes, and dig into spicy Mexican dishes with a Caribbean twist, such as margarita shrimp or *caracol al mojo de ajo* (grilled conch with garlic sauce). The local expat community often congregates here for lunch and a few piña coladas. Caliente Norte, a North Ambergris

> ### WORD OF MOUTH
>
> For lunch, the Blue Water Grill at the Sunbreeze Hotel is very good and the location can't be beat.
>
> –RBCal
>
> The Blue Water is a wonderful place to eat lunch or dinner. If you like seafood, try the seafood pasta. It is so good!
>
> –Linda137

branch of the restaurant, is at Essene Way. ⊠*Beachfront, Barrier Reef Dr. in Spindrift Hotel* ☎226/2170 ⊟*MC, V* ⊘*Closed Mon.*

$-$$$ ✕**Cocina Caramba.** You'll quickly sense the frenetic energy of this noisy and often packed restaurant operated by Rene Reyes, who worked in restaurants in Miami and San Pedro before opening his own spot. There's nothing very fancy on the menu here—just basics like grilled snapper (BZ$15), fried shrimp, pork chops, and Mexican fajitas and burritos—but everything is well prepared, and the service is snappy and enthusiastic. ⊠*Pescador Dr.* ☎603/1652 ⊟*MC, V* ⊘*Closed Wed.*

$-$$$ ✕**Fido's Courtyard.** Sooner or later you're sure to end up at Fido's (pronounced Fee-dough's), sipping something cold and contemplating the sea views, under what the owners claim is the largest thatch palapa in Belize. If not the largest, it may at least be the tallest. This casual restaurant and bar is one of San Pedro's most popular places, serving burgers, fish-and-chips, and pizza. Upstairs is the Rice 'n Roll sushi bar. Fido's is open every day for lunch and dinner, and most nights, depending on the season, there's live music. A southern outpost of Fido's opened in 2006 at the Royal Caribbean resort. ⊠*Beachfront, Barrier Reef Dr., just north of Catholic church* ☎226/3176 ⊟*MC, V.*

$-$$$ ✕**Wild Mango's.** Noted local chef Amy Knox moved here from Victoria
★   House and quickly made Wild Mango's one of the top dining choices on the island. Many of the dishes have a Mexican base but with Knox's sophisticated twist. She calls her cooking "New Wave Latin," Caribbean food infused with spicy Latin flavors from Cuba, Argentina, and Mexico. It's good enough to have earned her Belize Chef of the Year honors twice. Try the pulled pork taquitos, or the huge fish burritos (enough for two). Seating is beach casual, with stools at tables on a covered, open-air veranda. ⊠*Beachfront, at south end of Barrier Reef Dr.* ☎226/2859 ⊟*MC, V.*

$-$$ ✕**Estel's Dine by the Sea.** This is San Pedro's best place for a hearty American-style breakfast of bacon, fried potatoes, fry jacks, and freshly squeezed juice. Later in the day you can order burgers, Mexican meals, and excellent seafood dishes. The little white-and-aqua building is on the beach, as you might infer from the sandy floor and porthole-shaped windows. There's a terrace outside where you can sit under a thatch umbrella and watch pelicans. ⊠*Beachfront, Barrier Reef Dr.* ☎226/2019 ⊟*No credit cards.*

¢-$ ✕**DandE's Frozen Custard.** Dan and Eileen (DandE, get it?) Jamison, who used to run the local weekly paper, the *San Pedro Sun,* opened this custard and sorbet shop in 2005. For something with an island flavor, try the mango sorbet or the soursop frozen custard. ⊠*Pescador Dr. next to Cocina Caramba* ☎608/9100 ⊟*No credit cards* ⊘*Closed Wed.*

$$$$ ⊡**The Phoenix.** Bold geometric forms and massive concrete walls with deeply recessed windows mark this new luxury beachfront condominium resort, designed by architect Gui Trotti, who also designed part of NASA's space station. The Phoenix is at the north end of town, on the former site of a nun's retreat; at this writing it was partially complete, with its remaining units set to open in 2008. **Pros:** Deluxe, beautifully designed condo apartments. **Cons:** In-town location. ⊠*Beachfront, Barrier Reef Dr.* ⊕*www.ambergriscaye.com/phoenix* ⊸32 2-bedroom *apartments* &In-room: kitchen, Wi-Fi. In-hotel: restaurant, bar, 2 pools, beachfront, Wi-Fi, no elevator, airport shuttle ⊟MC, V.

$$$ 🏨 **Caye Casa.** Novelist and long-time Belize resident Julie Babcock built three new beachfront condos, which opened in 2007, to go with her two small casitas, at the north end of town. The small complex was designed to have a colonial atmosphere—with thatched roofs on the porches, wooden shutters, and traditional hardwood railings—but built to modern architectural standards. The great rooms in the condo units have cathedral ceilings, track lighting, and tile floors. There's a small pool and a new pier. **Pros:** Pleasant, well-designed small condo colony, quiet, beachfront spot. **Cons:** A few management wrinkles still need to be worked out. ⊠*Boca del Rio Dr., beachfront, at north end of town* ☎226/2880 ⊕*www.cayecasa.com* ➾*2 3-bedroom units, 1 2-bedroom, 2 casitas* &In-room: kitchen, Wi-Fi. In-hotel: Beachfront, pool, no elevator, laundry facilities ⊟MC, V.

$$$ 🏨 **Mayan Princess.** Sitting pretty in the middle of town, this pink three-story condo hotel has rattan furniture covered with pastel-color fabrics. Sliding doors open onto verandas, where you can eat meals prepared in your well-equipped kitchenette. There's no pool; guests do have access to the pool at San Pedro Fitness Center, but it's not nearby. All units have lovely sea views. In the low season—and sometimes even the high season—room prices drop significantly. It doesn't hurt to ask for a deal when making reservations. **Pros:** Central location, pleasant one-bedroom efficiencies with sea views, near good dive shop. **Cons:** No swimming pool on-site, beach area has heavy boat and pedestrian traffic. ⊠*Beachfront, Barrier Reef Dr.* ☎226/2778 or 800/850–4101 ⊕*www. mayanprincesshotel.com* ➾*23 apartments* &In-room: kitchenettes. In-hotel: beachfront, public Internet, no elevator ⊟AE, MC, V.

$$$ 🏨 **SunBreeze Hotel.** A midsize resort across from the airstrip at the town's busy southern edge (but there's no issue with aircraft noise), the SunBreeze has large rooms that surround a U-shaped, plant-filled courtyard. Five deluxe rooms (BZ$428 double including tax and service) have whirlpool baths; all are equipped for guests with disabilities, a rarity in Belize. The hotel was upgraded and renovated in 2004–05. There's a small beach area (with a seawall, though), and a shaded pool next to the Blue Water Grill. Also under the same ownership is the former AquaMarina Suites, at the north end of town, now called Sun-Breeze Suites. **Pros:** Comfortable, motel-like lodging, rooms are handicap-accessible, excellent restaurant on-site. **Cons:** Not much of a beach here. ⊠*Coconut Dr. across from Tropic Air* ☎226/2191, 800/688–0191 in U.S. and Canada ⊕*www.sunbreeze.net* ➾*42 rooms* &In-room: refrigerator (some). In-hotel: restaurant, bar, pool, beachfront, no elevator, laundry service, no-smoking rooms ⊟AE, MC, V.

$$ 🏨 **San Pedro Holiday Hotel.** Trimmed in cheery pink-and-white colors, this spic-and-span quartet of colonial-style houses is in the center of San Pedro. Though much has changed now, it opened in 1965 as the first hotel on the island. All rooms have polished wood floors, and many have views of the in-town beach. Celi's Restaurant has casual beachfront dining. **Pros:** Central location, affordable clean rooms. **Cons:** No pool, in-town beach isn't good for swimming. ⊠*Beachfront, Barrier Reef Dr.*

☎226/2014 ⊕*www.sanpedroholi-day.com* ⇱*16 rooms, 1 apartment* ⌂*In-room: no phone, refrigerator (some), no TV (some). In-hotel: restaurant, bar, beachfront, diving, water sports, no elevator, laundry service* ▤*AE, MC, V.*

$$ 🖼**The Tides Beach Resort.** If diving is your reason for being, and you don't want to spend a ton of money, you couldn't do better than this hotel, owned by Patojo Paz, one of the island's most experienced dive masters, and his wife. The three-story wood-frame structure recalls a time before everyone built with reinforced concrete. Top picks here are the second- and third-floor oceanfront rooms, which have bal-

WORD OF MOUTH

We stayed at The Tides hotel and it has its own dive shop, Patajo's. We did most of our tours through them. It is a small family-run place. Very friendly, clean, and close to the town. It isn't a big glitzy place, so you feel more connected with the locals. Everyone else there loved it and would definitely go back. On our last night there the owners, Sabrina and Patajo, treated some of the guests to a free BBQ'd meal.

—JanieC

conies overlooking the beach. The hotel is north of town, but you can walk along the beach to San Pedro's bars and restaurants. This is one of the island's better values, with beachfront rooms BZ$273 in season, including tax and a full breakfast. **Pros:** All rooms face the sea, respected dive shop on-site, good value. **Cons:** Rooms aren't overly large. ⊠*Beachfront, Boca del Rio Dr., north of town* ☎226/2283 ⊕*www.ambergriscaye.com/tides* ⇱*12 rooms* ⌂*In-room: no phone, refrigerator, no TV (some). In-hotel: bar, pool, beachfront, diving, no elevator, laundry service, airport shuttle* ▤*MC, V* ⦿*BP.*

¢–$ 🖼**Ruby's.** No wonder budget-minded travelers flock to this clean, simple hotel on the beach: air-conditioned rooms with private baths and balconies facing the ocean go for BZ$100, while the original rooms with fans, facing the street, are only BZ$70 for a double. Try the breakfast burritos at the hotel's little restaurant, Ruby's Café, which opens by 6 am for the fishing and diving crowd. **Pros:** Best budget accommodations in town. **Cons:** Bring earplugs as it can be noisy. ⊠*Beachfront, south end of Barrier Reef Dr. at Tarpon St.* ☎226/2063 ⊕*www. ambergriscaye.com/rubys* ⇱*23 rooms, 21 with bath* ⌂*In-room: no a/c (some), no phone, no TV. In-hotel: restaurant, beachfront, no elevator* ▤*MC, V.*

NORTH OF SAN PEDRO

Unless you are staying near one of the North Ambergris restaurants listed below, you'll want to take a water taxi or the Island Ferry to these restaurants, especially after dark. There are no cabs on the north end of the island; the golf cart path is bumpy and buggy at best and sometimes impassable after rains.

$$$$ ✕**Capricorn.** After a brief downturn in quality, Capricorn has regained ★ its sea legs and once again is one of the most consistently excellent and certainly one of the most popular restaurants on the island. If there's a weakness, it is that the chef stays with proven winners, such as filet mignon and grilled lobster (BZ$75) and rarely opts for innovation. The seaside setting is romantic. Reservations essential. Although the focus here has always been on the restaurant, there are three cute little cabañas. ⊠ *3 mi (5 km) north of San Pedro* ☎ *226/2809* ⊟ *AE, MC, V* ⊙ *Closed Wed.*

$$$$ ✕ **Rojo Lounge.** With a chef who was formerly a punk rock record pro-
Fodor$Choice   ducer, this is the hippest restaurant and bar on the cayes. Rojo Lounge,
★   in a sultry open-air palapa on a beautiful beach, is definitely red hot. Lunch offers a selection of sophisticated snacks like chili-dusted cold shrimp, grilled lobster salad, and conch pizza, from BZ$24 to BZ$50. Dinner is romantic and delicious, with surprising combinations such as chorizo shiitake and lobster pot stickers with mango starfruit ponzu (BZ$54) and guava-glazed baby back ribs (BZ$64). The bar serves killer frozen mojitos. Reservations essential. ⊠ *Beachfront, North Ambergris, 5 mi (8 km) north of town* ☎ *226/4012* ⊟ *AE, MC, V* ⊙ *Tues.–Sun. noon–10:30 PM.*

$$$–$$$$ ✕ **Rendezvous Restaurant & Winery.** Belize's only Thai–French restaurant
★   combines local seafood with Thai spices and presentation methods. The menu changes frequently. Our favories include pad thai (BZ$36) and spider crabs served with a hot Singapore sauce or chilled with a dill yogurt sauce (BZ$58). Try not to miss the chocolate truffle cake with Belizean *wongla* (sesame seed) candy (BZ$14). The owners, Glen and Colleen Schwenginger, who have lived and worked in Thailand and Singapore, also produce and bottle their own wines using imported grape concentrate. It's not bad. There's a new beach bar underneath the restaurant and a small butterfly farm, Butterfly Jungle, out back (BZ$20 Daily 10–5). ⊠ *4 mi (7 km) north of San Pedro* ☎ *226/3426* ⊟ *AE, MC, V.*

$$$$ ▦ **Mata Chica.** Casitas in shades of mango, banana, and blueberry offset by brilliant white sand give this resort a Gauguin-like quality. Inside, the fabric, artwork, and tiles echo the outdoor colors. New manage-ment is bringing much-needed new energy and improvements to the property, such as renovations of the cabañas and the addition of a swimming pool. For extra space, choose a two-bedroom villa or the 5,000-square-foot "Beach Mansion." Delectable though pricey seafood is served at Mambo, and one of the best restaurants in Belize, Rojo Lounge, is next door. There's a swimming pool. **Pros:** Charming col-lection of casitas on the beach, friendly staff, postcard-pretty beach. **Cons:** Smallish pool, restaurant and bar prices are steep. ⊠ *5 mi (8 km) north of San Pedro* ☎ *220/5010* ⊕ *www.matachica.com* ⟿ *12 casitas, 2 2-bedroom villas, 1 beach house* ⌂ *In-room: no phone, no TV. In-hotel: restaurant, bar, pool, spa, beachfront, water sports, no elevator, laundry service, public Internet, public Wi-Fi, airport shuttle (boat), no kids under 10* ⊟ *AE, MC, V.*

$$$$ ▦ **Azul Resort.** This resort has only two beach villas, but what beach
Fodor$Choice   houses they are! The two-level, 3,000 square feet, two-bedroom villas on
★   10 private acres of beachfront have an open floor plan, 20-foot ceilings, and beams of mylady wood. Custom kitchens have Viking appliances, and the stunning cabinets and most of the furniture are made of Belize's unique ziricote wood. Each villa has a 50-inch plasma flat-screen TV

and a Bose home-theater system. On the rooftop, you can laze in the hot tub or sunbathe in delicious privacy. There's a gorgeous circular infinity pool, and the hip Rojo Lounge is next door. The BZ$3,990 (double) or BZ$4,790 (for two couples) daily rate includes fabulous meals and drinks. If money isn't an object, the resort offers a plan that lets you fly to Belize City on a private jet and then transfer to Azul by helicopter. **Pros:** Amazing private beachfront villas with every luxury, fabulous food, five-star service. **Cons:** You'll spend a small fortune. ⊠*North Ambergris, 5 mi (8 km) north of San Pedro* ☎226/4012 ⊕*www.azulbelize.com* ⤳*2 beach houses* ⌂*In-room: kitchen, DVD. In-hotel: restaurant, room service, bar, pool, beachfront, water sports, no elevator, public Wi-Fi, helipad, airport shuttle (boat)* ▭*MC, V* ⦿*AI.*

$$$$ ⊞**Grand Caribe Suites and Residences.** Set in an arc on a 5-acre beachfront site, Grand Caribe's 74 luxury condos, in eight three-story, red-tiled-roof clusters, face the sea and a 500-foot stretch of sandy beach. Grand Caribe opened in 2008. The one, two- and three-bedroom suites have Brazilian floor tiles, kitchens with granite countertops and mahogany countertops, and high-quality furnishings. An unusual feature is the long, curving pier with berths for a number of boats. **Pros:** New luxury condos, all with views of the sea, short bike or golf cart ride to restaurants and to town. **Cons:** Final phases of project not set for completion until late 2008 or early 2009. ⊠*Tres Cocos area of North Ambergris, 1 mi (2 km) north of town* ☎226/4726 ⊕*www.grandcaribe.com* ⤳*74 condominium suites* ⌂*In-room: kitchen, Wi-Fi. In-hotel: bar, 3 pools, beachfront, diving, water sports, no elevator, airport shuttle (boat)* ▭*AE, MC, V.*

$$$$ ⊞**Portofino.** Even if you're not a newlywed, try the honeymoon suite at this tranquil North Ambergris resort, operated by a Belgian couple. Inside a thatch cabaña, the 800-square-foot suite has terrific sea views and a private whirlpool. The other cabañas, recently upgraded, have four-poster bamboo beds draped with linen mosquito nets (although mosquitoes are only occasionally a problem). "Tree house" suites are perched on wooden stilts above the sand, and a recently added house has suites on two levels. A circular swimming pool, which opened in 2008, has a footprint patterned after the Petronas Towers in Kuala Lumpur, Malaysia. Le Bistro restaurant serves seafood with Caribbean influences. **Pros:** Attractive small beachfront resort, gorgeous new pool. **Cons:** Restaurant isn't quite up to standards of top eateries on the island. ⊠*6 mi (10 km) north of San Pedro* ☎220/5096 ⊕*www.portofinobelize.com* ⤳ *8 rooms, 4 suites, 2 villa suites. In-room: no phone, no TV (some), kitchen (some), DVD (some), Wi-Fi. In-hotel: restaurant, room service, bar, pool, beachfront, water sports, no elevator, public Wi-Fi, laundry service* ▭*AE, MC, V* ⦿*CP.*

$$$$ ⊞**Blue Reef Island Resort.** Luxury in a remote setting is what you get at
★ this new resort located about 8 mi (13 km) north of town. All of the one- and two-bedroom condo suites were designed so as to enjoy views of either the sea or the infinity pool, or both. The condos, which sell for a cool half a million U.S., have 10-foot ceilings and granite floors. Still, you *are* really away from things here, about a 30-minute boat ride or a more than one-hour golf cart ride from town, so you can't

expect to easily pop out for a quick meal or shopping. **Pros:** Beautiful rooms, quiet far north location. **Cons:** Pesky mosquitoes at times, remote setting means it's not for those who want to try a different restaurant every night. ⊠*North Ambergris, 8 mi (13 km) north of San Pedro* ☎*866/825–8500* ⊕*www.bluereefresort.com* ⌕*23 units* ⌂*In-room: kitchen, DVD, no phone (guests are provided with cell phones). In-hotel: restaurant, bar, beachfront, pool, gym, water sports, no elevator, public Internet, laundry, airport shuttle (boat)* ▤*AE, MC, V.*

$$$$ **La Perla del Caribe.** Nine deluxe
★ villas command the beachfront about 6 mi (10 km) north of town. Varying in size from two to five-bedrooms, most of the units are named after precious jewels, such as Sapphire, Opal, and Emerald. The architecture is inspired by Mexican, Moroccan, and Mayan traditions. Villas are enhanced by distinctive touches such as mahogany floors, custom-made furniture, and gourmet kitchens. **Pros:** Very upscale villas with every amenity, lovely beach. **Cons:** Expensive, somewhat remote. ⊠*North Ambergris, 6 mi (10 km) north of San Pedro* ☎*220/5733* ⊕*www.laperlabelize. com* ⌕*9 beach houses* ⌂*In-room: kitchen, Wi-Fi. In-hotel: pool, beachfront, water sports, gym, no elevator, laundry, airport shuttle (boat)* ▤*MC, V.*

$$$$ **Seascape Villas.** Six posh homes spread across 4 beachfront acres are
★ among the island's most exclusive properties. Each 3,000-square-foot villa has a sunken living room, slate floors, an outdoor garden with hot tub, and unobstructed views of the sea. The villas are privately owned and available for rent when the owners aren't in residence. **Pros:** Deluxe private villas. **Cons:** No restaurant on-site. ⊠*North Ambergris, 4 mi (6 km) north of San Pedro* ☎*226/2119* ⊕*www. ambergriscaye.com/seascape/index.html* ⌕*6 beach houses* ⌂*In-room: kitchen, Wi-Fi. In-hotel: tennis court, pool, beachfront, water sports, no elevator* ▤*MC, V.*

$$$$ **Las Terrazas.** Developed by the owners of the nearby Journey's End Resort, Las Terrazas, which opened in late 2007, is a luxury condominium project with one- and two-bedroom suites available on a nightly basis. The condos have 9-foot ceilings, travertine tile floors, fully equipped kitchens with Brazilian granite countertops, and all the amenities including cable TV and high-speed Internet. An unusual, two-level pier sweeps out into the sea. When completed (set for late 2008), there will be a restaurant, fitness center, and two pools. **Pros:**

**NAVIGATING
AMBERGRIS CAYE**

Since places around here lack proper addresses, here's a list of hotels and restaurants in this area from north to south.

- Blue Reef Island Resort
- Belize Legacy Resort
- Portofino
- La Perla del Caribe
- Mata Chica/Mambo
- Azul Resort and Rojo Lounge
- Rendezvous
- Las Terrazas
- Seascape Villas
- Belizean Shores
- CapricornEl Pescador
- White Sands Cove/Belize Beach Suites
- Grand Caribe

Luxury condos on over 500 feet of beachfront. **Cons:** Project is still under development. ✉ *North Ambergris, 4 mi (62/3 km) north of town* ☎ *226/4249* ⊕ *www.lasterrazasbelize.com* ⌑ *39 condo suites (39 additional units planned)* ☖ *In-room: kitchen, Wi-Fi. In-hotel: bar, restaurant, pools, beachfront, water sports, gym, no elevator, airport shuttle (boat)* ☰ *AE, MC, V.*

$$$$ ☷ **El Pescador.** Nearly every place on Ambergris Caye claims that it offers fishing trips, but this hotel has the best angling resources. Loosely described as a "fishing camp," the main lodge is actually a handsome colonial house with comfortable, if not luxurious, rooms. Adjoining the lodge in two groupings, each with a pool, are deluxe two- and three-bedroom villas. You can enjoy a fine meal, served family style in the dining room, or a drink on the veranda. Most guests arrive as part of a fishing package; prices start at BZ$2,590 per person for three nights, including fishing guide, boat, and meals. Diving packages are also available. **Pros:** The place for salt water anglers. **Cons:** Rooms in original lodge are not overly large. ✉ *2½ mi (4 km) north of San Pedro* ☎ *226/2398* ⊕ *www.elpescador.com* ⌑ *14 rooms, 8 villas* ☖ *In-room: kitchen, no TV (some). In-hotel: restaurant, bar, pools, gym, beachfront, diving, water sports, no elevator, public Wi-Fi, laundry service, airport shuttle (boat)* ☰ *MC, V* ◉ *AI (some).*

$$$–$$$$ ☷ **Belizean Shores.** If you're looking for a peaceful setting and well-maintained rooms at reasonable prices, this condotel with one-bed-room units is a good choice. Kick back with a cool cocktail from the 24-hour pool's swim-up bar, or stay in and cook dinner in the pretty kitchens, which have mahogany cabinets, fridges, microwaves, and small butane stoves. If you want to eat out, skip the on-site restaurant—the food is so-so—and head instead for one of the nearby eateries, some of the island's best. Or, you can go into town on the resort's boat (BZ$10 per person each way). A new sister resort next door, Coco Beach, with 35 condos, mostly two-bedroom, opened in 2008. **Pros:** Comfortable condos, great pool, lots of on-site sports activities. **Cons:** Poor beach swimming, mediocre restaurant. ✉ *5 mi (8 km) north of San Pedro* ☎ *226/2355 or 800/319–9026* ⊕ *www.belizeanshores.com* ⌑ *48 suites* ☖ *In-room: kitchen, Wi-Fi. In-hotel: restaurant, bar, tennis court, pool, gym, beachfront, no elevator, public Internet, laundry service, airport shuttle (boat)* ☰ *MC, V.*

$$$–$$$$ ☷ **White Sands Cove.** This collection of one- and two-bedroom condos is housed in octagonal-shaped buildings near the beach. Suites have tile floors, cabinets and trim of cedar and mahogany, and full kitchens. There's 200 feet of beachfront, and a pier. **Pros:** Good value in a seaside condo, diving and other water sports available on-site. **Cons:** No restaurant on-site. ✉ *North Ambergris, 2½ mi (4 km) north of town* ☎ *226/3528, 888/362–2683 in U.S. and Canada* ⊕ *www.whitesand-scove.com* ⌑ *14 suites* ☖ *In-room: kitchen, Wi-Fi. In-hotel: bar, pool, beachfront, water sports, diving, bicycles, no elevator, airport shuttle (boat)* ☰ *AE, MC, V.*

$$$ ☷ **Belize Legacy Resort.** New in 2007, Belize Legacy enjoys a tranquil if somewhat remote setting over 7 mi (12 km) north of San Pedro. Its immediate neighbors are beach houses. The one- and two-bedroom condo suites, in two-story buildings with dark wood exterior walls, are well-equipped, with full kitchens, satellite TV, DVDs, and Wi-Fi. **Pros:** Comfortable condo suites at moderate rates, tranquil setting, friendly staff. **Cons:** If you don't like the on-site restaurant, the closest alternative is a 25-minute walk away; to go into town for dinner requires a BZ$50 per person round-trip water taxi ride. ⊠*North Ambergris, 7¼ mi (12 km) north of town* ☎*226/4600 or 866/210–2267* ⊕*www.belizelegacy.com* ⋑*32 condo apartments* ⌂*In-room: no phone, kitchen, DVD, Wi-Fi. In-hotel: bar, pool, beachfront, diving, water sports, bicycles, no elevator, airport shuttle (boat)* ⊟*AE, MC, V.*

SOUTH OF SAN PEDRO

$$-$$$ ✕**Casa Picasso.** Belizean artists created the Picasso-inspired art on the walls of this Spanish-influenced restaurant, which specializes in tapas like *gambas a la plancha* (sautéed shrimp with red pepper). Lasagna and other pasta dishes are also served, along with freshly baked rustic Italian bread. Martinis are a specialty. The restaurant has the island's largest selection of desserts, including a tangy key lime pie. ⊠*Sting Ray St. off Coconut Dr., on lagoon side* ☎*226/4507* ⊟*AE, MC, V.*

$$$$ ⊞**Brahma Blue.** Although in an unusual location, on the back of the lagoon, or "bayside," as it is being called, and a short boat ride away from San Pedro, Brahma Blue has ambitious plans to become one of the most upscale lodging choices on the island. As of this writing, the first phase of the development, a series of condominium units and a restaurant, was complete. The three-bedroom penthouse and two-bedroom condo suites have tile floors, granite countertops, verandas with water views, and deluxe furnishings. The Blue Lotus serves elegantly presented Indian dishes in a stunning, over-the-water setting. **Pros:** Luxury condos, striking views of San Pedro Town, restaurant with stunning top-of-water location. **Cons:** Location on the bayside requires boat access, project still under development. ⊠*On the bayside, across the lagoon from San Pedro* ☎*226/4567 or 888/699–8701* ⊕*www. brahmablue.com* ⋑*60 condo suites* ⌂*In-room: kitchen, Wi-Fi. In-hotel: restaurant, bar, pools, beachfront, spa, no elevator, laundry service, airport shuttle (boat)* ⊟*AE, MC, V.*

$$$$ ⊞**Grand Colony Villas.** These are some of the most upscale condos
★ on the island: two- and three-bedroom, two-bath apartments, ranging from 1,100 to more than 1,900 square feet, with tall ceilings, marble or hardwood floors, mahogany doors and cabinets, and luxurious furnishings. To top it all off, the beach here is as good as it gets on Ambergris Caye. **Pros:** Deluxe condo villas, beautifully finished and furnished, on good beach. **Cons:** Some units are time-shares, no restaurant on-site. ⊠*Coconut Dr., 1½ mi (3 km) south of town* ☎*226/3739* ⊕*www.grandcolonyvillas.com* ⋑*21 condo apartments* ⌂*In-room: kitchen, Wi-Fi. In-hotel: pool, beachfront, no elevator, laundry service* ⊟*AE, MC, V.*

$$$$ ⊞**Miramar Villas.** Small is beautiful, as long as it's not your hotel room. Here, at Miramar Villas, you enjoy the virtues of a small cluster of condos—10 units in a gated community that opened in late 2006—but with generous two- and three-bedroom spaces. From many rooms you'll enjoy views of the sea and the infinity-edge pool. A bi-level 2,400-

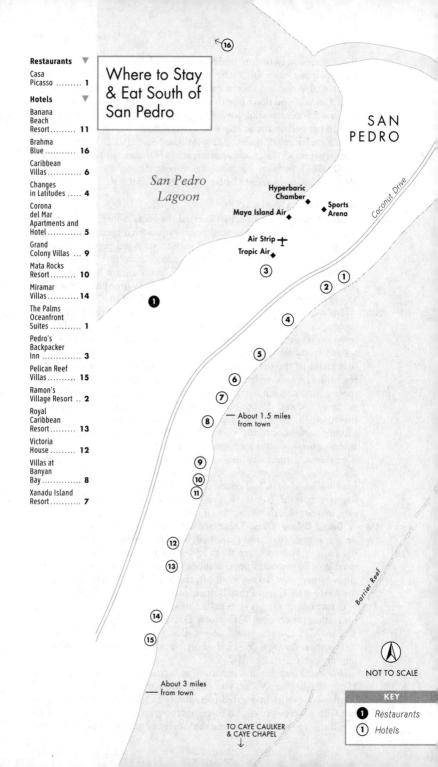

Where to Stay & Eat South of San Pedro

SAN PEDRO

San Pedro Lagoon

Coconut Drive

Hyperbaric Chamber ◆

Sports Arena ◆

Maya Island Air ◆

Air Strip ✚

Tropic Air ◆

About 1.5 miles from town

About 3 miles from town

Barrier Reef

NOT TO SCALE

TO CAYE CAULKER & CAYE CHAPEL ↓

KEY

● *Restaurants*

① *Hotels*

square foot penthouse suite has an oversize bedroom overlooking the sea, with tropical hardwood floor. There is a three-night minimum stay. **Pros:** Small upscale beachfront condo with nicely furnished two- and three-bedroom suites. **Cons:** No restaurant or bar on-site. ✉*S. Coconut Dr., 3 mi (5 km) south of San Pedro* ☎*877/288–1011* ⊕*www.miramarvillas.com* ⤳*10 units* ♿*In-room: kitchen. In-hotel: pool, beachfront, no elevator, public Wi-Fi* ▭*MC, V.*

$$$$ 🖫**Pelican Reef Villas.** Swimming in the beautiful palm-shaded pool, ★ you're enchanted by a waterfall that appears to come out of a stone cave. Unexpected touches like this are what have made Pelican Reef one of the most popular condotels on the island. It has 24 2-bedroom (BZ$872 including tax for up to four people) and 3-bedroom (BZ$1,255 for up to six) deluxe units in low-rise alabaster buildings with butter-yellow trim, about 2½ mi (4 km) south of town. Fully equipped kitchens have granite countertops and mahogany cabinets. In the bedrooms, sleigh beds have pillow-top mattresses. **Pros:** Well-run condo colony in quiet south-end location, luxurious accommodations, stunning pool, and good beach area. **Cons:** No restaurant on-site. ✉*Coconut Dr., 2½ mi (4 km) south of town* ☎*226/2352 or 281/394–3739 in the U.S.* ⊕*www.pelicanreefvillas.com* ⤳*24 condo apartments* ♿*In-room: kitchen, Wi-Fi. In-hotel: bar, pool, beachfront, water sports, no elevator, laundry service, airport shuttle* ▭*MC, V.*

$$$$ 🖫**Villas at Banyan Bay.** If you enjoy little luxuries like a whirlpool bath ★ in your room, this red tile–roofed complex about 1½ mi (2½ km) south of town will suit you splendidly. You won't feel cramped here—stylishly furnished two-bedroom condos with verandas overlooking the sea have cathedral ceilings with tropical hardwoods. The kid-friendly pool is one of the island's largest, and Mar de Tumbo tops the short list of the island's best beaches. Rico's Bar & Grill has one of the island's most beautiful seaside restaurant settings, and the food happily has improved of late, so you'll have a good dining experience, especially at breakfast or lunch, without having to leave the grounds. **Pros:** Well-maintained two-bedroom condos, ideal for families or two couples, one of island's best beaches. **Cons:** Restaurant is expensive. ✉*Coconut Dr., 1½ mi (2½ km) south of San Pedro* ☎*226/3739* ⊕*www.banyanbay. com* ⤳*42 apartments* ♿*In-room: kitchen. In-hotel: restaurant, room service, bar, pool, beachfront, diving, no elevator, laundry service, public Internet, airport shuttle* ▭*AE, MC, V.*

$$$–$$$$ 🖫**The Palms Oceanfront Suites.** Stay here for the gorgeous sea views from the oceanfront units. The one- and two-bedroom apartments are spacious, with earth-tone furnishings and kitchens, including full-size fridges. The tiny pool is in a shady spot at the back of the property and can be a little cool in winter. The Palms is at the south edge of town, a short stroll away from most of the restaurants and activities in San Pedro, five minutes from the airport (airport noise is not an issue, though), and five minutes from the largest grocery on the island. **Pros:** Comfortable beachfront apartments, convenient location near town, next to best in-town beach. **Cons:** Small, shaded pool, not as upscale as some of the island's new condo developments. ⊠*Coconut Dr.* ☎*226/3322* ⊕*www.belizepalms.com* ⊄*8 2-bedroom apartments, 5 1-bedroom apartments* ⅍*In-room: kitchen, Wi-Fi. In-hotel: pool, beachfront, water sports, no elevator* ▤*MC, V.*

$$$–$$$$ 🏨 **Ramon's Village Resort.** One of the first resorts on the cayes, Ramon's has grown into one of its largest, but still retains its thatch-and-sand atmosphere. A five-minute stroll from town, the very popular resort attracts an active crowd who take their margaritas by the pool. The beachfront units are attractive, but those in the back are dark and can be noisy, even though Ramon's has built high walls to screen off street noise. You may find room prices surprisingly high for the size and amenities, but you're paying for the terrific setting and location. The 500-foot beach is the best in town (though not the best on the island), and snorkeling is pretty good off the 420-foot pier, with its artificial reef. The hotel also manages a collection of cottages across the street called Steve and Becky's Cute Little Hotel. Skip the restaurant. **Pros:** Good in-town beach, has island atmosphere many are looking for. **Cons:** Pricey for what you get, busy location across from the airstrip, getting increasingly congested, some rooms are showing their age. ⊠*Coconut Dr.* ☎*226/2071, 800/624–4315 in U.S.* ⊕*www.ramons. com* ⊄*61 rooms, 8 cottages* ⅍*In-room: kitchen (some), refrigerator (some), no TV (some). In-hotel: restaurant, room service, bar, pool, beachfront, diving, water sports, no elevator, public Internet, laundry service* ▤*AE, MC, V.*

$$$–$$$$ 🏨 **Victoria House.** With its bougainvillea-filled gardens, this property 2½
Fodor's Choice   mi (4 km) south of San Pedro has the style and seclusion of a diplomatic
★   residence. In 2006, stunning new villas, some of the most luxurious accommodations in Belize, opened, and the casitas and other units were upgraded. Victoria House also debuted a new infinity swimming pool with a black marble waterfall. In the white colonial-style house with airy verandas and tile walkways are three ample suites with mahogany furnishings. If a suite's not your thing, you have a wide choice of other accommodations here, from motel-like rooms to a five-bedroom house. Service is always spot-on. **Pros:** Quiet and lovely grounds away from bustle of town, variety of gorgeous beachside accommodations, idyllic spot for breakfast outside overlooking the pool and beach. **Cons:** Restaurant hasn't regained eminence it had under former chef Amy Knox. ⊠*Coconut Dr., 2 mi (3 km) south of San Pedro* ☎*226/2067, 800/247–5159 in U.S.* ⊕*www.victoria-house.com* ⊄*14 rooms, 4 casitas, 3 suites, 8 villas* ⅍*In-room: no phone (some), kitchen (some), no TV (some), Wi-Fi. In-hotel: restaurant, room service, bar, pools, beachfront, diving, water sports, no elevator, laundry service, airport shuttle* ▤*AE, D, MC, V.*

$$$–$$$$ 🏨 **Xanadu Island Resort.** It's billed as the "world's first monolithic dome
★   resort," a description that might appeal only to engineers. Happily, these domes look much nicer than they sound, with thatch roofs over

2

the domes, and the result is a structure that can withstand winds up to 300 mph. There's a mélange of one-, two-, and three-bedroom units. All are attractively furnished in earth tones and have modern amenities. Palm trees surrounding the pool make it feel nicely tropical; there's also a 350-foot pier and a stretch of sand, but it has a seawall. You also get free access to bikes, canoes, and kayaks. **Pros:** Friendly management, attractive suites, tropically perfect pool. **Cons:** Seawall at beach, no restaurant or bar on-site. ⊠ *Coconut Dr., 1 mi (2 km) south of San Pedro* ☎ *226/2814* ⊕ *www.xanaduresort-belize.com* ⇨ *19 suites* ⼕ *In-room: safe, kitchen, Wi-Fi. In-hotel: pool, beachfront, water sports, bicycles, no elevator, no-smoking rooms, airport shuttle* ⊟ *AE, MC, V.*

$$$ 🏨 **Royal Caribbean Resort.** The small canary-yellow cabins lined up in tidy rows at this new resort may remind you of army barracks, except for the thatch roofs, but inside the rooms are comfortable, with tile floors, wicker furniture, and small kitchenettes. There's a pool and 400 feet of beach on 12 acres just south of Victoria House, and the price, just BZ$250 double, is right. Fido's has opened a branch at the resort. **Pros:** Good value, large pool, quiet seaside location. **Cons:** Army-barrack design, motel-like service. ⊠ *1 Seagrape St., 2¼ mi (3½ km) south of town* ☎ *226/4220* ⇨ *45 cabins* ⼕ *In-room: no a/c, no phone, kitchen. In-hotel: restaurant, pool, beachfront, no elevator, laundry service* ⊟ *AE, MC, V.*

$$–$$$ 🏨 **Banana Beach Resort.** Thanks to its friendly staff's accommodating
★ attitude and affordable rates, this resort has one of the island's highest guest occupancy rates. The original section, built around an interior courtyard, has one-bedroom suites; a newer section has regular rooms at bargain prices, plus deluxe "flex suites" that expand from one to four bedrooms, depending on your needs. The restaurant, El Divino (named after a beloved staffer who passed away), is a steak house and martini bar. **Pros:** Good value, friendly staff. **Cons:** Older rooms have somewhat dated furnishings. ⊠ *Coconut Dr., 1½ mi (2½ km) south of San Pedro* ☎ *226/3890* ⊕ *www.bananabeach.com* ⇨ *24 rooms, 45 suites* ⼕ *In-room: kitchen (some), Wi-Fi. In-hotel: restaurant, bar, 2 pools, beachfront, diving, no elevator, public Internet, laundry service, no-smoking rooms* ⊟ *AE, D, MC, V* �ⓄⅠ *CP.*

$$–$$$ 🏨 **Mata Rocks Resort.** Squeaky-clean rooms at this intimate, midlevel hotel right on the beach, about a 25-minute walk from town, have perfect sea views and breezes. Mata Rocks has the quintessential thatch tropical beach bar, and you're a short stroll away from several good restaurants. Bikes are complimentary. **Pros:** Small beachside resort, good value. **Cons:** Sometimes slow to respond to e-mails, no restaurant on-site. ⊠ *Coconut Dr., 1½ mi (3 km) south of town* ☎ *226/2336, 888/628–2757 in U.S. and Canada* ⊕ *www.matarocks. com* ⇨ *17 rooms* ⼕ *In-room: kitchen (some), refrigerator. In-hotel: bar, pool, bicycles, no elevator, public Internet, laundry service* ⊟ *AE, MC, V* ⓄⅠ *CP.*

$$ 🏨 **Changes In Latitudes.** Owners Renita and Cindy have spruced up the only true B&B on the island. The tranquil inn is near San Pedro's restaurants and bars, but isn't directly on the beach. Guests have access to the pool and pier (and free Wi-Fi) at the Belize Yacht Club resort next door. Although they're all on the small side, the rooms are clean and attractive. The three garden-side rooms get the most light. A full breakfast is served in the common room, but you can prepare your own meals. **Pros:** Helpful owners, good value, cheerful B&B atmosphere. **Cons:** Smallish rooms, not on water, close to busy street. ⊠*36 Coconut Dr., ¼ mi (½ km) south of San Pedro* ☎*226/2986 or 317/536–5160* ⊕*www.ambergriscaye.com/latitudes* ⤳*6 rooms* ⌂*In-room: no phone, no TV. In-hotel: bicycles, no elevator, laundry service* ⊟*MC, V* ⑩*BP.*

$$ ⬚**Corona del Mar Apartments and Hotel.** One of the best values on the island, Corona del Mar has lagoon-view rooms for BZ$180, and the apartment suites for BZ$300 can sleep six. Seafront units have balconies. Though there's no pool, it's right on the beach, and has the only elevator on the island. Most rooms are handicap-accessible. **Pros:** Top value, pleasant seafront rooms, friendly staff. **Cons:** No pool. ⊠*Coconut Dr., 1 mi (1½ km) south of town* ☎*226/2055* ⊕*www.ambergriscaye.com/coronadelmar/* ⤳*12 rooms, 4 suites* ⌂*In-room: kitchen (some), refrigerator (some). In-hotel: beachfront, water sports, public Wi-Fi* ⊟*AE, MC, V* ⑩*CP.*

$-$$ ⬚**Caribbean Villas.** It lacks some of the perks of newer, larger properties, such as a pool or room TVs, but Caribbean Villas, with its 2½ acres of gardens, a bird sanctuary, and quiet beachfront, is a low-key alternative to some of the glitzier developments. Choose from a small studio without air-conditioning (BZ$156 plus tax) to lofted suites for families (BZ$540). All but the studio have a sea view. The dock has a small artificial reef. Minimum stay in-season is four nights. **Pros:** Haven of quiet in developed area, good value, good beach. **Cons:** Lacks amenities such as pool, no restaurant. ⊠*Coconut Dr., 1 mi (1½ km) south of town* ☎*226/2715 or 866/522–9960 in U.S. and Canada* ⊕*www.caribbeanvillashotel.com* ⤳*5 rooms, 9 suites* ⌂*In-room: no a/c (some), no phone, kitchen (some), no TV. In-hotel: beachfront, water sports, no elevator, laundry service, public Internet, airport shuttle* ⊟*MC, V.*

¢-$ ⬚**Pedro's Backpacker Inn.** Gregarious British expat Peter Lawrence opened the island's only hostel-style accommodations in 2003. He's since added a sports bar, which has become a local expat hangout, and a bistro serving some of the best pizza in town. A single bed and shared bath in this white frame house go for as little as BZ$20 (plus tax), or you can get a double with private bath and air-conditioning for BZ$70 plus tax. Additional air-conditioned rooms are planned. **Pros:** Very good value, handy to the bar, the inimitable owner. **Cons:** Not on water, a bit of a hike to town, the inimitable owner. ⊠*Seagrape Dr. south of San Pedro* ☎*226/3825* ⊕*www.backpackersbelize.com* ⤳*20 rooms* ⌂*In-room: no a/c (some), no phone, no TV, Wi-Fi. In-hotel: restaurant, bar, no elevator, public Internet* ⊟*MC, V.*

CAYO ESPANTO

$$$$ ⬚**Cayo Espanto.** Espanto means fright in Spanish, but there's nothing
Fodor'sChoice   to be frightened of on this tiny island 3 mi (5 km) west of Ambergris
★   Caye, except possibly the wallop in your wallet if you stay here. This super-luxury resort, all there is on the island, has a staff-to-guest ratio of two to one. Each villa comes complete with a splash pool, Egyptian

2

cotton linens, and a personal houseman. Several villas have walls that literally fold back to let in the Caribbean sun. As a guest, you meet with the chef to plan your day's meals, which are delivered to your own waterside table. For all this personal care you'll pay a small fortune, up to BZ$5,692 a night, including 24% service and tax. There's a four-night minimum. Many guests arrive by helicopter; Astrum Helicopters in Belize City provides transport for BZ$2,500 for up to four persons. **Pros:** Over-the-top luxury and service. **Cons:** Island is on the back side of Ambergris Caye, not on the main Caribbean Sea. ⌂ *3 mi (5 km) west of Ambergris Caye* ✉ *Box 90, San Pedro* ☎ *221/3001, 888/666–4282 in U.S.* ⊕ *www.aprivateisland.com* ↪ *5 villas* ⚘ *In-room: refrigerator, Wi-Fi. In-hotel: room service, pools, beachfront, water sports, no elevator, laundry service, airport shuttle (boat)* ▤ *AE, MC, V* ◯|*AI.*

NIGHTLIFE San Pedro has the most active nightlife scene in Belize, but, still, don't expect Miami Beach. Beach bars abound, and you can get sloshed just walking from your South End hotel into town. A few spots have live music. Generally, the action starts late (after 10 or 11). Karaoke is big in Belize, and some bars and clubs in San Pedro have karaoke nights, which are more for locals than visitors. In late January and early February, singer Jerry Jeff Walker holds "Camp Belize," two weeklong events in San Pedro during which Walker puts on shows for his loyal fans.

BARS & CLUBS

Known for its burgers, **BC's Beach Bar** (✉ *South of SunBreeze Hotel*) is a popular oceanfront bar that hosts all-you-can-eat barbecues on Sunday afternoon. **Big Daddy's** (✉ *Barrier Reef Dr., north side of Central Park*) is the scene of much of the action in downtown San Pedro. Since it's right on the water, there's a beachside barbecue some nights. The music and real boozing don't get started until late, usually around 11.

Across the street from Big Daddy's is **Jaguar's Temple,** (✉ *Barrier Reef Dr.*) a popular San Pedro dance club.

If all you want is to enjoy a cold drink and watch sports on TV, **Pedro's Sports Bar** (✉ *Seagrape Dr.*) is your spot. It attracts a lot of island expats, and there are poker games a few nights a week.

Several popular bars are on piers out in the water, including **Wet Willy's** (✉ *At Hustler's pier*) and **Tackle Box** (✉ *At Shark's pier*). Under a giant thatch palapa, **Fido's** (✉ *Barrier Reef Dr.*) is always jumping and has live music most nights. On the odd side of the nightlife spectrum is the Chicken Drop, held on Wednesday starting around 6 PM at the **Pier Lounge** (✉ *At Spindrift Hotel, Barrier Reef Dr.*). Bet a buck on a numbered square, and if the chicken poops on your square, you win the pot of US$100.

Casino gambling is still fairly small time in San Pedro. Don't expect glitzy, Las Vegas-style action. **Casino Belize** (*Coconut Dr. at Belize Yacht Club* ☎ *226/2777*), the island's newest gaming venue, has live blackjack and poker games as well as slot machines. **Coconuts Caribbean Hotel** (*Coconut Dr., 1/3 mi (1/2 km) south of town* ☎ *226/3500*) has a small casino with slots, a sports book desk, and a few live games.

SHOPPING

Barrier Reef Drive, formerly sandy Front Street, but paved with concrete cobblestones in 2007, is San Pedro's Street of Shopping Dreams—it's lined with souvenir shops complemented by restaurants, small hotels, banks, and other anchors of tourist life on the island. Stores with more of a local appeal are on Pescador Drive (Middle Street) and Angel Coral Street (Back Street), especially at the north end of town. Barrier Reef is closed to golf carts and vehicles on weekends, starting around 6 PM Friday, and local vendors set up shop selling locally made jewelry and wood carvings (they're also out sometimes during the week in high season). Except for these items, few are made on the island. Most of the souvenir shops sell crafts from Guatemala and Mexico, along with carved wood and slate from the mainland.

Belizean hot sauces, such as Marie Sharp's and Gallon Jug's Lissette Sauce, along with local rums, make good souvenirs; they're cheaper in groceries (try Pescador Drive and Angel Coral Street) than in gift shops. To avoid worsening the plight of endangered sea life, avoid buying souvenirs made from black coral or turtle shell.

BEST SHOPS

At the long-established **Belizean Arts** (⊠ *Fido's Courtyard off Barrier Reef Dr.* ☎ *226/3019*), you'll find works by important local painters including Walter Castillo, Nelson Young, and Pen Cayetano. Also on display are handicrafts from the region, including hand-painted animal figures from Mexico, masks and fabrics from Guatemala, and brilliantly colored tropical fish made of coconut wood.

Ambar (⊠ *Fido's Courtyard off Barrier Reef Dr.* ☎ 226/3101) offers locally made jewelry of jade, silver, and gold. **Isla Bonita Designs** (⊠ *At north end of Barrier Reef Dr.* ☎ 226/4258) sells original clothing made on the island. **Orange Gift Shop** (⊠ *Coconut Dr. across from the Belize Yacht Club* ☎ 226/4066) is a higher-end gift shop, with crafts, original art, and better souvenirs. For gaudy geegaws and unabashedly touristy souvenirs, the **Toucan Gift Shops** (⊠ *Barrier Reef Dr.* ☎ 226/2431), including Toucan Too and Di Bush Toucan, all sporting the bright green, yellow, and red Toucan logo, are hard to miss.

Island Supermarket (⊠ *Coconut Dr., south of town* ☎ 226/2972) has the largest selection of groceries, liquor, and beer, along with hot sauces and other Belizean-produced items. Prices generally are 30% to 75% higher than in supermarkets in the United States, except for a few items, such as rum, produced in Belize, and Island Supermarket's prices are high even by San Pedro standards.

One of the less expensive places to buy groceries is **San Pedro Supermarket** (⊠ *Pescador Dr., at north end of town* ☎ 226/3446). They have free delivery and a 7% discount if you spend BZ$100 or more. Many local residents buy their groceries at Super Buy (⊠ *Back St.*) or Marina's Store (⊠ *Coconut Dr. about 1 mi (1½ km) south of town*), which have good prices but a small selection. **Caye Coffee** (⊠ *In San Pablo residential area south of town [follow signs]* ☎ 226/3568), the island's only coffee roaster, sells Belizean and Guatemalan coffees. **Wine De Vine**

(✉ *Vilma Linda Shopping Center across from primary school at south end of town* ☎226/3430) has a good selection of wines, many from Chile and Argentina, and imported cheeses, at prices (due to import taxes) roughly double the cost in the United States.

For those chartering a sailboat, **Lagniappe Provisioning** (⊕*www. lagniappe-belize.com* ☎226/3587) will deliver provisions to your boat for only a little more than you'd pay in a grocery.

CAYE CAULKER

5 mi (8 km) south of Ambergris Caye, 18 mi (29 km) northeast of Belize City.

A half hour away from San Pedro by water taxi and sharing essentially the same reef and sea ecosystems, Caye Caulker is very different from its big sister island, Ambergris Caye. It's smaller, with a population of around 1,200, less developed, way more relaxed, and less expensive.

Caye Caulker long has been a stop on the Central America backpacker trail, and it remains Belize's most popular budget destination. Yet, its more charming aspects are breaking through as more upscale lodgings open up in town. Flowers outnumber cars ten to one (golf carts, bicycles, and bare feet are the preferred means of transportation).

As you might guess from all the NO SHIRT, NO SHOES, NO PROBLEM signs at the bars, the living is relatively easy here. This is the kind of place where most of the listings in the telephone directory give addresses like "near football field." However, Caye Corker, as it's often called in Belize (or Cayo Hicaco in Spanish, a reference to the coco plums on the island), isn't immune to change. Many hotels have added air-conditioning, and the island now has cybercafés and several upmarket restaurants; there are even a couple of condos, with more under construction. Still, Caye Caulker remains the epitome of laid-back, and as development continues at a fevered pace on neighboring Ambergris Caye, Caulker's simpler charms exercise considerable appeal to those who seek an affordable and relaxing island experience.

Like Ambergris Caye, Caye Caulker can be used as a base to explore part of the mainland. It's only about 45 minutes by water taxi, or 15 minutes by air, to Belize City. Tours run from Caulker to the Mayan ruins at Lamanai and Altun Ha, and other tours go to the Belize Zoo and to the Caves Branch River for cave tubing.

For those used to researching and booking everything online, here's a caution about Caye Caulker: As is common with budget destinations, some of the tour and sports operators and cheaper lodging choices on Caulker don't have Web sites. In fact, some tour operators work from a spot on the beach and have only a cell phone, if that. Those that are online often have Web sites that are done on the cheap, with poor graphics and servers that are down intermittently. Consider it part of the charm of Caye Caulker.

WATER ACTIVITIES & TOURS

When you see the waves breaking on the Barrier Reef just a few hundred yards from the shore, boats full of eager snorkelers and divers, and the colorful sails of windsurfers dashing back and forth in front of the island, you know you've come to a good place for water sports and activities. You can dive, snorkel, and fish the same areas of the sea and reef as you can from San Pedro, but usually for a little less dough. One area where Caulker suffers by comparison with its neighboring island is in the quality of its beaches. Caulker's beaches, though periodically nourished by dredging to replenish the sand, are modest at best, mostly narrow ribbons of sand with shallow water near the shore and, in places, a mucky sea bottom. You can swim at "the Split," a channel cut through the island by Hurricane Hattie in 1961, at the north end of the village, or from the end of piers.

SCUBA DIVING & SNORKELING

Hol Chan Marine Reserve at the southern tip of Ambergris Caye *(see Ambergris Caye section, above)* is a popular destination for snorkel and dive trips from Caye Caulker. At Hol Chan, you can swim with nurse sharks and stingrays and see hundreds of tropical fish, some quite large due to the no-fishing restrictions in the reserve. On the way, your boat may be followed by a pod of frolicking dolphins, and you may spot sea turtles or even a manatee. Boats from Caulker also go to Lighthouse and Turneffe atolls.

The Caye Caulker Marine Reserve north and east of Caye Caulker, with its coral canyons, is a favorite of divers, especially for night dives. Caulker has its own mini version of San Pedro's Shark-Ray Alley, called Shark-Ray Village.

CHARTERS & EQUIPMENT A plethora of dive and snorkel operators offer reef tours (some of them are "cowboys"—unaffiliated and unreliable—so make sure you use a reputable company). Plan on spending about BZ$30–BZ$40 for a snorkel trip around the island or BZ$70–BZ$100 for a six-hour snorkel trip to Hol Chan Marine Reserve.

Local two-tank reef dives typically run about BZ$150, and those to Hol Chan or other nearby areas cost about BZ$160–BZ$180. Day trips to Lighthouse or Turneffe atoll, with three dives, cost around BZ$250–BZ$300. If you stop at Half Moon Caye, there's an additional BZ$80 park fee. At Hol Chan, the park fee is BZ$20, and at Caye Caulker Marine Reserve, BZ$10. These park fees, which apply for divers and snorkelers, are sometimes not included in the quoted prices for dive and snorkel trips. The 10% Goods and Services Tax (GST) instituted in mid-2006 also may—or may not—be included in the price you're quoted. Ask, to be sure.

Go out for a snorkel on a sailboat with **Raggamuffin Tours** (✉ *Front St.* ☎226/0348 ⊕*www.raggamuffintours.com*), which goes to Hol Chan for BZ$70, including the park entrance fee. **Tsunami Adventures** (✉*Front St. at Split* ☎226/0462 ⊕*www.tsunamiadventures.com*) (also known as Coral Adventures) runs full-day snorkeling trips to Hol Chan for BZ$98 including the park entrance fee and lunch. This

2

company also offers a number of other snorkel trips, including one to swim with dolphins at Spanish Lookout Caye (BZ$300) and a trip to Turneffe Atoll (BZ$135). **Carlos Tours** (⊠ *Front St.* ☎ *226/0058*) runs snorkel trips to Hol Chan Marine Reserve and elsewhere, manatee spotting trips to Swallow Caye, and full-day snorkel and sightseeing trips with several stops on the Barrier Reef, at San Pedro, and at small cayes. Prices vary according to the destination but range from around BZ$50 to $150 per person. **Anwar Tours** (⊠ *Front St.* ☎ *226/0327*) runs snorkel trips to Sargeant's Caye, with stops to see manatees at Swallow Caye and, often, lunch at St. George's Caye. Rates for this full-day trip are around BZ$120. Anwar, like other tour operators, provides various snorkel and other tour options, depending on demand. Stops and length of trips vary depending on weather and sea conditions. Established in 1978, **Belize Diving Services** (⊠ *Back St., near the football [soccer] field* ☎ *226/0143* ⊕ *www.belizedivingservice.com*) has been around long enough to know all the best spots. If you're looking for someone to take you out to the reef for diving, **Frenchie's Diving Services** (⊠ *Front St., north of public pier* ☎ *226/0234* ⊕ *www.frenchiesdiving-belize.com*) is a respected local operator.

SAILING

A few small sailboats offer sailing and snorkeling trips to nearby areas. One company, Raggamuffin Tours, also offers multiday combination sailing and camping trips to Lighthouse Atoll and to Placencia.

CHARTERS, LESSONS & EQUIPMENT

Raggamuffin Tours (⊠ *Front St.* ☎ *226/0348* ⊕ *www.raggamuffintours. com*) has day sails and sunset and moonlight sails for BZ$40–BZ$70. Longer charter trips are also available. Two-night camping and sailing trips to Lighthouse Reef are BZ$550 per person, and two-night/three-day camping and sailing trips to Placencia, with nights at Tobacco Caye and Ranguana Caye, also are BZ$550 per person. **Seahawk Sailing** (⊠ *Front St. next to Real Macaw* ☎ *607/0323* ⊕ *www.nickmela. com/seahawk*) offers snorkeling, overnight camping, and charter trips on a 30-foot sailboat.

WINDSURFING AND KITESURFING

With brisk easterly winds most of the year, Caye Caulker is one of Belize's premier centers for windsurfing. The island gets winds over 12 knots most days from November to July. The best windsurfing is in the morning and afternoon, with lulls around midday. In the late winter and spring, winds frequently hit 20 knots or more. Windsurfing and kitesurfing rental outfits quickly come and go on Caye Caulker; ask locally who is currently offering rentals and lessons.

CHARTERS, LESSONS & EQUIPMENT

Opened in 2004 by Michael Femrite, an aerospace engineer from Minnesota, **Michael's Windsurf & Water Sports** (⊠ *Beachfront, just north of main public pier* ☎ *226/0457*) has an excellent selection of long and short boards, with rental rates of BZ$40–BZ$50 an hour, BZ$90–BZ$110 for a half day, BZ$130–BZ$150 a day, and BZ$410–BZ$450 a week. Lessons are BZ$70–BZ$90. Michael's also has some kitesurfing equipment. An eight-hour, private introduction to kitesurfing course is

BZ$420. **Kitexplorer** (✉ *Beachfront* ☎ *602/9207*) offers beginning and advanced kitesurfing lessons.

FISHING

Caye Caulker was a fishing village before it was a visitor destination. From Caulker, you can fly-fish for bonefish or permit in the grass flats behind the island, troll for barracuda or grouper inside the reef, or charter a boat to take you to blue water outside the reef for deep-sea fishing. Blue marlin weighing more than 400 pounds have been caught off Caye Caulker, along with big sailfish, pompano, and kingfish. For blue-water deep-sea fishing, you'll pay BZ$500–BZ$1,200 and up for a full-day's fishing for up to four people.

For a guide and boat for flats and reef fishing, you'll pay around BZ$400–BZ$600 a day for one or two people. Bring all the fishing gear and tackle you think you'll need to Caye Caulker, as little is available on the island. If you're a do-it-yourself type, you can fish off the piers.

CHARTERS, LESSONS & EQUIPMENT **Porfilio "Piggy" Guzman** (✉ *Calle Almendro* ☎ *226/0152*) is the best-known fishing guide on the island, and he may charge a little more than others. **Raggamuffin Tours** (✉ *Front St.* ☎ *226/0348* ⊕ *www.raggamuffintours.com*) arranges full-day fishing charters with boat, guide, and spinning tackle for BZ$500, half day BZ$400. **Tsunami Adventures** (✉ *Front St. at Split* ☎ *226/0462* ⊕ *www.tsunamiadventures.com*) offers reef, deep-sea, and flats fishing trips starting at BZ$350 for a half day, including boat and guide.

MANATEE SPOTTING

Several operators do boat trips to see West Indian manatees. It's illegal in Belize to get into the water with the gentle sea cows, but some tour operators do permit it. Tours typically cost around BZ$70–BZ$80 per person. Some stop at Goff's Caye, which has excellent snorkeling.

CHARTERS, LESSONS & EQUIPMENT **Carlos Tours** (✉ *Front St.* ☎ *226/0058*), one of the most recommended tour operators on Caye Caulker, runs snorkeling trips with stops at some of the best snorkel spots near Caye Caulker, and also at Hol Chan Marine Reserve and other places, along with manatee-spotting tours. **Anwar Tours** (✉ *Front St.* ☎ *226/0327*) runs snorkel and manatee-spotting trips, and also does tours to the Altun Ha Mayan site. **Chocolate** (✉ *Front St.* ☎ *226/0151*), which pioneered manatee tours, only occasionally goes out on tours.

EXPLORING CAYE CAULKER

Caye Caulker is a fairly small island, only 5 mi (8 km) long and a little over 1 mi (2 km) wide at the widest point—most of the island is only a few hundred feet wide. The island itself is divided by "the Split," the small gulf of water separating the north area and the south area. The area north of the Split is mostly mangroves and lagoons, accessible only by boat, while the only village occupies most of the area south of the Split. From the Split to the airstrip, which is at the south end of the island, is about a mile (2 km). Directions in the village usually use the public pier or dock, where you come in on the water taxi, as the reference point. Things are either north of the pier or south of it. The village has only three main streets: Front, Middle, and Back (sometimes they're referred to as roads) running north and south; Back Street just runs on the south side of the village. All of the streets on the island are hard-packed sand. On the east side, you can also walk along the beachfront. Officially, the streets are named, from front to back, Avenida Hicaco, Avenida Langosta, and Avenida Mangle, but rarely does anyone use these names. There are more than a dozen short east–west streets, mostly unnamed.

The busiest part of the village is Front Street, especially around the area where the east–west street, officially Calle del Sol, comes from the public pier. Generally, the north end of the village bustles more than the south end, which is primarily residential. At the south end of the village, on the seafront before you get to the airstrip, is a small littoral forest with interpretive trails and a library and conference center operated by the Belize Tourism Industry Association. For tourist information, visit ⊕ *www.gocayecaulker.com*, the official site of the Caye Caulker chapter of the BTIA.

Other than a few emergency vehicles and several private cars that were recently permitted to be brought on the island, there are no cars on Caye Caulker. Most locals and visitors get around on foot, although you can rent a golf cart or bike.

North of the Split there are only a few homes, without electricity, but private land there is being sold, and more homes are planned. The Caye Caulker Forest Reserve, about 100 acres at the northern tip of the island, is a protected area consisting mostly of red, black, and white mangroves. A designated marine reserve, comprising the grassy lagoons, the Barrier Reef, and the sea out about a mile east of the reef, adjoins the forest reserve.

WHERE TO STAY & EAT

Caye Caulker has more than 40 hotels, mostly small places with just a few rooms. The older budget hotels are mostly clapboard, with fans but no air-conditioning, and usually without TV or room phones. If they're not on the water where they can catch the prevailing sea breezes, they are often burning hot during the day. Hotels built in the last decade or so are generally constructed with concrete, and an increasing number have air-conditioning. There are only three swimming pools on the island.

Once your dining choice on Caulker was fish, fish, or fish, but now you can enjoy Italian, Mexican, and Thai, as well as wonderful fresh seafood and lobster. Several restaurants serve wholesome natural foods and vegetarian dishes. Prices for meals here are generally lower than on other islands, and even a lobster dinner is usually less than BZ$40.

$$-$$$ ✕ **Don Corleone Caribbean Trattoria.** If you're tired of fried seafood and beans and rice, the authentic Italian at Don Corleone is an offer you can't refuse. On the wall is a poster of *The Godfather,* naturally, and you can get Italian wines and espresso and cappuccino. Try the pasta

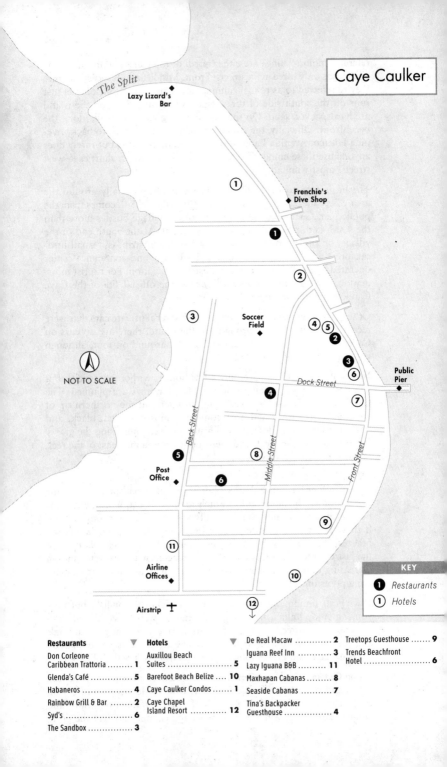

Caye Caulker

The Split

Lazy Lizard's Bar

Frenchie's Dive Shop

Soccer Field

NOT TO SCALE

Dock Street

Public Pier

Back Street

Middle Street

Front Street

Post Office

Airline Offices

Airstrip

KEY

① Restaurants

① Hotels

2

carbonara, cooked al dente as it should be, or the seafood linguine. The snapper, cooked simply in olive oil with capers (BZ$30) is excellent. ⊠ *Front St., halfway between public pier and Split, on west side of street* ☎ 226/0025 ⊟ *MC, V* ⊘ *Closed Sun.*

$-$$$ ✕**Habaneros.** On the front door is a hand-painted drawing of a habanero pepper plant, but you shouldn't feel threatened—not everything here is super spicy. When you taste the Snapper Santa Fe or the vegetable lasagna, you'll know why this is considered one of the best restaurants between San Pedro and Belize City. The specialty at lunch is "Mayan pizza," a thin-crusted pizza with a variety of topping options. ⊠ *Front St.* ☎ 226/0486 ⊟ *AE, MC, V* ⊘ *Closed Thur.*

$-$$$ ✕**Rainbow Grill & Bar.** To catch the sea breezes, the Rainbow is built out over the water. It serves some of the tastiest, freshest seafood on the islands—our favorites are the grilled or fried fish dishes. This place is always buzzing. ⊠ *On beachfront between public pier and Split* ☎ 226/0281 ⊟ *MC, V* ⊘ *Closed Mon.*

$-$$$ ✕**Syd's.** If you ask a local resident for a restaurant recommendation, chances are you'll get a vote for Syd's. It serves Belizean and Mexican favorites like beans and rice, stew chicken, *garnaches,* and tostadas (BZ$1.50), along with (in-season) lobster and conch at prices lower than you'll pay at most other eateries. If you have a choice, dine outside on the patio rather than inside. ⊠ *Middle St., south of public pier* ☎ 226/0294 ⊟ *MC, V* ⊘ *Closed Sun.*

$-$$ ✕**The Sandbox.** Whether outside under the palms or indoors under the lazily turning ceiling fans, you'll always have your feet in the sand here. Open from 7 AM to 10 PM, the Sandbox has a large menu, with tasty items such as lobster omelet with fry jacks for breakfast, lobster fritters or barbecue chicken for lunch, and red snapper for dinner. The chowders are also very good. Prices are reasonable, and portions are large. At night the bar gets lively. ⊠ *Front St. near public pier* ☎ 226/0200 ⊟ *AE, MC, V.*

¢-$ ✕**Glenda's Café.** The menu here is on a chalkboard, short and sweet, and you place your order at the window. At breakfast, when this café is most popular, you can get a hearty breakfast of eggs, bacon, beans, homemade cinnamon roll or johnnycakes and fresh orange juice for a pittance. It opens at 7:30 AM. ⊠ *Back St., north of post office* ☎ 226/0148 ⊟ *No credit cards* ⊘ *Closed Sun. No dinner.*

$$-$$$ 🏨**Iguana Reef Inn.** One of Caye Caulker's most upmarket lodgings,
★ Iguana Reef has just about everything but a concierge. The suites are colorfully furnished with handmade furniture and local artwork and have air-conditioning. Upstairs suites have vaulted ceilings with skylights. New in early 2007 is a third-story 2,000-square-foot penthouse suite with two bedrooms (BZ$763), and a swimming pool. Because the inn is on the island's lee or west side, you have the benefit of sunset views from your veranda, but you're not on the Caribbean-side beaches. **Pros:** Attractive, well-

---

WORD OF MOUTH

We liked the location of Iguana Reef: away from the main strip, but easy walking distance to everything. Caye Caulker is a very casual "barefoot" destination.–Kay5

Permanent Vacations

That well-tanned lady relaxing under a palm tree on the beach may not be a tourist after all. She could be an expatriate who decided to chuck it all and move to Belize. Thousands of Americans, Canadians, Europeans, and Asians have already done so or have bought property and plan to move later, perhaps after retirement.

Attracted by low real estate prices, a frost-free climate, and an awesome spectrum of activities, many expats are drawn to Belize, especially to Ambergris Caye, Corozal, Placencia, and the Cayo. Ambergris Caye has an idyllic Caribbean island atmosphere. Corozal Town and its environs have Belize's lowest living costs, and Mexico is right next door. The Cayo appeals to those who want land for growing fruit trees or keeping a few horses. Placencia has some of the best beaches in Belize.

With houses renting for as little as BZ$400 a month (though some in San Pedro go for 10 times that amount), and land selling at prices last seen in the United States in the 1970s, retirement dollars can stretch far here. Beachfront building lots go for as little as BZ$100,000–BZ$150,000—still pricey, but cheap in comparison to oceanfront lots in Florida or California. There are no major restrictions against foreigners owning land in Belize. Moreover, with English as an official language and English Common Law forming the basis of Belize's legal system, Belize is very accommodating to expats.

In late 2001 the government unveiled a program called the Qualified Retired Persons Incentive Program to attract retirees to Belize. In exchange for depositing BZ$4,000 a month in a Belize bank for living expenses, and proving that you have the resources to do so, anyone aged 45 and older can get official residency, along with the right to import household goods, a car, boat, and even an airplane tax-free. The application costs about BZ$2,900 and is relatively painless. After getting Qualified Retired Persons status, you have many of the rights of a Belize citizen except you can't vote or work for pay. The Belize Tourist Board (BTB) administers the program, and details are available on its Web site, ⊕ www.travelbelize.org.

Only a few hundred QRP applications have been approved to date. It's a wonder that more people haven't applied: 70 million baby boomers in the United States alone are expected to retire over the next 5 to 20 years. Many of them will be looking for alternatives to cold winters and high prices up north.

For those not quite ready to retire, it's still possible to move to Belize, although work permits are difficult to obtain, and salaries are a fraction of those in the United States, Canada, or Western Europe. The best option may be to invest in or start a business in Belize that employs Belizean workers, thus paving the way for a self-employment work permit and fast-track residency.

Of course, Belize isn't for everyone. And Belize, as seen from the perspective of a full-time resident, isn't the same as the Belize that's experienced by vacationers. Expats anywhere face culture shock, and Belize presents some special situations, including lack of high-tech medical care and a higher risk of theft and burglary than back home.

designed lodging, with pool. **Cons:** On back side of island. ✉*Near end of Middle St., next to soccer field* ☎*226/0213* ⊕*www.iguanareefinn. com* ↪*12 1-bedroom suites and 1 2-bedroom penthouse suite* ♿*In-room: safe, no phone, refrigerator, no TV. In-hotel: bar, pool, water sports, no elevator, no kids under 10* ▭*D, MC, V* ⅼⓄⅼ*CP.*

$$ 🏨**Auxillou Beach Suites.** Smack in the middle of Caulker, on the beach-front north of the public pier, is this collection of eye-catching green, coral, and blue houses. Inside, the one-bedroom suites are more toned down, with neutral-color walls, tile floors, and kitchenettes. Each unit has a deck or balcony, and you're only about 50 feet from the sea. **Pros:** Spacious beachfront rooms. **Cons:** Owner often not in residence. ✉*Front St. north of public pier* ☎*226/0370* ⊕*www.auxilloubeach suites.com* ↪*10 apartments* ♿*In-room: no phone, kitchenette, Wi-Fi. In-hotel: beachfront, no elevator* ▭*MC, V.*

$$ 🏨**Caye Caulker Condos.** If you want a full kitchen to prepare some of your own meals, these new condos are a good choice. The luxe units are done in cheerful tropical colors and have tile floors, full air-conditioning, Wi-Fi, and private verandas facing the water. Ask for a second-floor room (BZ$260, plus tax)—the view is better. Bikes are complimentary. **Pros:** Small apartments with kitchens, good location near water and most restaurants. **Cons:** Units are not particularly large. ✉*At north end of island, near Split* ☎*226/0072* ⊕*www.cayecaulker condos.com* ↪*8 apartments* ♿*In-room: safe, no phone, kitchen, Wi-Fi. In-hotel: beachfront, bicycles, no elevator* ▭*MC, V.*

$$ 🏨**Lazy Iguana B&B.** This B&B may be the tallest structure on the island. The views of the sunsets from the fourth-level rooftop terrace are ter-rific, though the hotel's location on the island's back side, away from the sea and sea breezes, means you may need to swat an occasional mosquito while you watch. The rooms are furnished with attractive wicker and tropical hardwood furniture. Feel free to make yourself at home in the common room, which has TV and Internet access—owner Mo Miller says no shoes are required. **Pros:** Laid-back, nicely furnished B&B. **Cons:** Not on sea, back-of-island location is 10-minute walk to main restaurant area. ✉*Back St., north of airstrip* ☎*226/0350* ⊕*www.lazyiguana.net* ↪*4 rooms* ♿*In-room: no phone, no TV, Wi-Fi. In-hotel: public Wi-Fi, no elevator, no kids under 10, no-smoking rooms* ▭*MC, V* ⅼⓄⅼ*CP.*

$$ 🏨**Seaside Cabañas.** If your Belizean dreams include lounging poolside, ★ Belikin in hand, get thee to Seaside, a delightful beachfront inn with one of only three swimming pools on the island. Seaside, which has three sunset orange–color thatch-roof buildings arranged in a U-shape around the pool, commands a prime location just south of the pub-lic pier. Bathrooms feel bare-bones (showers don't have curtains), but other creature comforts (air-conditioning, cable TV, and a mini-refrig-erator) make up for it. Four of the rooms (numbers 1, 2, 3, and 4) have private rooftop terraces for sunning or watching the sea—they're not much more a night and worth the extra money. The Una Mas bar serves drinks and coffee. **Pros:** Top choice on the island, pool, convenient location. **Cons:** Beach swimming in front of hotel is not good. ✉*At public pier* ☎*226/0498* ⊕*www.seasidecabanas.com* ↪*16 rooms, 1*

2-bedroom suite ♿*In-room: no phone, refrigerator. In-hotel: bar, pool, water sports, no elevator, no kids under 10* ▭*MC, V.*

$ 🖭**Barefoot Beach Belize.** Formerly the Seaview Guest House, the current owners, Kim and Susan Briggs, have turned this little seafront hotel into one of the most popular spots on Caulker. There are three rooms and a suite in a pastel blue, concrete building with pink and yellow trim and three cottages (BZ$194–BZ$316 a day). **Pros:** Choice of attractive accommodations, pier is nice spot to enjoy the water. **Cons:** Short walk from main restaurant area. ✉*Caye Caulker* ☎*226/0205* ⊕*www.barefootbeachbelize.com* ⤵*3 rooms, 1 suite, 3 cottages* ♿*In-room: refrigerator, kitchen (some), Wi-Fi. In-hotel: beachfront, water sports, no elevator, laundry services* ▭*MC, V.*

$ 🖭**De Real Macaw.** De Real Macaw represents the "new Caulker" trend in guesthouses: better service, bigger rooms, more amenities like air-conditioning and cable TV, and all at a good value. You have a choice of six rooms or two larger apartment suites. A two-bedroom "condo" with air-conditioning is BZ$284. **Pros:** Clean and well-run, good location near water and most restaurants. **Cons:** Not many frills. ✉*Front St. north of public pier* ☎*226/0459* ⊕*www.derealmacaw.biz* ⤵*6 rooms, 2 suites, 1 2-bedroom condo* ♿*In-room: no a/c (some), no phone (some), refrigerator (some), Wi-Fi. In-hotel: beachfront, no elevator, laundry service* ▭*MC, V.*

$ 🖭**Maxhapan Cabañas.** This little spot is in the center of the village and not on the water, but it makes up for it by being neat and clean, and set in a small, sandy garden. Each of the three rooms, two in a two-story cabaña and one in a one-level building, has tile floors and a veranda. The owner, Louise, is a charmer. **Pros:** Inexpensive, clean rooms. **Cons:** Not on the water. ✉*Caye Caulker* ☎*226/0118* ⤵*3 rooms* ♿*In-room: refrigerator. In-hotel: bicycles, no elevator, laundry services* ▭*MC, V.*

$ 🖭**Treetops Guesthouse.** Austrian owner Doris Creasey brings interna-
★   tional flair to this seaside guesthouse, which is so well run and such a good value that it's almost always full. One room has an East African theme, with authentic masks and spears, and another has art from Malaysia and Indonesia. Two third-floor suites, Sunset and Sunrise, have king-size beds and private balconies with views of the water. A few people rankle at the house rules and regulations enforced by the owner: rooms are cleaned at 8:30 AM, no ifs, ands, or buts; no cooking in rooms, not even hot water for coffee or tea; no outside guests; check-out required by 9:30 AM, but most find this one of the best guesthouses in Belize. **Pros:** Meticulously clean and well run, quiet location near water, excellent value. **Cons:** Some guests complain they are treated like children. ✉*Caye Caulker* ☎*226/0240* ⊕*www.treetopsbelize.com* ⤵*4 rooms, 2 with shared bath, 2 suites* ♿*In-room: no a/c (some), no phone (some), refrigerator. In-hotel: beachfront, water sports, no elevator, laundry service, no kids under 12, no-smoking rooms* ▭*MC, V.*

¢   🖭**Tina's Backpacker Guesthouse.** If you're looking for the cheapest place to stay on the island, look no further: You can have a hammock here for BZ$20 per person, plus tax. Though the two-story lodgings are very basic, you're right on the beach, and the price and location mean this place is usually packed with young people. Tina Auxillou, one of the Auxillou sisters who have many tourism-related businesses on the island, runs it. **Pros:** One of the least expensive lodging options on island, seafront location, convivial hostel atmosphere. **Cons:** Not always the cleanest spot, backpacker-level comfort. ☎226/0351 ⌂2 *rooms, 3 dorms, all with shared baths* ♿*In-room: no a/c, no phone, no TV. In-hotel: beachfront, no elevator* ⊟*MC, V.*

¢ 🔲**Trends Beachfront Hotel.** One of the first things you see when you arrive at the island's pier is this little hotel, painted tropical pink and turquoise. Thanks to its location and bright rooms, it's often booked full. TVs are available on request. **Pros:** Central location, comfortable no-frills rooms. **Cons:** Busy area can occasionally be noisy. ✉*Near Front St., at public pier* ☎226/0094 ⊕*www.trendsbze.com* ⌂6 *rooms, 1 cabaña* ♿*In-room: no a/c, no phone, refrigerator, no TV (some). In-hotel: beachfront, no elevator* ⊟*MC, V.*

$$$$ 🔲**Caye Chapel Island Resort.** Designed as a corporate retreat by the
Fodor's Choice   owner, a Kentucky coal baron, this resort now accommodates any-
★   one who's got the cash. The expansive villas, which stand at imperial attention along the seafront, are similar to what you might see in exclusive gated communities in Boca Raton, Florida. Inside you'll find every luxury—whirlpool baths, expansive wet bars, and kitchens with the latest German appliances. A dozen "budget" casitas, with single and double suites (BZ$750 including tax, service, and fees) have a price tag that's significantly less than the villas. Rates include use of a golf cart and unlimited golf. The golf course's clubhouse has a restaurant with indoor and open-air dining and stunning views of the sea. Meal plan is BZ$150 per day per person, plus 25% service, tax, and fees. **Pros:** It's like having your own private island with a golf course, stunning villas, beautiful setting. **Cons:** It's like being in a country club 24/7, very expensive. ✉*Caye Chapel* ☎226/8250 or 800/901–8938 ⊕*http://www.cayechapel.com/* ⌂8 *villas, 12 casitas* ♿*In-room: refrigerator, kitchen (some), DVD. In-hotel: restaurant, bar, golf course, tennis courts, pool, gym, beachfront, diving, no elevator, laundry service, no-smoking rooms, public Internet* ⊟*AE, D, MC, V.*

VACATION HOME RENTALS

A handful of privately owned homes are available for rent on the island, either daily or by the week. Expect to pay around BZ$80–BZ$200 a night or BZ$800–BZ$1,200 a week. In most cases, credit cards are not accepted.

GOLF GETAWAY

Not since the days of British colonialism has Belize had a real 18-hole golf course. But now Caye Chapel provides a beautiful par-72 course with challenges that include brisk prevailing winds and an occasional crocodile. If you just want to come play golf, the daily cost is BZ$400, including airfare from Belize City or San Pedro, greens fees, golf cart, and club rental. Reservations are required and must be made a week or less in advance. It is best to call the resort once you arrive in Belize. ☎226/8250 or 800/901–8938 ⊕*http://www.cayechapel.com/*

One of the larger rental agencies, **Caye Caulker Rentals** (⊠ *Front St.* ☎ *226/0485* ⊕ *www.cayecaulkerrentals.com*) has more than a dozen houses for rent, some daily from BZ$80 a night, and others, including beachfront houses, from around BZ$800 a week. Owned by Diane Auxillou Kuylen, **Diane's Beach House** (⊠ *Front St.* ☎ *226/0083* ⊕ *www.staycayecaulker.com/beachhouse.html*) has two nice suites—a one bedroom and a two bedroom—in a mango-color house with views of the sea. Rates are BZ$260–BZ$300 nightly. **Heredia's Apartments & House Rentals** (⊠ *Calley del Sol, about a block from public pier* ☎ *226/0132* ✍ *mr.heredia001@hotmail.com*) has several budget apartments and houses on the lagoon side, most under BZ$500 a week.

NIGHTLIFE

You don't come to Caye Caulker for the hot nightlife, but the island does have its share of laid-back bars.

Knock back a Belikin or two to the beat of reggae music at **I&I Reggae Bar** (⊠ *Off Front St., south of public pier, go south on Front St. to dead end, then turn right* ☎ *No phone*). Swings hang from the ceiling, replacing bar stools, in one area, and the top floor has hammocks and a thatch roof. There's really nothing else like this three-story bar in Belize. For live music, your best bet is **Oceanside** (⊠ *Front St., near public pier* ☎ *226/0233*). "Sunny place for shady people" is the slogan of the **Lazy Lizard** (⊠ *At Split* ☎ *226/0368*), but after dark there's a spotlight pointed into the water, so you can see fish, small sharks, and occasionally even a crocodile swimming around. **Herbal Tribe** (⊠ *Front St.* ☎ *226/0110*) is an open-air bar, heavy on the reggae. It also serves meals, including pizza, and there's a small art gallery.

SHOPPING

You won't find nearly as many shops here as in San Pedro, but there are a few stand-out stores to poke around for some interesting souvenirs.

Caribbean Colors (⊠ *Front St.* ☎ *226/2206*) has colorful watercolors and silk screenings by the owner, Lee Vanderwalker-Kroll, along with handmade jewelry, scarfs, and art by other artists. Also in the shop is the Coco Loco Café. **Annie's Boutique** (⊠ *North end of island near Split* ☎ *226/0151*) has some of Belize's best clothing for women and children. Here you'll find dresses and sarongs made with fabrics from Bali, unique silver jewelry, and Guatemalan bags.

Chan's (⊠ *Middle St., at corner of street coming from public pier* ☎ *226/0165*) is the largest grocery in the village. Look for Marie Sharp's here.

SOUTHERN CAYES

TOBACCO CAYE

11 mi (18 km) southeast of Dangriga.

If you don't want to pay a lot for your place in the sun, Tobacco Caye may be for you. It's a tiny island—barely 4 acres, and a walk around the entire caye takes 10 minutes—but it's right on the reef, so you can

National Symbols of Belize

National TREE: **Mahogany** (*Swietenia macrophilla*)

This prized tree has been heavily logged in Belize, and large specimens are found in only a few areas. The "big leaf" mahogany tree can grow more than 150 feet high and takes 80 years to reach maturity. The wood has a coppery red sheen, a tight, knot-free grain, and a single mature tree can be worth US$100,000 or more.

National FLOWER: **Black Orchid** (*Encyclia cochleatum*)

The name is deceiving. Only the lip of the flower is black, and the long, slender sepals and petals are yellow-green. These fragrant little flowers bloom year-round and can be found growing on trees in damp areas.

National BIRD: **Keel-Billed Toucan** (*Ramphastos solfurantus*)

Every cereal lover is familiar with this bird. The toucan, with its huge canoe-shape beak and bright yellow cheeks, can be found in open areas all over the country and loves to eat fruit.

National ANIMAL: **Baird's Tapir** (*Tapir-ello bairdii*)

Called the mountain cow by most Belizeans, the tapir is actually related to the primitive horse and rhinoceros. A beefy vegetarian, it can weigh up to 600 pounds and is often found in heavy bush, near rivers and streams.

National MOTTO: *Sub Umbra Florero*

"Under the Shade I Flourish" refers to the shade of the mahogany tree, which is on Belize's coat of arms and flag.

National DRINK: **Orange Fanta** and **Belikin Beer**

Unofficially, of course.

---

wade in and snorkel all you want. Though the snorkeling off the caye is not as good as in some other areas of Belize (some of the coral is dead and most of the fish are small), you can see spotted eagle rays, moray eels, octopuses, and other sea life. All the accommodations—Tobacco Caye Lodge, Reef's End, Lana's on the Reef, Tobacco Caye Paradise, and Gaviota Coral Reef Resort—are budget places, basically simple wood cabins, some not much larger than sheds. Since a half-dozen hotels vie for space, the islet seems even smaller than it is. Periodically the hotels get blown away by storms but are rebuilt, usually a little better than they were before.

Though some places are increasing rates, most prices remain affordably low, around BZ$80–BZ$145 a day per person, including meals. In 2007, several hotels on the island, including Tobacco Caye Lodge and Reef's End, began charging on the European Plan (EP), with meals extra. This—surprise!—generally had the effect of increasing total rates. At Reef's End, for example, a couple pays around BZ$300 for a back-packer style room and mediocre food.

A word of caution: Hotels can be very casual about reservations. After making reservations months in advance, you may arrive to find that your reservation has been lost and the hotel is fully occupied. Fortunately, it's usually easy to find a room in another hotel. Lana's on the

Reef, Gaviota Coral Reef Resort, and Tobacco Caye Paradise are the cheapest hotels, with rates starting around BZ$55 per person, including meals, but with tiny rooms and shared baths. The island has no shops, bars, or restaurants, except those at the hotels, but there is one dive shop. Boats leave from the Riverside Café in Dangriga for the 30-minute, BZ$35 trip to Tobacco Caye. Get to the Riverside by 9 AM; most boats leave around 9:30 (though at busy times such as Easter they come and go all day long). You can get information on the boats, as well as breakfast, at the Riverside Café. F See Southern Coast chapter.

Tobacco Caye is at the northern tip of the South Water Caye Marine Reserve, a 62-square-mi (160-square-km) reserve that's popular for diving and fishing and has some of the most beautiful islands in Belize. Visitors to the South Water Caye Marine Reserve pay BZ$10 a day, for up to three days, or BZ$30 a week, park fee. Rangers come around and collect it from guests at the Tobacco Caye hotels.

WHERE TO STAY

$ 🖼 **Gaviota Coral Reef Resort.** On this island, you're often locked into a meal plan at your hotel, so the quality of food matters. Here, the food, served family-style at fixed times, is very good. You'll enjoy fresh fish, beans and rice, and even salads. The clapboard rooms and cabins are tiny, but the location on the east side of the caye provides cooling breezes. At BZ$70per person, plus tax, including all meals, it's a good value. **Pros:** Friendly service, good value, good food. **Cons:** Backpacker-level accommodations. ⊠*Tobacco Caye* 🕾*509/5032* ⬤*4 rooms, 5 cabins, all with shared baths* ⬧*In-room: no a/c, no phone, no TV. In-hotel: restaurant, beachfront, water sports, no elevator* ⊟*MC, V* ⎮⊚⎮*AI.*

$ 🖼 **Tobacco Caye Lodge.** This cluster of pastel blue cabins is a few feet from the turquoise sea. There's a bit more room here for stretching out than at the island's other lodges, as the property extends from the sea on the east to the back side of the caye. A thatch-roof bar is set away from the cabins. Double rooms go for BZ$174. Meals are now extra. **Pros:** Most "upscale" of Tobacco hotels. **Cons:** Still pretty basic. ⊠*Tobacco Caye* 🕾*520/5033* ⬤*www.tclodgebelize.com* ⬤*6 cabins* ⬧*In-room: no a/c, no phone, no TV. In-hotel: restaurant, bar, beachfront, water sports, no elevator* ⊟*MC, V.*

SOUTH WATER CAYE

Fodor'sChoice *14 mi (23 km) southeast of Dangriga.*
★

This is one of our favorite underrated spots in Belize. The 15-acre South Water Caye has good off-the-beaten-reef diving and snorkeling in a stunning tropical setting, and the beach at the southern end of the island is one of Belize's sandy beauties. The reef is only a short swim from shore. The downside of the small caye? The sand flies here can be a nuisance, and there aren't any facilities other than those at the island's two resorts and the International Zoological Expeditions' student dorm.

The nearby **Smithsonian Institution's Marine Research Laboratory** (⊠ *Carrie Bow Caye*) welcomes visitors by appointment; contact the Blue Marlin Lodge for more information.

WORD OF MOUTH

For relaxation [and] snorkeling South Water Caye is great—just don't expect luxurious accommodations anywhere on the island.

—christhetraveler

WHERE TO STAY

$$$$ 🖼 **Blue Marlin Lodge.** An excellent, though pricey, base for fishing, snorkeling, and diving trips, this Belizean-owned resort at the north end of the island is only 50 yards from the reef. Accommodations, which spread out over half the caye, range from rooms with plywood walls to cozy wood cabins to a trio of aquamarine-color concrete dome buildings. Rooms are so close to the sea that wave sounds may lull you to sleep. Some of the rooms could use a major upgrade. The resort has its own dive shop and two boats for diving and fishing. The restaurant and bar are great places to swap stories with other travelers. Packages start at BZ$2,330 per person for three nights, including meals, transfers, and taxes. **Pros:** Great snorkeling and diving nearby, friendly staff. **Cons:** Some rooms need upgrades. ⊠*South Water Caye* ☎*522/2243, 800/798–1558 in U.S.* ⊕*www.bluemarlinlodge.com* ➲*9 rooms, 8 cottages* ♿*In-room: no a/c (some), no phone, no TV. In-hotel: restaurant, bar, beachfront, diving, water sports, no elevator* ☰*MC, V* ¶⊙¶*AI.*

$$$$ 🖼 **Pelican's Pouch South Water Caye.** Steps from one of Belize's best
★   beaches, where you can swim, snorkel, dive from shore, and fish to your heart's content, , is this former convent-turned-peaceful island retreat. The colonial-era main house has a dining room serving fresh seafood and Belizean-style dishes on the ground floor, and five large rooms on the second floor. You can also stay in one of four no-frills but pleasant cottages: Egret's Escape, a honeymoon cottage; Osprey's Nest, which sleeps six; Sandpiper Suites; and Heron's Hideaway, which has a porch over the water. Power here is solar, showers are rainwater, and toilets are the composting kind. **Pros:** On great little beach, with snorkeling from shore, tasty Belizean food, comfortable accommodations. **Cons:** You have to make your own entertainment. ⊠*South Water Caye* ☎*522/2044* ⊕*www.pelicanbeachbelize.com* ➲*5 rooms, 4 cottages with 7 suites, 1 student dorm* ♿*In-room: no a/c, no phone, no TV. In-hotel: restaurant, beachfront, diving, water sports, no elevator* ☰*AE, MC, V* ¶⊙¶*AI.*

SOUTHERN CAYES OFF PLACENCIA AND SOUTHERN COAST

8–18 mi (13–30 km) east of Placencia.

A few miles off the coast of Stann Creek District are several small islands with equally small tourism operations. If Placencia and Hopkins aren't far enough away from civilization for you, consider an overnight or longer visit to one of these quiet little paradises surrounded by fish.

WHERE TO STAY

$$$$ ⚏ **Coco Plum Caye.** It all comes down to this: relax in a hammock on the veranda of your private cottage, sip a cold drink, and gaze at the Caribbean. This 16-acre island has only five cottages, all air-conditioned and painted in bright tropical colors. Rates include meals, drinks, and use of snorkeling equipment and kayaks, with a minimum four-night stay. The snorkeling off the shore is only so-so, but rates include snorkel trips to the reef a few miles farther out. Four-night minimum stay. **Pros:** Air-conditioned cabins on tranquil island. **Cons:** Only fair snorkeling off beach, not on reef, sand flies can be a real nuisance. ⊠ *Coco Plum Caye, 8 mi (13 km) from Hopkins village* ⌖ *Box 239, Dangriga* ☎ *522/2200 or 512/786–7309* ⛵ *4 cottages* ⚲ *In-room: no phone, no TV. In-hotel: restaurant, bar, beachfront, water sports, no elevator, airport shuttle (by boat, from Dangriga)* ☰ *MC, V* ⚑ *AI.*

$$$$ ⚏ **Robert's Caye.** This tiny—it's less than one acre—spit of sand has four thatch cabañas perched partly over the water, Bora Bora–style. It's operated by the Inn at Robert's Grove on the Placencia peninsula. You might go batty if you had to spend a long time on such a small space, but for a couple of nights it's a delightful getaway. Robert's Caye operates on an all-inclusive basis, with all meals, drinks, boat transfers, and use of snorkeling equipment and kayaks. Cost is BZ$1,600 double for a one-night stay. Inn at Robert's Grove also manages Ranguana Caye, a 3-acre island with three very simple cottages about 18 mi [30 km] from Placencia; it's close to the reef, so the snorkeling is terrific. **Pros:** Cute, thatch Bora Bora-style cabañas, good food. **Cons:** Island is really, really tiny. ⊠ *Robert's Caye, 10 mi (17 km) from Placencia village* ⌖ *Inn at Robert's Grove, Placencia* ☎ *523/3565 or 800/565–9756* ⊕ *www.robertsgrove.com* ⛵ *4 cabañas* ⚲ *In-room: no a/c, no phone, no TV. In-hotel: restaurant, bar, beachfront, water sports, no elevator* ☰ *AE, MC, V* ⚑ *AI.*

$$$$ ⚏ **Whipray Caye Lodge.** Whipray Caye (also called Whippari Caye) lures anglers with some of the best permit and bonefish fishing in Central America, and owner Julian Cabral (he claims he is descended from a pirate who stopped off in Belize in the 17th century) is a top-flight fishing guide and fly fisherman. If you don't fish, you'll find excellent snorkeling here, and plenty of peace and quiet on this little 3-acre island. There are only four rooms in two wood cottages steps from the sea. Fishing packages start at around BZ$3,000 per person for four nights. **Pros:** Good choice for hard-core anglers. **Cons:** Very basic accommodations. ⊠ *Whipray Caye, 9 mi (15 km) from Placencia village* ⌖ *General Delivery, Placencia village* ☎ *610/1068* ⊕ *www.whipraycayelodge.com* ⛵ *4 rooms in two cottages* ⚲ *In-room: no a/c, no phone, no TV. In-hotel: restaurant, beachfront, water sports, no elevator* ☰ *PayPal* ⚑ *AI.*

THE ATOLLS

There are only four atolls in the Western Hemisphere, and three of them are off Belize (the fourth is Chinchorro Reef, off Mexico's Yucatán). The atolls—Turneffe, Lighthouse, and Glover's—are oval-shape masses of coral. A few small islands, some sandy and others mostly mangrove, rise up along the atolls' encircling coral arms. Within the coral walls are central lagoons, with shallow water 10 to 30 feet deep. Outside the walls, the ocean falls off sharply to 1,000 feet or more, deeper than any diver can go.

Unlike the more common Pacific atolls, which were formed from underwater volcanoes, the Caribbean atolls began forming millions of years ago, atop giant tectonic faults. As giant limestone blocks slowly settled, they provided platforms for coral growth.

Because of their remoteness (they're 25 mi [40 km] to 50 mi [80 km] from the mainland) and because most of the islands at the atolls are small, the atolls have remained nearly pristine. Only a few small dive and fishing resorts are here, and the serious divers and anglers who favor the area know that they have some of the best diving and fishing in the Caribbean, if not the world. The atolls are also wonderful for beachcombing, relaxing, and snorkeling—just bring plenty of books, as there are no shops or restaurants other than at the hotels.

Of course, paradise has its price: most of the atoll resorts are expensive and have minimum-stay requirements. Getting here also usually requires a long boat ride, sometimes rough enough to bring on *mal de mer*. Try to take one of the scheduled boats to the lodges or ride out on a dive or snorkel boat with a group; otherwise, you'll likely pay BZ$600 or more to charter a boat.

TURNEFFE ATOLL

25 mi (40 km) east of Belize City.

The largest of the three atolls, Turneffe, is the closest to Belize City. It's one of the best spots for diving, thanks to several steep drop-offs. Only an hour from Lighthouse Reef and 45 minutes from the northern edge of Glover's Reef, Turneffe is a good base for exploring all of the atolls.

The best-known attraction, and probably Belize's most exciting wall dive, is the **Elbow,** at Turneffe's southernmost tip. You may encounter eagle rays swimming nearby. As many as 50 might flutter together, forming a rippling herd. Elbow is generally considered an advanced dive because of the strong currents, which sweep you toward the deep water beyond the reef.

Though it's most famous for its spectacular wall dives, the atoll has dives for every level. The leeward side, where the reef is wide and gently sloping, is good for shallower dives and snorkeling; you'll see large concentrations of tube sponges, soft corals such as forked sea feathers and sea fans, and plenty of fish. Also on the atoll's western side is the wreck of the *Sayonara*. No doubloons to scoop up here—it was a small passenger and cargo boat that sank in 1985—but it's good for wreck dive practice.

Fishing here, as at all of the atolls, is world-class. You can fly-fish for bonefish and permit in the grassy flats, or go after migratory tarpon from May to September in the channels and lagoons of the atoll. Jack, barracuda, and snappers lurk in the mangrove-lined bays and shorelines. Billfish, sailfish, and other big creatures are in the blue water around the atoll.

WHERE TO STAY

$$$$ ⊞ **Turneffe Flats.** The sound of the surf is the only thing you'll hear at these smart blue-and-white beachfront cabins. The rooms, fitted with elegant hardwoods, are a far cry from the bare-bones fishing camp that occupied this site in the early '80s. You can dive here—a Pro 48 dive boat is on standby and the reef is only 200 yards from shore—but the ubiquitous fishing-pole racks suggest that snook, bonefish, and permit are still the dominant lure. You pay a pretty penny to indulge your passion, however—a weekly fishing package for two in-season is around BZ$16,000 including meals, taxes, and guided fishing. Most of the time, there's a minimum one-week stay. **Pros:** Focus here is on fishing. **Cons:** Focus here is on fishing. ⊠ *Northern Bogue Caye* ✆ *Box 10670 Bozeman, MT 59719* ☎ *888/512–8812* ⊕ *www. tflats.com* ➮ *8 cottages* ⌂ *In-room: no phone, no TV, no a/c (during daytime). In-hotel: restaurant, bar, beachfront, diving, water sports, public Internet, no elevator, no kids under 12, airport shuttle (boat)* ▭ *D, MC, V* ⎟◎⎟*AI.*

$$$$ ⊞ **Turneffe Island Lodge.** White dive tanks serving as fence posts and
★   a rusty anchor from an 18th-century British warship set the tone at this south end resort. This was Turneffe Atoll's first dive lodge, and it bagged the best spot a few hundred yards from the legendary Elbow. If you came to Belize for the diving, this is an ideal base. The rooms, in palm-shaded cottages with sea views, have been refurbished without spoiling the cozy feeling created by the varnished hardwood fittings. Eight beachfront cabañas are solid mahogany inside. The two-story colonial-style house holds the bar and the dining room. The resort isn't for penny-pinchers: a week-long beachcombing package is BZ$4,600 per person, and dive and fishing rates are higher. **Pros:** Beautiful atoll setting near great diving and snorkeling, delicious and varied meals. **Cons:** Very expensive. ⊠ *Coco Tree Caye* ☎ *713/313–4670 or 800/874–0118* ⊕ *www.turneffelodge.com* ➮ *12 rooms, 8 cabañas* ⌂ *In-room: no phone, no TV. In-hotel: restaurant, bar, diving, water sports, no elevator, airport shuttle (boat)* ▭ *AE, MC, V* ☉ *Closed Sept. and Oct.* ⎟◎⎟*AI.*

LIGHTHOUSE REEF ATOLL, THE BLUE HOLE & HALF MOON CAYE

50 mi (80 km) east of Belize City.

If Robinson Crusoe had been a man of means, he would have repaired here for a break from his desert island.

Lighthouse Reef is about 18 mi (29 km) long and less than 1 mi (2 km) wide and is surrounded by a seemingly endless stretch of coral. Here you'll find two of the country's best dives.

Blue Hole. From the air, the Blue Hole, a breathtaking vertical chute that drops several hundred feet through the reef, looks like a dark blue eye in the center of the shallow lagoon. The Blue Hole was first dived by Jacques Cousteau in 1970 and has since become a diver's pilgrimage site. Just over 1,000 feet wide at the surface and dropping almost vertically to a depth of 412 feet, the Blue Hole is like swimming down a mineshaft, but a mineshaft with hammerhead sharks. This excitement is reflected in the thousands of stickers reading, "I Dived the Blue Hole."

Half Moon Caye. The best diving on Lighthouse Reef is at this classic wall dive. Half Moon Caye begins at 35 feet and drops almost vertically to blue infinity. Floating out over the edge is a bit like free-fall parachuting. Magnificent spurs of coral jut out to the seaward side, looking like small tunnels; they're fascinating to explore and invariably full of fish. An exceptionally varied marine life hovers around this caye. On the gently sloping sand flats behind the coral spurs, a vast colony of garden eels stirs, their heads protruding from the sandlike periscopes. Spotted eagle rays, sea turtles, and other underwater wonders frequent the drop-off.

Half Moon Caye National Monument. Belize's easternmost island offers one of Belize's greatest wildlife encounters, although it's difficult to reach and lacks accommodations other than camping. Part of the Lighthouse Reef system, Half Moon Caye owes its protected status to the presence of the red-footed booby. The bird is here in such numbers that it's hard to believe it has only one other nesting ground in the entire Caribbean (on Tobago Island, off the coast of Venezuela). Some 4,000 of these birds hang their hats on Half Moon Caye, along with iguanas, lizards, and loggerhead turtles. The entire 40-acre island is a nature reserve, so you can explore the beaches or head into the bush on the narrow nature trail. Above the trees at the island's center is a small viewing platform— at the top you're suddenly in a sea of birds that will doubtless remind you of a certain Alfred Hitchcock movie. Several dive operators and resorts arrange day trips and overnight camping trips to Half Moon Caye. The park fee here is a steep BZ$80 per person.

At this writing, visiting Lighthouse Reef is best done as a side trip from Ambergris Caye, Caye Caulker, or another location in northern Belize. Lighthouse Reef Resort on Northern Caye, a long-established dive lodge, is closed for rebuilding until 2008 or 2009. Planned lodges and restaurants, which were announced in connection with the sale of lots on Long Caye, a 650-acre island, are in a state of limbo, as is the development of Long Caye itself.

You may be able to stay at **Calypso Beach Retreat** (⊠ *Long Caye, Lighthouse Atoll* ☎ *303/523–8165* ⊕ *www.calypsobeachretreat.com*), which is open occasionally, when there is demand from dive groups.

GLOVER'S REEF ATOLL

70 mi (113 km) southeast of Belize City.

Named after the pirate John Glover, this coral necklace strung around an 80-square-mi (208-square-km) lagoon is the southernmost of Belize's three atolls. There are five islands at the atoll. Visitors to Glover's Reef are charged a BZ$20 park fee (BZ$25 for fly-fishing).

Emerald Forest Reef. Although most of the best dive sites are along the atoll's southeastern side, this is the exception. It's named for its masses of huge green elkhorn coral. Because the reef's most exciting part is only 25 feet down, it's excellent for novice divers.

Long Caye Wall. This is an exciting wall with a dramatic drop-off hundreds of feet down. It's a good place to spot turtles, rays, and barracuda.

Southwest Caye Wall is an underwater cliff that falls quickly to 130 feet. It's briefly interrupted by a narrow shelf, then continues its near-vertical descent to 350 feet. This dive gives you the exhilaration of flying in blue space, so it's easy to lose track of how deep you are going. Both ascent and descent require careful monitoring.

Kayaking is another popular sport here; you can paddle out to the atoll's many patch reefs for snorkeling. Most hotels rent kayaks.

WHERE TO STAY

$$$$ **Isla Marisol.** At Isla Marisol you can sip a cold Belikin in a bar perched at the end of a pier, a hundred feet out in the Caribbean. After a breakfast of mango and johnnycake, you can dive "The Pinnacles," where coral heads rise 40 feet from the ocean floor. After a lobster or fish dinner, wander back to your cabin, a breezy retreat built of tropical hardwoods. A three-bedroom "Reef House" was added in 2007. Beachcomber packages including meals and transport to the island start at BZ$1,600 per person for three days, diving at BZ$2,100, and fishing at BZ$3,200. This is a good base from which to see whale sharks in the late spring. Bring plenty of bug juice, as sand flies can be irksome here. **Pros:** Beautiful setting, great diving. **Cons:** Food and accommodations are adequate, prices aren't a bargain, and sand flies often are terrible. ⊠*Southwest Caye* 🕾*520/2056 or 866/990–9904* ⊕*www.islamarisol resort.com* ➪*10 cabins, 1 2-bedroom house* △*In-room: no phone, no TV. In-hotel: restaurant, bar, beachfront, diving, water sports, no elevator, airport shuttle (by boat from Dangriga)* ⊟*AE, MC, V* ⏣*AI.*

$$$$ **Off the Wall Dive Center & Resort.** Though this resort focuses on diving, there's excellent snorkeling and fishing as well. Depending on your point of view, you'll find the small wood cabins, composting toilets, and outdoor rainwater showers either rustic or basic. The resort focuses on diving, but snorkelers and anglers have excellent options as well. Meals are served in a beachfront thatch palapa with sand floor. There's a seven-day minimum. **Pros:** Good value (for an atoll lodge), easy access to great diving, highly knowledgeable dive staff. **Cons:** Bugs can be a nuisance. ⊠*Long Caye* 🕾*614/6348* ⊕*www.offthewall belize.com* ➪*4 cabañas* △*In-room: no a/c, no phone, no TV. In-hotel:*

restaurant, bar, beachfront, diving, water sports, no elevator, airport shuttle (by boat from Dangriga) ☰MC, V ⦿AI.

$ 🖥**Glover's Atoll Resort.** This little group of cabañas, including several built over the water, is a lesson in laid-back living. Forget about electricity, running water, and indoor bathrooms, and surrender to a life of fishing, diving, snorkeling, and swimming. You bring your tackle for boat or shore fishing and your own food supplies, though simple meals and a few basics such as bottled water are sold, at fairly steep prices (a loaf of French bread is BZ$8), at the 9-acre island. Coconuts are free. Also available are beds in a bunkhouse and camping—however, tents have seen better days, and the bunkhouse is sometimes not clean. If you're camping, you should bring your own tent. This is as close as they come to a *Gilligan's Island*–style vacation spot, but, remember, the denizens of Gillgan's Island sometimes faced problems. Unless you come out on the free weekly boat from Sittee River on Sunday, you'll pay BZ$600 or more for transportation. **Pros:** Cheapest way to enjoy the atolls, access to great diving, snorkeling, and fishing. **Cons:** On-site management gets mixed reviews, some facilities are dirty, you must be able to rough it. ✉*Northeast Caye* 🖋*Box 2215, Belize City* ☎*520/5016* ⊕*www.glovers.com.bz* 🛏*12 cabins with shared bath, 1 dorm, campground* ⚍*In-room: no a/c, no phone, no TV. In-hotel: beachfront, diving, water sports, no elevator* ☰MC, V ⊗*Closed Sept. and Oct. most years.*

THE CAYES & ATOLLS ESSENTIALS

TRANSPORTATION

BY AIR

Maya Island Airways and Tropic Air operate flights to Ambergris Caye and Caye Caulker from both the municipal and international airports in Belize City. Each has hourly service every day to Ambergris Caye between about 7:30 AM and 5:30 PM. In high season, additional flights are added to accommodate demand. Round-trip fares for the 15- to 20-minute flight are about BZ$121 (municipal) and BZ$218 (international). Maya Island often offers a 25% discount if you pay cash rather than use a credit card.

The airstrip on Ambergris Caye is at San Pedro's southern edge. You'll always find taxis waiting at the airstrip, and most hotels run shuttles. If you're proceeding on foot, it's about five minutes to the hotels in town. The airstrip on Caye Caulker is at the island's south end. Hotels may send a golf cart to pick you up. Otherwise, you'll find that golf-cart taxis are available. Whether you arrive in San Pedro by air or by ferry from Belize City, you'll be met by a small crowd of friendly, but pushy, cab drivers touting cheap lodging deals. Note that hotels pay these drivers a commission, which is reflected in the hotel rate. For the best rates call the hotel directly upon your arrival.

There are no scheduled flights to the other cayes, although flights will stop at Caye Chapel on demand.

Contacts Maya Island Airways (⌂ *Box 458, Municipal Airport, Belize City* ☎ *223/1140, 800/225–6732 in U.S.* ⊕ *www.mayaislandair.com*). **Tropic Air** (⌂ *Box 20, San Pedro* ☎ *226/2012, 800/422–3435 in U.S.* ⊕ *www.tropicair.com*).

BY BOAT & FERRY

A variety of boats connect Belize City with Ambergris Caye and Caye Caulker. The cost to Ambergris Caye is BZ$20 one way for the 75-minute trip. The most dependable, operated by the Caye Caulker Water Taxi Association, leave from the Belize Marine Terminal on North Front Street. To San Pedro, the speedy open boats depart Belize City at 8, 9, 10:30 AM, noon, 1:30, 3, and 4:30 PM and return from San Pedro, from Shark's Pier, at 7, 8, 9:30, and 11:30 AM, and 1, 2:30, and 3:30 PM. There's an additional return boat at 4:30 PM on weekends and holidays.

Caye Caulker Water Taxi Association boats from Belize City take 45 minutes to reach Caye Caulker and cost BZ$15 each way. Departures are 8, 9, and 10:30 AM, noon, 1:30, 3, 4:30, and 5:30 PM, with return trips departing the public pier in Caye Caulker at 6:30, 7:30, 8:30, and 10 AM, noon, 1:30, 3, and 4 PM. There's an additional return boat at 5 PM on weekends and holidays. Boats can drop you at Caye Chapel as well.

To reach the more remote cayes, you're left to your own devices. You can charter boats in either San Pedro or Belize City, but they're not cheap. The resorts on the atolls run their own flights or boats, but these aren't available to the general public. Ask your hotel if it provides transportation. For the southern cayes, inquire about boats departing from Dangriga. Dangriga's Pelican Beach Hotel sends a boat to its resort on South Water Caye. If transportation to South Water Caye isn't included in your hotel package, you'll pay around BZ$110 per person.

Several boats make the run from Dangriga to Tobacco Caye for BZ$35 per person one way. Most boats leave Dangriga around 9:30 AM and return from Tobacco Caye midmorning. Check at the Riverside Restaurant in Dangriga or ask at your hotel on Tobacco Caye. Captain Buck is a dependable operator. Charter boats from Belize City, Dangriga, and elsewhere charge from BZ$500 to BZ$600, or more, one way to the atolls.

BY WATER TAXI

There aren't any cabs on North Ambergris; to get there from San Pedro, you can take a water taxi. Scheduled service is available roughly hourly on the Island Ferry during the day until 10 PM. Rates are BZ$14 to $50, depending on the destination. After 10, you can arrange a custom pick-up. Rates are BZ$40–BZ$100, or more, depending on your destination, the time of night, and the number in your party. Call Island Ferry or San Pedro Water Taxi.

Contacts Caye Caulker Water Taxi Association (✉ *Marine Terminal, N. Front St. at Swing Bridge, Belize City* ☎ *223/5752* ⊕ *www.cayecaulkerwatertaxi.com*). **Riverside Café** (✉ *South Riverside Dr., Dangriga* ☎ *501/502–3449*).**Island Ferry** (✉ *Barrier Reef Dr., San Pedro* ☎ *226/3231*). **San Pedro Water Taxi** (✉ *Beachfront, San Pedro* ☎ *226/2194*).

2

BY GOLF CART

On Ambergris Caye and Caye Caulker, there are no car rentals, but you can rent a golf cart. If you have a choice, get a gas cart rather than an electric so you don't run out of juice at an inopportune time; gas carts have a much longer range. Golf-cart rentals cost about as much as a car rental in the U.S.—around BZ$100–BZ$120 a day, or BZ$500 a week. Compare prices and ask for discounts.

To drive a cart, you'll need a valid driver's license from your home country. On Ambergris Caye, there are a half-dozen cart-rental companies; Moncho's, Castle Cars, and Cholo's are three of the largest. Your hotel can also arrange a cart rental. If crossing the new bridge to North Ambergris, golf carts are charged BZ$10 round-trip, and pedestrians BZ$2. The bridge is open 24 hours. On Caye Chapel, golf carts are included in the daily rate. Bicycles are for rent on Ambergris Caye and Caye Caulker for around BZ$10–BZ$12 a day, or BZ$80 a week.

GOLF-CART RENTALS **Castle Cars** (✉ *Barrier Reef Dr., San Pedro* ☎ *226/2421*). **Cholo's** (✉ *San Pedro* ☎ *226/2406* ⊕ *www.choloscarts.com*). **Moncho's** (✉ *Sea Star St., San Pedro* ☎ *226/3262* ⊕ *www.monchosrentals.com*).

BY TAXI

Regular taxi cabs are available in San Pedro and in the developed area south of town on Ambergris Caye. For a taxi, you can call Island Taxi, have your hotel arrange for a cab, or hail one of the cabs cruising the downtown area.

Contact **Island Taxi** (✉ *Pescador Dr., San Pedro* ☎ *226/3125*).

CONTACTS & RESOURCES

BANKS

Atlantic Bank, on Barrier Reef Drive in San Pedro, is open weekdays 8–2. Belize Bank, on Barrier Reef Drive in San Pedro, is open Monday–Thursday 8–3 and Friday 8–4:30. Alliance Bank in San Pedro is open 8–3 weekdays. ScotiaBank, on Coconut Drive, is open Monday–Thursday 8–2:30, Friday 8:30–4, and Saturday 9–noon. First Caribbean International Bank in San Pedro is open Monday–Thursday 8–2:30 and Friday 8–4:30.

On Caye Caulker, there's just one bank with an ATM machine that accepts foreign-issued ATM cards, Atlantic Bank on Back Street, in a new building near Chan's Market. It's open weekdays 8–2:30. On Ambergris Caye, all the banks except Alliance Bank accept ATM cards issued outside Belize on the VisaPLUS system. Cash advances on your Visa or MasterCard are also available at these banks. Caye Bank, an international bank, has an office in San Pedro, but it doesn't offer retail banking services to local residents or island visitors.

Contacts **Atlantic Bank** (✉ *Barrier Reef Dr., San Pedro* ☎ *226/2195* ✉ *Back St., Caye Caulker* ☎ *226/0207*). **Alliance Bank** (✉ *33 Barrier Reef Dr., San Pedro* ☎ *226/2136*). **Belize Bank** (✉ *49 Barrier Reef Dr., San Pedro* ☎ *226/2482*). **First Caribbean International Bank** (✉ *Barrier Reef Dr., San Pedro* ☎ *226/0355*). **Scotia Bank** (✉ *12 Coconut Dr., San Pedro* ☎ *226/3730*).

EMERGENCIES

The San Pedro Lions Polyclinic, which opened in 2005 on Ambergris Caye, has two physicians, three nurses, a pharmacist, and a health officer. The clinic has services just short of a full-scale hospital and is open weekdays from 8 to 8 and Saturdays 8 to noon. A doctor and nurse are on 24-hour call. Two other clinics, several doctors, three pharmacies, a dentist, and a hyperbaric chamber are also on the island.

On Caye Caulker, the Caye Caulker Health Center, usually staffed by a volunteer doctor, is open weekdays 8–11:30 and 1–4:30. For dental care or serious ailments you need to go to Belize City. There are no medical facilities on any of the other cayes, but if you have an emergency, call your embassy or contact Karl Heusner Memorial Hospital, the nation's main referral hospital, in Belize City, or a private hospital in Belize City, Belize Medical Associates. If you're on an island with an airstrip, Wings of Hope provides emergency airlift services, as does Astrum Helicopters.

For police emergencies, call 911 or 90. On marine radios, channel 16 is the international distress channel.

Clinics San Pedro Lions Polyclinic (✉ *Near airstrip, San Pedro* ☎ *226/4052 or 600/9071*). **Caye Caulker Health Center** (✉ *Front St., near Lena's Hotel, Caye Caulker* ☎ *226/0166*). **San Pedro Hyperbaric Chamber** (✉ *Near airstrip, San Pedro* ☎ *226/2851*).

Other Emergency Contacts Astrum Helicopters (✉ *Mile 3½, Northern Hwy., Belize City* ☎ *223/9462*)**Belize Medical Associates** (✉ *5791 Thomas St. Belize City* ☎ *223/0302*). **Karl Heusner Memorial Hospital** (✉ *Princess Margaret Dr., Belize City* ☎ *223/1548*). **United States Embassy** (✉ *Floral Park Rd., Belmopan City* ☎ *822/4011*). **Wings of Hope** (✉ *1675 Sunrise Ave., Belize City* ☎ *223/0078*).

MAIL & SHIPPING

On Ambergris Caye the post office in San Pedro is open weekdays 8–noon and 1–4. On Caye Caulker the post office is on Back Street on the south side of town. It's open 9–noon and 2–5 weekdays and 9–noon Saturday. There are no post offices on other cayes. Your hotel or lodge can arrange to mail letters and postcards for you. FedEx has a service desk at the Tropic Air cargo office in San Pedro, and the Belize Postal Service offers an international express mail service.

Post Offices Caye Caulker (✉ *Back St.* ☎ *226/0325*). **San Pedro** (✉ *Alijua Bldg., Barrier Reef Dr.* ☎ *226/2250*).

TOURS

From Ambergris and Caulker, and from smaller cayes with advance planning, you can do day trips to the mainland to see Mayan ruins, try cave tubing, visit the Belize Zoo, and do other activities. However, because you have to get from the islands to the mainland, and then to your destination, the cost will be higher than if you did the tour from a closer point.

From Ambergris Caye, a full-day cave tubing trip, combined with lunch and a visit to the zoo, runs around BZ$300 per person. A trip to

2

Lamanai, including lunch and drinks, costs about BZ$270. A visit to Altun Ha, combined with lunch and a stop at Maruba Spa, is around BZ$150–BZ$200. Tours are slightly less expensive from Caye Caulker. A Lamanai trip runs about BZ$220, and one to Altun Ha and Maruba about BZ$160, not including lunch at Maruba. All tour guides in San Pedro and on Caye Caulker should be members of their respective associations—if in doubt, ask to see identification. Among San Pedro's top tour operators are Tanisha Tours, which offers excellent trips to Altun Ha and Lamanai, along with manatee-spotting trips, cave tubing, and others.

SEAduced by Belize is unrivaled for its nature and kayak tours. SEAduced and SEArious Adventures both do other trips, including manatee spotting, visits to Altun Ha, and others. On Caye Caulker, Chocolate is the best-known guide and tour operator, though he is semiretired. He and the people he has trained are known for their full-day manatee trips. Carlos Tours offers excellent snorkeling trips. Raggamuffin Tours runs snorkeling, sailing, and other sea trips. Tsunami Adventures and Anwar Tours also run trips to the mainland. *(See F Caye Caulker and Ambergris Caye sections.)*

Contacts **Anwar Tours** (⊠ *Front St., Caye Caulker* ☎ *226/0327*). **Carlos Tours** (⊠ *Front St., Caye Caulker* ☎ *226/0058*). **Chocolate Tours** (⊠ *Front St., Caye Caulker* ☎ *226/0151*). **Raggamuffin Tours** (⊠ *Front St., Caye Caulker* ☎ *226/0348*). **SEAduced by Belize** (⊠ *Tarpon St., San Pedro* ☎ *226/2254*). **SEArious Adventures** (⊠ *Beachfront, San Pedro* ☎ *226/4202*). **Tanisha Tours** (⊠ *Middle St., San Pedro* ☎ *226/2314* ⊕ *www.tanishatours.com*). **Tsunami Adventures** (⊠ *Front St. at Split, Caye Caulker* ☎ *226/0462* ⊕ *www.tsunamiadventures.com*).

VISITOR INFORMATION

The Caye Caulker chapter of the Belize Tourism Industry Association has an office, staffed irregularly, at the Caye Caulker Mini-Reserve at the south end of the island. The official San Pedro Visitor Information Center, next to the Town Hall, is open 10–1 and 2–7, Monday through Saturday. Avoid other information booths, as they are likely fronts for time-shares.

The best source of information on the islands is online. Operated by Marty Casado, AmbergrisCaye.com (⊕ *www.ambergriscaye.com*) has more than 8,000 pages of facts and figures on San Pedro. Caye Caulker's official Belize Tourist Industry Association (BTIA) Web site is ⊕ *www. gocayecaulker.com*. The Toucan Trail Web site (⊕ *www.toucantrail. com*) is another excellent source of information, especially for those looking for information on the less-expensive end of the spectrum, as is the Web site of the Caye Caulker village council (⊕ www.cayecaulkerbelize.net). The *San Pedro Sun* newspaper publishes a free weekly tabloid-size visitor newspaper, *The San Pedro Sun Visitor Guide.*

Contacts **Caye Caulker Belize Tourism Industry Association** (⊠ *Mini-Reserve Caye Caulker village* ☎ *227/5717* ⊕ www.gocayecaulker.com) is at the south end of the island just northeast of the airstrip. **San Pedro Visitor Information Center** (⊠ *Barrier Reef Dr., near Town Hall, San Pedro* ☎ *226/2903*) is open 10–1 and 2–7 Monday–Saturday.

Northern Belize

WORD OF MOUTH

"This summer we went to Lamanai with Lamanai Eco-Adventures. Errol Cadle was our guide, and we had a terrific time! We went on Sunday and had the place to ourselves (no cruise ship folks)."

—Cayman Sue

"We can't recommend Chan Chich enough. We saw close to 100 species of birds (and we aren't birders so I am sure we missed many), mammals, amphibians, insects, lizards, spiders (yes, they are big) and lots of rainforest plants and flowers. One of the guides, Ruben, calls Chan Chich paradise. We would have to agree with him."

—EDH Traveler

RAZZAMATAZZ AND BLING ARE IN short supply in northern Belize. Here you'll find more orange groves than beach bars, more sugarcane than sugary sand, and more farms than restaurants. Yet, if you're willing to give in to the area's easygoing terms and slow down to explore back roads and poke around small towns and villages, this northern country will win a place in your traveler's heart. You'll discover some of Belize's most interesting Mayan sites, several outstanding jungle lodges, and a sprinkling of small, inexpensive inns with big personalities.

Northern Belize includes the northern part of Belize District and all of Orange Walk and Corozal districts. All together, this area covers about 2,800 sq mi (7,250 sq km) and has a population of around 80,000. The landscape is mostly flat, with mangrove swamps on the coast giving way to savannah inland. Scrub bush is much more common than broadleaf jungle, although to the northwest near the Guatemala border are large, wild tracts of land with some of the world's few remaining old-growth mahogany trees. The region has many cattle ranches, citrus groves, sugarcane fields, and, in a few areas, marijuana fields.

The only sizable towns in the region are Orange Walk, about 53 mi (87 km) north of Belize City, with about 18,000 residents, and the slightly smaller Corozal, with a population around 9,000, 85 mi (139 km) north of Belize City. Both are on the Northern Highway, a paved two-lane road that runs 95 mi (156 km) from Belize City up the center of the region, ending at the Mexican border.

Northern Belize gets less rain than anywhere else in the country (roughly 50 inches annually in Corozal), a fact that's reflected in the sunny disposition of the local population, mostly Mayas and Mestizos. Both Orange Walk and Corozal towns have a Mexican ambience, with central plazas the focus of the downtown areas. Most locals speak Spanish as a first language, though many also know English. Offering little in the way of tourism facilities itself, Orange Walk Town is a jumping-off point for trips to Lamanai and other Mayan ruins, to Mennonite farmlands, and to several well-regarded jungle lodges in wild, remote areas. Corozal Town, next door to Chetumal, Mexico, is a place to slow down, relax, and enjoy the laid-back atmosphere of a charming small town on the beautiful Corozal Bay (or, as Mexico calls it, Chetumal Bay).

If you tire of small-town pleasures, the Belize side of the Mexican border has three casinos, including one called Las Vegas that claims to be the largest casino in Central America, and a duty-free zone. Corozal has begun to draw foreign expats looking for inexpensive real estate and proximity to Chetumal, the Quintana Roo Mexican state capital, whose population is about the same as the entire country of Belize. Sarteneja Village, in the far northeastern part of Corozal District, about 35 mi (57 km) from Corozal Town, is a still undiscovered fishing village at the edge of the sea, near the Shipstern Wildlife Reserve. On the way are several pristine lagoons, including the lovely Progresso Lagoon.

TOP REASONS TO GO

MAYAN SITES

Several of the most interesting Mayan sites in the region are in northern Belize. These include Altun Ha, Lamanai, La Milpa, and Cerros. Altun Ha gets the most visitors of any Mayan site in Belize (about 75,000 a year), and Lamanai, on the New River Lagoon, and Cerros, on Corozal Bay, are notable in part because of their beautiful locations. Less accessible but also of interest to Mayan enthusiasts are sites at La Milpa, the third largest Mayan site in Belize, Cuello, and Nohmul. There's also a small site, Santa Rita, in Corozal Town.

WILD, OPEN SPACES

This part of Belize has some of the country's wildest and most remote tracts of land. The quarter-million acres of Rio Bravo Conservation and Management Area host only a few thousand visitors each year. Although people are scarce, Rio Bravo teems with wildlife. The area has 250 species of trees, including some of the largest mahogany trees in Belize, 70 species of mammals including jaguars, and more than 400 types of birds. Other large tracts of land rich with flora and fauna include the adjoining Gallon Jug lands, 130,000 privately owned acres around Chan Chich Lodge. The Shipstern Reserve is a 22,000-acre expanse of swamps, lagoons, and forests on the Sarteneja peninsula. Huge numbers of birds nest at the Crooked Tree Wildlife Sanctuary, a network of inland lagoons and swamps.

JUNGLE LODGES

Northern Belize is home to several first-rate lodges, including Chan Chich Lodge, a paradise for birders and the place where you're most likely to spot the reclusive jaguar in the wild. Lamanai Outpost, on the banks of the New River Lagoon, is a center for crocodile research. The exotic Maruba Resort Jungle Spa focuses on bringing Mother Earth to you in the form of natural spa treatments.

ORIENTATION & PLANNING

ORIENTATION

The Northern Highway, a paved two-lane road, is the transportation spine of the region, running about 95 mi (156 km) from Belize City to the Mexican border at Chetumal, passing the two main towns in northern Belize, Orange Walk and Corozal. Mile marker signs begin in Belize City at the traffic circle where Princess Margaret Drive, Freetown Road, and Central American Boulevard meet, and increase going north. However, the markers are not well maintained and many are missing.

In 2005 a bypass around Orange Walk Town opened, providing a way to avoid the congested downtown. Buses between Belize City and Corozal run frequently—roughly hourly during daylight hours—in both directions. About one-half of the buses continue on to Chetumal, Mexico.

Branching off the Northern Highway are a number of tertiary roads, mostly unpaved, including the road to Crooked Tree Wildlife Sanctuary; the Old Northern Highway that leads to the Altun Ha ruins and Maruba Spa; a road to Shipyard, a Mennonite settlement, which also connects with roads to the Lamanai ruins and to the La Milpa ruins and Gallon Jug; the San Estevan Road that is a route to Progresso, Copper Bank, and the Cerros Maya ruins, or, via a different branch, to Sarteneja. Another route to Sarteneja runs from Corozal Town and requires crossing the New River twice on hand-pulled auto ferries.

PLANNING

WHEN TO GO
Corozal Town and the rest of northern Belize get about the same amount of rain as Atlanta, Georgia, so the "rainy season"—generally June to November—here is not to be feared. It's hot and humid for much of the year, except in waterfront areas where prevailing breezes mitigate the heat. December to April is usually the most pleasant time, with weather similar to that of south Florida. In winter, cold fronts from the north occasionally bring rain and chilly weather, and when the temperature drops to the low 60s, locals sleep under extra blankets.

RESTAURANTS & CUISINE
With the exception of dining rooms at upscale jungle lodges, where four-course dinners can run BZ$70 or more, restaurants are almost invariably small, inexpensive, family-run places, serving simple meals such as stew chicken with rice and beans. Here, you'll rarely pay more than BZ$20 for dinner, and frequently much less. If there's a predominant culinary influence, it's from Mexico, and many restaurants serve tacos, tamales, *garnaches* (small, fried corn tortillas with beans, cabbage, and cheese piled on them), and soups such as *escabeche* (onion soup with chicken). A few places, mostly in Corozal Town, cater to tourists and expats, with burgers and steaks.

ABOUT THE HOTELS
As with restaurants, most hotels in northern Belize are small, family-run spots. In Corozal and Orange Walk towns, hotels are modest affairs with room rates generally under BZ$150 for a double, a fraction of the cost of hotels in San Pedro or other more popular parts of Belize. Generally, the hotels are clean, well maintained, and offer a homey atmosphere. They have private baths and plenty of hot and cold water, and many also have air-conditioning. Hotels and lodges in Crooked Tree, Sarteneja, Copper Bank, and Progresso are also small and inexpensive; few have air-conditioning. The jungle lodges near Lamanai, Gallon Jug, and Altun Ha, however, are a different story. Several of these, including Chan Chich Lodge, Maruba Jungle Lodge and Spa, and Lamanai Outpost Lodge, are upscale accommodations, with gorgeous settings in the jungle or on a lagoon and prices to match, typically BZ$500 or more for a double in-season; meals and tours are extra.

WHAT IT COSTS IN BELIZE DOLLARS				
¢	$	$$	$$$	$$$$
RESTAU-RANTS	under BZ$8	BZ$8–BZ$15	BZ$15–BZ$30	BZ$30–BZ$50	over BZ$50
HOTELS	under BZ$100	BZ$100–BZ$200	BZ$200–BZ$300	BZ$300–BZ$500	over BZ$500

Restaurant prices are per person for a main course at dinner. Hotel prices are for two people in a standard double room, including tax and service, in high season.

3

CROOKED TREE WILDLIFE SANCTUARY

33 mi (54 km) north of Belize City.

A paradise for birders and animal lovers, this wildlife sanctuary encompasses a chain of inland waterways around the Northern Lagoon covering about 3,000 acres. Traveling through by canoe, you're likely to see iguanas, crocodiles, coatis, and turtles. The sanctuary's most prestigious visitors, however, are the jabiru storks, several of

WORD OF MOUTH

"Do you like birds, nature, and the simple life? I would recommend Crooked Tree Sanctuary. It is so close to Belize City.

—rbo

which usually visit between November and May. With a wingspan up to 12 feet, the jabiru is the largest flying bird in the Americas. For birders the best time to come is in the dry season, roughly from February to early June, when lowered water levels cause birds to group together to find water and food, making them easy to spot. Birding is good year-round, however, and the area is more scenic when the lagoons are full. Snowy egrets, snail kites, ospreys, and black-collared hawks, as well as two types of duck—Muscovy and black-bellied whistling—and all five species of kingfisher native to Belize can be spotted. Even on a short, one- to three-hour tour, you're likely to see 20 to 40 species of birds. South of Crooked Tree, on Sapodilla Lagoon and accessible by boat, is a small Mayan site, Chau Hiix.

At the Crooked Tree **visitor center,** at the end of the causeway where you pay your BZ$8 sanctuary admission fee, you can arrange a guided tour of the sanctuary or rent a canoe (around BZ$10 per person per hour) for a do-it-yourself trip. You can also walk through the village and hike birding trails around the area. If you'd prefer to go by horseback, you'll pay around BZ$20 an hour. The visitor center has a free village and trail map. If you're staying overnight, your hotel can arrange canoe or bike rentals and set up tours and trips. A typical tour takes about three hours and costs around BZ$160–$200 for up to four persons. It starts at your hotel or the visitor center with a boat ride on the lagoon, then up Spanish Creek, where you are met by a car and returned to your hotel or visitor center. Although tours can run at any time, the best time is early in the morning, when birds are most active.

GREAT ITINERARIES

IF YOU HAVE 3 TO 5 DAYS IN NORTHERN BELIZE

If starting in Belize City, rent a car and drive to Crooked Tree Wildlife Sanctuary, which has great birding and offers the chance to see the jabiru stork, the largest flying bird in the Americas. Spend a few hours here, canoeing on the lagoon and hiking trails near Crooked Tree Village. If you have an interest in birding, you'll want to overnight here at one of the simple lagoon-side lodges, such as Bird's Eye View. Otherwise, drive on to Maruba, an upscale jungle lodge and spa. The drive from Crooked Tree takes about 45 minutes. While you're at Maruba, visit the Altun Ha Mayan site, which you can see in a couple of hours. On the second day, drive to Corozal Town, about 1½ hours from Maruba or Crooked Tree. Base here in Corozal Town for two days, at one of the small hotels on Corozal Bay, making day trips by boat to Lamanai and Cerros ruins (or you can drive). If you have additional days in the north, you can add a visit to Sarteneja or cross the border into Chetumal, Mexico. Alternatively, after the first night in Crooked Tree or at Maruba, drive to the Lamanai Mayan site, and spend the night there at one of the lodges on the New River Lagoon, or, for a different experience, proceed to Blue Creek Village, a Mennonite area, and spend the night at Hillside B&B. Then, continue on through Programme for Belize lands to Chan Chich Lodge, and spend the rest of your time in northern Belize at this classic jungle lodge. If money isn't much of an object and you want one of the best jungle lodge experiences in Central America, then ditch the car and fly from Belize City to Chan Chich, where you can spend all your time looking for jaguars and listening to the howler monkeys.

IF YOU HAVE 1 DAY IN NORTHERN BELIZE

With only one day, head to Lamanai, which with Caracol in the Cayo District, is the most interesting of Belize's Mayan sites. Although you can drive, the most enjoyable way to get to Lamanai is by a 1½-hour boat trip, up the New River. Tour boats (BZ$80 per person) leave around 9 AM from the Tower Hill bridge over the New River just south of Orange Walk Town. If you're staying overnight at Lamanai, your hotel can arrange boat transportation.

One of Belize's oldest inland villages, established some 300 years ago, **Crooked Tree** is at the reserve's center. With a population of about 900, most of Creole origin, the community has a church, school, and one of the surest signs of a former British territory: a cricket pitch. There are many large cashew trees around the village, which are highly fragrant when in bloom in January and February. Villagers make and sell cashew wine.

✉ *Turn west off Northern Hwy. at Mile 30.8, then drive 2 mi (3 km)* ☎ *223/4987 for Belize Audubon Society* ⊕ *www.belizeaudubon.org/ parks/ctws.htm* ☞ *BZ$8.*

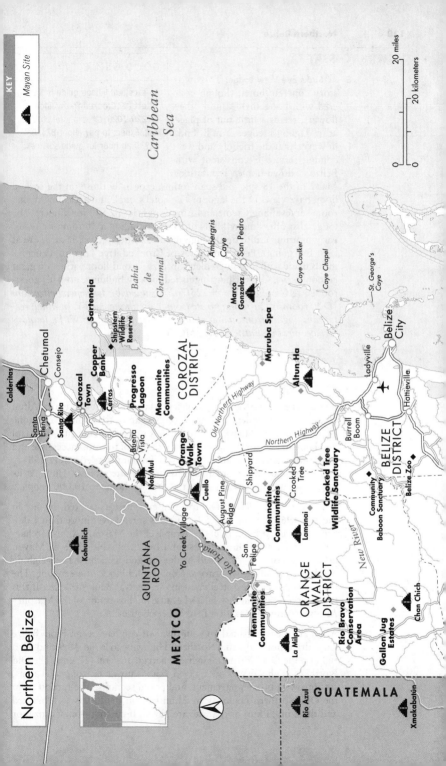

WHERE TO STAY

$ Bird's Eye View Lodge. This two-story concrete hotel, though covered with bougainvillea and other flowers, seems a little out of place at a lagoon's edge. You'll find, however, that the friendly and welcoming service is consistent with Belize's down-home reputation.

Many of the 18 spic-and-span rooms, especially those on the second floor, have views of the lagoon. The hotel's small and appealing dining room serves filling Creole and American fare (BZ$30 for dinner). The lodge also offers many kinds of tours, including a "birding-by-boat" early morning cruise on the lagoon (BZ$50 per person, if there are at least five going). **Pros:** On shores of Crooked Tree Lagoon, delicious meals made with local ingredients, breezy second-floor patio with great lagoon views. **Cons:** Undistinguished, blocky building, no-frills guestrooms. ✉ *Crooked Tree* ☎ *225/7027* ⊕ *www.birdseyeviewbelize.com* ⇨ *20 rooms* ⚐ *In-room: no a/c (some), no phone, no TV. In-hotel: restaurant, lagoonfront, water sports, no elevator, public Wi-Fi, laundry service, airport shuttle* ⊟ *AE, MC, V.*

ALTUN HA

🕓 *45 km (28 mi) north of Belize City.*

If you've never experienced an ancient Mayan city, make a trip to Altun Ha, which is a modern translation in Mayan of the name "Rockstone Pond," a nearby village. It's not Belize's most dramatic site—Caracol and Lamanai vie for that award—but it's one of the most accessible and most thoroughly excavated. The first inhabitants settled before 300 BC, and their descendants finally abandoned the site after AD 1000. At its height during the Classic period the city was home to 10,000 people.

A team from the Royal Ontario Museum first excavated the site in the mid-1960s and found 250 structures spread over more than 1,000 square yards. At Plaza B, in the Temple of the Masonry Altars, archaeologists unearthed the grandest and most valuable piece of Mayan art ever discovered—the head of the sun god Kinich Ahau. Weighing nearly 10 pounds, it was carved from a solid block of green jade. The head is kept in a solid steel vault in the Central Bank of Belize. If this temple looks familiar to you, it's because an illustration of the Masonry Altars structure appears on Belikin beer bottles.

Altun Ha is easily visited on your own—if you have a car. From Belize City, drive north on the Northern Highway to Mile 18.9 and turn right on the *Old* Northern Highway and go 10½ mi (17 km). The Old Northern Highway was once paved, but it's now a mix of gravel areas, sections with broken pavement, and paved sections. The turnoff from the Old Northern Highway to Altun Ha, on the left, is well marked and the 2 mi (3 km) of roadsite are paved. If coming from Corozal or

Orange Walk, you can also enter the Old Northern Highway at Carmelita Village, Mile 49 of the Northern Highway. Because the site is small, it's not necessary to have a tour guide, but licensed guides may offer their services when you arrive.

Tours from Belize City, Orange Walk, and Crooked Tree also are options. Altun Ha is a regular stop on cruise ship excursions, and on days when several ships are in port in Belize City, typically midweek, Altun Ha may be overrun with cruise passengers. Cruise Calendar Web site (⊕ *www.cruisecal.com*) provides information on days when cruise ships are in port. There's limited bus service from Belize City to Maskall Village on the Old Northern Highway, but buses are infrequent and drop you only at the entrance road, so it's a long hike to the ruins.

Several tour operators in San Pedro and Caye Caulker also offer day trips to Altun Ha, often combined with lunch at Maruba Jungle Resort Jungle Spa *(see ⇨ Maruba below)*. Most of these tours are by boat, landing at Bomba Village. From here, a van makes the short ride to Altun Ha.

⊕ *From Belize City, take the Northern Hwy. north to Mile 18.9. Turn right (east) on the Old Northern Hwy., which is only partly paved, and go 10½ mi (17 km) to the signed entrance road to Altun Ha on the left. Follow this paved road 2 mi (3 km) to the visitor center* ☎609/3540 ⌨*BZ$10* ☉*Daily 9–5.*

MARUBA RESORT JUNGLE SPA

40 mi (65 km) northeast of Belize City.

Though essentially a jungle lodge, Maruba Resort Jungle Spa has nearly become a tourist destination in itself, thanks to its exotic and somewhat sensual atmosphere. Maruba's spa touts its "Mood Mud" therapy, using six different mud baths. One, the red Daji mood mud, is supposed to arouse sexual passion.

Day visitors can have lunch or another meal at Maruba, take a swim (a second pool is reserved for overnight guests only), go horseback riding (BZ$60 per person for a 1½-hour ride), and have spa treatments. A day-spa package, including lunch and two treatments, is BZ$370. Individual spa treatments are BZ$60–BZ$300. For something a little different, in the late afternoon the lodge puts out food for black vultures, and about 200 show up. If you want a more tangible souvenir of your visit, residents of Bomba Village, a small riverside village nearby, have made a modest trade out of carving bowls and other items from zericote, mahogany, rosewood, and other tropical hardwoods.

WHERE TO STAY & EAT

$$$–$$$$ ☒ **Maruba Resort Jungle Spa.** "Neo-primitive tribal chic" is how Maruba describes its style. We don't know about that, but the resort definitely delivers an exotic experience in a jungle setting, complete with 24-hour electricity, air-conditioned cabañas, fresh flowers in the rooms, high thread-count sheets, and, in some suites, hot tubs. The decor is

HISTORY

The Maya settled this area thousands of years before the time of Christ. Cuello, near Orange Walk Town, dates from 2500 BC, making it one of the earliest known Mayan sites in all of Mesoamerica (the region between central Mexico and northwest Costa Rica). In the Pre-Classic period (2500 BC–AD 300), the Maya expanded across northern Belize, establishing important communities and trading posts at Santa Rita, Cerros, Lamanai, and elsewhere.

During the Classic period (AD 300–AD 900), Santa Rita, Lamanai, Altun Ha, and other cities flourished. To feed large populations perhaps totaling several hundred thousand, the Maya developed sophisticated agricultural systems, with raised, irrigated fields along the New River and other river bottoms. After the mysterious collapse of the Mayan civilization by the 10th century AD, the region's cities went into decline, but the Maya continued to live in smaller communities and rural areas around the many lagoons in northern Belize, trading with other settlements in Belize and in Mexico. Lamanai, perched at the edge of the New River Lagoon, was continuously occupied for almost three millennia, until late in the 17th century.

The Spanish first set foot in these parts in the early 1500s, and Spanish missionaries made their way up the New River to establish churches in Mayan settlements in the 16th and 17th centuries. You can see the remains of a Spanish church at the entrance of Lamanai near Indian Church Village. About this same time, small groups of shipwrecked British sailors established settlements in Belize but the Battle of St. George's Caye in 1789 effectively put an end to Spanish control in Belize.

In the second half of the 19th century, the so-called Caste Wars (1847–1904), pitting Maya insurgents against Mestizo and European settlers in Mexico's Yucatán, had an important impact on northern Belize. Refugees from the bloody wars moved south from Mexico, settling in Corozal Town, Orange Walk Town, Sarteneja, and also on Ambergris Caye and Caye Caulker.

Today, more than 40,000 acres of sugarcane are harvested by 4,000 farmers in northern Belize. Mennonites, who came to the Blue Creek, Shipyard, and Little Belize areas in the late 1950s, have contributed greatly to agriculture in the region, producing rice, corn, chickens, milk, cheese, and beans. And tourism, foreign retirement communities, and casino gaming are becoming important, especially in northern Corozal District.

near, if not actually over, the top, with gold-painted stucco walls, mock stained-glass windows made from old bottles, and bold fabric prints. The restaurant boasts "nouveau jungle" cuisine, which means that it's not rice and beans, but rather a selection of fish, shrimp, and pork dishes, sometimes interestingly prepared, with salads and vegetables from local gardens. At night the restaurant and bar are bathed in black light. Maruba probably gets more mixed reactions from guests than any other hotel in Belize; some love it while others think it's tacky and overpriced, so look at it carefully before booking. **Pros:** Exotic, sexy, hip. **Cons:** Can be buggy, in the middle of nowhere, Maruba has been in trouble with naturalists for its "Viper Rum," bottled with a snake coiled at the bottom. ✉*Mile 40½ Old Northern Hwy., Maskall Village* ☎*225/5555, 800/627–8227 in U.S.* 🌐*www.maruba-spa.com* *8 rooms and 10 suites* *In-room: no phone, DVD, Wi-Fi. In-hotel: restaurant, bar, 2 pools, gym, no elevator, laundry service, airport shuttle* 💳*AE, MC, V.*

NORTHWEST ORANGE WALK DISTRICT

This district borders both Mexico and Guatemala and holds four areas well worth the time it takes to visit them: Lamanai Archeological Reserve, at the edge of the New River Lagoon; the Mennonite communities of Blue Creek, Shipyard, and Little Belize; the 260,000-plus acres of the Río Bravo Conservation Area; and Gallon Jug lands, 130,000 acres in which the Chan Chich Lodge nestles. Mennonites immigrated to Belize in the 1950s, and the most accessible and interesting community for visitors is Blue Creek Village, which is on the way to Río Bravo and Gallon Jug.

These areas, especially Río Bravo and Gallon Jug, are best visited on an overnight or multinight stay. You can visit Lamanai on a day trip by boat or road from Orange Walk Town, or from Corozal Town (and guided day tours are also available from Belize City, San Pedro, and Caye Caulker), though it's well worth at least an overnight stay. If you're staying in Blue Creek, you can go to Río Bravo, Lamanai, and even Gallon Jug and Chan Chich on a day trip, but the poor roads will slow you down, and you'll have little time to explore. Both the Gallon Jug and Programme for Belize (Río Bravo) lands are private, with gated entrances, so you'll need advance permission to visit.

ORANGE WALK TOWN

52 mi (85 km) north of Belize City.

Orange Walk Town is barely on the radar of tourists, except as a jumping-off point for boat trips to Lamanai, road trips to Gallon Jug and Río Bravo, or as a place to gas up en route from Corozal to Belize City. Though its population of around 18,000, mostly Mestizos, makes it the third-largest urban center in Belize (after Belize City and San Ignacio), it's more like a "county seat" in an agricultural area than a city. In this case, it's the county seat of Belize's sugarcane region and you'll see big tractors and trucks hauling sugarcane to the Tower Hill refinery. Happily, the new bypass around Orange Walk Town has reduced through-traffic.

The town's atmosphere will remind you a little of Mexico, with signs in Spanish, a central plaza, and sun-baked stores set close to the streets. The plaza, near the Orange Walk Town Hall, has a small market (daily except Sunday and holidays) with fruits, vegetables, and inexpensive local foods for sale. This was once the site of Fort Cairns, which dates to the Caste Wars of the 19th century.

CLOSE UP

What's in a Name?

The name Belize is a conundrum. According to *Encyclopaedia Britannica,* it derives from *belix,* an ancient Maya word meaning "muddy water." Anyone who's seen the Belize River swollen by heavy rains can vouch for this description. Others trace the name's origin to the French word *balise* (beacon), but no one can explain why a French word would have caught on in a region once dominated by the English (Belize was known as British Honduras). Perhaps nothing more than a drinker's tale, another theory connects Belize to the Maya word *belikin* (road to the east), which also happens to be the name of the national beer. Some say Belize is a corruption of Wallace, the name of a Scottish buccaneer who founded a colony in 1620; still others say the pirate wasn't Wallace but Willis, that he wasn't Scottish but English, and that he founded a colony not in 1620, but in 1638.

There was indeed a pirate named Wallace, a onetime lieutenant of Sir Walter Raleigh who later served as Tortuga's governor. Perhaps it was liquor or lucre that turned him into a pirate, but at some point in the early to mid-1600s, he and 80 fellow renegades washed up near St. George's Caye. They settled in and lived for years off the illicit booty of cloak-and-dagger raids on passing ships. In 1798, a fleet of 31 Spanish ships came to exterminate what had now blossomed into an upstart little colony. Residents had a total of one sloop, some fishing boats, and seven rafts, but their maritime knowledge enabled them to defeat the invaders in two hours. That was the last Spanish attempt to forcibly dislodge the settlement, though bitter wrangles over British Honduras's right to exist continued for nearly a century.

We may never know if Wallace and Willis were one and the same, but what's in a name, anyway? Grab a Belikin and come up with a few theories of your own.

⏱ **Las Banquitas House of Culture** is worth an hour of your time. This small museum—the name refers to the little benches in a nearby riverside park—presents changing exhibitions on Orange Walk District history and culture. It's one of three government-supported Houses of Culture in Belize; the other two are in Belize City and Benque Viejo del Carmen. ⊠ *Main and Bautista Sts.* ☎ *322/0517* ⧆ *Free, some exhibits have small fees* ⊗ *Tues.–Fri. 8:30–5:30, Sat. 8–1.*

WHERE TO STAY & EAT

$-$$ ✕ **El Establo Bar & Grill.** This friendly, family-run eatery near the northern end of the Orange Walk bypass opened in mid-2005. Your hosts are Albino and Ada Vargas, and it's a great place to stop on a trip between Belize City and Corozal Town. Enjoy local dishes such as cow-foot soup, *escabeche,* and, of course, rice and beans. ⊠ *Indian Hill, Northern Hwy.* ☎ *322/0094* ⊟ *No credit cards.*

$ ⌂ **Lamanai Riverside Retreat.** It's many miles from Lamanai (so much for truth in Belizean advertising), but this restaurant is pleasantly set right beside the New River, the water route to the famous Mayan ruins. The outdoor restaurant boasts a menu of 50 different items, including well-prepared local dishes such as stew chicken with rice and beans. While you sip a beer, you may even see a crocodile in the river, and unfortunately, if there's no breeze, you may also see mosquitoes. There are three cabañas—simple wooden affairs with air conditioning. Tent camping is also available. **Pros:** Relaxing riverside setting, friendly and environmentally conscious owners, open-air dining. **Cons:** It's a short hike into town, pesky mosquitoes. ✉*Lamanai Alley, Orange Walk Town* ☎*302/3955* ✉ *lamanairiverside@hotmail.com* ⌂*3 cabañas* ⛄*In-room: no phone. In-hotel: no elevator, Internet* ☐*MC, V.*

¢-$ 🏨**Hotel de la Fuente.** Orlando de
★ la Fuente's place is a step up from the other hotels in Orange Walk Town, and the remarkably low room rates, starting at BZ$50 with air-conditioning, put it among the best values in northern Belize. It won the 2006 Small Hotel of the Year award from the Belize Tourism Industry Association. All rooms have air-conditioning, complimentary wireless Internet, coffeemakers, and comfortable new beds. Two suites (BZ$120–BZ$140) have separate bedrooms and kitchenettes. The hotel arranges trips to Lamanai for BZ$80 per person, including lunch, admission, and pick-up and drop-off at the hotel. **Pros:** Great value, attractive and modern rooms, central location. **Cons:** Not much atmosphere, no pool. ✉*14 Main St., Orange Walk Town* ☎*322/2290* ⊕*www.hoteldelafuente.com* ⌂*8 rooms, 2 suites* ⛄*In-room: no phone, refrigerator, kitchen (some), Wi-Fi. In-hotel: no elevator, Internet, laundry service* ☐*MC, V.*

¢ 🏨**St. Christopher's Hotel.** On a quiet street near the Banquitos House of Culture and backing up on the New River, this family-run hotel has simple but clean rooms, with tile floors and brightly colored bedspreads, at reasonable rates. It's owned by the Urbina family, one of the oldest and largest families in the area, with roots in Orange Walk dating back to the early 1800s. The back gardens are attractive and alive with tropical plants, and you can relax in a thatch palapa with picnic tables next to the river. **Pros:** Unpretentious, family-run hotel, central location near market and the river, a good value. **Cons:** No-frills rooms. ✉*10 Main St., Orange Walk Town* ☎*322/2420 or 302/1064* ⊕*www.stchristophershotelbze.com* ⌂*25 rooms* ⛄*In-room: no a/c (some), no phone. In-hotel: restaurant, no elevator, laundry service* ☐*MC, V.*

3

LAMANAI

▲
Fodor'sChoice
★

About 2½ hours northwest of Belize City, or 24 mi (39 km) south of Orange Walk Town.

Lamanai ("submerged crocodile") is Belize's longest-occupied Mayan site, inhabited until well after Christopher Columbus discovered the New World in 1492. In fact archaeologists have found signs of continuous occupation from 1500 BC until AD 1700.

Lamanai's residents carried on a lifestyle that was passed down for millennia, until the Spanish missionaries arrived. You can still see the ruins of the missionaries' church in the nearby village of Indian Church. The same village also has an abandoned 19th-century sugar mill. With its immense drive wheel and steam engine—on which you can still read the name of the manufacturer, Leeds Foundry of New Orleans—swathed in strangler vines and creepers, it's a haunting sight.

A SPECIAL PLACE

What makes Lamanai so appealing is its setting on the west bank of a beautiful 28-mi-long (45-km-long) lagoon, one of only two waterside Mayan sites in Belize (the other is Cerros, near Corozal Town). Nearly 400 species of birds have been spotted in the area and a troop of howler monkeys visits the archaeological site regularly. Lamanai Outpost Lodge and other hotels offer guided tours of the ruins, but you can also explore the site on your own.

In all, 50 to 60 Mayan structures are spread over this 950-acre archaeological reserve. The most impressive is the largest Pre-Classic structure in Belize—a massive, stepped temple built into the hillside overlooking the New River Lagoon. Many structures at Lamanai have only been superficially excavated. Trees and vines grow from the tops of temples, and the sides of one pyramid are covered with vegetation. On the grounds you'll find a new visitor center with educational displays on the site, and pottery, carvings, and small statues, some dating back 2,500 years. Local villagers from the Indian Church Village Artisans Center set up small stands on the grounds to sell handmade carvings, jewelry, and other crafts, along with T-shirts and snacks. ⊠ *Near Indian Church Village, Orange Walk District* ⌦ *BZ$10* ⊗ *Daily 9–5.*

GETTING HERE   There are several ways to get here. One option is to drive on the well-maintained but mostly unpaved road from Orange Walk Town. Turn west at the Orange Walk fire station. From here go to Yo Creek, then southwest to San Felipe Village, a total of 24 mi (39 km). In San Felipe go straight (the road to Chan Chich turns to the right) for another 12 mi (19 km) to reach the ruins. Another route by road is via Shipyard—the unpaved road to Shipyard is just south of Orange Walk Town, so watch for a sign. The best way to approach the ruins, however, is by boat, which takes about an hour and a half from Orange Walk. Boats leave around 9 AM from the Tower Hill bridge over the New River on the Northern Highway, about 6 mi (10 km) south of Orange Walk. The cost is BZ$80 per person. Some hotels in Orange Walk Town arrange Lamanai tours, with pick up and drop off at the hotel, also for around BZ$80 per person. You can also take a 15-minute charter plane trip from Belize City. Charter flights are around BZ$400 for up to four persons. If staying overnight at Lamanai, your hotel or lodge can arrange transport by boat or plane.

WHERE TO STAY & EAT

$$$$ ⊞ **Lamanai Outpost Lodge.** Perched
★ on a low hillside on the New River Lagoon, this eco-lodge's well-designed thatch cabañas sit amid lovely gardens and have porches with lagoon views. The Lamanai ruins are within walking distance. There's a pricey, near all-inclusive plan with all meals, transfers, and activities, such as boat trips to catch and tag crocodiles, included. A room-only (EP) plan is also offered. The restaurant, Bushey's Place, serves excellent, filling meals. A dock extends 130 feet into the lagoon and is a good, safe place for swimming. A jarring recent addition is the lodge's airboats, which break the stillness of the lagoon with the loud roar of airplane props. **Pros:** Gorgeous setting on the New River Lagoon, easy access to Lamanai ruins, good tours. **Cons:** High rates, not easy to get to. ⊠*Indian Church* ☎672/2000, 888/733–7864 in U.S. ⊕*www.lamanai.com* ⇆*20 cabins* ⚷*In-room: no a/c (some), no phone, refrigerator, no TV. In-hotel: restaurant, bar, laundry service, public Internet, Wi-Fi, no elevator, airport shuttle* ⊟*AE, MC, V* ❙⊙❙*EP or AI.*

$$$ ⊞ **Lamanai South Lodge.** Lamanai South is a less-expensive alternative for overnighting near the Lamanai ruins. On 52 acres adjoining the New River Lagoon, the lodge has four rooms in a coral-color concrete building, with thatch roof, steps from the water. The rooms, with cream-color stucco walls, have furniture made of local hardwoods, screen windows front and back for ventilation, and verandas with views of the lagoon. Above the rooms is a 2,000 square-foot, thatched second level with a restaurant and bar, not always open. When available, meal packages are BZ$90 per person per day. **Pros:** Right at the edge of the New River Lagoon, lower prices than the better-known Lamanai Outpost. **Cons:** Long hike to Lamanai ruins, often just a caretaker on site, not well set up for tours. ⊠*Indian Church Village* ☎615/1892 ⊕*www. lamanaisouth.com* ⇆*4 rooms* ⚷*In-room: no a/c, no phone, no TV. In-hotel: restaurant, bar, no elevator* ⊟*MC, V* ❙⊙❙*MAP.*

MENNONITE COMMUNITIES

2½ hrs northwest of Belize City.

The Mennonite religion emerged in Holland during the Protestant Reformation in the 16th century. These Anabaptists (so called for the practice of baptizing adults) first moved to Germanic lands—many in Belize still speak Low German, which combines elements of German and Dutch—and then to Prussia, the United States (mainly Pennsylvania), and Manitoba, Canada. In the 1950s some 3,000 Mennonites emigrated to Belize, where they established communities in the Orange Walk and Cayo districts. Today, there are an estimated 8,000 Mennonites in Belize.

The Blue Creek Mennonite community, about midway between Orange Walk Town and Chan Chich Lodge—it's 33 mi (54 km) from Orange Walk Town via Yo Creek, August Pine Ridge, and San Felipe, and 36 mi (59 km) from Chan Chich—is predominantly progressive, which means the Mennonites accept modern conveniences such as automobiles and electricity.

Near the Linda Vista shopping center is a small bed-and-breakfast where you can stay and learn a little about Mennonite life in Belize. About 6 mi (10 km) beyond Blue Creek, you'll enter the Río Bravo reserve managed by Programme for Belize.

Most of the Mennonites in Shipyard, which you reach via an unpaved road that turns west off the Northern Highway just south of Orange Walk Town, and Little Belize, which you can visit by driving northeast from Orange Walk Town via San Estevan, are conservative; they shun the use of cars and motorized farm equipment. Both Little Belize and Shipyard are primarily farming areas and have no hotels or tourist facilities, but the unexpected sight, on dusty rural roads, of pale-skin folks in old-fashion dress—the women in long plaid dresses and the men with suspenders and straw hats—in horse-pulled buggies will remind you of how diverse Belizean culture really is.

WHERE TO STAY

$ ☒ **Hillside Bed and Breakfast.** After Mennonites John and Judy Klassen finished raising their 10 children, they opened this small B&B. It has clean motel-like rooms with 24-hour electricity on a hill overlooking Blue Creek Village, with two larger thatch cabañas nearby, down steep wood steps. Kitchen facilities are available. The breakfast (BZ$10) is huge and delicious, with homemade bread, fresh-squeezed orange juice, and locally produced milk and eggs. **Pros:** Beautiful vistas over Blue Creek, nice way to get to know a little of the Mennonite community. **Cons:** Basic, motel-like rooms, accessible only if you have your own transport. ☒ *General Delivery, Blue Creek Village* ☎ *323/0155* ☞ *5 rooms, 2 cabañas* ☪ *In-room: no a/c, no phone, kitchen (some), no TV. In-hotel: no elevator, laundry service* ☒ *No credit cards.*

RÍO BRAVO CONSERVATION & MANAGEMENT AREA

2½ hrs northwest of Belize City.

Created with the help of distinguished British naturalist Gerald Durrell, the Río Bravo Conservation & Management Area spans 260,000 acres near where Belize, Guatemala, and Mexico meet. The four-hour drive from Belize City takes you through wildlands where you may encounter a troupe of spider monkeys, wildcats, flocks of ocellated turkeys, a dense shower of butterflies—anything but another vehicle.

Managed by Belize City–based Programme for Belize, a not-for-profit organization whose mission is the wise use and conservation of Belize's natural resources, the Río Bravo Conservation Area contains some 400 species of birds, 70 species of mammals, and 200 types of trees. About one-half of Río Bravo is managed as a nature reserve, and the rest is managed to generate income, from forestry and other activities, including tourism.

Within the reserve's borders are more than 60 Mayan sites; many have yet to be explored. The most important is **La Milpa,** Belize's largest site beside Caracol and Lamanai. At its height between AD 400 and 830, La Milpa was home to almost 50,000 people. The suburbs of this city spread out some 3 mi (5 km) from the city center, and the entire city encompassed some 30 square mi (78 square km) in area. So far, archaeologists have discovered 20 large courtyards and 19 stelae.

Visiting Río Bravo, like the other areas of northwestern Orange Walk, is best done in a four-wheel-drive vehicle. You must make arrangements to visit in advance with **Programme for Belize** (☎ *227/5616 in Belize City* ⊕ *www.pfbelize.org*), as the entire Río Bravo conservation area is managed by this private, nonprofit organization, and the main road through its lands is gated. You also need advance reservations to stay at La Milpa Field Station *(see below)*. Staying overnight or longer at this field station is the best way to see Río Bravo, but you can visit it briefly on a day trip. From Belize City or Corozal Town, drive to Orange Walk Town, going into town rather than taking the bypass. Turn west at the crossroads near the Orange Walk fire station toward Yo Creek. Continue on through Yo Creek, following the road that turns sharply south and goes through San Lazaro, Trinidad, and August Pine Ridge villages. At San Felipe, 24 mi (40 km) from Orange Walk Town, the road turns sharply to the west (right) at a soccer field. Follow this road for about 7 mi (12 km) to the Río Bravo bridge and into Programme for Belize lands. If you don't have your own car, contact Programme for Belize and ask if they can arrange transportation for you from Orange Walk Town or elsewhere.

Guides and information are available at La Milpa Field Station. Chan Chich Lodge, Lamanai Outpost Lodge, and other hotels also can arrange visits with guides to La Milpa and the Río Bravo Conservation & Management Area. *Emory King's Driver's Guide to Beautiful Belize,* updated annually and available at many gift shops and hotels in Belize, has helpful maps and directions to this and other destinations in Orange Walk and other parts of Belize. The Programme for Belize Web site *(see above)* also has driving directions to La Milpa Field Station.

WHERE TO STAY

$$ 🏠 **La Milpa Field Station.** About 3 mi (5 km) from La Milpa Mayan site, this field station is a combination of hotel and summer camp. Stay in a rustic thatch cabañas with private bath or in a dorm that sleeps 30. Since you're in a remote area, you'll take all your meals, generally simple Belizean-style dishes such as rice and beans with stew chicken or pork, at the field station. Nine hiking trails are maintained around the lodge, and guides are available to take you to La Milpa and other Mayan sites. In spring and summer you can visit archaeological teams working at La Milpa. **Pros:** You'll feel like an archaeologist here, quiet and remote setting surrounded only by nature, serves filling Belizean dishes. **Cons:** Not for the party crowd, not easy to get to. ⊠ *1 Eyre St.,*

☎227/5616 ⊕*www.pfbelize.org* ⇝*8 rooms in 4 cabins, 1 dormitory (30 beds) ⚤In-room: no a/c, no phone, no TV. In-hotel: restaurant, no elevator* ⊟*MC, V* ⦿*FAP.*

GALLON JUG

3½ hrs northwest of Belize City.

The 130,000 acres of Gallon Jug Estates is owned by Sir Barry Bowen, one of Belize's wealthiest businessmen. Living among the old-growth mahogany trees and many other tropical hardwoods are more than 350 species of birds and many mammals and reptiles. Jaguar sightings are fairly common around the lodge Chan Chich, averaging around one a week. You're likely to see toucans, many different hummingbirds, and flocks of parrots.

This is a working farm that produces coffee and raises cattle, cacao, and corn. It's the only truly commercial coffee operation in Belize—elevations in Belize are too low to grow high-quality Arabica coffees that thrive at over 4,000 feet—producing Gallon Jug Estates coffee from coffee trees on more than 100 acres. Gallon Jug Estates also produces hot sauces and delicious mango jams, which are for sale in Belize and elsewhere. Tours of the coffee plantings and the production facility, along with other farm tours, can be arranged through Chan Chich Lodge.

Chan Chich, also owned by Bowen, is one of the best jungle lodges in Central America, if not the world. This is the only place to stay in the area. It's possible to visit on a day trip from La Milpa Field Station, Blue Creek Village, or even Lamanai or Orange Walk Town, but you need your own transportation and advance permission to come on the gated Gallon Jug lands.

The easiest and fastest way to get here is by charter airplane (about BZ$500, depending on the number of people, to Gallon Jug Estates' own 3,000-foot airstrip). Javier Flying Service in Belize City has several flights a week on a three-seater airplane, and flights are also available through Maya Island Air and Tropic Air. Chan Chich will arrange the flights for you. You can also drive to Chan Chich, about 3½ hours from Belize City. Follow the route to Río Bravo *(see above)* and continue on through Programme for Belize lands to the Cedar Crossing gatehouse and into Gallon Jug lands. It's a long but beautiful drive, and you're almost certain to see a considerable amount of wildlife along the dirt road. An alternate route is from the Cayo District in western Belize. However, at present, Chan Chich only occasionally grants permission to come via the Cayo, as most of the route is through private lands, and the roads are not well marked. In any case, you need to ask the lodge in advance for permission to visit by car, and the lodge will provide detailed driving directions.

WHERE TO STAY & EAT

$$$$

Fodor's Choice

★

🖼 **Chan Chich Lodge.** Coca-Cola and Belikin "Belizeanaire" Sir Barry Bowen, knighted by Queen Elizabeth in 2008, built these cabañas, which are at once rustic yet eminently comfortable with thatch roofs, rich hardwood floors and furnishings, and wraparound verandas. Recently renovated, the deluxe cabañas have king beds and huge new bathrooms with miles of marble, granite, glass, and even bidets. The gorgeous new two-bedroom villa (BZ$1,790 for up to five persons) has two king beds, two baths, and air-conditioning. The lodge sits smack dab in the middle of a Mayan archaeological site, and regardless of how you feel about that, Chan Chich is simply one of the best jungle lodges in Central America. Former president Jimmy Carter is counted among the lodge's many illustrious previous guests. Guides lead wildlife excursions into the thousands of acres of surrounding bush. Tour options include bird-watching treks and horseback rides to Mayan ruins that remain undisturbed. Howler monkeys welcome you with reverberating bass calls. You're more likely to see an elusive jaguar here than anywhere else outside the Belize Zoo. A gorgeous pool is screened to keep out insects. An all-inclusive option with meals, most tours, and local beers is BZ$1,040–BZ$1,100 double, plus tax, in-season. **Pros:** Arguably the best birding and wildlife spotting in Belize, so safe you don't lock your cabañas door, magnificent setting within Mayan site, understated but eminently comfortable accommodations. **Cons:** Difficult to get to, definitely splurge prices. ⬨ *Box 37, Belize City* 🖀 *223/4419, 800/343–8009 in U.S.* ⊕ *www.chanchich.com* 🗏 *12 cabañas, 1 2-bedroom villa* ⬨ *In-room: no a/c (some), no phone, no TV. In-hotel: restaurant, bar, pool, no elevator, public Internet, Wi-Fi, laundry service* ⊟ *AE, MC, V* 🍽 *EP or AI.*

3

COROZAL BAY

Corozal Bay, or Chetumal Bay as it's called on most maps, has turquoise waters. It provides a beautiful waterside setting for Corozal Town and a number of villages along the north side of Corozal District. Tarpon, bonefish, permit, and other game fish are not hard to find. The drawback is that there are few natural beaches in Corozal District, although some hotels have trucked in sand to build human-assisted beach areas. Also, there's no good snorkeling or diving locally, and the Belize Barrier Reef is several long hours away by boat. However, the Mexican border and the city of Chetumal is only 9 mi (14½ km) away. Chetumal, capital of Quintana Roo state, with a modern mall and air-conditioned multiplex movie theaters, provides a bustling counterpoint to easygoing Corozal.

At the border, the Commercial Free Zone (usually called the Corozal Free Zone, though that's not its official name) promises duty-free goods and cheap gas. The reality is a little less appealing. Most of the duty-free items are cheap trinkets from China and Taiwan, and the gasoline, while one-third cheaper than in Belize, is more expensive than in Mexico. Plus, to sample the questionable enticements of the Free Zone, visitors have to formally exit Belize, paying exit taxes and fees.

Casinos have sprung up on the Belize side of the border, at the edge of the Commercial Free Zone. There are three casinos: the **Princess Casino,** the larger **Royal Princess Casino** (both associated with the Princess Hotel & Casino in Belize City), and the largest of the three, the **Las Vegas Casino,** which opened in late 2006. The Las Vegas casino has 54,000 square feet of gaming area, making it, according to management, the largest in Central America. In addition to more than 300 slot machines, plus blackjack, roulette, and poker, the casino has gaming areas designed to appeal to visitors from Asia, with Pai Gow, mahjongg, and other games. There's also a private club area for high rollers from Mexico and elsewhere. The Las Vegas Casino has broken ground on a new 385-room hotel, expected to open in 2009. If it actually does, it will be by far the largest hotel in Belize.

COROZAL TOWN

95 mi (153 km) north of Belize City.

Settled by refugees from the Yucatán during the 19th-century Caste Wars, Corozal is the last town before Río Hondo, the river separating Belize from Mexico. Though thoroughly ignored by today's travelers, this friendly town is great for a few days of easy living. It's hard not to fall into the laid-back lifestyle here—a sign at the entrance of a local grocery used to advertise STRONG RUM, 55 BELIZE DOLLARS A GALLON.

English is the official language in Corozal, but Spanish is just as common here. The town was largely rebuilt after Hurricane Janet nearly destroyed it in 1955, so it's neat and modern. Hurricane Dean in 2007 sideswiped Corozal Town, blowing off some roofs and knocking down trees, but otherwise did no serious damage. Many houses are clapboard, built on wooden piles, and other houses are simple concrete-block structures, though the growing clan of expats is putting up new houses that wouldn't look out of place in Florida. One of the few remaining colonial-era buildings is a portion of the old fort in the center of town.

The history of Corozal, including a graphic portrayal of the brutality of colonial rule on the indigenous people, is depicted in a strikingly beautiful mural by Manuel Villamar Reyes on the wall of the **Corozal Town Hall.** ⊠ *1st St. S* ☎ *422/2072* ▦ *Free* ☉ *Mon.–Sat. 9–noon and 1–5.*

A landmark 1886 former lighthouse near the market houses the **Corozal Cultural Center,** along with a museum and the Belize Tourist Industry Association information center. You can still see the spiral staircase and parts of the original beacon. On display are handblown rum bottles and a traditional Mayan thatch hut. ⊠ *Off 1st Ave. at edge of Corozal Bay* ☎ *422–3176* ▦ *BZ$10* ☉ *Daily 8–5.*

Not far from Corozal are several Mayan sites. The closest, **Santa Rita,** is a short walk from the town's center. It's on a low hill across from the Coca-Cola plant. Only a few of its structures have been excavated, and there's currently no visitor center open, so it takes some imagination to picture this settlement, founded in 1500 BC, as one of the district's major trading centers. It isn't currently officially open, but you can walk around the site.

A twice-daily water taxi service, the *Thunderbolt,* runs from Corozal Town to San Pedro, Ambergris Caye, with a stop on demand at Sarteneja.

WHERE TO STAY & EAT

$-$$ ✕**RD's Diner.** A gregarious Belizean from Punta Gorda owns and runs this inexpensive new restaurant. The focus here is seafood, but the menu runs the gamut, from a double cheeseburger (BZ$10) to baked ribs with mushroom sauce (BZ$15.) The conch steak, lightly cooked in garlic butter and served with potatoes and salad (BZ$18),

> ### HOT PROPERTY
>
> Corozal District has become a hot spot for expats seeking property for retirement and for snowbirds looking for a vacation home at prices considerably lower than at beach areas such as Ambergris Caye or Placencia. Several hundred foreign expats live in Corozal District, and the numbers are growing. They're attracted by home prices that sound as if they're from the 1970s—a two-bedroom, modern home in a nice area can go for less than US$100,000, though you can always pay more.

is a must. You'll enjoy almost anything else on the menu, but avoid the nachos drowning in pseudo-cheese. ⊠*4th Ave.* ☎*422/3796* ◷Closed Tues. ⊟*MC, V.*

¢-$$ ✕**Patti's Bistro.** Although Patti's is next door to an undertaker and the street address is the unlucky number 13, you don't have to worry—the food here is among the best in town, the service is sprightly and friendly, and prices are low. A delicious fried-chicken dinner with salad and mashed potatoes is only BZ$9 and a T-bone steak dinner BZ$15. Sit inside or at one of the handful of outdoor tables. ⊠*13 4th Ave.* ☎*402/0174* ◷Closed Sun. ⊟*MC, V.*

¢-$ ✕**Cactus Plaza.** For a great bargain, grab a seat and order a plateful of tacos, tostadas, *salbutes* (stuffed tortillas), and other Mexican finger foods. You won't be stuck with a big check: most entrées are less than BZ$8. Everything is freshly made and tasty. On weekends, this becomes more of a nightclub, and it can be noisy. ⊠*6 6th St. S, 2 blocks west of bay* ☎*442/0394* ◷Closed Sun.– Tues. ⊟*No credit cards.*

$-$$ ▩**Casablanca by the Sea.** It's worth a short trip to Consejo just to see ★ the hand-carved mahogany doors gracing many of the room entrances at this inn. Beverly Temte, an expat from New England, created this appealing, small hotel. In a quiet village, with views of Chetumal across Corozal Bay, this is a fine place to get away. Be warned, though: The location is off the beaten path, the TVs get only a few Spanish-language channels, and there's not much to do around the hotel. The best rooms are the second-floor units (BZ$210) facing the bay. The first-floor restaurant serves tasty Belizean and American food, and the waterside area with a palapa and a pier is perfect for sipping drinks on the bay. **Pros:** Charming bayside setting, great place to get away, well-maintained. **Cons:** Taxi or your own transportation required to visit town, no pool or beach, bay swimming is only so-so. ⊠*8 mi (18 km) northeast of Corozal Town, Consejo* ☎*423/1018 or 888/790–5264* ⊕*www.*

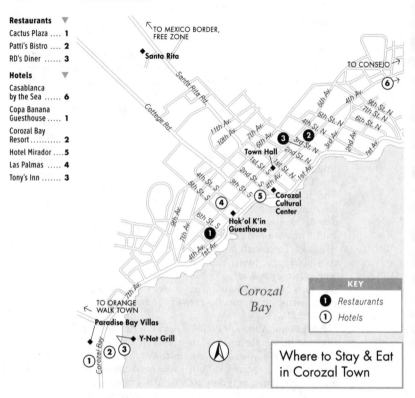

Where to Stay & Eat
in Corozal Town

casablanca-bythesea.com ➷7 rooms, 3 suites ♨In-room: mini-fridge
(some), DVD, no phone. In-hotel: restaurant, bar, bayfront, no elevator ▤AE, MC, V.

$ ▦**Copa Banana Guesthouse.** This homelike hotel, painted bright yellow,
has five sunny suites carved out of two houses across the street from
Corozal Bay. Guests share a kitchen, dining room, and living room. A
two-bedroom apartment also is available for longer-term rental. The
owners, who run a real estate agency in Corozal, also rent cars. Bikes
are complimentary. **Pros:** Handy to have kitchen privileges, tastefully
decorated, close to bay. **Cons:** Bike ride or long walk to heart of town, it
may seem a little crowded. ✉409 Bay Shore Dr. ☎422/0284 ⊕www.
copabanana.bz ➷5 rooms, 1 apartment ♨In-room: no phone. In-
hotel: bicycles, no elevator, no-smoking rooms ▤MC, V.

$ ▦**Corozal Bay Resort.** With more than an acre of beachfront on Coro-
zal Bay, the hotel's large beach is courtesy of its owners, Doug and
Maria Podzun, who trucked in tons of sand. The bayside resort has
nicely done thatch cabañas in pastel colors and a restaurant and bar,
both recently spruced up. The glass-walled palapa nightclub and restaurant, adjacent to the pool, have views of the bay. **Pros:** Nice tropical
feel to thatch cabañas, breezy bayside setting, room prices have been
reduced. **Cons:** Pool needs TLC, beach has seawall. ✉Almond Dr. off

Northern Hwy. at south end of Corozal Town ☎*422/2691* ⊕*www. corozalbayinn.com* ⇆*10 cabañas* ⌂*In-room: no phone, refrigerator, Wi-Fi. In-hotel: restaurant, bar, pool, beachfront, public Wi-Fi, no elevator* ⊟*MC, V.*

$ ⊡**Tony's Inn.** One of the oldest hotels and restaurants in Corozal, Tony's Inn is still going strong, despite the passing of its founder, Tony Castillo. His family now runs the motel. The rooms have been upgraded—but perhaps not enough—and now all have air-conditioning, phones, and mahogany furniture. At the inn's popular restaurant, Y Not Grill & Bar, in a breezy bayside thatch palapa, fajitas (chicken, beef, shrimp, or combo) are the way to go. **Pros:** Breezy bayside setting, excellent restaurant on-site, safe guarded parking. **Cons:** Long walk into the heart of town, rooms have been here a long time and while updated could still use some work. ⊠*South End, Corozal Town* ☎*422/2055, 800/447–2931 in U.S.* ⊕*www.tonysinn.com* ⇆*24 rooms* ⌂*In-hotel: 2 restaurants, bar, bayfront, no elevator, laundry service, no-smoking rooms, public Internet, public Wi-Fi* ⊟*AE, MC, V.*

¢-$ ⊡**Hotel Mirador.** Breathless as you may be, when you reach the fifth-level terrace of this new hotel—the highest point in Corozal Town—the views of Corozal Bay and town are breathtaking. The owners also operate a furniture store in Corozal, and they've outfitted the tiled and plastered rooms with beds and furnishings from their store. A Chinese eatery called Romantic Restaurant (which, sadly, it is not) occupies part of the first floor. **Pros:** No need for a Stairmaster, beautiful views from top-floor patio, good value in the heart of town. **Cons:** Layout of stairs precludes bay views from many rooms, mediocre food at Chinese restaurant, sometimes less than customer-friendly service. ⊠*4th Ave. and 2nd St. S.* ☎*422/0189* ✎*miradorhotel-coro@hotmail.com* ⇆*24 rooms* ⌂*In-room: no a/c (some), no phone, Wi-Fi. In-hotel: restaurant, bar, no elevator, public Internet* ⊟*AE, MC, V.*

¢-$ ⊡**Las Palmas.** Formerly the budget-level Nestor's Hotel, new owners have totally renovated and rebuilt, bringing the whole property upmarket. The three-story concrete hotel is right in the middle of town, inside a walled courtyard. The rooms, with whitewashed stucco walls, have new beds, linens, and brightly colored bedspreads, and all have air-conditioning, TVs, and mini-refrigerators. Doubles start at BZ$90 plus tax. **Pros:** Handy location in town, good value. **Cons:** Not on the water, limited secure parking. ⊠*123 5th Ave.* ☎*422/0196* ⊕*www.laspalmashotelbelize.com* ⇆*20 rooms* ⌂*In-room: no phone, Internet, refrigerator. In-hotel: restaurant, bar, no elevator, laundry service* ⊟*MC, V.*

COPPER BANK

12 mi (20 km) southeast of Corozal Town.

Copper Bank is a tidy and small (population around 500) Mestizo fishing village on Corozal Bay. The village is something of a footnote to the nearby Mayan site, Cerros.

Like the Tulum site in Mexico, the small site of **Cerros** is unusual in that it is directly on the water. With a beautiful setting on Corozal Bay, the late Pre-Classic center dates to 2000 BC and includes a ball court, several tombs, and a large temple. One way to get here is by boat from Corozal, which costs around BZ$120–BZ$180 for up to four people. You can also drive from Corozal Town, crossing the New River on the hand-pulled ferry. To get to the ferry from Corozal, take the Northern Highway south toward Orange Walk Town to just south of Jal's Travel and Paula's Gift Shop. Turn left and follow this unpaved road for 2½ mi (4 km) to the ferry landing. After crossing the river, you'll come to a T-intersection. Turn left for Copper Bank; the right turn takes you to Progresso. The trip to Copper Bank takes about a half hour, but longer after heavy rains, as the dirt road can become very bad, even impassable. As you enter Copper Bank, watch for signs directing you to "Cerros Maya." ⊠ *2½ mi (4 km) north of Copper Bank* ☎ *No phone* 🖃 *BZ$10, although at times there's no caretaker to collect* ⊙ *Daily 8–4.*

WHERE TO STAY & EAT

¢-$ 🍽 **Cerros Beach Resort.** New in 2006, Cerros Beach Resort is an off-the-beaten-path option for good food and simple lodging on Corozal Bay, near the Cerros ruins. Expat owners Bill and Jen cook up a mean chicken Cordon Bleu, pumpkin cheesecake, and other surprisingly sophisticated dishes (given the out-of-the-way location). On Sundays, there's usually a beach barbecue, and in-season a weekly gourmet dinner by reservation only. Guests typically come by boat from Consejo or Corozal Town, but except after heavy rains, you can also drive here. If you want to stay overnight, four small solar-powered cabañas go for as little as BZ$80, less off-season. **Pros:** Low-key, crowd-free small resort on the bay, tasty food, good value. **Cons:** Easiest to get to by boat, resort lost some of its trees in Hurricane Dean in 2007. ⊹ *Near Cerros Maya site on north side of Cerros peninsula; entering Copper Bank village, watch for signs to Cerros Beach Resort; the resort will arrange for a pick up by boat from Consejo or Corozal Town for parties of 5 or more* ☎ *623/9766* ⊕ *www.cerrosbeachresort.com* ⌑ *4 cabañas* ⌂ *In-room: no a/c, no TV, no phone. In-hotel: restaurant, bar, beachfront, no elevator, public Internet* ☐ *MC, V.* ⊙ *Restaurant closed Mon.; irregular hrs.*

$ 🍽 **Copper Bank Inn.** Open in 2004, Copper Bank Inn is housed in what is probably the largest building in the village, a white, two-story 10,000-square-foot house. There's a small bar and restaurant on the first floor. The guest rooms are pleasant, with tile floors, mahogany furniture, wooden shutters, and white plaster walls. **Pros:** You'll likely be the only guest in this big old house. **Cons:** You'll be the only guest. ⊠ *Copper Bank Village* ☎ *608/0838* ⊕ *www.copperbankinn.com* ⌑ *10 rooms* ⌂ *In-room: no phone. In-hotel: restaurant, bar, no elevator, laundry service* ☐ *MC, V.*

SARTENEJA

40 mi (67 km) from Corozal Town.

This small Mestizo and Creole community enjoys a bay setting that makes it one of the most relaxed and appealing in all of Belize. Lobster fishing and pineapple farming are the town's two main industries, though Sarteneja is also a center for building wooden boats. Most residents speak Spanish as a first language, but many also speak English.

Visitors and real estate buyers are beginning to discover Sarteneja, and while tourism services are still minimalist, several small guesthouses are now open, and there are several places to get a simple, inexpensive bite to eat.

Driving to Sarteneja from Corozal Town takes about 1½ hours via the New River ferry and a second, bayside ferry across the mouth of the river. The road is unpaved and can be very muddy after heavy rains. You can also drive to Sarteneja from Orange Walk Town, a trip of about 40 mi (67 km) and 1½ hours. There are several Perez Bus Line buses a day, except Sunday, from Belize City via Orange Walk Town. The trip from Belize City takes 3½ to 4 hours and costs BZ$10.

The twice-daily water taxi between Corozal Town and San Pedro will drop you at Sarteneja, on request (BZ$25 from Corozal, around 45 minutes, and BZ$45 from San Pedro, about 75 minutes). You also can hire a private boat in Corozal to take you and your party to Sarteneja; the cost is negotiable but likely will be BZ$200 or more. You may be able to hitch a ride on one of the skiffs that travels between Corozal and Sarteneja or between Chetumal, Mexico, and Sarteneja.

There is no immigration office in Sarteneja, so if you're coming from Mexico, you can go to the Sarteneja police station to get your Belize entry permit. Sarteneja has a recently opened airstrip, with two flights daily on Tropic Air from San Pedro (BZ$164 round-trip).

About 3½ mi (6 km) west of Sarteneja on the road to Orange Walk or Corozal is the ⚠ **Shipstern Wildlife Reserve.** You pass the entrance and visitor center as you drive into Sarteneja. The 31 square mi (81 square km) of tropical forest forming the reserve are, like the Crooked Tree Wildlife Sanctuary, a paradise for bird-watchers. Currently, Shipstern is owned and operated by a Swiss conservationist nongovernmental organization, but it is slated to become a Belize national park managed by the Belize Audubon Society. More than 250 species of birds have been identified here. Look for egrets (there are 13 species), American coots, keel-billed toucans, flycatchers, warblers, and several species of parrots. Mammals are in healthy supply as well, including pumas, jaguars, and raccoons. The butterfly farm next to the visitor center is now a small education area, and butterflies are being repopulated.

Nearby, the museum at Mahogany Park focuses on the history and uses of this beautiful tropical hardwood. There is a botanical trail leading from the visitor center, with the names of many plants and trees identified on small signs. Admission, a visit to the butterfly center, and a one-hour guided tour of the botanical trail is BZ$10 per person. You can add a tour of the Mahogany Park for BZ$5. Other tours are available, including a full-day lagoon tour for BZ$150 for a group of up to six. ✉*Sarteneja* ☎*223/4533* ⊕*www.belizeaudubon.org.*

WHERE TO STAY

$ Krisamis Bayview Lodge. This little single-story hotel, steps from the sea, has three rooms, each with two double beds. Meals are available if ordered in advance. Shipstern and boat tours are offered. The restaurant has a colorful mural, by local artist Cluterio Carillo, depicting some of the history of Sarteneja. **Pros:** Breezy bayfront location. **Cons:** A little more expensive than most other options in Sarteneja. ⊠*North Front St., Sarteneja Village, on the seafront at the west end of the village* ☎*423/2283* ⊕*www.krisamis.com* ⬎*3 rooms* ⚬*In-room: no a/c, no phone, Wi-Fi. In-hotel: Seafront, restaurant, no elevator, laundry service* ☰*MC, V.*

¢–$ Fernando's Seaside Guesthouse. Lounge on the second-floor veranda of this small guesthouse and watch the fishing boats anchored just a few hundred feet away. The best room is at the front of the hotel, with a window looking toward the sea, a king-size bed, air-conditioning, and cable TV. Owner Fernando Alamilla is a licensed guide and can arrange trips to Bacalar Chico National Park & Marine Reserve at the north end of Ambergris Caye. The owner's mother prepares meals for guests, if requested in advance. **Pros:** Seaside location, water views from the comfy second-floor porch. **Cons:** Rooms at back lack a sea view and those without air-conditioning can be hot. ⊠*North Front St., Sarteneja Village* ☎*423/2085* ⊕*www.cybercayecaulker.com/sarteneja.html* ⬎*4 rooms* ⚬*In-room: no a/c (some), no phone. In-hotel: restaurant, bar, beachfront, no elevator, laundry service* ☰*MC, V.*

¢ Backpackers Paradise. A young Canadian-Swiss couple offer hostel-like accommodation near Sarteneja village, and it's a bargain—BZ$10 for a small cabañas or BZ$5 per person for camping. Be aware that the cabañas are barely large enough for a double bed, lacking chairs, closet, and any frills. All but one cabin share a communal bathroom. The restaurant is equally wallet-friendly, with prices from BZ$2 to BZ$8. **Pros:** Friendly, inexpensive, you can pick your own tropical fruit from the owners' trees. **Cons:** Truly basic, best suited for hard-core backpackers. ⊠*Bandera Rd., Sarteneja Village* ☎*403/2051* ⊕*www.cabanasbelize. com* ⬎*4 rooms, 3 with shared bath* ⚬*In-room: no a/c, no TV, no phone. In-hotel: restaurant, no elevator* ☰*No credit cards*

¢ Candalie's Seaside Cabañas. Our picks for the best, and best-value, lodging in Sarteneja are two seaside cottages at Candalie's: Named Wood Stork and Brown Pelican, the high-ceilinged cabins each have double beds, cable TV, and plenty of space. Wood Stork, closer to the water and with a large mural of the stork on the side, has air-conditioning, while Brown Pelican has a fan. Both are bargains, at BZ$80 plus tax. The two share a restaurant, where meals must be ordered in advance. **Pros:** Spacious private cottages, seaside location, good value. **Cons:** Mattresses are thin, furnishings wouldn't win any interior design awards, limited hot water. ⊠*North Front St., Sarteneja Village, on the seafront at the west end of the village* ☎*423/2005* ✉ *candaliescabanas@yahoo.com* ⬎*2 cottages* ⚬*In-room: no a/c (some), no phone. In-hotel: seafront, no elevator, laundry service* ☰*No credit cards.*

NORTHERN BELIZE ESSENTIALS

TRANSPORTATION

BY AIR

Corozal Town has flights only to and from San Pedro (Ambergris Caye), and some of these flights stop at Sarteneja. Airstrips at Lamanai and Gallon Jug have charter service. Tropic Air and Maya Island Air each fly four or five times daily between Ambergris Caye and the airstrip at Corozal, about 2 mi (3 km) south of town off the Northern Highway. The journey takes 20 minutes and costs BZ$86 one way. There's no direct service to Belize City or other destinations in Belize. Charter service is available to Chan Chich Lodge and the Indian Church/Lamanai area. An airstrip has opened at Sarteneja, and from San Pedro to Corozal, two Tropic Air flights daily stop at Sarteneja. The one-way fare is BZ$86.

Contacts **Tropic Air** (☎ *226/2012, 800/422–3435 in U.S.* ⊕ *www.tropicair.com*).
Maya Island Air (☎ *422/2333, 800/225–6732 in U.S.* ⊕ *www.mayaairways.com*).

BY BOAT & FERRY

An old, hand-pulled sugar barge ferries passengers and cars across the 100-yard-wide New River from just south of Corozal Town to the road to Copper Bank, Cerros, and the Shipstern peninsula. The ferry is free from 6 AM to 9 PM daily. To get to the ferry from Corozal, take the Northern Highway toward Orange Walk Town to just south of Jal's Travel and Paula's Gift Shop. Turn left and follow the unpaved road to the ferry landing. A bridge over the New River has been promised, but there's no word on when it may be built. A second, hand-pulled auto ferry has been added between Copper Bank and Sarteneja. From Copper Bank, follow the ferry signs. Near Chunox, at a T-intersection, turn left and follow the unpaved road 20 mi (32 km) to Sarteneja.

A twice-daily water taxi operates between Corozal Town and Ambergris Caye, with a stop on demand at Sarteneja. The *Thunderbolt* boats depart from Corozal at the pier near Reunion Park behind Corozal Cultural Center at 7 AM and 3 PM and go from San Pedro also at 7 AM and 3 PM, leaving from the *Thunderbolt* dock on the back side of the island. Fare is BZ$45 one way. The boats have three 250-horsepower outboards, a canopy cover with sliding windows, and bus-style seats. The trip usually takes about two hours but may be longer if there's a stop at Sarteneja.

From Chetumal, Mexico, you can arrange to have a skiff bring you directly to Sarteneja; the boat trip takes less than an hour and avoids a long bus ride. The charge is negotiable but is usually around US$20 per person. You can have your passport stamped at the police station in Sarteneja.

Tour boats run from near Orange Walk, and less frequently from Corozal, on the New River to Lamanai. Boats from San Pedro and Caye

Caulker bring visitors from those islands to Altun Ha and environs via Bomba, a small coastal village.

Contact **Thunderbolt** (⊠ *San Pedro Town* ☎ *610/4475* ✍ *thunderbolttravels@ yahoo.com*).

BY BUS

Bus service to the villages and other sites off the Northern Highway is limited, so to reach them you're best off with a rental car or a guided tour. Air service to northern Belize is spotty. Several small bus lines, including Northern Transport, Gil Harry, Tillett's, T-Line, and others, make the 3- to 3½-hour journey between Belize City and Corozal Town, approximately every hour. About half the buses continue on to Chetumal, Mexico. Any nonexpress bus will stop and pick up almost anywhere along the highway. The cost is about BZ$10, or BZ$12 for express service. There's limited bus service on the Old Northern Highway and from Orange Walk to Sarteneja. Two daily buses go from Chetumal to Sarteneja.

In addition to regular buses, a Guatemalan tourism bus operator, Línea Dorada, operates a daily bus from the main Chetumal bus terminal, currently leaving at 5 AM and going all the way to Flores, Guatemala, near Tikal, with a stop at the Marine Terminal in Belize City. The trip takes about 8 hours and costs BZ$50–BZ$60.

BY CAR

Corozal is the last stop on the Northern Highway before you hit Mexico. The 95-mi (153-km) journey from Belize City will probably take about two hours, unless you're slowed by sugarcane trucks. The Northern Highway is a two-lane paved road in good condition. Other roads, including the Old Northern Highway, roads to Lamanai, Río Bravo, and Gallon Jug, and the road to Sarteneja are mostly unpaved. Because tour and long-distance taxi prices are high, especially if you're traveling with family or in a group, you likely will save money by renting a car, despite the relatively high cost of car rental and fuel in Belize.

Car rental agencies in Belize City will deliver vehicles to Corozal and Orange Walk for a small fee, around BZ$80–BZ$100. Corozal Bay Inn in Corozal Town and Copa Banana (⇨ *above*), and one small local car rental agency, Corozal Cars, have a few cars to rent. Corozal police enthusiastically ticket cars from other parts of Belize for such minor violations as parking the wrong way on a one-way street, so be especially cautious.

BY TAXI

To get around Corozal, call the Taxi Association or ask your hotel to arrange for transportation. Likewise, in Orange Walk call the Taxi Association or ask your hotel to arrange a taxi.

Contacts **Corozal Cars** (⊠ *Mile 85, Northern Hwy., Corozal* ☎ *422/3339* ⊕ *www. corozalcars.com*). **Taxi Association** (⊠ *1st St. S, Corozal* ☎ *422/2035*). **Taxi Association** (⊠ *Queen Victoria Ave., Orange Walk* ☎ *322/2560*).

CONTACTS & RESOURCES

BANKS & EXCHANGE SERVICES

Although American dollars are accepted everywhere in Corozal and Orange Walk, money changers at the Mexico border and in Corozal Town exchange Belize dollars for U.S. and Mexican currency, usually for better rates than in banks. The three banks in Corozal—Atlantic Bank, Belize Bank, and ScotiaBank—have ATMs, and all three now accept ATM cards issued outside Belize. Orange Walk Town also has branches of Belize Bank and ScotiaBank with ATMs that accept foreign ATM cards. There are no banks in Sarteneja or the Copper Bank area.

Contacts **Atlantic Bank** (⊠ *1 Park St. S, Corozal* ☎ *422/3473*). **Belize Bank** (⊠ *5th Ave. at 1st St. S, Corozal* ☎ *422/2087* ⊠ *Main and Park Sts., Orange Walk* ☎ *322/2019*). **ScotiaBank** (⊠ *4th Ave., Corozal* ☎ *422/2046* ⊠ *Main and Park Sts., Orange Walk* ☎ *322/2194*).

EMERGENCIES

For dental and medical care, many of Corozal's residents go to Chetumal, Mexico. In Corozal call Bethesda Medical Centre if you need medical care or Dr. Glenda Major if you require a dentist. The Corozal Hospital, with only limited facilities, is on the Northern Highway. In Orange Walk, the Northern Regional Hospital doesn't look very appealing, but it provides emergency and other services. Consider going to Belize City for medical and dental care, if possible.

Doctors & Dentists **Bethesda Medical Centre** (⊠ *Mile 85½, Northern Hwy.), Corozal* ☎ *422/2129*). **Glenda Major, D.D.S** (⊠ *1st St. S, Corozal* ☎ *422/2837*).

Hospitals **Corozal Hospital** (⊠ *Northern Hwy., Corozal* ☎ *422/2076*). **Northern Regional Hospital** (⊠ *Northern Hwy., Orange Walk* ☎ *322/2752*).

Pharmacies **V-Mart Pharmacy** (⊠ *4th Ave. and 1st St. N, Corozal* ☎ *422/2597*). **de la Fuente Drugstore** (⊠ *16 Main St., Orange Walk* ☎ *322/2035*).

INTERNET, MAIL & SHIPPING

The Corozal post office, on the west side of the main town plaza, is open 8:30–noon and 1–4:30. The Orange Walk post office has the same hours and is at the north end of town on the main road through town, Queen Victoria Avenue (locally known as Belize-Corozal Road, which is the same as the Northern Highway). Internet cafés in Corozal open and close frequently. The Belize Telecommunications Ltd. office has Internet access for BZ$5 per half hour. Most Corozal Town hotels have Internet of some kind, either Wi-Fi or a computer connected to the Internet. Contacts **Belize Telecommunications Ltd.** (⊠ *115 5th Ave.* ☎ *422/2196*)

Post Offices **Corozal** (⊠ *5th Ave.* ☎ *422/2462*). **Orange Walk** (⊠ *Queen Victoria Ave.* ☎ *322/2345*).

TOURS

As Corozal Town gets relatively few tourists, except those en route from Mexico or looking for real estate, it doesn't have many tour operators or guides. Your hotel can usually arrange tours to Lamanai, Cerros, and other sites. Henry Menzies of Belize VIP Transfers arranges trips to Mexico as well as to sites around Corozal. He'll also meet you in Chetumal and bring you across the border, or take you from Corozal to Chetumal (BZ$60 for up to three persons, or BZ$20 per person for four or more). To or from Cancun, Belize VIP Transfers charges BZ$800 for up to four persons. To or from Belize City, the charge is BZ$250 for up to four persons. In Orange Walk, Jungle River Tours and J. Avila & Sons run boat trips (BZ$80 per person) up the New River to Lamanai and can help arrange other tours and trips.

Contacts **J. Avila & Sons River Tours** (⊠ *42 Riverside St., Orange Walk* ☎ *322/3068*). **Henry Menzies, Belize VIP Transfers** (⊠ *Caribbean Village, South End, Corozal* ☎ *422/2725* ⊕ *www.belizetransfers.com*). **Jungle River Tours** (⊠ *20 Lovers La., Orange Walk* ☎ *302/2293*).

VISITOR INFORMATION

Brochures and visitor information are available in the Corozal Cultural Center, near the market. The service is provided by the local chapter of the Belize Tourism Industry Association. An excellent source of general information on northern Belize is the Web site Northern Belize, ⊕ *www. northernbelize.com*, and another is Belize North ⊕ *www.belizenorth. com*. A good source of online information about Corozal is ⊕ *www. corozal.com*, put together by students at a local community college. A site with some local information on Orange Walk is managed by the Orange Walk Town Council, ⊕ *www.owtowncouncil.com*.

Tourist Information **Corozal Cultural Center** (⊠ *1st Ave.* ☎ *422/3176*).

The Cayo

WORD OF MOUTH

"If you have a rental car, and you start from Cayo early, you can actually do all of Mountain Pine Ridge in one day. First check in for the trip to Caracol, and then go take some pics of Rio Frio Cave, which is an open-ended cave just made for pics. Then do Caracol, and spend a few hours there. Then do Rio On Pools for a couple of hours. Then do Big Rocks for a couple of hours. Then stop at Mystic Mountain for a couple of homemade liqueur shots (yeah, they rock), or go to Five Sisters for an early dinner, before heading back to Cayo. You can do it all, and not feel rushed!"

—DrFeelAwesome

By Lan Sluder   **WHEN THE FIRST JUNGLE LODGES** opened in the early 1980s in the Cayo, Belize's largest district, not many people thought this wild area would become a tourist magnet. The mountainous region on the country's western border was too remote. Today, more than half of those touring Belize visit the Cayo during their trip, making this the country's second most popular destination after Ambergris Caye.

El Cayo is Spanish for "the caye" or key. Local residents still call San Ignacio Town "El Cayo," or just "Cayo," which can potentially create some confusion for outsiders. The name is thought to have originally referred to the small island formed where the Macal and Mopan rivers meet at San Ignacio.

You'll know when you've entered the Cayo a few miles east of Belmopan, Belize's capital. Running along the Belize River for miles, the road winds out of the valley and heads into a series of sharp bends. In a few minutes you'll see cattle grazing on steep hillsides and horses flicking their tails.

Other things change as you enter the Cayo. The Creole people who live along the coast give way to Maya and Mestizos; English is replaced by Spanish as the predominant language; and off the main roads four-wheel-drive vehicles become a necessity. The lost world of the Maya comes alive through majestic, haunting ruins. And the Indiana Jones in you can hike through the jungle, ride horseback, canoe down the Macal or Mopan River, and explore incredible caves.

ORIENTATION & PLANNING

ORIENTATION

The Cayo's main connection to the coast is the Western Highway, a paved two-lane road running 78 mi (128 km) between Belize City and the Guatemala border. The highway is in generally good condition, but shoulders are narrow, and parts of the highway can be slick after rains. Secondary roads, mostly unpaved and sometimes difficult to drive on, branch off the Western Highway, leading to small villages and to the Mountain Pine Ridge, the Spanish Lookout Mennonite area, and various jungle lodges. The Mountain Pine Ridge is crisscrossed by an extensive network of gravel and dirt roads, some formerly logging trails.

At Belmopan, the paved Hummingbird Highway is Belize's most scenic road, cutting 54 mi (90 km) southeast through the Maya Mountains to Dangriga, passing Five Blues Lake and Blue Hole national parks. Mile markers on the Hummingbird start in Dangriga.

PLANNING

WHEN TO GO

The best time to visit the Cayo is late fall and winter, when temperatures generally are moderate. During the dry season, late February or March to May or early June, at the lower elevations around San Ignacio and Belmopan, daytime temperatures can reach 100°F, though it does cool off at night. Seasonal rains usually reach the Cayo in June. In summer, after the rains begin, temperatures moderate a little, but humidity increases. Year-round the Mountain Pine Ridge is noticeably cooler and less humid than anywhere else in Belize.

SAFETY IN THE CAYO

Although most visitors report feeling completely safe in the Cayo, in 2005 and 2006 there was a series of robberies by armed bandits. Alleged ringleaders of the gang were caught in Guatemala and turned over to Belizean authorities, and no further incidents have occurred since mid-2006. At this writing, the U.S. Embassy had issued a warning about highway banditry on unpaved roads near the Guatemala border, and trips to Caracol may be made only in convoys accompanied by Belize Defence Forces soldiers. Ask locally about any recent incidents before starting road trips to remote areas.

RESTAURANTS & CUISINE

San Ignacio is the culinary center of the Cayo, with close to 20 restaurants. Most are small spots, with only a few tables. Restaurants offer Indian, French, German, and even Sri Lankan, fare as well as burritos and beans. Prices, designed to appeal to the budget and midlevel travelers who stay in town, rarely rise above the moderate level. At the jungle lodges outside San Ignacio, prices are much higher. Some lodges charge BZ$65 or $70, or more, for a mediocre dinner, leaving some guests to wonder if the expense is justified.

ABOUT THE HOTELS

In the Cayo you have two very different choices in accommodations: jungle lodges and regular hotels. Jungle lodges, regardless of price or amenities, offer a close-to-nature experience, typically next to a river or in a remote mountain setting. Most lodges house their guests in thatch cabañas, patterned after traditional Mayan houses. At the top end, lodges such as Blancaneaux and Chaa Creek deliver a truly deluxe experience, with designer toiletries, thick, imported mattresses, and decor that wouldn't be out of place in *Architectural Digest*. At the other end, some budget lodges have outdoor bathrooms and thin foam mattresses. In between are a number of midlevel lodges providing an off-the-beaten-path experience at moderate prices.

Whereas the district's lodges are back-a-bush (a Belizean expression for "out in the jungle"), the Cayo's hotels are in towns or along the Western Highway. The area's least expensive hotels are clustered in San Ignacio, one of the backpacker centers of Belize. Hotels in and around Belmopan are a little more expensive, since they cater to people in the capital on government business. Whether hotel or jungle lodge, most properties in the Cayo are small, typically run by the owner.

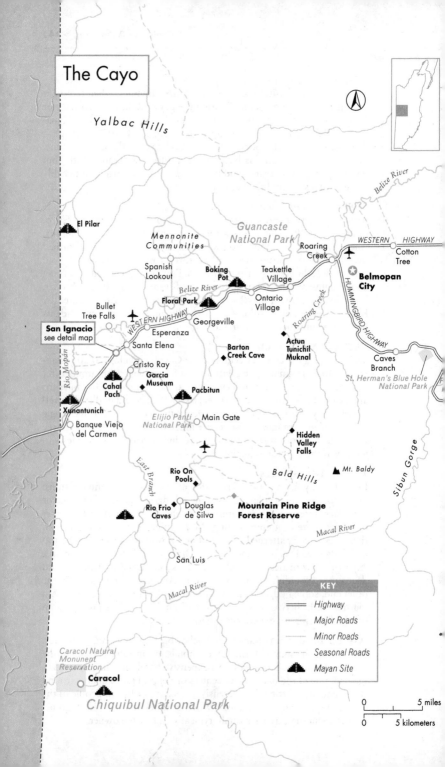

TOP REASONS TO GO

NATIONAL PARKS & RESERVES

About 60% of the Cayo District is national parks and reserves, which is good news if you like hiking, birding, wildlife spotting, canoeing, or other outdoor activities. The Mountain Pine Ridge, at more than 127,000 acres, is the largest forest reserve in Belize. Other protected areas include the Elijio Panti National Park, St. Herman's Blue Hole National Park, and Guanacaste National Park.

CAVES

Although there are caves in Toledo and elsewhere in Belize, the Cayo has the biggest and most exciting ones. Actun Tunichil Muknal is the top caving experience in Belize; explore huge underground chambers on foot or float on subterranean rivers through the underworld of the ancient Maya.

MAYAN SITES

The Cayo is home to the largest and most important Mayan site in Belize; Caracol has more than 35,000 buildings over 30 square mi (78 square km). It also has the most easily accessible Mayan sites in the country, Cahal Pech and Xunantunich, along with dozens of smaller ones.

JUNGLE LODGES

With more than 30 jungle lodges, the Cayo has far more than all the other districts of Belize combined. There's a lodge for every budget, from bare-bones cabins along the Mopan River to ultradeluxe villas on the Macal River and in the Mountain Pine Ridge.

MOUNTAINS

The Cayo's 2,000–3,000 foot mountains provide a welcome respite from the heat and humidity of lowland Belize. Though lacking the craggy heights of the volcanic mountains of Guatemala or Costa Rica, the Mountain Pine Ridge and the north end of the Maya Mountain range make up for it with a dramatic lineup of natural wonders—waterfalls, caves, rivers, and a new lake created by dams on the Macal.

Generally, inexpensive hotels and lodges maintain the same rate year-round, though some may discount a little in the off-season (generally mid-April to early December). More expensive places have off-season rates 30% to 40% less than high season.

WHAT IT COSTS IN BELIZE DOLLARS					
	¢	1	2	3	4
RESTAU-RANTS	under BZ$8	BZ$8–BZ$15	BZ$15–BZ$25	BZ$25–BZ$50	over BZ$50
HOTELS	under BZ$100	BZ$100–BZ$200	BZ$200–BZ$300	BZ$300–BZ$500	over BZ$500

Restaurant prices are per person for a main course at dinner. Hotel prices are for two people in a standard double room, including tax and service.

GREAT ITINERARIES

IF YOU HAVE 3 DAYS IN THE CAYO

Upon arrival at the international airport, immediately head to the Cayo by rental car, bus, or shuttle van. If you have time, stop en route at the Belize Zoo. Stay at one of the jungle lodges around San Ignacio, if it's in your budget. On your first full day in the Cayo, explore the area around San Ignacio, visiting the Xunantunich Mayan ruins, the Belize Botanic Gardens on the grounds of duPlooy's Lodge, and Green Hills Butterfly Farm. Assuming you have the energy, walk the Rainforest Medicine Trail and spend a few minutes at the Natural History Center, both at the Lodge at Chaa Creek. On the second day, if you're not planning to move on to Tikal in Guatemala after your stay in the Cayo, at least take a day tour there. Guided tours from San Ignacio usually include van transportation to the Tikal park, a local guide at the site, and lunch. Alternatively, if you're heading to Tikal later, take a day trip to Caracol in the Mountain Pine Ridge. Bring a picnic lunch and make stops at Río On pools, the Río Frio cave, and a waterfall, such as Five Sisters. On your final day, take a full-day guided tour of Actun Tunichil Muknal. Have dinner at a restaurant in San Ignacio.

IF YOU HAVE 5 DAYS IN THE CAYO

Rent a car at the international airport and drive to a jungle lodge near Belmopan. If you have time, stop en route at the Belize Zoo and do a quick driving tour of the capital. On your first full day, go cave tubing and take a zip-line canopy tour at Jaguar Paw Lodge. Alternatively, for a more strenuous day, take a trip with Caves Branch Adventure Camp, or do their cave-tubing trip. End your day with dinner at your lodge and a night wildlife-spotting tour. On your second day, drive down the Hummingbird Highway and take a dip in the inland Blue Hole. Also, visit St. Herman's Cave or go horseback riding at Banana Bank Lodge. On the third day, move on to a jungle lodge near San Ignacio or in the Mountain Pine Ridge and follow the three day itinerary.

BELMOPAN CITY

50 mi (80 km) southwest of Belize City.

It used to be said that the best way to see Belize's capital was through the rearview mirror as you head toward San Ignacio or south down the Hummingbird. It's a dreary cluster of concrete office buildings plunked in the middle of nowhere, proving that cities can't be created overnight. However, with the opening of the main campus of the University of Belize in Belmopan in 2002, the relocation of several embassies (including the U.S. embassy) from Belize City to Belmopan, and new commercial activity around the capital, Belmopan—finally—is showing some signs of life. The population has grown to more than 15,000. Commercial and retail activities are booming, and there's a minor real estate gold rush going on. Despite all this, however, we recommend you spend most of your time at nearby sites rather than in the city itself.

The **Belize Zoo** (⇨ See Chapter 1), one of the country's top sights, is only a half hour east of Belmopan via the Western Highway.

Worth a quick visit on the way out of Belmopan is Belize's small nature reserve, **Guanacaste National Park,** named for the huge guanacaste trees that grow here. Also called monkey's ear trees because of their oddly shaped seedpods, the trees tower more than 100 feet. (Unfortunately, the park's tallest guanacaste tree had to be cut down in 2006, due to safety concerns that it might fall.) The 50-acre park has a rich population of tropical birds, including smoky brown woodpeckers, black-headed trogons, red-lored parrots, and white-breasted wood wrens. You can try one of the eight daily hourly tours, or you can wander around on your own. After, cool off with a refreshing plunge in the Belize River; there's also a small picnic area. ☒ *Mile 47.7, Western Hwy.* ☎ *223/5004 Belize Audubon Society in Belize City* ☞ *BZ$5* ⊙ *Daily 8:30–4:30; tours every hr 8:30–3:30.*

🌣 Less than a half hour south of Belmopan, the 575-acre **St. Herman's Blue Hole Natural Park** has a natural turquoise pool surrounded by mosses and lush vegetation, excellent for a cool dip. The Blue Hole is actually part of an underground river system. On the other side of the hill is St. Herman's Cave, once inhabited by the Maya. A path leads up from the highway, right near the Blue Hole, but it's quite steep and difficult to climb unless the ground is dry. To explore St. Herman's cave beyond the first 300 yards or so, you must be accompanied by a guide (available at the park), and no more than five people can enter the cave at one time. With a guide, you also can explore part of another cave system here, the Crystal Cave (sometimes called the Crystalline Cave), which stretches for miles; the additional cost is BZ$20 per person for a two-hour guided tour. The park visitor center is 12½ mi (20½ km) from Belmopan. ☒ *Mile 42.5, Hummingbird Hwy.* ☞ *BZ$8* ⊙ *Daily 8–4:30.*

A WACKY TALE

At Five Blues Lake National Park, you used to be able to hike 3 mi (5 km) of trails, explore several caves, and canoe and swim in this lake with five shades of blue. The lake was a *cenote,* a collapsed cave in the limestone. In July 2006, despite heavy rains, the water level in the lake began to recede. On July 20, 2006, local residents heard a strange noise "as if the lake were moaning." A giant whirlpool formed, and most of the water in the lake was sucked into the ground. Many of the fish died, and now the lake is mostly dry. Researchers believe that a sediment "plug" dissolved and the lake drained, like water from a bathtub, into underground sinkholes and caves. As of this writing, the lake has partially refilled with water, but the park is not officially operating and there are no park rangers on hand. The park entrance is about 3½ mi (5¾ km) from the Hummingbird Highway, via a narrow dirt road. Bikes can be rented in St. Margaret's Village, and homestays and overnight camping in the village also can be arranged. ☒ *At end of Lagoon Rd., off Mile 32, Hummingbird Hwy.*

HISTORY

The Maya began settling the Belize River Valley of the Cayo some 4,000 years ago. At the height of the Maya civilization, AD 300 to 900, Caracol, El Pilar, Xunantunich, Cahal Pech, and other cities and ceremonial centers in what is now the Cayo were likely home to several hundred thousand people, several times the population of the district today.

Spanish missionaries first arrived in the area in the early 17th century, but they had a difficult time converting the independent-minded Maya, some of whom were forcibly removed to the Petén in Guatemala.

The first significant Spanish and British settlements were logwood and mahogany logging camps. The town of San Ignacio and its adjoining sister town, Santa Elena, were established later in the 1860s. Though only about 70 mi (115 km) from Belize City, San Ignacio remained fairly isolated until recent times, because getting to the coast by horseback through the bush could take three days or longer. The Western Highway was paved in the 1980s, making it easier to get here. The first jungle lodges began operation, and tourism now vies with agriculture as the main industry.

WHERE TO STAY & EAT

In addition to the restaurants listed here, the food and produce stalls at the market (open Monday–Saturday, off Bliss Parade next to the bus terminal on Constitution Drive) are good places to buy snacks and fruit at inexpensive prices—for example, you can get 5 to 10 bananas for BZ$1.

$-$$$ ✕ **Caladium.** In business since 1984 and operated by the Del Valle family, the Caladium is one of the oldest businesses in this young capital. Most Belizeans know it, since it's next to the bus station at Market Square. Here you'll find many of the country's favorites on the menu, including fried chicken, tender barbecued pork ribs, traditional rice and beans with chicken, beef, or pork, and cow-foot soup. It's clean, well-run, and air-conditioned. ⊠ *Market Sq.* ☎ *822/2754* ⊟ *MC, V* ⊘ *Closed Sun.*

$-$$ ✕ **Ristorante Puccini's.** Ostensibly Italian, and with good pasta dishes, this popular restaurant and bar has branched out to serve a wide variety of other dishes, from fajitas to steaks. You can eat inside in the Spartan but air-conditioned dining room, or enjoy a table outside in the evening cool. ⊠ *Constitution Dr.* ☎ *822/1366* ⊟ *MC, V* ⊘ *Daily.*

$$$ ▥ **Jaguar Paw.** Although this lodge is down a long dirt road, it's anything but rustic. Eye-popping Mayan murals, by American painter Pamela Braun, adorn the inner walls of the main lodge, which also has a 25-foot indoor waterfall. Each room has air-conditioning and a theme—the Victorian Room has a country armoire and sheer curtains; the Pioneer Room has a pebble-lined shower and rough-hewn wooden bed. Surrounding all this are 215 acres of jungle containing 9 mi (15 km) of hiking trails, a butterfly farm, a zip-line canopy tour, and caves that you (and at times hundreds of day-trippers) can float through on

an inner tube. **Pros:** One of the few jungle lodges with air-conditioning, lots of activities on-site including cave tubing, zip lining, and rock climbing. **Cons:** Can be busy with cruise ship groups. ✛ *Off Western Hwy., turn south at Mile 37 and follow dirt road 7 mi (11 km)* ☎ *820/2023, 877/624–3770 in U.S.* ⊕ *www.jaguarpaw.com* ⇆ *16 rooms* ⌂ *In-room: no phone, no TV. In-hotel: restaurant, bar, pool, no elevator, public Wi-Fi, public Internet, airport shuttle* ▭ *AE, DC, MC, V.*

> **WORD OF MOUTH**
>
> "I always loved Jaguar Paw's cave tubing. It's so prehistorically beautiful. Some of it is pitch black, and there is a cave you can hike way back into. Sweet place!"
>
> —DrFeelAwesome

$$$ ★ ⚏ **Pook's Hill.** When the lamps are lighted each night on the polished rosewood veranda, this low-key jungle lodge, on 300 remote acres adjoining the 6,700-acre Tapir Mountain Reserve (open only to researchers) and Actun Tunichil Muknal National Monument, is one of the most pleasant places in the Cayo. The stone-and-thatch cabañas are laid out on a grassy clearing around a small, partially excavated Mayan site. During the day you can swim, ride horses, go birding, or boat up the Roaring River to a series of caves. Dine family-style by lantern light (the cabañas do have 24-hour electricity, though some water for showers is heated by wood fires). You can hike from here to Actun Tunichil Muknal. **Pros:** Jungle lodge in true jungle setting, on doorstep of Actun Tunichil Muknal. **Cons:** Insects can be a nuisance. ✛ *At Mile 52 of Western Hwy., head south for 5 mi (8 km)* ☎ *820/2017* ⊕ *www.pookshillbelize.com* ⇆ *11 cabañas* ⌂ *In-room: no a/c, no phone, no TV. In-hotel: restaurant, bar, no elevator, public Internet, airport shuttle* ▭ *MC, V.*

$$–$$$ ★ ⚠ ⚏ **Caves Branch Adventure Co. & Jungle Camp.** Budget-minded guests at this jungle lodge on a 58,000-acre private reserve will head to the bunkhouse (BZ$30 per person) or the campground (BZ$10 per person), while those in search of creature comforts will appreciate the new mahogany and bamboo bungalows and suites. The lodge also has new 800-square-foot hillside "treehouse suites" 20 feet above the ground (BZ$390, plus 9% tax). Owner Ian Anderson and his highly trained jungle guides offer more than a dozen wilderness adventures, priced from BZ$150 to BZ$350 per person for day trips. On the tubing expedition to Footprint Cave you spend hours floating around underground lakes and crawling past stalagmites into dry chambers. Cold Belikins await you when you return, followed by a delicious dinner (BZ$36). **Pros:** Some of the best adventure tours in Belize; lush jungle setting; Lodge House view makes it the perfect spot for dinner. **Cons:** Not for couch potatoes. ✉ *12 mi (19½ km) south of Belmopan at Mile 41½ of Hummingbird Hwy.* ☎ *822/2800* ⊕ *www.cavesbranch.com* ⇆ *8 suites, 3 bungalows, 10 cabañas, 7 with shared bath, 8 beds in bunkhouse, riverside campsites* ⌂ *In-room: no a/c, no phone, no TV. In-hotel: restaurant, bar, no elevator, laundry service, public Internet, airport shuttle* ▭ *MC, V.*

$$ 🏨**Banana Bank Lodge.** Along the banks of the Belize River, this jungle lodge is one of the best spots for families. Equestrians of all skill levels can choose from 80 horses. Owners John and Carolyn Carr (he's a cowboy from Montana; she's a noted artist) arrange canoe trips and hikes on the lodge's 4,000 acres. Deer and a spider monkey roam the grounds, along with many birds in an aviary. The aging resident jaguar, Tika, died in 2007, but she has been replaced by a new young jaguar named Tikatoo. Thatch cabañas with curving walls are modest but comfortable (no air-conditioning, though), and there are three air-conditioned rooms and two suites in the three-story Chateau Brio, and four budget rooms in the Chalet. Hearty, simple meals are served family-style. **Pros:** Good choice for families and horse lovers; lodge now has a swimming pool; guests and owners mingle at meals. **Cons:** Pesky mosquitoes. ⊹ *From Western Hwy., turn north at Mile 46.9 and cross bridge over Belize River. Follow gravel/dirt road 3 mi (5 km) to Banana Bank sign. Turn right and follow dirt road for 2 mi (3 km)* ☎820/2020 ⊕*www.bananabank.com* ☞*7 rooms, 7 cabañas, 2 suites* ♿*In-room: no a/c (some), no phone, no TV, Wi-Fi (some). In-hotel: restaurant, no elevator, swimming pool, public Internet, airport shuttle* ▭*MC, V* ⋮◎*BP.*

$$ 🏨**Belize Jungle Dome.** Although the original owners are no longer in residence, the Belize Jungle Dome's manager does a good job of making guests welcome at this well-appointed small inn near the Belize River. Choose from an extensive selection of tours—including caving, cave tubing, horseback riding, and kayaking—or you can just laze by the pool, sip a cold Belikin (the national beer), and listen to the howler monkeys. The four suites and standard room here have tile floors, lots of windows, and an uncluttered look. **Pros:** Large selection of tours; access to hiking trails, horseback riding, and other facilities at nearby Banana Bank Lodge; intimate upscale accommodations. **Cons:** Owners no longer in residence; mosquitoes can be a nuisance. ⊹ *From Western Hwy., turn north at Mile 46.9 and cross bridge over Belize River. Follow gravel/dirt road 3 mi (5 km) until you see Banana Bank sign. Turn right and follow dirt road 2 mi (3 km)* ☎822/2124 ⊕*www.belizejungledome.com* ☞*1 room, 4 suites* ♿*In-room: no phone, kitchen (some), Wi-Fi. In-hotel: restaurant, bar, pool, no elevator, public Wi-Fi, airport shuttle* ▭*MC, V.*

$ 🏨**Bull Frog Inn.** More of a mom 'n' pop motel than an inn, with retro-style furnishings reminiscent of the 1960s, the Bull Frog caters mainly to government workers and Belizeans on business in Belmopan. Your bed may sag a bit and the TV picture may roll, but it's all part of the Belmopan experience. Certainly, the open-air restaurant, serving Belizean comfort food like pork chops and escabeche (onion soup with chicken), is a decent choice in the capital; the bar usually has live music on Fridays. **Pros:** Cheerful service, pleasant restaurant. **Cons:** Furnishings are a bit run down; rooms are more expensive than they should be. ✉*25 Half Moon Ave.* ☎822/3425 ⊕*www.bullfroginn. com* ☞*25 rooms* ♿ *In-hotel: restaurant, bar, no elevator, public Internet* ▭*AE, MC, V.*

TO AI OR NOT TO AI

Many lodges and resorts in Belize offer a tweaked version of the sort of all-inclusive you often find in Mexico or Jamaica: optional packages that include nearly everything, such as all meals, guided tours, and sports (fishing, diving, or sometimes even golfing). So when is it worth your money to choose one of these over selecting room, meals, and activities à la carte?

The answer is, it depends. If you're going to a remote caye resort or jungle lodge, you may not have a choice. When you're an hour away from the nearest restaurant, you're pretty much stuck eating at your hotel. On the other hand, at a destination such as Ambergris Caye, Caye Caulker, or Placencia, there are many excellent restaurants to choose from. It would be a shame to lock yourself into a single dining experience. A few resorts on Ambergris Caye, mainly those located on the far north end of the island (a long boat ride away from San Pedro), do offer all-inclusive or near all-inclusive packages; however, for most people,

one of the main reasons for coming to Ambergris Caye is the opportunity to sample the variety of restaurants.

The main advantage of an all-inclusive or mostly inclusive package is that you don't have to worry about the details of travel planning. Once you've paid your fixed price, all you have to do is show up at the airport with your bags packed. The resort or lodge picks you up at the Belize International Airport, takes you on guided tours, provides your meals, and practically holds your hand. It's almost like being on a cruise, with few decisions to make. If you're the type of person who likes a fairly rigid, organized travel experience, an AI package is probably a good bet for you.

Before you book, be sure to total up the value of what you expect to get at the all-inclusive, and compare that with what you probably would pay on an à la carte basis. If some of the included activities don't appeal to you, it might actually be more expensive to go with an AI.

$ **Yim Saan.** On the Hummingbird Highway near the entrance to the Ring Road, this Chinese-owned motel and restaurant is the newest lodging choice in Belmopan. The 10 rooms on the second floor will make you think you're in an interstate motel in Alabama rather than in Belize's capital, but they're sparkling clean, with tile baths, air-conditioning, cable TV, and in-room phones. The restaurant on the first floor, probably the fanciest in town (which says a lot about Belmopan), serves tasty and inexpensive, if uninspired, Chinese food, mostly Cantonese-style. **Pros:** Clean rooms; good meal option downstairs. **Cons:** Not very atmospheric. ⊠*4253 Hummingbird Hwy.* ☎*822/1356* ⇌*10 rooms* △ *In-hotel: restaurant, bar, no elevator* ☐*MC, V.*

THE OUTDOORS

Belmopan and San Ignacio offer a similar lineup of outdoor activities, and since they're only about 20 mi (33 km) apart, you can stay in one area and enjoy the activities around the other.

BIRDING

Although there's good birding in many areas around Belmopan, **Pook's Hill Lodge** (☎822/2017), 5½ mi (9 km) off the Western Highway at Mile 52½ is in a league of its own. The birding list from Pook's Hill includes the Mealy Parrot, Spectacled Owl, Aztec Parakeet, and Keel-billed Toucan.

CANOEING & KAYAKING

The Belize River, wide and mostly gentle (Class I–II) offers good canoeing and kayaking. It was once used by loggers to transport mahogany to Belize City and hosts the annual La Ruta Maya Mountains to the Sea Canoe Race. The multiday race is held in March during the Baron Bliss holiday. You can also canoe or kayak portions of the Caves Branch River (also Class I–II). Many hotels and lodges arrange canoe or kayak trips, including **Caves Branch Adventure Co. & Jungle Lodge** (☎822/2800), off the Hummingbird Highway, and **Crystal Paradise Resort** (☎824/2772), in Cristo Rey Village near San Ignacio. Full-day canoe or kayak trips start at around BZ$120 per person.

CANOPY TOURS

You may feel a little like Tarzan as you dangle 80 feet above the jungle floor, suspended by a harness, moving from one suspended platform to another. **Jaguar Paw Lodge** (☎820/2023), off Mile 37 of the Western Highway, has eight platforms set 100 to 250 feet apart. At the last platform you have to rappel to the ground. The cost is BZ$110–BZ$150, depending on whether lunch and transportation are included. There's a 240-pound weight limit.

CAVING

The area around Belmopan, with its karst limestone topography, is a paradise for cavers. At **St. Herman's Blue Hole National Park**, at Mile 42 of the Hummingbird Highway, there are two large caves, St. Herman's and the Crystal Cave. Both require a guide to explore (guides are available at the national park visitor center).

Fodor'sChoice ★ The most rewarding caving experience, and one of the most amazing experiences of any kind in Belize, is **Actun Tunichil Muknal,** or "Cave of the Crystal Sepulchre," southwest of Teakettle Village in the 500-acre Actun Tunichil Muknal National Monument. You hike about 45 minutes—crossing the Roaring River three times and even swimming in it a few yards—and enter the cave's hourglass-shape opening. Once inside, you scramble over large boulders and squeeze through tight passageways (though not too tight: even a large person can get through). Tours easily last three hours or longer. This is a real caving experience, with no lighting except what your guide provides and no well-marked walkways or roped-off platforms. If you're physically active and can swim, don't hesitate. You'll see amazing limestone formations, thousand-year-old human calcified skulls and skeletons, and many Mayan artifacts including well-preserved pottery. Only a few licensed guides are authorized to run tours of the cave. The best is PACZ Tours, operated by Emilo Awe and Jaamal Crawford, with help by Bob Jones, formerly of Eva's. **PACZ Tours** (✉- *30 Burns Ave., San*

Ignacio ☎824/0536 ⊕www.pacztours.net). The Belize government is training additional guides for the ATM (Actun Tunichil Muknal) tour, and more options may be available when you're in Belize. The tour costs around BZ$160—including lunch, if you book directly with PACZ. Your hotel or lodge can arrange an ATM or other caving trip but may add on an additional fee.

CAVE TUBING

The most popular outdoor activity around Belmopan is cave tubing. You float down the Caves Branch River in an inner tube, at points going through dark limestone caves in the subterranean sections of the river.

Caves Branch River has two main entry points: near **Jaguar Paw Lodge** (✉Off Mile 37 of Western Hwy. ☎820/2023) and near **Caves Branch Adventure Co. & Jungle Lodge** (✉Off Hummingbird Hwy. ☎822/2800). The Jaguar Paw access attracts more people, and when several cruise ships are in port at Belize City, the river here can be jammed. There's a parking area about ½ mi (1 km) from Jaguar Paw, BZ$4 parking fee, and here you'll find a number of tour guides for cave tubing tours, which vary in length, generally costing from BZ$80 to BZ$150. ⇨See tour operators in Belize City Essentials and San Ignacio section of this chapter. Cave tubing trips from Caves Branch Lodge are longer, require more hiking, and cost more. For example, the "River of Caves" trip, through 7 mi (12 km) of underground caves, takes much of a day and costs BZ$190 per person.

Cave tubing is subject to changes in the river levels. In the dry season (February–May or June), the river levels are often too low for cave tubing. Also, after heavy rains, the water level in the river is too high to safely float through caves, so in the rainy season (June–November) cave tubing trips may occasionally be canceled. Always call ahead to check if tours are operating.

HORSEBACK RIDING

The best equestrian operator in this part of Belize is **Banana Bank Lodge & Jungle Equestrian Adventure** (☎820/2020), off the Western Highway near Belmopan. Run by John Carr, a former Montana cowboy and rodeo rider, Banana Bank has about 80 horses, mostly quarter horses, a large round-pen riding arena, stables, and miles of jungle trails on a 4,000-acre ranch. A two- to three-hour ride costs BZ$120.

SAN IGNACIO

23 mi (37 km) southwest of Belmopan.

When you hear the incredible commotion made by black grackles in the town square's trees, and see the Hawksworth Bridge, the only public suspension bridge in Belize, you'll know you've arrived at San Ignacio, the hub of the Cayo district. San Ignacio is an excellent base for exploring western Belize. Nearby are three Mayan ruins, as well as national parks and a cluster of butterfly farms.

With its well-preserved wooden structures, dusty little San Ignacio is a Belizean town where you might want to linger. Evenings are cool and mosquito-free, and the colonial-era streets are lined with funky bars and restaurants. It's worth coming at sunset to listen to the eerily beautiful sounds of these iridescent grackles.

On Saturday mornings, **San Ignacio Market,** in an open field across from the soccer stadium, comes alive with farmers selling local fruits and vegetables. Vendors also hawk crafts, clothing, and household goods. A much smaller vegetable and fruit market is open weekdays on Burns Avenue, closer to town. ☉*Sat. 7–noon, though some vendors stay later.*

NEARBY SITES

★ Yours truly can ask to work the crank yourself as you ride a hand-pulled
�™ ferry across the Mopan River, near the village of San José Succotz, toward the archaeological site of **Xunantunich** (pronounced *shoo-nan-too-nitch*), which means "stone maiden." As you hike through the profusion of maidenhair ferns to the ruins, you'll encounter numerous butterflies flitting through the air. A magnificent avenue of cohune palms announces your arrival at an important ceremonial center from the Maya Classic Period. Drinks and snacks are available at a visitor center that provides the history of the site. El Castillo, the massive 120-foot-high main pyramid, was built on a leveled hilltop. The pyramid has a spectacular 360-degree panorama of the Mopan River valley into Guatemala. On the eastern wall is a reproduction of one of the finest Mayan sculptures in Belize, a frieze decorated with jaguar heads, human faces, and abstract geometric patterns telling the story of the Moon's affair with Morning Light. ⊠*Near San José Succotz Village, 6½ mi (11 km) southwest of San Ignacio on Benque Rd., Western Hwy.* ☎*No phone* ☜*BZ$10* ☉*Daily 8–4.*

El Pilar, a less frequented archaeological site, is still being excavated under the direction of Anabel Ford, a professor at the University of California. Excavations of Mayan ruins have traditionally concentrated on public buildings, but at El Pilar the emphasis has been on reconstructing domestic architecture—everything from houses to gardens with crops used by the Maya. El Pilar, occupied from AD 700 to 1000, shows evidence of sentry posts in some areas, suggesting that this was a community of high-ranking officials surrounded by a hostile population. Two well-marked trails take you around the site. Because the structures haven't been stripped of vegetation, you may feel like you're walking through a series of shady orchards. Don't forget binoculars: in the 5,000-acre nature reserve there's some terrific bird-watching. Behind the main plaza, a lookout grants a spectacular view across the jungle to El Pilar's sister city, Pilar Poniente, on the Guatemalan border. Note that several incidents of robbery have occurred at or near this site. ⊠*8 mi (13 km) west of Bullet Tree Falls, Western Hwy.* ☎*No phone.* ☜*BZ$10* ☉*Daily 8–5.*

�™ Just outside San Ignacio is a third major Mayan ruin, the unfortunately named **Cahal Pech** ("place of the ticks"). It was occupied from around

900 BC to AD 1100. At its peak, in AD 600, Cahal Pech was a medium-size settlement with some three dozen structures huddled around seven plazas. It's thought that it functioned as a guard post, watching over the nearby confluence of the Mopan and Macal rivers. It may be somewhat less compelling than the area's other ruins, but it's no less mysterious, given that these structures mark the presence of a civilization we know so little about. Look for answers at the small visitor center. ⊠ *On hill at edge of San Ignacio* ☎ *No phone* ⌨ *BZ$10* ⊙ *Daily 8–5.*

On private land, **Actun Chechem Ha,** which means "Cave of the Poisonwood Water," is a Mayan burial cave with artifacts that date back two millennia. There are many pots and a stela used for ceremonial purposes. To examine some of the pottery, you'll have to climb ladders, and getting to the cave requires a 35-minute walk, mostly uphill. Tour companies visit here from San Ignacio. ⊠ *10 mi (17 km) south of Benque Viejo* ☎ *820/4063 to arrange a visit* ⌨ *BZ$50 for guided tour for up to 3 people, if arranged with owner; tours including transportation from San Ignacio or your lodge and often including lunch and swimming at Vaca Falls are around BZ$100 per person* ⊙ *By appointment.*

One of the most unusual attractions in Belize, **Poustinia Land Art Park** is a collection of 30 original works of art by artists from about a dozen countries, including Belize, Norway, Guayana, Brazil, Guatemala, and England, scattered about some 60 acres of a former cattle ranch. It's owned by Luis Alberto Ruiz, a Belmopan architect, who calls Poustinia an "environmental project." Poustinia is a Russian word for "desert of the soul." Among the works of outdoor art, which some would call funky and others fascinating, are "Downtown," by Venezuelan artist Manuel Piney, and "Returned Parquet," a visual reference in mahogany parquet flooring to Belize's colonial history by Tim Davies, a British artist. Getting around the park, which is open by appointment only, to see the art requires many hours of sometimes strenuous hiking. Be sure to bring insect repellent. Two simple cabins at the site are available for rent "to artists and short-term visitors" for BZ$80 double a night. Electricity is provided three hours a day, with extra hours of power available at additional cost. ⊠ *Hydro Rd., 2½ mi (5 km) south of Benque Viejo, 8 mi (13 km) southwest of San Ignacio* ☎ *822/3522 to arrange a visit* ⌨ *BZ$10* ⊙ *By appointment.*

☁ The **Rainforest Medicine Trail** gives you a quick introduction to traditional Mayan medicine. The trail takes you on a short, self-guided walk through the rain forest, giving you a chance to study the symbiotic nature of its plant life. Learn about the healing properties of such indigenous plants as red gumbo-limbo and man vine and see some endangered medicinal plants. The shop here sells Mayan medicinal products like Belly Be Good and Flu Away. ⊠ *Next to Lodge at Chaa Creek* ☎ *824/2037* ⌨ *BZ$12 for Rainforest Medicine Trail, BZ$16 including Natural History Center and Blue Morpho Breeding Center; free to Chaa Creek guests* ⊙ *Daily 9–5.*

☾ The **Chaa Creek Natural History Center** has a tiny library and lots of displays on everything from butterflies to snakes (pickled in jars). Outside is a screened-in blue morpho butterfly-breeding center. If you haven't encountered blue morphos in the wild, you can see them up close here and even peer at their slumbering pupae, which resemble jade earrings. Once you're inside the double doors, the blue beauties, which look boringly brown when their wings are closed, flit about or remain perfectly still, sometimes on your shoulder or head, and open and close their wings to a rhythm akin to inhaling and exhaling. Tours are led by a team of naturalists. ⊠ *The Lodge at Chaa Creek* ☎ *824/2037* ⊕ *www.chaacreek.com* ☎ *BZ$10 or BZ$16 combined with Rainforest Medicine Trail; free to Chaa Creek guests* ☾ *Daily 9–4.*

☾ The life's work of Ken duPlooy, an ornithologist who died in 2001, and the personable Judy duPlooy, is the **Belize Botanical Gardens,** a collection of hundreds of trees, plants, and flowers from all over Central America. Enlightening tours of the gardens, set on a bank of the Macal River, are given by Heather, daughter of Ken and Judy, who is the director of the gardens, and by local Maya who can tell you the names of the plants in Maya, Spanish, and English as well as explain their varied medicinal uses. An orchid house holds the duPlooys' collection of more than 100 orchid species. ✢ *duPlooy's Lodge; from San Ignacio, head 4¾ mi (7½ km) west on Benque Rd., turn left on Chial Rd., San Ignacio* ☎ *824/3101* ⊕ *www.belizebotanic.org* ☎ *BZ$10 self-guided tour, BZ$15 guided tour* ☾ *Daily 9–5.*

☾ Besides thoughtful displays on the Cayo flora and fauna, **Tropical Wings,** a little nature center, raises 20 species of butterfly including the blue morpho, owl, giant swallowtail, and monarch varieties. The facility, at the Trek Stop *(⇨ see below),* has a small restaurant and gift shop. ⊠ *Benque Rd., Western Hwy., 6 mi (10 km) west of San Ignacio* ☎ *823/2265* ☎ *BZ$5* ☾ *Daily 9–5.*

The mission of **Benque House of Culture,** one of three government-sponsored houses of culture in Belize (the others are in Belize City and Orange Walk Town), is "promoting beauty and goodness." Who could argue with that? This tiny museum has displays on the history of Benque Viejo, which celebrated its centennial in 2004, and also offers arts and crafts classes for local schoolchildren and their teachers. ⊠ *64 Joseph St., 7 mi (11½ km) west of San Ignacio, Benque Viejo del Carmen* ☎ *823/2697* ☎ *BZ$2* ☾ *Weekdays 8–5.*

The small hilltop community of **Spanish Lookout,** about 5 mi (8 km) north of the Western Highway (the easiest access is via the paved Route 30 at Mile 57½ of the Western Highway), is one of the centers of Belize's Mennonite community. The village's blond-haired, blue-eyed residents may seem out of place in this tropical country, but they're actually responsible for many of Belize's major projects. They built nearly all the area's resorts, and most of the eggs and milk you'll consume during your stay come from their farms. The women dress in cotton frocks and head scarves, and the men don straw hats, suspenders, and dark trousers. Some still travel in horse-drawn buggies, though

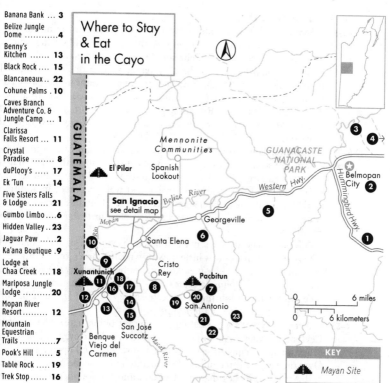

**Where to Stay
& Eat
in the Cayo**

many Mennonites around Spanish Lookout have embraced pickup trucks and modern farming equipment. The cafés and small shopping centers in Spanish Lookout offer a unique opportunity to mingle with these sometimes world-wary people, but they don't appreciate being gawked at or photographed any more than you do. Stores in Spanish Lookout are modern and well-stocked, the farms wouldn't look out of place in the U.S. Midwest, and many of the roads are paved. Oil in commercial quantities was discovered in Spanish Lookout in 2005, and several wells now pump about 5,000 barrels of black gold daily.

WHERE TO STAY & EAT

The lodges along the Mopan River, a dark jade-color river that winds into Belize from Guatemala, tend to be in the moderate to budget range, the exception being the Mopan River Resort. Lodges on the Macal River, with some exceptions, are typically more upmarket. A number of new, mostly moderately priced lodges have recently opened on the Cristo Rey and Chiquibul roads en route to the Mountain Pine Ridge, and also in and near Bullet Tree. It remains to be seen whether these lodges can attract enough guests to stay in business.

SAN IGNACIO

$-$$$ ✕ **Sanny's Grill.** Owner Sanny Herrera Ruiz's democratic motto proclaims: PRICES ANYONE CAN AFFORD. With a hot grill and sizzling spices, this restaurant transforms Belizean basics, like chicken or pork chops, beyond standard fare. Try the champagne shrimp or lime-thyme red snapper, along with the tastiest, spiciest rice and beans in the Cayo. Eat them in the casual dining room or out on the covered deck. In a residential area off Benque Road, the place can be hard to find after dark. ⊠ *23rd St., heading west of San Ignacio, look for sign just beyond Texaco station* ☎ *824/2988* ▭ *MC, V* ☉ *No lunch.*

$-$$ ✕ **Hannah's.** This is one of San Ignacio's most popular restaurants, and
★ deservedly so. It's far from fancy—you eat on simple tables in what is essentially a large shed that's open to busy Burns Avenue—but service is cheerful, and the food inexpensive and well-prepared. In addition to the usual Belizean beans-and-rice dishes, Hannah's serves salads, andwiches, burritos, and Indian curries. ⊠ *5 Burns Ave.* ☎ *824/3014* ▭ *MC, V* ☉

¢-$$ ✕ **Café Sol.** No need to wilt in the sun here, as you can sit in the shade of a large mango tree at this little downtown café and enjoy healthy vegetarian, vegan, and white-meat dishes. For breakfast, try the vegetarian sausages and rich banana pancakes. The fresh-made guava, mango, lime, and watermelon juices are refreshing. ⊠ *West St.* ☎ *824/2166* ▭ *MC, V* ☉ *Closed Sun. and Mon.*

¢-$$ ✕ **Serendib.** What's a Sri Lankan restaurant doing here? The original Ceylonese owner came to Belize with the British Army, and like many other squaddies (enlisted men), decided to stay on and open a business. Over the years, the menu here has migrated more to Belizean, Chinese, and American dishes than Sri Lankan, and the founder has sold the property to new management, but you can still get authentic curries. The restaurant is a comfortable, cool escape from the crowds on the street outside. ⊠ *27 Burns Ave.* ☎ *824/2302* ▭ *MC, V* ☉ *Closed Sun.*

¢-$ ✕ **Eva's.** Not merely a bustling café-bar, this Cayo institution, established by the legendary Bob Jones though now under new ownership, also acts as an Internet café, bulletin board, information center, trading post, tour center, and meeting place. In addition to the bacon, eggs, and sandwiches, Eva's serves authentic Belizean fare. The food may not always be as good as at some other restaurants in town, but the atmosphere makes up for it. Mugs of wickedly strong black tea are always available, along with copious quantities of Belikin. ⊠ *22 Burns Ave.* ☎ *824/2267* ⊕ *www.evasonline.com* ▭ *No credit cards.*

¢-$ ✕ **Hode's Place Bar & Grill.** With a large shaded patio next to a citrus
★ grove and swings, slides, and an ice cream bar for the kids in the back, Hode's is even bigger than it looks from the outside; it's popular for cold beers, karaoke, and billiards and often the busiest place in town. Oh yes, it also has good food in large portions and at modest prices. The escabeche is terrific, and the fried chicken with French fries (BZ$9) is the best in Cayo. ⊠ *Savannah Rd., across from sports field* ☎ *824/2522* ▭ *MC, V.*

¢-$ ✕ **Old French Bakery.** All the tasty French temptations that you can't get elsewhere in Belize are available at this little bakery, run by Sean and

Blanco Bachet. Pick up a crusty baguette and an authentic croissant for only a couple of Belize dollars. It's open from 7 AM to 8 PM every day. ✉*Main Sq., across from taxi stand* ☎604/4651 ▭*No credit cards.*

$$$ ⌂**La Casa del Caballo Blanco.** New in late 2007, Caballo Blanco (it is named after a white horse belonging to the former owner of the land, and the horse has remained on the property) is a small eco-lodge. There are six rooms with tile floors, decorated with Guatemalan fabrics, in three duplex thatch cabañas. The main lodge building evokes the style of a 19th-century hacienda. A knoll-top location provides lovely views of San Ignacio and the hills beyond, and at night the meadow below the lodge comes alive with thousands of flickering fireflies. Delicious dinners (BZ$36) are served in a small dining room, but there is no bar. The lodge is home to Casa Avian Support Alliance (CASA), a "rehab center" for birds recovering from injury, illness, and captivity, and the lodge's 23 acres are a bird sanctuary.**Pros:** Beautiful hilltop views, comfortable new accommodations, friendly staff. **Cons:** Roadside location means some noise; owners aren't in residence full-time. ✉*Bullet Tree Rd., next to San Ignacio Hospital* ☎707/974–4942 ⊕*www.casacaballoblanco.com* ⌦*6 rooms* ♿*In-room: No a/c, no TV, no phone. In-hotel: restaurant, laundry service, public Wi-Fi, public Internet, no elevator* ▭*MC, V.*

$$$ ⌂**Windy Hill Resort.** The cabañas at this lodge all have private verandas and are perched on a low hill across the landscaped grounds. Furnishings are custom-made from local hardwoods, and decorations include handwoven Guatemalan rugs. Each cabaña is cooled by a ceiling fan. You can lounge around the swimming pool and enjoy the nice views across the valley. The resort is on 100 acres at the edge of San Ignacio, right beside the highway. It runs many tours to Tikal, Caracol, and other destinations. Windy Hill has many packages with tours and meals included, starting at around BZ$2,250 for a double for two nights. **Pros:** Handy roadside location, offers many tours, pleasant cabins on hillside. **Cons:** Not a jungle lodge, so-so food. ✉*Benque Rd., Western Hwy., 1 mi (1½ km) west of San Ignacio* ☎824/2017 or 800/946–3995 ⊕*www.windyhillresort.com* ⌦*25 cabañas* ♿*In-room: no a/c (some), no phone. In-hotel: restaurant, pool, public Internet, no elevator, airport shuttle* ▭*AE, MC, V.*

$$-$$$ ⌂**San Ignacio Resort Hotel.** Queen Elizabeth visited here once, and while you may not feel like royalty, you'll appreciate the spacious and comfortable (though arguably a bit stark) rooms with verandas facing a hillside. The Running W Restaurant specializes in steak from the owners' Running W ranch (the filet is the way to go, as the sirloin, from grass-fed cattle, is chewy), and the Stork Bar is one of the best places in town to get a drink. Birding and other excursions can be arranged by the staff. There's an iguana hatchery on the property, and next door is a small casino, a branch of the Princess casinos in Belize City and Corozal, packed with video poker machines, one-armed bandits, and a few live tables. **Pros:** Safe, comfortable choice at the edge of town. **Cons:** A bit expensive considering the concrete block walls. ✉*Buena Vista Rd.* ☎824/2034 ⊕*www.sanignaciobelize.com* ⌦*24 rooms, 1 suite* ♿*In-hotel: restaurant, bar, pool, laundry service, public Internet, no elevator, airport shuttle* ▭*AE, MC, V.*

$-$$ ⊞**Cahal Pech Village.** You'll enjoy the best views in the Cayo at this
★   resort set on a high hill at the western edge of San Ignacio, near the
Cahal Pech Maya site. Local owners Daniel and Miriam Silva opened
the hotel in 1994 and have been expanding and improving it ever since.
The latest additions are new cottages and rooms and a gorgeous two-
level swimming pool, watched over by a giant statue of a pterodactyl.
You have a choice here of thatch cabañas or air-conditioned rooms.
The restaurant, while not a gourmet spot, serves tasty Belizean and
American fare (such as grilled fish, pork chops, spaghetti, and steaks) in
an open-air space with views of the valley below. It usually bustles with
guests and locals stopping in for a bite and a Belikin. **Pros:** Great views,
enticing pool, good value. **Cons:** Some rooms are a bit dowdy. ⊠ *Cahal
Pech Rd., 1 mi (2 km) west of town, off Western Hwy.* ☏ *824/3740*
⊕ *www.cahalpechvillageresort.com* ⇆ *20 rooms, 5 suites, 20 cabañas*
⌂ *In-room: no phone, no TV (some). In-hotel: restaurant, bar, pool,
public Internet, no elevator, airport shuttle* ⊟ *MC, V.*

$-$$ ⊞**Maya Mountain Lodge.** Designed with the nature lover in mind, this
hilltop lodge aspires toward comfort rather than luxury. Owners Bart
and Suzi Mickler designed the nature trails. One trail passes 150 edible
jungle plant species; the other focuses on ornamental plants. In summer they run workshops on ecology, birding, and other subjects. The
whitewashed, newly renovated cottages all have private patios. A large
wooden building has rooms, recently renovated with air-conditioning
added, for budget-conscious guests. The pleasant open-air dining room
serves tempting, wholesome food. There's an aboveground pool, and
the lodge runs a variety of tours and trips. **Pros:** Comfortable, unpretentious; good food. **Cons:** Roadside location. ⊠ *Cristo Rey Rd., 1 mi (2
km) outside San Ignacio* ☏ *824/2164* ⊕ *www.mayamountain.com* ⇆ *8
cottages, 6 rooms* ⌂ *In-room: no phone, no TV. In-hotel: restaurant,
pool, laundry service, public Internet, no elevator* ⊟ *AE, MC, V.*

¢-$ ⊞**Martha's Guesthouse and Restaurant.** With spic 'n' span rooms, a popu-
lar restaurant, handy laundry, and convenient tours, Martha's provides
just about everything you need, in an affordable package right in the
heart of downtown San Ignacio. The regular rooms, most with shared
bath, have white walls and polished wood floors, but for a little more
you can get a larger room with cable TV, fridge, and balcony. The
First Lady Suite is worth the climb up to the fourth floor, as it's large
enough for a family, has a kitchenette, and a huge veranda with views
of the hills. In 2006, an annex called the Inn at Martha's about a block
away added six rooms. The original location can be noisy, due to traffic and barking dogs; the annex is quieter. Martha's Restaurant, with
local art on the walls and a sweet garden patio, is open 7 AM–10 PM
every day, serving pizza, sirloin steak (BZ$20), and local dishes such as
chaya tamales (chaya is a type of greens grown around Cayo). Martha's
stays booked, even off-season. **Pros:** Handy downtown location; good
value. **Cons:** Can be noisy. ⊠ *10 West St.* ☏ *804/3647* ⊕ *www.marthas
belize.com* ⇆ *16 rooms, 7 with shared baths, 1 suite* ⌂ *In-room: no a/c
(some), no phone, kitchen (some), refrigerator (some), no TV (some).
In-hotel: restaurant, bar, laundry service, public Internet, no elevator*
⊟ *AE, MC, V.*

¢-$ 🖼Aguada Hotel & Restaurant. Budget travelers jump at the opportunity to stay in this tidy, attractive, and cheap hotel in Santa Elena, a low-key town adjoining San Ignacio. Aguada became so popular that the owners, a Belizean-American couple, added more rooms overlooking the pool. There's a friendly restaurant with Belizean dishes and American standards like burgers. In the large common room are a TV and games. The hotel has a van that runs to and from the airports in Belize City for around BZ$80 a person. **Pros:** Clean, inexpensive, safe rooms with air-conditioning, one of the few budget hotels in Belize with a pool. **Cons:** Location is a bus or taxi ride away (though the ride's short) from downtown San Ignacio. ⊠*Santa Elena* 📞*824/3609* ⊕*www.aguadahotel. com* ➱*14 rooms* ⌂*In-room: no phone, no TV. In-hotel: restaurant, pool, public Internet, no elevator, airport shuttle* ▭*MC, V.*

¢-$ 🖼Casa Blanca Guest House. Though it's in the center of San Ignacio, on
★ bustling Burns Avenue, this small hotel is an oasis of quiet and one of Belize's top budget choices. The rooms, with cool white, mahogany-trimmed walls and locally made wood furniture, are a big step above typical budget lodging. You can prepare yourself snacks or full meals in the shared kitchen, and you're within walking distance of a dozen or more restaurants. Casa Blanca is often fully booked, even off-season. **Pros:** Central downtown location, extremely clean, appealing rooms, good value. **Cons:** Limited parking nearby. ⊠*10 Burns Ave.* 📞*824/2080* ⊕*www.casablancaguesthouse.com* ➱*9 rooms* ⌂*In-room: no a/c (some), no phone, no elevator* ▭*MC, V..*

¢ 🖼Falconview Backpackers Adventure Hostel. For BZ$24 per person, including hotel tax, you get a bunk bed or hammock in a small dormitory, kitchen privileges, and the company of co-owner Ray Auxillou, one of the great characters in Belize. Canadian by birth, Ray (now in his early 70s) has spent much of his life in Belize. Among other things, he has been a fisherman and tourism pioneer on Caye Caulker, a teacher, an adventurer, and a novelist. His current passion is growing organic vegetables hydroponically. Ray's wife, Silvia, is from Colombia. Falconview also has a one-bedroom apartment with kitchenette, for BZ$98 a night, or BZ$427 weekly, including hotel tax. **Pros:** Bargain rates; interesting company. **Cons:** Backpacker-level comfort. ⊠*2964 Pluto St., Hillview Santa Elena* ✛*At Mile 66½ Western Hwy. go south toward Hillview about ½ mi (1 km)* 📞*663/5580* ⊕*http://folkmusicfl. tripod.com/adventuresinbelize/* ➱*dormitory, 1 1-bedroom apartment* ⌂*In-room: no a/c, no phone, no TV, kitchenette (some). In-hotel: public Internet, no elevator* ▭*MC, V.*

ALONG THE MOPAN RIVER

¢-$ ✕Benny's Kitchen. This little open-air restaurant near Xunantunich has won many fans who come for hearty Mayan and Creole dishes at rock-bottom prices. Most items on the menu are BZ$8 or less, including *chilimole* (chicken with mole sauce), cow-foot soup, *escabeche*, and stewed pork with rice and beans and plantains. The classic Mayan pibil (pork cooked in an underground oven), when available, is BZ$12. The banana *licuados* (milk shakes) are delicious. ⊠*San José Succotz Village, across Benque Rd., Western Hwy., from ferry to Xunantu-*

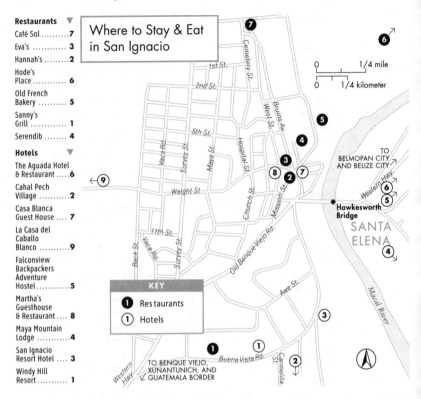

Where to Stay & Eat in San Ignacio

nich ⊕ *Turn south just west of ferry and follow signs about 3 blocks* ☎ *823/2541* ▭ *No credit cards.*

$$$$ **Ka'ana Boutique Resort and Spa.** A large infusion of cash by Irish inves-
★ tors who struck it rich with oil wells in the Spanish Lookout area of
the Cayo has turned a failed mid-level tour hotel into a well-designed,
upscale boutique resort. With tranquil gardens, a wine cellar, spacious
rooms outfitted with iPod docks, espresso machines, high-end toiletries, and LCD TVs, Ka'ana, which opened in 2007, brings a new level
of luxury, not to mention high prices, to San Ignacio. The restaurant,
while beautiful, is very expensive—for example, breakfast is BZ$40,
and several entrees at dinner are BZ$60 or more, all plus tax and tip.
Oddly, since Ka'ana is more than 70 miles from the sea, the pool is
salt water. **Pros:** Terrifically comfortable beds; attractive and convivial
staff. **Cons:** Roadside location; very expensive. ✉ *Mile 69¼, Western
Hwy.* ☎ *824/3350 or 877/522–6221 in the U.S.* ⊕ *www.kaanabelize.
com* ⌁ **$£** *rooms* ✎ *In-room: Wi-Fi, mini-bar. In-hotel: restaurant, bar,
pool, spa, laundry service, no elevator* ▭ *AE, MC, V.*

$$$$ **Mopan River Resort.** Belize's first truly all-inclusive resort is one of the
★ best values in the Cayo. Once you've taken the short ferry trip across
the Mopan River to the resort's manicured palm-studded grounds,
you're in your own private bit of paradise, and everything except bor-

der fees and site admission charges is included in the price, from meals and drinks to trips to Tikal and Barton Cave, transfers from Belize City, and even tips. A week's stay including everything is BZ$2,925–BZ$3,220 per person. The thatch cabañas have traditional facades, but have modern amenities like cable TVs, air-conditioning, and refrigerators with gratis soft drinks and beer. The swimming pool, lighted by constantly changing fiber-optic lights, provides a romantic setting for a late-night swim. Buffet meals are taken family-style, so you get to know the other guests. Co-owner Pamella Picon is an ordained minister who can marry you in the resort's wedding chapel. **Pros:** Excellent value in a true All-Inclusive, charming hosts, beautiful grounds. **Cons:** Not a jungle lodge; location near Benque Viejo town can be noisy. ⊠ *Benque Viejo del Carmen* ☎ *823/2047* ⊕ *www.mopanriverresort.com* ⊋ *12 cabañas* ⚒ *In-room: no phone, kitchen (some), refrigerator. In-hotel: pool, laundry service, no-smoking rooms, public Wi-Fi, public Internet, no elevator, airport shuttle* ⊟ *D, MC, V* ⊘ *Closed July–Oct.* †○†*AI*

$$ ⚠ ⊞ **Clarissa Falls Resort.** The low gurgle of nearby Mopan River rap-
☺ ids is the first and last sound of the day at Clarissa Falls Resort. Warm and friendly owner Chena Galvez has spent her life on a cattle ranch here, on a rolling 800-acre expanse of grassy pasture. Over the years Chena and family have built a small colony of homey thatch cabañas. Prices are a little high considering the basic nature of the accommodations, but you're also paying for the idyllic setting. If you're on a tight budget, there's camping (BZ$15 per person) and, for students only, rooms in a bunkhouse and three meals daily for BZ$90. A shuttle to and from the international airport near Belize City is available for BZ$180 one way for up to four persons. Pros: Quiet, pastoral riverside setting; you'll want to hug the owner. Cons: Resort is on a ranch and not in a true jungle setting. ⊠ *Benque Rd., Mile 70, Western Hwy.,* ⊹*5½ mi (9 km) west of San Ignacio* ☎ *824/3916* ⊕ *www.clarissafa-lls.com* ⊋ *11 cabañas, 1 bunkhouse with 10 beds* ⚒ *In-room: no a/c, no phone, no TV. In-hotel: restaurant, laundry service, no elevator, airport shuttle* ⊟ *MC, V..*

$–$$ ⊞ **Clarissa Falls Resort.** This is a well-known place among Belizeans, who come for tasty enchiladas (BZ$3), chicken with rice and stewed beans (BZ$12), and Relleno Negro (spicy soup with chicken, boiled egg and meatballs, served with freshmade tortillas, BZ$18). Meals are served in an open-air thatch-roofed palapa overlooking the river. Vegetarian and vegan dishes available. *Benque Rd., Mile 70, Western Hwy.,* ⊹*5½ mi (9 km) west of San Ignacio* ☎ *824/3916* ⊟ *MC,V.*

$ ⊞ **Cohune Palms River Cabañas.** This charming spot has five thatched
★ cabañas set among palms on a small peninsula on the Mopan River. Cooled by breezes from the river, you can lounge in a hammock while checking your e-mail by Wi-Fi, and then swing into the water on a rope. Get your questions about El Pilar and other nearby Mayan sites answered by the co-owner, Bevin Waight, an American anthropologist who originally came to Belize on an archeological dig. The open-air restaurant serves Belizean dishes using local ingredients, along with pasta and seafood, and vegetarian options are available. The lodge offers free pickup from San Ignacio. **Pros:** Excellent moderately priced

lodge, knowledgeable owners. good food. **Cons:** May be tough to leave. ⊠*Bullet Tree Falls* ☎824/0166 *or 609/2738* ⊕*www.cohunepalms.com* ⇌*5 cabañas* ⚿*In-room: no a/c, no phone, no TV. In-hotel: restaurant, bar, laundry service, Wi-Fi, public Internet, no elevator* ▤*MC, V.*

WORD OF MOUTH

"Check out The Trek Stop—they have a nice butterfly enclosure near Xunantunich and it's one of my favorite places in the area."
—hopefulist

¢ ⚠ ▣**The Trek Stop.** After a day out
★ and about, a cold Belikin and filling Mexican and Belizean dishes await you at this cluster of neat-as-a-pin cabins. Tent camping (BZ$10 per person) is also available, as is a common kitchen for preparing your own grub. Michigan expats and their Belizean partners opened this spot on top of a hill near Xunantunich in 1998. It's an exceptional find, particularly for budget travelers, as cabins (with showers and composting toilets around the corner) start at just BZ$24 per person or BZ$40 double. Large new double cabins with private bath are BZ$70. Here you can also hike nature trails, visit the butterfly farm, and play Frisbee golf at the only disc golf course in Belize. **Pros:** Top value for the money, friendly owners. **Cons:** Just a couple steps up from camping; location means you'll have to take a bus or taxi to most sights. ⊠*San José Succotz Village, 6 mi (9 km) west of San Ignacio* ☎823/2265 ⊕*www. thetrekstop.com* ⇌*9 cabins, 7 without private bath* ⚿*In-room: no a/c, no phone, no TV. In-hotel: restaurant, bar, public Wi-Fi, no elevator, airport shuttle* ▤*MC, V.*

ALONG THE MACAL RIVER

$$$$ ▣**The Lodge at Chaa Creek.** This was the first jungle lodge in the Cayo,
Fodor'sChoice and owners Mick and Lucy Fleming have spent 30 years polishing
★   Chaa Creek to a fine, rich patina. To start, the gracefully landscaped grounds, surrounded by 340 acres of rolling hills above the Macal River, are magnificent. On the grounds are the Rainforest Medicine Trail, Natural History Centre, and butterfly farm. There's a friendly and competent staff of 100. The whitewashed stone cottages with thatch roofs and custom-made furnishings are both simple and elegant. Ideal for honeymooners are the "tree top" and other suites (BZ$1,170) with whirlpools. A new two-bedroom villa suite (BZ$1,370 for up to four persons) is located above the spa, which incidentally is widely considered the best spa in Belize. For cost-conscious travelers there's the Macal River Camp, with small A-frame rooms on individual wooden platforms (BZ$220 double, including meals). Dinner (BZ$64) is a special event, and a full breakfast is included in the rates. Additionally, Chaa Creek's tours are among the country's finest, and horseback riding is available. **Pros:** Stunningly beautiful grounds, excellent staff and service, lovely cabañas and suites. **Cons:** Lodging and meal prices have jumped in recent years. ⊠*Chial Rd., southwest of San Ignacio* ⊕*From San Ignacio go 4¾ mi (7½ km) on Benque Rd., Western Hwy., turn left on Chial Rd.* ☎824/2037 ⊕*www.chaacreek.com* ⇌*14 rooms in duplex cottages, 6 suites, 4 villas, 10 casitas, 1 2-bedroom suite* ⚿*In-room: no a/c (some), no phone, no TV. In-hotel: restaurant, spa, bicy-*

cles, no elevator, laundry service, public Wi-Fi, public Internet, airport shuttle ⊟*AE, D, MC, V* ⍝❙*BP.*

$$$ 🏠 **duPlooy's Lodge.** High above a bend in the Macal River called Big
⟳ Eddy is this remarkable, relaxing lodge whose grounds include the 45-
★ acre Belize Botanic Gardens. From your vantage point on the covered
deck and 200 feet of canopied walkway, 30 feet above the forest floor,
you'll see iguanas sunning in the trees and, perhaps while sipping a
beer, you can do your bird-watching in comfort. You can swim and dive
off the rocks from the sandy river beach below. Bungalows are filled
with hardwood furnishings. The two-story La Casita has wraparound
porches, king-size beds, whirlpool bath, fridge, and great views. There
are private bungalows and less expensive rooms in the jungle lodge,
and the River House has family suites (BZ$536 for a three- or four-
bedroom suite). The food is terrific (full meal plan is BZ$96 a person,
including 10% tax and 10% service), and there's always a vegetar-
ian option. **Pros:** Variety of lodging choices, excellent food, botanic
gardens on-site, eco-conscious management. **Cons:** Costs for meals,
transfers, and tours add up. ⊹*Head 4¾ mi (7½ km) west on Benque
Rd., turn left on Chial Rd., San Ignacio* ☎*824/3101* ⊕*www.duplooys.
com* ↪*1 house, 4 cabañas, 3 suites, 15 rooms* ⌂*In-room: no a/c, no
phone, no TV. In-hotel: no elevator, laundry service, public Internet,
no-smoking rooms, airport shuttle* ⊟*MC, V.*

$$$ 🏠 **Ek' Tun.** At Ek' Tun, sapphire blue water gushes from natural mineral
springs into a rock-lined pool among towering palms. You're immersed
in complete solitude here at owner Phyllis Lane's private paradise—you
can even skinny-dip, if you like—with only the howler monkeys for
company. Arrive by river skiff to the 200-acre grounds, which have
giant ceiba trees and flowering shrubs. With only two rustic but lovely
thatch-roof cottages, this is more of a bed-and-breakfast in the jungle
than a traditional lodge. On the extensive network of trails you can
spot orange-breasted falcons and toucans. Meals (breakfast and dinner total BZ$67 per person including tax and service) are served in a
stucco-and-thatch dining room overlooking the Macal River. There's
a three-night minimum stay. **Pros:** Stunning, remote location. **Cons:**
Ek'Tun does not accept single travelers or guests under 18. ⊠*On
Macal River, 12 mi (20 km) upriver from San Ignacio* ☎*820/3002*
⊕*www.ektunbelize.com* ↪*2 cabañas* ⌂*In-room: no a/c, no phone,
no TV. In-hotel: no elevator, bar, pool, no kids under 18, no-smoking
rooms, airport shuttle* ⊟*MC, V.*

$-$$$ 🏠 **Black Rock River Lodge.** Some 800 feet above limestone cliffs and the
Macal River gorge, Black Rock may have the most beautiful setting
of any lodge in the country. The well-shaded cabins, which come in
deluxe, river-view, and shared-bath versions, have stone floors and cus-
tom-made hardwood furniture and views across Black Rock canyon.
New ownership appears eco-conscious, running the lodge on hydro
and solar power, and also safety-conscious, helping alleviate concerns
about a couple of crime incidents that took place several years ago
under previous management. Since you're a 35-minute drive (about
BZ$50 by taxi) from San Ignacio, partly on a narrow, single-lane dirt
trail, by necessity you'll take all your meals here (the full meal plan

is BZ$101 per person including tax and service) and do most tours with the lodge. **Pros:** Remote, beautiful setting, eco-conscious management. **Cons:** You're stuck here for meals and tours unless you have a car. ⊠ *On Macal River, 13 mi (22 km) upriver from San Ignacio, Box 48, San Ignacio* ☎ *824/2341* ⊕ *www.blackrocklodge.com* ➩ *13 cabins* ⚬ *In-room: no a/c, no phone, no TV. In-hotel: no elevator, public Internet, laundry service* ☰ *AE, MC, V.*

THE OUTDOORS

San Ignacio is the center for touring in western Belize. Just walk along busy Burns Avenue and you'll see signs for all kinds of tours and find the offices of several tour operators. Individual tour guides, who by law must be Belizean citizens and be licensed by the government, may work for tour operators, for a lodge or hotel, or they may freelance on their own. Many hang out at Eva's downtown, or at other restaurants in town. You can stop in and sign up for the next day's tours, usually at lower rates than from the larger operators. Obviously, the more layers of costs involved, the higher the price for you, but on the other hand larger operators have more resources, and they have their long-term reputations to protect, so they *may* be more reliable. Tours from lodges usually are more costly than if booked with an independent tour operator. Also, some lodges try to sell packages of tours rather than individual ones.

Most jungle lodges offer a full range of day trips, using either their own guides or working with independent guides and tour companies. The largest lodge-affiliated tour operations are Chaa Creek Expeditions and Windy Hill Tour Company, but Crystal Paradise, duPlooy's, Maya Mountain, Cahal Pech Village, San Ignacio Resort Hotel, and other hotels and lodges also do many tours and trips.

If you have a rental car, you can visit all of the Mayan sites in the Cayo on your own, along with other attractions such as the butterfly farms, the Belize Botanic Gardens, Rainforest Medicine Trail, and many of the attractions in the Mountain Pine Ridge. However, for most caving tours, you'll need a guide, and for canoe and kayak trips, you'll need drop-off and pick-up. Local guides also are critical for nature hikes and birding trips, as many of these guides have remarkable local knowledge and ability to spot things you probably wouldn't see otherwise.

BIRDING

The area around San Ignacio is very good for birding because it contains such a variety of habitats—river valleys, foothills, lagoons, agricultural areas, and broadleaf jungle—each of which attracts different types of birds. For example, Aguacate Lagoon near Spanish Lookout attracts waterbirds such as Night Herons, Neotropic Cormorants, and Whistling Ducks. Open land and pastures are good for spotting Laughing Falcons, Vermillion Flycatchers, Eastern Meadowlarks, and White-tailed Kites.

BUDGETING YOUR TRIP

Here are a range of rates you can expect to pay for selected trips. These charges are per person and usually include transportation, lunch (on full-day trips), and in the case of river trips, drop-off and pick-up. Admission to Mayan sites, border fees (BZ$37.50 to go from Belize and to Guatemala), and gratuities to guides are usually extra. On some trips, such as to Tikal or Caracol, there's often a flat fee for one to four persons, so the more going together, the cheaper.

■ Guided nature walk, at lodge: BZ$20–BZ$60

■ Morning birding walk, at lodge: BZ$10–BZ$30 (sometimes free)

■ Day trip to Tikal: BZ$150–BZ$300 (cheaper for larger parties)

■ Overnight trip to Tikal: BZ$300–BZ$500

■ Day trip to Caracol: BZ$100–BZ$200 (cheaper for larger parties)

■ Half-day tour of Xunantunich: BZ$40–BZ$100

■ Mountain Pine Ridge tour: BZ$70–BZ$120

■ Actun Tunichil Muknal: BZ$160–BZ$200

■ Barton Creek Cave with canoe: BZ$75–BZ$100

■ Self-guided canoe or kayak trip on Macal or Mopan rivers: BZ$50–BZ$70

■ Half-day horseback riding: BZ$60–BZ$120

■ Mountain bike rental: BZ$25–BZ$70 a day (complimentary at some lodges)

■ Overnight camping trip, with guide: BZ$300 per night for up to three persons, plus supplies

There's good birding on the grounds of most of the lodges along the Mopan and Macal rivers, including **Chaa Creek, Ek 'Tun, duPlooy's, Crystal Paradise,** and **Clarissa Falls.** In addition, local guides and tour companies run birding trips. One of the best known is **Paradise Expeditions,** which is associated with Crystal Paradise (☎824/2772 ✍ info@birdingin-belize.com).

CANOEING & KAYAKING

The Cayo's rivers, especially the Mopan and Macal, make it an excellent place for canoeing and kayaking. Most of the larger resorts, like **Chaa Creek** and **duPlooy's,** have canoes or inflatable kayaks. Generally you put in in the Macal around Chaa Creek and paddle and float down to the Hawksworth Bridge at San Ignacio, a trip that takes about two hours. You'll pay about BZ$50 a person for canoe rental and pick-up. You'll see iguanas and bird life on the banks, and if you dip in for a swim, don't be surprised if tiny (toothless) fish school around you to figure out if you're food. In San Ignacio you can rent canoes from **Toni's River Adventures** (☎824/3292), which also organizes guided Macal River trips and overnight camping trips. **River Rat** (☎625/4636 ⊕www.riverratbelize.com) arranges half-day and full-day kayaking trips, both for beginners and experienced river runners, as well as custom caving and jungle trips. If you'd rather float down the Mopan on an inner tube, **The Trek Stop** (☎823/2265) rents them for BZ$20, a rate that includes drop-off and pick-up; inflatable kayaks rent for BZ$50, including drop-off and pick-up.

Do exercise caution. You won't believe how fast the rivers, especially the Macal, can rise after a heavy rain. Following rains in the Mountain Pine Ridge, it can reach

> **DON'T MISS**
>
> In town, **Arts & Crafts of Central America** (✉ *24 Burns Ave.* ☎ *824/2253*) has a small selection of crafts, at competitive prices.

a dangerous flood stage in just a few minutes. Also, in the past there have been some incidents of visitors in canoes being stopped and robbed on the Macal. Watch weather forecasts, and ask locally about safety on the rivers.

CAVING

Fodor's Choice
★
Over the millennia, as dozens of swift-flowing rivers bored through the soft limestone, the Maya Mountains became pitted with miles of caves. The Maya used them as burial sites and, according to one theory, as subterranean waterways that linked the Cayo with communities as far north as the Yucatán. Previously, the caves fell into a 1,000-year slumber, disturbed only by the nightly flutter of bats. In recent years the caves have been rediscovered by spelunkers. First on the scene was Ian Anderson, owner of **Caves Branch Adventure Co. & Jungle Camp** (✉ *12 mi [19½ km] south of Belmopan* ☎ *822/2800* ⊕ *www.cavesbranch.com*). He and his friendly staff of trained guides run exhilarating adventure-theme caving, tubing, and hiking trips from a tiki-torchlighted jungle camp just south of Belmopan. (⇨ *See Belmopan lodging, above.*) **PACZ Tours** (✉ *30 Burns Ave., San Ignacio* ☎ *824/0536*) specializes in tours to the spooky, wonderful Actun Tunichil Muknal near Belmopan. David A. Simpson, of **David's Adventure Tours** (✉ *San Ignacio* ☎ *824/3674* ⊕ *www.davidsadventuretours.com*), was the first to do tours of the now-popular Barton Creek Cave. You can canoe through Barton Creek, 8 mi (13 km) southeast of San Ignacio.

HIKING

Most of the lodges have hiking trails. **Black Rock River Lodge, Ek' Tun, Chaa Creek, Maya Mountain, Crystal Paradise,** and **duPlooy's** all have especially good areas for hiking. If you want even more wide-open spaces, head to the Mountain Pine Ridge, which offers hundreds of miles of hiking trails, mostly old logging roads. (⇨ *See Mountain Pine Ridge, below.*)

For more adventurous hikes and overnight treks, you'll want to go with a guide. Among the best adventure guides in the Cayo is **Winston Harris** (✉ *60 Cristo Rey Rd., Cristo Rey village* ☎ *809/4016*), a former British Army tracker and member of the British Special Armed Services elite force. He is an expert on jungle survival. **Marcus Cucul** (✉ *Box 485, Belmopan* ☎ *600/3116* ⊕ *www.mayaguide.bz*), is a Kekchi Mayan who is trained in cave and wilderness rescue.

HORSEBACK RIDING

When it comes to horseback riding adventures, whether on the old logging roads of the Mountain Pine Ridge or on trails in the Slate Creek Preserve, the undisputed local experts are found at the lodges of

Mountain Equestrian Trails (✉ *Pine Ridge Rd.* ☎ 669/1124 ⊕ *www.met-belize.com*) and **Lodge at Chaa Creek** (✉ *Chial Rd.* ☎ 824/2037 ⊕ *www.chaacreek.com*). **Easy Rider** (✉ *Collins Ave., San Ignacio* ☎ 824/3734) also runs equestrian tours of the Mayan ruins and other points of interest in the region.

MOUNTAIN PINE RIDGE

❸ *17 mi (27 km) south of San Ignacio.*

★ The Mountain Pine Ridge Forest Reserve is a highlight of any journey to Belize and an adventure to reach. It's in the high country of Belize—low mountains and rolling hills are covered in part by vast pine forests and crisscrossed with old logging roads. The higher elevations provide cooler temperatures and, of course, outstanding views. The best way to see this area is on a mountain bike, a horse, or your own feet, not bouncing around in an Isuzu Trooper.

Aside from pines, you'll see lilac-color mimosa, Saint-John's-wort, and occasionally a garish red flower known as hotlips. Look out for the craboo, a wild tree whose berries are used in a brandylike liqueur believed to have aphrodisiacal properties. Birds love this fruit, so any craboo is a good place to spot orioles and woodpeckers.

WHAT TO SEE

Inside the Mountain Pine Ridge Forest Reserve is **Hidden Valley Falls.** Also known as the Thousand Foot Falls (it actually drops nearly 1,600 feet), it's the highest in Central America. A thin plume of spray plummets over the edge of a rock face into an ostensibly bottomless gorge below. The catch is that the viewing area (admission BZ$3), where there is a shelter with some benches and a public restroom, is some distance from the falls. Many visitors find the narrow falls unimpressive from this vantage point. To climb closer requires a major commitment: a steep climb down the side of the mountain is several hours.

At the nearby **Río On** you can sunbathe on flat granite boulders or dunk yourself into crystal-clear pools and waterfalls.

☾ **Río Frio Caves** are only a few miles by car down a steep track, but ecologically speaking, these caves are in a different world. In the course of a few hundred yards, you drop from pine savanna to tropical forest. Nothing in Belize illustrates its extraordinary geological diversity as clearly as this startling transition. A river runs right through the center and over the centuries has carved the rock into fantastic shapes. Swallows fill the place, and at night ocelots and margays pad silently across the cold floor in search of slumbering prey. Seen from the dark interior, the light-filled world outside seems more intense and beautiful than ever. Rising vertically through the cave's mouth is a giant hardwood tree, *Pterocarpus officialis*. Its massive paddle-shape roots are anchored in the sandy soil of the riverbank and its green crown strains toward the blue sky.

More than 30,000 pupae are raised annually at the **Green Hills Butterfly Ranch and Botanical Collections,** the largest and best of Belize's butterfly farms open to the public. For a closer look at the creatures, the facility, located outside the Mountain Pine Ridge reserve, has about 30 species in a huge flight area. Jan Meerman, who's published a book on Belize's butterflies, runs the place with Dutch partner Tineke Boomsma. On the grounds also are many flowers, including passionflowers, bromeliads, heliconias, and orchids. ⊠ *Mile 8, Chiquibul Rd. (also called Mountain Pine Ridge Rd.)* ☎ *820/4017* ⊠ *BZ$10 for guided tour* ⊙ *Daily 8–4, last tour 3:30.*

Named after the famed Guatemala-born herbal healer who died in 1996 at the age of 106, **Elijio Panti National Park** is a wonderful addition to Belize's already extensive national parks system. It spans 13,000 acres around the villages of San Antonio, Cristo Rey, and El Progreso and into the Mountain Pine Ridge. The hope is that with no hunting in this park, more wildlife will return to western Belize. As it only opened in 2001, the park boundaries are ill-defined, no admission fee is charged, and an official welcome center and other park formalities do not exist.

The **Chalillo Dam Lake** was created in late 2005 by the controversial damming of the Macal River for a power plant. Since then, another dam has been completed and a third dam is under construction. The original 150-foot-high dam with a span width of 420 feet, along with its sisters, destroyed a habitat for endangered species such as the Scarlet Macaw and was opposed by environmentalists in Belize and around the world. It is unknown how many Mayan sites were flooded. However, the dams may eventually have an upside: providing a new lake ecosystem for birds (Scarlet Macaws are still present in the area around the dam) and wildlife, not to mention recreational activities on the reservoir. The lake, which initially flooded some 2,500 acres, will eventually extend some 12 mi (20 km) along the Macal and Raspacula river valleys, in some places over a half-mile wide. As of this writing, however, some of the area looks like a campaign ad against clear-cutting. Submerged logs and debris in the still-filling reservoir and continuing construction on dams mean that the lake and dams are not yet open to the public.

WHERE TO STAY & EAT: NEAR MOUNTAIN PINE RIDGE

In addition to the lodges in the Mountain Pine Ridge itself, which include the top-end Blancaneaux Lodge and Hidden Valley Inn, along with the moderate Five Sisters Lodge, several jungle lodges, some newly opened and all in the moderate price category, are located on the two roads leading to the Mountain Pine Ridge—the Chiquibul Road from Georgeville (also sometimes called the Mountain Pine Ridge Road) and the Cristo Rey Road from Santa Elena. Of the lodges en route to the Mountain Pine Ridge, Table Rock Lodge and Crystal Paradise Resort are on the Macal River, while Mariposa Jungle Lodge, Gumbo Limbo Village Resort, and Mountain Equestrian Trails are not.

$$$ 🏠**Mariposa Jungle Lodge.** Two retired American lawyers, Jim and Sharyn Brinker, opened this small, intimate lodge in late 2007. Six well-designed cabañas are set in the shade on a low hill, with pimento walls, thatch roofs, and furniture handmade at the lodge and elsewhere in Belize. They're outfitted with everything you'll need, down to flashlights, purified water coolers, and umbrellas. Meals are served in the main lodge building, which also has a bar, an art-filled guest study, and a gift shop. Dinners are themed, with international touches from the owners' travels, and cost BZ$56 for a four-course meal, plus tax and service. **Pros:** Personalized service, attractive cabañas. **Cons:** Pricey meals, bumpy 30-minute drive from San Ignacio. ✉*Cristo Rey Rd., near junction with Chiquibul Rd., San Antonio Village* ☎*670/2113 or 304/933–1793 in the U.S.* ⊕*www.mariposajunglelodge.com* ⇆*6 cabañas* ⚙*In-room: no a/c, no phone, no TV. In-hotel: restaurant, no elevator, public Wi-Fi, laundry service, no-smoking rooms, airport shuttle* ⊟*MC, V.*

$$$ 🏠**Mountain Equestrian Trails.** If horses are your thing, this is your place. MET, as most people call it, is one of Belize's top equestrian spots. You can do full-day rides (BZ$166 per person) into the Mountain Pine Ridge to waterfalls and river caves, or half-day rides (BZ$122) to Pacbitun Maya site. Five-night room and riding packages are BZ$2,342 per person, plus 19% tax and service. Rustic comfort is the watchword here; you relax by kerosene lamplight, as the thatch cabañas have no electricity. Meals (dinner is BZ$40) are served in the cantina. **Pros:** Very horsey. **Cons:** Expect rustic. ✉*Mile 8, Chiquibul Rd., San Antonio Village* ☎*669/1124* ⊕*www.metbelize.com* ⇆*10 cabañas,* ⚙*In-room: no a/c, no phone, no TV. In-hotel: no elevator, laundry service, airport shuttle* ⊟*MC, V.*

$$ 🏠**Gumbo Limbo Village Resort.** Well-priced, with a lovely hilltop setting, and amenities such as a pool, this new lodge is an attractive option just 2 mi (3 km) from the Western Highway at Georgeville. Four flat-roofed cottages (BZ$240 in-season, BZ$170 off-season, plus tax), each with floor-length windows and a patio offering views of the jungle canopy, flank the open-air restaurant/bar palapa and nearby swimming pool. **Pros:** Attractive new cottage accommodations, lovely views from hilltop setting, reasonable prices. **Cons:** Steep hill on dirt access road is a doozy. (✉*Mile 2, Chiquibul Rd., Georgeville* ☎*665/3112* ⊕*www. gumbolimboresort.com* ⇆*4 cottages* ⚙*In-room: no a/c, no phone, no TV, Wi-Fi. In-hotel: restaurant, bar, pool, no elevator, public Wi-Fi, laundry service, airport shuttle* ⊟*MC, V.*

$$ ⚠ 🏠**Table Rock Lodge.** Located on a small working farm and surrounded by almost 100 acres of jungle, Table Rock has only three thatch cottages—but all have tile floors, four-poster beds, and Guatemalan crafts and fabrics. You can explore winding pathways and cut trails down to the Macal River, or visit with the resident donkeys. The lodge also provides tents (including set-up, breakdown, and firewood) for riverside camping (BZ$60). **Pros:** Low-key, relaxing, off-the-beaten-path lodge. **Cons:** Not a party spot. ✉*Cristo Rey Rd., San Antonio Village* ☎*670/4910* ⊕*www.tablerockbelize.com* ⇆*3 cottages* ⚙*In-room: no a/c, no phone, no TV. In-hotel: no elevator, laundry service* ⊟*MC, V* ⊗*Closed May and Oct.*

$-$$ ⬚ **Crystal Paradise Resort.** This lodge is operated by the Tut (pro-
nounced Toot) family—Mom and Dad Tut and 10, yes, 10, children.
Mom and the daughters cook and run the lodge, and several of the
sons are accomplished guides for birding, caving, and river expeditions. There's a range of lodging, from simple rooms to traditional
thatch cabañas with views of the Macal River Valley. Rates, starting
at BZ$185 double including tax, are affordable, but are made even
more so as delicious, fresh-made breakfasts and dinners, served in an
open palapa, are included in the price. **Pros:** With meals included, this
is one of the best buys in the Cayo; good guided tours. **Cons:** No-frills
rooms and cabañas. ⊠ *Cristo Rey Rd., Cristo Rey Village* ⊕ *www.
crystalparadise.com* ⬚ *12 cabañas, 8 rooms* ⬚ *In-room: no a/c, no
phone, no TV. In-hotel: no elevator, public Internet, laundry service,
airport shuttle* ☰ *MC, V.*

WHERE TO STAY & EAT: MOUNTAIN PINE RIDGE

$$$$ ⬚ **Blancaneaux Lodge.** As you sweep down this upscale resort's hibis-
Fodor'sChoice cus- and palm-lined drive, past the big, new swimming pool, opened in
★ 2008 where the croquet lawn used to be, you may get a whiff of Beverly
Hills. Indeed, the lodge is owned by director Francis Ford Coppola.
Spread on a hillside above Privassion River, the villas with their soaring thatch ceilings, Japanese-style tile baths, plunge pools, and screened
porches overlooking the river have appeared in *Architectural Digest.*
The filmmaker's own villa, with private pool, is available (BZ$1,607
double, including tax and service) when he isn't in residence. A newly
completed house, "The Enchanted Cottage," (BZ$2,380) of local stone
and with a red Guatemalan tile roof, is set on a hill apart from the
other villas; it comes with its own golf cart. A fleet of four-wheel-
drive vehicles takes you to remote Mayan ruins or on shopping trips
to Guatemala. Those with their own planes can fly into the resort's
landing strip, or you can come on a charter flight from Belize City. The
main restaurant is one of the best in the Cayo, specializing in Italian
dishes and serving wines from Coppola's wineries. A second restaurant,
opened in 2008, serves Guatemalan food, by reservation only. You
can swim off large boulders in the Privassion River, relax in a giant
hot tub, swim in the new infinity pool or, if you have a villa, your private plunge pool. **Pros:** Fabulous grounds, deluxe cabañas and villas,
wonderful food and service. **Cons:** Many steep steps may pose problems for the infirm or elderly; very expensive. ⊠ *Mountain Pine Ridge
⊹ Turn right at Blancaneaux sign 4½ mi (7½ km) from Mountain Pine
Ridge entrance gate* ☎ *824/4912 or 824/3878, 800/746–3743 in U.S.*
⊕ *www.blancaneaux.com* ⬚ *10 cabañas, 7 villas, 1 house* ⬚ *In-room:
no a/c, no phone, safe, kitchen (some), no TV, Wi-Fi (some). In-hotel:
2 restaurants, bar, spa, bicycles, 2 pools, no elevator, laundry service,
public Internet, airport shuttle* ☰ *AE, MC, V* ⊚ *CP.*

$$$ ⬚ **Hidden Valley Inn.** Owned by a prominent Belize City family, Hidden
★ Valley Inn sits on 7,200 acres and has more than a dozen waterfalls
and 90 mi (150 km) of hiking and mountain biking trails. The estate
grounds, including the waterfalls, are exclusively for guests and not
open to the public. Romantics can enjoy a catered champagne lunch at

their own private waterfall. The cottages have mahogany furnishings, tile floors, and fireplaces. Dinner (BZ$72 including tax and service) is served in the main house, which has vaulted ceilings and four fireplaces. After dinner, sip coffee grown on the premises. They've recently added a private airstrip. **Pros:** Charming lodge atmosphere, wonderful waterfalls, excellent birding. **Con:** Loss of many mature pines due to the pine beetle means it can be hot and dry on the trails. ⊠ *Mountain Pine Ridge* ⚜ *Turn left at Hidden Valley Inn sign 3¾ mi (6¼ km) from Mountain Pine Ridge entrance gate* ☎ *822/3320, 866/443–3364 in U.S.* ⊕ *www. hiddenvalleyinn.com* ⇆ *12 cottages* ⚟ *In-room: no a/c, no phone, no TV. In-hotel: restaurant, bar, bicycles, pool, no elevator, public Wi-Fi, public Internet, laundry service, airport shuttle* ⊟ *AE, MC, V.*

$$ ⊞ **Five Sisters Falls & Lodge.** With a laid-back and romantic style, this Belizean-owned lodge is perched on a steep hill above the five small waterfalls that give the place its name. A small, open-air hydraulic lift will take you down to the river if you're eager to avoid the 286 steps. After your swim, the thatch-roof bar is a great place to unwind. Accommodations are in attractive suites or thatch cabañas with screened porches. A privately owned villa, managed by the lodge, with a stunning riverside setting below the falls (BZ$600 with tax and service), is the top choice here. Its driveway allows you to avoid the steep steps. The lodge's restaurant, with a beautiful view of the falls, prepares savory Belizean food at reasonable prices (dinner BZ$25 to $40). **Pros:** Appealing combination of value and comfort in the Mountain Pine Ridge; no need for a gym if you walk the steps up from the river. **Cons:** Some standard cabañas lack a view. ⊠ *Mountain Pine Ridge* ⚜ *Turn right at Blancaneaux and Five Sisters signs 4½ mi (7½ km) from Mountain Pine Ridge entrance gate. Continue past airstrip about 1 mi (1½ km)* ☎ *820/4005, 800/447–2931 in U.S.* ⊕ *www. fivesisterslodge.com* ⇆ *14 cabañas, 4 suites, 1 2-bedroom villa* ⚟ *In-room: no a/c, no phone, no TV. In-hotel: restaurant, bar, no elevator, public Internet, laundry service, airport shuttle* ⊟ *MC, V* ⑩ *CP.*

THE OUTDOORS

BIRDING

Birding is great in the Mountain Pine Ridge, and, surprisingly, it's even better now that many of the pines were felled by the southern pine beetle. Without the tall pines, it's much easier to spot Orange-breasted Falcons, Blue Crown Motmots, White King Vultures, Stygian Owls, and other rare birds. Some of the best birding is at **Hidden Valley Inn,** a destination for numerous birding tours, and open only to guests.

CAVING

Easily accessible in the Cayo is the Río Frio Cave (⇨ *see above)*. You can also do trips to Barton Creek Cave, about 8 mi (13 km) northwest of Mountain Pine Ridge entrance gate, off Mountain Pine Ridge Road, and to Actun Tunichil Muknal from Mountain Pine Ridge. Hidden Valley Inn has two caves open only to guests of the inn.

A Crime of Flowers

A rather plain looking palm leaf has become a big-money target for poachers in Belize—and a huge problem for the Forestry Department. The leaves in question, Xate (pronounced Sha-tay), are widely used in the floral industry because they stay fresh looking for 45 to 60 days after harvest. They come from three *Chamaedorea* palm species: *C. elegans*, known as parlor palm; *C. oblongata*, called Xate macho; and *C. ernesti-augustii*, or fishtail. The latter is the most sought after, fetching up to one US$1 at its final destination, though poachers get only a fraction of that.

Xate grows wild in Belize, and also in parts of Guatemala and Mexico. Guatemalan Xate collectors, called *xateros*, have stripped much of their own El Petén jungles and have now moved on to Belize, crossing the border into the Chiquibul and other remote areas. *Xateros* earn more collecting Xate than working at regular jobs, if they can even find work in the economically depressed rural areas of El Petén. Not surprisingly, Belizeans are increasingly joining the ranks of Xate poachers. The harvesters sweep through the jungle, removing the palm leaves with a pocket knife or machete. Each palm plant produces two to five usable leaves.

Unfortunately, the poachers do more than just collect Xate. They sometimes stumble across Mayan sites and loot them for priceless artifacts. Some trap toucans, parrots, and the endangered

Scarlet Macaw for sale on the black market, and they hunt wild animals, including protected tapirs, for food. The Belize Forestry Department has reported significant depletion of native wildlife in areas with large numbers of Xate collectors. In a few cases, *xateros* have been implicated in robberies or in attacks on researchers and on Belize Defence Forces soldiers.

In early 2006 Belize Forestry Department officers came across 13 men close to the Hummingbird Highway near Belmopan loading Xate leaves onto a tractor. They arrested three of the men, two Belizeans and a Guatemalan, and confiscated more than 80,000 Xate leaves, with a street value of US$84,000. Two of the men were convicted of illegal harvesting but were fined only US$425 total. With little chance of getting caught and only modest fines if they are, Xate poachers are working at minimal risk.

What can you do to reduce the damage done by illegal Xate collectors? First, avoid buying flower arrangements that contain Xate, unless you're sure that the Xate was harvested legally. You can also support an effort by the Natural History Museum in London, in cooperation with the Belize Ministry of Natural Resources and the Belize Botanic Gardens at duPlooy's Lodge near San Ignacio, to encourage sustainable, organic growing of Xate by Belizean farmers.

—Lan Sluder

HIKING

With its karst limestone terrain, extensive network of old logging trails and roads, and cooler temperatures, the Mountain Pine Ridge is ideal for hiking. All of the lodges here have miles of marked trails. You can also hike along the roads (mostly gravel or dirt), as there are very few cars in the Pine Ridge. Most people find this more pleasant than trying to fight their way through the bush. The mountain area around Baldy Beacon is especially beautiful; it may remind you of part of the Highlands of Scotland.

All of the Mountain Pine Ridge and Chichibul Wilderness is lightly populated, and some of the residents, such as unemployed squatters who have moved into this remote area, may not always have your best interests at heart. Cell phones don't usually work here, although there has been talk of installing some cell phone towers as a security measure. Lodges such as Hidden Valley Inn provide radio phones to guests who are hiking. Always leave word with a responsible party about your hiking plans and time of expected return. Carry plenty of water, food, a compass, and basic medical supplies, especially on long hikes to remote areas. You may want to hire a guide.

HORSEBACK RIDING

In this remote area with virtually no vehicular traffic and many old logging roads, horseback riding is excellent. **Blancaneaux Lodge** and **Hidden Valley Inn** offer horseback riding, and **Mountain Equestrian Trails** (⊠ *Pine Ridge Rd.* ☎ *820/4041* ⊕ *www.metbelize.com*) runs riding trips into the Pine Ridge. A full-day trip costs around BZ$160.

MOUNTAIN BIKING

Mountain Pine Ridge has the best mountain biking in Belize on hundreds of miles of remote logging roads. Blancaneaux and Hidden Valley Inn provide complimentary mountain bikes to guests. Mountain bikes can also be rented in San Ignacio at **The Trek Stop** (⊠ *San José Succotz* ☎ *823/2265* ⊕ *www.thetrekstop.com*) for BZ$24 a day.

SHOPPING

The village of San Antonio, on the way to the Mountain Pine Ridge reserve, is home to the Garcia sisters' **Tanah Art Museum** (⊠ *San Antonio* ☎ *824/3310*), run by four sisters with clever hands and great business acumen. Look for their eye-catching slate carvings. At the other end of the village is the Magana family's arts-and-crafts shop, **Magana Zaactunich Art Gallery** (⊠ *San Antonio* ☎ *No phone*), which specializes in wood carvings.

CARACOL

40 mi (65 km) south of San Ignacio, a 3-hr journey by road.

Fodor'sChoice
★

Caracol (Spanish for "snail") is the most spectacular Mayan site in Belize, as well as one of the most impressive in Central America. It was once home to as many as 200,000 people (two-thirds the population of modern-day Belize). It was a metropolis with five plazas and 32 large structures covering almost a square mile. Altogether there are some 35,000 buildings at the site, though only a handful has been excavated. Once Caracol has been fully excavated it may dwarf even the great city of Tikal, which is a few dozen miles away in Guatemala. The latest evidence suggests that Caracol won a crushing victory over Tikal in the mid-6th century, a theory that Guatemalan scholars haven't quite accepted. Until a group of *chicleros* (collectors of gum base) stumbled on the site in 1936, Caracol was buried under the jungle of the remote Vaca Plateau. It's hard to believe it could have been lost for centuries, as the great pyramid of Caana, at 140 feet, is Belize's tallest structure.

✢ *From Mountain Pine Forest Ridge reserve entrance, head south 14 mi (23 km) to village of Douglas DiSilva, turn left and go 36 mi (58 km)* ▨ *BZ$15* ☉ *Daily 8–4.*

THE RUINS

The main excavated sections are in four groups, denoted on archaeological maps as A, B, C, and D groups. The most impressive structures are the B Group at the northeast end of the excavated plaza. This includes Caana, or "Sky Palace," listed as Structure B19-2nd, along with a ball court, water reservoir, and several large courtyards. The A Group, on the west side of the plaza, contains a temple, ball court, and a residential area for the elite. The Temple of the Wooden Lintel (Structure A6) is one of the oldest and longest-used buildings at Caracol, dating back to 300 BC. It was still in use in AD 1100. To the northwest of the A Group is the Northwest Acropolis, primarily a residential area. The third major plaza forming the core of the site is at the point where a causeway enters the "downtown" part of Caracol. The D Group is a group of structures at the South Acropolis.

Near the entrance to Caracol is a small but interesting visitor center. If you've arrived on your own, a guide usually can be hired at the site, but you can also walk around on your own. A brochure on Caracol is sold for BZ$4. Seeing all of the excavated area involves several hours of hiking around the site. Be sure to wear comfortable shoes and bring insect repellent, as occasionally mosquitoes and other bugs are a nuisance. Also, watch for anthill mounds and, rarely, snakes. This part of the Chiquibul Forest Reserve is a good place for birding and wildlife spotting. Around the ruins are troops of howler monkeys and flocks of oscellated turkeys, and you may also see deer, coatimundis, foxes, and other wildlife at the site or on the way.

TIPS

Advance permission to visit Caracol is no longer required. Although only a short section of the road to Caracol from San Ignacio is paved, it's in generally good shape. Currently, due to bandit incidents in 2005 and early 2006 (there have been none since), visits to Caracol may be made only in a convoy, protected by Belize Defence Forces soldiers. The convoys leave two or three times a day from Augustine/Douglas DiSilva village. Check with your hotel for current departure times of the convoys. You can drive your own rental vehicle in the convoy or go on a tour van.

TOURS

Most visitors to Caracol come as part of a tour group from San Ignacio, or from one of the lodges in the Mountain Pine Ridge. Full-day tours, which often include a picnic lunch and stops at Río Frio Cave, Río On, and other sights in the Mountain Pine Ridge, cost from about BZ$100–BZ$175 per person, depending on what is included and the number of people going. Tours from independent operators generally cost less than those from lodges. Because of its remote location, Caracol gets only about 12,000 visitors a year. That's about one-tenth the number who visit Altun Ha, one-fifth the number who visit Xunantunich, and a small fraction of the number who see Tikal. Thus, you're in a small, exclusive company, and on some slow days you may be one of only a handful of people at the site. Excavations usually are carried out in the winter, typically January through March.

THE CAYO ESSENTIALS

TRANSPORTATION

BY AIR

Most people bound for the Cayo fly into Belize City, but there are no longer any scheduled flights on to San Ignacio. Many Cayo hotels and lodges have van transportation from both airports in Belize City for about BZ$250–BZ$300 for up to four people, one way. Several hotels run shuttle vans, both for their own guests and for other visitors coming to the Cayo, between Belize City and San Ignacio, for around BZ$60–BZ$70 a person. Among them are Aguada and Cahal Pech Village.

A taxi from the international airport near Belize City to San Ignacio will cost around BZ$180–BZ$250 (for the cab, not per person), depending on your bargaining ability.

Shuttle Vans Aguada (⊠ *Santa Elena* ☏ *804/3609* ⊕ *www.aguadahotel. com*). **Cahal Pech Village** (⊠ *San Ignacio* ☏ *824/3740* ⊕ *www.cahalpech villageresort.com*).

BY BUS

Although the largest bus line in the country, Novelo's, shut down in 2005, a number of bus lines have taken its place, and once again there is frequent service—about once every half hour during daylight and early evening hours—between Belize City and the Cayo. National Transportation is the successor company to Novelo's and uses its old terminals, but there are several smaller lines that operate on the Western Highway routes, including T-Line, BZ Bus (a drivers' co-op), Tillet's, and others. Cost between Belize City and San Ignacio is about BZ$6 on a local, and BZ$8 on an express. Buses are typically old U.S. school buses and are not air-conditioned. Except for National Transportation Services (usually called National Transport), some of the smaller bus companies do not have regular offices or bus terminals. Ask locally about where to catch buses, or simply flag down the next bus you see.

Information **National Transportation Bus Terminal** (✉ *Savannah St., San Ignacio* ☎ *227/6372*)

BY CAR

Other than the well-maintained two-lane Western Highway, most roads in the Cayo are unpaved and dusty in the dry season, muddy in the rainy season. To get to the Cayo, simply follow the Western Highway from Belize City. Watch out for "sleeping policemen" (speed bumps) near villages along the route.

Coming into San Ignacio is a little confusing. As you go through the "twin town" of Santa Elena and head into San Ignacio, you'll see the Hawksworth Bridge straight ahead. The bridge is one way coming from the west but this is not well marked; those coming from the east and unfamiliar with the area often try to drive across the bridge the wrong way. A sign noting a detour has now been erected, directing vehicles to another bridge.

To keep from running afoul of traffic rules, turn right before the Hawksworth Bridge, following the detour to what is called the "lower bridge" or "low lying bridge." Cross this and follow Savanah Road around the sports stadium and, if you're lucky, you'll soon end up back on Western Highway just to the west of San Ignacio. Alternatively, after you cross the river, you can turn left and go through to Burns Avenue, the main street in town.

From San Ignacio, the Western Highway continues on about 9 mi (15 km) to the Guatemala border. This stretch is locally known as the Benque Road.

From the Western Highway, there are two routes into the Mountain Pine Ridge, both just east of San Ignacio: the Mountain Pine Ridge Road (also sometimes called the Chiquibul Road or the Georgeville Road), at Georgeville at Mile 61.6 of the Western Highway, and the Cristo Rey Road, with the turnoff at Mile 66.5 of the Western Highway. From the Western Highway, the entrance to the Mountain Pine Ridge is 10.2 mi (17 km) via the Mountain Pine Ridge Road and 14.8 mi (25 km) via the Cristo Rey Road. Both roads, cut through limestone, are rough, but currently the Georgeville Road is rougher. The first mile of the Cristo Rey Road is paved, as well as a few short sections farther on. If coming from Belmopan you'll save a little time by taking the first road you see, at Georgeville, but if coming from San Ignacio or points west, take the Cristo Rey Road. Large green road signs clearly mark both turns.

Heading southeast from San Ignacio on the Cristo Rey Road, a little beyond San Antonio, the Cristo Rey Road meets the Mountain Pine Ridge Road coming from Georgeville. Turn right to go into the Mountain Pine Ridge. After 2½ mi (4 km), a guard at a gatehouse will record your name, destination, and license plate number. The main road through the Mountain Pine Ridge to Caracol is being improved, partly to provide better access to Caracol and also due to the construction of the Challilo Dam and other dams on the Macal River (➪ *see below).* Some of the roads in the Pine Ridge have names, but most have numerical monikers, like A10. The main road through the Mountain Pine Ridge that passes the four area lodges and Douglas DiSilva village (also known as Augustine village) is mostly a dirt road that can become almost impassable after heavy rains.

To get to Spanish Lookout, the Mennonite area, from the Western Highway there are two options. One is to turn north off the Western Highway at about Mile 63. This road is unpaved and requires you to cross the Belize River on a hand-pulled ferry. The other option is what the Mennonites call Route 30. It heads north at about Mile 57½ of the Western Highway, is beautifully paved, and has a bridge over the river.

The Bullet Tree Road from San Ignacio to Bullet Tree village is now paved.

4

Information **Cayo Auto Rentals** (⊠ *81 Benque Rd., San Ignacio* ☎ *824/2222* ⊕ *www.cayoautorentals.com*). **Safe Tours Belize** (⊠ *Western Hwy., Santa Elena* ☎ *824/3731*).

BY TAXI

Taxis are plentiful in and around San Ignacio, but they're expensive if you're going to a remote lodge. For example, a taxi from San Ignacio to one of the Mountain Pine Ridge lodges is likely to be around BZ$80–BZ$100, and to one of the lodges west of San Ignacio, about BZ$40–BZ$50 (rates are negotiable). Taxis within San Ignacio shouldn't be more than BZ$6 to most points. Collective taxis (they pick up as many passengers as possible) run to the Guatemala border for around BZ$5. You can find taxis at Market Square in the middle of town, around Burns Avenue, or call **Cayo Taxi Association** at ⊠ *824/2196* or **San Ignacio Taxi** at ⊠ *824/2155*, or have your hotel call one.

CONTACTS & RESOURCES

BANKS & EXCHANGE SERVICES

Although American dollars are accepted everywhere, you can exchange money at the border crossing in Benque Viejo del Carmen. Banks in San Ignacio include Atlantic, Belize Bank, and ScotiaBank. They are all downtown on Burns Avenue. All have ATMs, and all now accept ATM cards issued outside the country.

Banks **Atlantic Bank** (⊠ *17 Burns Ave., San Ignacio* ☎ *824/2596*). **Belize Bank** (⊠ *16 Burns Ave., San Ignacio* ☎ *824/2031*). **ScotiaBank** (⊠ *Burns Ave. at Riverside St., San Ignacio* ☎ *824/4190*).

EMERGENCIES

In case of emergency, there's the private La Loma Luz Hospital, in Santa Elena, east of San Ignacio, as well as the public hospital, San Ignacio Hospital.

Hospitals **La Loma Luz Hospital** (⊠ *Western Hwy., Santa Elena* ☎ *824/3253*). **San Ignacio Hospital** (⊠ *Bullet Tree Rd., San Ignacio* ☎ *824/2066*).

Hot Lines **Police** (☎ *911 or 824/2111*).

Pharmacies The Pharmacy (✉ *24 West St., San Ignacio* ☎ *824/2510*).

INTERNET, MAIL & SHIPPING

The San Ignacio post office is on Hudson Street near the vegetable market. It's open weekdays 8–noon and 1–4:30 and Saturday 8–noon.

Contacts San Ignacio Post Office (✉ *Hudson St., San Ignacio* ☎ *824/2049*). **Eva's** (✉ *22 Burns Ave.* ☎ *824/2267*) is a busy café with Internet.

SAFETY

Being close to Guatemala's El Petén region, thousands of Cayo visitors take short trips across the border to view the fantastic ruins of Tikal. Its proximity to this tourist attraction is a boon for the Cayo but also a burden, as the poverty-stricken population of northern Guatemala spills over into relatively affluent Belize. On several occasions armed gangs from Guatemala have robbed tourists around San Ignacio, especially near the El Pilar Mayan site. Several tour groups were attacked and robbed en route to Caracol in 2005 and early 2006 and there have been other incidents, including some on the Macal River. However, most visitors to the Cayo say they feel quite safe. As a visitor, you're unlikely to encounter any problems.

VISITOR INFORMATION

There is no official tourism information office in the Cayo. The best way to find out what's going on in the San Ignacio area is to stop by **Eva's** in San Ignacio, a café that doubles as an unofficial visitor center. You can also contact local tour operators. The Belize Tourism Board Web site, ⊕ *www.travelbelize.org*, has some information on visiting the Cayo. Another Web site, Toucan Trail, ⊕ *www.toucantrail.com*, supported by the Belize Tourism Board, has excellent information on budget travel in Belize, including the Cayo. Belize Explorer, ⊕ *www. belizex.com*, formerly operated by BTIA but now a private Web site affiliated with Cahal Pech Village hotel in San Ignacio and a few other hotels, still has some useful information on tours, attractions, and travel services in the Cayo.

Information Eva's (✉ *22 Burns Ave., San Ignacio* ☎ *824/2267*).

The Southern Coast

WORD OF MOUTH

"Placencia is very different from the cayes. If you want a beach where waves roll up, Placencia is the place to go in Belize. The cayes don't have this really."

—jmike

"Check out the Jaguar Reef Lodge in the Hopkins area. It's an adventure lodge. I'd split my time between it and Ambergris Caye, if possible."

—LvSun

By Lan Sluder

AS ALWAYS IN BELIZE, THE transition from one landscape to another is swift and startling. As you approach the Hummingbird Highway's end in coastal Dangriga, the lush, mountainous terrain of the north gives way to flat plains bristling with orange trees. Farther south the Stann Creek Valley is Belize's San Fernando Valley, where bananas, the nation's first bumper crop, and most other fruit is grown. Equally startling to the change in scenery is the cultural segue: whereas San Ignacio has a Spanish air, the southern coast is strongly Afro-Caribbean.

Tourist dollars, the staple of contemporary Belize, have largely bypassed Dangriga to land 35 mi (56 km) south in Placencia, the region's most striking destination. Several years ago there were only three small resorts north of Placencia village. Now there are about 20, stretching up to the village of Seine Bight, Maya Beach, and beyond. Plans are in the works for hundreds of new condos and a number of hotels. Owners of small beach resorts and inns are cashing in, selling out to developers, who are in turn combining several small tracts into one, hoping to put together larger residential or resort projects. Many believe that the tipping point for the Placencia peninsula has been reached and that the new wave of resorts will be larger, more upscale, and more multinational.

The paving of the Southern Highway from Dangriga all the way to Punta Gorda (except for a short stretch near Golden Stream) has made the region much more accessible. Off the main highway, however, most roads consist of red dirt and potholes, and the road from the Southern Highway to Placencia is one of the worst.

Real estate sales are a driving force in Placencia, Hopkins, and elsewhere along the coast. The lure is the beaches. The Southern Coast has the best beaches on the mainland, although as elsewhere inside the protecting Barrier Reef, the low wave action means the beaches are narrow and there's usually sea grass in the water close to shore. (Sea grass—not seaweed, which is an algae—may be a nuisance for swimmers, but it's a vital part of the coastal ecosystem, acting as a nursery for sea life.) Much of the seafront land north of Placencia village has been divided into lots awaiting development; if things continue at this pace, the area will one day rival Ambergris Caye as Belize's top beach destination.

ORIENTATION & PLANNING

ORIENTATION

Coming from the north, two roads lead to the Southern Coast: the Hummingbird Highway from Belmopan, and the Coastal Road (also sometimes, misleadingly, called the Coastal Highway) from La Democracia on the Western Highway. The Hummingbird Highway is paved and is the most scenic drive in all of Belize. The Coastal Road is unpaved, dusty, or muddy depending on the amount of rain. Despite the name, it does not hug the coast, and in fact you never glimpse the

TOP REASONS TO GO

BEACHES

The mainland's best beaches are on the Placencia peninsula and around Hopkins. Although they're narrow ribbons of khaki rather than wide swaths of talcum-powder sand, they're ideal for lazing in a hammock under a cocopalm. And you don't have to fight the crowds for a spot—at least not yet.

JAGUARS

The world's first and only jaguar preserve is the Cockscomb Basin Wildlife Sanctuary. Chances are you won't actually see one of these big, beautiful cats in the wild, as they roam the high bush mainly at night, but you may see tracks or hear a low growl in the darkness.

WATER SPORTS

Anglers won't be disappointed by the bonefish, tarpon, and other sports fishing. The Barrier Reef here is 15 mi (25 km) or more off the

coast, so it's a long trip out, even with the fast boats the dive shops use, but there are patch reefs around closer islands, with excellent snorkeling. Serious divers will find two of Belize's three atolls, Turneffe and Glover's, within reach. In a charter sailboat you can island-hop in the protected waters inside the reef.

CULTURAL EXPERIENCES

The Southern Coast isn't so much a melting pot as a tropical stew full of different flavors. A seaside Garífuna village recalls Senegal, while just down the road, a Creole village evokes the Caribbean. Inland, Maya live much as they have for thousands of years next door to Mestizos from Guatemala and Honduras who've come to work the banana plantations or citrus groves. Sprinkled in are expats from the northern climes, looking for a retirement home or trying to make a buck in tourism.

sea from it. Also, the loose gravel roadway is an accident waiting to happen. In short, if you're driving, take the Hummingbird.

The Hummingbird runs 54 mi (89 km) from Belmopan to Dangriga. As it approaches Dangriga, it technically becomes the Stann Creek District Highway, but most people simply refer to the entire road as the Hummingbird Highway. About 6 mi (10 km) from Dangriga is the junction with the Southern Highway, another good, mostly paved road running 100 mi (164 km) to Punta Gorda. The Southern Highway is not as scenic as the Hummingbird, although for much of its length the low Maya Mountains are visible to the west.

Off the spine of the Southern Highway, various shorter, mostly unpaved, roads lead to villages on the coast and inland: from the highway, it's about 4 mi (7 km) on partly paved roads to Hopkins and also to Sittee Village; 25 mi (42 km) to Placencia Village; 5 mi (8 km) to Big Creek; 13 mi (21 km) to Monkey River.

The road everyone loves to hate is the road to Placencia from the Southern Highway. The first section is sometimes called the Riversdale Road, after the small settlement where the road reaches close to the sea. The rest of the route, down to Placencia village, is referred to as the Peninsula Road; though most just call it "the Road." Only short sections—at Seine Bight and Placencia villages and at the Coco Plum development—are paved, and after heavy rains it can be mucky. Even in the best conditions, it's a 45-minute drive from Placencia Village back to the junction with the Southern Highway. For years, plans were floated to pave the road down the Placencia peninsula. At this writing, the Caribbean Development Bank has loaned Belize the money to pave the road, and work is slated to begin any day. Locals, however, say they'll believe it when they see it.

PLANNING

WHEN TO GO

The weather on the Southern Coast is similar to that in central and northern Belize, only a little wetter. On average, for example, the Cayo District has rain, or at least a shower, on 125 days a year, while in Stann Creek District there's some rain on 183 days—usually thanks to late fall and winter cold fronts or summer tropical fronts passing through. Of course, these showers are generally followed by sunshine.

Summer daytime temperatures along the coast reach the high 80s, occasionally the 90s, falling at night to the mid-70s. In winter, daytime temperatures are in the low to mid-80s and drop to the mid- or high 60s at night. On or near the sea, it feels cooler due to the prevailing breezes, which calm only occasionally, usually for a few days at a time in summer. Humidity is high most of the year, typically 80% or more. Water temperatures from November to March are usually in the high 70s. For the rest of the year they're in the low 80s.

RESTAURANTS & CUISINE

Broiled, grilled, fried, sautéed, cooked in lime juice as ceviche, or barbecued on the beach: anyway you eat it, seafood is the life-stuff on the Southern Coast. Restaurants serve fish, lobster, conch, and shrimp, often fresh from the boat, or, in the case of shrimp, straight from the shrimp farms near Placencia.

Expect mostly small, locally owned restaurants; some breezy beachside joints with sand floors, others wood shacks. Placencia has by far the largest number of eateries, with Hopkins a distant second. Most upscale restaurants are in resorts, such as Inn at Robert's Grove and Turtle Inn. The Bistro at Maya Beach Hotel is one of the country's best. And it's worth making a trip to Placencia just to sample the incredible gelato at Tutti-Frutti.

Off-season, especially in late summer and early fall, restaurants in Placencia and Hopkins may close for a few weeks, and on any day the owners may decide to close early if there are no customers, so call ahead. It's also a good idea to make reservations so the cooks will have enough food on hand.

GREAT ITINERARIES

IF YOU HAVE 3 DAYS ON THE SOUTHERN COAST

Base yourself in Placencia. On your first full day, walk the sidewalk in Placencia Village, hear the latest gossip, and get to know a little of village life. Hang out on the beach at your hotel and get on Belize time, then have drinks and dinner in the village. On your second day, take a snorkel trip to Laughing Gull Caye or another snorkel area, or, if you dive, do a full-day dive trip to Turneffe or Glover's atoll. On your final day, drive, or take a guided tour, to Cockscomb Basin Wildlife Sanctuary. Be sure to stop at the Maya Centre craft cooperative for gift shopping. If there's time, also visit the Mayflower Mayan site and waterfall. End the day with dinner at the Bistro at Maya Beach Hotel.

IF YOU HAVE 5 DAYS ON THE SOUTHERN COAST

Drive or fly to Dangriga (the closest airport to Hopkins). While in Dangriga, stop by the Garífuna museum, then proceed by taxi or rental car to Hopkins to stay at one of its beach resorts. On your first full day, relax on the beach in the morning, then tour Cockscomb Basin Wildlife Sanctuary and hike the jungle trails. Be sure to stop at the Maya Centre craft cooperative. Have dinner at one of the local restaurants in Hopkins Village. On your second full day, visit the Mayflower Mayan site and waterfall in the morning, and spend the rest of the day on the beach. On your third day, rise early and drive (or go by taxi) to Placencia. If the weather's good, take a snorkel trip. Have dinner in Placencia Village. On your fourth day, if you dive, do a day dive trip to Turneffe or Glover's Atoll, or go fishing for permit or tarpon. If you catch anything edible, have one of the local restaurants prepare it for you for dinner. Or, simply spend a lazy day in a hammock at the beach and around the pool. On your final day, if you're interested in Mayan sites, do a day trip to Lubaantun and Nim Li Punit near Punta Gorda, or else go on a tour of Monkey River.

WHAT IT COSTS IN BELIZE DOLLARS					
	¢	$	$$	$$$	$$$$
RESTAU-RANTS	under BZ$8	BZ$8–BZ$15	BZ$15–BZ$25	BZ$25–BZ$50	over BZ$50
HOTELS	under BZ$100	BZ$100–BZ$200	BZ$200–BZ$300	BZ$300–BZ$500	over BZ$500

Restaurant prices are per person for a main course at dinner. Hotel prices are for two people in a standard double room, including tax and service.

There are two kinds of lodging to choose from on the Southern Coast: small, basic hotels, often Belizean-owned, and upscale beach resorts, usually owned and operated by Americans or Canadians. The small hotels are clustered in Placencia Village, Hopkins Village, and in Dangriga town. The beach resorts are on the Placencia peninsula north of Placencia Village and also near Hopkins. Several of these resorts, including Francis Ford Coppola's Turtle Inn and the Inn at Robert's Grove on the Placencia peninsula, Kanantik between Hopkins and Placencia, and Hamanasi in Hopkins, are among the best hotels in Belize. There also are a small number of vacation rental houses near Hopkins and on the Placencia peninsula.

At least a dozen condo developments have opened, are under construction, or are in the planning stages on Placencia peninsula and near Hopkins. Only time will tell whether all these plans will fully materialize or whether supply will outstrip demand, but it's clear that this area has reached the point where development by large international companies is inevitable.

FROM GALES POINT TO PLACENCIA

DANGRIGA

99 mi (160 km) southeast of Belmopan.

With a population of around 12,000, Dangriga is the largest town in the south and the home of the Garífuna or Black Caribs, as they're also known (though some view the latter term as a remnant of colonialism). The plural is Garinagu. There's not much to keep you in Dangriga. Though the town is on the coast, there are no good beaches, no first-class hotels, few restaurants, and, except for a small museum on Garífuna culture in the outskirts of town, not much to see. Rickety clapboard houses on stilts and small shops line the downtown streets, and the town has a kind of end-of-the-road feel. Dangriga isn't really dangerous, though it has a rough vibe, a little like Belize City, that's off-putting for many visitors.

Each year, on November 19 and the days around it, the town cuts loose with a week of Carnival-style celebrations. Garífuna drumming, costumed Jonkunu dancers, punta music, and a good bit of drinking make up the festivities of Garífuna Settlement Day, when these proud people celebrate their arrival in Belize and remember their roots.

WHAT TO SEE
Billy Barquedier National Park is a 1,500-acre park along the Hummingbird Highway in Stann Creek District. Managed by the Belize Forest Service and established in 2001, the park is still in its infancy. While it offers no spectacular sights, it does have primitive hiking trails and the Barquedier Waterfall (locally sometimes called Bac-a-Der Waterfall). It's part of a community co-management program for parks and reserves, in this case with the Steadfast Tourist and Conservation group of Steadfast village. It's best to enter the park via the northern entrance at Mile 16½ of the Hummingbird Highway. ⊠ *Main entrance at Mile 16½, Hummingbird Hwy., and a second entrance is at Mile 17½* ⊙ *9– 4:30 daily.*

Getting to **Davis Falls** requires a four-wheel-drive vehicle and an arduous 2 mi (3 km) hike, but the falls here are about 500 feet high and are the second highest in the country (after 1,000-Foot Falls in the Mountain Pine Ridge), and the natural pool at the base of the falls is 75 feet

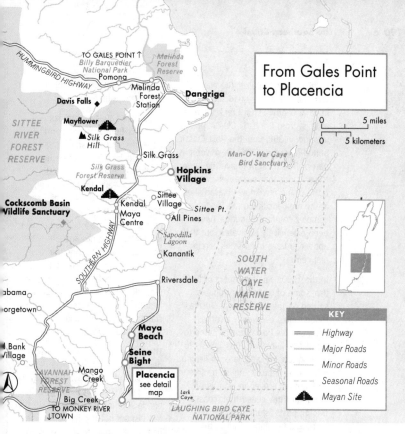

Placencia
see detail
map

From Gales Point to Placencia

KEY

═══	Highway
──	Major Roads
──	Minor Roads
┄┄	Seasonal Roads
▲	Mayan Site

deep. The swimming is wonderful, and the undisturbed forest around the falls is great for a picnic or enjoying nature. Before going to Davis Falls, stop at the Citrus Products of Belize plant (Mile 42) or at Awe & Sons store in Alta Vista village (Mile 40), for late-breaking information and to pay your admission fee. ⊠ *Off Mile 42, Hummingbird Hwy.* ⊠ *BZ$10* ☉ *9–4:30 daily.*

☖ Named after a Garífuna heroine who came to Belize with her 13 children, founding the village of Punta Negra in Toledo District, the **Gulisi Garífuna Museum,** opened in late 2004, has a number of displays on Garífuna history and life. Three exhibits are on Garífuna migration from Africa to St. Vincent, then to Roatan and Belize. Another exhibit is on Thomas Vincent Ramos, a visionary Garífuna leader who, in 1941, established the first Garífuna Settlement Day. Other displays are on Garífuna food, clothing, and music and dance. The museum also displays paintings by Garífuna artists including Benjamin Nicholas. ⊠ *Mile 2, Hummingbird Hwy.* ☎ *502/0639* ⊠ *BZ$10* ☉ *Weekdays 10–5, Sat. 8–noon.*

Declared a national park in 2001, **Mayflower Bocawina National Park** has three minor Mayan ceremonial sites: Mayflower, T'au Witz, and Maintzunum, near Silk Grass Creek. Nearby are the three waterfalls Bocawina Falls, Three Sisters Falls, and Antelope Falls. To get to

HISTORY

As elsewhere in Belize, the Maya were here first. They had settlements in what is now Stann Creek District at least from the Early Classic period (around AD 300) until the Post-Classic period (about AD 1200). However, this part of Belize did not have the large Mayan cities that existed elsewhere. None of the few known Mayan sites in the area, including the Mayflower complex south of Dangriga, have been extensively excavated, but they appear to have been small ceremonial centers.

In the 1600s small numbers of English, some of whom were pirates, settled on the Placencia peninsula, though most eventually left the area. Creoles from Jamaica came to Stann Creek in the 1700s, mainly to work in logging, and, later, in fishing. In the next century English traders and farmers arrived in what is now Dangriga. They called their coastal trading posts "stands," which was corrupted to "stann." Hence, the name Stann Creek. On November 19, 1823, a group of Garinagu from the Bay Islands of Honduras, former African slaves who had intermarried with Carib Indians in the southern Caribbean, arrived at the mouth of the Stann Creek River, at what was then called Stann Creek Town. This date is still celebrated in Belize as Garífuna Settlement Day. Later, the name of Stann Creek Town (but not the district) was changed to Dan-griga, which means "sweet water" in the Garífuna language.

In the late 1800s, several families, originally from Scotland, Portugal, Honduras, and elsewhere, arrived in Placencia. The names of these families—Garbutt, Leslie, Westby, and Cabral—are still common on the peninsula. In the 19th and early 20th century, the fertile soils of the coastal plain were found to be ideal for growing bananas and citrus, and soon agriculture became the most important industry in the region. The first railroad in Belize, the Stann Creek Railway, built by the United Fruit Company to transport bananas, started operation around World War I. The railroad closed in the 1950s.

The first small tourist resorts were developed on the Placencia peninsula as well as at Maya Beach in the 1960s and '70s, but the bad roads and lack of infrastructure meant that few visitors got this far south. The first fishing cooperative was established in Placencia in 1962. Although fishing is still a way of life for a few people on the coast, the big money now is in shrimp farming.

Hurricane Iris in October 2001 devastated much of the Southern Coast south of Maya Beach, but the area has bounced back stronger than ever. Today, tourism and real estate count for much of the region's development.

Bocawina and Three Sisters Falls, which are close together, it's an easy hike of about 1¼ mi (2 km) on the marked Bocawina Falls trail. The trail to Antelope Falls, about 1¾ mi (3 km), is somewhat more difficult due to some steep sections that can be slick after rains. Maps of the trails are available at the small visitor center. So far, little excavation has been conducted at the Mayan sites, but the parklike setting at the base of the Maya Mountains is beautiful. Another ½ mi (1 km) takes you to Mama Noots, a lodge where you can buy drinks and snacks.

⊠*Off Mile 6* ⊹*From Southern Hwy. go 4½ mi (7½ km) west on dirt road to park visitor center* ⊒*BZ$10* ⊙*Daily 8–4.*

One of the most beautiful lagoons in Belize, **Southern Lagoon,** is about 25 mi (41 km) north of Dangriga—a 45-minute car ride. This lagoon is home to many West Indian manatees, and on beaches nearby, hawksbill turtles nest May to October. The Northern and Western lagoons also are in this area.

The small Creole village of **Gales Point,** population about 500, set beside the lagoon, is home to several drum makers, including Boombay Andrewin and Emmeth Young. They both give Creole-style drumming lessons (about BZ$16 an hour) at the Maroon Creole Drum School. You can find Young at his snack and gift shop, the **Sugar Shack** (⊠*Gales Point Village* ☎*603/6051* ⊙*Hrs vary but generally Mon.–Sat. 9–5*). Handmade drums of coconut wood, cashew wood, or mahogany cost BZ$100–BZ$800. ☎*209/8031 community phone for Gales Point* ⊹*To Gales Point: from Dangriga, go northwest on Hummingbird Hwy. 8½ mi (14 km) to village of Melinda; turn right on Manatee Hwy. (Coastal Rd) and follow 13 mi (21 km) to turnoff, a sharp right turn. This dirt road to Gales Point Village runs about 2½ mi (4 km) until it ends at lagoon and Manatee Lodge.*

WHERE TO STAY & EAT

Unless you have a special interest in Garífuna culture or are heading out to Tobacco, Southwater, or other offshore cayes, you'll probably not spend much time in Dangriga. Several sights of interest are near Dangriga, though these can also be easily visited from Hopkins, another Garífuna settlement.

NEAR DANGRIGA

$$ 🏨**Manatee Lodge.** This colonial-era lodge, just feet from the Southern Lagoon and surrounded by flowers, has a stunning setting. With its fading white facade like something out of a Graham Greene novel and sometimes lackadaisical service, the lodge may not quite live up to its location, but in minutes you can be on a boat looking for manatees (BZ$110 for a two-person tour) or on a deserted beach. Rooms on the second floor are simple but have polished wood floors and views of the lagoon. The dining room serves tasty Belizean fare and international dishes. **Pros:** Beautiful waterside setting, interesting colonial atmosphere. **Cons:** Off-the-beaten-path location, à la carte tours fairly expensive. ⊠*Gales Point Village* ☎*220/8040* ⊕*www.manateelodge. com* ⇔*8 rooms* ⌂*In-room: no a/c, no phone, no TV. In-hotel: restaurant, bar, no elevator, public Internet, no-smoking rooms, airport shuttle* ⊟*AE, MC, V.*

$–$$ 🏨**Mama Noots Backabush Lodge.** Being environmentally conscious doesn't have to come at the expense of comfort. A combination solar, wind, and hydro system generates this resort's electricity. Most of the produce served in the open-air dining room is grown on the grounds. Rooms, in thatch cabanas or a modern concrete lodge building, have views of the rugged Maya Mountains. Because the resort is *backabush* (in the jungle), owners Nanette Denny and family advise guests to bring lightweight "jungle clothing," plus plenty of insect repellent and an adventuresome spirit. Nearby are the Mayflower archaeological site and miles of jungle trails and waterfalls. **Pros:** Hard-to-beat location near national park, lots of wildlife and birds, well-maintained grounds. **Cons:** You need lots of bug spray. ⊠*Near Mayflower archaeological site, 5 mi (8 km) off Mile 6, Southern Hwy., 6 mi (10 km) south of junction of Hummingbird and Southern Hwys.* ☎*670/8019* ⊕*www.mamanoots.com* ⬎*6 rooms, 2 cabanas* ⬚*In-room: no a/c, no phone, no TV. In-hotel: restaurant, bar, no elevator, public Wi-Fi, no-smoking rooms* ▭*MC, V.*

DANGRIGA

$-$$ ×**Riverside Café.** Information, rather than the food or atmosphere, is what you usually come here for, although the Creole and Garífuna dishes are hearty and tasty, too. Fishermen and the guys who run boats out to Tobacco Caye and other offshore cayes hang out here, and if you're going to the islands you can arrange transportation while you're sipping a beer or having a plate of rice and beans. ⊠*S. Riverside Dr.* ☎*523/9908* ▭*No credit cards.*

¢-$$ ×**King Burger.** Formerly called Burger King, but a far cry from the chain of the same name, this is the best place in Dangriga to get an honest plate of stew chicken and rice and beans. The fresh fish is good, and, yes, so are the hamburgers. Everything's affordable, too. ⊠*Commerce St.* ☎*522/2476* ▭*No credit cards* ⊙*Closed Sun.*

$$ 🏨**Pelican Beach Resort.** This waterfront hotel on the north end of Dangriga, near the airstrip, is the best the town has to offer. Most rooms are in a two-story colonial-style building with a veranda. Some have porches with sea views. The restaurant has dependable food and service, and the staff is knowledgeable. Though there's a pier and small beach area, the water's not very appealing for swimming. It's about a half-hour stroll to the center of town. The resort has an annex on Southwater Caye, an hour away by boat. **Pros:** Charming colonial-era main building, breezy seaside location, the best lodging in Dangriga. **Cons:** Not the beach of your dreams, rooms only a couple of steps up from basic. ⊠*Scotchman Town, North End* ⬚*Box 2, Dangriga* ☎*522/2044* ⊕*www.pelicanbeachbelize.com* ⬎*20 rooms* ⬚*In-room: no a/c (some), no phone (some), Wi-Fi. In-hotel: restaurant, bar, beachfront, no elevator, laundry service, public Internet, airport shuttle* ▭*AE, MC, V.*

$ 🏨**Bonefish Hotel.** If you're overnighting in Dangriga before heading out to Tobacco Caye or another offshore caye, this little hotel, painted aquamarine and white, is an acceptable option. It's near the sea and the riverside area where the boats go out and under the same management as Blue Marlin Lodge on Southwater Caye. Rooms are carpeted and clean. There's a restaurant on the first floor. **Pros:** Handy location, clean rooms. **Cons:** Won't win any interior-design awards, staff not as friendly as they could be. ⊠*15 Mahogany St.* ☎*522/2243* ⊕*www.bluemarlinlodge.com* ⬎*7 rooms* ⬚*In-room: no phone, refrigerator (some). In-hotel: no elevator, restaurant, laundry service* ▭*AE, MC, V.*

¢ 🏨**Ruthie's Cabañas.** This is the closest you can come to staying in a Garífuna home in Dangriga. Owners Ruthie and Meeto Flores built the

The Garífuna Struggle

Perhaps the most unusual of the ethnic groups calling Belize home, the Garífunas have a story that is both bizarre and moving, an odyssey of exile and dispossession in the wake of the confusion wrought in the New World by the Old. The Garífuna are descended from a group of Nigerian slaves who were shipwrecked on the island of St. Vincent in 1635. The Caribs, St. Vincent's indigenous population, fiercely resisted the outsiders at first, but they eventually overcame their distrust.

In the eyes of the British colonial authorities, the new ethnic group that developed after years of intermarriage was an illegitimate and troublesome presence. Worse still, the Garífuna sided with, and were succored by, the French. After nearly two centuries of guerrilla warfare, the British decided that the best way to solve the prob-lem was to deport them en masse. After a circuitous and tragic journey across the Caribbean, during which thousands perished of disease and hunger, the exiles arrived in Belize.

That the Garífuna have preserved their cultural identity testifies to Belize's extraordinary ability to encourage diversity. They have their own religion, a potent mix of ancestor worship and Catholicism; their own language, which, like Carib, has separate male and female dialects; their own music, a percussion-oriented sound known as punta rock; and their own social structure, which dissuades young people from marrying outside their community. In writer Marcella Lewis, universally known as Auntie Madé, the Garífuna also had their own poet laureate. In 2002 the United Nations designated the Garífuna as a World Heritage culture.

tiny thatch cabanas themselves, live in a two-story building next door, and go out of their way to make you feel at home. The small rooms all have private baths and are steps from the sea, so you get a nice breeze, though the swimming is not good here. Ruthie is a good cook and prepares traditional Garífuna dishes such as *hudut* (fish cooked in coconut milk) and, for breakfast, delicious coconut bread. **Pros:** Almost a cultural experience, seaside location. **Cons:** Really, really basic, small rooms. ✉31 Southern Foreshore ☎502/3184 ➷2 cabanas, 3 rooms ⚒In-room: no a/c, no phone, no TV. In hotel: restaurant, no elevator ▭No credit cards.

HOPKINS VILLAGE

10 mi (17 km) south of Dangriga on the Southern Hwy., then 2 mi (3 km) east on a partially paved road.

Hopkins is an intriguing Garífuna coastal village of about 1,000 peo-ple, halfway between Dangriga and Placencia. Garífuna culture is more accessible here than in Dangriga. Hopkins has the same toast-color beaches as those in Placencia, and a number of new resorts have opened to take advantage of them. Americans, Canadians, and Europeans are snapping up beachfront land here at prices somewhat lower than in Placencia or on Ambergris Caye, but so far only a few vacation homes and condos have been built. If there's a downside to the area, it's the biting sand flies, which can be vicious.

In the center of town you can watch local Garífuna boys hone their drumming skills at the **Lebeha Drumming Center** (☎608/3143). *Lebeha* means "the end" in the Garífuna language, a reference to the school's location at a small guesthouse and bar near the north end of the village. Visitors are welcome. The drums, mostly made by a noted drum maker in Dangriga, Austin Rodriquez, are of mahogany or mayflower wood, with deerskin on the drumhead. Other instruments include *shakas,* or shakers, calabash gourds filled with fruit seeds, and turtle shells. The boys, mostly in their early teens, usually play punta rock, first made famous by Andy Palacio, a Garífuna from Barranco village in Toledo, rather than the more traditional Garífuna music. The drumming goes on nightly, though the most activity is on weekends. Donations are accepted, and you can purchase a CD of Lebeha drumming.

WHERE TO STAY & EAT

In addition to the resorts and hotels listed below, Hopkins has about 20 small guesthouses, mostly run by local villagers but also by some expats who have found the easygoing Hopkins life suits them. Typically just two or three rooms are built next to the home of the owner, who has an eye to tapping the growing tourism market in Hopkins. Most don't look like much from the outside but have the necessities including electricity and, usually, private baths. Among the better ones are **Wabien Guest House** (☎523/7010), **Yugadah Inn** (☎503/7089), **Seagull's Nest Guest House** (☎522/0600), **Whistling Seas Vacation Inn** (☎608/0016), **Ransoms Seaside Gardens** (☎*No phone*), and **Laruni Cabins** (☎523/7026). Rates in almost all cases are less than BZ$100 for a double, with the least expensive ones, usually a block or two back from the water, costing less than BZ$50 for a double. At these guesthouses, it's usually not necessary to make reservations. When you arrive in the village, just walk around until you find one that suits you.

$$$ ✕**Barracuda Bar & Grill.** Owners Tony and Angela Marsico traded running a restaurant in Alaska for operating a beachside bistro in Belize. They've turned this restaurant, part of Beaches and Dreams Seafront Inn, into one of the best eateries on the southern coast, with delicious dishes like fig-stuffed pork chops. Catch the breezes on the covered, open-air deck while you munch a hand-made pizza or enjoy a burger. Inside, there's a bar with satellite TV. ⊠*Sittee Point* ☎523/7259 ▭*MC,V* ⊘*Closed Apr.–Oct.*

¢–$$$ ✕**King Cassava Cultural Restaurant and Bar.** Some call this bar and restaurant the soul of Hopkins. At the very least, it has some of the best soul food, Garífuna-style. The tasty, fresh fish, barbecued lobster, and spicy shrimp, plus friendly service, helped earn this place the "Small Vendor of the Year" award from the Belize Tourism Board in 2007. Located at the entrance to the village on the road from the Southern Highway, it doesn't look like much, but when the rum and beer start flowing, the drums start drumming, and the action at the pool table in the back room gets hot, this is the place to be in Hopkins. ⊠*Hopkins, at the main crossroads entering the village* ☎503/7305 ▭*No credit cards.*

$-$$ ✕**Yugadah Inn.** A family of sisters, all good cooks, runs this small hotel and restaurant on the sea (*Yugadah* means "coastal village" in the Garífuna language). They prepare food in a traditional, freestanding kitchen. ⊠*Hopkins* ☎*502/7089.*

¢-$$ ✕**Innies Restaurant.** At Innies, as at most of the other local restaurants in Hopkins, you're eating in a spot that was once somebody's house or back porch. In this pink dining room with linoleum floor, you dine on picnic tables with oilcloths, and the inexpensive food is well prepared. Fried chicken with rice and beans or french fries is around BZ$6, and fish dinners are a little more. Traditional Garífuna dishes such as *hudut* (fish cooked in coconut milk and served with mashed plantains) are also available. ⊠*Hopkins, south end of village* ☎*523/7026* ▭*No credit cards.*

¢-$$ ✕**Iris's Place Restaurant.** Iris's little dining room in a small, blue concrete building has only four tables. Don't let the appearance or hand-lettered sign put you off. Inside it's clean, and the food is tasty. Besides the ubiquitous stew chicken with rice and beans, you can get seafood, including lobster and conch in season. For breakfast, bacon and eggs and fry jacks cost around BZ$5. ⊠*Hopkins, south end of village* ☎*523/7019* ▭*No credit cards.*

$$$$ ▥**Belizean Dreams.** This collection of three-bedroom, three-bath condos is among the most upmarket accommodation choices on the Southern Coast. All villas have exactly the same floor plans and furnishings, but units 1 and 9 are directly on the beach, and the others have sea views. The units, with hardwood and natural stone floors and custom-made cedar and mahogany furniture, can be reserved as a complete villa, or choose a single bedroom or two-bedroom suite. The bedrooms have vaulted ceilings with exposed beams and four-poster king beds. You can dine at nearby resorts or have a cook prepare a private meal for you at the condo. Some units have a five-day minimum stay. The same developer also owns Hopkins Bay, a condo colony at the north end of Hopkins village with similar accommodations at similar prices. **Pros:** Deluxe condo apartments, units can be combined and configured to meet your needs. **Cons:** No on-site restaurant, don't expect the same kind of hands-on management as at a small inn. ⊠*Hopkins* ☎*523/7272, 800/456–7150 in U.S. and Canada* ⊕*www.belizeandreams.com* ⇱*9 3-bedroom villas (available as 1-, 2-, or 3-bedroom units)* ⚙*In-room: kitchen (some), refrigerator (some), Wi-Fi. In-hotel: room service, beachfront, pool, no elevator* ▭*MC, V.*

$$$$ ▥**Hamanasi.** With beautifully landscaped grounds, top-notch accommodations, and an excellent dive program, Hamanasi (Garífuna for "almond") is among Belize's superior beach and dive resorts. Upon your arrival, you'll notice that the grounds are manicured and the

Fodor's Choice
★

5

lobby is filled with local artwork, including distinguished paintings by Benjamin Nicholas. The "zero effect" pool seems to stretch to infinity. Choose from regular rooms, gorgeous suites with king-size four-poster beds of barba jolote wood, and "tree houses" on stilts, the most popular (and expensive) accommodations. There's a five-night minimum stay in high season. Most people come here for the diving opportunities—Hamanasi has three large, well-equipped dive boats and is the leading operator in the Hopkins area—but you won't feel out of place if you want to snorkel or just laze around the pool. The restaurant, which has a romantic outdoor dining area, serves delicious seafood and other dishes. Dinner is BZ$70. **Pros:** Well-run, deluxe lodging in beautiful beachside setting, excellent dive trips and inland tours. **Cons:** Expensive restaurant, diving requires a long boat trip to the reef or atolls. ⊠ *Hopkins* ✆ *Box 265, Dangriga* ☎ *520/7073, 877/552–3483 in U.S.* ⊕ *www.hamanasi.com* ➪ *8 rooms, 13 suites* ⌂ *In-room: no phone, refrigerator, Wi-Fi (some), no TV. In-hotel: restaurant, bar, pool, beachfront, diving, no elevator, public Internet, public Wi-Fi, no-smoking rooms, airport shuttle (from Dangriga)* ☰ *MC, V* ⊺◎⊺ *CP.*

$$$$ 🖻 **Jaguar Reef Lodge and Spa.** At night, with a row of torches burning
★ on the beach and the waterside thatch-covered dining room glowing in lamplight, this lodge has an East African feel. Nestled on the coast, it has views over the water in one direction and of the Maya Mountains' green slopes in the other. The whitewashed duplex cabanas with thatch roofs have soaring pitched ceilings with exposed wooden beams. The newer Colonial suites and rooms have local artwork, salt-tile floors, and custom-made hardwood furnishings. For those who aren't excited about swimming in the sea, there are two seaside pools. Meals are served in a glassed-in beachside restaurant. The Butterflies Spa offers a variety of treatments and packages (the day package, for instance, includes three treatments and lunch). **Pros:** Attractive and well-kept grounds, lovely beachside location, good selection of tours. **Cons:** Diving and snorkeling requires a long boat trip out to the reef, restaurant can be inconsistent. ⊠ *Hopkins* ✆ *Box 297, Dangriga* ☎ *520/7040, 800/289–5756 in U.S. and Canada* ⊕ *www.jaguarreef.com* ➪ *8 rooms, 9 suites, 1 2-bedroom suite, 7 duplex cabanas* ⌂ *In-room: no phone, safe, kitchen (some), refrigerator, no TV, Wi-Fi. In-hotel: restaurant, bar, 2 pools, gym, spa, beachfront, diving, water sports, bicycles, no elevator, laundry service, airport shuttle (from Dangriga), no-smoking rooms* ☰ *MC, V.*

$$$$ 🖻 **Kanantik Reef & Jungle Resort.** At this all-inclusive luxury resort, you
★ can experience the Barrier Reef without having to make decisions more complicated than whether to have fish or steak for dinner. You can frolic on a palm-lined private beach and snorkel, sail, or kayak at your leisure. Kanantik—a Mopan Maya word meaning "to take care"—has air-conditioned cabanas tucked onto 300 acres south of Hopkins. Echoing African themes, the large and luxuriously outfitted cabanas are striking round structures with conical roofs. Everything except motorized fishing and imported liquors is included in the daily rate. **Pros:** Stunning beachside setting, stress-free all-inclusive. **Con:** Remote location keeps you isolated from local people and culture. ⊠ *Off Southern*

Hwy., between Hopkins and Placencia peninsula ✉*Box 1482, Belize City; Box 150, Dangriga* ☎*520/8048, 800/965–9689, 877/759–8834 in U.S.* ⊕*www.kanantik.com* ⤢*25 cabanas* ♿*In-room: refrigerator, no TV. In-hotel: restaurant, bar, pool, beachfront, diving, water sports, no elevator, laundry service, public Internet, airport shuttle (from Dangriga), no kids under 14* ▭*MC, V* ⏻*AI.*

$$$ ✕**Beaches and Dreams Seafront Inn.** Refugees from Alaska's harsh winters purchased this small beachfront inn, originally opened in 1998, and have spruced up the two octagonal cottages. Each cottage has two rooms, with vaulted ceilings and rattan furniture, just steps from a nice beach. A fifth unit has been added in the back. From mid-April through October, the restaurant is closed, and the hotel operates with minimal staff, but room rates drop to a bargain BZ$120. **Pros:** Kick-off-your-shoes atmosphere, steps from the sea, good restaurant. **Con:** In summer, hotel goes barebones and restaurant closes. ✉*Sittee Point* ☎*523/7259* ⊕*www.beachesanddreams.com* ⤢*5 rooms* ♿*In-room: no a/c, no phone, no TV. In-hotel: restaurant, bar, beachfront, bicycles, public Wi-Fi, no elevator* ▭*MC, V* ⏻*BP*

$$$ ▦**Parrot Cove Lodge.** Under new ownership, which has improved the property, this small beachfront resort, with rooms in earth tones arranged around a courtyard with a pool, is an option if you don't need all the amenities of the larger resorts but want more than a guesthouse offers. Pleasure Cove also has beachside apartments, including luxuriously appointed two-bedroom villa suites (BZ$800). **Pros:** Casual, quiet location, variety of lodging choices. **Con:** Bit of a hike to restaurants and activities in Hopkins village. ✉*Sittee Point, 1 mi (1½ km) south of Hopkins* ☎*520/7089, 612/221–0603 in U.S.* ⊕*www. pleasurecovelodge.com* ⤢*5 rooms, 1 suite, 3 1-bedroom apartments, 2 2-bedroom villa apartments* ♿*In-room: no phone, kitchen, no TV, Wi-Fi (some). In-hotel: restaurant, beachfront, pool, bicycles, no elevator, public Internet, public Wi-Fi* ▭*MC, V.*

$-$$ ▦**Hopkins Inn.** Greg and Rita Duke are helpful hosts at their little beachfront cottage colony in Hopkins. The four cozy cabins have tile floors, ceilings paneled in local hardwoods, and porches with sea views. A Continental breakfast with fruit and locally baked bread is brought to your cabin each morning. **Pros:** On the beach, helpful owners. **Con:** You may be awakened by roosters crowing. ✉*Hopkins* ☎*523/7283* ⊕*www. hopkinsinn.com* ⤢*4 cottages* ♿*In-room: no phone, refrigerator, no TV. In-hotel: beachfront, no elevator* ⏻*CP* ▭*No credit cards.*

$ ▦**Jungle by the Sea.** Although not actually in the jungle, this group ★ of wood cabanas on stilts, also known as Jungle Jeanie's, is on about 2 acres of beachfront nicely shaded by coconut palms. You can rent kayaks and windsurfers here, or just relax in a hammock. You can also pitch your tent for BZ$14 per person. "Jungle Jeanie" Barkman and husband "Jungle John" are actually Canadians who have lived in Belize for years. **Pros:** Comfortable cabañas, lovely stretch of beach, quiet location. **Con:** Short hike to other resorts or to in-town restaurants and bars. ✉*Hopkins* ☎*523/7047* ⊕*www.junglebythesea.com* ⤢*6 cabanas* ♿*In-room: no phone, refrigerator, kitchen (some), no TV. In-hotel: beachfront, no elevator* ▭*No credit cards.*

¢–$ 🖼️**All Seasons Guest House.** The three small but immaculate guest rooms here are designed around a theme. The Jungle Room has a zebra motif and mosquito net on the bed; the Butterfly Room has accents in the deep blue of the Blue Morpho; the Bamboo Room has, well, bamboo and a ceiling fan. Although the guesthouse isn't directly on the beach, there's a sunny patio and garden, and you can rent a motor scooter (BZ$75 a day). **Pros:** Pleasant rooms, lovely garden. **Con:** Not directly on the sea. ⊠*Hopkins* 🕾*Box 251, Dangriga* 🖀*523/7209* ⊕*www.allseasons belize.com* 🗩*3 rooms* ⌂*In-room: no a/c (some), no phone, refrigerator, no TV. In-hotel: no elevator* 🖃*No credit cards.*

DISTANCES

Hopkins is less than 10 minutes by road (about one-half paved) from the paved Southern Highway and is ideally situated for a variety of outdoor adventures, both land and sea. Here's the distance from Hopkins to selected points of interest:

■ Belize Barrier Reef: 10 mi (17 km)

■ Cockscomb Basin Wildlife Sanctuary: 10 mi (17 km)

■ Glover's and Turneffe Atolls: 25 mi (42 km)

■ Mayflower Bocawina National Park: 15 mi (25 km)

¢–$ 🖼️**Tipple Tree Beya Hotel.** This tiny beachfront guesthouse provides a comfortable, no-frills alternative to the coast's upmarket resorts. Run by friendly Patricia Sturman, the inn has rooms that are simple but immaculately clean, as well as a separate private cabin with a kitchenette. Kayaks are available for rent. **Pros:** Steps from the water, hammocks on the porch. **Cons:** Basic, not overly large rooms; can be hot in summer. ⊠*Hopkins* 🖀*520/7006* ⊕*www.tippletree.com* 🗩*4 rooms, 1 with shared bath, 1 cabin* ⌂*In-room: no a/c, refrigerator (some), no phone, no TV. In-hotel: beachfront, water sports, bicycles, no elevator* 🖃*MC, V.*

THE OUTDOORS

BIRD-WATCHING

Cockscomb Basin Wildlife Sanctuary has excellent birding, with some 300 species identified in the reserve. You can also sometimes see the jabiru stork, the largest flying bird in the Western Hemisphere, in the marsh areas just to the west of Hopkins Village. Keep an eye out as you drive into the village from the Southern Highway. North of Hopkins is Fresh Water Creek Lagoon and south of the village is Anderson Lagoon. These lagoons and mangrove swamps are home to many waterbirds, including herons and egrets. A kayak trip on the Sittee River should reward you with kingfishers, toucans, and various flycatchers. About 30 minutes by boat off Hopkins is Man-o-War Caye, a bird sanctuary that has one of the largest colonies of frigate birds in the Caribbean, more than 300 nesting birds. **Hamanasi, Jaguar Reef,** and other hotels arrange bird-watching trips. Costs for guided birding tours run from BZ$50 to BZ$200 per person, depending on where you go and the length of time.

CANOEING & KAYAKING

When kayaking or canoeing on the Sittee River, you can see many birds and, possibly, manatees and crocodiles. Manatees also are often spotted in the sea just off the Hopkins shore. If you go on a tour with a licensed guide from a local lodge, expect to pay BZ$100–BZ$150 per person. Several hotels in Hopkins, including **Tipple Tree Beya Hotel, Hopkins Inn, Jungle by the Sea,** and **All Seasons Guest House,** rent kayaks, canoes, and other water equipment by the hour or day. Although it's possible to do sea kayaking from Hopkins, often the water is choppy. Long sea-kayaking trips should be tried only by experienced kayakers, preferably with a guide.

CAVING

Caving tours from Hopkins typically go to St. Herman's Cave and the Crystal Cave at Blue Hole National Park on the Hummingbird Highway. Cost is around BZ$120 per person.

DIVING

Diving off Hopkins is very good to terrific. The Barrier Reef is closer here—about 10 mi (17 km) from shore—than it is at Placencia. Diving also is fairly costly here. Half-day, two-tank dive trips to the reef or the South Water Caye Marine Reserve are around BZ$180–BZ$200, not including regulator, BCD, wet suit, and other equipment rental, which can add BZ$50. Dive shops with fast boats can also take you all the way to the atolls—Turneffe, Glover's, and even Lighthouse. These atoll trips generally start early in the morning, at 6 or 7 AM, and last all day. Costs for three-tank atoll dives are around BZ$280–BZ$340 for Glover's and Turneffe, and BZ$500 for Lighthouse. In late spring, when whale sharks typically show up, local dive shops offer dives to see the Belizean behemoths at Gladden Spit Marine Reserve for around BZ$350–BZ$400. Marine park fees (not usually included in dive trip charges) are BZ$10 each for South Water Caye and Glover's marine reserves, and BZ$30 for Gladden Spit.

One of the best diving operations in Southern Belize is at **Hamanasi** (☎520/7073 ⊕*www.hamanasi.com*). Here you'll find the newest equipment and the biggest boats. **Second Nature Divers** (⊠*At Jaguar Reef Lodge* ☎520/7040 ⊕*www.secondnaturedivers.com*) has a good reputation as well.

HIKING

Most hiking trips go to Cockscomb Basin Wildlife Sanctuary, where there are a dozen short hiking trails near the visitor center. Full-day trips to Cockscomb generally cost about BZ$120–BZ$150 per person from Hopkins and can be booked through your hotel. If you're a glutton for punishment, you can go on a guided hike to Victoria Peak, the second-highest mountain peak in Belize. The 40-mi (67-km) hike from the visitor center at Cockscomb Basin Wildlife Sanctuary to the top entails inclines of 45 to 60 degrees. Most of these trips require three to five days up and back and cost in the range of BZ$500 per person (minimum of two people). One guide who will take you is **Marcos Cucul**

(⊕*www.mayaguide.bz*). He is a jungle survival guide who is a member of the Belize National Cave and Wilderness Rescue Team.

HORSEBACK RIDING

Local lodges arrange horseback-riding trips, working with ranches near Belmopan and Dangriga. A full-day horseback trip, including transportation to the ranch and lunch, is around BZ$150 per person.

MANATEE-WATCHING TOURS

Local lodges offer trips to Gales Point and the Southern Lagoon to try to spot Antillean manatees, a subspecies of West Indian manatees. These large aquatic mammals—adults weigh 800 to 1,200 pounds—are related to elephants. They're found in shallow waters in lagoons, rivers, estuaries, and coastal areas in much of Belize, and are especially common in the lagoons around Gales Point. These gentle herbivores can live 60 years or longer. The cost of manatee-spotting trips varies but is around BZ$150 per person. Under Belize government guidelines, you're not permitted to feed manatees, to swim with them, or to approach a manatee with a calf.

SNORKELING

Snorkeling off Hopkins is excellent, though expensive compared with the Northern Cayes. Half-day snorkeling trips from Hopkins to the Belize Barrier Reef, usually a pristine section of it in the South Water Caye Marine Reserve, cost from BZ$100 to BZ$150 per person, depending on whether you're snorkeling from an island on the reef or from a boat (the boat costs more). These snorkel trips are about twice as pricey as those to Hol Chan from Ambergris Caye or Caye Caulker, partly because the trip out and back to snorkel sites here is much longer, and also because there's less competition to hold prices down. Full-day snorkel trips to Glover's Atoll, which has some of the best snorkeling in the Caribbean, are around BZ$150–BZ$200.

WINDSURFING

Windsurfing is a growing sport in Hopkins, as the wind is a fairly consistent 10 to 15 knots, except in August and September when it sometimes goes calm. The best winds are in April and May. **Windschief** (☎523/7249 ⊕*www.windschief.com*) rents well-maintained equipment for BZ$10 for the first hour, then BZ$5 for additional hours, or BZ$60 a day. Private lessons are BZ$60 an hour. Several hotels also rent windsurfing equipment.

SHOPPING

Shopping is limited in Hopkins, where the local "shopping center" is a small clapboard house with a few dozen items for sale. Locals traditionally make much of what they use in daily life, from cassava graters to fishing canoes and paddles, and drums and *shakas* (shakers made from a calabash gourd filled with seeds). Around the village, you'll see individuals selling carvings and other local handicrafts made from shells and coconuts. Also, several small shops or stands, including **JoyJah's Gift Shop, Kulcha Gift Shop,** and **Tribal Arts,** none of which have phones, sell locally made crafts. You can bargain for the best price, but remember that there are few jobs around Hopkins and that these craftspeople are trying to earn money to help feed their families. **Jaguar Reef Resort** (☎ 520/7040) has a fine little gift shop filled with pottery and embroidery as well as Garífuna crafts. The store also carries Marie Sharp's superb hot sauces, New Age music, and drugstore items like sunscreen and the crucial no-see-um bug repellent. **Hamanasi** (☎ 520/7073) also has a well-stocked gift shop.

COCKSCOMB BASIN WILDLIFE SANCTUARY

10 mi (17 km) southwest of Hopkins.

★ The mighty jaguar, once the undisputed king of the Central and South American jungles, is now endangered. But it has a haven in the Cockscomb Basin Wildlife Sanctuary, which covers 128,000 acres of lush rain forest in the Cockscomb Range of the Maya Mountains. Thanks to this reserve, as well as other protected areas around the country, Belize has the highest concentration of jaguars in the world.

Some visitors to Cockscomb are disappointed that they don't see jaguars and that wildlife doesn't jump out from behind trees to astound them as they hike the trails. The experience at Cockscomb is indeed a low-key one, and seeing wildlife usually requires patience and luck. You'll have the best chance of seeing wild animals, perhaps even a jaguar or one of the other large cats, if you stay overnight, preferably for several nights, in the sanctuary. You may also have better luck if you go for an extended hike with a guide. Several nearby lodges, such as **Hamanasi**, offer night hikes to Cockscomb, departing around dusk and returning around 9 PM.

Cockscomb Basin also has native wildlife aside from the jaguars. You might see other cats—pumas, margays, and ocelots—plus coatis, kinkajous, deer, peccaries, and, last but not least, tapirs. Also known as the mountain cow, this shy, curious creature appears to be half horse, half hippo, with a bit of cow and elephant thrown in. Nearly 300 species of birds have been identified in the Cockscomb Basin, including the Keel-Billed Toucan, the King Vulture, several hawk species, and the Scarlet Macaw.

Within the reserve is Belize's best-maintained system of jungle and mountain trails, most of which lead to at least one outstanding swimming hole. The sanctuary also has spectacular views of Victoria Peak and the Cockscomb Range. Bring serious bug spray with you—the reserve swarms with mosquitoes and tiny biting flies called no-see-ums—and wear long-sleeve shirts and long pants. The best times to hike anywhere in Belize are early morning, late afternoon, and early evening, when temperatures are lower and more animals are on the prowl.

You have to register in a thatch building at Maya Centre on the Southern Highway before proceeding several miles to the visitor center. In the same building is an excellent gift shop selling baskets, wood and fabric crafts, and slate carvings by local Maya craftspeople, at good prices. Buying crafts at this shop, which is run as a co-op by local residents, generally gets more of the money into local hands than if you buy from a commercial gift shop. At Maya Centre also is a small butterfly farm.

The road from Maya Centre to the Cockscomb ranger station and visitor center winds 6 mi (10 km) through dense vegetation—splendid cahune palms, purple mimosas, orchids, and big-leaf plantains—and as you go higher the marvelous sound of tropical birds, often resembling strange windup toys, grows stronger and stronger. This is definitely four-wheel-drive terrain. You may have to ford several small rivers as well as negotiate deep, muddy ruts. At the end, in a clearing with hibiscus and bougain-villea bushes, you'll find a little office, where you can buy maps of the nature trails, along with restrooms, several picnic tables, cabins, and a campground.

> ## ON JAGUARS
>
> Jaguars are shy, nocturnal animals that prefer to keep their distance from humans, so the possibility of viewing one in the wild is small. The jaguar, or *el tigre*, as it's known in Spanish, is a supremely independent creature that shuns even its own kind. Except during a brief mating period and the six months the female spends with her cubs before turning them loose, jaguars roam the rain forest alone. At certain times of year, however, jaguars are spotted here almost every day, especially just before sunrise.

Altogether there are some 20 mi (33 km) of marked trails. Walking along these 12 nature trails is a good way to get to know the region. Most are loops of ½–1½ mi (1–2 km), so you can do several in a day. The most strenuous trail takes you up a steep hill; from the top is a magnificent view of the entire Cockscomb Basin. ⊠ *Outside Maya Centre* ☎ *227/7369* 🖮 *BZ$10* ⊙ *Daily 8–5.*

WHERE TO STAY

Although most visitors come to Cockscomb on day trips and stay in Hopkins, Placencia, or Dangriga, you can camp in the reserve for BZ$10 a night per person, or for a little more money, you can stay in pleasant new rooms in a dormitory with solar-generated electricity for BZ$37 per person. Also, a small house and three cabins, each with private bath, can accommodate up to four or six people (BZ$107 per house/cabin). An old, primitive cabin with 10 bunk beds is BZ$16 per person. There's a communal kitchen for cooking. No fishing or hunting is allowed in the reserve, and pets are prohibited. Book in Belize City through the **Belize Audubon Society** (☎ *223/5004* ⊕ *www.belizeaudubon.org*).

¢ 🖫 **Tutzil Nah Cottages.** Gregorio Chun and his family, including brothers Ouscal and Julian, Mopan Maya people who've lived in this area for generations, provide accommodations in simple thatch cabanas. Meals also are available, for BZ$12–BZ$24, and the Chuns provide a range of tours to Cockscomb and Mayan sites. **Pros:** Near Maya Centre, owners highly knowledgeable about Cockscomb, interesting tours available. **Con:** Basic accommodations with shared baths. ⊠ *Near*

Maya Centre, Mile 13½, Southern Hwy. ☎520/3044 ⊕*www.maya-center.com* ➪*2 cabanas with outdoor shared baths* ⚘*In-room: no a/c, no phone, no TV. In-hotel: no elevator, airport shuttle (from Dangriga)* ▭*No credit cards.*

MAYA BEACH

36 mi (61 km) south of Dangriga by road.

Dusty in dry weather and a muddy slop after rains, the largely dirt road that runs 25 mi (41 km) from the Southern Highway to Placencia Village is the only artery down the peninsula. Beginning at Riversdale—about 8½ mi (14 km) from the Southern Highway, at the elbow where the peninsula joins the mainland—you'll get a quick glimpse through mangroves of the startlingly blue Caribbean. As you go south, the Placencia Lagoon is on your right, and behind it in the distance rise the low Maya Mountains. On your left, a few hundred feet away, beyond the remaining mangroves and a narrow band of beach, is the sea.

The northern peninsula from Riversdale south to Maya Beach, which is about 7 mi (12 km) south of Riversdale, once had just a few small seaside houses, and Maya Beach was a sleepy beach community. Now, "For Sale" signs dot the roadside, supersized beach mansions are going up, and several new condominium communities and resorts are open or are being planned. These new resorts and condo developments join a small group of laid-back seaside hotels and cabins.

Traveling from Riversdale to Maya Beach to Seine Bight and Placencia, you'll find no clear delineation between one area and another. Even local residents may not be entirely sure exactly where one community ends and another begins.

If you stay at the northern end of the peninsula, you may want a rental car because public transportation is limited to an on-again, off-again shuttle and a few buses bound to or from Dangriga. Taxis are expensive (about BZ$50 to Placencia village from Riversdale, and BZ$40 from Maya Beach).

WHERE TO STAY & EAT

$$–$$$$ ✕**Maya Beach Hotel Bistro.** Before ending up here, owners John and Ellen
Fodor'sChoice Lee (he's Australian, she's American) traveled the world and worked in
★ 20 countries. They obviously figured out what travelers love, because their bistro by the beach is one of our favorite restaurants in all of Belize. The Bistro menu changes occasionally, but among the standards you'll go gaga over are five-onion cioppino, mixed seafood in a robust tomato and vegetable stew; ultrafresh ceviche; delicious snapper stack; and cocoa-dusted pork chop on a risotto cake. We weren't thrilled, though, by the new lobster shooters——who likes to drink lobster-flavored tequila? ⊠*Maya Beach* ☎520/8040 ▭*MC, V* ☉*Bistro closed Mon. and for part of July.*

$ ✕**Mango's of Maya Beach.** The big beachfront, two-story thatch cabana was an institution for years in Maya Beach, before going through a series of changes and finally closing. Then, in 2007, to the delight of thirsty Maya Beachers, Mango's reopened, with a new thatch roof, new kitchen, and new owners. Besides serving beer, snacks, and gossip, Mango's occasionally does fish fries. ⊠*Maya Beach* 📇

$$$$ 📺**Bella Maya Resort and Residences.** After a long series of delays, this long-anticipated condominium resort, stretching across the narrow Placencia peninsula from sea to lagoon, finally opened in late 2007. Only about half of the 60 condo units——those on the sea side——are complete. The rest, across the road on the lagoon side, are promised to be finished by late 2008, as are a spa and gym. The two-bedroom, two-bath, 1,100 square foot suites here are luxuriously outfitted, with

travertine marble floors, Wi-Fi, and custom kitchens with granite countertops. **Pros:** Large, luxurious condo suites, beautiful swimming pool. **Cons:** Check to confirm that all facilities and amenities are available during your visit. ⊠*4 mi (6 2/3 km) north of Seine Bight* 📞*523/8113, or 800/343–2008 in the U.S., 44 (0) 2077312200 in the U.K.* ⊕*www.bella mayaresort.com* 🛏*60 condo apartments* ⌂*In-room: kitchen, Wi-Fi, no TV (some). In-hotel: restaurant, bar, pool, beachfront, water sports, no elevator, laundry service, public Internet, airport shuttle* ▭*AE, MC, V.*

$$$ 📺**Green Parrot Beach Houses.** This resort has Mennonite-built cottages, now showing a little wear, along a nice stretch of beach, each with a kitchenette and dining area. The sleeping quarters are upstairs in a loft-like space with a pitched wooden roof. One nifty feature is an octagonal wall panel, operated by pulleys that you can open for a bedside view of the ocean. Two of the smaller thatch cabanas have outdoor showers. The beachfront restaurant has a limited menu. **Pros:** Good option for families, pleasant beach area. **Con:** No swimming pool. ⊠*No. 1 Maya Beach, 4 mi (6½ km) north of Seine Bight* 📞*523/2488* ⊕*www. greenparrot-belize.com* 🛏*6 cabins, 2 cabanas* ⌂*In-room: no a/c, no phone, no TV. In-hotel: restaurant, bar, beachfront, water sports, no elevator, laundry service, airport shuttle* ▭*MC, V* ⊙*CP.*

$$$ 📺**Ocean's Edge Beach Houses.** The two beach houses at this seaside hideaway each have a loft bedroom on the second level——with views of the water from the jalousie windows——and a living area and kitchen on the first floor. The houses have rustic exteriors of local woods. You can sit on your deck and see False Caye, a nice snorkeling area about 30 minutes by kayak (complimentary) from the beach. The property is managed by the owners of Barnacle Bill's (⊃ *see below*). **Pros:** Pleasant, self-catering beach houses. **Cons:** You're on your own here, five-day minimum stay. ⊠*49 Maya Beach Way, north end of Maya Beach, 3 mi (5 km) north of Seine Bight* 📞*523/8010, 866/367–7679 in U.S.*

and Canada ⊕www.oceansedge-belize.com ➴2 houses △In-room: no a/c, no phone, kitchen, refrigerator, no TV. In-hotel: beachfront, water sports, bicycles, no elevator ☰MC, V.

$$$ 🏨**The Placencia.** Transplant an upscale Texas condo community to Belize, and you might end up with something like the Placencia, formerly called Zeboz. The resort offers such amenities as tennis courts; an upscale restaurant with a 9,000-bottle wine cellar; the nation's largest swimming pool; and a sandy, 1,000-foot beach with a dock that goes out some 200 feet. The one-bedroom apartments have a whirlpool bath and tile floors. The Capriccio restaurant serves Italian and some Belizean dishes, and there are two other small open-air restaurants. If you don't want to leave, you can buy a condo here, starting at about US$308,000. The developers are building additional condos as well as huge, McMansion-style houses in a gated community on the lagoon side. **Pros:** Beautiful beach, huge pool, attractive condos. **Cons:** Sprawling complex lacks personality, rarely many guests, a BZ$50 cab ride to Placencia village. *✉6 mi (10 km) north of Seine Bight ☎520/4110 ⊕www.theplacencia.com ➴92 condo apartments △In-room: kitchen (some), Wi-Fi. In-hotel: 3 restaurants, bar, tennis courts, pool, spa, beachfront, diving, water sports, no elevator, laundry service, public Internet, airport shuttle ☰AE, MC, V.*

$$-$$$ 🏨**Calico Jack's Village.** Co-owner Chester Williams developed a new hurricane-resistant technique, employing foam-filled concrete blocks, to build this small beachfront resort at the peninsula's far north end. Nine rustic, cohune-palm thatched cabanas, some of which have air-conditioning, are set about 60 feet from the sea. New additions are a two-bedroom "treehouse" villa nestled in palm trees and two-bedroom villas located behind the cabanas. Most units are accessible to people with disabilities, unusual in Belize. Service is eager, and the beach is pretty, though as elsewhere on the peninsula sand flies occasionally can be irksome. Jutting from the shore are two tempting private piers with thatch palapas and hammocks. **Pros:** Rooms accessible to people with disabilities, a good value. **Cons:** BZ$50 cab ride from Placencia village, entrance looks a little junky due to old parked vehicles. *✉5½ mi (9 km) north of Seine Bight ☎523/8009 ⊕www.calicojacksvillage.com ➴9 cabanas, 3 2-bedroom villas △In-room: no a/c (some), no phone, no TV, kitchenette (some). In-hotel: restaurant, bar, pool, beachfront, water sports, bicycles, no elevator, public Internet, public Wi-Fi, airport shuttle ☰AE, MC, V ◉CP.*

$-$$$ 🏨**Maya Beach Hotel.** This is the kind of small, unpretentious hotel that
★   many come to Belize to enjoy, but few actually find. Rooms are simple and small but pleasant, with polished wood floors. Most are only steps from the water, and many have views of False Caye and the sea. In addition, the hotel rents several apartments and houses nearby with access to a pool. Some have minimum stay requirements. The on-site restaurant is one of Belize's best. **Pros:** Like a small beach hotel should be, excellent restaurant. **Con:** Rooms are only a couple of steps up from basic. *✉Maya Beach ☎520/8040, 800/503–5124 in U.S. ⊕www.mayabeachhotel.com ➴6 rooms, 4 apartments, 2 houses △In-room: no a/c (some), no phone, kitchen (some), no TV (some), Wi-Fi (some).*

In-hotel: restaurant, bar, beachfront, water sports, no elevator, public Wi-Fi ▭MC, V ⊗Bistro closed Mon. and for part of July.

$-$$$ 🏨 **Maya Breeze Inn.** Choice is what it's about at this small resort. You can choose from three cabins and two apartments on the sea side of the road, or take a room in the lagoon-side hotel. The cabins are older, wood units, painted a sunshine yellow, while the hotel rooms are in a modern concrete building with terra-cotta floors and private balconies. One of the apartments has a cathedral ceiling and a third-floor loft with a terrific view of the sea. **Pros:** Variety of accommodations, attractive pool. **Con:** Lagoon-side rooms don't have the best views. ⊠*Maya Beach, 2 mi (3 km) north of Seine Bight* ☎*523/8012, 888/458–8581 in U.S.* ⊕*www.mayabreezeinn.com* ⇌*3 cabins, 2 apartments, 4 rooms* ⌂*In-room: no phone, safe (some), kitchen (some), refrigerator. In-hotel: beachfront, water sports, pool, no elevator, laundry service, public Internet, airport shuttle* ▭*MC, V.*

$$ 🏨 **Barnacle Bill's Beach Bungalows.** "Barnacle Bill" Taylor, known as the
★ wit of Maya Beach, and wife Adriane rent a pair of wooden Mennonite bungalows set among palm trees about 60 feet from the sea. Each cottage is on stilts and has a private bath and a kitchen where you can prepare your own meals. Bill and Adriane can arrange to stock your fridge and pantry in advance, if you like. There are complimentary bikes and kayaks. On a calm day, it's about a 20-minute kayak ride to False Caye, where you can enjoy some of the peninsula's best free snorkeling. **Pros:** Friendly spot, helpful owners, nice place just to relax. **Con:** Don't expect luxury. ⊠*23 Maya Beach Way* ☎*523/8010* ⊕*www.gotobelize.com/barnacle* ⇌*2 cottages* ⌂*In-room: no a/c, no phone, no TV. In-hotel: beachfront, water sports, bicycles, no elevator, airport shuttle, no kids under 12* ▭*MC, V.*

$-$$ 🏨 **Beachfront Suites.** Think small, act independently: there are only two self-catering suites at this private home, painted a tropical pink and blue. Both are on the second floor, and both have full kitchens, ice-cold air-conditioning, double doors opening to a veranda with views of the water, custom-made hardwood furnishings, and Wi-Fi. **Pros:** Attractive suites, good value for the money. **Con:** In a remote area so you need a rental car. ⊠*253 Plantation, 1½ mi (3 km) south of Riversdale in the Plantation development* ☎*606/1521* ⊕*www. beachfrontinbelize.com* ⇌*2 suites* ⌂*In-room: kitchen, Wi-Fi. In-hotel: beachfront, water sports, no elevator, laundry service, no-smoking rooms* ▭*AE, MC, V, D.*

$-$$ 🏨 **Singing Sands.** The six wood-and-thatch cabanas here are small and simply decorated with Guatemalan needlecrafts. Cabins 1 and 2 are closest to the beach. There's a dock with a nice area for swimming, and a pool for those who'd rather take a dip in fresh water. **Pros:** Small, owner-run beach hotel, pleasant cottages. **Cons:** Smallish rooms, no a/c. ⊠*Maya Beach* ☎*520/8022* ⊕*www.singingsands.com* ⇌*6 cabanas* ⌂*In-room: no a/c, no phone, no TV. In-hotel: restaurant, bar, pool, beachfront, no elevator, laundry service, public Internet, airport shuttle* ▭*MC, V* ◎*CP.*

A Creole Primer

The Creole language is associated with the Creole or black people of Belize, especially those around Belize City. But people all over Belize know the Creole language and speak it daily. You'll hear Creole spoken by Mennonite farmers, Chinese shopkeepers, and Hispanic tour guides. Creole was brought to Belize by African slaves and former slaves from Jamaica and elsewhere in the Caribbean. Creole words are primarily of English origin, with some words from several West African tongues, Spanish, Miskito (an indigenous language of Central America, spoken by some 200,000 people in Honduras, Nicaragua, and Belize), and other languages.

Spoken in a lilting Caribbean accent and combined with a grammar and syntax with West African roots, the language, despite English word usage, is difficult for foreigners to understand. Plurals aren't used often in Creole. For some, knowing how to speak Creole is a test you have to pass before you can become a "real" Belizean. However, with the increasing number of Hispanic immigrants in Belize, it's heard less and less, while Spanish is heard more and more.

Here are a few Creole words and phrases. If you want to learn more, get the Kriol-Inglish Dikshineri (Paul Crosbie, Editor-in-Chief) published by the Belize Kriol Project and available in gift shops and bookstores in Belize.

Ah mi gat wahn gud guf taim: I had a really good time

Bwah: Boy

Bashment: Party

Chaaly prise: A large rat, after Sir Charles Price, an 18th-century Jamaican planter

Chinchi: A little bit

Dis da fi wi chikin: This is our chicken (well-known slogan of Mennonite chicken company)

Dollah: A Belize dollar

Fowl caca white and tink eh lay egg: A chicken sees its white droppings and thinks it laid an egg (said of a self-important person)

Grind mean: Ground meat

Gyal: Girl

Humoch dis kaas?: How much is this?

Ih noh mata: It doesn't matter

Madda rass: Foolishness (literally, mother's ass)

Tiga maga but eh no sic: Tiger's skinny but he's not sick (that is, don't judge a book by its cover)

Waawa: Foolish

Wangla: Sesame seed or candy made from sesame seeds

Weh di beach deh?: Where's the beach?

Yerrisso: Gossip, from "Ah her so" (so I hear)

SEINE BIGHT

47 mi (77 km) south of Dangriga.

Like Placencia, its Creole neighbor to the south, Seine Bight is a small coastal fishing village. It may not be for long, though, as Placencia's resorts are stretching north to and through this Garífuna community, one of six predominantly Garífuna villages in Belize. The beach, especially south of Seine Bight, is great, though near the village garbage sometimes mars the view. Hotels do rake and clean their beachfronts, and several community cleanups have been organized in an effort to solve this problem. All the businesses catering to tourists are along the main road (actually, it's the only road) that leads south to Placencia Village. The name Seine Bight derives from a type of net, called a seine, used by local fishermen. Bight means an indentation or inward bend in the coastline.

Like Placencia Village, Seine Bight was devastated by Hurricane Iris in October 2001, and many of the village's simple wooden homes were destroyed. However, any traces of the storm have been erased by expanding resorts and new residential construction.

Several small resorts and tracts of beachfront near Seine Bight have been sold, and there are plans for the development of a large, but low-rise resort.

WHERE TO STAY

$$$$
Fodor'sChoice
★
The Inn at Robert's Grove. Energetic New Yorkers Bob and Risa Frackman invite you to stay at their place on a beautiful, palm-lined stretch of beach. You can play tennis and swim in the sea or in one of the three beachside pools. Their chef, Frank DaSilva, packs lunches for boat rides to deserted cayes and serves delicious dinners in the seaside dining room. The Saturday night pool-side barbecue——think grilled lobster (in season), fresh fish, and tons of shrimp——attracts crowds from up and down the peninsula. Such personal attention makes this one of Belize's top beach resorts. Although the regular rooms and junior suites have been beautifully refurbished, if possible opt for the deluxe suites, most with verandas overlooking the ocean and some with kitchens. The hotel has a dive center and two private cayes, Bob's Caye and Ranguana Caye, for picnics or overnight trips. Robert's Grove was voted "Belize Hotel of the Year " in 2008 by members of Belize's Tourism Industry Association. **Pros:** Well-run, personal attention, gorgeous seaside rooms and suites, lots of on-site activities. **Cons:** Nothing particularly exotic here, not inexpensive. ⊠½ *mi (1 km) south of Seine Bight* ☎*523/3565, 800/565–9757 in U.S.* ⊕*www.robertsgrove.com* ⌐*20 rooms, 32 suites* ♿*In-room: kitchen (some), refrigerator (some), Wi-Fi. In-hotel: 2 restaurants, bars, tennis courts, 3 pools, gym, spa, beachfront, diving, water sports, bicycles, no elevator, laundry service, public Internet, airport shuttle* ⊟*AE, MC, V.*

$$–$$$
Nautical Inn. The rooms at this inn are in two-tier octagonal buildings shipped from North Carolina. They have American-style fixtures, firm mattresses, phones, cable TV, air-conditioning, and glass-wall showers. On Wednesday evening the hotel hosts Garífuna drummers, coconut bowling, and a beach barbecue. **Pro:** Good room amenities despite moderate price. **Con:** Buildings have some odd angles. ⊠*Seine Bight* ☎*523/3595, 800/688–0377 in U.S.* ⊕*www.nauticalinnbelize.com*

⯈12 rooms ♿In-room: refrigerator (some). In-hotel: restaurant, pool, beachfront, no elevator, public Internet, airport shuttle ▭MC, V.

$$ 📺**Laru Beya Villas.** Laru Beya, a condo colony whose name means "on the beach" in the Garífuna language, sits on seven beachfront acres. Rooms are bright and sunny, with tile floors and bamboo furniture. The larger villa units, with up to three bedrooms, have full kitchens, and some have rooftop Jacuzzis and verandas with sea views. **Pros:** Well-designed rooms and suites, a good value. **Con:** Not a full-service resort, though you can walk to nearby restaurants and bars. ✉½ mi (1 km) south of Seine Bight, south of Robert's Grove 📞523/3476, 800/813–7762 in U.S. and Canada ⊕www.larubeya.com ⯈24 units ♿In-room: kitchen (some). In-hotel: bar, pool, beachfront, no elevator, public Internet, airport shuttle ▭MC, V.

SHOPPING

Painter and writer Lola Delgado moved to Seine Bight from Belize City in the late 1980s. Her workshop, **Lola's Art** (📞601/1913 🕗8 AM–9 PM), displays her cheerful acrylic paintings of local scenes (BZ$100 and up). She also sells hand-painted cards and some of her husband's wood carvings. Espresso and pastries are available. The workshop is up a flight of steps in a tiny wooden house off the main street, behind the football field.

PLACENCIA

5 mi (8 km) south of Seine Bight, 52 mi (85 km) south of Dangriga.

On a sheltered half-moon bay with crystal-clear water and almost 3 mi (5 km) of palm-dotted white sand, this fishing village is straight out of a Robert Louis Stevenson novel. Founded by pirates, the community is now inhabited by an extraordinary mélange of people. To the west, the Cockscomb Range ruffles the tropical sky with its jagged peaks; to the east, a line of uninhabited cayes grazes the horizon. From here you can dive along the reef, hike into the jungle, look for Scarlet Macaws in Red Bank Village to the southwest (between December and February), explore the Mayan ruins at Mayflower or, on a day trip, at Lubaantun and Nim Li Punit, or treat yourself to some of the best sportfishing in the country. Once you arrive you'll probably just want to lie in a hammock with a good book, perhaps getting up long enough to cool off in the waves.

Sometimes billed as the world's narrowest street, a single concrete path through the village is just wide enough for two people. Setting off purposefully from the southern end of the village, the path meanders through everyone's backyard, passes wooden cottages on stilts overrun with bougainvillea and festooned with laundry, then, as if it had forgotten where it was headed in the first place, peters out abruptly in a little clearing filled with lovely white morning glories. Stroll along the sidewalk, and you've seen the village. If you don't mind it being a little rough around the edges, you'll be utterly enchanted by this rustic village, where the palm trees rustle, the waves lap the shore, and no one is in a hurry.

Along the path are most of the village's quaint guesthouses and palapa-covered cafés, which serve mainly burgers, rice and beans, and a bit of seafood. With the opening of more and more small resorts up the peninsula, Placencia's restaurants are beginning to compete with those in Ambergris Caye.

WHERE TO STAY & EAT

$$$ ✕**French Connection.** A young European couple has brought modern
★ French cooking back to the peninsula. The menu changes frequently, but you can try first courses such as lobster and crab bisque or baby octopus and chorizo, then a main course of smoked mackerel and snapper fishcake or grilled pork chop with wild mushrooms and brandy sauce. Although the wine list is small and pricey, the London-trained chef's reach sometimes exceeds his grasp, and the beef dishes aren't the best, this is a sophisticated addition to Placencia dining. Reservations are suggested. The owners sometimes close for a week or two during slow periods. ⊠*Placencia village near center of village* ☎*523/3656* ⊟*MC, V* ⊗*Closed Mon. and Tues; no dinner Sun.*

$-$$$ ✕**La Dolce Vita.** In a slightly Fellini-esque setting, upstairs over Wallen's Store, La Dolce Vita brings authentic antipasti, bruschetta, and pasta dishes to Placencia. The Rome-born chef-owner, Simone DeAngelis, imports his own Italian pastas, olive oils, and wines to make sure everything is first quality. With opera music playing in the background, it's like being in a small, family-run restaurant in Italy. ⊠*On main road in Placencia village, above Wallen's Store* ☎*523/3115* ⊟*MC, V* ⊗*No lunch.*

$-$$$ ✕**De Tatch Café.** This open-air bar and restaurant with a "tatch" (thatch) roof long has been one of the most popular hangouts in the village. Try the huge shrimp burrito and wash it down with a few cold Belikins. If you go fishing and catch something, the restaurant will prepare it for you. Breakfasts are good here, too. ⊠*In village near Seaspray Hotel* ☎ *503/3385* ⊟*MC, V* ⊗Closed Wed.

$-$$$ ✕**Pickled Parrot Bar & Grill.** This popular feet-in-the-sand restaurant and bar is in the heart of Placencia. Fresh seafood is the main draw, but owner Wende Bryan also offers pizza, fajitas, and burgers. ⊠*Off main road, behind Wallen's Market* ☎*604/0278* ⊟*V* ⊗*No lunch Sun.*

$-$$$ ✕**Purple Space Monkey.** Everybody's favorite Internet café—formerly in a big thatch-roofed building that burned down in 2006—is now under new ownership and has come back, bigger and better than ever, in a brightly painted building, wisely sans the thatch. The new version is more of a restaurant than a cybercafé, serving well-prepared Belizean and American food all day long. It's especially popular for breakfast. There's free Wi-Fi access for customers, plasma TVs to watch sports, and a used-book exchange. ⊠*On main road, next to new BTIA office.* ☎*523/4094* ⊟*MC, V*

$-$$$ ✕**Trattoria Placencia.** You can parla Italiano, Americano, or Creole at this Italian and seafood place on the beach. Owner Cris is from Rome,

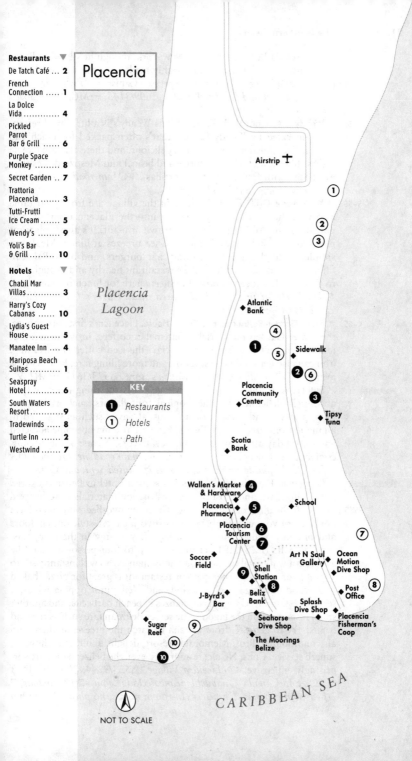

Placencia

Placencia Lagoon

Airstrip ✝

Atlantic Bank

Sidewalk

Placencia Community Center

Tipsy Tuna

Scotia Bank

KEY

① Restaurants

① Hotels

..... Path

Wallen's Market & Hardware

Placencia Pharmacy

Placencia Tourism Center

School

Soccer Field

Art N Soul Gallery

Ocean Motion Dive Shop

Shell Station

Beliz Bank

Post Office

J-Byrd's Bar

Splash Dive Shop

Placencia Fisherman's Coop

Sugar Reef

Seahorse Dive Shop

The Moorings Belize

CARIBBEAN SEA

NOT TO SCALE

and "Greg da Barman" is from New York, though he's lived in Belize for many years. The pastas are freshly made—try the seafood fettuccine or ravioli. They even have espresso. Capisce? ⊠*In village, near Seaspray Hotel and De Tatch Café* ☎609/3143 ▭*MC, V* ⊘*Closed Sun. No lunch.*

$-$$ ✗**Wendy's.** No, not that Wendy's. This Wendy's is a little local restau-
★ rant, operated by Wendy Lemus, that's often packed for lunch and dinner. The grilled fish is fresh and delicious, and there also are Creole dishes (like stew chicken with rice and beans) and Mestizo dishes (like escabeche with freshmade flour tortillas). ⊠*Main road near dock in Placencia Village* ☎523/3335 ▭*MC, V.*

$-$$ ✗**Yoli's Bar & Grill.** The best views in the village are from your table at Yoli's. Built on a pier jutting out into the Placencia harbor, and new in 2006, Yoli's attracts a big crowd at night. It's also a pleasant place to sip a Belikin and enjoy the sea breezes at lunch. Meals are simple, highlighting local seafood, hamburgers, and basic Belizean fare. Food is cooked at Merlene's restaurant nearby and brought out to the pier. The local Rotary club meets here for lunch on Mondays. ⊠*Harborfront in the Bakader area, near Harry's Cozy Cabañas* ☎523/3183 ▭*MC, V.*

¢-$$ ✗**Secret Garden Restaurant and Coffee House.** Placencia's first coffeehouse, the Secret Garden brews rich Guatemalan coffees. In warm weather (and when isn't it warm in Placencia?) the iced coffee is refreshing. You can also get sandwiches, soups, and more filling fare. Free Wi-Fi is available. ⊠*In village, behind Wallen's store* ☎523/3617 ▭*MC, V*

FodorśChoice ✗**Tutti-Frutti.** Authentic, Italian-style gelato is the thing here, and it's
★ absolutely delicious. Try the tropical fruit flavors, such as banana,
¢ lime, papaya, and mango, or an unusual flavor such as sugar corn, all made from natural ingredients. Beware: You may become addicted and return day after day to sample new flavors. A cone of the luscious confection is super cheap. ⊠*In village on main road, next to the BTIA office.* ☎*No phone* ▭*No credit cards* ⊘*Closed Sept. and Oct.*

FodorśChoice ▯**Turtle Inn.** Francis Ford Coppola's second hotel in Belize is exotic.
★ Furnishings, art, and most of the construction materials were selected
$$$$ in Bali by the director and his wife. The seven two-bedroom villas have not one or two, but three bathrooms (two Japanese-style ones indoors and one in a walled outdoor garden). If you stay in the Coppolas' personal villa (BZ$4,284 per night for up to four persons), you'll be assigned a walkie-talkie-carrying "houseman" who will instantly see to any of your requests. The open-air restaurant is great for pizza (baked in a wood-burning oven), seafood, and Neibaum-Coppola wines; a second restaurant, Gauguin, specializes in beach barbecue, and another small restaurant on the lagoon side serves Belizean fare such as rice and beans. Try to get a seafront cabana to catch the breeze, as there's no air-conditioning. **Pros:** Memorable resort, delightful outdoor showers, superb service. **Cons:** No a/c; restaurants, even the Belizean one, are surprisingly expensive. ⊠*Placencia Village* ☎*523/3244, 800/746–3743 in U.S. and Canada* ⊕*www.blancaneauxlodge.com* ⊅*17 cabanas, 7 2-bedroom cabanas, 1 house* ⅃*In-room: no a/c, no phone, Wi-Fi, no*

TV. In-hotel: 3 restaurants, 2 pools, spa, beachfront, diving, no eleva-tor, airport shuttle, no-smoking rooms ☰AE, MC, V ❛❍❜CP.

$$$$ 🏨**Chabil Mar Villas.** Chabil Mar means "beautiful sea" in Ketchi
★ Mayan, and the sea and almost 400 feet of beach here are indeed gorgeous at this gated condo development. The villas are tastefully designed and luxuriously furnished, down to wine corkscrews and ser-vice for eight. Although each unit is different, they're all upscale, with features such as marble floors, original art, and four-poster king beds. There's no restaurant, but you can have meals prepared and brought to your condo. **Pros:** Beautiful grounds, luxurious condos, lovely stretch of beach, every comfort and convenience is at hand. **Con:** No on-site restaurant. ✉*Peninsula Rd. north of Placencia Village* 📞*523/3606* ⊕*www.chabilmarvillas.com* 🛏*3 1- and 18 2-bedroom condos* ⌂*In-room: kitchen, DVD, Wi-Fi. In-hotel: pool, beachfront, water sports, no elevator, airport shuttle, no-smoking rooms* ☰AE, MC, V ❛❍❜CP.

$$$ 🏨**Mariposa Beach Suites.** Wings painted on posts in the gardenlike grounds signal that you've arrived at Mariposa (Spanish for "butter-fly"). The ground floor of this beachfront home has a brace of suites, each with a queen bed and kitchen. Pamela Braun, a Belize-based Amer-ican artist, painted the Mayan decorations on the walls. Out back is a small cottage, and on the 175-foot beach are thatch palapas with ham-mocks for lounging. **Pros:** Opposite of a big resort, a home away from home. **Con:** Restaurants and bars are a short taxi ride away. ✉*1½ mi (2½ km) north of Placencia* 📞*523/4069* ⊕*www.mariposabelize.com* 🛏*2 suites, 1 cottage* ⌂*In-room: no a/c, no phone, kitchen, no TV. In-hotel: beachfront, no elevator* ☰MC, V.

$$ 🏨**South Waters Resort.** This harborside resort has three condo units with full kitchens, air-conditioning, cable TV, DVD players, and walk-in clos-ets. There are also four cabanas without air-conditioning. The hotel's restaurant and bar, the Crow's Nest, is under a big thatch palapa with views of the sea. It has live entertainment at times and, with its ship's hull-shaped bar, has become a popular drinking spot. **Pros:** Variety of accommodations, Belizean-owned. Con: No parking nearby. ✉*In Bakader area, on beach* 📞*523/3308* ⊕*www.southwatersresort.com* 🛏*4 cabanas, 3 suites* ⌂*In-room: no a/c (some), no phone, kitchen (some), refrigerator (some), no TV (some). In-hotel: restaurant, bar, beachfront, watersports, no elevator* ☰MC, V.

$-$$ 🏨**Tradewinds.** If you're yearning for a cottage right on the beach but
★ don't want to spend a lot of money, then this little cottage colony is for you. Nine cabins, painted in Caribbean pastels, are small but pleasant. They have the best spot in the village, secluded about 20 feet from the sea at the peninsula's south point. Two of the cabins are "deluxe," with king beds and fully equipped kitchens; they go for BZ$222 dou-ble in-season. **Pro:** Charming cottages by the sea. **Cons:** Rooms are small, beach sand nearby is coarse, no parking nearby. ✉*South Point* 📞*523/3122* 🛏*9 cabins* ⌂*In-room: no a/c, no phone, refrigerator, no TV. In-hotel: beachfront, water sports, no elevator* ☰MC, V.

$-$$ 🏨**Westwind.** A favorite with anglers and beachcombers, this is a depend-able, no-frills spot to rest your head. The rooms are plain but spotlessly clean, and owner George Westby has a wealth of Placencia stories to

VACATION RENTAL HOUSES

In addition to hotels and beach resorts, Placencia has a growing number of vacation rentals, private homes, and apartments that are available on a weekly, sometimes daily, basis. Among these are:

Captain's House (☎ 523/4018) is a three-bedroom house on the beach on the north end of Placencia village, constructed almost entirely of mahogany (BZ$400 a night or BZ$2,500 weekly).

Casa del Sol (☎ No phone ⊕ www.casadelsolbelize.com), one of the most luxurious houses on the peninsula, has a swimming pool, beach, and four bedrooms and four baths, renting for BZ$1,400 a night (one- and two-bedroom sections of it are also available, starting at BZ$500 a night).

Colibri Beach Villa (☎ 523/3125 ⊕ www.colibribelize.com) is a lovely efficiency apartment at the north end of Placencia Village, with furniture and fixtures from Italy (BZ$340 a night).

Easy Living Apartments (☎ 523/3524 ⊕ www.easyliving.bz) consists of four modern, two-bedroom apartments in the center of the village, with fully equipped kitchens. Rates are BZ$300 nightly for two persons, BZ$465 for four persons.

Garden Cabanas (☎ 523/3481 ⊕ www.gardencabanas.com) are two small cottages with full kitchens tucked away in a garden setting in the village, a few minutes from the beach; BZ$540 weekly, BZ$90 nightly. Often full in season.

Las Amigas (☎ No phone ⊕ www.lasamigasbelize.com), two cabanas near the water in the village, with kitchenettes, bedroom, and veranda (BZ$800 weekly).

Toucan Lulu (☎ 523/3069 or 714/710–4905 in the U.S. ⊕ www.toucanlulu.com), has six beachfront, self-catering units in a quiet area of Placencia village, from BZ$90 to BZ$200 nightly in-season.

share. All rooms have a balcony, patio, or terrace with at least a partial view of the sea. **Pros:** What a beachcomber looks for, friendly and secure. **Con:** Not for the luxury-minded. ⊠ *Beachfront, near middle of Placencia Village* ☎ 523/3255 ⊕ *www.westwindhotel.com* ⟳ *12 rooms, 1 suite, 1 house* ⌂ *In-room: no a/c (some), no phone, refrigerator, no TV. In-hotel: beachfront, no elevator, public Internet* ☰ *MC, V.*

$ ⛱ **Harry's Cozy Cabañas.** Harry Eiley's three varnished-wood cabanas in the "Bakader" area with screened porches are as nice as Harry is, though they don't have quite as much character. Each has a kitchenette with a refrigerator. The hotel is in a quiet area away from the main part of the village. **Pro:** Comfortable, self-catering cabanas. **Cons:** Borders on funky, time for refurbishing. ⊠ *Placencia Harbor in Bakader area* ☎ 523/3234 ⊕ *www.cozycabanas.com* ⌂ *In-room: no a/c, no phone, kitchen, no TV. In-hotel: no elevator* ☰ *MC, V.*

¢–$ ⛱ **Seaspray Hotel.** There's no whirlpool or room service at this blue-and-white, wooden hotel. You just get a clean room (14 of them are on the beach) at a fair price. Your choice of rooms includes budget ones in the back to deluxe rooms with a porch, kitchenette, TV, and lovely sea views. There's also one cabin with a porch and kitchenette, about 30 feet from the sea. **Pros:** Good value, right in the middle of things. **Con:** Can be noisy at times. ⊠*Near middle of PlacenciaVillage* ☎*523/3148* ⊕*www.seasprayhotel.com* ↝*19 rooms, 1 cabin* ⚡*In-room: no a/c, no phone, kitchen (some), refrigerator (some), no TV (some). In-hotel: restaurant, beachfront, no elevator* ⊟*AE, D, MC, V.*

¢ 🏨**Lydia's Guest House.** For cheap and cheerful, plus friendly and clean, stay at this budget guesthouse in Placencia Village. Many guests become regulars. You can use the refrigerator and basic shared kitchen to prepare your meals. Owner Lydia Villaneuva also manages two nearby cabanas and one house, if you need more space. **Pros:** Can't beat the price, you have kitchen privileges. **Con:** Basic, backpacker-style accommodations. ⊠*North end of Placencia Village* ☎*523/3117* ⊕*www.placencia.com/members/lydiasguesthouse.htm* ↝*8 rooms, all with shared bath, 2 cabanas, 1 house* ⚡*In-room: no a/c, no phone, no TV* ⊟*MC, V.*

¢ 🏨**Manatee Inn.** Run by a friendly young Czech couple, the Manatee Inn is good value for your money. The rooms on the second floor of this wood-frame, two-story lodge are simply furnished, extremely clean, and have hardwood floors and private baths. Larger apartments, perfect for families, are on the first floor. **Pro:** Comfortable budget accommodations. Con: Beach is a couple of hundred feet away. ⊠*At north end of Placencia Village* ☎*523/4083* ⊕*www.manateeinn. com* ↝*6 rooms, 2 apartments* ⚡*In-room: no a/c, no phone, no TV (some)* ⊟*AE, MC, V.*

SHOPPING

The highlight of shopping on the Placencia peninsula is going to the grocery store, and the largest (Wallen's Market) is about the size of convenience store, so you get the picture. The larger resorts, including Inn at Robert's Grove and Turtle Inn, do have nice gift shops. In Placencia village, a few small gift shops, including Beach Bazaar and Sunova Beach Gift Shop, are on the sidewalk. **Beach Bazaar** (⊠*On sidewalk opposite Westwind Hotel* ☎*523/3113* ⊙*9 AM–1 PM and 4–7 PM*) has everything from souvenir shot glasses to arts and crafts.

Sunova Beach Gift Shop (⊠*On sidewalk near Tipsy Tuna* ☎*523/4060* ⊙*Mon.–Sat. 8:30 am–noon and 1– 6 pm)* sells T-shirts, wood carvings, and local art.

The oldest grocery in Placencia, **Wallen's Market** (⊠*Peninsula Road, across from soccer field* ☎*523/3128* ⊙*9 AM–5 PM*), has the basics, and it's even air-conditioned. Wallen's also has a pharmacy and hardware store.

NIGHTLIFE

Nightlife in Placencia is generally limited to drinking at a handful of local bars, although you may hear live music on weekends at the Tipsy Tuna or J-Byrds. **Barefoot Beach Bar at the Tipsy Tuna** (⊠*Beachfront, Pla-*

cencia ☎*523/3515* ⊙*Open 11:30* AM*–10* PM) is an open-air beach bar that draws the crowds. Live music some weekend nights.

Crows Nest (⊠*At South Waters Resort, Placencia Village in Bakader area* ☎*523/3412*) is in an open-air thatch palapa with a nautical theme. The bar, made to look like part of a ship's hull, is a pleasant spot to sip a cold one with a view of the water. **J-Byrds Bar** (⊠*At docks, Placencia Village* ☎*523/3412*) attracts a fairly hard-drinking crowd, and there's a dance party on Friday nights.

The popular **Tipsy Tuna Sports Bar** (⊠*Placencia Village, on beach* ☎*523/3515*) has live music some weekend nights, and you can always shoot pool or watch sports on a big-screen TV. There's karaoke every Thursday; the place is dark on Tuesday.

THE OUTDOORS

FISHING

The fly-fishing on the flats off the cayes east of Placencia is some of Belize's best. This is one of the top areas in the world for permit. The area from Dangriga south to Gladden Caye is called "Permit Alley," and the mangrove lagoons off Punta Ycacos and other points south of Placencia are also terrific permit fisheries. You'll encounter plentiful tarpon—they flurry 10 deep in the water at times—as well as snook. You can also catch king mackerel, barracuda, wahoo, and cubera snapper. However, a lingering impact of Hurricane Iris in 2001 is that there are no longer any good bonefish flats close to shore at Placencia. Bonefish are still around, but they're now several miles away, off the cayes.

GUIDES

Most of the better hotels also can arrange guides, many of whom pair with specific hotels. For example, Arthur Vernon works almost exclusively for Turtle Inn. Fishing guides in Placencia are down-to-earth, self-taught guys who have fished these waters for years. They use small skiffs called pangas. The many excellent guides in Placencia include Wyatt Cabral, Julian Cabral, Egbert Cabral, Bruce Leslie, Eworth Garbutt, Daniel Cabral, Dermin Shivers, and Arthur Vernon. For more information and help matching a local guide to your specific needs, get in touch with **Mary Toy at Destinations Belize** (☎*523/4018* ⊕*www.destinationsbelize.com*). You may also want to talk with **Wyatt Cabral** (☎*523/3534* ⊕*www.wyattsfishing.com*). He's a native of Placencia who is considered one of the best fly-fishing guides. Another well-known fly-fishing guide is **Julian Cabral** (☎*610/1068*). Or contact **Bill Kiene at Kiene's Fly Shop** (☎*916/486–9958, 800/400–0359 in U.S.* ⊕*www.kiene.com*), who has been to Placencia many times and is very familiar with fishing conditions here.

Expect to pay around BZ$500–BZ$750 for a full day of fly-fishing, spin casting, or trolling. That includes your guide, boat, and lunch. If you're on a budget, you can rent a canoe and try fishing the Placencia lagoon on your own, where you may catch snook, barracuda, and possibly other fish.

GEAR

The guides usually provide trolling gear for free, but they charge about BZ$40 a day for light spin-casting tackle gear, and you may be happier with your own spinning gear. If you're serious about fly-fishing, of course you'll want to bring your own gear. For fly-fishing for snook, permit, and tarpon, the experts recommend you bring a 9/10 weight rod, 9-foot, 20-pound leader (80-pound shock leader for tarpon), clear slow-sinking line, and extra spool weight-forward floating line. Bring Clouser Half and Half, Berke's Juvineel, Cockroach, Black Death, Bluewater Mullet, Del's Merkin, Mangrove Critter, and other flies. For bonefish, you'll want a 7- to 9-weight rod, 7- to 9-weight floating line, and Boggle Head, Bonefish Bitters, and Flash Shrimp flies.

If you fish with live bait, the primary baitfish are silversides, shrimp, and crab. Lures and plastic baits should mimic these baitfish.

For reef and tarpon spin fishing, you'll need some fairly heavy reels, such as a Penn Spinfisher 5500 or 6500 Saltwater Spinning Reel with 25-pound test line. For tarpon, bring gummy minnows, in all colors. For bones, bring a Penn 4500 SS or similar with 6- to 10-pound test line. Leave your surf rod at home, as it will be of little use in Placencia. Don't forget to bring polarized sunglasses, a good fishing hat, insect repellent, lots of sunscreen and lip salve, and, if you're wading, thick-soled flats boots.

SAILING

The Moorings (⊠*Placencia Harbor, Placencia* ☎*523/3206, 888/952–8420 in U.S.* ⊕*www.moorings.com*) offers bareboat catamaran charters, with a week's sailing going for around BZ$8,000–BZ$14,000. **Next Wave Sailing** (⊠*Placencia Harbor, Placencia* ☎*523/3391* ⊕*www.nextwavesailing.com*) offers day and sunset cruises, with snorkeling, along with private charters, on a 50-foot catamaran. Day sails are BZ$176 per person and include drinks, lunch, and snacks. Sunset cruise is BZ$99. *Talisman* (⊠*Placencia Harbor, Placencia*) is a 52-foot ketch offering day sailing trips for BZ$240 per person or longer trips from BZ$540 to BZ$650 including meals and drinks. Also available are fully crewed charters on several other boats, from BZ$1,000 to BZ$2,300 per night for 2 to 12 persons. **TMM Placencia** (⊠*Placencia Harbor, Placencia* ☎*523/3586, 800/633–0155 in U.S.* ⊕*www.sailtmm.com*), also in San Pedro, expanded into Placencia in 2003. Rates vary, depending on boat type and time of year, but range from BZ$5,400 to more than BZ$18,000 a week, not including provisions, cruising fee (BZ$30 per person), and incidentals. Skippers and cooks are each an additional BZ$200 per day.

SCUBA DIVING

This far south, the reef is as much as 20 mi (33 km) offshore, necessitating boat rides of at least 45 minutes to reach dive sites. Because this part of the reef has fewer cuts and channels, it's also more difficult to get out to the seaward side, where you'll find the best diving. As a result, most of the diving in this region is done from offshore cayes, which are surrounded by small reefs, usually with gently sloping drop-offs of about 80–100 feet. This isn't the place for spectacular wall dives—you're better off staying in the north or heading out to the atolls. Near Moho Caye, southeast of Placencia, you'll find brilliant red-and-yellow corals and sponges that rarely appear elsewhere in Belize. Laughingbird Caye, Belize's smallest marine reserve, is a popular spot for snorkeling. Whale sharks, gentle giants of the sea, appear off Placencia, in the Gladden Spit area, in late spring and early summer. You can snorkel or dive with them on day trips (around BZ$160–BZ$300) from Placencia. The best time to see whale sharks is three or four days before and after a full moon, April through early June.

Diving costs a little more in Placencia than elsewhere. All-day trips, including two-tank dive, all gear, and lunch, run BZ$150–BZ$210. Snorkeling trips start at around BZ$80, and a snorkeling tour is about BZ$100–BZ$120 for a trip that lasts almost all day.

GUIDES

Most of the larger resorts, like the Inn at Robert's Grove and Turtle Inn, have good dive shops and also offer snorkel trips at competitive prices. Brian Young runs the respected **Seahorse Dive Shop** (☎ *523/3166*). **Splash Dive Shop** (☎ *523/3345*) offers dive and snorkel trips.For snorkeling trips and gear there's also **Ocean Motion** (☎ *523/3363*), on the sidewalk in the heart of Placencia Village (by the grocery store). **South Belize Reef and Jungle** (☎ *523/3330*), across from Atlantic Bank in the village and at Laru Beya resort, also runs dive and snorkel trips.

THE SOUTHERN COAST ESSENTIALS

TRANSPORTATION

BY AIR

You'll arrive fresher if you fly. From Belize City (both international and municipal airports) there are frequent flights to Dangriga and Placencia. There are more than 20 flights daily between Belize City and Placencia. Both Tropic Air and Maya Island Air fly from Belize City (BZ$140 one way from the municipal airport, BZ$164 from the international airport). The airstrip is about 2 mi (3 km) north of Placencia's center, so you'll probably want to take a taxi (BZ$12 from the center of the village) if your hotel doesn't provide a shuttle.

The same airlines also fly from Belize City to Dangriga (around BZ$72 from the municipal airport, BZ$109 from the international airport). Maya Island Air also has flights to Savannah airstrip across the Placencia Lagoon at Independence/Big Creek (about BZ$150 from the municipal airport, BZ$173 from the international airport) and will stop at the airstrip near Kanantik on demand. There's no airstrip at Hopkins. If going there, fly to Dangriga.

Maya Island Air offers flights between the Savannah airstrip and San Pedro Sula, Honduras. They cost BZ$250 one way.

Tropical Storm Arthur

Hurricane and tropical storm season isn't supposed to start in Belize until June 1, but in 2008 the season started a day early, to devastating effect. Tropical Storm Arthur, which formed just off the coast of Belize on May 31, 2008, and quickly moved ashore, in a few hours dumped up to 15 inches of rain on the country, from the far north to far south. At least seven Belizeans in southern Belize were reported drowned. Early estimates of the financial cost range up to US$50 million and higher.

Government officials said the flooding from the storm was the worst in Belize in at least three decades, with some areas under water that had never been flooded before. Several villages, including Gales Point in Belize District and Sittee in Stann Creek District, were inundated with flood waters. A number of villages in Orange Walk and Corozal districts along the Northern Highway also received flooding. Ambergris Caye and Caye Caulker had some moderate flooding, and several dozen small

boats sank. A large part of Belize's rice crop was destroyed.

Happily, Belize's tourism industry escaped mostly unscathed. Nearly all hotels, lodges and resorts stayed open or quickly reopened after the storm. Roads and other infrastructure in popular tourist areas were generally undamaged. One impact for visitors may be the loss of the Kendall Bridge over the Sittee River, at Mile 13.7 of the Southern Highway. This major bridge, located between Maya Centre and Hopkins, was washed away, for a few weeks severing the only road access to points south, including Placencia and Punta Gorda. At this writing, a temporary causeway is in place over the Sittee River, allowing vehicular traffic including buses to cross. A permanent new bridge is expected to be completed in mid-2009. Check locally before driving south of the Hopkins area. Air service to all airstrips in the south continues normally.

—Lan Sluder

You'll generally fly in small turbine or prop aircraft, such as the 13-passenger Cessna Caravan C208. Some flights from Belize City make multiple stops—at Dangriga, Placencia, and sometimes Big Creek—as they fly south to Punta Gorda, while others are nonstop. In any event, the total time you'll spend in the airplane is short, less than an hour to Placencia. Contacts **Maya Island Air** (⊠ *Placencia airstrip* ☎ *523/3475* ⊕ *www.mayaairways.com*). **Tropic Air** (⊠ *Placencia airstrip* ☎ *523/3410* ⊕ *www.tropicair.com*).

BY BOAT & FERRY

There are no scheduled boat or ferry services from Belize City to points along the Southern Coast, nor are there any scheduled water taxis or ferries between those points or to offshore cayes. However, there's a scheduled water taxi, a small boat named the *Hokey Pokey*, between Placencia Village and Mango Creek and Independence, two adjacent villages on the west side of Placencia Lagoon. With a combined population of about 3,000, the villages of Mango Creek and Independence are home to residents who work at Big Creek, a nearby deep-water port that ships bananas, citrus, and, now, oil from Belize's new wells in Spanish Lookout, Cayo. There's little of interest to most tourists here. Currently the boat departs the M&M Texaco dock in Placencia Village at 6:45 AM, 10 AM, 12:30 PM, 2:30 PM, 4 PM, 5 PM, and 6 PM (the 6 PM boat doesn't run on Sundays.). From Independence/Mango Creek it departs at 6:30 AM, 7:30 AM, 8 AM, 11 AM, noon, 2:30 PM, and 4:30 PM. One-way fare is BZ$5. For information, call 523/2376. The schedule changes frequently, so ask locally.

From Placencia, a weekly boat, the *Express,* runs to Puerto Cortes, Honduras, with a stop in Big Creek across the lagoon to clear immigration and customs. The boat departs Placencia at 9:30 AM Friday, arriving in Honduras at 2 PM. It returns Monday from Puerto Cortes at 10 AM, arriving in Placencia at 2 PM. Fare is BZ$100 per person one way. You can purchase tickets and make reservations directly or at the BTIA Placencia Tourism Center.

From Dangriga, another boat charter service runs twice weekly to Puerto Cortes. The boats are the *Nesymein Neydy,* a 47-foot cabin cruiser that can accommodate 60 people, and *Nesymein Neydy II,* a 32-foot cruiser that can carry up to 30. One boat departs from the North Riverside dock in Dangriga at 9 AM Thursday, stopping in Placencia to pick up passengers at the M&M Texaco dock at 11 AM, and arriving in Puerto Cortes around 2 PM. On Saturday, the boat boards in Dangriga at 8:30 AM and does not stop in Placencia. Boats return from Puerto Cortes from the fish market in Laguna at 8:30 AM on Monday and 9 AM on Tuesday. The trip costs BZ$100 per person one way.

The boat trips to Puerto Cortes can be very rough and wet. If you're prone to seasickness, take antinausea medications and avoid the trip entirely in stormy weather.

Also from Dangriga, boats go out daily to Tobacco Caye. There are no fixed schedules, but the boats generally leave around 9 to 9:30 AM, and the fare is BZ$35 per person one way. Ask at the Riverside Café.

Contacts **Hokey Pokey** (⊠ *Placencia* ☎ *523/2376*). **Express** (⊠ *Placencia* ☎ *523/4045*). **Nesymein Neydy Charter Boats** (⊠ *North Riverside, Dangriga* ☎ *522/3227* ⊕ *www.belizenet.com/boatcharters*).

BY BUS

In the south, National Transport and James Bus Line run from Belize City via Belmopan to Dangriga and Independence and then Punta Gorda. Other, smaller lines also cover this route. Schedules are subject to change, but James Bus Line has about five to six buses daily, with departures starting at 5:30 AM and ending at 5:30 PM. Two of the James Line buses leave Dangriga at 11:30 AM and 5:15 PM daily and stop in Placencia, while the other buses stop in Independence across the lagoon, en route to Punta Gorda. National Transport also has several buses a day from Belize City to Dangriga, with two buses (at 10:30 AM and 4 PM) daily from Dangriga to Placencia. Fares from Belize City are around BZ$15 to Dangriga and BZ$20 to Placencia (BZ$5 from

Dangriga to Placencia). *(See Hokey Pokey ferry schedule above, in the Boat & Ferry Travel section.)*

With connections, the trip from Belize City to Dangriga and Hopkins is three to four hours; Placencia is around five to six hours or more, depending on the number of stops. Buses are usually old U.S. school buses or ancient Greyhound buses, are often crowded, and don't have air-conditioning or restrooms. The James Bus Line buses generally are in the best condition. You'll arrive much more refreshed if you go by air—the flight's less than an hour.

The main bus stop in Placencia is in the village near the Shell station. Some buses also stop at Hopkins, near the T-intersection from the Southern Highway. The bus station in Dangriga is seven blocks south of town on the main road, near the Texaco and Shell stations.

Contacts **James Bus Line** (⊠ *7 King St., Punta Gorda* ☎ *702/2049).* **National Transport Services** (⊠ *West Collet Canal, Belize City* ☎ *227/6372).*

BY CAR

To get to Placencia, head southeast from Belmopan on the Hummingbird Highway. The highway is one of Belize's best roads, as well as its most scenic. On your right rise the jungle-covered Maya Mountains, largely free of signs of human habitation except for the occasional field of corn or beans. As you approach Dangriga you'll see large citrus groves.

Although the so-called Manatee Highway or Coastal Road (it actually runs several miles from the coast), which begins at Mile 30 of the Western Highway, is a shortcut to Dangriga and points south, the road is unpaved. It's dusty in dry weather and muddy after rains. Occasionally the wood bridges on the road wash out. The road is so accident-prone that some car rental companies prohibit renters from driving the road, and others increase the deductible you pay if you have a wreck on the road. Our advice: take the Hummingbird Highway.

The Southern Highway is now beautifully paved from Dangriga south, except for a short section near Golden Stream. Work began in early 2008 on paving this section. The turnoff to Hopkins is at Mile 10 of the Southern Highway, and the turn to Placencia is at Mile 22.2. From the Southern Highway to Placencia most of the 25-mi (42-km) road is unpaved and can be treacherous after rains, even for four-wheel-drive vehicles.

There are now two gas stations in Placencia Village, and one at Riversdale. Dangriga has several gas stations.

Two small local outfits, Barefoot Rentals and Peninsula Rentals rent cars in Placencia. Rates are around BZ$160 a day for a Geo Tracker or Isuzu Trooper. Barefoot will drop the car to you at your hotel or the Placencia airstrip. Also, Budget and other rental agencies in Belize City will deliver a car to Placencia, Hopkins, or Dangriga for a fee of around BZ$100–BZ$140.

Contact **Barefoot Rentals** (⊠ *Placencia* ☎ *607/5125* ⊕ *www.barefootrentals.net).*

BY TAXI

If you need a ride to the airport in Dangriga, call Neal's Taxi. Fare from downtown to the airstrip at the town's north end costs about BZ$6–BZ$8. Taxis are more expensive in Placencia, given the relatively short distances involved. It's BZ$50 one way for one to three persons and BZ$15 per person for four or more from Placencia Village to the north end of the peninsula (where The Placencia is); BZ$40 one way from Placencia Village to Maya Beach for one to three persons and BZ$15 per person for four or more; BZ$12 for one person and BZ$6 per person for two or more from Placencia Village to the airstrip. Your hotel can arrange a taxi for you, or call Percy Neal or Samuel Burgess.

A shuttle van service runs from time to time up and down the peninsula. When the van operates, fare is around BZ$4 per person. Ask at your hotel if it's running, but don't count on it.

Contacts **Neal's Taxi** (⊠ *1 St. Vincent St., Dangriga* ☎ *522/3309*). **Percy Neal** (⊠ *Placencia* ☎ *523/3131*). **Samuel Burgess** (⊠ *Placencia* ☎ *607/2711*).

CONTACTS & RESOURCES

BANKS & EXCHANGE SERVICES

There are three banks in Placencia. Atlantic Bank has an office on the road just north of Placencia Village, as well as a second ATM in Placencia village, and Scotia Bank is also in the village. Belize Bank has an office at Placencia Point. All three banks have ATMs that accept foreign-issued cards.

Belize Bank in Dangriga accepts foreign-issued ATM cards on the PLUS, CIRRUS, and Visa Electron networks. First Caribbean International Bank in Dangriga has an ATM that accepts foreign cards on the Visa Electron network. There are no banks in Hopkins.

Banks **Atlantic Bank** (⊠ *Peninsula Rd., Placencia* ☎ *523/3386*). **Belize Bank** (⊠ *24 St. Vincent St., Dangriga* ☎ *522/2903* ⊠ *Placencia Point, Placencia* ☎ *523/3144*). **First Caribbean International Bank** (⊠ *Commerce St., Dangriga* ☎ *522/2015*). **Scotia Bank** (⊠ *Main St., Placencia* ☎ *523/3277*).

EMERGENCIES

Although Placencia has a small medical clinic with a physician and nurse, plus an acupuncturist, a part-time chiropractor, and a natural healer, and Seine Bight, Hopkins, and Independence have medical clinics, for serious medical attention you should go to Dangriga or Belize City. The Belize Emergency Response Team, based in Belize City, provides air transportation all over the country in emergency cases. A pharmacy with very limited supplies is at Wallen's store in Placencia.

Hospitals **Belize Emergency Response Team** (⊠ *Placencia* ☎ *223/3292*). **Dangriga Regional Hospital** (⊠ *Stann Creek District Hwy., Dangriga* ☎ *522/2078*). **Independence Medical Center** (⊠ *Independence* ☎ *523/2167*). **Placencia Medical Clinic** (⊠ *In center of village near primary school, Placencia* ☎ *523/3326*).

INTERNET, MAIL & SHIPPING

The Placencia post office is on the second floor of a wooden building at the south end of the sidewalk. It's usually open 8:30–noon and 1–4 weekdays. The Dangriga post office is near the Bonefish Hotel, at the south end of town. Currently there's no post office in Hopkins.

Many resorts on the Southern Coast now offer Internet access, either wireless or in Internet rooms. In addition, there are several Internet cafés in Placencia Village, and in Dangriga and near Hopkins. In Placencia, the Secret Garden offers free Wi-Fi for customers of the restaurant and coffeehouse. The Purple Space Monkey also offers free Wi-Fi for customers. Elsewhere, you'll pay around BZ$10 an hour for access.

Contacts **Dangriga Post Office** (⊠ *Near Bonefish Hotel* ☎ *522/2035*). **Placencia Post Office** (⊠ *South end of sidewalk* ☎ *523/3104*). **De Tatch** (⊠ *In center of village, Placencia* ☎ *503/3385*). **Placencia Office Supply** (⊠ *Placencia* ☎ *523/3205*). **Purple Space Monkey** (⊠ *Placencia* ☎ *523/4094*). **Secret Garden Restaurant and Coffeehouse** (⊠ *Placencia, behind Wallen's Market* ☎ *523/3617*). **Sittee River Internet** (⊠ *Sittee River Village* ☎ *603/8358*). **Val's Laundry** (⊠ *Mahogany and Sharp Sts., Dangriga* ☎ *502/3324*).

SAFETY

Most visitors say they feel safe on the Placencia peninsula and in Hopkins. However, petty theft is a perennial problem, especially in Placencia Village. Many budget travelers report thefts from their hotel rooms. A few Placencia hotels, and most of the more upscale resorts up the peninsula and in Hopkins, have security guards. Visitors may get hassled a little on the streets of Dangriga, and care should be exercised if walking around town after dark.

TOURS

Altogether, Placencia has about 75 licensed tour guides. Most of the guides, except the fishing guides, work on a contract basis for resorts or tour operators. These tour guides and operators offer dive and snorkel trips to Laughing Bird or other cayes and to the Barrier Reef, wildlife tours to Monkey River, birding tours to Red Bank, hiking trips to Cockscomb Basin Wildlife Sanctuary, and excursions to Mayan ruins such as Mayflower, Nim Li Punit, or Lubaantun.

The larger resorts on the peninsula, including Inn at Robert's Grove, Turtle Inn, Nautical Inn, Rum Point Inn, and others, offer a variety of tours and trips, using tour guides they have come to trust. ⇨ *See Where to Stay & Eat sections, above, for contact information.*

Mary Toy's Destinations Belize is a full-service tour and travel operation, offering fishing, boating, sailing, and other trips with some of the best guides in the region, along with hotel reservations. Mary is a former attorney from St. Louis who left the practice of law to practice her fishing and beachcombing skills in Belize. Other tour operators include Caribbean Tours and Joy Tours.

For first-time visitors, taking a couple of sea and land tours is a good way to become familiar with what the area offers. If you have a rental car, you can do some of the trips, such as to Cockscomb, Mayflower, and the ruins near Punta Gorda, on your own. To book tours and trips, check with your hotel or walk along the sidewalk in Placencia Village, where several of the tour operators have small shops. You can also check with the Belize Tourism Industry Association (BTIA) visitor information office. You'll probably pay a little less by booking in the village instead of at your hotel, but the savings may not be worth the effort.

For the more adventurous traveler, Toadal Adventures, one of the top operators on the Southern Coast, has excellent biking, hiking, and kayaking tours.

Day trips to Nim Li Punit and Lubaantun Mayan sites near Punta Gorda cost around BZ$150–BZ$160 per person, while day trips to the Mayflower ruins and waterfalls run about BZ$120. Half-day snorkeling trips inside the reef, to Laughing Bird Caye and other snorkel spots, are around BZ$100–BZ$110. A full day of snorkeling on the reef is around BZ$120–BZ$130. Boat trips to Monkey River are around BZ$90, while a boat excursion on the Placencia Lagoon to look for manatees is around BZ$80. Cockscomb trips run about BZ$60. Most full-day trips include a picnic lunch. If you're going to an area with an admission fee, such as Cockscomb, the fee is additional.

Contacts **Caribbean Tours** (⊠ *Placencia* ☎ *253/3481* ⊕ *www.ctbelize.com*). **Destinations Belize** (⊠ *Placencia* ☎ *253/4018* ⊕ *www.destinationsbelize.com*). **Joy Tours** (⊠ *Placencia* ☎ *253/3325* ⊕ *www.belizewithjoy.com*). **Toadal Adventures Belize** (⊠ *Point Placencia, Placencia* ☎ *253/3207* ⊕ *www.toadaladventure.com*).

VISITOR INFORMATION

The Placencia office of the Belize Tourism Industry Association is in a new location on the main road between the Purple Space Monkey and Tutti-Fruitti Gelato. The BTIA publishes the *Placencia Breeze,* an informative monthly newspaper, and has a very helpful Web site listing all accommodations, restaurants, and bars, ⊕ *www.placencia.com.* Another extremely helpful site on Placencia is put together by local resident Mary Toy, ⊕ *www.destinationsbelize.com.* Hopkins has several interesting Web sites put together by local residents, including ⊕ *www.hopkinsbelize.com* and ⊕ *www.cometohopkins.com.*

Information **Belize Tourism Industry Association** (⊠ *In a new location on the main road in Placencia village, next to Tutti-Fruitti Placencia* ☎ *523/4045*).

The Deep South

WORD OF MOUTH

"There are trips daily from Placencia to Lubaantun and Nim Li Punit, both in the Maya villages
of the Toledo District. I think both are impressive.
Lubaantun for its beauty and Nim Li Punit for its
extraordinary stelae."

—Katie Valk

By Lan Sluder   **FOR MANY YEARS, ILL-MAINTAINED ROADS,** spotty communications, and the country's highest annual rainfall—as much as 180 to 200
inches—kept Belize's southernmost region off-limits to all but the most
adventurous of travelers. The precipitation hasn't changed (you'll need
boots and an umbrella in the rainy season), but with improvements to
the Southern Highway—all of the highway has been beautifully paved,
except for a short stretch near Golden Stream—and the opening of new
lodges and hotels, the riches of Toledo District (often pronounced with
a short "e," Toh-LEH-doh, by local residents, though others pronounce
it with a long "e") are finally becoming accessible.

Toledo has Belize's only extensive, genuine rain forest, and its canopy
of trees conceals a plethora of wildlife, including jaguars, margays,
tapirs, and loads of tropical birds. The area's rich Mayan heritage is
just being unearthed, with archaeologists at work at Pusilha, Nim Li
Punit, Uxbenká, and elsewhere. Contemporary Maya—mainly Mopan
and Ketchi—still live in villages around the district, as they have for
centuries, along with the Garífuna, Creoles, East Indians, and others
who constitute the Toledo population of 30,000.

Don't expect to come to Toledo and lounge on the sand. The area
doesn't have good beaches except a few accessible only by boat: the
coastal waters of the Gulf of Honduras are almost invariably muddy
from silt deposited by numerous rivers flowing from the Maya Mountains. What *can* you expect? Exceptional fishing (Toledo has one of
the world's best permit fisheries) and cayes off the coast that are well
worth exploring. The closest are the Snake Cayes; farther out are the
Sapodilla Cayes, the largest of which is Hunting Caye. A horseshoe-
shape bay at the caye's eastern end has beaches of white coral where
turtles nest in late summer.

Besides all the usual luscious tropical fruits, rice and cacao (chocolate) are grown in Toledo. Around local Mayan villages sizable quantities of organic cacao are cultivated. Most is shipped abroad and used
in the Maya Gold brand of chocolate bars. In 2007, a cacao festival
was organized, and it will continue annually in May (dates vary—see
⊕ www.toledochocolate.com).

ORIENTATION & PLANNING

ORIENTATION

The main road to the Deep South is the newly paved Southern Highway, which runs 100 mi (164 km) from the intersection of the Hummingbird Highway to Punta Gorda (PG). Only a 9-mi (15-km) section,
from Golden Stream at Mile 68.6 to Big Falls at Mile 77.6, is unpaved
and sometimes rough going. For the paving of this last stretch, con-
tracts have been signed, work has begun, and by the time you get to
Toledo the road work should have been completed.

TOP REASONS TO GO

RAIN FORESTS

The greenest, lushest jungles in Belize are in Toledo, fed by heavy rains and temperatures that stay mostly above 70°F. Red Ginger, bright yellow-and-orange Lobster Claw, masses of pink on Mayflower trees, and orchids of all colors splash the emerald green landscape. Scarlet-rumped Tanagers, Black-headed Trogans, Green Kingfishers, and Roseate Spoonbill join hundreds of other birds in the rain forest cacophony.

OUTPOST ATMOSPHERE

Punta Gorda has that end-of-the-road feel, as if this is the last outpost on Earth. Yes, the Southern Highway does end here—but it's more than that. Here you get the feeling that even in today's world of almost 7 billion people, there are still places where you could, if you needed to, hide out for awhile and not be found.

FISHING

Among serious anglers, Southern Belize has a reputation for having one of the world's great permit fisheries, and for its large populations of tarpon and bonefish. The flats off Punta Ycacos are prime permit and bonefish grounds, and freshwater lagoons near Punta Negra hold snook, small tarpon, and other fish.

MAYA & GARÍFUNA CULTURE

Other areas of Belize (not to mention Guatemala and Honduras) may have more spectacular ruins than Toledo, but where the Deep South shines is in its contemporary Mayan culture. Dozens of Mopan and Ketchi villages exist much as they have for centuries, as do the Garífuna villages of Punta Negra and Barranco and the town of Punta Gorda (PG). You can visit some of the villages and even stay awhile in guesthouses or homestay programs.

As you travel south on the Southern Highway, the Great Southern Pine Ridge is on your right, starting at about Mile 55. Farther in the distance are the Maya Mountains. On your left is the Caribbean Sea, and farther south, beyond Punta Negra, the Gulf of Honduras.

Branching off the Southern Highway are mostly unpaved roads, some barely more than muddy trails, that go to small villages. On the Southern Highway about 33 km (20 mi) north of Punta Gorda, at about Mile 83, you'll come to an intersection. If you turn left you'll stay on the Southern Highway to PG; if you turn right on the San Antonio Road, you'll go to Lubaantun, San Antonio Village, and other Mayan villages. To reach PG directly, continue to Mile 95, turn right on Saddleback Road, and go 5 mi (8 km). To enter from the prettier Bay of Honduras side, stay straight and go the same distance.

PLANNING

SAFETY

Punta Gorda is generally a safe, friendly town. Indeed, Toledo District has the lowest murder rate in Belize, and one of the lowest rates of other serious crimes. With normal precautions, you should have no problem walking around, even after dark. The nearby Mayan villages

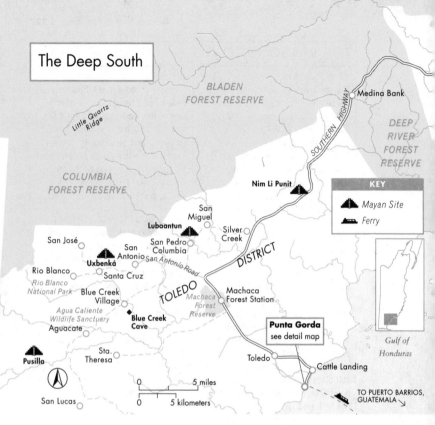

The Deep South

BLADEN FOREST RESERVE

Little Quartz Ridge

COLUMBIA FOREST RESERVE

Medina Bank

DEEP RIVER FOREST RESERVE

SOUTHERN HIGHWAY

Nim Li Punit

San Miguel

Lubaantun

Silver Creek

San José

San Pedro Columbia

San Antonio

San Antonio Road

DISTRICT

KEY

Mayan Site

Ferry

Uxbenká

Rio Blanco

Rio Blanco National Park

Santa Cruz

Blue Creek Village

Agua Caliente Wildlife Sanctuary

Aguacate

Blue Creek Cave

TOLEDO

Machaca Forest Reserve

Machaca Forest Station

Punta Gorda
see detail map

Pusilla

Sta. Theresa

Toledo

Cattle Landing

Gulf of Honduras

San Lucas

0   5 miles

0   5 kilometers

TO PUERTO BARRIOS, GUATEMALA

are also relatively free of crime. Guatemala's Caribbean coast, just a short boat ride away, has a reputation for lawlessness, which can occasionally spill over into Toledo.

WHEN TO GO

June through September is the peak of the rainy season in Toledo. Unless you love a good thunderstorm, come between December and April, when most of Toledo gets only about an inch of rain a week.

RESTAURANTS & CUISINE

With relatively few tourists coming to the region, and most local residents unable to afford to eat out regularly, restaurants in Toledo often are here today and gone tomorrow. Those that do make it are usually simple, mostly basic spots serving local fish and staples like stew chicken with beans and rice. Prices are low—you'll rarely pay more than BZ$20 for dinner. Nearly all Toledo restaurants are in PG.

ABOUT THE HOTELS

The entire Toledo District has only about 30 hotels, most of them in and around Punta Gorda. Most are small and owner-run. You can usually show up without reservations and look for a place that suits you. Clean rooms are under BZ$100, and for BZ$150–BZ$200 you can stay at a charming small inn. Several jungle lodges have rates of BZ$300 or more.

WHAT IT COSTS IN BELIZE DOLLARS				
¢	$	$$	$$$	$$$$
RESTAU-RANTS	under BZ$8	BZ$8–BZ$15	BZ$15–BZ$25	BZ$25–BZ$$50	over BZ$50
HOTELS	under BZ$100	BZ$100–BZ$200	BZ$200–BZ$300	BZ$300–BZ$500	over BZ$500

Restaurant prices are per person for a main course at dinner. Hotel prices are for two people in a standard double room, including tax and service.

PUNTA GORDA

102 mi (164 km) south of Placencia.

Most journeys south begin in the region's administrative center, Punta Gorda. PG (as it's affectionately known) isn't your typical tourist destination. Though it has a wonderful setting on the Gulf of Honduras, it has no real beaches. There are few shops of interest to visitors, only one tiny museum, a few simple restaurants, and little nightlife. Don't expect many tourist services.

So why, you ask, come to PG? First, simply because it isn't on the main tourist track. The accoutrements of mass tourism are still, refreshingly, missing here. Schoolchildren may wave at you, and residents will strike up a conversation with you. Toledo has stunning natural attractions too, such as clean rivers for swimming and cave systems with Mayan artifacts that rival those in the Cayo district. Also, with several new hotels to choose from, it's a comfortable base from which to visit surrounding Mayan villages, offshore cayes, and the high bush of the Deep South.

Founded in 1867 by Confederate immigrants from the United States and later settled by missionaries, Punta Gorda once had 12 sugar estates, each with its own mill. After World War II, Great Britain built an important military base here, but when that closed in 1994, the linchpin of the local economy was yanked out. With some increase in tourist dollars and foreigners' growing interest in real estate here, PG is starting to pick up again but hasn't lost its frontier atmosphere.

☾ If you're interested in learning more about the Creole culture, stop by the **Kriol Museum.** It's just a room in the house of popular singer Lila Vernon, but it has some interesting displays about Creole history and music, along with some items typical of Creole households. FYI: Kriol is the spelling of Creole used by the National Kriol Council of Belize. ⊠*6 Front St.* ☎*702/2140* ✉*Donations accepted.*

THE OUTDOORS

Punta Gorda and Toledo offer great opportunities for outdoor activities—fishing, diving, snorkeling, sea and river kayaking, and caving. The problem has been that due to so few visitors to the Deep South, and the limited number of tour operators, visitors often arrived to find that few tours were actually available on a given day, or if they were running, tended to cost much more than in other parts of Belize. An attempt to schedule tours to always run on specific days—for example, to Port Honduras Marine Reserve for snorkeling on Mondays and to Blue Creek for caving on Tuesdays—has fizzled out. Still, with tourism slowly increasing, more tours are being offered and most prices are reasonable. Try to go with a group of four to six, as many tours have a price based on a group of up to six people, not per person.

> ### TO MARKET, TO MARKET
>
> On market days—Monday, Wednesday, Friday, and Saturday, with Wednesday and Saturday usually being the largest—the town comes to life with vendors from nearby Mayan villages and even from Guatemala. They pack the downtown market area with colorful fruit and vegetable stands. Fresh fish also are sold in a building at the market, daily except Sunday, and for a small fee you can have your fish cleaned.

Among the most popular tours are those to the Snake Cayes. An all-day trip of snorkeling, fishing, and beach bumming costs around BZ$500 for up to four people, plus the BZ$10 per person Port Honduras Reserve entrance fee. Another popular tour combines Blue Creek caves and Agua Caliente Wildlife Sanctuary; it's around BZ$130 per person, with a minimum of two people. Tours to Lubaantun, often in combination with a visit to Rio Blanco National Park and its waterfall, are around BZ$130 a person (two-person minimum).

ALL THINGS GREEN

☼ Hot springs, fresh-water lagoons, caves, and hiking trails dot the **Agua Caliente Wildlife Sanctuary,** a good-size nature preserve. You can fish here as well. ⊠ *About 13 mi (21 km) west of Punta Gorda* ✛ *From Punta Gorda, take Southern Hwy. 10 mi (16 km) north. Turn left on Laguna Rd. and go 3 mi (5 km). The trail to the wildlife sanctuary begins in the village. Ask a local resident to show you where it begins.*

☼ Ever been fresh-water snorkeling? Check out the Bladen River in the **Bladen Forest Reserve.** The river snakes through the reserve, allowing for excellent kayaking, canoeing, swimming, and, yes, freshwater snorkeling. Tours are given by interns from the Belize Foundation for Research and Environmental Education (BFREE), which is on the reserve's grounds. Camping and simple bunkhouse accommodations are available at BZ$60 per person, meals included. To visit Bladen Forest Reserve, contact BFREE. ⊠ *Off Mile 59, Southern Hwy.* ☎ *614/3896.*

☼ One of the largest undisturbed tropical rain forest areas in Central America is the **Columbia Forest Reserve.** It's in a remote area north of San José Village, and the karst terrain—an area of irregular limestone in which erosion has produced sinkholes, fissures, and underground streams and caves—is difficult to navigate, so the only way to see this area is with a guide and with advance permission from the Belize Forestry Department. It has extremely diverse ecosystems because the ele-

HISTORY

The Maya, mostly a group called the Manche Chol Maya, established sizable ceremonial centers and midsize cities in Toledo beginning almost 2,000 years ago. Uxbenká is one of the oldest centers, dating to AD 200. In the Classic period, Lubaantun, which flourished in the 8th and 9th centuries, is thought to have been the administrative center of the region, but for reasons still unclear it was abandoned not long after this. In Southern Belize as elsewhere in Mesoamerica, the Mayan civilization began a long, slow decline a little more than 1,000 years ago.

Spanish conquistadores, including Hernándo Cortés himself in 1525, came through Southern Belize in the early 16th century, but the Maya resisted the Spanish and, later, Britain's attempts to control and tax them. The British, who arrived as loggers, tried to put the Maya in "reservations" and eventually, in the 18th and 19th centuries, moved nearly the entire Manche Chol population to the highlands of Guatemala.

In the late 19th century, groups of Mopan and Ketchi Maya began moving into Southern Belize from Guatemala, establishing more than 50 villages around Toledo. Around the same time, Garífuna from Honduras settled in Punta Gorda, Barranco, and Punta Negra.

Southern Belize, with its rain and remoteness from Belize City, has languished economically for most of the 20th century. The paved Southern Highway may help boost tourism in the region in coming years.

vation ranges from about 1,000 to over 3,000 feet, with sinkholes as deep as 800 feet. You'll find areas of true "high bush" here: old-growth tropical forest with parts that have never been logged at all. Much of the rich flora and fauna of this area has yet to be documented. For example, one brief 12-day expedition turned up 15 species of ferns never found before in Belize, along with several new species of palms, vines, and orchids. ✉*North of San José Village* ☎*722/2765.*

☾ **Rio Blanco National Park** is a tiny national park (105 acres) with a big waterfall. The Rio Blanco waterfall splashes over rough limestone boulders into a deep pool, which you can jump into for a refreshing swim. You reach the waterfall after hiking a well-marked trail. Upstream a short distance from the falls is a nice area for a picnic, shaded by trees and flowering bushes. ✉*30 mi (49 km) west of Punta Gorda between Santa Cruz and Santa Elena villages, on road to Jalacte.*

☾ One of the wildest and most remote areas of Belize is the **Sarstoon-Temash National Park,** between the Temash and Sarstoon rivers in the far south of Toledo District on the border of Guatemala. Red mangroves grow along the river banks; animals and birds rarely seen in other parts of Belize, including white-faced capuchin monkeys, can be spotted here, along with jaguars (if you're lucky), ocelots, and tapirs. The only way to see this area is with a guide by boat. ✉*About 13 mi (21 km) south of Punta Gorda by boat.*

✪ **Toledo Botanical Arboretum** is an organic farm with a growing collection of fruit trees (now more than 50 varieties) and hundreds of other local plants and trees. The farm and gardens are part of the Dem Dats Doin' organization run by Yvonne and Alfredo Villoria. For a tour, call in advance, or go with one of the Thursday tours (F see above) that include a visit to the farm. ⊠ 1¼ mi (2 km) from turnoff to Lubaantun ☎ 772/2470 ≌ BZ$10.

> **ON SET**
>
> In keeping with its evangelical origins, many PG visitors are missionaries who vie for the souls of the Maya by offering them free dentistry or medicine. *The Enemy God*, a movie with a religious theme, was filmed near Punta Gorda in late 2006 and early 2007.

FISHING

For bonefish and tarpon, head to the estuary flats in the Port Honduras marine reserve at the end of the Río Grande, or go northward to Punta Ycacos. In the Marine Reserve, anglers pay a day-park fee of BZ$20, or BZ$60 for three to seven days. There is no fee for the Punta Ycacos, unless you fish in the Port Honduras reserve. For a full day's fly-fishing with a local guide and boat, you'll pay around BZ$500–BZ$600 for two anglers. **Machaca Hill Lodge** (☎ 722/0050, 800/242–2017 in U.S. ⊕ www.machacahill.com) is a leading soft adventure and fishing lodge in Toledo and provides good local guides. **John "Jackie" Young** (⊠ Front St., Punta Gorda ☎ 702/0061 ⊕ www.puntagordabelize.com/jackie young) runs fly-fishing and spin-casting trips in the Port Honduras Marine Reserve and on Toledo rivers and lagoons. **TIDE Tours** (⊠ Prince and Main Sts., Punta Gorda ☎ 722/2129 ⊕ www.tidetours.org) offers six-night fishing and camping packages, including meals, gear, and air transfers from Belize City, for around BZ$3,400 per person.

SCUBA DIVING

This far south the reef has pretty much broken up, but individual cayes have their own small reef systems. The best of the bunch is at the Sapodilla cayes, seven cayes with great wall dives. Lime Caye here has camping, and Hunting Caye has a lighthouse. The only drawback is that because they're 40 mi (64 km) off the coast, a day's dive trip costs around BZ$300 per person or more, depending on how many people go. The Snakes Cayes, with several notable dive sites, are closer in, about 30 km (18 mi) northeast of Punta Gorda. The four Snakes—East, West, South, and Middle—are so named because of boa constrictors that once lived there. **Reef Conservation International** (⊠ Franks Caye, Punta Gorda ☎ 702/2117 ⊕ www.reefci.com) operates marine conservation trips from Franks Caye in the Sapodilla Cayes Marine Reserve. You can stay there in basic accommodations. There's plenty of snorkeling and diving, but you can also assist marine biologists and other Reef CI staff in monitoring and preserving the Barrier Reef.

TIDE Tours (⊠ Prince and Main Sts., Punta Gorda ☎ 722/2129 ⊕ www.tidetours.org) can arrange diving, snorkeling, and other trips to the Sapodilla and Snakes Cayes.

SNORKELING

The turquoise waters lapping up the shores of the usually deserted white-sand beach on Snake Caye are good for snorkeling. **TASTEE Tours** (⊠ *Front St., Punta Gorda* ☎ *722/2070*) runs day trips to the Port Honduras Marine Reserve that include manatee watching at Frenchman Lagoon, an island picnic, snorkeling around the Snake Cayes and Abalone Caye, and trolling for fish (either catch-and-release or for your dinner). Tours run Monday and Wednesday; cost is BZ$186 per person.

Garbutt's Marine (⊠ *Punta Gorda* ☎ 604/3548 ✍ *garbuttsmarine@ yahoo.com*) does day-long snorkeling trips to the Snakes Cayes for around BZ$500 for up to four persons. **TIDE Tours** (⊠ *Prince and Main Sts., Punta Gorda* ☎ *722/2129* ⊕ *www.tidetours.org*) offers full-day trips to Snake Caye. For two people, it's BZ$250 per person.

WHERE TO STAY & EAT

$-$$ ✕ **Emery Restaurant.** Management at Emery's has changed several times recently, but the same cooks stay on, dishing out good Belizean fare at low prices. The grilled fish is always fresh and delicious, and the expansive open-air section (but with a roof to keep out the rain) is pleasant. ⊠ *North St.* ☎ *No phone* ▭ *No credit cards.*

$-$$ ✕ **Grace's.** An established spot, Grace's has genuine value and serves a hearty plate of beans and rice and other Belizean staples. Get a seat near the entrance and eye the town's street life. This is PG's best place for a full breakfast of eggs, bacon, fry jacks (a Belizean version of a sopaipilla), and, of course, beans. For lunch and dinner you can always get chicken, but you can usually get fresh fish, too, plus pizza, chow mein, hamburgers, and several dozen other dishes. ⊠ *19 Main St.* ☎ *702/2414* ▭ *No credit cards.*

$ ✕ **Mangrove Inn at Casa Bonita.** You walk through the owner's living ★ room to get to your table, and the meals served here are definitely home cooked. The cook and co-owner here, Iconie Williams, formerly operated one of PG's best restaurants, also called Mangrove Inn, and she has reopened it here in the B&B in her home. She cooks different dishes every evening, but you'll usually have a choice of seafood (snapper, snook, or shrimp, BZ$14– BZ$18) or hearty fare like lasagna (BZ$15) or roasted chicken (BZ$10). It's all delicious and inexpensive. ⊠ *Front St.* ☎ *722/2270* ▭ *No credit cards.*

$$$-$$$$ ⛺ **Machaca Hill Lodge.** Formerly the fishing lodge known as El Pescador ★ PG, Machaca Hill Lodge now focuses more on soft adventure trips and tours in the Laughing Falcon Reserve, an 11,000-acre private nature reserve managed by the lodge's owners. Fishing trips, however, are still offered. Set on a high hill above the Rio Grande River (you can ride a new tram car to the bottom), the lodge has awesome views of the sea and jungle. Howler monkeys troop by regularly. After a day exploring the Toledo rain forest, dive into the pool, then sup on fish and fresh vegetables from the lodge's organic farm. Tables on the restaurant's veranda offer the best views. The spacious cottages (renovated and upgraded in 2006) have vaulted ceilings, tile floors, and ice-cold air-conditioning. All-inclusive packages including meals, drinks, taxes, and tours start at

6

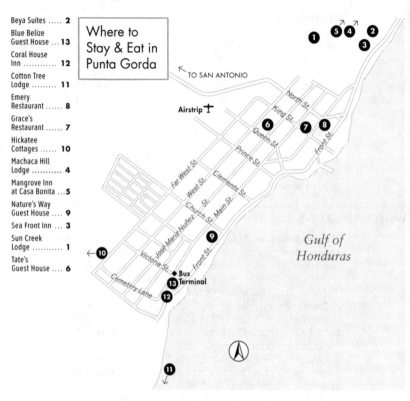

Where to
Stay & Eat in
Punta Gorda

TO SAN ANTONIO

Airstrip

Gulf of
Honduras

Bus
Terminal

BZ$1,480 per person for three nights. **Pros:** Great views of sea and jungle from hilltop location, the top lodge option near PG. **Con:** Not a bargain. ✉*5 mi (8 km) north of Punta Gorda* ✆*Box 135, Punta Gorda* ☎*722/0050* ⊕*www.machacahill.com* ⇲*12 cottages* ☝*In-room: no phone, no TV, Wi-Fi. In-hotel: restaurant, bar, pool, room service, no elevator, laundry service, airport shuttle* ▭*AE, MC, V.*

$–$$ ▥**Coral House Inn.** Americans Rick and Darla Mallory renovated this

★   1938 British colonial-era house and turned it into one of the most pleasant small guesthouses in the country. It's near the sea at the end of Front Street, about as far south as you can go on paved roads in Belize. You'll recognize the house by coral-color paint and the vintage VW van parked in front. The four guest rooms have tile floors, new beds, air-conditioning, and wireless high-speed Internet. There's a small pool and complimentary bikes. Breakfast is included in rates. Owners also manage a nearby, newly renovated private rental home, available for BZ$200–$250 nightly (plus 9% tax), depending on length of stay. **Pros:** One of the best small inns in Belize; most comfort amenities provided, from a/c to pool to wireless. **Con:** No restaurant, so you'll have to go out for dinner. ✉*151 Front St.* ☎*722/2878* ⊕*www.coralhouseinn.net* ⇲*4 rooms* ☝*In-room: no phone, no TV, Wi-Fi. In-hotel: pool, bicycles, public Wi-Fi, no elevator, airport shuttle, laundry service* ▭*MC, V.* ⦿*CP*

$ ⊞**Beya Suites.** From the verandas on the second floor of this bright pink, waterfront hotel, you have expansive views of the Gulf of Honduras. Despite the name, the hotel has rooms rather than true suites, but they're modern, with tile floors, plaster walls, cable TV, and air-conditioning. The Belizean-owned hotel has a restaurant and bar. **Pros:** Views of the water, Belizean-owned. **Cons:** Not really suites. ⊠*Front St., #6, Hopeville* ☎722/2188 ⊕*www.beyasuites.com* ⤳*6 rooms* △*In-room: no phone. In-hotel: restaurant, bar, public Internet, no elevator, laundry service* ▤*AE, D, MC, V.*

$ ⊞**Blue Belize Guest House.** At this welcome new addition to PG lodging choices, you can settle in and do your own thing in one of the two self-catering flats, with kitchenettes (fridges and microwaves), spacious bedrooms, and a shared veranda with hammocks. One of the owners is a PhD marine biologist, and the other is a well-known fishing and tour guide. **Pros:** Spacious one-bedroom apartments, breezy seafront location, well-guided tours and fishing trips. **Cons:** No a/c, kitchenettes are tiny. ⊠*139 Front St.* ☎722/2678 ⊕ *www.bluebelize.com* ⤳*2 1-bedroom apartments* △*In-room: no a/c, no phone, kitchenettes, Wi-Fi, no TV. In-hotel: no elevator* ▤*MC, V.*

$ ⊞**Hickatee Cottages.** A charming and enthusiastic young British couple, Ian and Kate Morton, opened this lodge at the edge of PG in 2005. Three Caribbean-style cottages have zinc roofs and private verandas and are nestled in lush foliage. They're outfitted with locally made furniture and hardwood floors. Bikes are complimentary, and delicious meals made with fruits and vegetables from the owners' organic nurseries next door are available (dinner is around BZ$30). A special treat: Once a week (at this writing, on Wednesday) you can go with Ian to visit the nearby Fallen Stones butterfly farm, which he manages. Fallen Stones is one of the largest commercial butterfly operations in Central America, and closed to the public, except for guests of Hickatee. **Pros:** Lovely cottages, some of the best food in Toledo, helpful, friendly owners. **Cons:** A longish hike or bike ride from town. ⊠*Ex-Servicemen Rd.* ⊹*Coming into PG, turn right at the Texaco station. Continue past school on Main to the PG hospital. Bend right on Cemetery. From Front St. turn right at Texaco station and follow Main St. through town. At PG Hospital, turn right on Cemetery La. After 3 blocks, turn half-left on Ex-Servicemen Rd. Follow road for 1 mi (1½ km); Hickatee Cottages is on left* ☎662/4475 ⊕*www.hickatee.com* ⤳*3 cottages* △*In-room: no a/c, no phone, no TV. In-hotel: restaurant, bar, bicycles, public Internet, no elevator, airport shuttle* ▤*MC, V.*

Fodor's Choice ★

$ ⊞**Sea Front Inn.** With its pitched roofs and stone-and-wood facade, this 4-story hotel may remind you of a Swiss ski lodge. Directly overlooking the Gulf of Honduras with the green humps of the Saddle Back Mountains as a backdrop, its top floors command especially spectacular views. There are a dozen single and double rooms and two suites with kitchenettes. Each is unique, fitted with Belizean hardwoods. A third-floor restaurant (open only for breakfast) has a roof supported by rosewood tree trunks etched with Mayan carvings. For longer stays, there are six apartments in the back for BZ$1,639–BZ$3,000 a month, plus 9% tax. **Pros:** Appealing waterfront location, one-of-a-kind rooms.

6

Cons: Upper story rooms require climbing a lot of steps, service some-times less helpful than it could be. ⊠*Front St.* ☏*722/2300* ⊕*www.seafrontinn.com* ⤦*12 rooms, 2 suites,5 1-bedroom apartments, 1 2-bedroom apartment* ⌂*In-room: no phone. In-hotel: restaurant (break-fast only), bar, public Wi-Fi, no elevator* ▭*MC, V.*

¢ 🖫**Nature's Way Guest House.** In this funky, ramshackle house near the water is an assortment of rooms for backpackers on a budget. It feels a bit like a hostel, as it serves as a sort of meeting place for travel-ers exploring the frontier or heading on to Guatemala or Honduras. Choose from one of the spartan rooms or a bunk in one of the dorm-style rooms. On the breakfast-only menu are tofu, yogurt, and granola. The owner is glad to share with you his strong opinions on Toledo and just about anything else. Pros: International travelers congregate here; inexpensive, pleasant waterfront location. Cons: Cleanliness may not be up to your standards. ⊠*83 Front St.* ☏*722/2119* ⤦*17 rooms with shared bath* ⌂*In-room: no a/c, no phone, no TV. In-hotel: restaurant, no elevator* ▭*No credit cards.*

¢ 🖫**Tate's Guest House.** If you don't demand luxury, you couldn't find a nicer spot in PG. Run by longtime PG post office worker William Tate and his family, this guesthouse on a quiet residential street is an excellent value. The rooms are immaculate, and the atmosphere's friendly and cheerful. One room has a kitchenette, and there's also a small common kitchen with refrigerator and microwave. Pros: Pleasant accommodations at near backpacker rates. Cons: Few frills. ⊠*34 José Maria Nuñez St.* ☏*722/0147* ⤦*5 rooms* ⌂*In-room: no a/c (some), no phone, kitchen (some). In-hotel: no elevator* ▭*No credit cards.*

THE MAYA HEARTLAND

Drive a few miles out of town, and you find yourself in the heartland of the Maya people. Half the population of Toledo is Maya, a far higher proportion than any other region. The Toledo Maya Cultural Council has created an ambitious network of Maya-run guesthouses, and in 1995 it initiated the Mayan Mapping Project. By collating oral history and evidence of ancient Mayan settlements, the project hopes to secure rights to land that the Maya have occupied for centuries, but that the Belizean government have ceded to multinational logging companies. There's also a separate, privately run Mayan homestay program, where you stay in local homes rather than in guesthouses. *See Where to Stay, below, for information on these two programs.*

The Maya divide into two groups: Mopan Maya– and Ketchi-speak-ing peoples from the Guatemalan highlands. Most of the latter are recent arrivals, refugees from repression and overpopulation. Each group tends to keep to itself, living in separate villages and preserv-ing unique traditions. Among the Ketchi villages in Toledo are Crique Sarco, San Vincente, San Miquel, Laguna, San Pedro Columbia, Santa Teresa, Sunday Wood, Mabelha, and Corazon. Mopan Maya villages include San Antonio, Pueblo Viejo, and San José.

Belize's Multicultural Gumbo

The celebration of Belize's historic multiculturalism begins on its flag: the two strapping young men—one black and the other white—are woodcutters standing beneath a logwood tree. Under them is a Latin inscription: *sub umbra floreat*—"In the shade of this tree we flourish."

Belize is a rich gumbo of colors and languages. Creoles, once the majority, now make up only about one-fourth of the population. Creoles in Belize are descendants of slaves brought from Jamaica to work in the logging industry. By the early 18th century, people of African descent came to outnumber those of British origin in Belize. The two groups united early in the country's history to defeat a common enemy, the Spanish. Most of the Creole population today is concentrated in Belize City and Belize District, although there are predominantly Creole villages elsewhere, including the villages of Gales Point and Placencia. English is the country's official language and taught in school, although, an English dialect, Creole, is widely spoken.

Mestizos are the fastest growing group in Belize and make up about one-half of the population. These are persons of mixed European and Maya heritage, typically speaking Spanish as a first language and English as a second. Some migrated to Belize from Mexico during the Yucatán Caste Wars of the mid-19th century. More recently, many "Spanish" (as they're often called in Belize) have moved from Guatemala or elsewhere in Central America. Mestizos are concentrated in northern and western Belize.

Numbering close to a million at the height of the Mayan kingdoms, the Maya today constitute only about one-tenth of the Belize population of 314,000. There are concentrations of Yucatec Maya in Corozal and Orange Walk districts, Mopan Maya in Toledo and Cayo districts, and also Ketchi Maya in about 30 villages in Toledo. Most speak their Mayan dialect, and either English or Spanish, or both.

About 1 in 20 Belizeans is a Garífuna. The Garinagu (the plural of Garífuna) are of mixed African and Carib Indian heritage. Most originally came to Belize from Honduras in the 1820s and 1830s. Dangriga and Punta Gorda are towns with large Garífuna populations, as are the villages of Seine Bight, Hopkins, and Barranco. Besides their own tongue—an Arawakan-based language with smatterings of West African words—many Garinagu speak English and Creole.

Other groups include several thousand Mennonites, sizable communities of East Indians, and Chinese, mostly from Taiwan and Hong Kong. Belize's original white populations were English, but today's "gringos" are mostly expats from the United States and Canada, with some from the United Kingdom. All these groups find in this tiny country a tolerant and amiable home.

Whatever the background of its citizens, Belize's population is young. More than two out of five Belizeans are under 15 years of age, and the median average age is around 20 years, more than 16 years younger than the median age in the United States.

EXPLORING

MAYA VILLAGES

The Mopan Maya village of **San Antonio,** a market town 35 mi (56 km) west of Punta Gorda, is Toledo's second-largest town, with a population of more than 2,000. It was settled by people from the Guatemalan village of San Luis, who revere their former patron saint. The village church, built of stones carted from surrounding Mayan ruins, has a stained-glass window donated by another city with a connection to the saint: St. Louis, Missouri. The people of San Antonio haven't forgotten their ancient heritage, though, and each June 13 they take to the streets for a festival that dates back to pre-Columbian times.

Farther west is the Ketchi village of **San Pedro Columbia,** a cheerful cluster of brightly painted buildings and thatch houses. One of the most eye-catching is a raspberry-red grocery called the People Little Store.

On the way to San Pedro Columbia, don't miss **Blue Creek,** a beautiful stretch of river dotted with turquoise swimming holes. A path up the riverbank leads to dramatic caves. The Hokeb Ha Cave is fairly easy to explore on your own, but others require a guide or a tour. International Zoological Expeditions, a Connecticut-based student travel organization, has established a **jungle lodge** at Blue Creek, with seven rustic cabañas and a restaurant. To visit this part of Blue Creek, you have to get permission from the **IZE jungle lodge** (☎508/655–1461, 800/548–5843 in U.S.). Don't swim in the river at night—a highly poisonous snake called the fer-de-lance likes to take nocturnal dips.

MAYAN RUINS

⟳ **Nim Li Punit,** a Late Classic site discovered in 1976, has 26 unearthed stelae, including one, Stela 14, that is 30 feet tall—the largest ever found in Belize and the second largest found anywhere in the Mayan world. Nim Li Punit, which means "Big Hat" in the Ketchi Mayan language, is named for the elaborate headgear of a ruler pictured on Stela 14. Shady trees cool you off as you walk around the fairly small site (you can see it all in an hour or so). Stop by the informative visitor center on the premises to learn more about the site. Nim Li Punit is near the Ketchi village of Indian Creek, and children (and some adults) from the village usually come over and offer jewelry and crafts for sale. ⊠*27 mi (44 km) northwest of Punta Gorda off Mile 72½, Western Hwy.* 🔘*BZ$10.*

⟳ **Lubaantun,** which lies beyond the village of San Pedro Columbia, is a Late Classic site discovered in 1924 by German archaeologist Thomas Gann, who gave it a name meaning "place of fallen stones." Lubaantun must have been an awe-inspiring sight: on top of a conical hill, with views to the sea in one direction and the Maya Mountains in the other, its stepped layers of white-plaster stone would have towered above the jungle like a wedding cake. No one knows exactly what function the structures served, but the wealth of miniature masks and whistles found suggests it was a center of ceramic production. The trio of ball courts and the central plaza with tiered seating for 10,000 spectators seems like a Maya Madison Square Garden. There's a small visitor center at the site.

In the last century Lubaantun became the scene of the biggest hoax in modern archaeology. After it was excavated in the 1920s, a British adventurer named F. A. Mitchell-Hedges claimed to have stumbled on what became known as the Crystal Skull. Mitchell-Hedges described the incident in a potboiler, *Danger, My Ally*, in 1951. According to the book, the Crystal Skull was found under an altar at Lubaantun by his daughter Anna. Mitchell-Hedges portrayed himself as a serious archaeologist and explorer: in truth, he was a magazine hack who was later exposed in England as a fraud and a grave robber. The Crystal Skull made good copy; also known as the Skull of Doom, it was supposedly used by Mayan high priests to zap anyone they didn't care for. Mitchell-Hedges claimed it was 3,600 years old and had taken 150 years to fashion by rubbing a block of pure rock crystal with sand. A similar skull, in the possession of the British Museum, shows signs of having been manufactured with a dentist's drill. Anna Mitchell-Hedges, who today lives in Ontario, has promised to one day reveal the secret. So far, she has adamantly refused to allow the Crystal Skull to be tested and has denied all requests by the Belizean government to return it. ✉ *20 mi (33 km) northwest of Punta Gorda, about 1 mi (1½ km) from village of San Pedro Columbia* 🎫*BZ$10.*

☙ **Pusilha,** a Classic-period ceremonial site with a plaza and several stelae on the banks of the Moho River, about 1 mi (1½ km) from the Guatemala border, is currently under excavation by Dr. Geoffrey Braswell and other archeologists from the State University of New York at Buffalo. The site is not open to the public, but you may be able to visit by asking permission of the *alcalde* (mayor) of San Benito village or of the archaeologists, if they're on-site. Ask a villager to direct you to the home of the alcalde, but note that many in this remote village speak only Ketchi Maya and perhaps Spanish. The Pusilha remains are at the back of the village along the Moho River. By road from Punta Gorda, go 13 mi (21 km) north on the Southern Highway to the San Antonio junction. Turn left on the San Antonio Road and go 3¾ mi (6¼ km). Turn left on the road to Blue Creek village and go past Blue Creek and Jordan village to Santa Teresa village, about 13 mi (22 km). Take a right on San Benito Poité Road for 7 mi (11 2/3 km) to San Benito Poité village. It's easier to reach by boat up the Moho River, and most visitors will want to arrange a guided trip from PG. Except for the Southern Highway and a section of the San Antonio Road, these roads are unpaved and may be impassable after heavy rains. ✉ *About 2 hours by back roads from Punta Gorda, near village of San Benito Poité on banks of Moho River* 🕾*772/2470.*

☙ **Uxbenká,** or "ancient place," is near Santa Cruz Village, about 3 mi (5 km) west of San Antonio. This small ceremonial site has a main plaza with six structures, and a series of smaller plazas. More than 20 stelae have been found here, six of them carved. This site is not officially open to visitors, but if you ask a villager in Santa Cruz, you can probably get an informal guided tour.

HELPING OUT IN BELIZE

Want to help others less fortunate than you? Want to make the world a better place? Then you may want to investigate volunteer opportunities in Belize. There are basically three kinds of volunteer opportunities available:

Church and mission trips. This typically involves a week to several weeks of volunteer work in a medical or dental clinic, or building churches or homes, or other hands-on assistance. Usually these volunteer groups are based outside of Belize, often at a church or school or as a part of a local medical society. In most cases, volunteers pay for their own transportation to Belize, along with personal expenses in the country, but food and lodging sometimes are provided by the mission. Your best bet is to contact your church, college, or local medical society and ask if they know of upcoming mission trips to Belize.

Independent volunteering. Find a worthwhile organization and volunteer your services. Conservation organizations, churches, libraries, medical clinics, humane societies, and schools are among those that may welcome volunteers. You typically won't receive any lodging or food in return for your volunteer activities. To arrange this kind of independent volunteer work, you usually need to be in Belize and make personal contact with the organization you are seeking to help.

Organized volunteer programs. These volunteer programs often revolve around conservation, such as working with wildlife or reef preservation. A few programs offer volunteer opportunities in education, animal care, or social work.

Some programs require volunteers to pay a placement fee, which can be several hundred dollars or more, plus pay for room, board, and transportation to Belize. In other programs, volunteers do not pay a fee and they may receive food and lodging in exchange for their volunteer work, but they usually have to pay transportation and incidental expenses out of pocket. For longer-term volunteering, consider the U.S. Peace Corps, which has a significant presence here.

Some organizations that accept volunteers in Belize:

Belize Zoo and Tropical Education Center. The Belize Zoo, one of the great conservation organizations in Central America, and the adjoining Tropical Education Center have a wide range of education and outreach programs. A few motivated volunteers are accepted to assist Belize Zoo and TEC programs. ✆ Box 1787, Belize City ☎ 220/8003 ⊕ www.belizezoo.org.

Cornerstone Foundation. This nonprofit's programs include cultural, community service, and peace-related volunteer programs in Cayo District. Volunteers commit for a minimum of three weeks and up to three months. For longer-term programs, individuals pay US$300 to US$400 a month for housing; couples and families, US$600. There is a US$100 application fee, a weekly meal fee of around US$15, and other fees. Those involved in three-week programs such as the AIDS Education or Natural Healing programs pay a fee of around US$550 to US$650. At any one time, the foundation may have from 1 to 18 volunteers in Belize, plus local staff. ✉ 90 Burns

Ave., San Ignacio ☎*824/2373* ⊕*www.peacecorner.org.*

Green Reef. Green Reef is a private, nonprofit group based in San Pedro, devoted to protecting the marine and coastal resources. Green Reef currently doesn't have a volunteer coordinator, but it says it is interested in hearing from prospective volunteers, especially those with skills in photography, fund-raising, community involvement, and education. ✉*100 Coconut Dr., San Pedro* ☎*226/3254* ⊕*www.green reefbelize.org.*

Monkey Bay Wildlife Sanctuary. Monkey Bay is a private wildlife sanctuary and environmental education center on 1,070 acres near the Belize Zoo. It has some volunteer opportunities in conservation and community service. Monkey Bay also offers homestay programs, as well as 12- to 21-day education and adventure programs for students (middle school to university). The education programs are at rates starting at about US$75 a day. ✪*Box 187, Belmopan City* ☎*820/3032* ⊕*www. monkeybaybelize.org.*

Mount Carmel High School. Many of the faculty members at this high school are volunteers. Volunteers, who must be four-year university graduates and be "willing to teach in a Catholic environment," commit to teach for a period of one to two years. In return, they receive room, board, and US$12.50/week in spending money. ✉*Benque Viejo del Carmen* ☎*823/2024* ⊕*www. mchsbenque.org.*

Plenty International. Plenty, founded in 1974, places 8 to 10 volunteers annually in Toledo District and elsewhere. Volunteers should have medical, midwifery, marketing, and other skills. The minimum commitment is three months, and a nominal (US$30) placement fee is charged. There are no stipends or other payments to volunteers, but in some cases volunteers may receive food and housing. ✉*Box 394, Summertown, TN 38483* ☎*913/964– 4323* ⊕*www.plenty.org.*

—Lan Sluder

6

WHERE TO STAY

$$$$ ⬚ **Belize Lodge & Excursions.** One of the most unexpected sites on the Southern Highway is Indian Creek Lodge, which rises out of nowhere beside the road as a high-walled compound with cabañas lined up a hillside. Once inside the compound, though, you see that the thatch cabañas have delightful views of two freshwater lagoons and of part of a sprawling 13,000-acre private preserve. Nearby is another lodge, Balaam Na (Ketchi Maya for House of the Jaguar), which, at this writing, is expected to be home to two jaguars, one spotted and the other black. All-inclusive rates here are BZ$800 per person per night. These lodges are two of the four properties in southern Belize being developed by Ken Karas and his company, Belize Lodge & Excursions. The two others include the Jungle Camp, reachable only by river boat, and Moho Cay Lodge off the coast of Toledo. All the properties operate as all-inclusives, usually with a five-night minimum. **Pros:** Remote, beautiful lodging in a choice of settings. **Cons:** High rates, these lodges are still a work in progress. ⊠*Southern Hwy., 25 mi north of Punta Gorda* ☎*223/6324 or 888/292–2462 in the U.S.* ⊕*www.belizelodge. com* ⇴*18 cabañas, 3 suites, 8 tents on platforms* ⬚*In-room: no a/c, no phone, no TV. In-hotel: restaurant, bar, no elevator, Wi-Fi, laundry service* ▭*MC, V* ⦿*AI.*

$$$ ⬚ **Cotton Tree Lodge.** This jungle lodge is named after the silk cotton tree (also called the kapok or ceiba), a giant specimen of which stands near the main lodge building. Fittingly, the lodge strives to provide a silky smooth experience for guests. Opened in late 2006, it sits beside the Moho River about 15 mi (24 km) from Punta Gorda. Guests are usually brought in by boat (though you can also come by road) and stay in one of 10 thatch cabañas ranged among wild fig trees along the river's edge. The property's walkways are raised; in the summer rainy season the Moho floods, and at times the grounds become a large lake, with water lapping at the walkways. The lodge is off the grid, and everything here is solar- or generator-powered. Good meals (dinner BZ$48) are served in a huge thatch palapa (stand-alone gazebo-like thatched roof). All-inclusive rates in-season start at BZ$390 per person per day, plus 9% hotel tax and 10% service, and include accommodations, meals, horseback riding, tours, taxes, and transfers, but not dive and snorkel trips. Discounts are sometimes available, so shop around. **Pros:** Stunning riverside setting, complete with rope swing to play Tarzan in the river; lots of activities. **Cons:** Sometimes buggy, no swimming pool. ⊠*San Felipe village* ☎*670/0557, 866/480–4534 in the U.S.* ⊕*www.cottontreelodge.com* ⇴*10 cabañas* ⬚*In-room: no a/ c, no TV, no phone. In-hotel: restaurant, bar, water sports, bicycles, no elevator, public Wi-Fi, public Internet, laundry service, airport shuttle, no kids under 4* ▭*AE, D, MC, V* ⦿*EP or AI.*

$$$ ⬚ **The Lodge at Big Falls.** Relax beside a meandering jungle river, listen to otters splash, and admire colorful butterflies at this small lodge on 30 placid acres beside the Rio Grande River. This is a birder's paradise: 350 species have been recorded within 5 mi (8 km) of the lodge. Owners Marta and Rob Hirons—she's an American who has lived abroad since she was 21, and he's English—built the six pleasant thatch cabañas with tile floors and private baths. After dinner (around BZ$64), read up on naturalist lore in the lodge's Resource Center, where you can use satellite Internet. **Pros:** It's fun to tube or swim in the river; excellent birding, good food. **Cons:** Meals are pricey; you're nickled and dimed on kayaks, inner tubes, and Internet service; setting near Big Falls village with a large rice processing plant nearby may not be the jungle you expected. ⊠ *Off Mile 79, Southern Hwy.* ☏ *Box 103, Punta Gorda* ☎ *501/671–7172* ⊕ *www. thelodgeatbigfalls.com* ⇋ *6 cabañas* ⚷ *In-room: no a/c, no phone, no TV. In-hotel: restaurant, bar, pool, water sports, bicycles, public Internet, no elevator, airport shuttle, laundry service* ⊟ *MC, V.*

☾ ¢–$ ▦ **Sun Creek Lodge.** This little lodge, open since 2004, is run by Bruno and Melissa Kuppinger. He's German; she's Belizean. Bruno runs adventure tours, and Melissa focuses on the lodge and does the cooking. The thatch cabañas are simple but comfortable, with outdoor showers surrounded by plants. The grounds are nicely landscaped with flowering shrubs. Car rentals are available. **Pros:** Inexpensive, landscaped setting, excellent tours available. **Cons:** Somewhat remote setting, basic accommodations. ⊠ *About 14 mi (23 km) northwest of Punta Gorda, off Mile 86, Southern Hwy.* ☎ *604/2124* ✍ *suncreek@hughes.net* ⇋ *4 cabañas with shared baths* ⚷ *In-room: no phone, no TV. In-hotel: restaurant, no elevator, public Internet, airport shuttle* ⊟ *MC, V* ⊙ *CP.*

¢ ▦ **T.E.A.** The Toledo Ecotourism Association arranges stays in one of eight participating Mayan and Ketchi villages, including Blue Creek, San Antonio, Pueblo Viejo, and Medina Bank, and also one Garífuna village, Barranco. You stay in a simple but clean guesthouse, typically with thatch roof, bunk beds, and outside bathroom, then visit Mayan homes for breakfast, lunch, and dinner. During the day there are walks to the nearby ruins or to waterfalls that empty into shimmering pools. Before you book this kind of stay, though, know that the point of it is ₹ to get an authentic feel for the region—this can be a rare opportunity to learn about the culture, but if the thought of chickens running in and out of your digs isn't your idea of a nice vacation, this isn't the stay for you. **Pros:** True cultural experience, rare opportunity to participate in Mayan village life. Cons: Extremely basic lodging and facilities. ⊠ *Front St., Punta Gorda* ☎ *722/2096* ✍ *ttea@btl.net* ⚷ *In-room: no a/c, no phone, no TV. In-hotel: no elevator* ⊟ *No credit cards* ⊙ *FAP.*

¢ ▦ **Village Homestay Network.** Run by Dem Dats Doin' ecofarm, the Village Homestay Network arranges for visitors to stay with one of about 20 Mayan families in one of three Toledo villages: Aguacate, a Ketchi village; San José, a Mopan village; and Na Luum Ca, also Mopan. You sleep in a hammock in a traditional thatch hut with dirt floor, help with daily activities such as making tortillas, and eat meals with the host family. Bathrooms are outhouses, and you bathe in a river. Rates are a bargain at BZ$12 per person per night for lodging plus BZ$15 per person for three meals daily; there's also a one-time administration fee of BZ$14 per person. **Pros:** Unique opportunity to get up close and personal with the indigenous community. **Cons:** Basic lodging even by backpacker standards. ⊠ *53 Main Middle St., Punta Gorda* ☎ *722/2470* ✍ *demdatsdoin@btl.net* ⚷ *In-room: no a/c, no phone, no TV* ⊟ *No credit cards* ⊙ *FAP.*

THE DEEP SOUTH ESSENTIALS

TRANSPORTATION

BY AIR

Maya Island Air and Tropic Air fly south to Punta Gorda from both the municipal (BZ$178 one way) and international (BZ$207 one way) airports. There are about five flights daily on each airline. The Punta Gorda airstrip is on the town's west side from the town square; walk four blocks west on Prince Street.

Contacts **Maya Island Air** (⊠ *Punta Gorda airstrip* ☎ *722/2856* ⊕ *www.maya airways.com*). **Tropic Air** (⊠ *Prince St.* ☎ *722/2008* ⊕ *www.tropicair.com*).

BY BOAT

Requena's, the most reliable operator, provides daily boats departing at 9:30 AM from the docks on Front Street, Punta Gorda, to Puerto Barrios, Guatemala. The trip takes about an hour. The fare is BZ$40 one way. Requena's returns to PG at 2 PM. Two other water taxi services, Pichilingo and Marisol, run afternoon water taxis for BZ$43 one way. The Pichilingo boat departs at 2 PM and Marisol at 4 PM. You must pay a BZ$7.50 conservation fee when departing PG, and about a US$10 exit fee when departing Guatemala for Belize. To make a reservation, you need to provide your full name, date of birth, nationality, and passport number. If you're flying to PG just to catch the water taxi to Puerto Barrios, take the 8 AM Maya Island flight from the municipal airstrip in Belize City. Requena's will pick you up at the airstrip.

Contact **Requena's Charter Service** (⊠ *12 Front St., Punta Gorda* ☎ *722/2070* ⊕ *www.puntagordabelize.com/requena/* ✎ *watertaxi@btl.net*).

BY BUS

Several bus lines, including James Bus Lines, National Transport, Usher's, and Belize Bus Drivers Co-op, run the routes south to Dangriga, Placencia, and Punta Gorda. James buses generally are in the best condition and are the most comfortable. From Belize City to Punta Gorda it's a six- to -seven-hour trip via Belmopan and Dangriga, depending on connections and whether it's an express or local bus. It costs around BZ$15 to Dangriga, BZ$20 to Placencia, and BZ$$22–BZ$30 to PG. Most buses are old U.S. school buses—they're usually crowded and have no air-conditioning. If you have the budget, fly.

Buses run frequently—generally about every one to two hours during daylight hours—on the Southern Highway between Dangriga and PG, but public transportation is very limited off the highway. On market days (generally Monday, Wednesday, Friday, and Saturday) buses leave the main plaza in PG around noon. Different buses, mostly old American school buses operated by local entrepreneurs, go to different villages, returning on market days very early in the morning. There's no published schedule—you have to ask locally. Fares are modest, BZ$2–BZ$4. As of this writing, buses served the villages of Barranco, Big Falls, Crique Jute, Crique Sarco, Golden Stream, Indian Creek, Jalacte,

Laguna, San Antonio, San Marcos, San Miquel, San Pedro Columbia, Pueblo Viejo, and Silver Creek.

Information James Bus Line (⊠ 7 King St., Punta Gorda ☎ 702/2049).

BY CAR

The journey to Punta Gorda via the Hummingbird and Southern highways used to be a chiropractor's nightmare: a bone-shuddering marathon via Belmopan and Dangriga across some of Belize's worst roads. The paving of the Hummingbird and Southern highways has made the trip much shorter and more pleasant. At this writing, only a short section of the Southern Highway near Golden Stream was unpaved, and work was underway to complete this section. The Southern Highway is now one of Central America's best roads.

Off the Southern Highway, most roads are unpaved. In dry weather they're bumpy yet passable, but after heavy rains the dirt roads can turn into quagmires even for four-wheel-drive vehicles. Most tertiary roads are not well marked, so you may have to stop frequently for directions. Despite this, expensive taxis and infrequent bus service to and from the Mayan villages are arguments for renting a car.

BY TAXI

Taxis in the Deep South are available mostly in PG. You can find taxis at Central Park in PG, or your hotel can call one for you. Any trip within PG should cost around BZ$6, with additional charges for extra stops. You can also hire a taxi to take you to nearby villages, but negotiate the rate in advance; it could be anywhere from BZ$20 to BZ$150, or more, depending on the destination. If you want a car and driver, a taxi likely will charge you around BZ$300 a day. There are no major car rental companies in Punta Gorda, but Sun Creek Lodge has a few rental cars. They cost around BZ$140 per day.

Contact Sun Creek Lodge (⊠ About 14 mi [23 km] northwest of Punta Gorda, off Mile 86, Southern Hwy. ☎ 604/2124).

CONTACTS & RESOURCES

BANKS & EXCHANGE SERVICES

The only banks in Punta Gorda are Belize Bank and ScotiaBank. Happily, both have ATMs that accept foreign-issued ATM cards (on the PLUS, CIRRUS, and Visa Electron systems).

Banks & ATMs Belize Bank (⊠ 30 Main St., at Hospital St. ☎ 722/2324). **ScotiaBank** (. ☎ 722/0098).

EMERGENCIES

Hospital Punta Gorda Hospital (⊠ Main St. at south end of town ☎ 722/2026).

HEALTH

Malaria is a problem in southern Belize, especially in rural areas outside Punta Gorda. If you're going to spend any time in the bush, discuss with your physician whether to use chloroquine or other malaria prophylaxis. The municipal water supply in Punta Gorda is treated and is safe to drink. In rural areas the water is often from community wells; here you should drink bottled water.

MAIL & SHIPPING

The Punta Gorda post office is on Front Street across from the ferry dock. Hours are 8:30–noon and 1–4:30 weekdays.

Post Office **Punta Gorda post office** (⊠ *Front St.* ☎ *722/2087*).

TOURS

TIDE Tours, a subsidiary of the Toledo Institute for Development and Environment, a nonprofit organization promoting ecotourism in Toledo, does not itself run tours but instead acts as a clearinghouse for several good tour operators. It can arrange fishing, kayaking, snorkeling, trips to Mayan ruins, and cultural tours. Bruno Kuppinger at Sun Creek Lodge and IBTM Tours specializes in adventure tours, some definitely not for couch potatoes, including the weeklong Maya Divide hiking trip. Garbutts Marine offers dependable boat trips to the Snakes Cayes. Another sizable tour operator is TASTEE Tours, associated with Requena's Water Taxi Service. Romero's Charters and Tours, while not a tour operator, has a driver service that can take you to any of the inland destinations. For birding, it's hard to beat George Alford, who can be contacted through TIDE. Several of the hotels, including Hickatee Cottages, offer kayaking on the Moho River. The Toledo Tour Guide Association has about 20 members. All are licensed by the Belize government. Some of these tour guides work for the larger tour operators, and others work independently.

Contacts **Bruno Kuppinger, Sun Creek Lodge and IBTM Tours** (⊠ *Sun Creek Lodge, Mile 86, Southern Hwy.* ☎ *604/2124* ✍ *suncreek@hughes.net*).**Garbutt's Marine** (⊠ *Punta Gorda* ☎ *604/3548* ✍ *garbuttsmarine@yahoo.com*).**Romero's Charter and Tours** (⊠ *Forest Home* ☎ *614/3998* ✍ *rcharters@btl.net*). **TASTEE Tours** (⊠ *12 Front St., Punta Gorda* ☎ *722/2795* ⊕ *www.puntagordabelize.com*). **TIDE Tours** (⊠ *Prince and Main Sts., Box 150, Punta Gorda* ☎ *722/2129* ⊕ *www. tidetours.org*). **Toledo Tour Guide Association** (⌂ *Box 147, Punta Gorda* ⊕ *www. puntagordabelize.com/ttga/index.htm*).

VISITOR INFORMATION

The office of the Belize Tourism Industry Association (BTIA), on Front Street near the water taxi dock, is open Tuesday–Saturday 9–noon and 1–4:30, and Sunday 9–noon.

Information **Belize Tourism Information Center** (⊠ *Front St.* ☎ *722/2531*).

Tikal & Environs

WORD OF MOUTH

"Tikal is fabulous. We hired a guide who gave us a great overview and the confidence to explore on our own the following day. We climbed to the top of all the pyramids (sore legs!), including the one in El Mundo Perdido to watch the sunset. Beautiful."

—msteacher

"Do the overnight in Tikal. So worth it! Spending the night gives you the advantage of being in the park first thing in the morning and late in afternoon without day-trippers. A sunset and sunrise on the temples is breathtaking."

—Fry69

By Lan Sluder   **THE JUNGLES OF EL PETÉN** were once the heartland of the Mayan civilization. The sprawling empire—including parts of present-day Mexico, Belize, Honduras, and El Salvador—was once made up of a network of cities that held hundreds of thousands of people, but a millennium ago this fascinating civilization went into a mysterious decline and soon virtually disappeared. The temples that dominated the horizon were swallowed up by the jungle.

Today, ancient ruins seem to just crop up from El Petén's landscape. In comparison with the rest of Guatemala, which has 15 million people in an area the size of Tennessee, El Petén is relatively sparsely populated, although this is changing. Fifty years ago, El Petén had fewer than 20,000 residents. Due to massive immigration from other areas of Guatemala, El Petén now has more than half a million people (almost twice the population of the entire country of Belize). Still, nature reigns supreme, with vines and other plants quickly covering everything that stands still a little too long. Whatever your primary interest—archaeology, history, birding, biking—you'll find plenty to do and see in this remote region.

Four-wheel-drive vehicles are required to get to many of the archaeological sites, while others, such as those in the Mirador Basin, are reachable only by boat or on foot. The difficulty doesn't just enhance the adventure, it gives you time to take in the exotic scenery and rare tropical flora and fauna that are with you all the way.

If you drive instead of fly from Belize, you'll notice the difference in Guatemala almost the instant you cross the border. Spanish replaces English, and except in some hotels and other tourist businesses, very little English is spoken. Prices for everything from beer to meals to lodging are considerably lower. Starting at the border, where you may be asked for a small fee to enter Guatemala (there is no such entry fee), bribes and petty corruption are a way of life. Extreme poverty is much more evident, and by comparison with this part of Guatemala, Belize looks middle-class.

HISTORY

At its peak, the Mayan civilization developed one of the earliest forms of writing, the very first mathematical system use zero, complex astronomical calculations, advanced agricultural systems, and an inscrutable belief system. It was during this zenith that spectacular cities such as Tikal were built. By the time the Europeans arrived, the Mayan civilization had already mysteriously collapsed.

Until the 1960s the El Petén region was a desolate place. This all changed when the Guatemalan government began offering small tracts of land in El Petén for US$25 to anyone willing to settle it. The landless moved in droves, and today the population is more than 500,000—a 25-fold increase in around 50 years.

Unemployment in El Petén is high and tourism—mostly associated with Tikal and other Mayan sites—is the main industry. Many make ends meet through subsistence farming, logging, hunting for *xate* (palm leaves used in the floral industry) in the wild, and marijuana cultivation. Exploration for oil is underway in a few areas as well.

EXPLORING TIKAL & ENVIRONS

Guatemala is a rugged country where major roads are few and far between and highways are all but nonexistent. But because there are only two airports—one in Guatemala City, the other in Flores—you're forced to do most of your travel by land. All but the hardiest travelers will want to stay in the larger towns and explore the more isolated regions on day trips. Most of the roads in El Petén are still unpaved, the exceptions being the road from Santa Elena–Flores to Tikal, the road from Río Dulce in the south to Santa Elena–Flores, and a few others.

From the Belize border, it's about 62 mi (100 km) by road to Tikal, and from the Belize border to Flores it's slightly longer (70 mi [112 km]). This road, except for some dusty streets in the scruffy Guatemalan border town of Melchor de Mencos, is in good condition. At El Cruce, also known as Ixlu, the road splits, turning north to Tikal and southwest to Santa Elena and Flores. If, instead of going on to Tikal, you turn west near the village of El Remate, the road (unpaved here) takes you around the north end of Lake Petén Itzá, passing the villages of San José and San Andrés, and eventually ending up at the town of San Benito, adjoining Santa Elena. Driving, by car or van, the trip to Tikal from the Belize border is roughly 1½ hours, depending on road and weather conditions.

WHEN TO GO

The weather around Tikal is similar to that in the Cayo—very hot in spring, with some rain; hot and always humid in summer and fall; and a little cooler and more pleasant but still often hot and a bit muggy in winter. Most people visit Tikal from June to August and from Christmas to April. The busiest time of year in all of Guatemala is *Semana Santa,* the week from Palm Sunday to Easter Sunday, though it's not as busy in El Petén as elsewhere.

ABOUT THE RESTAURANTS

In El Petén, you have a couple of choices for dining: *comedores,* which are small eateries along the lines of a U.S. café or diner, with simple and inexpensive local food; and restaurants, that, in general, are a little nicer and serve a wider selection of food, often with an international or American flavor. Restaurants are mostly in Flores and other towns. Elsewhere you'll probably eat in hotel or lodge dining rooms. You can also eat at street stalls (if you don't have a sensitive tummy), and buy cheap and wonderful fruits, breads, cheeses, and other items for picnics at markets and groceries.

The basis of Guatemalan, especially Mayan, food is corn, usually eaten as a tortilla, as a tamale, or on the cob. Black beans accompany most meals, either whole beans cooked in a broth or mashed and refried. Meats are often served in *caldos* (stews) or cooked in a spicy chili sauce. Thin and tender *lomito,* a popular cut of beef, is on the menu in most restaurants. The most popular fish is the delicious *robálo,* known elsewhere as snook. The *queso fundido* (melted cheese with condiments and tortillas) is a good choice for light eaters. El Petén has a few regional specialties, including *palmito* (heart of palm) in salads and *escabeche de pescado* (fish with a pickled relish).

Though garden-fresh *ensaladas* (salads) may be tempting, avoid them unless you're absolutely sure they have been thoroughly washed in boiled and chlorine-treated water—and, even then, think twice.

Breakfast is usually tortillas, eggs, and beans. Lunch is the biggest meal of the day, and you can save money by ordering *comidas corridas,* two- or three-course specials. Dinner is usually a little more expensive than lunch, even for the same items.

In El Petén, some restaurants serve wild game, or *comida silvestre.* Although often delicious, the game has usually been taken illegally. You might see *venado* (venison), *coche del monte* (mountain cow or peccary), and *tepezcuintle* (paca, a large rodent) on the menu.

A tip of about 10% is standard at most Guatemalan restaurants.

ABOUT THE HOTELS

El Petén now has a wide range of lodging options, from suites at luxurious lakeside resorts to stark rooms in budget hotels. Flores has many lodging choices, and the number of hotels there keeps prices competitive. The hotels in the much larger Santa Elena, the gateway to the island town of Flores, are generally larger and more upscale than the places in Flores, but with less atmosphere. El Remate, about 22 mi (35 km) from Flores on the road to Tikal, is a pleasant alternative, with several excellent small, mostly inexpensive hotels. At Tikal itself are three lodges, all somewhat overpriced (by Guatemalan, but not Belizean, standards) and often catering to groups. They have the great advantage of being right at the park. On the north side of Lago de Petén Itzá are several hotels, including a couple of the most upscale in the region: Francis Ford Coppola's La Lancha and the largest resort hotel in the area, Hotel Camino Real Tikal. Bellhops and maids expect tips only in the more expensive hotels.

WHAT IT COSTS IN GUATEMALAN QUETZALES					
	¢	$	$$	$$$	$$$$
RESTAU- RANTS	under Q40	Q40–Q70	Q70–Q100	Q100–Q130	over Q130
HOTELS	under Q160	Q160–Q360	Q360–Q560	Q560–Q760	over Q760

Restaurant prices are per person for a main course at dinner. Hotel prices are for two people in a standard double room, including tax and service. Remember that most hotels in El Petén charge a total of 22% tax on top of the room rate.

As in Belize, many hotels in El Petén have high and low seasons. They charge higher rates during the dry season, December through April, and sometimes also during the July to August vacation season. Advance

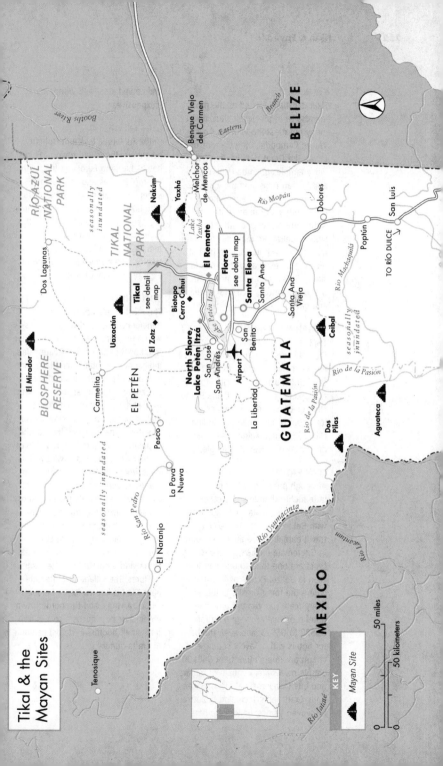

Tikal & the Mayan Sites

TOP REASONS TO GO

TIKAL

Tikal is usually ranked as the most impressive of all Mayan sites, and many put it—along with Angkor Wat in Cambodia, the pyramids of Egypt, the Great Wall of China, the Petra temples in Jordan, the Greek and Roman ruins, and the Machu Picchu Inca site in Peru—among the wonders of the ancient world. Although Caracol and other Mayan sites in Belize are magnificent, none truly rivals Tikal in visual impact. It's much more excavated than any large site in Belize, and you'll never forget the jungle setting, rich with wildlife and birds.

OTHER MAYAN RUINS

Tikal is the best known, but hardly the only important, Mayan site in El Petén. El Mirador, close to the Mexican border, was a giant city-state, perhaps larger than Tikal, and in the Mirador Basin are the remains of at least four other centers, including Nakbé, El Tintal, Xulnal, and Wakná; most are still covered in jungle.

LOW PRICES

Although prices in El Petén are a little higher than in some other areas of Guatemala, in comparison with Belize, the area is rife with travel bargains. Overall, price levels in Guatemala for hotels, meals, and tours are one-third to one-half less than in Belize. Except at Tikal Park, where the three on-site hotels are overpriced, you can get a decent hotel room with private bath for US$20 to US$25, and even the better hotels with a lovely setting and charm are rarely more than US$100. Simple meals are a couple of dollars, and bus travel costs about US$1 an hour. Craft items, including beautiful woven fabrics, handmade hats, and carved slate and wood, are inexpensive.

FLORES & PETÉN ITZÁ

Unlike its larger, less atmospheric neighbors, the island town of Flores has a charming European feel, with red-roof houses and cobblestone streets. You can dine in little bistros with lakeside views or stay in simple, inexpensive inns. Lago de Petén Itza is the second-largest lake in Guatemala. You can kayak around the lake or take a *lancha* (small boat) to explore its distant corners.

SHOPPING FOR HANDICRAFTS

The most famous of Guatemala's handicrafts are handwoven fabrics—women in nearly every village weave traditional patterns. But Guatemala's indigenous population creates countless other kinds of handicrafts, such as ceramics, wood carvings, baskets, toys, statues, bags, or hats. Guatemala's markets are a wonderful way to witness the everyday lives of the population. Vendors line a jumble of narrow passages and hawk everything from fruits and vegetables to toiletries. Although other areas of Guatemala, especially the highlands where many of the crafts are created, have better shopping and more markets than you'll find in El Petén, there's an open-air market in Santa Elena, and a number of little shops in Flores. The village of El Remate near Tikal is known for its unique wood carvings, and the border town of Melchor de Mencos also has *tiendas* (small booths or stores) catering to crafts-hungry tourists.

reservations are a good idea during these periods, especially at Tikal park lodges.

TIKAL

22 mi (35 km) north of El Remate, 42 mi (68 km) northeast of Flores.

Fodor'sChoice
★

You rise shortly before dawn. It isn't long before you hear the muffled roars of howler monkeys in the distance. After a quick cup of coffee, you and your fellow adventurers follow your guide through the deserted plazas toward the pyramid that towers over everything else. The climb up the side is difficult in the dark, but after scrambling up rickety ladders and over roots and vines you find yourself at the top. You glance to the east, past the endless expanse of jungle, just as the sun starts to rise.

Tikal is one of the most popular tourist attractions in Central America—and with good reason. Smack in the middle of the 222-square-mi (575-square-km) Parque Nacional Tikal, the towering temples are ringed on all sides by miles of virgin forest. The area around the ruins is great for checking out creatures that spend their entire lives hundreds of feet above the forest floor in the dense canopy of trees. Colorful birds like yellow toucans and Scarlet Macaws are common sights.

Although the region was home to Maya communities as early as 600 BC, Tikal itself wasn't established until sometime around 200 BC. One of the first structures to be built here was a version of the North Acropolis. Others were added at a dizzying pace for the next three centuries. By AD 100 impressive structures like the Great Plaza had already been built. But even though it was a powerful city in its own right, Tikal was still ruled by the northern city of El Mirador. It wasn't until the arrival of a powerful dynasty around AD 300 that Tikal arrogated itself to full power. King Great Jaguar Paw sired a lineage that would build Tikal into a city rivaling any of its time. It's estimated that by AD 500, the city covered more than 18 square mi (47 square km) and had a population of close to 100,000.

The great temples that still tower above the jungle were at that time covered with stucco and painted with bright reds and greens, and the priests used them for elaborate ceremonies meant to please the gods and assure prosperity for the city. What makes these structures even more impressive is that the Maya possessed no metal tools to aid in construction, had no beasts of burden to carry heavy loads, and never used wheels for anything except children's toys. Of course, as a hierarchical culture they had a slave class, and the land was rich in obsidian, a volcanic glass that could be fashioned into razor-sharp tools.

By the 6th century Tikal governed a large part of the Mayan world, thanks to a leader called Caan Chac (Stormy Sky), who took the throne around AD 426. Under Caan Chac, Tikal became an aggressive military and commercial center that dominated the surrounding communities

7

GREAT ITINERARIES

IF YOU HAVE 1 DAY

You can visit **Tikal** on a day trip from the San Ignacio area and get a good sense of its grandeur, although if you have the time it's better to spend at least one or two nights. Take a bus or taxi to the border and walk across, and then go by Guatemalan taxi or minibus to Tikal; if you don't want to worry about the logistics, take one of the many Tikal day tours offered by tour operators and hotels in the Cayo. You'll have several hours to explore Tikal before returning to Belize. Hire a guide at the park to show you around (services of a park guide are usually included on tours from San Ignacio).

IF YOU HAVE 2 DAYS

If you're in Belize City, take the Linéa Dorada bus from the Marine Terminal to **Flores**, or from the San Ignacio area cross the border (take a bus or taxi to the border and walk across) and then go by minibus or taxi to Tikal. Depending on your schedule, you may choose to spend the night either at Tikal park so you can see the ruins in the morning (a must for birders), or in Flores, El Remate, or elsewhere along the shores of **Lake Petén Itzá**. If you arrive at the park after 3 PM, your ticket will be good for admission the next day as well. You can easily spend two days, or longer, exploring the ruins. You may want to hire a guide for your first day, then wander about on your own on the second. If you have additional time, consider an extension in El Petén. The town of Flores, with its lakeside bistros and cobblestone streets, merits at least a half-day stroll. With scores of other ruins in the region, you could spend weeks traveling off the beaten track.

with a power never before seen in Mesoamerica. The swamps protected the city from attack and allowed troops to spot any approaching enemy. Intensive agriculture in the *bajos* (lowlands) provided food for the huge population. A valuable obsidian trade sprang up, aided by the city's strategic position near two rivers.

Tikal thrived for more than a millennium, forming strong ties with two powerful centers: Kaminal Juyu, in the Guatemalan highlands, and Teotihuacán, in Mexico City. The city entered a golden age when Ah-Cacao (Lord Chocolate) ascended the throne in AD 682. It was Ah-Cacao and his successors who commissioned the construction of the majority of the city's most important temples. Continuing the tradition of great structures, Ah-Cacao's son commissioned Temple I, which he dedicated to his father, who is buried beneath it. He also ordered the construction of Temple IV, the tallest temple at Tikal. By the time of his death in 768, Tikal was at the peak of its power. It would remain so until its mysterious abandonment around AD 900.

For almost 1,000 years Tikal remained engulfed by the jungle. The conquistadors who came here searching for gold and silver must have passed right by the overgrown ruins, mistaking them for rocky hills. The native Peténeros certainly knew of the ancient city's existence, but no one else ventured near until 1848, when the Guatemalan government dispatched archaeologists to the region. Tikal started to receive

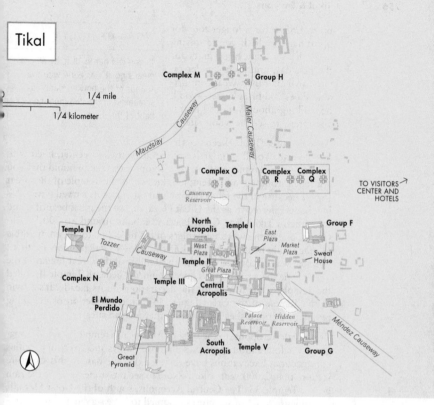

Tikal

Complex M   Group H

1/4 mile

1/4 kilometer

Maudslay Causeway

Maler Causeway

Complex O

Complex R   Complex Q

TO VISITORS
CENTER AND
HOTELS

Causeway
Reservoir

North
Acropolis   Temple I

East
Plaza

Market
Plaza

Group F

Temple IV

Tozzer Causeway

West
Plaza

Sweat
House

Complex N

Temple II

Great Plaza

Temple III

Central
Acropolis

El Mundo
Perdido

Palace
Reservoir

Hidden
Reservoir

Méndez Causeway

South
Acropolis   Temple V

Group G

Great
Pyramid

international attention in 1877, when Dr. Gustav Bernoulli commissioned locals to remove the carved wooden lintels from across the doorways of Temples I and IV. These items were sent to a museum in Basel, Switzerland.

In 1881 and 1882 English archaeologist Alfred Percival Maudslay made the first map showing the architectural features of this vast city. As he began to unearth the major temples, he recorded his work in dramatic photographs—you can see copies in the museum at Tikal. His work was continued by Teobert Maler, who came in 1895 and 1904. Both Maler and Maudslay have causeways named in their honor. In 1951 the Guatemalan air force cleared an airstrip near the ruins to improve access for large-scale archaeological work. Today, after more than 150 years of digging, researchers say that Tikal includes some 3,000 buildings. Countless more are still covered by the jungle. ⊠ *Parque Nacional Tikal* ☎ *No phone* ⊕ *www.tikalpark.com* ⊠ *Q150 (increased from Q50 in 2007)* ⊙ *Daily 6–6.*

THE TIKAL RUINS

You can tour Tikal on your own or with local guides. The guides, which can be booked at the guide-booking desk near the visitor center, make the visit more interesting, though don't believe everything they tell you. Expect to pay about US$20 for a half-day tour for two, and up to US$50 for a longer tour for up to five people. If you're staying more than one day, hire a guide for the first day, and then wander on your own after that. Wear comfortable shoes and bring water—you'll be walking about 6 mi (10 km) if you intend to see the whole site.

As you enter Tikal, keep to the middle trail. You'll soon arrive at the ancient city's center, filled with awe-inspiring temples and intricate acropolises. The pyramid that you approach from behind is **Temple I,** known as the Temple of the Great Jaguar because of the feline represented on one of its carved lintels. It's in what is referred to as the **Great Plaza,** one of the most beautiful and dramatic in Tikal. The Great Plaza was built around AD 700 by Ah-Cacao, one of the wealthiest rulers of his time. His tomb, comparable in magnitude to that of Pa Cal at the ruins of Palenque in southern Mexico, was discovered beneath the Temple of the Great Jaguar in the 1960s. The theory is that his queen is buried beneath **Temple II,** called the Temple of the Masks for the decorations on its facade. It's a twin of the Temple of the Great Jaguar. In fact, construction of matching pyramids distinguishes Tikal from other Mayan sites.

The **North Acropolis,** to the west of Ah-Cacao's temple, is a mind-boggling conglomeration of temples built over layers and layers of previous construction. Excavations have revealed that the base of this structure is more than 2,000 years old. Be sure to see the stone mask of the rain god at Temple 33. The **Central Acropolis,** south of the Great Plaza, is an immense series of structures assumed to have served as administrative centers.

If you climb to the top of one of the pyramids, you'll see the gray roof combs of others rising above the rain forest's canopy but still trapped within it. **Temple V,** to the south, underwent a $3 million restoration project and is now open to the public. **Temple IV,** to the west, is the tallest-known structure built by the Maya. Although the climb to the top is difficult, the view is unforgettable.

To the southwest of the plaza lies the **South Acropolis,** which hasn't been reconstructed, and a 105-foot-high pyramid, similar in construction to those at Teotihuacán. A few jungle trails, including the marked Interpretative Benil-ha Trail, offer a chance to see spider monkeys and other wildlife. Outside the park, a somewhat overgrown trail halfway down the old airplane runway on the left leads to the remnants of old rubber-tappers' camps and is a good spot for bird-watching.

At park headquarters are two small archaeological museums that display Mayan artifacts. They are a good resource for information on the enigmatic rise and fall of the Maya people, though little information is in English.

Museo Lítico or Stelae Museum has stelae found at Tikal and interesting photos from early archaeological excavations. ⊠*Near visitor center* 🎫*Q10 ($1.30)* ⊙*Daily 9–5.*

Museo Tikal, also known as the Tikal Sylvannus G. Morley Museum, has a replica of Ha Sawa Chaan K'awil's burial chamber and some ceramics and bones from the actual tomb (the jade, however, is a replica). ⊠*Near visitor center* 🎫*Free with ticket from Museo Lítico* ⊙*Daily 9–5.*

WHERE TO STAY & EAT

There are three hotels on the park grounds: Tikal Inn, Jungle Lodge, and Jaguar Inn. At all of these you pay for the park location rather than good amenities and great service. Electric power is from generators, which usually run from around 5 or 6 AM to 10 or 11 PM. Since the hotels here have a captive audience, service is not always as friendly or helpful as it could be, and reservations are sometimes "lost," even if you have confirming e-mail. Camping is also available, at the park campsite (US$4–US$7) or at the Jaguar Inn. Several *comedores* are at the entrance to the park, Comedor Tikal currently being the best, and you can also get food in the park and at the hotels. All of the hotels have room-only rates, but if you are booking through a travel agent you may be required to take a package that includes meals and a Tikal tour.

$$$$ 🏨 **Jungle Lodge.** Built fifty years ago to house archaeologists working at Tikal, this hotel has cute duplexes with porches but not much privacy. The bungalows are spacious, with double beds and tile floors. There are whirling ceiling fans, but the generator is shut off from 11 PM to 5 AM, so you may be hot at night. Two new suites have king beds and whirlpool baths. If your budget allows, choose one of the bungalows or suites. The restaurant was rebuilt in late 2006 and serves unremarkable food. **Pros:** Best of the three lodges in the park, clean and adequate accommodations. **Cons:** You are paying for location; food is mediocre. ⊠*Parque Nacional Tikal* ☎*7861–0447* ⊕*www.jungle lodge.guate.com* ➾*12 rooms with shared baths, 34 bungalows, 2 suites* ♿*In-room: no a/c, no phone, no TV. In-hotel: restaurant, bar, pool, no elevator, public Internet, laundry service* ⊟*MC, V* ⟦◎⟧*BP.*

$$$$ 🏨 **Tikal Inn.** This cluster of comfortable bungalows, set farthest from the park entrance, wraps around a well-manicured garden and a pool. It's set apart from the other lodgings, affording a bit of privacy. The rooms have a modern feel, yet they have thatch roofs and stucco walls decorated with traditional fabrics. Avoid the rooms near the parking lot, as guests who want to watch the sunrise over the park gather there and can be noisy. A restau-

> **WORD OF MOUTH**
>
> "In Tikal we stayed at the Jungle Lodge. Try to get up very early in the morning to watch the sunrise from the top of one temple (bring a flashlight for an early morning walk from the lodge) and listen to a real jungle sounds before other tourists start arriving around 9 AM. We had our late breakfast around 10 AM, then returned to investigate the temples more closely. Nothing like staying in Tikal overnight."—z

Dancing with the Dead

Colorful cemeteries, with their turquoises and pinks, mauves and sky blues, play an integral part in the living fabric of contemporary Guatemalan society. It's not uncommon to see entire families visiting their deceased relatives on Sunday. But a visit to the cemetery need not be mournful, and they often bring a bottle of alcohol to share among themselves, occasionally tipping the bottle to the earth, so that their dead relatives also get their share. Incense is burned and shamans perform ancient rites alongside Catholic and evangelical priests. Day of the Dead gives family members their greatest chance to celebrate and honor their deceased relatives with music, dance, song, festivals and, yes, much drinking and merriment.

Celebrating the dead rather than mourning their passing is a Mayan tradition that reaches back to pre-Columbian times. The *Popol Vuh*, or Mayan Bible as it's sometimes referred to, looks toward an active relationship with deceased friends and relatives. "Remember us after we have gone. Don't forget us," reads the *Popol Vuh*. "Conjure up our faces and our words. Our image will be as dew in the hearts of those who want to remember us."

It is unknown who authored the *Popol Vuh*, which was translated into Spanish in the early 18th century by Father Francisco Ximénez, but the practices and myths of the sacred book of the Maya still make their way into the Day of the Dead celebrations across Guatemala. The book has also been integral in understanding the traditions, cosmology, and mythology of the Quiché. According to scholars, it's one of the finest surviving aboriginal American manuscripts.

The country's two most fascinating Day of the Dead celebrations take place in Santiago Sacatepéquez and Todos Santos Chuchumatán on November 1. In Santiago Sacatepéquez, a Cakchiquel pueblo located 19 mi (30 km) from Antigua, the villagers gather in the early morning hours and have a procession through the narrow streets to the cemetery. Once there, they take part in what is one of Guatemala's most resplendent ceremonies, flying giant kites of up to 2 meters in diameter to communicate with those who have passed away. The villagers tie messages to the kite tails to let the dead know how they are doing and to ask God for special favors. The colorful celebration is finished with a lunch feast of *fiambre*, a traditional dish of cold cuts, boiled eggs, vegetables, olives, and other delicacies.

The color scheme of the cemeteries is more than just decorative: turquoise and green tombs signify an adult member of the family was recently interred in the aboveground crypts, whites and yellows indicate the passing of an elderly family member, and pinks and blues are reserved for deceased children.

Whether or not you're lucky enough to see Guatemala's cemeteries during the Day of the Dead celebrations, they are still worth a visit. Although foreigners are welcome in the cemeteries, it's important to respect the traditions and dignity of those visiting deceased relatives—tread softly and leave your camera behind.

—Gregory Benchwick

rant has a menu that changes daily. **Pros:** Good location in the park, has a swimming pool. **Cons:** Poor service at times, rooms are hot, limited hot water and electricity. ⊠*Parque Nacional Tikal* ☎*7926–1917 or 7926–0065* ✆*hoteltikalinn@itelgua.com* ↩*18 rooms, 18 bungalows* ⌂*In-room: no a/c, no phone, no TV. In-hotel: restaurant, bar, pool, no elevator, laundry service* ▬*AE, DC, MC, V.*

$$ ▦▲**Jaguar Inn.** Although this small hotel won't win any travel awards and has the feel of a backpacker's place, it's considerably less expensive than the other two hotels in the park and has a good restaurant. The small rooms have tile floors and wooden furnishings, with Guatemalan fabrics. You can also camp here for Q40 ($5) per person, including rental of a hammock and mosquito net. **Pros:** Cheapest lodging at the park, camping available. **Cons:** Basic rooms somewhat jammed together. ⊠*Parque Nacional Tikal* ☎*No phone* ↩*13 rooms in cabins, 1 dorm* ⌂*In-room: no a/c, no phone, no TV. In-hotel: restaurant, public Internet, no elevator* ▬*MC, V.*

TIKAL ENVIRONS

FLORES

★ *133 mi (206 km) north of Río Dulce, 38 mi (61 km) northeast of Sayaxché.*

The red-roof town of Flores, on an island surrounded by the waters of Lago Petén Itzá, is on the site of the ancient city of Tatyasal. This was the region's last unconquered outpost of Mayan civilization, until finally falling to the Spanish in 1697. The conquerors destroyed the city's huge pyramids.

Today the provincial capital is a pleasant place to explore, with its narrow streets lined with thick-walled buildings painted pink, blue, and purple. Flowering plants droop over balconies, giving the town a tropical flavor. There's a central square presided over by a colonial church. Connected to the mainland by a bridge and causeway, Flores serves as a base for travelers to El Petén. It's also the center of many nongovernmental organizations working for the preservation of the Mayan Biosphere, an endangered area covering nearly all of northern Petén. Flores is also one of the last remaining vestiges of the Itzá, the people who built Mexico's monumental Chichén Itzá.

In the 1800s, before it was a departure point for travelers headed for the ruins, Flores was called Devil's Island because of the prison on top of the hill (a church stands there now). Since 1994 the building has been home to the **Centro de Información sobre la Naturaleza, Cultura, y Artesanía de Petén** (⊠*North side of Parque Central* ☎*7926–0718* ☉*Weekdays 8-5*). This center has a small museum with photographs of the region and information about local resources, such as allspice, chicle (a chewing-gum base made from tree sap), and *xate* (a shade palm used in floral decorations). A gift shop sells wood carvings, woven baskets, cornhusk dolls, and even locally made peanut butter.

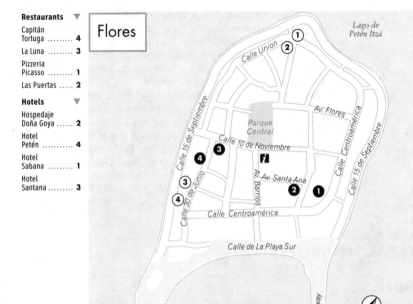

KEY

❶ *Restaurants*

① *Hotels*

🛈 *Tourist info.*

WHERE TO STAY & EAT

$-$$$ ✕ **La Luna.** With its homemade paper lamp shades illuminating lovely
★ blue walls, La Luna inspires romance on any moonlit night. But you
can just as easily fall in love with what we think is the most creative
restaurant in town when you stop in for a delicious lunch. Choose
from inventive dishes, including wonderful vegetarian options like
the stuffed squash in white sauce. Many people drop by for a drink
at the bar. ⊠ *Calle 30 de Junio* ☎ *7926–3346* ▤ *AE, DC, MC, V*
☽ *Closed Sun.*

¢-$$$ ✕ **Capitán Tortuga.** The large, cartoonlike Capitán Tortuga sign may fool
you into thinking this restaurant is just for kids, but the excellent grilled
steak and seafood options make this one of Flores' best restaurants.
The *pinchos* (grilled kebabs) are cooked on an open barbecue, sending
enticing aromas throughout the restaurant. There's a nice patio out
back, which offers tremendous sunset views of the lake. ⊠ *Calle 30 de
Junio and Callejón San Pedrito* ☎ *7926–0247* ▤ *MC, V.*

¢-$ ✕ **Las Puertas.** On a quiet side street, Las Puertas was named for its six
screened doors. It's a favorite hangout for locals and travelers alike. The
friendly couple who run the place take great pride in serving only the
freshest foods. Notable are the delicious sandwiches made with homemade bread and mozzarella cheese and the giant goblets of incredible
iced coffee. In the afternoon you can relax with a fruit drink as you

play one of the many board games. Don't forget to stop back at night for a hearty dinner and live music. ⊠ *Calle Central at Av. Santa Ana* ☏ *7926–1061* ⊟ *AE, DC, MC, V* ⊗ *Closed Sun.*

¢–$ ✗ **Pizzeria Picasso.** If you find yourself returning to Pizzeria Picasso, it's because the brick-oven pizza is incomparably hot and delicious. The decor, featuring a print of Picasso's *Guernica,* is another draw. If you're not in the mood for pizza, there is a variety of pastas as well. Save room for cheesecake or tiramisu and a cup of steaming cappuccino. ⊠ *Calle Centroamérica* ☏ *7926–0673* ⊟ *AE, DC, MC, V* ⊗ *Closed Mon.*

$$ ⌂ **Hotel Petén.** Take a dip in this lovely hotel's arabesque plunge pool to escape the midday heat. Rooms are simply furnished, but if you ask for one facing the lake (only five do not), you'll have an incredible view of Lake Petén Itza. The same owners also operate several other hotels and a reliable tour company. **Pros:** Modern hotel with great sunset views of the lake. **Cons:** Four flights of stairs to get to top-floor rooms. ⊠ *Calle Centroamérica, off Calle 30 de Junio* ☏ *7926–0692* ⊅ *21 rooms* ⌂ *In-hotel: restaurant, bar, pool, public Internet, no elevator, laundry service* ⊟ *AE, DC, MC, V* ⫯ *BP.*

$–$$ ⌂ **Hotel Sabana.** This small hotel, with four floors in one section and five in another, offers simple rooms that open onto a terrace overlooking the pool. A sundeck has nice views of the lake. This is a reliable choice if you need some creature comforts such as air-conditioning and a TV. **Pros:** Dependable choice with some amenities. **Cons:** A lot of stairs to climb. ⊠ *Calle Union and Av. Libertad* ☏ *7926–1248* ⊕ *www.hotelsabana.com* ⊅ *28 rooms* ⌂ *In-hotel: restaurant, bar, pool, no elevator, laundry service* ⊟ *AE, DC, MC, V.*

$–$$ ⌂ **Hotel Santana.** Sitting right on the water, this bright pink hotel is the
★ best lodging on the island. All the rooms open up onto wide balconies with wicker chairs where you can enjoy the view. Rooms at the back have lake views. The sunny central courtyard surrounds a pleasant pool. **Pros:** Best lodging in Flores, lovely views of the lake. **Cons:** Mishmash of building styles and materials, but it seems to work. ⊠ *Calle 30 de Junio, Playa Poniente* ☏ *7926–0662* ⊕ *www.santanapeten.com* ⊅ *35 rooms* ⌂ *In-room: safe. In-hotel: restaurant, pool, public Internet, no elevator, laundry service* ⊟ *AE, DC, MC, V.*

¢ ⌂ **Hospedaje Doña Goya.** A rooftop terrace with hammocks swinging in the breeze is the best part of this budget lodging. If you prefer, grab a good book and sink into one of the comfortable lounge chairs. The hotel is clean and well run, which explains why it is so popular. Arrive early in the day to secure a room. A bed in the dorm is Q25. ⊠ *Calle Union* ☏ *7926–3538* ⊅ *6 rooms, 3 with bath, dormitory* ⌂ *In-room: no a/c (some), no TV. In-hotel: no elevator* ⊟ *No credit cards.*

NIGHTLIFE

Discoteca Raices (⊠ *Av. Periférico*) is the island's only true disco. The bar at the **Maya Princess** (⊠ *Av. La Reforma and Av. 14 de Noviembre*) shows nightly movies on a big-screen TV.

Las Puertas (⊠ *Calle Central at Av. Santa Ana* ☏ *7926–1061*) has live music every night. The artsy **La Luna** (⊠ *Calle 30 de Junio* ☏ *7926–3346*) has a pleasant atmosphere.

SPORTS & THE OUTDOORS

BOATING

Boat trips on Lake Petén Itzá can be arranged through most hotels in Flores or by haggling with boat owners who congregate behind the Hotel Santana. Tours often include a stop at Paraíso Escondido, a small mainland park northwest of Flores.

SANTA ELENA

¼ mi (½ km) south of Flores.

Although it lacks the charms of neighboring Flores, gritty Santa Elena is pretty much unavoidable. Most services that you'll need for your trip to El Petén, from currency exchange to travel planning, are usually offered here. There are also more upscale hotels here than in Flores.

WHERE TO STAY & EAT

$$$$ **Petén Espléndido.** You're not on Flores, but the views of that pretty island from your private balcony are the next best thing. The pool, surrounded by palm trees, is a great place to spend an afternoon sunbathing. Sit at one of the shaded tables on the terrace or in the pretty dining room and enjoy the *especial del día* (daily special). The hotel is popular among business travelers, who appreciate the fully equipped convention center. Families enjoy the paddleboats on the lake. **Pros:** The top full-service hotel in Santa Elena, only elevator in the Petén, nice views of Flores. **Cons:** A bit formal, smallish rooms. ⊠ *At foot of bridge leading to Flores* ☎ *7926–0880* ⊕ *www.petenesplendido.com* ⇆ *62 rooms* ⌂ *In-room: safe. In-hotel: restaurant, room service, bar, pool, public Internet, airport shuttle, parking (no fee)* ⊟ *AE, DC, MC, V.*

$$$$ **Villa Maya.** You could lie in bed and count the birds flying by your
★ window at these modern villas at Lake Petenchel, east of Santa Elena. Some 50 species have been spotted in the area. If you're more interested in wildlife, ask an attendant where to find the troop of spider monkeys that roams the grounds and the adjacent rain forest. All 56 rooms, in two-level bungalows spread out around the grounds, are tastefully decorated with colorful weavings and mahogany accents, and have terrific views. Vans shuttle you to and from Tikal. **Pros:** Beautiful lake views, quiet and peaceful setting. **Cons:** Not convenient to a selection of restaurants and shopping. ⊠ *5 mi (8 km) east of Santa Elena* ☎ *5415–1592, 2334–8136 in Guatemala City* ⊕ *www.villasdeguatemala.com* ⇆ *56 rooms* ⌂ *In-room: no TV, no phone. In-hotel: restaurant, bar, room service, 2 pools, bicycles, laundry service, parking (no fee), public Internet, no elevator* ⊟ *AE, DC, MC, V.*

> **WORD OF MOUTH**
>
> "We really enjoyed a couple of nights at the Villa Maya and will stay there again. They have their own private lagoon and the pools were very nice. They also have a hot tub. It is only a 20-minute cab ride into Flores if you want to go there to eat. The food at Maya was very good, we thought."
>
> —Suzie2

SPORTS & THE OUTDOORS

There are several caves in the hills behind Santa Elena with interesting stalactite and stalagmite formations and subterranean rivers. The easiest to visit is Aktun Kan, just south of town.

🐚 **Ixpanpajul Parque Natural** (✉*Ruta a Santa Elena, Km 468* ☎*2336–0576* ⊕*www.ixpanpajul.com*) is a private nature reserve sitting on a large stand of primary rain forest. Hiking the suspended bridges of the skyway will give you a bird's-eye view of the indigenous flora and fauna that make the rain forest the most biodiverse ecosystem on the planet. The park also offers myriad adventure opportunities from nighttime ATV tours to horseback rides to mountain-bike excursions. The entrance to the reserve is 6 mi (10 km) south of Santa Elena.

EL REMATE

18½ mi (30 km) northeast of Flores.

A mellow little town on the eastern shore of Lago Petén Itzá, El Remate is known mostly for its wood carvings, made by families that have dedicated themselves to this craft for generations. Just west of El Remate is the Biotopo Cerro Cahuí, and you can rent a canoe or kayak (around Q10 or $2 an hour) at El Remate to explore the lake. Because it's less than one hour from both Tikal and Yaxhá, El Remate makes a good base for exploring the area.

With more than 1,500 acres of rain forest, **Biotopo Cerro Cahuí** (✉*West of El Remate* ☎*Q20*) is one of the most accessible wildlife reserves in El Petén. It protects a portion of a mountain that extends to the eastern edge of Lago Petén Itzá, so there are plenty of opportunities for hiking. Two well-maintained trails put you in proximity of birds like ocellated turkeys, toucans, and parrots. As for mammals, look up to spot the long-armed spider monkeys or down to see squat rodents called *tepezcuintles*. Tzu'unte, a 4-mi (6-km) trail, leads to two lookouts with views of nearby lakes. The upper lookout, Mirador Moreletii, is known by locals as Crocodile Hill because, from the other side of the lake, it looks like the eye of a half-submerged crocodile. Los Ujuxtes, a 3-mi (5-km) trail, offers a panoramic view of three lakes. Both hikes begin at a ranger station, where English-speaking guides are sporadically available. Some robberies and attacks on tourists have taken place in the reserve, so ask locally about safety conditions before you explore on your own.

WHERE TO STAY & EAT

¢–$ ✕**La Estancia Cafetería.** Owner Victor Morales's specialty is an exquisite whitefish served with vegetables sautéed in butter on a wooden platter. Every once in a while he cooks up some fresh venison. Even though the driveway is usually filled with cars, this eatery is easy to miss—look for the Orange Crush sign. ✉*1¼ mi (2 km) south of El Remate* ☎*No phone* ⊟*No credit cards.*

$$–$$$ 🛏**La Mansión del Pájaro Serpiente.** Perched high on the hillside, La Mansión del Pájaro Serpiente has some of the prettiest accommodations in

El Petén. You have a choice of rooms in either standard or deluxe bungalows. Canopy beds grace the larger bedrooms, which are furnished in dark tropical woods and have big windows that let in lots of light. You can throw open the windows to catch the lake breezes, so sleeping is comfortable. Up a nearby hill is a swimming pool, and farther up you'll find a covered terrace with several hammocks. The open-air restaurant serves local and international dishes. **Pros:** Pretty little cabins set on a hillside, lake views, swimming pool. **Cons:** Not for those who can't walk up and down hills. ⊠*On main hwy. south of El Remate* ☎*7926–4246* ↩*10 rooms* ↻*In-room: no a/c, no phone, no TV. In-hotel: restaurant, bar, pool, no elevator, laundry service* ▭*MC, V.*

$-$$ 📺 **La Casa de Don David.** As you chat with David Kuhn, the owner of this cluster of bungalows, keep an eye out for his pet parrot. The little fellow sometimes gets jealous. But talking with Kuhn is worth it, as he and his wife, Rosa, have lived in the area for almost 30 years and are a great source of travel tips. Rooms are simple and clean, with private baths. Perhaps La Casa is most famous for its second-story restaurant which has good home cooking. Have dinner for two in a booth, or eat at the "friendship table" and make some new acquaintances. One meal is included in the room rate—you can choose to have breakfast or dinner here. **Pros:** Knowledgeable host, attractive grounds, good restaurant. **Cons:** Not a lot of frills. ⊠*On road to Biotopo Cerro Cahuí* ☎*5306–2190 or 7928–8469* ⊕*www.lacasadedondavid.com* ↩*15 rooms* ↻*In-room: no a/c (some), no TV. In-hotel: restaurant, public Internet, no elevator, laundry service* ▭*MC, V* ⊙*BP.*

SPORTS & THE OUTDOORS

The fun folks at **Tikal Canopy Tour** (⊠*Near entrance to Tikal* ☎*708–0674* ✎ *tikalcanopy@hotmail.com*) have expeditions that take you to the true heart of the rain forest—not on ground level, but more than 100 feet up in the air. In the canopy you'll see monkeys and maybe even a sloth. The tour, which costs US$30 per person, ends with an exhilarating 300-foot-long ride down a zip line.

SHOPPING

Although most souvenirs here are similar to those found elsewhere in Guatemala, the beautiful wood carvings are unique to El Petén. More than 70 families in this small town dedicate themselves to this craft. Their wares are on display on the side of the highway right before the turnoff for the Camino Real hotel on the road to Tikal.

NORTH SHORE, LAKE PETÉN ITZÁ

8 mi (13 km) west of El Remate.

The small villages of San Pedro, San José, and San Andrés, on the northwest shore of Lake Petén Itzá, have beautiful views of the sparkling lake. Several upscale lodges and hotels have opened here, and the area is accessible via bus or car on an improved dirt road either from El Remate or from Santa Elena.

WHERE TO STAY & EAT

$$$$ 🏠**Camino Real Tikal.** To experience the natural beauty of the jungles surrounding Lago Petén Itzá without sacrificing creature comforts, many people head to Camino Real Tikal. It's possible to spend several days at the hotel without exhausting the possibilities—kayaking on the lake, hiking in a private reserve, swimming in the pool, lounging in the lakeside hammocks, and experiencing a traditional Mayan sauna. A dozen three-story thatch-roof villas set high on the hillside hold the rooms, all of which have porches with views of the sparkling lake. **Pros:** Most upscale large hotel in El Petén, beautiful setting. **Cons:** Somewhat remote, rooms a bit dated. ✉ *Lote 77, Parcelamiento Tayasal, 3 mi (5 km) west of El Remate, San José* ☎*7926–0204* ⊕*www.caminoreal. com.gt* ⇨*72 rooms* ♨*In-room: safe, refrigerator. In-hotel: 2 restaurants, bars, pool, gym, water sports, bicycles, public Internet, no elevator, airport shuttle* ▭*AE, DC, MC, V* ❙◉❙*BP.*

$$$$ 🏠**La Lancha.** Francis Ford Coppola's latest lodging venture isn't quite
★ as luxe as his two properties in Belize, but everything is done in exquisite taste. Guatemalan and Balinese textiles and handmade furniture make rooms cozy. All the casitas glimpse Lake Petén Itzá, though the pricier, larger lake-view units have the stunning, splurge-worthy views. **Pros:** Lovely lake views, all done in good taste. **Cons:** Expensive (for Guatemala), somewhat remote, lots of steep stairs. ✉*8 mi (13 km) west of El Remate, San José* ☎*7928–8331, 800/746–3743 in U.S.* ⊕*www.blancaneauxlodge.com* ⇨*10 casitas* ♨*In-room: no phone, no TV. In-hotel: restaurant, bar, pool, bicycles, no elevator, airport shuttle* ▭*AE, MC, V* ❙◉❙*CP.*

$$$$ 🏠**Ni'tun Ecolodge.** After hiking through the jungle, you'll love returning
Fodor'sChoice to this charming cluster of cabins, owned by a former coffee farmer.
★ The point is to disturb the environment as little as possible, so the buildings are constructed of stone and wood left behind by farmers clearing land for fields. The common areas, including a massive kitchen downstairs and an airy bar and reading room upstairs, are delightful. Ni'tun also runs Monkey Eco Tours, so you can choose from itineraries ranging from one-day trips to nearby villages to a seven-day journey to El Mirador. **Pros:** Small, very personal lodge experience, excellent food, engaging owner. **Cons:** Somewhat off the beaten path. ✉*1 mi (2 km) west of San Andres, northwest of Flores* ☎*5201–0759* ⊕*www.nitun. com* ⇨*4 cabins* ♨*In-room: no a/c, no TV. In-hotel: restaurant, bar, no elevator, public Internet* ▭*AE, DC, MC,* ⊘*Closed late May–early June. V* ❙◉❙*BP.*

OTHER MAYAN SITES IN EL PETÉN

Although Tikal is the most famous, El Petén has hundreds of archaeological sites, ranging from modest burial chambers to sprawling cities. The vast majority have not been explored, let alone restored. Within a few miles of Tikal are several easy-to-reach sites. Because they're in isolated areas, it's a good idea to go with a guide *(see Tours in Tikal & the Mayan Ruins Essentials, below).*

SIGHTS TO SEE

Nakúm lies deep within the forest, connected to Tikal via jungle trails that are sometimes used for horseback expeditions. You cannot visit during the rainy season, as you'll sink into mud up to your ankles. Two building complexes and some stelae are visible. ✉*16 mi (26 km) east of Tikal.*

The 4,000-year-old city of **Uaxactún** (pronounced Wah-shank-TOON) was once a rival to Tikal's supremacy in the region. It was conquered by Tikal in the 4th century and lived in the shadow of that great city for centuries. Inscriptions show that Uaxactún existed longer than any other Mayan city, which may account for the wide variety of structures. Here you'll find a Mayan observatory.

Uaxactún is surrounded by thick rain forest, so the trip can be arduous, but as it's difficult to get here, you most likely won't have to fight the crowds as you do at neighboring Tikal, leaving you free to enjoy the quiet and mystic air of the ruins. The rock-and-dirt road is passable during the drier seasons and nearly impossible at other times without a four-wheel-drive vehicle. You'll need to secure a permit to visit Uaxactún. The administration building in Tikal is on the road between the Jaguar Inn and the Jungle Lodge. Obtaining a permit is sometimes easier said than done, but with a little persistence and perhaps a small *mordida* (bribe), you should be able to get past the guards into the administration area where they grant the free permits. Sometimes police will ask to accompany you on the trip, which is helpful for two reasons: it prevents potential robberies and, most important, will give you an extra person to push if your vehicle gets stuck. The police may ask you for some money; a Q20 tip goes a long way toward making your trip smooth. ✉*16 mi (24 km) north of Tikal.*

Overlooking a beautiful lake of the same name, the ruins of **Yaxhá** are divided into two sections of rectangular structures that form plazas and streets. The city was probably inhabited between the Pre-Classic and Classic periods. The ruins are being restored by a German organization. Lake Yaxhá, surrounded by virgin rain forest, is a good bird-watching spot. During the rainy season only a four-wheel-drive vehicle—or setting out on horseback, motorcycle, or on foot—will get you to Yaxhá; the rest of the year the road is passable. ✉*30 km (48 km) south of Flores, 19 mi (30 km) east of Tikal.*

A popular ecotourism destination, **El Zotz** is where you'll find the remnants of a Mayan city. On a clear day you can see the tallest of the ruins at Tikal from these unexcavated ruins. The odd name, which means "the bat" in Q'eqchí, refers to a cave from which thousands of bats make a nightly exodus. Troops of hyperactive spider monkeys seem to have claimed this place for themselves, swinging through the treetops and scrambling after each other like children playing a game of tag. Unlike those in Tikal, however, these long-limbed creatures are not used to people and will shake branches and throw twigs and fruit to try to scare you away. Mosquitos are fierce especially in rainy season; bring your strongest repellent. ✉*15 mi (24 km) west of Tikal.*

El Mirador, once equal in size and splendor to Tikal, may eventually equal Tikal as a must-see Mayan ruin. It's just now being explored, but elaborate plans are being laid to establish a huge park four times the size of Tikal. The Mirador Basin contains the El Mirador site itself, four other known Mayan cities that probably were as large as Tikal (Nakbé, El Tintal, Xulnal, and Wakná), and many smaller but important sites—perhaps as many as 80 to 100 cities. The Mirador Basin is home to an incredible diversity of plant and animal life, including 200 species of birds, 40 kinds of animals (including several endangered ones, such as jaguars), 300 kinds of trees, and 2,000 different species of flora. It has been nominated as a UNESCO World Heritage Site. Currently, fewer than 2,500 visitors get to El Mirador annually, as it's a difficult trek requiring five or six days of hiking (round-trip). The jumping-off point for the trek is Carmelita Village, about 50 mi (84 km) north of Flores. There are no hotels in the Mirador Basin, and no roads except for dirt paths. Local tour companies *(see below)* can arrange treks. ✉ *40 mi (66 km) northwest of Tikal.*

TIKAL & THE MAYAN RUINS ESSENTIALS

TRANSPORTATION

BY AIR

Aeropuerto Internacional Santa Elena (FRS), often referred to as the Flores airport, is less than ½ mi (1 km) outside town. Taxis and shuttles meet every plane and charge about 20 quetzales to take you into town. The airport has service to and from Belize City, Guatemala City, and Cancún.

In mid-2008, flights on Tropic Air and Maya Island Air between the international airport in Belize City and Flores, which had been suspended for eight months, resumed. Fares are around US$225 (BZ$450) round-trip. The airlines also resumed their day and overnight tours from Belize City and San Pedro, Ambergris Caye. Day and overnight tours from Belize City range from around US$330 (BZ$660) to US$350 (BZ$700), including round-trip air, security and exit fees, meals and, in some cases, lodging. ours from San Pedro are higher.

When flying out of Flores internationally, you'll pay the US$30 Guatemalan exit fee, plus the US$3 tax imposed on all flights from Flores.

Contacts Maya Island Air (☎ *501/223–1140 in Belize City, 7926–3386 in Flores* ⊕ *www.mayaairways.com*). **Tropic Air** (☎ *501/226–2012 in Belize, 800/422–3435 in U.S. and Canada* ⊕ *www.tropicair.com*).

BY BUS

Linea Dorada runs daily buses (US$20 one way from the Marine Terminal in Belize City), departing at 9:30 AM, all the way to Flores, via San Ignacio, Belize, and Melchor de Mencos, Guatemala. The 146 mi (235 km) trip takes four to five hours, including border crossing. San Juan Travel also runs two small buses daily from Belize City's Marine Terminal (US$15 to US$20), at 9:30 AM and 2:30 PM (note that times may change). Agents with desks in the Marine Terminal, including Mundo Maya Deli and S&L Travel, can book the buses for you.

A less expensive option, but one that requires more time and effort, would be to take regular Belize buses to San Ignacio, and then a bus (or collective or a taxi) to the border just beyond the town of Benque Viejo del Carmen.

Numerous local chicken buses and minibuses run roughly hourly during the day between Melchor de Mencos at the Belize border and Santa Elena–Flores. The chicken buses are always packed and cost around US$3. These buses won't take you all the way to Tikal, however; for that, you must get off in Ixlu (also known as El Cruce, the crossroads), and change buses. A minibus to Tikal from Ixlu is around US$2.50.

A better if slightly more expensive option from Melchor to Flores is to take one of the collective minibuses or vans. They wait until they are full and charge around US$10 per person. If there are no collectives available, you can hire a taxi for around US$50 to US$60 (for the taxi, not per person.)

When leaving Belize by land, there's a US$18.75 exit fee. The 42-mi (70-km) paved route between Flores–Santa Elena and Tikal is served by scheduled minibus shuttles, operated by San Juan Travel and other companies. They cost around Q25 one way or Q50 round-trip per person and leave from the San Juan Hotel, stopping at other hotels. The trip takes about 1½ hours. Buses leave at 5, 6, 7, 8, 9, and 10 AM and 2 PM and return at 12:30, 2, 3, 4, 5, and 6 PM. Note that schedules are subject to frequent change and you should check with your hotel before making plans. Local buses serving other destinations depart from the market in Santa Elena near Calle Principal. They are inexpensive but very slow.

Contacts Linea Dorada (✉ *4a Calle, Santa Elena* ☎ *7926–0528* ✉ *Calle de la Playa, Flores* ☎ *2232–9658*). **Mundo Maya Deli** (✉ *Marine Terminal, Belize City* ☎ *223/1235*. **San Juan Travel** (✉ *Calle 2, Santa Elena* ☎ *7926–0042*).

S & L Travel (✉ *Marine Terminal, Belize City* ☎ *227/7593*).

BY CAR

Roads in El Petén are often in poor repair and not very well marked. Some roads are impassable during the rainy season, so check with the tourist office before heading out on seldom traveled roads, such as those to the more remote ruins surrounding Tikal. A four-wheel-drive vehicle, *doble-tracción,* is highly recommended.

To be on the safe side, never travel at night. If you come upon a fallen tree across the road, do not get out of your car to remove the debris. Robbers have been known to fell trees to get tourists to stop. Turn around as quickly as possible.

If you're not booked on a tour, the best way to get around El Petén is by renting a four-wheel-drive vehicle. The major rental agencies, including Budget and Hertz, have offices at Aeropuerto Internacional Santa Elena. Koka, a local company, also rents vehicles from an office in the airport, as does Tabarini, which usually has a good selection. You need a valid driver's license from your own country to drive in Guatemala. Crystal Auto Rental in Belize City permits its vehicles to be taken into Guatemala (the El Petén/Tikal area only).

Local Agencies **Budget** (⊠ *Aeropuerto Internacional Santa Elena* ☎ *7950–0741*). **Crystal** (⊠ *Mile 5, Northern Hwy., Belize City* ☎ *501/223–1910*). **Hertz** (⊠ *Aeropuerto Internacional Santa Elena* ☎ *7950–0204*). **Koka** (⊠ *Aeropuerto Internacional Santa Elena* ☎ *7926–1233*). **Tabarini** (⊠ *Aeropuerto Internacional Santa Elena* ☎ *7926–0253 or 7926–0277*).

BORDER FORMALITIES

The Belize border is about 9 mi (15 km) from San Ignacio, just west of the town of Benque Viejo del Carmen. Belize has built a new customs and immigration building at the border. Border crossings here are usually quick and easy.

Upon arrival at the border, you'll be approached on the Belize side by money changers asking if you want to exchange U.S. or Belize dollars for Guatemalan quetzales. The rate given by money changers will be a little less than you'll get at an ATM or bank, but you may want to exchange enough for your first day in Guatemala. There's a bank in Melchor de Mencos, but it does not have an ATM and doesn't exchange money. While U.S. dollars are usually accepted in El Petén, it's easier to deal in quetzales, and the exchange rate at shops and restaurants may be poor. There also are money changers on the Guatemalan side.

Belize formalities include paying your US$18.75 exit fee. Guatemalan officials often ask for a Q10 or US$2 entrance fee. There's no such fee, but many visitors pay this small bribe just to keep things going smoothly. Most visitors to Guatemala, including citizens of the United States, Canada, and European Union, do not need visas, and passports are normally stamped with a permit to enter for 90 days. Customs officials rarely check baggage.

Melchor de Mencos is a scruffy border town with unpaved streets. Shops on the main drag sell Guatemalan crafts. Other than extremely basic hotels (some of which are brothels), the only place to stay nearby is the Río Mopan Lodge (US$70 double). The Swiss owner, Marco Gross, can help smooth any border problems, arrange good tours anywhere in El Petén, exchange money, and provide a good night's sleep at his lodge. Among his tours: a day trip to Tikal, including lunch, entrance fee, guide, and transfers (US$50), and an overnight tour, including a one-night stay at the Jungle Lodge in the park, along with guide, entrance fees, lunch, and transfers (US$100 per person, double occupancy).

There's no safe long-term parking at the border, so if you are driving a rental car, you should arrange to park it elsewhere. Only a handful of Belize rental companies allow their vehicles to be taken into Guatemala (try Crystal in Belize City). Note, however, that Belize insurance isn't valid in Guatemala, and Guatemalan insurance currently isn't sold at the border. The nearest place to buy it is Flores.

BY TAXI

After you cross the border from Belize into Melchor de Mencos, you can hire a taxi or minivan to take you and your party direct to Tikal or, if you prefer, to Flores–Santa Elena. You'll pay US$40–US$60 (for the van-taxi, not per person), depending on your bargaining ability and your fluency in Spanish. Taxis from the Santa Elena–Flores airport to Tikal are around US$40.

CONTACTS & RESOURCES

BANKS & RESOURCES

Guatemalan currency is called the quetzal, after the resplendent national bird. There are 1-, 5-, 10-, and 25-centavo coins. Bills come in denominations of one-half, 1, 5, 10, 20, 50, and 100 quetzales. At this writing, US$1 was worth roughly Q7.69, but at most hotels and money changers in El Petén you'll get a little less.

While U.S. dollars are seldom refused in Guatemala and the U.S. dollar is officially a parallel currency, using quetzales will make transactions easier and less confusing. You can exchange U.S. dollars at any bank and in high-end hotels. It's far more difficult to exchange other currencies. If you're traveling with currency other than U.S. dollars, it would be wise to change the money into dollars or quetzales before you arrive. Traveler's checks are accepted mainly in larger hotels. If you need to exchange money, do so before heading off on your jungle adventure.

There are several banks in Santa Elena, but few anywhere else in the region. Those on Calle 4, the main street, have ATMs that work with foreign ATM cards with MasterCard or Visa logos on the PLUS or CIRRUS systems. You may have to try more than one ATM before you find one that works with your card. Flores has one bank, but it does not have an ATM. Make sure you only have a four-digit pin number, as many ATMs only take four digits.

Banks **Banrural** (⊠ *Calle 4 at Av. 3, Santa Elena* ☎ *7926–1002*). **Banco Industrial** (⊠ *Calle 4, Santa Elena* ☎ *7926–0281*).

HEALTH

If you've been traveling in Belize, where you can generally drink the water and usually eat even street food with no problem, Guatemala's health and hygiene standards come as an unpleasant surprise. Tap water is rarely potable, and even better restaurants may not pass a health inspection. To prevent traveler's diarrhea, drink only bottled water and avoid raw vegetables—on their own or in salads—unless you know they've been thoroughly washed and disinfected with *agua pura* (purified water) and bleach. Be wary of strawberries and other unpeeled fruits. Heat stroke is another risk, but one that can easily be avoided. The best way to avoid it is to do as the locals do (wake early and retire at midday for a siesta) and drink lots of water.

EMBASSIES

Contacts **Canada** (⊠ *Edificio Edyma Plaza, 8th fl., 13 Calle 8–44, Guatemala City* 🕾 *2363–4348*). **United Kingdom** (⊠ *16 Calle 0–55, Edificio Torre Internacional, 11th fl., Guatemala City* 🕾 *2367–5425*). **United States** (⊠ *Av. La Reforma 7–01, Guatemala City* 🕾 *2326–4000*).

EMERGENCIES

Medical facilities in El Petén are not as modern as in the rest of the country. If you're really sick, consider getting on the next plane to Guatemala City. Centro Médico Maya in Santa Elena has physicians on staff, though little or no English is spoken.

Contact **Centro Médico Maya** (⊠ *Av. 4, Santa Elena* 🕾 *7926–0180*).

Pharmacy **Farmacia Nueva** (⊠ *Av. Santa Ana, Flores* 🕾 *7926–1387*).

SAFETY

Most crimes directed at tourists in El Petén have been pickpocketings, muggings, and thefts from cars. There have been a number of incidents over the years involving armed groups stopping buses, vans, and private cars, both at Tikal park and on the road from Tikal to the Belize border. The bandits take passengers' valuables; occasionally, passengers have been assaulted. Ask locally about conditions before you leave Belize, but keep in mind that some 300,000 international visitors come to Tikal every year, and the vast majority of them have no problems with crime.

In town, don't wear flashy jewelry and watches, keep your camera in a secure bag, and don't handle money in public. Hire taxis only from official stands at the airport, outside hotels, and at major intersections. If you can avoid it, don't drive after sunset. One common ploy used by highway robbers is to construct a roadblock, such as logs strewn across the road, and then hide nearby. When unsuspecting motorists get out of their cars to remove the obstruction, they are waylaid. If you come upon a deserted roadblock, don't stop; turn around.

Avoid participating in local rallies, as protesters are not always treated well. A few years ago, several Guatemalans were killed protesting a bus fare increase.

The increase in adoption of Guatemalan children has caused many people—particularly rural villagers—to fear that children will be abducted by foreigners. Limit your interaction with children you do not know, and be discreet when taking photographs.

Emergency Services **Police** (🕾 *7926–1365*).

MAIL & SHIPPING

The main post office in Flores is a half block east of the main square. In Santa Elena the post office is a block east of the bridge leading to Flores. Post offices are open Monday–Friday 8–5. Tikal also has a small post office. Mail service is slow, so expect to get back home before your letter does.

Post Offices **Flores** (⊠ *Av. Barrios, Flores*). **Santa Elena** (⊠ *Calle Principal Santa Elena*). **Tikal Park** (⊠ *Near visitor center*).

TELEPHONES

Public phones are few and far between in Guatemala, but most towns have offices where you can place both national and international calls. The easiest way to place a call is from your hotel. Guatemala's country code is 502; there are no local area codes. Guatemala recently switched from a seven-digit to an eight-digit telephone system. All numbers in Guatemala City now have a prefix of 2, and all numbers outside Guatemala City have a prefix of 7. The exception is cell-phone numbers, which have a prefix of 5.

TOURS

Flores-based Martsam Travel, run by Lileana and Benedicto Grijalva, offers many different types of tours in the area. Tikal Travel in Melchor de Mencos at the Belize–Guatemala border has well-priced tours of Tikal and other Mayan sites in El Petén. Tip tour guides about 10% of the tour price.

Contacts **Martsam Travel** (⊠ *Calle Centroamérica and Av. 30 de Junio, Flores* ☎ *7926–0346* ☎ *7926–3225*). **Tikal Travel at Río Mopan Lodge** (⊠ *Melchor de Mencos* ☎ *7926–5196* ⊕ *www.tikaltravel.com*).

FROM BELIZE

Many tour operators in the San Ignacio, Belize, area operate day and overnight or multinight Tikal tours. You'll pay more in Belize than in Guatemala, but you reduce the hassle factor—you'll probably be picked up at your Cayo hotel, whisked across the border, provided with a guide to Tikal, and fed lunch (hotel accommodations are arranged if you're staying overnight). You'll typically pay US$75 to US$100 for a day trip to Tikal from San Ignacio, and US$150 to US$200 for an overnight tour. Tours from Belize typically don't include the Belize and Guatemala exit fees. *See* ⇨ *The Cayo and Adventure Vacations chapters for more information.*

VISITOR INFORMATION

Arcas, which returns illegally captured animals to the wild, is a great resource on the flora and fauna of El Petén. The staff at Inguat, Guatemala's tourism promotion agency, is courteous, professional, and knowledgeable. Inguat has two offices in El Petén, one in Flores at the central plaza and one at Aeropuerto Internacional Santa Elena. CINCAP (Centro de Información sobre de Naturaleza, Cultura y Artesanías), on the central plaza in Flores, also has tourism information and historical exhibits on the Petén.

Contacts **Arcas** (⊠ *6 mi [10 km] east of Santa Elena in San Benito* ⊕ *www. arcasguatemala.com*). **CINCAP** (⊠ *Parque CentralFlores* ☎ *7926–0718*). **Inguat** (⊠ *On Parque Central, Flores* ☎ *7926–0669* ⊠ *Aeropuerto Internacional Santa Elena* ☎ *7926–0533 at airport*).

Mayan Sites

WORD OF MOUTH

"Stay around San Ignacio and see Caracol, see Xunantunich and enjoy the jungle and river there, find someone to take you up the river and canoe down yourself."

—macnamara

"We had to walk a mile through a jungle trail to get to the [Tikal] ruins. The weather was perfect: 75°, cloudy. Wow, what a site! The courtyard area in the grand Plaza was surrounded by temples and Mayan housing. [We] saw spider monkeys, colorful birds, coatimundis, and finally, howler monkeys. The howlers were so loud. Just amazing how the Mayans built these magnificent temples in 600 AD without our modern ways."

—puckettt

By Lan Sluder

VISITING BELIZE WITHOUT TOURING ANY Mayan sites is like going to Greece and not seeing the Acropolis and the Parthenon. For at least five millennia, the Maya left their imprint on what is now Belize, and today some of the Mayan world's most awe-inspiring ruins are yours to explore. Archaeologists have identified more than 600 significant Mayan sites in Belize, and doubtless many more are yet to be discovered. You can choose from among more than a dozen major excavated sites that are open to visitors, in all parts of the country, from Corozal and Orange Walk districts in the north to Cayo in the west and Toledo in the south. Some, such as Cahal Pech or Xunantunich, are by the roadside and easily reached; others, such as La Milpa or Cerros, will have you tramping the bush like Indiana Jones. Even the most accessible sites aren't overrun with hordes of travelers—at some you may be the only visitor, other than perhaps a troop of howler monkeys or a flock of parrots. This chapter fills you in on the fascinating history of the Maya in Belize, exposes some of the secrets of their great architecture, suggests itineraries for visiting the most interesting sites, and provides tips for touring the realm of the Maya.

NOTABLE MAYAN SITES IN BELIZE

The following are our picks for the most notable Mayan sites in Belize. See the destination chapters for detailed information on the sites, including hours and admission fees.

NORTHERN BELIZE

Altun Ha. The most-visited Mayan site in Belize, though not the most impressive, is popular with cruise ship passengers and for those staying on Ambergris Caye or Caye Caulker. It's a little more than an hour's drive north of Belize City. One of the temples at Altun Ha is prominently pictured on Belikin beer bottles.

Cerros. Although the few remaining original structures here are weathered, and there's no museum or visitor center, Cerros—like Tulum in the Yucatán—enjoys a glorious location right beside the water.

Chan Chich. The lodge of the same name was built literally on top of this minor ceremonial site. It can be reached by car or charter flight and is best visited in connection with a stay at the lodge.

Cuello. It's one of the oldest Mayan sites in the region, settled more than 2,500 years ago. It's on the property of a rum distillery near Orange Walk Town, and you have to get permission in advance to visit it.

La Milpa. The third-largest Mayan site in Belize (only Caracol and Lamanai are larger), La Milpa is in the early stages of exploration and excavation. It can be visited through advance arrangement with Programme for Belize, on whose land it sits.

★ **Lamanai.** Boat your way up the New River to the shores of the New River Lagoon to see this ruin, which has the most beautiful setting of any Mayan site in Belize. You can also reach it by road from Orange Walk Town. Lamanai has a small museum and a resident troop of howler monkeys.

Noh Mul. This ruin, settled around 350 BC, is about 10 mi north of Orange Walk Town on private land.

Santa Rita. Corozal Town is built on what was the large Mayan trading center known as Chactemal (or Chetumal, as the capital of Quintana Roo, Mexico, is known today). A part of the ruins, now called Santa Rita, is on a hill on the outskirts of town.

THE CAYO

Fodor'sChoice **Actun Tunichil Muknal.** "ATM" near Belmopan provides the most reward-★ ing Mayan cave experience in Belize. To see the cave, you have to take a 45-minute hike and a brief swim, and be a part of a guided tour.

Cahal Pech. This small Late Classic site, with a lovely location on a hill overlooking San Ignacio, is easily accessible from town. It has a little museum.

★ **Barton Creek Cave.** You can canoe through part of this 7-mi (11 km) wet cave system once used by the Maya for human sacrifices. It's about a half hour off the Chiquilbul Road on the way to the Mountain Pine Ridge.

Caracol. The largest and most significant site in Belize is a must if you're in Cayo. It's an all-day trip from San Ignacio through the Mountain Pine Ridge, but it's well worth the time. There's a museum and visitor center, and extensive excavations have been underway for more than 20 years.

Che Chem Ha. This cave on private land south of Benque Viejo has artifacts dating back 2000 years.

El Pilar. Set on low hills above the Mopan River at the Guatemalan border is one of the largest sites in Belize, but little of it has been excavated.

Pacbitun. Near San Antonio village on the road to the Mountain Pine Ridge, Pacbitun dates back to at least 1000 BC. It's on private land.

★ **Xunantunich.** Though it's not one of the largest sites in Belize, Xunantunich is one of the easiest and most pleasant to visit. To reach it, you cross the Mopan River on a quaint, hand-pulled ferry. There's a well-done museum and visitor center. For views of Cayo and part of Guatemala, be sure to climb to the top of El Castillo. It's off the Western Highway, west of San Ignacio.

PETÉN, GUATEMALA

Fodor'sChoice **Tikal.** Along with Copán in Honduras and Palenque in Mexico, Tikal is ★ considered by many to be the most impressive of all Mayan sites. The Petén area is home to several other ruins, including **Nakúm, El Ceibal,**

8

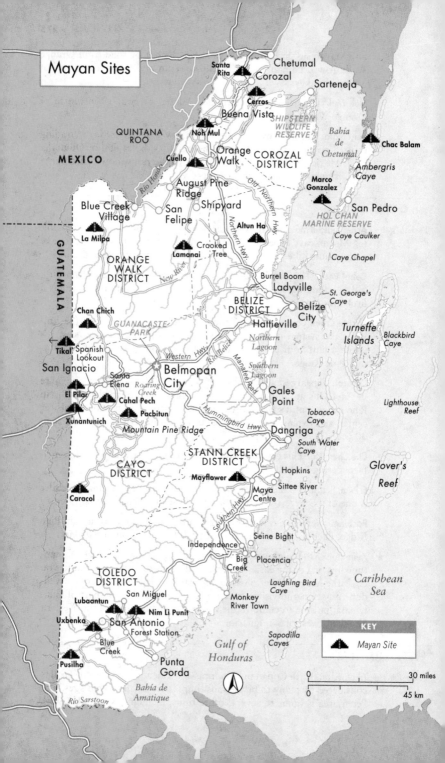

Mayan Sites

MEXICO

QUINTANA ROO

GUATEMALA

Santa Rita
Chetumal
Corozal
Sarteneja
Cerros
Buena Vista
SHIPSTERN WILDLIFE RESERVE
Bahía de Chetumal
Noh Mul
Chac Balam
Cuello
Orange Walk
COROZAL DISTRICT
Ambergris Caye
August Pine Ridge
Marco Gonzalez
Blue Creek Village
San Felipe
Shipyard
Old Northern Hwy
San Pedro
HOL CHAN MARINE RESERVE
La Milpa
Altun Ha
Caye Caulker
ORANGE WALK DISTRICT
Lamanai
Crooked Tree
Caye Chapel
New River
Burrel Boom
Ladyville
St. George's Caye
Chan Chich
BELIZE DISTRICT
Belize City
GUANACASTE PARK
Hattieville
Turneffe Islands
Blackbird Caye
Tikal
Spanish Lookout
Western Hwy
Rio Belize
Northern Lagoon
San Ignacio
Santa Elena
Roaring Creek
Belmopan City
Manatee Road
Southern Lagoon
El Pilar
Cahal Pech
Lighthouse Reef
Xunantunich
Pacbitun
Hummingbird Hwy
Gales Point
Mountain Pine Ridge
Dangriga
Tobacco Caye
CAYO DISTRICT
South Water Caye
Glover's Reef
STANN CREEK DISTRICT
Caracol
Mayflower
Hopkins
Maya Centre
Sittee River
Southern Hwy
Seine Bight
Independence
Big Creek
Placencia
TOLEDO DISTRICT
Laughing Bird Caye
Caribbean Sea
Lubaantun
San Miguel
Uxbenka
Nim Li Punit
San Antonio
Forest Station
Monkey River Town
Blue Creek
Sapodilla Cayes
Pusilha
Punta Gorda
Gulf of Honduras
Rio Sarstoon
Bahía de Amatique

KEY

▲ *Mayan Site*

0 — 30 miles
0 — 45 km

Uaxactún, Yaxhá, Yaxchilán, El Zotz, and **El Mirador.** Some, like El Mirador, are extremely remote, requiring a multiday jungle trek.

SOUTHERN BELIZE

Lubaantun. Occupied for less than 200 years in the Late Classic period, Lubaantun is unusual in that no stelae were ever found here, and the precisely fitted building stones, laid without mortar, have rounded corners. The controversial "Crystal Skull" supposedly was found here. Lubaantun is near San Pedro Columbia village, about 20 mi (32 km) from Punta Gorda.

Mayflower. This Classic period site, off the Southern Highway just south of Dangriga, is in the early stages of excavation. Waterfalls nearby make the setting appealing.

Nim Li Punit. Off the Southern Highway north of Punta Gorda is Nim Li Punit ("Big Hat" in Ketchi), a small but pretty site. There's a visitor center.

Pusilha. At a site near Aguacate Village on the Moho River is this collection of extensive but low-lying structures on a small hill. You can also see the remains of a stone bridge. Because of its remote location off the main highway, there aren't many tourists who make the trip out here.

AMBERGRIS CAYE

Although there are no large Mayan sites on the cayes, Ambergris Caye has several small ruins. **Chac Balam** can be visited on a boat tour to Bacalar, at the far north end of the island. **Marco Gonzalez,** at the south end of the island, is difficult to find without a local guide.

SEEING THE RUINS

Most visitors to Belize are not serious "Maya buffs" who spend all their time touring ruins. Instead, they opt to visit Mayan sites as just one aspect of their beach or mainland vacation. If this is your first trip to Belize, we recommend you do the same. Following are the sites that are easily visited from the most popular areas.

Ambergris Caye & Caye Caulker. Tour operators on these islands run trips to **Lamanai** (usually a full day trip by boat and road) and to **Altun Ha** (normally a half day trip, although it may be longer if it includes lunch and a spa visit at Maruba Spa). You can also visit **Tikal** on an overnight trip by air to Flores, Guatemala, with a change of planes in Belize City. It's also possible to arrange boat tours of small ruins on Ambergris Caye, including **Chac Balam** at Bacalar.

Belize City. Tour operators based in Belize City, most of which cater to cruise ships, offer day trips by road, boat, or air to **Lamanai** and by road to **Altun Ha,** and also by road to **Xunantunich** and other ruins, including **Cahal Pech** near San Ignacio. The Altun Ha tour often is combined with a brief tour of Belize City. The tours to San Ignacio may be combined with a stop at the Belize Zoo. You can also visit **Tikal** on a day or overnight trip by air from the international airport in Belize City to Flores.

Corozal Town. Tour operators in Corozal Town can arrange a full-day trip by road and boat to **Lamanai.** They also offer boat trips to **Cerros** or a visit to nearby **Santa Rita** by road. By advance arrangement, tour operators may be able to offer road tours of **Cuello, La Milpa, Noh Mul,** or other less-visited sites.

San Ignacio, Belmopan & Mountain Pine Ridge. Tour operators in the San Ignacio, Belmopan, and Mountain Pine Ridge areas focus on the

> **TIPS**
>
> Tour operators in each area offer day or part-day trips (and in a few cases, overnight trips) to the sites. Tours may not operate every day, especially off-season, and there may be a minimum number of participants required for the tour to run. Tour operators may be able to provide tours to lesser-visited sites with an advance arrangement. Except for certain caves such as Actun Tunichil Muknal, which can be visited only with a guide, most Mayan sites can be visited independently—you just need a rental car, or, in a few cases, bus fare.

many Mayan sites in Cayo, including **Caracol, Xunantunich, Cahal Pech,** and **El Pilar.** Tours to Caracol typically require a full day, while the other sites can each be done in a half-day or less. There are also guided tours of notable caves, including **Actun Tunichil Muknal** (full day) and **Che Hem Ha** (half-day). Day and overnight tours by road to **Tikal** are also offered.

Hopkins & Placencia. Tour operators in Hopkins and Placencia offer half-day tours to the **Mayflower** ruins (sometimes combined, on a full-day trip, with a visit to the Cockscomb Basin Wildlife Sanctuary). They also offer full-day trips by road to the ruins near Punta Gorda, mainly **Lubaantun** and **Nim Li Punit.** You can also fly from Dangriga or Placencia, via Belize City, to Flores to see **Tikal.**

Punta Gorda. Tour operators in Punta Gorda and nearby focus on trips by road to the ruins of **Lubaantun, Nim Li Punit,** and, less commonly, **Pusilha.** These tours usually include visits to modern Maya villages near Punta Gorda. You can also fly from Punta Gorda, with a change of planes in Belize City, to Flores to see **Tikal.**

A MAYAN PRIMER

CHRONOLOGY

Traditionally, archaeologists have divided Mayan history into three main periods: Pre-Classic, Classic, and Post-Classic. Although some academics question the validity of such a uniform chronology, the traditional labels are still in use.

GREAT ITINERARY: MAYAN SITES BLITZ

If you want to see the top Mayan sites in one trip, base yourself in Cayo for a few days. Information on tour operators and guides, and on admissions to specific sites, are in destination chapters.

If, after a few days in western Belize and Guatemala you still haven't had your fill of things Mayan, you can add extensions to northern Belize and to Punta Gorda in southern Belize.

DAY 1: SAN IGNACIO

San Ignacio is an easy jumping-off spot to see several small but fascinating nearby ruins. If you get an early start, you can take in **Xunantunich, Cahal Pech,** and **El Pilar.** Both Cahal Pech and Xunantunich can be reached by bus (albeit with a short hike after the bus ride in both cases), but a taxi or rental car is needed to get to El Pilar. Guided tours of all these sites can be arranged in San Ignacio or at lodges and hotels in the area. (⇨ See The Cayo, Chapter 4)

DAY 2: CARACOL

Caracol, the most important Mayan site in Belize, deserves a full day. You can drive yourself—or go on a tour. There is no bus transportation in the Mountain Pine Ridge. Even if you arrive independently, you can hire a guide to show you around once you're at the site, or you can tour it on your own. There's an informative museum and visitor center. Due to a series of bandit incidents in 2005 and early 2006, at press time trips to Caracol are being done in convoys, protected by Belize Defense Forces soldiers. Since there have been no further incidents since mid-2006, this convoy system may be discontinued. Check locally for updates. (⇨ See The Cayo, Chapter 4)

DAYS 3 & 4: TIKAL

Tikal is by far the most impressive Mayan site in the region and shouldn't be missed. Many operators offer day tours of Tikal from the San Ignacio area. (⇨ See Tikal, Chapter 7)

TIPS

Altun Ha, the ruin closest to Belize City, gets crowds of cruise ship day-trippers; so if you go, try to avoid days when there are several cruise ships in port.

Be aware of your surroundings, and before heading anywhere remote by yourself, check with the locals to find out if there have been any recent safety issues.

On your visit to Tikal, stay at one of the lodges at the park if possible—you'll be able to visit the ruins early in the morning or late in the afternoon, when howler monkeys and other animals are active and most day visitors have left.

Pack plenty of bug juice with DEET. Mosquitoes are especially bad around Cerros and at the ruins near Punta Gorda.

8

The **Pre-Classic** (circa 3,000 BC–AD 250) period is characterized by the influence of the Olmec, a civilization centered on the Gulf Coast of present-day Mexico. During this period, cities began to grow, especially in the southern highlands of Guatemala and in Belize, and it's at this time that Belize's Cuello, Lamanai, Santa Rita, Cahal Pech, Pacbitun, and Altun Ha sites were first settled.

By the **Late Pre-Classic** (circa 300 BC–AD 250) period, the Maya had developed an advanced mathematical system, an impressively precise calendar, and one of the world's five original writing systems. In Belize, Cerros was established during the Late Pre-Classic period.

During the **Classic** (circa 250 BC–AD 900) period, Maya artistic, intellectual, and architectural achievements literally reached for the stars. Vast city-states were crisscrossed by a large number of paved roadways, some of which still exist today. The great cities of Caracol (Belize), Palenque (Mexico), Tikal (Guatemala), and Quirigu (Guatemala) were just a few of the powerful centers that controlled the Classic Maya world. In AD 562, Caracol—which, at its height, was the largest city-state in Belize, with a population of about 150,000—conquered Tikal. Other notable Classic period sites in Belize include Xunantunich, El Pilar, and Lubaantun.

The single largest unsolved mystery about the Maya is their rapid decline during the **Terminal Classic** (AD 800–900) period and the centuries following. Scholars have postulated that climate change, pandemic disease, drought, stresses in the social structure, overpopulation, deforestation, and changes in the trade routes could have been responsible. Rather than a single factor, several events taking place over time could well have been the cause.

The Maya of the **Post-Classic** (AD 900–early 1500s) period were heavily affected by growing powers in central Mexico. Architecture, ceramics, and carvings from this period show considerable outside influence. Although still dramatic, Post-Classic cities such as Chichén Itzá and Uxmal pale in comparison to their Classic predecessors. By the time the Spanish conquest reached the Yucatán, the Maya were scattered, feuding, and easy to conquer. Several sites in Belize, including Lamanai, were continuously occupied during this time, and even later.

KEY DATES

Here are some key dates in the history of the Maya in Belize and in the El Petén area of Guatemala. Most of the dates are approximate, and some dates are disputed.

BC

3114	Date of the creation of the world, or 0.0.0.0.0 according to the Long Count calendar
3000	Early Olmec and Mayan civilizations thought to have begun
2500	Cuello established
2000	Santa Rita established
1500	Lamanai established
1000	Cahal Pech established
900	Olmec writing system developed; Caracol established
800	Tikal established
700	First written Mayan language
500	First Mayan calendars carved in stone
250	Altun Ha established
200	First monumental buildings erected at Tikal and El Mirador

AD

400–600	Tikal becomes leading city-state, with population of perhaps 200,000
553	Accession of Lord Water as Caracol ruler
562	Caracol conquers Tikal
599	Accession of Lord Smoke Ahau as Caracol ruler
618	Accession of Kan II as Caracol ruler
631	Caracol defeats Naranjo; Caracol's population is 150,000
700	Lubaantun established
800	Cahal Pech abandoned
895	Xunantunich abandoned
899	Tikal abandoned
900	Classic period of Mayan history ends
900–1500	Maya civilization in decline, many cities abandoned
1000	Southern Belize Mayan centers mostly abandoned
1050	Caracol abandoned
1517	Spanish arrive in Yucatán and begin conquest of Maya
1517–1625	Diseases introduced from Europe cause death of majority of Maya
1524–25	Hernán Cortés passed through Belize en route to Honduras, after leading expeditions to conquer the Aztecs in Mexico
1546–1600s	Maya in Belize rebel against Spanish
1695	Tikal ruins rediscovered by Spanish
1700s	Lamanai continuously occupied over 3,000 years
1724	Spanish abolish *encomienda* system of forced Maya labor
1839	John Lloyd Stephens and Frederick Catherwood visit Belize
1847	Caste Wars in Yucatán begin
1881	Early archaeological work begins at Tikal, by Alfred Maudslay
1894	Thomas Gann begins exploring Xunantunich and other Belize ruins
1936	Caracol ruins rediscovered by a lumberman
1956	William Coe and others begin excavations at Tikal
1992	Rigoberta Menchu, a Maya from Guatemala, wins Nobel Peace Prize
2006	Mel Gibson's *Apocalypto,* set in a crumbling Mayan civilization, and with actors speaking Yucatec Maya, was filmed in Veracruz
2012	The predicted end of the world, 13.0.0.0.0 in the Long Count calendar

8

HISTORY IN BRIEF

Anthropologists believe that humans from Asia crossed a land bridge, in what is now the Bering Strait in Alaska, into North America more than 25,000 years ago. Gradually these Paleoindians, or "Old Indians," whose ancestors probably were Mongoloid peoples, made their way down the continent, establishing Native American or First Nation settlements in what is now the United States and Canada. Groups of them are thought to have reached Mesoamerica, which includes, besides Belize, much of central Mexico, Guatemala, Honduras, and Nicaragua, around 20,000 to 22,000 years ago.

These early peoples were hunter-gatherers. The Olmec civilization, considered the mother culture of later Mesoamerican civilizations including that of the Maya, arose in central and southern Mexico 3,000 to 4,000 years ago. The Olmecs developed the first writing system in the New World, dating from at least 900 BC. They also had sophisticated mathematics and created complex calendars. The Olmecs built irrigation systems to water their crops.

As long ago as around 3000 BC—the exact date is in question and has changed as archaeologists have made new discoveries—the Maya began to settle in small villages in Belize and elsewhere in the region. They developed an agriculture based on the cultivation of maize (corn), squash, and other fruits and vegetables. Some archeologists believe that the Maya—like other Indians in the region as well as in the South American Amazon—augmented soils with charcoal, pottery fragments, and organic matter to create terra preta (Portugese for dark soil), very fertile earth that stood up to hard tropical rains. In Belize, settlements were established as early as 2500 BC at Cuello in what is now Orange Walk District in northern Belize. Then, over the next 1,000 years or so, small settlements arose at Santa Rita in Corozal and Lamanai in Orange Walk, and at Cahal Pech, Caracol, and elsewhere in Cayo District in western Belize. What would become the great city-states of the region, including Tikal in today's Petén region of Guatemala and Caracol in Cayo, was first settled around 900 to 700 BC.

Two or three centuries before the time of Christ, several Mayan villages grew into sizable cities. The Maya began to construct large-scale stone buildings at Tikal and elsewhere. Eventually, Tikal, Caracol, and other urban centers each would have thousands of structures—palaces, temples, residences, monuments, ball courts, even prisons. Although the Maya never had the wheel, and thus no carts or wagons, they built paved streets and causeways, and they developed crop irrigation systems.

At its height, in what is known as the Classic period (250 BC to AD 900), the Maya civilization consisted of about 50 cities, much like ancient Greek city-states. Each had a population of 5,000 to 100,000 or more. Tikal, the premier city in the region, may have had 200,000 residents in and around the city during its heyday, and Caracol in Belize probably had nearly as many. The peak population of the Maya civilization possibly reached 2 million or more, and as many as a million may have lived in Belize alone—nearly four times the current population.

The Mayan culture put a heavy emphasis on religion, which was based on a pantheon of nature gods, including those of the sun, moon, and rain. The Mayan view of life was cyclical, and Mayan religion was based on accommodating human life to the cycles of the universe.

Contrary to what scholars long believed, however, Mayan society had many aspects beyond religion. Politics, the arts, business, and trade were all important and dynamic aspects of Mayan life. Dynastic leaders waged brutal wars on rival city-states. Under its ruler Lord Smoke Ahau, Caracol, the largest city-state in Belize, conquered Tikal in AD 562, and less than a hundred years later, conquered another large city, Naranjo (also in Guatemala).

The Maya developed sophisticated mathematics. They understood the concept of zero and used a base-20 numbering system. Astronomy was the basis of a complex Mayan calendar system involving an accurately determined solar year (18 months of 20 days, plus a 5-day period), a sacred year of 260 days (13 cycles of 20 days), and a variety of longer cycles culminating in the Long Count, based on a zero date in 3114 BC, or 0.0.0.0.0—the date that the Maya believed was the beginning of the current cycle of the world.

The Mayan writing system is considered the most advanced of any developed in Mesoamerica. The Maya used more than 800 "glyphs," small pictures or signs, paired in columns that read from left to right and top to bottom. The glyphs represent syllables and, in some cases, entire words, that can be combined to form any word or concept. There is no Mayan alphabet. Mayan glyphs can represent either sounds or ideas, or both, making them difficult to accurately interpret. The unit of the writing system is the cartouche, a series of 3 to 50 glyphs, the equivalent of a word or sentence in a modern language.

As in most societies, it's likely that the large majority of the Maya spent much of their time simply trying to eke out a living. In each urban area the common people lived in simple thatch dwellings, similar to those seen in the region today. They practiced a slash-and-burn agriculture. Farmers cleared their small plots by burning the bush, then planting maize, squash, sunflowers, and other crops in the rich ash. After two or three years, when the soil was depleted, the plot was left fallow for several years before it could be planted again.

Beginning around AD 800, parts of the Mayan civilization in Belize and elsewhere in Mesoamerica began to decline. In most areas the decline didn't happen suddenly, but over decades and even centuries, and it took place at different times. For example, the cities in the Northern Lowlands of the Yucatán, such as Chichén Itzá, flourished for several more centuries after Tikal and Caracol were abandoned.

Scholars are still debating the reasons for the decline. Climatic change, lengthy droughts, overpopulation, depletion of arable land, social revolutions by the common people against the elites, epidemics, and the impact of extended periods of warfare all have been put forth as reasons. It may well have been a combination of factors, or there may have been different causes in different regions.

Whatever the reasons, the Mayan civilization in Belize and elsewhere in Mesoamerica never regained its Classic period glory. By the time the Spanish arrived in the early 1500s, only a few of the Mayan cities, mainly in the Highlands of Guatemala, were still thriving. Most of the great cities and trading centers of Belize and Guatemala, including Caracol and Tikal, had long been abandoned. Lamanai and a few other urban settlements were still inhabited.

Seeking gold and other plunder, the Spanish began their conquest of the Maya in the 1520s. Some Mayan states offered fierce resistance, and the last Mayan kingdom, in Mexico, was not vanquished until almost 1700. The Maya in Belize rebelled against the Spanish several times, but there was one enemy against which the Maya were defenseless: European disease. Smallpox, chicken pox, measles, flu, and other infectious diseases swept through the Mayan settlements. Scientists believe that within a century, nearly 90% of the Maya had been wiped out by "imported" diseases.

Maya resistance to European control continued from time to time. In 1847 Mayan Indians in the Yucatán rose up against Europeans in the bloody Caste Wars, which lasted until 1904. This had a major impact on Belize, as many Mexican Mestizos (persons of mixed Indian and European heritage) and Maya moved to northern Belize to escape the violence. Sarteneja, Orange Walk Town, and Ambergris Caye were among the areas at least partly settled by refugees from the Yucatán.

Much of the Mayan civilization was buried under the tropical jungles for centuries, and Westerners knew little about it. In the process of trying to convert the Maya to Christianity in the 16th century, the Spanish burned most of the codices, Mayan "books" made of deer hide or bleached fig-tree paper. Only in the last few decades have scholars made progress in deciphering Mayan glyphic writing.

In 1839 two British adventurers, John Lloyd Stephens and Frederick Catherwood, visited Central America, including Belize, and explored a number of the Mayan sites. Their books, especially *Incidents of Travel in Central America, Chiapas, and Yucatán,* with text by Stephens and illustrations by Catherwood, brought the attention of the world to the Mayan past.

In the late 1800s the first systematic archaeological excavations of Tikal and Mayan sites in Belize were begun. Alfred Maudslay, an Englishman, conducted excavations at Tikal in 1881–82, and Harvard's Peabody Museum did fieldwork there between 1895 and 1904. Sylvanus Morley, a well-known Maya expert, conducted work at Tikal at times between 1914 and 1928. In 1956 the University of Pennsylvania began the first large-scale excavation project at Tikal. In Belize, Thomas Gann, a British medical officer stationed in what was then British Honduras, carried out the first excavations of several major Belize Mayan sites, including Santa Rita, Xunantunich, Lubaantun, sites on Ambergris Caye, and others, starting in 1894. Since then, many university and museum teams, including ones from the University of Pennsylvania, the Royal Ontario Museum, Tulane University, the University of Texas, the University of California, and the University of Central Florida, have conducted extensive fieldwork in Belize. Drs. Diane and Arlen Chase, of the University of Central Florida, have been at work at the largest site in Belize, Caracol, since 1983.

About 35,000 Maya live in Belize today. In southern Belize they're predominantly Ketchi and Mopan Maya; in western Belize, Mopan Maya; and in northern Belize, Yucatec Maya. The largest concentration of Maya in Belize is in the small villages in Toledo District near Punta Gorda.

The end of the world, or at least its current cycle, will take place on December 21, 2012, according to the Long Count calendar of the ancient Maya.

DOS & DON'TS FOR VISITING RUINS

■ **Don't ever take any artifact from a Mayan site, not even a tiny pottery fragment.** The theft of Mayan antiquities is a serious crime. Luggage is often searched at the international airport, and if any Mayan artifacts are found, you could be in hot water.

■ **Do climb the temples and enjoy the views from the top.** At most sites, you're free to climb the ruins. The views from El Castillo at Xunantunich, from structures at Cerros of Chetumal Bay, and from Lubaantun to the sea, are among the most memorable. Be warned, though: most of the steps are very steep.

■ **Do descend into Xilbalda.** The Maya called the underworld Xilbalda. You can experience it by visiting one of the caves once used by the Maya. Actun Tunichil Muknal, "The Cave of the Stone Sepulchre," near Belmopan, is our favorite. Che Chem Ha near San Ignacio is another cave with many Mayan artifacts. Ho Keb Ha, also known as Blue Creek Cave, is a cave system near Blue Creek village in Toledo. Barton Creek Cave, en route to the Mountain Pine Ridge and more than 7 mi (11½ km) long, was once used by the Maya for human sacrifices; today you can float it in a canoe. All of these caves are best visited with a guide. Actun Tunichil Muknal and Che Chem Ha, at the very least, absolutely require one. Private land, especially in Cayo and Toledo, often contains caves with Mayan artifacts.

■ **Do look for wildlife at the ruins and en route.** One of the best things about the ruins and their surroundings is that they're home to many birds and wild creatures. On the long drive to Caracol, for example, you'll pass through pine ridge and broadleaf jungle, and you may see brocket deer, oscellated turkey, and coatimundi. En route to Caracol, we once saw a small crocodile sunning at the bridge over the Macal River and, on another occasion, a fer-de-lance at DiSilva village. You're sure to see many beautiful butterflies. The trip up the New River to Lamanai is another good opportunity to see birds and wildlife on the riverbanks, and once you get to Lamanai, chances are good that you'll spot howler monkeys. Tikal is a great place to see howler and spider monkeys and other wild creatures.

8

■ **Don't be surprised to find Maya ruins in unexpected places.** There are at least 600 known Mayan sites in Belize, and the number of ruins out there probably runs into the thousands. Nearly every jungle lodge in Belize has some kind of Mayan site on the grounds, and some lodges, such as Pook's Hill, Nabitunich, Chan Chich, and Maya Mountain, have hosted archaeological digs. Mayan artifacts still remain in many caves, and pottery fragments can be as common as weeds in the backyards of many private homes. After all, at the height of the Maya kingdoms, there were perhaps a million Maya living in Belize, and their traces are everywhere.

ARCHITECTURE

One look at the monumental architecture of the Maya, and you might feel transported to another world (perhaps that's why Tikal was used as the rebel base in the original 1977 *Star Wars*). The breathtaking structures are even more impressive when you consider that they were built 1,000 to 2,000 years ago or more, without iron tools, wheels, or pulleys. The following is a brief explanation of the architecture you see at a Maya ruin.

INFLUENCES

Mayan architecture, even the great temples, may echo the design of the typical thatch hut ordinary Maya used for thousands of years. The rectangular huts had short walls made of a limestone mud and were topped by a steeply tilted two-sided thatch roof. Caves—ever-important Mayan ceremonial sites—were also influential. Many aboveground Mayan temples and other monumental structures have cavelike chambers, and the layout of Mayan cities probably reflected the Mayan cosmology, in which caves played a critical role.

BUILDING MATERIALS

With few exceptions, the large buildings in Mayan cities were constructed mostly from limestone, which was widely available in Belize and the Mexican Yucatán. Quarries were often established close to a building site so that workers didn't have to haul stone long distances. The Maya used limestone for mortar, stucco, and plaster. Limestone was crushed and burned in wood-fired kilns to make lime. A cement-like mortar was made by combining one part lime with one part of a white soil called *sahcab,* and then adding water.

The Maya also used wood, which was plentiful in Mesoamerica. In fact, some of the early temples were probably constructed of wood poles and thatch, much like the small houses of the Maya; unfortunately, these buildings are now lost.

TOOLS

The Maya were behind the curve with their tool technology. They didn't have iron tools, pulleys to move heavy weights, or wheels to build carts. They didn't have horses or other large animals to help them move materials. Instead, they used large numbers of laborers to tote and haul stones, mortar, and other building materials.

Obsidian, jade, flint, and other hard rocks were used to make axes, knives, and saws. The Maya had mason's kits to cut and finish limestone, and they had the equivalent of a plumb bob and other tools to align and level stones. The Maya were skilled stoneworkers, although the degree of finish varied from city to city.

CITY LAYOUT

In most Mayan cities, large plazas were surrounded by temples and large pyramids, probably used for religious ceremonies and other important public events. Paved causeways connected the plazas. Away from the city center were sprawls of "suburbs"—smaller stone buildings and traditional thatch huts.

Most cities had ball courts, and although the exact rules are unclear, players used a ball of natural rubber (rubber was discovered by the Olmecs) and scored points by getting the ball through a hoop or goalpost. "Sudden death" had a special meaning—the leader of the losing team was sometimes killed by decapitation.

8

Adventure Vacations

WORD OF MOUTH

"From Ambergris Caye, I would definitely recommend Lamanai, specifically with Tanisha Tours. Two different boat rides and a ride through the countryside in between. Light breakfast, lunch, and Belikin on the way home included. Lots of wildlife, in addition to the very beautiful ruins."

—JeanH

9

By Lan Sluder

THESE DAYS MORE TRAVELERS THAN ever are seeking trips with an active or adventure component, and tour operators are responding with an ever-increasing selection of exciting itineraries. Belize, with its opportunities for many different kinds of activities, is at the leading edge of the adventure-travel trend. In Belize you can select something easy, like cave tubing, snorkeling, fishing, horseback riding, hiking, birding, wildlife spotting, and canoeing. Or you can go for jungle trekking, caving, windsurfing, sea kayaking, or mountain-biking expeditions that require higher degrees of physical endurance and, in some cases, considerable technical skill. You can rough it or opt for comfortable, sometimes even luxurious, accommodations; put adventure at the center of your trip or make it only a sideline; go for a multiweek package or only a day trip. Study multiple itineraries and packages to find the trip that's right for you.

Choosing a tour package carefully is always important, but it becomes even more critical when the focus is adventure or sports. Below are selected trip offerings from some of the best adventure tour operators, both inside and outside Belize. When wisely chosen, special-interest vacations lead to distinctive, memorable experiences—just pack your curiosity along with the bug spray.

Tour prices operated by companies in Belize incur a 10% Goods and Services Tax. In many cases, the GST is not included in the tour prices shown.

For additional information about a specific activity or destination within Belize, contact the **Belize Tourist Board** (⊠ *Blue Horizons Bldg., Mile 3½, Northern Hwy.* ⏇ *Box 325, Belize City, Belize* ☎ *501/223–1913 or 800/624–0686* ⊕ *www.travelbelize.org*), or one of the tour operators listed in this section.

CHOOSING A TRIP

With dozens of options for special-interest and adventure tours in Belize, including do-it-yourself or fully guided package trips, it's helpful to think about certain factors when deciding which company or package will be right for you.

■ **Are you interested in adventure travel on the sea or the mainland or both?** Belize offers two very different adventure environments: the sea and the mainland. The Caribbean, various bays and lagoons, the Barrier Reef that runs 185 mi (303 km) along the eastern coast of the country, and three South Pacific–style atolls are perfect for activities such as fishing, sailing, diving, snorkeling, and windsurfing. Inland, you can rappel hundreds of feet into a limestone sinkhole, explore an underworld labyrinth of caves full of Mayan artifacts, hike the rain forest, ride horses or bikes to remote waterfalls, or tube through underground rivers. Some travelers prefer to concentrate on either water or land activities, but you can combine the two. Just be sure to give yourself enough time.

■ **How strenuous a trip do you want?** Adventure vacations commonly are split into "soft" and "hard" adventures. Hard adventures, such as

strenuous jungle treks and extended caving trips, usually require excellent physical conditioning and previous experience. Most hiking, biking, canoeing-kayaking, cave tubing, snorkeling, brief cave tours, and
similar soft adventures can be enjoyed by persons of all ages who are
in good health and are accustomed to a reasonable amount of exercise.
A little honesty goes a long way—recognize your own level of physical
fitness and discuss it with the tour operator before signing on.

■ **Would you like to pick up new skills?** Belize is a great place to pick up
new skills, whether it's how to paddle a kayak, how to rappel down a
cliff face, or how to dive. For example, you can take a quick resort diving course to see if you like scuba, or you can do a complete open-water
certification course, usually in three to four days. Before committing to
any program, do some research to confirm that the people running it
are qualified. Check to see if the dive shop or resort is certified by one
of the well-known international dive organizations, such as the Professional Association of Diving Instructors (PADI), the largest certification
agency in the world, or National Association of Underwater Instructors
(NAUI), the second-largest. Among the other how-to programs or lessons offered in Belize are kayaking, kayak surfing (riding the sea swells
driven through the Barrier Reef by prevailing trade winds), horseback
riding, snorkeling, and windsurfing. The sky's the limit, literally: you
can go parasailing and, at times, you can even score skydiving lessons.

■ **Do you want an "off-the-shelf" tour package or do you prefer to build your
own trip?** You can opt to buy a prepackaged adventure or special-interest
trip, complete with full-time guides who will do everything from meeting
your international flight to cooking your meals, or you can go the more
independent route, arranging local guides or tour operators on a daily, or
even hourly, basis. Because English is the official language in Belize and
most tour operators have e-mail and Web sites, it's easy to put together
an adventure package à la carte. Many package tour operators also offer
you the ability to combine two or more trips or to create a custom itinerary. It all comes down to whether you're happier doing it yourself or
having someone else take care of all the logistics and details.

■ **How far off the beaten path do you want to go?** As one of the least
densely populated countries in the hemisphere—more than two-fifths
of the country is devoted to nature reserves and national parks—Belize
offers many off-the-beaten-path experiences. Although many trips
described in this chapter might seem to be headed into uncharted territory, tour operators carefully check each detail before an itinerary goes
into a brochure. You won't usually be vying with busloads of tourists
for photo ops, but you'll probably run into occasional small groups of
like-minded travelers. Journeys into truly remote regions, such as Victoria Peak in the Maya Mountains, typically involve camping or the sim-
plest of accommodations, but they reward with more abundant wildlife
and locals who are less accustomed to the clicking of cameras.

■ **Are you ready for intellectual adventure?** Although Belize delivers great
physical adventures, don't overlook the opportunities for cerebral
exploration, too. Among the options for stimulating your little gray

cells are archaeological digs, ecology and nature programs, elder education, and homestays in a different cultural setting. You'll come back with recharged mental batteries and perhaps some new skills, too.

■ **How much are you willing to spend?** Belize has an adventure for nearly every budget. For penny-pinchers, homestay or local guesthouse programs and camping are among the low-cost options. At the high end, yacht charters and upmarket packaged nature tours can cost thousands of dollars per person per week. In general, the more planning, organizing, and booking you do yourself, and the more you rely on Belize-based operators, the lower the cost. As always, comparison shopping pays off. The cost of two tours of the same length can vary greatly, depending on accommodations, equipment, transportation options, and amount of hand-holding involved. The Internet has made comparing rates much easier, and nearly all tour operators have Web sites. Use the Web to check recent reviews of tours and tour operators.

CRUISES

CRUISES AROUND THE CAYES & ATOLLS

Few things in life compare with the experience of being on a sailboat in the Caribbean—the caress of the wind and the salt spray on your face, the sun on your back, and all around the mint green, turquoise, and vodka-clear sea. Companies listed below provide day sails as well as longer, multiple-night trips.

Season: Year-round

Locations: Most day sails and longer crewed trips start in San Pedro, Caye Caulker, Belize City, or Placencia. The boats visit nearby islands, snorkel spots, and dive destinations. Generally, they stay inside the Barrier Reef.

Cost: Day sails on a crewed boat start at under BZ$100 per person and may include lunch and drinks. Overnight and longer trips can run BZ$300–BZ$1,500 or more per day, depending on the size of the boat, the number in your party, and what's included.

Tour Operators: Belize Sailing Charters; El Gato; Next Wave; Raggamuffin Tours; Winnie Estelle

Raggamuffin Tours does day sails around the northern cayes, as well as a BZ$550-per-person, two-night/three-day island-hopping trip from Caye Caulker to Placencia. The nights are spent camping on Tobacco and Rendezvous cayes (camping equipment provided), with stops at Goff and Southwater cayes. Belize Sailing Charters does day and longer trips on the *Talisman* and other boats out of Placencia. *Next Wave* does day sails out of Placencia, and several boats, including *El Gato* and *Winnie Estelle,* do day trips out of San Pedro. Sailboat owners tend to be free spirits who may pick up and sail to another port at the drop of a yachting cap, so check locally to see what boats are still sailing.

CLOSE UP

Ecotourism in Belize

Central America is the original eco-tourism destination; as a result, you'll see the term used liberally everywhere. For lodging it can be used to describe a deluxe private cabaña on a well-tended beach or a hut in the middle of nowhere with pit toilets. It may also point to environmental conservation efforts by parks or tour companies that are conscious of natural resources and their role in not depleting them. Or it may mean just the opposite. Wildlife parks, butterfly farms, cloud forests, and Maya ruins are some of the incredible ecodestinations in this area. And mountain biking, bird-watching, jungle hiking, scuba diving, cave tubing, fishing, and white-water rafting are just some of the eco-activities.

You can do your part to protect the natural heritage of Belize and the Tikal area of Guatemala by being an ecologically sensitive traveler. Where possible, choose green hotels, those that have taken care to protect the environment and that have energy-efficient cooking, lighting, and cooling systems, and that recycle and dispose of waste responsibly. Be culturally sensitive, as both countries have highly diverse populations, each with different cultural attitudes and perspectives. Also, try to do business with companies that hire local people for positions at all levels, and where

possible choose local restaurants and hotels over chain properties. When diving or snorkeling, avoid touching or breaking coral, and don't take part in swim-with-dolphins or swim-with-manatees tours as most naturalists say these programs disturb the animals. Also, use ecofriendly sunscreen. On caving or hiking trips, take nothing but photographs and leave nothing of yours behind. When visiting Maya sites, never remove anything, not even a tiny shard of pottery.

For the most part, Belize has reaped the benefits of the growing tourism industry, drawing in much-needed capital to bolster national coffers. The costs of tourism are less obvious, however. Among other effects, indigenous communities are undermined by increasingly tourist-oriented economies—cultivating a plot of land may no longer support a family, but selling knickknacks in the streets just might. Where tourists come, expats often follow, and land, especially beachfront land, is quickly priced out of the reach of locals. There's no easy solution to this dilemma, and balancing the advantages of tourism against its drawbacks is, and will remain, a constant struggle for Belize. The long-term effects are as much dependent on the attitudes and behavior of visitors as they are on prudent national policies.

YACHT CHARTERS

A crewed or bareboat sailing charter lets you explore the Belize Barrier Reef and little-visited cayes at your own pace. Most charters are for a week, though shorter charters may be available off-season. Placencia and San Pedro are the two main sailboat charter bases in Belize. You sail inside the reef, protected from ocean swells. A typical day? Wake to a private sunrise over the Caribbean. Have breakfast and a quick swim. Dive or snorkel all morning, snag a lobster or conch, and then drop anchor at a remote island for a barbecue on the beach. In the afternoon, relax with a rum and tonic and enjoy the warm trade winds. Go ashore to a beachside restaurant for a seafood dinner. Then, relax on your boat before drifting off to sleep under Central American stars.

Season: Year-round
Locations: Inside the Barrier Reef—either the northern cayes from San Pedro, Ambergris Caye, or the southern cayes from Placencia.
Cost: Bareboat sailing charters range from about BZ$1,000 to BZ$2,000 per night for two to eight people (not all operators permit daily charters), and BZ$6,000–BZ$16,000 or more for weeklong charters for two to eight people, plus provisions. For crews, add about BZ$200–BZ$250 a day for a skipper and BZ$200 a day for a cook.
Tour Operators: Belize Sailing Charters; Katkandu; The Moorings; Raggamuffin Tours; TMM Belize

TMM Belize, with bases in San Pedro and Placencia, has around 40 catamarans for weekly bareboat or crewed charter. The Moorings, with a base in Placencia, has a selection of 37- to 47-foot catamarans. Among the smaller charter operations, Belize Sailing Charters offers crewed charters on the *Talisman* and other sailboats. Raggamuffin Tours provides multiday crewed charters from Caye Caulker to Placencia. *Katkandu,* based in San Pedro, runs weeklong and longer cruises to southern Belize and to the Rio Dulce in Guatemala.

LEARNING VACATIONS

ART & ARCHAEOLOGY

Some travelers want a quick look at a country's major sights, while others prefer to immerse themselves in the culture. In Belize this means participating in a "dig" at a Maya archaeological site, usually under the direction of a university archaeological team. Other tours don't get involved with archeological digs but focus on the history of the Maya civilization.

Season: Sessions run only a few weeks of the year, usually in spring or summer.
Locations: Archaeological digs that accept volunteer workers are mostly in Orange Walk District.
Cost: Archaeological programs start at around BZ$1,250 for one week, and BZ$2,300 for two weeks. These prices don't include transportation to Belize or incidental personal expenses.
Tour Operators: Elderhostel; Maya Research Program; University of Texas Mesoamerican Archaeological Research Laboratory

Elderhostel offers a 14-day program in Belize, Guatemala, and Honduras on the history of the Maya, with insight into modern-day issues affecting their community. The Maya Research Program, sponsored by the Blue Creek Regional Political Ecology Project, has one- and two-week volunteer programs in the Blue Creek area of Orange Walk District. The University of Texas Mesoamerican Archaeological Research

Laboratory (MARL) accepts volunteers at its field station in the Rio Bravo Conservation area of Orange Walk District, located on Programme for Belize lands. Volunteers (who pay a fee to participate) must commit for at least one week and may stay as long as three weeks, and in some cases longer. The program usually runs from February to April, with other options in summer, some for academic credit. Volunteers live in a rustic dorm setting and learn the basics of field archaeology through lectures and hands-on experience.

CULTURAL TOURS

A few programs offer the chance to live with the modern-day Maya or Garífuna at a homestay or village guesthouse program. You can also spend a week learning how to process cacao or spend four days learning to cook Belizean—including Mayan—recipes.

Season: Year-round
Locations: Homestay and village guesthouse programs are in Toledo District near Punta Gorda. There's also a homestay tour at Indian Church Village in Orange Walk District.
Cost: Village guesthouse programs start at BZ$45 per person per night, including lodging, activities, and meals. Homestays generally cost about the same. The Chocolate Week near Punta Gorda costs BZ$2,765 per person including lodging and meals. Belizean cooking classes cost BZ$1,300 including lodging and some meals.
Tour Operators: Beyond Touring; Cottontree Lodge; Dems Dats Doin'; Maya Centre Women's Group; Maya Mountain Lodge & Tours; Toledo Ecotourism Association

The Toledo Ecotourism Association (T.E.A.) program allows visitors to participate in the village life of the Maya while maintaining some personal privacy. You stay in small guesthouses in one of nine Mopan and Kek'chi Maya villages in Toledo District, including San Antonio, San Miguel, and Blue Creek. Barranco, a predominantly Garífuna village, also has a guesthouse. The guesthouses are very simple, with traditional thatch roofs and outdoor latrines. You take meals in the homes of villagers and participate in the routines of village life. The program, endorsed by the Belize Tourist Board, is a collective owned by more than 200 members and is designed to promote cultural exchange. The cost is only BZ$84 a day for two, including meals. A separate program, run privately by Dem Dats Doin' (which also operates an ecofarm and a private tourist information office in Punta Gorda) arranges stays for visitors in the homes of Toledo villagers. Again, the accommodations are extremely simple—you may share a room with the family in a small thatch building with dirt floor. Two people pay a total of less than BZ$75 a day, including meals. Homestays at Maya Centre at the entrance to the Cockscomb Wildlife Sanctuary can be arranged through the Maya Centre Women's Group, a group of about 50 Mopan women who have banded together to sell handicrafts. Beyond Touring also offers some homestay programs at Indian Church Village near Lamanai. Cottontree Lodge's Chocolate Week program lets you "work your way through the entire practical process from scratch, starting with the cacao fruit on the tree and ending with the chocolate in your mouth." Maya Mountain Lodge & Tours has a four-day/three-night cooking class that teaches you to prepare Maya and Belizean recipes, and some Thai dishes, too.

ECO-ORIENTED VOLUNTEER PROGRAMS

If you have more time than money, and want to help Belizeans, you may want to look into eco-oriented volunteer programs.

Season: Year-round
Locations: Throughout Belize
Cost: From BZ$770 a month, including food and lodging, but not including transportation to Belize, mandatory health insurance, and incidental personal expenses.
Tour Operators: Belize Audubon Society; Cornerstone Foundation; Green Reef Belize Coral Caye Conservation NGO

With the Belize Audubon Society (BAS), you can apply for volunteer jobs at its marine or mainland parks or at its office in Belize City. People with education, community development, and conservation experience and skills make especially good candidates. The BAS is Belize's premier conservation organization and manages or comanages eight national parks and monuments. Volunteers must commit for a minimum of three months (one month at marine areas) and in most cases must pay for their own accommodations and food. For example, volunteers at Half Moon Caye National Monument at Lighthouse Atoll pay BZ$30 a day. The nonprofit Cornerstone Foundation, based in San Ignacio, Cayo, provides volunteer opportunities in community development, ecology, health care, and other areas. Volunteers, who live in communal lodging, must commit for a minimum of three months. Cornerstone charges BZ$2,310 per person for a three-month program, and that fee includes lodging but not food, transportation, or personal expenses. Green Reef on Ambergris Caye is a nonprofit dedicated to the sustainable use of Belize's marine resources. It accepts volunteers, who usually pay nothing but must provide their own lodging, food, and transportation expenses.

THE OUTDOORS

BIRD-WATCHING TOURS

When selecting a bird-watching tour, ask questions. What species might be seen? What are the guide's qualifications? Does the operator work to protect natural habitats? How large are the birding groups? What equipment is used? (In addition to binoculars and a birding guidebook, this should include a high-powered telescope, a tape recorder to record and play back bird calls, which is a way of attracting birds, and a spotlight for night viewing.)

Season: Year-round, though more common from December to March, when birds from the north winter in Belize and there's less rain.

Locations: Cayo, Orange Walk, Stann Creek, and Toledo Districts
Cost: From BZ$1,600 per person for a six-day/five-night birding trip, including guides, lodging, and some meals. On an à la carte basis, short birding hikes with a local guide cost from BZ$30 per person.
Tour Operators: Chan Chich Lodge; Exotic Birding; Hidden Valley Inn; Nature Treks; Paradise Expeditions; Victor Emanuel Nature Tours; Wildside Tours

More than 575 species of birds have been spotted in Belize, and every year five or more additional species are found in the country. Birders flock to Belize to see exciting species such as the Jabiru Stork, the largest bird in the Western Hemisphere; the Harpy Eagle with its 7-foot wingspan; the beautiful Scarlet Macaw; the Keel-billed Toucan, the national bird of Belize; 21 species of hummingbirds; and endangered or rare species such as the Yellow-headed Parrot, Oscellated Turkey, Orange-breasted Falcon, and Chestnut-breasted Heron. Birding hot spots in Belize include Crooked Tree Wildlife Sanctuary, the Mountain Pine Ridge, the area around Chan Chich Lodge at Gallon Jug, and the Cockscomb Basin. *Birds of Belize,* by H. Lee Jones and Dana Gardner, is the bible of Belize birding, although some complain that the 484-page, 2.2-pound birding guide is heavy and cumbersome in the field. The operators listed above offer trips to the best birding areas in Belize.

ECOTRIPS

With about two-fifths of Belize dedicated to national parks and reserves, the country is a natural for ecotripping.

Season: Year-round
Locations: Throughout Belize
Cost: From BZ$100 for day trips
Tour Operators: Belize Audubon Society; Chaa Creek Expeditions; Chan Chich Lodge; G.A.P. Adventures; Hamansi Eco Tours; Hidden Valley Inn; International Expeditions; International Zoological Expeditions; TIDE Tours; Victor Emanuel Nature Tours

Park rangers and local guides at Cockscomb Basin Wildlife Sanctuary, managed by the Belize Audubon Society, provide guided nature tours of Cockscomb and can also arrange multiday treks to Victoria Peak, one of the highest mountains in the country. Hamanasi and other resorts in Hopkins and Placencia run day tours to Cockscomb. International Zoological Expeditions has bases at Blue Creek in Toledo District and on South Water Caye off Dangriga; from both areas it runs educational and nature programs for students, teachers, and others. Victor Emanuel Nature Tours runs tours, oriented to birding but including wildlife spotting, at Chan Chich Lodge, Hidden Valley Inn, and at Crooked Tree. TIDE runs nature tours in Bladen Nature Reserve and elsewhere in beautiful Toledo. G.A.P. Adventures' 15- to 60-day trips through Mexico and Central America, which offer a mix of Mayan ruins, cultural tours, birding, and beaching, include time in Belize. The 60-day Mexico & Central America Journey trip, which it calls "the Big Kahuna," includes about five days in Belize. International Expedition's

10-day Rainforest, Reef & Ruins trip has stops at Lamanai, Tikal, and Ambergris Caye. At many jungle lodges, including, notably, Chan Chich, Ek'Tun, Chaa Creek, duPlooy's, Blancaneaux, Lamanai Outpost, Lodge at Big Falls, Caves Branch, and Pook's Hill *(see individual chapters for details on these lodges)*, you can hire a local guide to take you on a guided nature walk or a longer wildlife spotting trip.

JUNGLE CAMPING & LODGES

Belize has a few developed campgrounds, and it does offer primitive camping on some cayes and at some national parks on the mainland. Several hotels and lodges also offer a camping option. Because there are dozens of jungle lodges in Belize, most are not covered in this section. *See* individual chapters for information on lodges.

Season: Year-round
Locations: Throughout Belize
Cost: Camping from BZ$5 per person per night
Tour Operators: Belize Audubon Society; Caves Branch Adventure Co.; Glovers Atoll Resort; IBTM; Inglewood Camping Grounds; Island Expeditions; Jungle Camp at Chaa Creek; Seakunga Adventures; Slickrock Adventures

Caves Branch Adventure Co. offers camping both at its base camp off the Hummingbird Highway and as a part of its many overnight jungle treks. For a more upscale camping experience, Chaa Creek has small casitas on raised platforms at its Jungle Camp, near its main lodge in Cayo. Several small hotels and lodges, including the Trek Stop in Cayo and Jungle Jeanies and Tipple Tree Beya Inn, both in Hopkins, allow camping for a small fee. Another camping option in Cayo is Inglewood Camping Grounds, which even has RV hookups. Seakunga Adventures specializes in kayaking and camping trips, with base camps in the Sapodilla Cayes, Glover's Atoll, and elsewhere. Both Slick Rock Adventures and Island Expeditions offer camping on the cayes and inland as part of their kayaking and other adventure trips. Glover's Atoll Resort provides primitive camping facilities at its beautiful island, Northeast Caye, on Glover's Atoll. Basic tent-camping facilities are available at several national parks and reserves, including Cockscomb and Half Moon Caye, both of which are managed by the Belize Audubon Society. Most of the remote islands off the Belize coast are now privately owned, and camping is allowed only with permission of the owner or caretaker. Bruno Kuppinger at IBTM runs extreme camping and trekking trips, including the week-long Maya Divide trip.

PHOTO SAFARIS

A photo safari can sharpen your photography skills while letting you visit some of the most scenic spots in Belize.

Season: Year-round
Locations: Cayo District, the Cayes
Cost: From BZ$4,400, plus airfare

Tour Operators: Exotic Birding; Nature Photography Adventure

Nature Photography Adventure runs annual photo safari trips to Belize. Typically, you stay in a midlevel lodge in Cayo and also visit one of the cayes. Exotic Birding, in addition to running birding trips to Belize, offers an annual 10-day Belize Photography Workshop. The trip begins with a class in Houston, then moves to Belize, with stays at Crooked Tree, San Ignacio, and Caye Caulker.

SPORTS

BICYCLING

Despite heat, humidity, bad drivers, and rough roads, cycling is a big sport in Belize, and you often see local cyclists risking life and limb to train on the Western or Northern highways. Mountain biking, however, is only beginning to take hold in Belize, mostly in the Mountain Pine Ridge.

Season: Year-round
Locations: Mountain Pine Ridge for mountain biking
Cost: From BZ$150 per person for a full-day mountain-biking expedition; some hotels and lodges rent bikes from BZ$10 to BZ$20 a day, or provide them free for guests.
Tour Operators: Tropical Expeditions Belize; Caves Branch Adventure Co.

Caves Branch offers what they call "jungle biking," a Belize version of mountain biking that involves a full-day bike trip. Belize Tropical Expeditions has a 9-day/8-night "Ride & Explore" trip that begins in Placencia and ends in Caye Caulker.

CANOEING & KAYAKING

Belize has some of the best sea kayaking in Central America. Thanks to the Barrier Reef, a literal barrier to big waves and swells, the sea inside the reef is much calmer than the open ocean. Belize also has good kayaking and canoeing on inland rivers and lagoons.

Season: Year-round
Locations: Sea kayaking around Ambergris Caye, Caye Caulker, and elsewhere along the coast inside the Barrier Reef; canoeing and kayaking on the Macal, Mopan, Sibun, Swasey, Hondo, New, Belize, and other rivers, and on the Progresso, Placencia, Northern, Southern, New, and other lagoons.
Cost: Day kayaking and canoe trips from BZ$150 a person; kayaking tours from BZ$1,600 per person for four days, BZ$2,800 per person for seven days.
Tour Operators: Caves Branch Adventure Co.; G.A.P. Adventures; International Zoological Expeditions; Island Expeditions; Mountain Travel Sobek; Seakunga; Slick Rock Adventures; Toadal Adventure

There are two types of kayaking trips: base kayaking and expedition kayaking. On a base kayaking trip, you have a home base—usually a caye—from which you take day trips (or longer). On an expedition-style trip, you travel from island to island or up mainland rivers. Typically, base kayaking is easier, but expedition kayaking is more adventurous.

Toadal Adventures, based in Placencia, provides top-notch sea and river expedition kayak trips that usually last for four to six days in southern Belize; they can customize trips to your specific schedule and interests. Island Expeditions and Slick Rock Adventures both do complete expedition packages, several of which combine sea and river kayaking and base and expedition aspects. They both focus on Glover's Atoll and land activities in central and southern Belize. Seakunga also runs both base camp and expedition-style kayaking trips at Glover's Atoll as well as the Sapodilla Cayes in southern Belize, and other locales. International Zoological Expeditions has eight- to ten-day trips, usually with an educational component such as ethnobotanical walks or mapping an island. IZE's trips combine time inland at Blue Creek in Toledo and at South Water Caye. Saddle Caye South offers self-guided kayak trips—in effect, kayak rentals—and five-day island-hopping expeditions with guide, kayaks, camping gear, meals, and support boat. About three days of Mountain Travel Sobek's nine-day "Rainforest to Reef" trip are spent kayaking around the Sapodilla Cayes and the Port Honduras Marine Reserve in Toledo District. G.A.P. Adventures has a weeklong island-hopping kayak trip, starting and ending in Placencia. You paddle for two to four hours a day, with stops at Pumpkin Caye, the Silk Cayes, and the Sapodilla Cayes. Most of the trips by all operators provide opportunities for snorkeling, fishing, hiking, and caving as well as kayaking. Several Belize-based operators, including Caves Branch Adventure Co., and a number of the other jungle lodges, run day and overnight kayaking trips in Cayo District. In addition, rental kayaks are available in Placencia, San Pedro, Caye Caulker, and elsewhere for do-it-yourselfers. Some hotels also provide kayaks for their guests.

CAVE TUBING

An activity you'll find in few places outside Belize is cave tubing. You drift down a river, usually the Caves Branch River in Cayo District, in a large rubber inner tube. At certain points the river goes underground, and you float through eerie underground cave systems, some with Maya artifacts still in place. The only light is from headlamps.

Season: Year-round, though seasonal rains June through November can sometimes raise water levels too high for tubing, and during dry season (February–May) some river levels may occasionally become too low.
Locations: Rivers in Cayo District, primarily the Caves Branch River and Barton Creek
Cost: From BZ$100 per person for a half-day trip
Tour Operators: Action Belize; Belize Jungle Dome Adventure Vacations; Belize Taxi Tour Guide Association (sometimes called Cave-Tubing in Belize); Belize Trips; Caves Branch Adventure Co.; Cayo Adventure

Tours; Chaa Creek Expeditions; Discovery Expeditions; Ecological Tours and Services; Green Dragon Adventure Travel; Ian Anderson's Caves Branch Adventure Co.; Jaguar Paw Lodge; Jungle Dome Adventure Vacations; Mayawalk; Windy Hill Tour Co.

In the last decade since Jaguar Paw Lodge and Ian Anderson's Caves Branch Adventure Co. first introduced it, cave tubing has become one of the most popular soft adventure activities in Belize. It's the number one mainland shore excursion of cruise-ship passengers, and on days when several large ships are docked in Belize City, you should expect inner-tube traffic jams. Several Belize City–based tour operators, including Action Belize, Ecological Tours, and Discovery Expeditions, cater to the cruise-ship day-trippers. In addition, Cayo-based tour operators, including Chaa Creek Expeditions, Ian Anderson's Caves Branch Adventure Co., Jaguar Paw Lodge, Cayo Adventure Tours, Green Dragon Adventure Travel, and Windy Hill Tour Co., run cave-tubing day trips. Belize Trips can arrange custom cave-tubing trips for individuals or groups. The drill with most of these operations is the same. You pile into a van or bus for a short drive to a parking area near the Caves Branch River off the Western Highway, hike a short distance, and then pop into the Caves Branch with your inner tube for a float on the river and through several caves. Depending on where you're launched into the river, you float through anywhere from three to seven caves, some of which have ancient pottery shards and other artifacts of the Maya. Most of the caverns are very dark, and guides normally provide headlamps. The activity level is usually light, and even some people who can't swim or who are in their seventies and eighties go cave tubing. Caves Branch Adventure Co. offers longer and more active (and more expensive) cave-tubing trips. In the "River of Caves" cave-tubing trip, you float underground for a total of nearly 7 mi (11 km). San Ignacio–based tour operators, including Cayo Adventure Tours, also offer tubing at Barton Creek Cave.

CAVING

Belize has some of the most extensive cave systems in Central America. One cave system in the Chiquibul Wilderness is 35 mi (56 km) long. Only serious, highly trained cavers need consider the remote, difficult caves of Belize, but more casual adventurers can find fairly easy day trips to caves like Actun Tunichil Muknal, frequently described by visitors as a highlight of their Belize vacation.

Season: Year-round
Locations: Cayo and Toledo districts
Cost: Day trips to caves from BZ$70 per person.
Tour Operators: Caves Branch Adventure Co.; PACZ Tours

A small number of tour companies, including PACZ, are permitted to take visitors into Actun Tunichil Muknal (ATM) cave. From a base camp off the Western Highway in Cayo District, you walk about 45 minutes to the "Cave of the Stone Sepulchre" in Roaring Creek Valley. Entering the cave requires a short swim. Once you make your way inside the cave formation, your headlamp reveals hundreds of Mayan artifacts—thought to have been used in rituals to *Chac,* the Rain God of the Maya—as well as human remains. Most visitors find visiting ATM an amazing experience. There are several other easy-to-moderate caves in Cayo that can be visited on day tours, including Che Chem Ha, Rio Frio, and Barton Creek. Caves Branch Adventure Co., widely considered the premier jungle guide operation in the country, conducts day and overnight caving trips. Some of the trips are rated moderate and others difficult.

FISHING

Drop your hook in Belize and you're almost guaranteed to catch something. Lagoons and shallow flats are ideal for bonefish. The Barrier Reef supports grouper, snapper, and jacks. In the blue water beyond the reef, anglers will find tuna, sailfish, and pompano. Some of the world's best permit fisheries are off the coast of southern Belize. The estuaries and river mouths are home to tarpon and snook. It's even possible to achieve a "grand slam" in Belize—that is, catch tarpon, permit, and bonefish, all in one day.

Season: Year-round, with best fishing for tarpon May–September; permit, January–November; snook, November–March; bonefish, April–November; sailfish, January–June.

Locations: All coastal areas and the Cayes

Cost: Local fishing guides charge from BZ$400 per day; complete fishing packages including meals, accommodations, and guides for seven days, from BZ$3,500 per person (not including airfare).

Tour Operators: Belize River Lodge; Destinations Belize; El Pescador; Fishing International; Glover's Atoll Resort; International Zoological Expeditions; Isla Marisol; Machaca Hill Lodge; Rod & Reel Adventures; Turneffe Flats Lodge; Turneffe Island Lodge

The best-known fishing lodges in Belize aren't skunky fishing camps but high-end resorts catering to affluent anglers who, after a hard day on the water, expect ice-cold cocktails, equally icy air-conditioning, and Sealy Posturepedic mattresses. El Pescador on North Ambergris Caye; Machaca Hill Lodge (formerly El Pescador PG) in Punta Gorda; two lodges on Turneffe Atoll (Turneffe Flats and Turneffe Island Lodge); several beach resorts in Placencia and Hopkins; and some lodges on Lighthouse and Glover's atolls offer fishing with a touch of luxury—everything from guides to cold drinks is included.

Belize River Lodge, the oldest fishing lodge in Belize (it's been in continuous operation since 1960) operates live-aboard boats including a 58-foot Hatteras yacht. It also runs fishing skiffs from its lodge on the Belize Olde River.

If you want a less-expensive fishing vacation, you can make your own arrangements for lodging and meals and hire your own local fishing guides in San Pedro, Placencia, Hopkins, Punta Gorda, and elsewhere. Mary Toy's Destinations Belize in Placencia is a compromise between

Adventures to Get Your Heart Rate Up

Most adventure tours and trips in Belize can be handled by anyone used to a reasonable amount of activity. Even couch potatoes can hack it. But a few are more physically challenging and require a higher level of fitness or skill. Here are three adventures that will send your heart rate soaring:

Climb Victoria Peak. This may be the toughest trek in Belize. You need a guide, and the trip takes a total of four to five days up and back. Though Victoria Peak is only 3,675 feet high, and the top of the mountain is just 17 mi (28 km) from the visitor center at Cockscomb Basin Wildlife Sanctuary, the going—through tropical jungle—is rough, hot, and humid, with slopes of up to 60 degrees.

Dive the Blue Hole. The bottom of Blue Hole, a large underwater sinkhole at Lighthouse Atoll, is more than 400 feet down. Although not an inherently difficult dive, it's deep, and it's best done only by experienced divers. Hammerhead, tiger, and other sharks prowl the hole. Be fore-warned: over the years, at least three divers have died making the dive. If you don't dive, you can snorkel the Blue Hole; most dive boats also welcome snorkelers.

Rappel the Black Hole. Caves Branch Adventure Co. runs a two-day jungle expedition that starts with a rappel more than 200 feet into the Actun Loch Tunich sinkhole, followed by a trip through more than 10 mi (6 km) of underground river. For a longer and even more intense jungle trek, consider Caves Branch's seven-day "Lost World Expedition."

a total package and doing it all yourself. She can help you arrange moderate accommodations, some meals, and guides for light-tackle or fly-fishing day trips (or for longer periods). She also puts together moderately priced packages for fishing in Placencia and elsewhere in southern Belize.

LIVE ABOARDS

If you're serious about diving and want to hit the best dive spots in Belize, morning, noon, and night, with as many as six dives a day, live-aboard dive boats are your best bet.

Season: Year-round

Locations: Live aboards concentrate on dives around Belize's three atolls—Lighthouse, Turneffe, and Glovers—with most dives at Light-house and Turneffe. The boats depart from Belize City.

Cost: Expect to pay about BZ$3,000–BZ$5,600 for six days of diving. That price includes all dives, meals, airport transfers, and stateroom accommodations on the dive boat. It does not include airfare to Belize, tips, alcoholic beverages, equipment rentals, Nitrox, marine park fees, and incidentals.

Tour Operators: Belize Aggressor;; Peter Hughes Diving

Peter Hughes Diving's 138-foot *Sun Dancer II*, which can hold up to 20 passengers in 10 staterooms, departs from Belize City on Saturday afternoon and moors at either Turneffe or Lighthouse Atoll. For the next six days, divers explore these two atolls, getting as many as five dives a day. The ship moves two or three times a day. (Twenty people died during Hurricane Iris in October 2001, near Placencia, when Peter Hughes Diving's *Wave Dancer* live aboard capsized.) The itinerary of the 18-passenger *Belize Aggressor* is similar to that of the *Sun Dancer II,* with passengers embarking in Belize City on a Saturday and spending time until the next Friday at Turneffe and Lighthouse atolls, with as many as five or six dives each day.

SCUBA DIVING & SNORKELING

Belize has the largest living coral reef system in the Western and Northern hemispheres, and three of the only four coral atolls outside the South Pacific. Here you can see more than 300 species of tropical fish, 100 types of coral, and many large sea creatures, including hammerheads, whale sharks, manatees, and manta rays. It's no wonder that the scuba diving and snorkeling in Belize are considered among the best in the world. Belize has more than 50 dive shops and snorkel tour operators, so only a representative sample of the top operators are included here. *(See individual chapters for more information on dive and snorkel shops and on specific dive destinations.)*

Season: Year-round

Locations: Serious divers focus on the three atolls—Lighthouse, Turneffe, and Glover's—all of which have dedicated dive lodges and are the destinations of most live-aboard dive boats. Good recreational diving options abound all around the northern cayes and off the southern coast. For snorkeling, Hol Chan Marine Reserve near Ambergris Caye is the most popular spot, and at Shark-Ray Alley, now a part of Hol Chan, you can swim with stingrays and nurse sharks. There's also excellent snorkeling along most of the Barrier Reef, patch reefs, and at the atolls.

Cost: Snorkel trips from BZ$40 per person; two-tank dives from BZ$100; one-week dive packages, including hotel, meals, and dives, from BZ$2,500 per person.

Tour Operators: Amigos del Mar; Belize Aggressor; Belize Dive Connection; Belize Trips; Destinations Belize; Ecologic Divers, Glover's Atoll Resort; Hamanasi Eco Tours; Isla Marisol; Peter Hughes Diving; Protech Belize; Reef Conservation International; Sea Horse Dive Shop; Sea Sports Belize; Turneffe Island Lodge

The largest concentration of dive shops and dive trip operators (and also snorkel boat operators) is on Ambergris Caye. It's a short boat ride to the spur-and-groove formations along the Barrier Reef and to Hol Chan Marine Reserve. Several San Pedro operators with speedboats, including Amigos del Mar, Ecologic Divers, and Protech Belize, can take you to the Blue Hole, the largest ocean sinkhole in the world, with depths of more than 400 feet. Paradise Down and other dive shops on Caye Caulker take divers to the same sites as the dive shops on Ambergris Caye. Almost a dozen dive lodges and hotels are on Belize's atolls, including Turneffe Island Lodge, Blackbird Caye Resort, Isla Marisol, Glover's Atoll Resort, and others. Live-aboard dive boats also dive the atolls, although the Belize Aggressor, Peter Hughes live aboards leave from and return to Belize City.

Almost a dozen dive lodges and hotels are on Belize's atolls, and live-aboard dive boats also cluster here. Off the southern coast—served by Hamanasi Eco Tours, Sea Horse Dive Shop, Reef Conservation International, and other operators—you can dive less-visited sites such as the Silk Cayes, home to large numbers of whale sharks in spring, and Belize's largest marine park, South Water Caye Marine Reserve.

Belize City–based dive operations generally concentrate on the cruise market. These include Belize Dive Connection and Sea Sports Belize. Dive Connection also has a swim-with-dolphins program, at a 4-acre lagoon at Spanish Lookout Caye. You spend about 20 minutes with four Atlantic bottlenose dolphins. Cost is BZ$200 per person including transportation to the island from Belize City.

HIKING, TREKKING & WALKING

See trips above and other multisport categories for more information.

HORSEBACK RIDING

Time to tack up and hit the trail! You can ride to waterfalls in the Mountain Pine Ridge or to Maya ruins and caves in the Cayo.

Season: Year-round
Locations: Cayo District
Cost: From BZ$1,400 per person for horseback riding packages for four days; from BZ$80 for a half-day ride.
Tour Operators: Banana Bank Lodge; Equitours; Mountain Equestrian Trails

Two well-established Belize outfits offer horseback-riding tours. At Banana Bank Lodge you can ride one of their 50 horses (predominantly quarter horses) on a 4,000-acre ranch that hugs the banks of the Belize River. At Mountain Equestrian Trails you can take day rides or multinight horseback trips into the Mountain Pine Ridge and the high bush of Cayo District. U.S.-based Equitours offers riding tour packages in Cayo, with extensions to Tikal. The Lodge at Chaa Creek, Cahal Pech Village, Caves Branch Adventure Camp, and duPlooy's Lodge, all in Cayo, as well as Inn at Robert's Grove in Placencia, Maruba Spa off the Old Northern Highway, and Cotton Tree Lodge in Toledo also arrange horseback-riding trips.

ZIP LINING

Zip lines allow you to experience the jungle at canopy level, suspended in a harness 50 to 80 feet in the air, zooming from one platform in the trees to another.

Season: Year-round

Tour Operators

Below is contact information for all tour operators mentioned in this chapter, including international Belize-based operators or those who are based in the United States or elsewhere. The list is selective—we've chosen established firms that offer a good selection of itineraries.

Action Belize. ✉ Mile 3½, Northern Hwy., Belize City, Belize ☎ 501/223–2987 or 888/383–6319 ⊕ www.actionbelize.com.

Adventure Center. ✉ 1311 63rd St., #200, Emeryville, CA ☎ 510/654–1879 or 800/228–8747 ⊕ www.adventurecenter.com.

Adventure Life. ✉ 1655 S. 3rd. St. W, Suite 1, Missoula, MT ☎ 406/541–2677 or 800/344–6118 ⊕ www.adventure-life.com.

Amigos del Mar. ✉ San Pedro, Belize ☎ 501/226–2706 ⊕ www.amigosdive.com.

Banana Bank Lodge & Jungle Equestrian Adventure. ⌂ Box 48, Belmopan City, Belize ☎ 501/820–2020 ⊕ www.bananabank.com.

Belize Aggressor. ✉ 7810 Hwy. 182 E, Morgan City, LA ☎ 985/385–2628 or 800/348–2628 ⊕ www.aggressor.com.

Belize Audubon Society. ✉ 12 Fort St., Box 1001, Belize City, Belize ☎ 501/223–4988 ⊕ www.belizeaudubon.org.

Belize Dive Connection. ✉ 71 N. Front St., Belize City, Belize ☎ 501/223–4526 ⊕ www.belizediving.com.

Belize River Lodge. ✉ Riverview Ladyville, Belize ☎ 501/225–2002 or 888/275–4843 ⊕ www.belizeriverlodge.com.

Belize Sailing Charters. ✉ Placencia, Stann Creek, Belize ☎ 501/523–3138 ⊕ www.belize-sailing-charters.com.

Belize Trips. ⌂ Box 1108, Belize City, Belize ☎ 501/223–0376, 561/210–7015 in the U.S. ⊕ www.belize-trips.com.

Beyond Touring. ✉ 3036 Lake Shore Dr., Deerfield Beach, FL ☎ 954/415–2897 or 866/393–2731 ⊕ www.beyondtouring.com.

Cave-Tubing in Belize. ✉ Belize City, Belize ☎ 501/605–1575, 501/222–5523 ⊕ www.cave-tubing.com.

Caves Branch Adventure Co. ⌂ Box 356, Belmopan City, Belize ☎ 501/822–2800 ⊕ www.cavesbranch.com.

Cayo Adventure Tours. ⌂ Box 88, San Ignacio, Cayo, Belize ☎ 501/824–3246 ⊕ www.cayoadventure.com.

Chaa Creek Expeditions. ⌂ Box 53, San Ignacio, Cayo, Belize ☎ 501/824–2037, 877/709–8708 in the U.S ⊕ www.chaacreek.com.

Chan Chich Lodge. ⌂ Box 37, Belize City, Belize ☎ 501/223–4419 or 800/343–8009 ⊕ www.chanchich.com.

Chukka Caribbean Adventures. ⌂ Box 698, Belize City, Belize ☎ 501/223–5194 ⊕ www.chukkacaribbean.com.

Cornerstone Foundation. ✉ 90 Burns Ave., San Ignacio, Cayo, Belize ☎ 501/824–2373 ⊕ www.peacecorner.org.

Cottontree Lodge. ✉ Moho River, San Felipe, Toledo, Belize ☎ 501/670–0557 ⊕ www.cottontreelodge.com.

Dems Dats Doin'. ⌂ Box 73, Punta Gorda, Belize ☏ 501/722–2470 ✉ demdatsdoin@btl.net.

Destinations Belize. ⌂ General Delivery, Placencia, Belize ☏ 501/523–4018 ⊕ www.destinationsbelize.com.

Discovery Expeditions. ✉ 5916 Manatee Dr., Belize City, Belize ☏ 501/223–0748 ⊕ www.discoverybelize.com.

Ecological Tours & Services. ⌂ Box 473, Belize City, Belize ☏ 501/223–4874 ⊕ www.ecotoursbelize.com.

Ecologic Divers. ✉ Beachfront, San Pedro, Belize ☏ 501/226–4118 or 847/234–5855 ⊕ www.ecologicdivers.com.

Elderhostel. ⌂ 11 Avenue de Lafayette, Boston, MA 02111 ☏ 800/454–5768 ⊕ www.elderhostel.org.

El Gato. ✉ San Pedro, Belize ☏ 501/226–2264 ⊕ www.ambergriscaye.com/elgato.

El Pescador. ⌂ Box 17, San Pedro, Ambergris Caye, Belize ☏ 501/226–2398 or 800/242–2017 ⊕ www.elpescador.com.

Equitours. ⌂ Box 807, Dubois, WY 82513 ☏ 307/455–3363 or 800/545–0019 ⊕ www.ridingtours.com.

Exotic Birding. ✉ 2727 Nelson Rd., #E207, Longmont, CO ☏ 877/247–3371 ⊕ www.exoticbirding.com.

Fishing International. ✉ 5510 Skylane Blvd., Suite 200, Santa Rosa, CA ☏ 707/542–4242 or 800/950–4242 ⊕ www.fishinginternational.com.

G.A.P. Adventures. ✉ 19 Charlotte St., Toronto, ON Canada ☏ 416/260–0999 or 800/708–7761 ⊕ www.gapadventures.com.

Glovers Atoll Resort. ⌂ Box 2215, Belize City, Belize ☏ 501/520–5016 ⊕ www.glovers.com.bz.

Green Dragon Adventure Travel. ✉ Banana Bank, Belmopan City, Belize ☏ 501/822–2124 ⊕ www.greendragonbelize.com.

Green Reef Belize Coral Reef Conservation NGO. ✉ 100 Coconut Dr., San Pedro, Ambergris Caye, Belize ☏ 501/226–2833 ⊕ www.ambergriscaye.com/greenreef/index.html.

Hamanasi Eco Tours. ✉ Hopkins/Sittee River Rd., Hopkins, Stann Creek, Belize ☏ 501/520–7073 ⊕ www.hamanasi.com.

Hidden Valley Inn. ⌂ Box 170, Belmopan City, Belize ☏ 501/822–3320 or 866/443–3364 ⊕ www.hiddenvalleyinn.com.

IBTM Tours (Bruno Kuppinger) ✉ Sun Creek Lodge, Mile 14, Southern Hwy. ☏ 501/614–2080 ✉ suncreek@hughes.net.

Inglewood Camping Grounds. ✉ Mile 68¼, Western Hwy., San Ignacio, Cayo, Belize ☏ 501/824–3555 ⊕ www.inglewoodcampinggrounds.com.

9

CLOSE UP

Tour Operators (continued)

International Expeditions.
⊠ 1 Environs Park, Helena, AL
☎ 205/428–1700 or 800/633–
4734 ⊕ www.ietravel.com.

International Zoological Expeditions (IZE). ⊠ 210 Washington St.,
Sherborn, MA ☎ 503/655–1461 or
800/548–5843 ⊕ www.ize2belize.com.

Isla Marisol. ⌂ Box 10, Dangriga,
Belize ☎ 501/520–2056 or 866/990–
9904 ⊕ www.islamarisolresort.com.

Island Expeditions. ⊠ 368–916
W. Broadway, Vancouver, BC Canada ☎ 604/452–3212 or 800/667–
1630 ⊕ www.islandexpeditions.com.

Jaguar Paw Lodge. ⌂ Box 1832,
Belize City, Belize ☎ 501/820–2023 or
888/775–8645 ⊕ www.jaguarpaw.com.

Jungle Camp at Chaa Creek.
⌂ Box 53, San Ignacio, Cayo,
Belize ☎ 501/824–2037, 877/709–
8708 in the U.S. ⊕ www.jungle
camp.com.

Katkandu. ⊠ San Pedro,
Belize ☎ 501/226–3168 ⊕ www.
ambergriscaye.com/katkandu/.

Machaca Hill Lodge. ⌂ Box 135,
Punta Gorda, Belize ☎ 501/722–
0050 ⊕ www.machacahill.com.

Maya Centre Women's Group.
⊠ Southern Hwy., Maya
Centre ⌂ Box 108, Dangriga,
Belize ☎ 501/603–9256.

Maya Mountain Lodge & Tours.
⊠ San Ignacio, Belize ☎ 501/824–
2164 ⊕ www.mayamountain.com.

Maya Research Program. ⊠ 209
W. 2nd St., #295, Ft. Worth, TX
☎ 817/350–4986 ⊕ www.maya
researchprogram.org.

The Moorings. ⊠ 19345 U.S. Hwy.
19N #4, Clearwater, FL ☎ 727/535–
1446 or 888/952–8420 ⊕ www.
moorings.com.

Mountain Equestrian Trails. ⊠ Mile
8, Mountain Pine Ridge Rd., Cayo,
Belize ☎ 501/820–4041 or 800/838–
3918 ⊕ www.metbelize.com.

Mountain Travel-Sobek. ⊠ 1266
66th St., Emeryville, CA ☎ 510/594–
6000 or 888/687–6235 ⊕ www.
mtsobek.com.

Nature Photography Adventure. ⌂ Box 752, Willard, MO
65781 ☎ 417/742–3470 ⊕ www.
naturephotography.us.

Nature Treks. ⌂ Box 64805, Tucson,
AZ 85728 ☎ 520/696–2002 ⊕ www.
naturetreks.net. **Next Wave.**
⊠ Placencia Harbor, Placencia Village
Belize ☎ 501/523–3391 ⊕ www.
nextwavesailing.com.

PACZ Tours. ⊠ c/o Eva's, Burns St.,
San Ignacio, Cayo, Belize ☎ 501/824–
2477 ⊕ www.evasonline.com.

Paradise Expeditions. ⌂ Box 126,
San Ignacio, Cayo, Belize ☎ 501/824–
2772 ⊕ www.birdinginbelize.com.

Peter Hughes Diving. ⊠ 5273 NW
158th St., Miami, FL ☎ 305/669–9391
or 800/932–6237 ⊕ www.peter
hughes.com.

Protech Belize. ⌂ Box 130,
San Pedro, Ambergris Caye,
Belize ☎ 501/226–3008 ⊕ www.
protechdive.com.

Raggamuffin Tours. ⊠ Front St.,
Caye Caulker, Belize ☎ 501/226–
0348 ⊕ www.raggamuffintours.com.

Reef Conservation International. ⊠ Parrot St., Punta Gorda,

Belize ☎ 501/702–2117 ⊕ www.
reefci.com.

Rod & Reel Adventures. ✉ 32617
Skyhawk Way, Eugene, OR
☎ 541/349–0777 or 800/356–
6982 ⊕ www.rodreeladventures.com.

SeaHorse Dive Shop. ✉ Harborfront,
Placencia Village, Stann Creek,
Belize ☎ 501/523–3166 or 800/991–
1969 ⊕ www.belizescuba.com.

Seakunga Adventures. ✉ 908–1112
W. Pender St., Vancouver, BC, Canada ☎ 604/893–8668 or 800/781–
2269 ⊕ www.seakunga.com.

Sea Sports Belize. ✉ 83 N. Front
St., Belize City, Belize ☎ 501/223–
5505 ⊕ www.seasportsbelize.com.

Slickrock Adventures. ⌂ Box 1400,
Moab, UT 84532 ☎ 435/259–4225 or
800/390–5715 ⊕ www.slickrock.com.

South American Experience.
✉ 38–44 Gillingham St., Victoria, London U.K. ☎ 0870/499–0683 ⊕ www.
southamericanexperience.co.uk.

TIDE. ✉ 14 Front St., Punta
Gorda, Toledo, Belize ☎ 501/722–
2129 ⊕ www.tidetours.org.

TMM (Belize) Ltd. ✉ Coconut Dr., San
Pedro, Belize ☎ 501/226–3026 or
800/633–0155 ⊕ www.sailtmm.com.

Toadal Adventure Belize. ✉ Pt.
Placencia, Placencia, Stann Creek,
Belize ☎ 501/523–3207 ⊕ www.
toadaladventure.com.

**Toledo Ecotourism Asso-
ciation.** ⌂ Box 157, Punta Gorda,
Belize ☎ 501/722–2096 ✎ ttea@btl.net.

Tropical Expeditions Belize.
✉ 1149 Coney Dr., Belize City,
Belize ☎ 501/223–6939 ⊕ www.
tropicalexpeditionsbelize.com.

Turneffe Flats Lodge. ⌂ Box 10670,
Bozeman, MT 59719 ☎ 623/298–2783
or 888/512–8812 ⊕ www.tflats.com.

Turneffe Island Lodge. ✉ 440
Louisiana, Suite 900, Houston, TX
☎ 713/236–7739 or 800/874–
0118 ⊕ www.turneffelodge.com.

**University of Texas Mesoamerican
Archaeological Research Laboratory.** ✉ 1 University Station R7500,
Austin, TX ☎ 512/232–7049 ⊕ http://
uts.cc.utexas.edu/~marl/.

Victor Emanuel Nature Tours.
✉ 2525 Wallingwood Rd., Suite
1003, Austin, TX ☎ 512/328–5221 or
800/328–8368 ⊕ www.ventbird.com.

Wilderness Travel. ✉ 1102 9th St.,
Berkeley, CA ☎ 510/558–2488 or
800/368–2794 ⊕ www.wilderness
travel.com.

Wildside Tours. ✉ 539 Prince
Frederick St. , King of Prussia, PA
☎ 888/875–9453 ⊕ www.wildside
toursinc.com.

Windy Hill Tour Co. ⌂ Box 85, San
Ignacio, Cayo ☎ 501/824–2017 or
800/946–3995 ⊕ www.windyhill
tours.com.

Winnie Estelle. ✉ San
Pedro ☎ 501/226–2394 ⊕ www.
ambergriscaye.com/winnieestelle/.

Locations: Cayo District
Cost: From BZ$110 per person
Tour Operators: Jaguar Paw Lodge; Chukka Caribbean Adventures

Jaguar Paw Lodge, which opened the first zip line in Belize, has eight platforms. Chukka has four platforms. There is also a zip line near the entrance of Tikal park, and there are two other zip lines nearby.

MULTISPORT

Multisport simply means that you can take part in a series of different activities—hiking, kayaking, cave tubing, birding, swimming, snorkeling. With so many land and water activities packed into one small country, Belize is ideal for multisporting, and many Belize-based and international tour operators provide trips that exercise nearly every muscle in your body.

Season: Year-round
Locations: Throughout Belize
Cost: Day tours from BZ$100 per person; package tours from BZ$800 for four days, and BZ$2,100 for 15 days.
Tour Operators: Adventure Center; Adventure Life; Beyond Touring; Caves Branch Adventure Co.; Cayo Adventure Tours; Chaa Creek Expeditions; Destinations Belize; G.A.P. Adventures; Hamanasi Eco Tours; International Zoological Expeditions; Island Expeditions; Mountain Travel Sobek; Nature Treks; PACZ Tours; Seakunga Adventures; Slick Rock Adventures; TIDE; Toadal Adventure Belize; Wilderness Travel; Windy Hill Tour Co.

Many Belize adventure trips include a bunch of different activities. For example, the 15-day Hummingbird Highway trip offered by Adventure Center starts with four days at and around Tikal, touring Maya sites; the next couple of days sends you caving and hiking in Cayo, followed by three days of canoeing on the Macal River, and ending with snorkeling or diving off Caye Caulker. Adventure Life offers a similar trip, but of eight days, beginning with Tikal, then moving to Belize to explore the Macal River and the caves of Cayo, ending with two days of water activities around Ambergris Caye. Island Expeditions' 10-night Ultimate Adventure trip begins with sea kayaking, diving, snorkeling, and boardsailing at Glover's Atoll, then switches to caving and kayaking on the mainland. Seakunga's multisport tour, Caves to Cayes, combines kayaking, mountain biking, and inflatable river-raft activities. The other tour companies listed above offer a similar variety of activities in many areas of Belize.

UNDERSTANDING
BELIZE

AT A GLANCE

FAST FACTS

Name: Officially changed from British Honduras to Belize in 1973

Capital: Belmopan City

Type of government: Parliamentary democracy

National anthem: "Land of the Free"

Administrative divisions: 6 districts (similar to U.S. states though not much larger than many U.S. counties)—Corozal, Orange Walk, Belize, Cayo, Stann Creek, and Toledo

Independence: September 21, 1981; Belize remains a member of the British Commonwealth

Constitution: September 21, 1981

Legal system: Based on English Common Law

Suffrage: 18 years of age; universal

Legislature: An elected House of Representatives and an appointed Senate

Population: 314,000 (2007)

Population density: 35 people per square mi, the lowest population density in Central America and one of the lowest population densities in the Americas

Median age: Male 19.9, female 20

Life expectancy: Male 66, female 70

Infant mortality: 24.38 deaths per 1,000 live births

Literacy: 77%

Language: English (official). Spanish is widely spoken. Creole, Garífuna, and several Mayan languages also spoken

Ethnic groups: Mestizo, 50%; Creole, 25%; Maya, 11%; Garífuna, 6%; other, 10%

Religion: Roman Catholic, 50%; Pentecostal, 7%; Seventh Day Adventist, 7%; Anglican 5%; Methodist, 4%; Mennonite, 4%; Jehovah's Witness, 2%

Discoveries & inventions: When Western Europe was still in the Dark Ages, the ancient Maya in Belize and elsewhere in Mesoamerica had developed astronomical, mathematical, agricultural, calendrical, medical, and hieroglyphic writing systems of extraordinary complexity.

GEOGRAPHY & ENVIRONMENT

Land area: 22,966 square km (8,866 square mi); about the size of Massachusetts

Coastline: 386 km (240 mi), bordered on the east by the Caribbean

Terrain: Low-lying coastal plains that give way to low mountains in the south

Islands: More than 400 islands offshore in the Caribbean, the largest of which is Ambergris Caye

Natural resources: Farm land, timber, fish, oil

Natural hazards: Hurricanes (June–November) and coastal flooding

Environmental issues: Deforestation, water pollution from sewage and agricultural runoff, deterioration of coral reefs

If the world had any ends, British Honduras would certainly be one of them.
–Aldous Huxley

The Macal River Valley is sacred land. It's worth fighting for. Everything is connected in the biological world. We have lost too much of the planet, bit by bit, piece by piece. And that is exactly how we have to save it, piece by piece.
–Sharon Matola, director of the Belize Zoo, on the fight against building hydropower dams on the Macal River, a fight lost as the dams were built

ECONOMY

Currency: Belize dollar

Exchange rate: BZ$2 = $1

GDP: US$2.3 billion (purchasing power parity)

Per capita income: US$8,300 (ppp)

Inflation: 4.3% (2006)

Unemployment: 12% (2007)

Work force: 122,000 (services 62%, agriculture 23%, industry 15%)

Debt: US$1.5 billion

Major industries: Tourism, agriculture, fishing

Agricultural products: Sugar cane, citrus fruit, bananas, cacao

Exports: US$427 million

Major export products: Sugar, oil, bananas, citrus, clothing, fish, cultured shrimp, wood

Export partners: U.S. 34%, U.K. 34%

Imports: US$612 million

Major import products: Machinery, manufactured goods, fuels, pharmaceuticals, food, beverages, tobacco

Import partners: U.S. 36%, Mexico 13%, Cuba 8%, Guatemala 7%, China 4%, Japan 4%

No wait till de man ded, fu tell am y good. (Creole for "Don't wait until a man is dead to tell him that he is good.")
—Lucio Alcocer, Belizean songwriter

POLITICAL CLIMATE

National elections, with 75% of registered voters participating, were held in February 2008. The United Democratic Party won 25 of 31 House seats, ousting the People's United Party, which had been in office since 1998. On February 9, 2008, Dean Barrow, an attorney from Belize City and head of the UDP, became prime minister.

The only major ongoing international dispute is with Guatemala, which claims Belize territory in the south and north; an agreement reached in late 2002 to resolve the issue has not yet been brought to a referendum in either country.

Our two countries (Belize and the United States) share the same side of planet Earth. We can draw wisdom and strength from the basic values of a common heritage, the same language and common law, a kindred parliamentary democracy, and a mixed economy.
—George Cadle Price, prime minister of Belize, 1983, to President Ronald Reagan

DID YOU KNOW?

- More than 40% of Belize's land is protected as national parks or reserves.

- Belize has the longest barrier reef in the Western and Northern hemispheres.

- The two tallest buildings in Belize, one at Caracol and one at Xunantunich, date back more than 1,000 years.

- Belize is thought to have the largest population of manatees in the world.

- Belize is the only country in Central America with English as the official language.

- Belize has fewer than 400 mi of paved roads.

- The expanse of Selva Maya (Maya Forest), which Belize shares with Guatemala and Mexico, covers some 25,000 square km, the largest block of tropical forest north of the Amazon Basin.

- At the height of the Mayan civilization, Belize may have had a population approaching 1 million people, almost four times the population of the country today.

- Belize is the only country in Central America without a border on the Pacific Ocean.

BELIZE Q&A

Here are answers to the 10 most frequently asked questions we receive about Belize:

Is Belize a safe place to visit? The best answer is "Yes, but . . ." Most visitors say they feel quite safe in Belize (except, they say, in some areas of Belize City). Tourist Police patrol areas of Belize City, Placencia, and Ambergris Caye, and many hotels and jungle lodges have security guards. Out of the hundreds of thousands of visitors, the numbers who are victims of any kind of crime is perhaps a few hundred. So, though this is still a developing country, enjoy yourself and and follow standard travel precautions: don't wander into areas that don't feel safe; avoid deserted beaches and streets after dark; and don't flash expensive jewelry or cash. Be aware that there have been a few carjackings and robberies on remote roads or at little-visited parks and Mayan sites; travel in a group or with a guide to less popular places.

Where can we snorkel from shore? Belize has world-class snorkeling, but most of it requires a boat ride to the barrier reef. There are exceptions—the small islands that are on or near the reef, such as South Water, Ranguana, and Tobacco cayes, or the areas around the atolls, especially Glover's. Of course, you can go snorkeling off almost any beach, even if there's no patch of coral nearby.

How much does it rain during the rainy season (May through November)? It depends on where you are in Belize and when you're there. Northern Belize gets about a third as much rain—around 50 inches—as the Deep South, which can get 150 inches or more. The seasonal rains begin in Toledo in early May, progress north over the next couple of months, and usually start in Corozal in late June. The cayes have different microclimates than the mainland and generally get less rain.

The rainy season typically peaks from June through August. By November, rainfall in nearly all areas of Belize averages 8 inches or less a month. The so-called rainy season is actually a good time to visit Belize, and that's not just a Tourism Board answer. Often the rains come overnight or in the early morning, and then the sun comes out. Many old Belize hands say they prefer traveling in summer or fall: prices are lower, hotel rooms are plentiful, the landscape is lush after rains. It's also a little cooler than in the dry season months of April and May, and water visibility is usually very good.

Are the beaches in Belize nice? Although there are lovely stretches of beaches, many of the beaches are not as good for swimming or sunbathing as the wide, sandy beaches of the main Caribbean or of Mexico's Yucatán. Belizean beaches are usually narrow ribbons of sand, with clear but shallow water and an often-mucky sea floor. The best beaches on the mainland are on the Placencia peninsula. Ambergris Caye has some beautiful beaches, though swimming often isn't good. Southwater Caye and Belize's three atolls have excellent (nearly deserted) beaches as well. Beach resorts keep their beach areas clean, but elsewhere you may see garbage on the beach, brought in by the tides from other areas and from boats.

Does Belize have "real" jungles? "High bush" in Belize means undisturbed wilderness, and there's plenty of that. However, not all bush in Belize is the kind of canopied, broadleaf jungle that you may be thinking about. The Deep South, with its plentiful rainfall, has lush tropical and semitropical rain forest. The Cayo also has wide swaths of broadleaf bush. Northern Belize and parts of the Cayo have little classic jungle—it's primarily dry rain forest and agricultural lands.

Why are airfares to Belize so high, and how can we find cheaper flights? Belize is not a mass-market tourist destination. Air service is still limited, and service is mostly from a few hubs in the United States. Charter flights are rare, so fares tend to stay high. To find the most affordable flights, stay flexible on your dates, check the meta fare comparison Web sites such as Kayak.com, avoid peak holiday travel (around Christmas and Easter), and sign up for Internet specials and e-mail fare alerts on the airlines flying to Belize—currently Continental, American, US Airways, Delta, and TACA.

While traveling around the country, should we rent a car, take a bus, fly, or hire a taxi? Each has advantages and disadvantages. With a rental car, you go when and where you want, including remote areas that don't have air or bus service or to sites that would otherwise require an expensive guided tour. However, auto rental costs are high, and gas is around US$5 a gallon. Buses provide a true local experience and fares are dirt cheap, but buses mainly run on the major roads and stop frequently to pick up and drop off passengers. Buses take up to twice as long as a private car. Flying is the fastest way to get around the country; service is frequent on most routes, and the views from low altitudes are often dramatic. The downside? Fares—especially if you're traveling with a family—can add up, and not all destinations have service. In some cases, transfers by taxi can be an option, although taxis generally are quite expensive. For most long-distance trips, there are no set fares, so the rate is a matter of negotiation and can vary considerably, depending on your bargaining skills. Drivers may also ask a little more if there are three or four going together, rather than just one or two. Expect to pay around BZ$3 a mile for longer trips in Belize. Here are some costs for taxi transfers, but remember, your mileage may vary:

International airport to San Ignacio: BZ$180–BZ$220

International airport to Placencia: BZ$300–BZ$400

San Ignacio to Mountain Pine Ridge (lodges): BZ$80–BZ$120

San Ignacio to Placencia: BZ$400–BZ$500

Dangriga to Hopkins: BZ$80–BZ$100

We're on a budget—can we just stay in a cheap hut on the beach or hang a hammock on a palm tree? Maybe. If you're looking for $5-dollar rooms on the beach or free camping on your own private island, you won't find that in Belize. However, there's camping at a few campgrounds in national parks and reserves, including Cockscomb and Half Moon Caye. Some beach hotels and lodges allow camping and may even rent you a tent. Expect to pay BZ$10 and up, per person, per night. Most people find that for only a few dollars more per night, they can stay at a budget hotel and avoid the problems with bugs, snakes, and potential thefts often faced by campers. Caye Caulker, Placencia Village, Hopkins, and San Ignacio all have budget hotels with double rooms starting at around BZ$30 a night.

We want to spend time at the beach and also in the jungle. Where should we go? On a first and relatively brief visit to Belize, sample the best "surf and turf" by splitting your time between one of the popular beach areas—Ambergris Caye, Caye Caulker, Hopkins, or Placencia—and the rest in the Cayo, which has the largest concentration of popular mainland activities.

How do we get to the Cayo from the international airport near Belize City? There's currently no scheduled air service from Belize City to San Ignacio. Though jungle lodges offer guest transfers, prices are high—typically BZ$300 or more for one to four people. You may want to try one of four other ways to do it:

■ **Rent a car.** It's about two hours from the international airport to downtown San Ignacio. The main roads, like the Western Highway, are in good condition, and directions are well marked. However, if you're going somewhere outside San Ignacio proper, such as Hidden Valley Inn or Blancaneaux Lodge, the roads aren't paved and can be difficult to navigate. There are about eight rental car companies at the airport, just across the parking lot from the main terminal.

■ **Take a shuttle van.** Several hotels and tour operators, including Cahal Pech Village Resort, Aguada Hotel, and Discovery Tours, have van service to Cayo from the international airport and other points in Belize City, including the Marine Terminal and the municipal airport. One-way trips cost around BZ$80–BZ$100 per person. Make reservations in advance. Service is sometimes discontinued in the off season. *For contact information,* ⇨ *see The Cayo, Chapter 4.*

■ **Bus it.** Though this is the cheapest option, it's a hassle, as you have to go into Belize City to catch a west-bound bus (BZ$50 for a taxi into town). From the downtown bus terminal, local buses take about three hours to get to San Ignacio and cost around BZ$8.

■ **Hire a taxi.** If you're traveling with several people, it may make sense to negotiate with a taxi at the airport to take you to your destination in Cayo. Licensed cabs have green plates. The exact price depends on exactly where you're going and your bargaining skills, but it will likely be less than BZ$200.

RETIRING IN BELIZE

So you fell in love with Belize, met some expats who bought their beachfront lot for a song, and want to do the same for your retirement years? Here's the scoop on what you can really expect if you decide to follow suit.

Belize can be enchanting for potential retirees. The climate is frost free. Land and housing costs are still moderate, especially compared with already popular areas of the Caribbean. The official language is English, and the historical and legal background of the country is more comparable to those in the United States, Canada, and Great Britain than most other parts of Latin America and the Caribbean. Belize has a stable and democratic, if sometimes colorful, tradition. Recreational activities, on land and in the Caribbean, are almost limitless.

But for all those positives, there are some drawbacks: high costs for food, gas, and household items; high import duties; crime and drug problems; culture shock for those unaccustomed to the ways of a semitropical, developing country with a true multicultural society; growing resentment of foreigners; plenty of red tape; increasing taxes; a 5% transfer tax on real estate purchases by foreigners, payable by the buyer (buyers of new condos or houses pay 5% transfer tax plus 10% sales tax); and, most importantly for many retirees, medical care that in many cases isn't up to first-world snuff. Sometimes, too, it's the little things that bother expats: They can't live without *The New York Times* and fresh bagels on Sunday or they experience unbearable cravings for an Arby's roast beef sandwich. If retirement in Belize still sounds like a good option for you, there are three options to look into:

The Qualified Retired Persons Incentive Program. It's run by the Belize Tourism Board, and anyone at least 45 years old is eligible to participate in the program.

Contact the tourism board for more information (⊕ *www.belizeretirement.org*).

Official Permanent Residency. Requirements and benefits are similar to those of the Retired Persons Incentive Act. With official residency, you can work in Belize. Before you can apply, you need to live in Belize for a year first, leaving for no more than two weeks. Permanent Residency approvals are handled by the Belize immigration department and often take a long time.

Regular Tourist Card. Many expats simply stay in Belize on a regular tourist card. Upon entry, you receive a free visitor permit, good for up to 30 days. This permit can be renewed for up to six months at BZ$50 a month. After that, renewals cost BZ$100 a month. After 12 months, it's necessary to leave the country for 72 hours and start the process again. Renewals are never guaranteed, and the rules could change at any time.

The best advice for anyone contemplating retiring or relocating? Try before you buy. Living in Belize is quite different from vacationing. If possible, rent an apartment or house for a few months and see how you like daily life. Be cautious about buying property. Real estate agents sometimes aren't licensed or regulated, and because the pool of qualified buyers in Belize is small, it's a lot harder to sell than to buy.

Living Abroad in Belize, by Lan Sluder (author of this book), is a handbook for those considering retiring or relocation in Belize. The author interviewed scores of expats and retirees in Belize to help provide readers with a realistic view of the pros and cons of living there.

WILDLIFE GLOSSARY

An amazing array of creatures make their homes in Belize and Guatemala. Many are not terribly difficult to see, thanks to their brilliant coloring. Others are likely to elude you completely. A rundown of some of the region's most attention-grabbing mammals, birds, reptiles, amphibians—even a few insects—are listed below. Common names, in English and Spanish, are given, so you can understand the local wildlife lingo.

Agouti (guanta, paca, tepezcuintle): A 20-inch-long tailless rodent with small ears and a large muzzle, the agouti is known locally as the *gibnut*. It's reddish brown on Guatemala's Pacific coast, more tawny orange on Belize's Caribbean slope. You might spot one sitting on its haunches and eating large seeds and fruit. Largely nocturnal, the agouti is more likely to be seen on a menu than in the wild. Known as the royal rat, it was served to Queen Elizabeth on her last visit to Belize.

Anteater (oso hormiguero): Three species—giant, silky, and collared—are found in this region. Only the collared, or vested, anteater is commonly seen (and too often as a roadkill). This medium-size anteater (30 inches long with an 18-inch tail) has long sharp claws for ripping into insect nests. You may spot one lapping up ants and termites with its long, sticky tongue.

Aracari (cusingo): These slender toucans, known for their strikingly colored bills, eat ripe fruit. They often travel in groups of six or more. Collared aracaris on the Caribbean coast have a chalky upper mandible.

Armadillo (cusuco): These are the same animals that are found in the southern United States. Mostly nocturnal and solitary, this edentate (a mammal with few or no teeth) roots in the soil with its long muzzle for a varied diet of roots, insects, and small animals. They are sometimes found on the menu in local restaurants.

Basilisk (gallego): Flaps of skin on their long toes enable the "Jesus Christ lizard" to run across water. The emerald basilisk in the Caribbean lowlands is marked with turquoise and black on its green body. Adult males grow to 3 feet and have crests on their heads, backs, and tails.

Caiman (cocodrilo): The spectacled caiman is a small crocodile that subsists mainly on fish. It's most active at night (its eyes glow red when illuminated by a flashlight), basking in the sun by day. It's distinguished from its American cousin by its sloping brow and smooth back scales.

Capuchin monkey (mono carablanca): With black fur and pink faces surrounded by wisps of white, capuchin monkeys are found singly or in groups of up to 20. They are extremely active foragers, sometimes even coming to the ground to search for food.

Coati (pizote): A long-nose relative of the raccoon, the coati has a slender, ringed tail it often holds straight up. Lone males or groups of females with young are active during the day, either on the ground or in the trees. They're omnivorous and feed on fruit and seeds as well as mice and rats. In Belize, they are known as Quash.

Cougar (puma): Growing to 5 feet in length, mountain lions are the largest unspotted cats in Central America. Rarely seen, they live in most habitats in the region and feed on vertebrates ranging from snakes to deer.

Crocodile (lagarto): Although often referred to as alligators, crocodiles reign supreme in this region. They are distinguished from the smaller caiman by their flat heads, narrow snouts, and spiky scales. The American crocodile can reach 16 feet in length, while the smaller Morelet's crocodile grows to 8 feet. The territories of both species overlap in estuaries and brackish coastal waters, but only the American crocodile is able to filter excess salt from its system, allowing it to venture to the more distant cayes. Crocodiles seldom attack humans, preferring fish, birds, and the occasional small mammal. Both species are endangered and protected by international law.

Ctenosaur (garrobo): Known in Creole as the wish willy, this 36-inch-long lizard is mostly tan with four dark bands on its body and a tail ringed with rows of sharp, curved spines. This cousin of the iguana sleeps in burrows or tree hollows and is most commonly seen along the coast of Belize. Though largely vegetarian, it won't turn its nose up at a meal of a small creature.

Dolphin (delfin): Several species are frequently spotted off the Pacific shores. They often travel in groups of 20 or more and play around vessels. Look for spotted dolphins, which are 6 feet long and have pale markings on their posterior.

Eagle Ray: One of the Caribbean's most graceful swimmers, these flat-bodied rays range in size from 6 to 8 feet. They have a white underside and numerous white spots and circular markings over their darker backs. Their pronounced heads have flattened, tapered snouts, and their long, thin tails have one to five venomous spines at the base. They prefer cruising sandy areas, occasionally stopping to dig for mollusks.

Fer-de-lance (barba amarilla): One of the most dangerous of all pit vipers, the fer-de-lance has a host of names, such as tommygoff in Belize and tomagasse in Guatemala. This aggressive snake grows up to 8 feet in length and is distinguished by the bright yellow patches on its head.

Frigate bird (tijereta del mar): These black birds with slender wings and forked tails are some of the most effortless and agile fliers of the avian world. Coastal dwellers, Frigate birds are more common on the Pacific than on the Atlantic. When mating season approaches, males inflate a scarlet pouch beneath their beaks in an effort to attract females.

Frog (rana): Over 30 species of frogs can be found in Belize. Most are nocturnal in an effort to avoid being eaten, but the brightly colored poison dart frogs—whose brilliant red, blue, and green coloration warns predators that they don't make a good meal—can be spotted during the day. Red-eyed leaf frogs are among the showiest of nocturnal species. They firmly attach themselves to plants with neon-orange legs, scarlet eyes bulging out from a metallic green body splashed with white dots and blue patches. Large brown marine toads are also common at night.

Howler monkey (mono congo): These chunky-bodied monkeys travel in troops of up to 20. A bit on the lethargic side, they eat leaves, fruits, and flowers. The deep, resounding howls of the males serve as communication among and between troops. Erroneously termed "baboons" by Belizeans, these dark-faced monkeys travel only from tree to tree, limiting their presence to dense jungle canopy. They are increasingly difficult to spot in the wild.

Iguana (iguana): The largest lizards in Central America, these scaly creatures can grow to 10 feet. They are good swimmers, and will often plop into a body of water when threatened by a predator. Only young green iguanas are brightly colored; adult females are grayish, while adult males are olive (with orangish heads during mating season). They are considered a delicacy among Belizeans, who call them "bamboo chicken."

Jacana (gallito de agua): These birds are sometimes referred to as "lily trotters" because their long toes allow them to walk on floating vegetation. They eat aquatic plants and animals and are found at almost any body of water. They expose their yellow wing feathers when in flight. The liberated females lay eggs in several floating nests tended by males.

Jaguar (tigre): The largest feline in the Western Hemisphere grows up to 6 feet long and can weigh up to 250 pounds. Exceedingly rare, this nocturnal predator is most often spotted near the Cockscomb Basin Wildlife Sanctuary in Belize.

Kinkajou (martilla): A nocturnal relative of the raccoon, kinkajous are known for their 20-inch-long prehensile tails. They actively and often noisily forage for fruit, insects, and the occasional sip of nectar. (If you're unsure that what you have spotted is a kinkajou, simply look at the picture on Belize's $20 note.)

Leaf-cutter ant (zompopa): Called wee wee ants in Creole, leaf-cutter ants are the region's most commonly noticed ants. They are found in all lowland habitats. Columns of these industrious little guys, all carrying clippings of leaves, sometimes extend for several hundred yards from plants to the underground nest. The leaves are used to cultivate the fungus that they eat.

Macaw (lapas): The beautiful Scarlet Macaw is the only species of this bird found in Belize. Huge, raucous birds with long tails, macaws use their immense bills to rip apart fruits to get to the seeds. Their nests are in hollow trees. They are endangered because of poachers and deforestation.

Manatee: An immense and gentle mammal, the manatee is often called the sea cow. Living exclusively in the water, particularly in shallow and sheltered areas, manatees are said to be the basis of myths about mermaids. Scarce today, these vegetarians have been hunted for thousands of years for their tasty flesh; their image frequently appears in ancient Maya art.

Margay (caucel): This nocturnal, spotted cat is similar to the somewhat larger ocelot, but has a longer tail. Mobile ankle joints allow it to climb down trunks head first. The margay eats small vertebrates.

Morpho (morfo): This spectacular butterfly doesn't fail to astound first-time viewers. Easy to overlook when resting, their color is only apparent when they take flight. One species has brilliant-blue wings, while another is distinguished by its intense violet color. Adults feed on fallen fruit, never flowers.

Motmot (pájaro bobo): Handsome birds of the forest, motmots sit patiently while scanning for large insects and small vertebrates. The species found in Belize make their nests in burrows.

Ocelot (manigordo): These medium-size spotted cats have shorter tails than their cousins the margays. They are active night and day, feeding on rodents and other small animals. Their forepaws are rather large in relation to their bodies, hence the Creole name that translates as "fat hand."

Oropéndola (oropéndola): These crow-size birds, members of the oriole family, have bright-yellow tails. They nest in colonies with the female building pendulous nests in isolated trees. Males make unmistakable gurgling calls. They are fairly omnivorous, but subsist mostly on fruit.

Parrot (loro): A prerequisite of any tropical setting, there are five species of parrot in Central America. All are clad in green, which means they virtually disappear upon landing in the trees. Most have a splash of color or two on their head or wings.

Pelican (pelicano): Their large size, big bills, and flapping throat pouches make brown pelicans unmistakable inhabitants of both coasts (although they are far more abundant on the Pacific side). A white American variety prefers freshwater locations. They often fly in V formations and dive for fish.

Red-footed Booby: This bird received its unflattering name because it was unafraid of humans, which made it easy prey for hungry sailors landing at Belize's Half Moon Caye, where 4,000 now live in a protected nature reserve. Look for nests with fuzzy white chicks.

Roseate spoonbill (garza rosada): Pink plumage and distinctive bills set this wader apart from all other wetland birds. They feed by swishing their bills back and forth in the water while using their feet to stir up bottom-dwelling creatures.

Sea turtle: Sea turtles on the coasts of Belize come in three varieties: green, hawksbill, and loggerhead. All have paddlelike flippers and have to surface to breathe.

Spider monkey (mono colorado, mono araña): These lanky, long-tailed monkeys hang out in groups of two to four. Their diet consists of ripe fruit, leaves, and flowers. These incredible aerialists can swing effortlessly through the trees using their long arms and legs and prehensile tails.

Caribbean and southern Pacific populations are dark reddish brown, while their cousins in the northwest are blond.

Tapir (danta): The national animal of Belize is also known as the mountain cow. Something like a small rhinoceros without the armor, it has a stout body, short legs, and small eyes. Completely vegetarian, it uses its prehensile snout for harvesting vegetation. The shy creature lives in forested areas near streams and lakes, where it can sometimes be spotted bathing.

Toucan (tucán, tucancillo): Recognizable to all who have ever seen a box of Fruit Loops, the toucan is common in Belize. The largest are the keel-billed and chestnut-mandibled toucans, growing to 22 inches long. The much smaller and stouter emerald toucanet and yellow-ear toucanet are among the most colorful. All eat fruit with their curved, multi-hued beaks.

—Elbert Greer

BOOKS & MOVIES

Two histories stand out: *The Making of Modern Belize*, by C. H. Grant, and *A Profile of the New Nation of Belize*, by W. D. Setzekorn. *Jaguar*, by Alan Rabinowitz, an interesting book about the creation of the Cockscomb Basin Wildlife Sanctuary, unfortunately tells you too much about the man and too little about the cat. Aldous Huxley, who wrote *Beyond the Mexique Bay*, is always hard to beat. If you're interested in the Maya, Ronald Wright's *Time Among the Maya* ties past and present together in one perceptive whole. Classic works on the Maya include *The Maya* by Michael Coe, a compendious introduction to the world of the Maya, and *The Rise and Fall of the Maya Civilization*, by one of the grand old men of Maya archaeology, J. Eric S. Thompson.

For natural history enthusiasts, four books belong in your suitcase: *Birds of Belize* by H. Lee Jones and Dana Gardner; *Guide to Corals and Fishes of Florida, the Bahamas and the Caribbean* by I. Greenberg; *The Ecotravellers' Wildlife Guide, Belize and Northern Guatemala* by Les Belesky; and *An Introduction to Tropical Rainforests* by T. C. Whitmore.

Our Man in Belize is a fascinating memoir of life in British Honduras in the 1950s and '60s. For beach reading, *Belize, a Novel* by Carlos Ledson Miller is a fast-paced saga of a Belizean family over four decades. Darker, but with insight into living in the jungle and also into the problem of domestic abuse, is *Belize Survivor*, a novel by Nancy R. Koerner.

Paul Theroux's novel, *The Mosquito Coast*, about an obsessed American who drags his family to Central America, was actually set in Honduras, but the movie by the same name, starring Harrison Ford, was filmed in Belize in 1986. The rip-roaring *The Dogs of War*, 1981, starring Christopher Walken, about soldiers of fortune in Africa, has wonderful scenes of Belize City, especially the lobby of the Chateau Caribbean Hotel. Emory King, film commissioner for the Belize government from 1998 until his death in 2007, has a bit part (as indeed he had in nearly all the TV shows and movies shot in Belize for the past three decades).

Heart of Darkness (1994, starring John Malkovich), and 2001's *After the Storm*, directed by Guy Ferland, were also filmed in Belize. One of the first reality TV shows, *Temptation Island*, was shot mostly on Ambergris Caye, at Mata Chica and Captain Morgan's resorts, in 2000–2001. He hasn't filmed anything in Belize, but Francis Ford Coppola *(The Godfather, Apocalypse Now)* owns two resorts in Belize, Turtle Inn in Placencia and Blancaneaux in the Mountain Pine Ridge, along with a third, La Lancha, near Flores, Guatemala. Although filmed in 2005 and 2006 in Mexico, not Belize, Mel Gibson's *Apocalypto* is notable because all the dialogue is in the Yucatec Maya language.

Travel Smart
Belize

GETTING HERE & AROUND

▮ BY AIR

TO BELIZE

The major U.S. departure gateways are Atlanta, with daily flights on Delta to Belize City (most flights are regional jets with one-class service); Charlotte, with daily nonstops on US Airways to Belize City (with fewer flights in the fall); Houston, with daily nonstop service to Belize City on TACA (Central American Air Transportation) and Continental; and Miami and Dallas-Fort Worth with daily nonstop service on American. TACA also flies to Belize City from several U.S. cities with a change of planes in San Salvador, El Salvador. Continental has a weekly nonstop from Newark.

To Belize City, it's roughly 2 hours from Miami and Atlanta; 2½ hours from Dallas, Houston, and Charlotte, and 4½ hours from Newark. Service from some of these gateways may be cut back during the off-season.

Airfares to Belize are often twice or more the cost of a ticket to Cancún or Cozumel, Mexico, so, if you have the time, it pays to fly into the Yucatán and take a bus to Belize. From the Yucatán, a first-class or deluxe bus costs US$25 or less, and takes five to six hours, to Chetumal, Mexico, a border town where you can transfer to a Belize bus.

WITHIN BELIZE

Domestic planes are single- or twin-engine island-hoppers. The main carriers are Tropic Air and Maya Island Air, both of which fly to San Pedro on Ambergris Caye and Caye Caulker as well as Caye Chapel, Corozal Town, Dangriga, Placencia, Punta Gorda, and Sarteneja. In July 2008, service between the international airport in Belize City and Flores, Guatemala, resumed, with round-trip flights for around BZ$450.

FLIGHT SAFETY 411

Belize is one of about 20 countries rated as Category 2, which means that the U.S. Federal Aviation Administration (FAA) has determined that the country's civil aviation authority doesn't provide safety oversight of its air carriers in accordance with minimum standards established by the International Civil Aviation Organization (ICAO). Belize has been working to resolve the issue through new legislation and oversight procedures. In mid-2008, negotiations with the Guatemalan government resulted in Belize carriers being permitted to fly to and from Flores, Guatemala. These flights had been discontinued since November 2007.

Maya Island Air has daily service between Savannah airstrip, near Independence across the lagoon from Placencia, and San Pedro Sula, Honduras, for BZ$650 round-trip. Belize domestic flights on Maya Island and Tropic from and to the international airport are between BZ$240 and BZ$470 round-trip and about BZ$135 to BZ$400 round-trip between the municipal airstrip in Belize City and domestic destinations.

Charter services such as Javier Flying Service and Cari Bee Air Service will take you almost anywhere for around BZ$400 per hour and up; Javier has flights to Chan Chich Lodge. Astrum Helicopters, based near Belize City, offers transfers, aerial property tours, and custom sight-seeing and photography tours anywhere in Belize. Costs for up to six people in the Bell 206 helicopters are around BZ$2,000 an hour. Fixed rates apply for transfers to specific resorts, starting at BZ$2,500 for four persons.

You'll save 10% to 45% on flights within Belize by flying to and from the municipal airport near downtown Belize City, rather than to or from the international airport north of the city in Ladyville. If you're arriving at the international airport, a transfer by taxi to the municipal airport is BZ$50 (for up to four persons, not per person), transferring to the municipal airport makes more sense for families or groups traveling together. If you need to fly between the Belize City area and another part of the country, it's always at least a little cheaper to fly to or from municipal.

Air Contacts American Airlines (☎ 800/433-7300, 501/223-2522 in Belize ⊕ www.aa.com). **Astrum Helicopters** (☎ 501/222-5100 ⊕ www.astrum-helicopters.com). **Cari Bee Air Service** (☎ 501/223-3542). **Javier Flying Service** (☎ 501/223-5360). **Continental Airlines** (☎ 800/523-3273 for U.S. and Mexico reservations, 800/231-0856 for international reservations, 501/822-1062 in Belize ⊕ www.continental.com). **Delta Airlines** (☎ 800/221-1212 for U.S. reservations, 800/241-4141 for international reservations, 501/225-3423 in Belize ⊕ www.delta.com). **Maya Island Air** (☎ 501/226-3838, 800/521-1247 in U.S. ✉ mayair@btl.net ⊕ www.mayaairways.com). **TACA** (☎ 800/535-8780, 501/227-7363 in Belize, 502/261-2144 in Guatemala). **Tropic Air** (☎ 501/226-2012, 800/422-3435 in U.S. ✉ tropicair@btl.net ⊕ www.tropicair.com). **USAirways** (☎ 800/428-4322 for U.S. and Canada reservations, 800/622-1015 for international reservations, 501/225-3589 in Belize ⊕ www.usairways.com).

Airlines & Airports Airline and Airport Links (⊕ www.airlineandairportlinks.com) has links to many airlines and airports.

Airline Security Issues Transportation Security Administration (⊕ www.tsa.gov).

AIRPORTS

International flights arrive at the Philip Goldson International Airport (BZE) in Ladyville, 9 mi (15 km) north of Belize City, probably the world's only airport with a mahogany ceiling. Small domestic airports (which comprise landing strips with a one-room check-in) in Belize are in Belize City (TZA), Caye Chapel (CYC), Corozal (CZH), Dangriga (DGA), Savannah (SVH) Placencia (PLJ), Punta Gorda (PND), San Pedro (SPR), Caye Caulker (CUK), and Sarteneja (SJX).

The international airport has security precautions similar to those in the United States; the domestic airstrips have limited security systems, but there has never been an airline hijacking in Belize. For international flights, arrive at the airport at least two hours before departure; for domestic flights, about half an hour. In Belize, domestic airlines with more passengers than seats sometimes simply add another flight.

Belize Belize Municipal Airstrip (✉ Belize City ☎ No phone). **Philip Goldson International Airport** (✉ Ladyville ☎ 501/225-2014).

■ BY BOAT

Since Belize has about 200 mi (325 km) of mainland coast and some 400 islands in the Caribbean, water taxis and passenger ferries, usually with a capacity of 40 to 45 people, are key. The Caye Caulker Water Taxi Association has scheduled service six or more times a day from Belize City to Ambergris Caye (BZ$20 one way, 1¼ hours), Caye Caulker (BZ$15, 45 minutes), and Caye Chapel (BZ$15 one way, 35 minutes) as well as between those cayes. A water taxi also runs twice daily between Corozal Town and San Pedro (BZ$45 one way, 2 hours). To reach the more remote cayes, you're basically left to your own devices, unless you're staying at a hotel where such transfers are arranged for you. The resorts on the atolls run their own flights or boats, but these aren't available to the general public.

Water taxis accept only cash in U.S. or Belize dollars. You can buy tickets at the Marine Terminal in Belize City or at the piers on Ambergris Caye and Caye Caulker. Schedules are posted at these locations and are available online. Most water taxis allow two pieces of luggage per person, along with miscellaneous personal items. Bicycles and other larger items may be permitted, if there's space, but you may be charged extra. Note that life jackets aren't typically provided, and seas can be rough. Postpone your trip if the weather looks bad or if the boat offered looks unseaworthy or crowded.

Information **Belize Marine Terminal** (⊠ N. Front St. at Swing Bridge, Belize City ☎ 501/223–1969). **Caye Caulker Water Taxis Association** (☎ 501/223–2969 ⊕ www.cayecaulkerwatertaxi.com).

TRAVEL TIMES FROM BELIZE CITY		
To	By Air	By Car or Bus
San Pedro	20 minutes	n/a
Caye Caulker	15 minutes	n/a
Corozal Town	1–2 hours (via San Pedro)	2–3 hours
San Ignacio	n/a	2–3 hours
Placencia	40 minutes	3½–5 hours
Punta Gorda	1 hour	4–6 hours
Cancún, Mexico	n/a	8–10 hours

▌ BY BUS

There's frequent bus service on the Northern and Western highways and to southern Belize via the Hummingbird and Southern highways. Elsewhere service is spotty. There's no municipal bus service in Belize City, except for points in the city along the Northern and Western highways.

Buses can get you just about anywhere cheaply (about BZ$2–BZ$30 for inter-town trips) and quickly. Expect to ride on old U.S. school buses or retired North American Greyhound buses. On some routes there are a few express buses with air-conditioning and other comforts. These cost a few dollars more.

Be prepared for tight squeezes—this can mean three people in a two-person seat—and watch for pickpockets. Large

bags are typically stowed on top, which may make you nervous, but theft from bus tops is rare. Drivers and *cobradors* or *ayudantes* (fare collectors, who call out the stops) are knowledgeable and helpful, if a bit gruff. They can direct you to the right bus, and tell you when and where to get off. To be sure you're not forgotten, try to sit near the driver.

Most buses on main routes run according to more-or-less reliable schedules; on lesser-traveled routes the schedules may not mean much. Buses operate mostly during daylight hours, but they run until around 9 PM on the western route between Belize City and San Ignacio. The Belize Tourism Board *(⇨ see Visitor Information above)* sometimes has schedules for popular routes. Buses in Belize accept only cash in U.S. or Belize dollars.

Inexpensive public buses, also of the converted school bus variety, crisscross Guatemala, but they can be slow and extremely crowded, with a three-per-seat rule enforced. Popular destinations, such as Tikal or Santa Elena, use Pullman buses, which are as well equipped as American bus lines. Your hotel or INGUAT office can help you make arrangements. Fares on public buses are a bargain at US25¢–US$3.

In Guatemalan cities, you pay the bus driver as you board. On intercity buses, fare collectors pass through the bus periodically. They have an amazing ability to keep track of all the paid and unpaid fares. Buses follow loose schedules, sometimes waiting to leave until the bus fills up. On some routes the day's very last bus isn't always a sure thing. Schedules for Pullman buses are usually observed.

Reservations are usually not needed or expected in Belize or Guatemala, even for Pullman departures. The terminals in Belize City and some towns have ticket windows where you can pay in advance and get a reserved seat. If you board at other points, you pay the driver's assistant and take any available seat. Arrive at terminals about a half hour before departure.

Belize Companies James Bus Line (⊠King St., Punta Gorda ☎501/702-2049). **National Transport** (⊠W. Collet Canal, Belize City ☎501/227-6372)

Guatemala Companies Autobuses del Norte (⊠Guatemala City ☎502/2251-0079) **Línea Dorada** (⊠Calle Principal, Santa Elena ⊠Calle de la Playa, Flores ☎501/2232-9658).

▌BY CAR

GASOLINE

Modern gas stations—Texaco, Esso, and Shell brands, some of them with convenience stores and 24-hour service—are in Belize City and most major towns. In more remote areas, especially in the south, fill up the tank whenever you see a station. Unleaded gas costs over BZ$11 a gallon. Diesel fuel is only slightly less. Attendants who pump gas for you don't expect a tip.

Prices at Guatemala's service stations aren't quite as high as in Belize. At most stations an attendant will pump the gas and make change. Plan to use cash, as credit cards sometimes aren't accepted.

PARKING

In Belize City, with its warren of narrow and one-way streets, downtown parking is often at a premium. For security, try to find a guarded, fenced parking lot, and don't leave your car on the street overnight. Elsewhere, except in some areas of San Ignacio and Orange Walk Town, there's plenty of free parking.

There are no meters in Belize. In most cities and towns, parking rules are laxly enforced, although cars with license plates from elsewhere may attract a ticket.

ROAD CONDITIONS

Three of the four main roads—the Western Highway, Northern Highway, and Hummingbird Highway—are completely paved. These two-lane roads are gener-

ally in good condition. The Southern Highway, from Dangriga to Punta Gorda, is completely paved except for a 9-mi (15-km) stretch near Big Falls that's expected to be paved by 2009. Signage is good along the main highways; large green signs direct you to major sights.

Elsewhere, expect fair to stupendously rough dirt, gravel, and limestone roads; a few unpaved roads may be impassable at times in the rainy season.

FROM/TO	ROUTE	DISTANCE
Belize City-Corozal Town	Northern Highway	99 mi (160 km)
Belize City-San Ignacio	Western Highway	72 mi (116 km)
Belize City-Placencia	Western, Hummingbird, and Southern highways	147 mi (237 km)
Belize City-Punta Gorda	Western, Hummingbird, and Southern highways	200 mi (323 km)
San Ignacio-Placencia	Western, Hummingbird, and Southern highways	113 mi (182 km)

Immense improvements have been made to Guatemala's ravaged roads. A highway from Río Dulce to Tikal has cut travel time along this popular route significantly. The road from the Belize border toward Tikal is unpaved for the first 19 mi (32 km). Roads in remote areas are frequently unpaved, rife with potholes, and treacherously muddy in the rainy season. Four-wheel-drive vehicles are recommended for travel off the beaten path. In cities, expect narrow brick streets. Road signs are generally used to indicate large towns, smaller towns may not be so clearly marked. Look for intersections where people seem to be waiting for a bus—that's a good sign that there's an important turn-off nearby.

ROADSIDE EMERGENCIES

When renting a car (⇨ *below*), ask the agency what they do if your car breaks down in a remote area. Most agencies in Belize send a driver with a replacement vehicle or a mechanic to fix the car. For help in Guatemala, your best bet is to call the National or Tourist Police. In either country, consider renting a cell phone (⇨ *Phones, under Communication in Essentials, below*).

Emergency Services Belize Police (☎911). **Guatemalan National Police** (☎110). **Guatemalan Tourist Police** (☎832–0532 Ext. 35 or 832–0533 Ext. 35).

RULES OF THE ROAD

Driving in Belize and Guatemala is on the right. Seat belts are required, although the law is seldom enforced. There are few speed limit signs, and speed limits are rarely enforced. However, as you approach villages and towns watch out for "sleeping policemen," a local name for speed bumps. Belize has about a dozen traffic lights, and only Belize City has anything approaching congestion.

Despite the relatively small number of private cars in Belize, traffic accidents are the nation's number one cause of death. Belizean drivers aren't always as skilled as they think they are, and drunk drivers can be a problem. Guatemala's narrow roads and highways mean you can be stuck motionless on the road for an hour while a construction crew stands around a hole in the ground. Always allow extra travel time for such unpredictable events, and bring along snacks and water. Otherwise, if you observe the rules you follow at home, you'll likely do just fine. Just don't expect everyone else to follow them.

RENTAL CARS

Belize City and the international airport in Ladyville have most major car rental agencies as well as several local operators. Prices vary, but all are high by U.S. standards (BZ$120–BZ$275 per day). Off-season, rates are a little lower. Note that agencies with their own pumps actu-

ally charge less for gas than you'd pay at service stations, so ask for fill-ups. Also, some hotels have all-terrain vehicles with guides for about BZ$400 per day. A few resorts have rental cars for about BZ$150–BZ$180 per day.

For serious safaris, a four-wheel-drive vehicle is invaluable. But since unpaved roads, mudslides in rainy season, and a general off-the-beaten-path landscape are status quo here, all drivers will be comforted with a four-wheel-drive vehicle.

Car rental has never really caught on in Guatemala, which, given the narrowness of the roads, is just as well. If you do rent a car opt for four-wheel drive, which will run around US$65 a day.

In Belize and Guatemala, rental car companies routinely accept driver's licenses from most other countries without question. Most car-rental agencies require a major credit card for a deposit, and some require you be over 25.

Most Belize agencies don't permit their vehicles to be taken into Guatemala or Mexico. Crystal in Belize City does permit its vehicles to be taken into Guatemala, although without any insurance coverage.

CAR-RENTAL INSURANCE

If you own a car, your personal auto insurance may cover a rental to some degree, though not all policies protect you abroad; always read your policy's fine print. If you don't have auto insurance, then seriously consider buying the collision- or loss-damage waiver (CDW or LDW) from the car-rental company, which eliminates your liability for damage to the car. Some credit cards offer CDW coverage, but it's usually supplemental to your own insurance and rarely covers SUVs, minivans, luxury models, and the like. If your coverage is secondary, you may still be liable for loss-of-use costs from the car-rental company. But no credit-card insurance is valid unless you use that card for *all* transactions, from reserving to paying the final bill.

All companies exclude car rental in some countries, so be sure to find out about the destination to which you are traveling.

In Belize CDW insurance costs BZ$20–BZ$40 a day, and you may still be liable for the first BZ$1,000–BZ$4,000 in damages.

Major Agencies Avis (☎800/331–1084 or 501/205–2629 in Belize ⊕ www.avis.com). **Budget** (☎800/472–3325 or 501/223–2435 in Belize ⊕ www.budget-belize.com). **Crystal** (☎501/223–1600 ⊕ www.crystal-belize.com). **Hertz** (☎800/654–3001 or 501/223–0886 in Belize ⊕ www.hertz.com).

BY CRUISE SHIP

The Belize government says that two-thirds of a million cruise passengers visit Belize annually, all arriving on big ships that call on Belize City. Because of shallow water near shore, passengers are brought ashore in small boats called tenders. Although Carnival Cruise Lines has agreed to build a new US$50 million cruise terminal in Belize City, construction has been delayed. Another cruise terminal on a caye off Belize City is also in the works.

On arrival in Belize City most passengers take snorkel or Maya ruin tours, or wander around the historic Fort George area, visiting the Fort Point Tourist Village.

Cruise Lines Carnival Cruise Line (☎305/599–2600 or 800/227–6482 ⊕ www. carnival.com). **Costa Cruises** (☎954/266–5600 or 800/462–6782 ⊕ www.costacruise. com). **Holland America Line** (☎206/281–3535 or 877/932–4259 ⊕ www.hollandamerica. com). **Norwegian Cruise Line** (☎305/436–4000 or 800/327–7030 ⊕ www.ncl.com). **Princess Cruises** (☎661/753–0000 or 800/774–6237 ⊕ www.princess.com). **Regent Seven Seas Cruises** (☎954/776–6123 or 800/477–7500 ⊕ www.rssc.com). **Royal Caribbean International** (☎305/539–6000 or 800/327–6700 ⊕ www.royalcaribbean.com).

Seabourn Cruise Line (☎305/463–3000 or 800/929–9391 ⊕ www.seabourn.com).

BY SHUTTLE

Belize has some shuttle service, primarily between Belize City and San Ignacio. Most hotels and lodges will arrange van transfers for guests to and from the international airport in Belize City for BZ$250–BZ$400 for up to four passengers. The Aguada Hotel is one of several Cayo operators that offer van service to and from Belize City, at around BZ$80–BZ$100 per person.

Línea Dorada and San Juan Travel run twice-daily vans or minibuses between Belize City and Flores, Guatemala, for BZ$30–BZ$40. Línea Dorada also has service between Chetumal and Flores, via Belize City, for BZ$70. These fares don't include exit fees of BZ$37.50 when leaving Belize by land.

Shuttles in Guatemala are private minivans that hold up to eight passengers. They're faster and more comfortable than public buses. Minivans from the Belize border to Flores or Tikal run US$50 to US$80, depending on your bargaining ability (in Spanish) and the number of passengers. Shuttles between Flores and Tikal charge a flat US$5 per person round-trip and run frequently, starting at 5 AM from Flores.

Reservations are generally required for shuttle service in both Belize and Guatemala. Some may ask for payment up front; before obliging, be sure you're dealing with a reputable company.

Belize Company Aguada Hotel (☎501/804–3609).

Guatemala Companies Línea Dorada (☎502/926–3649). **San Juan Travel** (☎502/7926–0042).

ESSENTIALS

▌ ACCOMMODATIONS

Traditional hotels, usually found in larger towns, can be basic budget places or international-style hotels such as the Radisson Fort George in Belize City.

Jungle lodges are concentrated in the Cayo, Toledo, and Orange Walk districts, but they can be found most anywhere except the cayes. Jungle lodges need not be spartan; most have electricity (though the generator may shut down at 10 PM), a number have swimming pools, and a few have air-conditioning. The typical lodge has a roof of bay-palm thatch and may remind you of a Maya house gone upscale.

Beach hotels range from a basic seaside cabin on Caye Caulker to a small, deluxe resort such as the Inn at Robert's Grove on the Placencia peninsula or Hamanasi near Hopkins. On Ambergris Caye, many resorts are "condotels"—small, low-rise condo complexes with individually owned units that are managed like a hotel.

Lodging choices on remote cayes appeal to the diving and fishing crowd. Amenity levels vary greatly, from cabins with outdoor bathrooms to simple cottages with composting toilets to comfortable villas with air-conditioning.

Regardless of the kind of lodging, you'll almost invariably stay at a small place of 2 to 25 rooms where the owners actively manage the property. Thus, Belize accommodations usually reflect the personalities of their owners, for better or worse.

In the off-season—generally May–November, though dates vary by hotel—most properties discount rates by 20% to 40%. Although hotels have published rates, in the off-season at least you may also be able to negotiate a better rate, especially if you're staying more than one or two nights. Walk-in rates are usually lower than pre-booked rates, and rooms booked direct on the Internet may be lower than those booked through agents.

As most hotels have only a few rooms, a last-minute cancellation can have a big impact on the bottom line. Most properties have a sliding scale for cancellations, with full refunds (minus a small administrative fee) if you cancel 60 or 90 days or more in advance, with reduced refund rates for later cancellations, and often no refunds at all for cancellation 30 to 45 days out. Practices vary greatly, so check on them.

Most hotels allow children under a certain age to stay in their parents' room at no extra charge, but others charge for them as extra adults; find out the cutoff age for discounts.

All prices for Belize are in Belize dollars for a standard double room in high season, based on the European Plan (EP) and excluding service charges and 9% hotel tax.

APARTMENT & HOUSE RENTALS

You can most easily find vacation rentals on Ambergris Caye. Its Web site has a good selection of rental houses and condos. There also are some vacation rental houses in Placencia and Hopkins and on Caye Caulker. Individual chapters in this guide direct you to vacation rental sources.

Information **Ambergris Caye Web Site** (⊕ www.ambergriscaye.com).

HOSTELS

The Belize Tourism Board doesn't go out of its way to encourage hostel stays, but a few hostel-type budget hotels and guest houses are available on Caye Caulker and Ambergris Caye as well as in Belize City, Punta Gorda, and San Ignacio.

Information **Hostelling International—USA** (☎ 301/495–1240 ⊕ www.hiusa.org).

▌ COMMUNICATIONS

INTERNET

Belize is wired. DSL high-speed Internet is available in most populated areas, and cable Internet is offered in Belize City and elsewhere. In more remote areas, there's the option of satellite Internet. An increasing number of hotels offer broadband, either wired or wireless, in rooms, and others have high-speed Internet in an Internet room. There may or may not be an extra charge.

There are Internet cafés in San Pedro, Caye Caulker, Belize City, San Ignacio, Placencia, Hopkins, Corozal Town, Punta Gorda, and other areas. Rates are usually BZ$10–BZ$20 an hour. Most offices of the main phone company, Belize Telecommunications, Ltd., have computers with DSL Internet connections (BZ$10 per half hour). BTL also has Wi-Fi hot spots at the international airport and elsewhere.

If you're traveling with a laptop, be aware that the power supply may be uneven, and most hotels don't have built-in current stabilizers. At remote lodges, power is often from fluctuating generators. Bring a surge protector and your own disks or memory sticks if you want to save your work.

Contacts Cybercafes (⊕ www.cybercafes.com) lists more than 4,000 Internet cafés worldwide.

PHONES

CALLING WITHIN BELIZE

All Belizean numbers are seven digits. The first digit is the district area code (2 for Belize District, 3 Orange Walk, 4 Corozal, 5 Stann Creek, 6 for mobile phones, 7 Toledo, and 8 Cayo). The second indicates the type of service (0 for prepaid services, 1 for mobile, 2 for regular landline). The final five digits are the phone number. Thus, a number such as 22x-xxxx means that it's a regular phone in Belize District.

WORD OF MOUTH

After your trip, be sure to rate the places you visited and share your experiences and travel tips with us and other Fodorites in Travel Ratings and Talk on www.fodors.com.

To dial any number in Belize, local or long distance, you must dial all seven digits. When dialing from outside Belize, dial the international access code, the country code for Belize (501), and all seven digits. When calling from the United States, dial 011/501–xxx–xxxx.

Belize has a good nationwide phone system. There are pay phones on the street in the main towns. All take prepaid phone cards rather than coins. Local calls cost BZ25¢; calls to other districts, BZ$1. Dial 113; for operator assistance, dial 115. You can get phone numbers in Belize on the Web site of Belize Telecommunications Ltd (BTL).

CALLING OUTSIDE BELIZE

To call the United States, dial 001 or 10-10-199 plus the area code and number. You'll pay around BZ$1.50 a minute. Pay phones accept only prepaid BTL phone cards, available in shops at BTL offices in denominations from BZ$5 to BZ$50. "USA Connect" prepaid cards, for sale in some stores in Belize City and elsewhere, come in denominations of BZ$5–BZ$20 and claim discounts of as much as 57% for calls to the United States only. BTL blocks many foreign calling cards and also attempts to block even computer-to-computer calls on Skype and similar services.

The country code is 1 for the United States and Canada, 61 for Australia, 64 for New Zealand, and 44 for the United Kingdom.

Resources Belize Telecommunications Ltd. (☎ 501/227–7960 ⊕ www.btl.net).

MOBILE PHONES

If you have a multiband phone and your service provider uses the GSM 1900 digital system (AT&T and T-Mobile phones do) you can use your phone in Belize. You'll need a new SIM card (your provider may have to unlock your phone for you to use a different SIM card), which will cost about BZ$50, and a prepaid BZ$10 phone card. Both items and rental cell phones (starting at BZ$10 a day or BZ$70 a week) are available at the BTL office at the international airport or in some cell phone stores in Belize City and elsewhere.

Another option is a small BTL competitor, Smart!, which operates a nationwide cell phone system that uses CDMA technology (like Verizon in the U.S.). At one of its offices—in Belize City, Corozal Town, Orange Walk Town, Belmopan City, San Ignacio, San Pedro, or Benque Viejo—you can reprogram your CDMA phone for use in Belize. There's an activation fee of BZ$40, and you'll need to purchase a prepaid plan with per-minute rates for outgoing calls of BZ55¢ to BZ70¢ (incoming calls, text messages, and voice mail are free).

Contacts **BTL International Airport Office** (☎ 225/4162 ⊕ www.btl.net) **Smart!** (☎ 280/1010 ⊕ www.smart-bz.com).

■ CUSTOMS & DUTIES

At the international airport, it rarely takes more than 15 to 30 minutes to clear immigration and customs.

Duty-free allowances for visitors entering Belize include 1 liter of liquor and one carton of cigarettes per person. Customs officials will confiscate beer, including beer from Guatemala or Mexico, as Belize protects its domestic brewing industry.

All electronic and electrical appliances, cameras, jewelry, or other items of value must be declared at the point of entry. You should have no trouble bringing in a laptop.

Firearms of any type are prohibited, as are fresh fruits and vegetables. Although a couple of dozen food items, including meats, rice, beans, sugar, and peanuts, require an import license, grocery items in small amounts for personal use, in their original packages, are usually allowed.

To take home fresh seafood of any kind from Belize, you must first obtain a permit from the Fisheries Department. There's a 20-pound limit.

You may enter Guatemala duty-free with a camera, up to six rolls of film, any clothes and articles needed while traveling, 500 mg of tobacco, 3 liters of alcoholic beverages, 2 bottles of perfume, and 2 kg of candy. Unless you bring in a lot of merchandise, customs officers probably won't even check your luggage, although a laptop may be somewhat scrutinized.

It's illegal to export most Maya artifacts. If you buy any such goods, do so only at a well-established store, and keep the receipt. You may not take fruits or vegetables out of Guatemala.

Information in Belize **Belize Fisheries** (☎ 501/224–4552).

U.S. Information **U.S. Customs and Border Protection** (⊕ www.cbp.gov). **U.S. State Department** (⊕ www.travel.state.gov).

■ EATING OUT

For information on food-related health issues, see ⇨ Health below.

MEALS & MEALTIMES

You can eat well in Belize thanks to a gastronomic gumbo of Mexican, Caribbean, Mayan, Garífuna, English, and American dishes (think fried chicken, pork chops, and T-bone steaks). On the coast and cayes, seafood—especially lobster, conch, snapper, and grouper—is fresh, relatively inexpensive, and delicious.

Try Creole specialties such as cowfoot soup (yes, made with real cows' feet), "boil up" (a stew of fish, potatoes, plan-

LOCAL DO'S & TABOOS

CUSTOMS OF THE COUNTRY

Patience and friendliness go a long way in Belize. Don't criticize local ways of doing things—there's usually a reason that may not be obvious to visitors—and, especially with officials, adopt a respectful attitude. Belizean officials usually are not looking for a bribe, but they do expect courtesy and respect.

GREETINGS

Belizeans are incredibly kind and friendly. Let them know you are, too, and always greet someone with a "Good morning" before asking for directions, for a table in a restaurant, or when entering a store or museum, for example. It will set a positive tone and you'll be received much more warmly for having done so.

SIGHTSEEING

Don't take pictures inside churches. Do not take pictures of indigenous people without first asking their permission. Offering them a small sum as thanks is customary.

OUT ON THE TOWN

With the exception of Pullman buses and shuttles, the seats on many buses often have three people seated abreast. Though tourists are often larger than the average local, you should respect the rule, and make room for others. It's fine to step into the aisle to let someone take a middle or window seat.

DOING BUSINESS

Business dress is casual. Men rarely wear suits and ties, and even the prime minister appears at functions in a white shirt open at the neck.

LANGUAGE

English is Belize's official language. Spanish also is widely spoken especially in northern and western Belize. Several Maya dialects and the Garífuna language are also spoken. Some Mennonite communities speak German. Creole, which uses versions of English words and a West African–influenced grammar and syntax, is spoken by many Belizeans, especially around Belize City.

Around Tikal, wherever tourist traffic is heavy, you'll find a few English speakers; you'll have considerably less luck in places off the beaten path. In general, very little English is spoken in El Petén, and in some small villages in the region, absolutely none. In addition, many Guatemalans will answer "yes" even if they don't understand your question, so as not to appear unkind or unhelpful. To minimize such confusion, try posing questions as "Where is so-and-so?" rather than asking "Is so-and-so this way?"

tains, cassava and other vegetables, and eggs), and the ubiquitous "stew chicken" with rice and beans. Many Creole dishes are seasoned with red or black *recado,* a paste made from annatto seeds and other spices.

In border areas, enjoy Mestizo favorites such as *escabeche* (onion soup), *salbutes* (fried corn tortillas with chicken and a topping of tomatoes, onions, and peppers), or *garnaches* (fried tortillas with refried beans, cabbage, and cheese).

In Dangriga and Punta Gorda or other Garífuna areas, try dishes such as *sere lasus* (fish soup with plantain balls) or cassava dumplings.

Breakfast is usually served 7 to 9, lunch from 11 to 2, and dinner from 6 to 9. Few restaurants are open late. Remember, though, that small restaurants may open or close at the whim of the owner. Off-season, restaurants may close early if it looks as if there are no more guests coming, and some restaurants close completely for a month or two, usually in September and October. Unless otherwise noted, the restaurants listed in this guide are open daily for lunch and dinner.

■TIP→**Other than at hotels, restaurants are often closed on Sunday.**

RESERVATIONS & DRESS

Reservations are rarely needed in Belize or the Tikal area. The exceptions are for dinner at jungle lodges and at small restaurants where the owner or chef needs to know in advance how many people are dining that night. We mention reservations only when they're essential.

A few restaurants in Belize City have a dress code, which basically means that you can't wear shorts at dinner. We mention dress only when men are required to wear a jacket or a jacket and tie, which is nearly unheard of in Belize.

WINES, BEER & SPIRITS

Many restaurants serve beer—almost always Belikin—and terrific, tropical mixed drinks; a growing number offer wine. Belikin is available in regular, stout, and premium versions. Lighthouse, a lighter lager by the same brewery, is also available at many bars and restaurants. American and other imported beers are available in some groceries, but prices are high. Due to restrictive import laws, the beers of neighboring Mexico and Guatemala are rarely available.

Several Belize companies manufacture liquors, primarily rum, but also gin and vodka. Traveller's "One Barrel" Rum, with a slight vanilla flavor, is a favorite, and Duurley's Gold or "Parrot" (so called for the parrot on the label) wins the stamp of approval from some aficionados.

Imported wines are available in supermarkets and better restaurants, at about twice the price of the same wines in the United States. There are wine stores in Belize City and San Pedro. One restaurant, Rendezvous on North Ambergris Caye, makes its own wines from imported grape juice, and cashew wine and other local wines are sometimes available around the country.

The drinking age in Belize is 18, although IDs are rarely checked. The official drinking age in Guatemala is 20.

▮ ELECTRICITY

There's no need to bring a converter or adapter as electrical current is 110 volts, the same as in the United States, and outlets take U.S.-style plugs. In a few remote areas, lodges and hotels may generate their own electricity, and after the generators are turned off at night, power, if there's any, comes only from kerosene lanterns or your flashlight.

∎ EMERGENCIES

In an emergency, call 911 or 90 nationwide. There are police stations in Belize City and in Belmopan City, in the towns of Benque Viejo, Corozal, Dangriga, Orange Walk, Punta Gorda, San Ignacio, and San Pedro, and in Placencia Village and a few other villages. Police try to respond quickly to emergencies, although lack of equipment, supplies, and training may sometimes reduce their effectiveness.

Police are generally polite, professional, and will do what they can to help. In Belize City and in most tourist areas, including Placencia and San Pedro, there are special tourist police whose job is to patrol areas where visitors are likely to go and to render any assistance they can, including providing directions.

Most Belizeans are extremely solicitous of the welfare of visitors to the country. In an emergency, it's likely that bystanders or people in the area will gladly offer to help, usually going out of their way to render any assistance they can.

Your hotel can provide the names of nearby physicians and clinics. You can also go to the emergency room of public hospitals in Belize City, Belmopan City, and major towns. Don't worry about payment—in an emergency, you'll be treated regardless of your ability to pay, though after being treated you may be asked to pay what you can. Private hospitals (there's one in Belize City and one in San Ignacio) may ask for some guarantee of payment. *For more information, see ⇨Health, below.*

American Embassy **Embassy of the United States** (⊠ Floral Park Rd., Belmopan City ☎ 501/822–4011).

∎ HEALTH

Many medicines requiring a doctor's prescription at home don't require one in Belize; drugstores often sell prescription antibiotics, sleeping aids, and painkillers.

However, pharmacies generally have a very small inventory, and only the most commonly prescribed drugs are available. In Belize, private physicians often own an associated pharmacy, so they sell you the medicine they prescribe. Some pharmacies are open 24 hours, and deliver directly to hotel rooms. Most hotel proprietors will direct you to such services.

Consider buying trip insurance with medical-only coverage. Neither Medicare nor some private insurers cover medical expenses anywhere outside of the United States. Medical-only policies typically reimburse you for medical care (excluding that related to pre-existing conditions) and hospitalization abroad, and provide for evacuation. You still have to pay the bills and await reimbursement from the insurer, though.

Another option is to sign up with a medical-evacuation assistance company. A membership in one of these companies gets you doctor referrals, emergency evacuation or repatriation, 24-hour hotlines for medical consultation, and other assistance. International SOS Assistance Emergency and AirMed International provide evacuation services and medical referrals. MedjetAssist offers medical evacuation.

Medical Assistance Companies **AirMed International** (⊕ www.airmed.com). **International SOS Assistance Emergency** (⊕ www.intsos.com). **MedjetAssist** (⊕ www.medjetassist.com).

Medical-Only Insurers **International Medical Group** (⊕ *www.imglobal.com*). **International SOS** (⊕ *www.internationalsos.com*). **Wallach & Company** (⊕ *www.wallach.com*).

CRITTERS

Sand flies (also sometimes referred to as no-see-ums, or as sand fleas, which are a different insect) are common on many beaches, cayes, and in swampy areas. They can infect you with leishmaniasis, a disease that can cause the skin to develop sores that can leave scars. In rare cases, the visceral form of leishmaniasis, if untreated, can be fatal.

Use repellent containing a high concentration of DEET or try Cactus Juice insect repellent to help deter sand flies. Some say lathering on Avon's Skin So Soft or any oily lotion such as baby oil helps, too, as it drowns the little bugs.

The botfly or beefworm is one of the most unpleasant of Central American pests. Botfly eggs are deposited under your skin with the help of a mosquito, where one can grow into larva, a large living worm. To rid yourself of your unwanted pal, cover the larva's airhole in your skin with Vaseline, and after it suffocates you can remove it with a sterile knife. Or see your doctor.

Virtually all honeybees in Belize and Guatemala are Africanized. The sting of these killer bees is no worse than that of regular bees, but the hives are much more aggressive. If attacked by Africanized bees, try to get into a building, vehicle, or under water.

Scorpions are common in Belize and around Tikal. Their stings are painful, but not fatal. There are many poisonous snakes in Belize and lowland Guatemala, including the notorious fer-de-lance and small but deadly coral snakes. However, most visitors never even see a snake, and if bitten, medical centers do stock antivenom.

Crocodiles (called alligators by Belizeans) are present in many lagoons and rivers, but very rarely are they known to attack humans.

Divers and snorkelers may experience "itchy itchy" or pica pica, a skin rash, in spring and early summer, when the tiny larvae of thimble jelly fish may get on the skin. Putting Vaseline or other greasy lotion on the skin before entering the water may help prevent the itch, and applying Benadryl, vinegar, or even Windex to the affected area may help stop the itch.

If you're a light sleeper, you might want to pack earplugs. Monkeys howling through the night and birds chirping at the crack of dawn are only charming on the first night of your nature excursion.

FOOD & DRINK

Belize has a high standard of health and hygiene, so the major health risk is sunburn, not digestive distress. You can drink the water in Belize City, the Cayo, Placencia, on Ambergris Caye, and in most other areas you're likely to visit, though you may prefer the taste of bottled water. In remote villages, however, water may come from shallow wells or cisterns and may not be safe to drink. The water on Caye Caulker often smells of sulfur.

On trips to Tikal or other areas in Guatemala, assume that the water isn't safe to drink. Bottled water—*agua mineral* or *agua pura* in Spanish—is available even at the smallest *tiendas* (stores) and is cheaper than in North America. Eating contaminated fruit or vegetables or drinking contaminated water (even ice) could result in a case of Montezuma's Revenge, or traveler's diarrhea. Also skip uncooked food and unpasteurized milk and milk products.

INFECTIOUS DISEASES

HIV/AIDS is an increasing concern in Central America. This is especially true in Belize, where the incidence on a per capita basis is the highest in the region.

According to the U.S. Centers for Disease Control and Prevention, there's a limited risk of malaria, hepatitis A and B, dengue fever, typhoid fever, and rabies in Central America. In most urban or easily accessible areas you need not worry. However, if you plan to spend a lot of time in the jungles, rain forests, or other remote regions, or if you want to stay for more than six weeks, check with the CDC's International Travelers Hotline.

In areas where malaria and dengue are prevalent, sleep under mosquito nets. If you're a real worrier, pack your own—it's the only way to be sure there are no tears. Although most hotels in Belize have screened or glassed windows, your room probably won't be completely mosquito-proof. Wear clothing that covers your arms and legs, apply repellent containing at least 30% DEET, and spray for flying insects in living and sleeping areas.

There's no vaccine for dengue, but you can take antimalarial pills; chloroquine (the commonly recommended antimalarial for Belize and Guatemala) is sold as Aralen in Central America. It must be started a week before entering an area with malaria risk. Malarone is prescribed as an alternative, and it can be started only two days before arrival in a risk area. Don't overstress about this: in Belize there are fewer than 1,000 reported cases of malaria a year, mostly in the far south, actually fewer cases than are reported in the United States. In Guatemala, El Petén is a risk area.

You should be up to date on shots for tetanus and hepatitis A and B. Children traveling to Central America should have current inoculations against measles, mumps, rubella, hepatitis, and polio.

Health Warnings **National Centers for Disease Control & Prevention** (CDC) ☎877/394–8747 international travelers' health line ⊕wwwn.cdc.gov/travel) **World Health Organization** (WHO) (⊕www.who.int).

▌ HOURS OF OPERATION

Belize has three local banks, Alliance Bank, Atlantic Bank, and Belize Bank, and two international ones, First Caribbean International (formerly Barclays) and Bank of Nova Scotia. Hours vary, but are typically Monday–Thursday 8–2 and Friday 8–4. The Belize Bank branch at the international airport in Belize City is open 8:30–4 daily.

Belize is a very laid-back place that requires a certain amount of flexibility when shopping or sightseeing. Stores tend to open according to the whim of the owner, but generally operate 8–noon and 2–8. Larger stores and supermarkets in Belize City and in towns such as San Ignacio and San Pedro don't close for lunch.

On Friday, some shops (and even the Belize Tourism Association main office in Belize City) close early, and many are only open a half day on Saturday. On Sunday, Belize takes it very easy: few shops are open, and many restaurants outside of hotels are closed. Most Mayan sites in Belize are open 8–4. Guatemala's Tikal ruins are open daily 6–6.

HOLIDAYS

New Year's Day (January 1); Baron Bliss Day (officially March 9, but date may vary); Good Friday; Holy Saturday; Easter Monday; Labour Day (May 2); Sovereign's Day (May 24); National Day (September 10); Independence Day (September 21); Columbus Day (October 12); Garífuna Settlement Day (November 19); Christmas Day; Boxing Day (December 26).

▌ MAIL

When sending mail to Central America, be sure to include the city or town and district, country name, and the words "Central America" in the address. Belizean mail service is very good, except to and from remote villages, and the stamps, mostly of wildlife, are beautiful. An airmail letter from Belize City takes about a week to reach the United States, longer from other areas.

An airmail letter to the United States is BZ60¢, a postcard, BZ30¢; to Europe, BZ75¢ for a letter, BZ40¢ for a postcard. The post office in Belize City is open Monday–Thursday 8–5 and Friday 8–4:30.

If you have to send something fast, use DHL or Federal Express, which are expensive but do the job right. In Belize City, Mail Boxes Etc. can wrap, mail, and deliver your packages.

Express Services **DHL** (⊠38 New Rd., Belize City, Belize 🕾501/223–4350). **FedEx** (⊠1 Map St., Belize City, Belize 🕾501/224–5221). **Mail Boxes Etc.** (⊠166 N. Front St., Belize City, Belize 🕾501/227–6046).

▎ MONEY

There are two ways of looking at the prices in Belize: either it's one of the cheapest countries in the Caribbean, or it's one of the most expensive countries in Central America.

A good hotel room for two will cost you upward of BZ$200; a budget one, as little as BZ$30. A meal in one of the more expensive restaurants will cost BZ$50–BZ$75 for one, but you can eat the classic Creole dish of stew chicken and rice and beans for BZ$8. Prices are highest in Belize City and on Ambergris Caye.

ITEM	AVERAGE COST IN BELIZE
Cup of Coffee	BZ$2
Glass of Wine	BZ$10–BZ$18
Glass of Beer	BZ$5–BZ$10
Sandwich	BZ$8–BZ$14
One-Mile Taxi Ride in Capital City	BZ$5
Museum Admission	BZ$10–BZ$20

Prices throughout this guide are given for adults. Substantially reduced fees are almost always available for children, students, and senior citizens.

ATMS & BANKS

Your own bank will probably charge a fee for using ATMs abroad; the foreign bank you use may also charge a fee. Nevertheless, you'll usually get a better rate of exchange at an ATM than you will at a currency-exchange office or even when changing money in a bank. And extracting funds as you need them is a safer option than carrying around a large amount of cash. That said, do *not* go to Belize expecting to get all your cash from ATMs, as machines frequently are down or out of money.

ATMs in Belize give cash in Belize dollars. Belize Bank's 15 offices around the country take ATM cards issued outside Belize on the CIRRUS, MasterCard, PLUS, and Visa Electron networks. Atlantic Bank's 12 ATMs, including those in Placencia, Caye Caulker, and the international airport (near the American Airlines check-in area) also accept foreign cards. Alliance Bank ATMs currently do not accept ATM cards issued outside Belize, but this could change.

First Caribbean International Bank ATMs (only in Belize City, Belmopan, and Dangriga) accept foreign cards with Visa and MasterCard logos. ScotiaBank has 11 ATMs around the country that accept foreign-issued ATM cards.

CREDIT CARDS

Throughout this guide, the following abbreviations are used: **AE**, American Express; **D**, Discover; **DC**, Diners Club; **MC**, MasterCard; and **V**, Visa.

It's a good idea to inform your credit-card company before you travel, especially if you're going abroad and don't travel internationally very often. Otherwise, the credit-card company might put a hold on your card owing to unusual activity—not a good thing halfway through your trip.

Record all your credit-card numbers—as well as the phone numbers to call if your cards are lost or stolen—in a safe place, so you're prepared should something go wrong. Both MasterCard and Visa have general numbers you can call (collect if you're abroad) if your card is lost, but you're better off calling the number of your issuing bank, since MasterCard and Visa usually just transfer you to your bank; your bank's number is usually printed on your card.

In Belize, MasterCard and Visa are widely accepted, American Express less so, and Discover hardly at all. Note that the American Express representative is **Belize Global Travel Services, Ltd.**

Hotels, restaurants, shops, and tour operators in Belize sometimes levy a surcharge for credit card use, usually 5% but ranging from 2% to 10%. If you use a credit card, ask if there's a surcharge.

Reporting Lost Cards American Express (☎800/992–3404 in the U.S. or 336/393–1111 collect from abroad ⊕www.americanexpress.com). **Belize Global Travel Services Ltd.** (✉41 Albert St., Belize City, Belize ☎501/227–7363 for Amex card-member services or 801/945–9163 collect for traveler's check refunds). **Diners Club** (☎800/234–6377 in the U.S. or 303/799–1504 collect from abroad ⊕www.dinersclub.com). **Discover** (☎800/347–2683 in the U.S. or 801/902–3100 collect from abroad ⊕www.discovercard.com). **MasterCard** (☎800/622–7747 in the U.S. or 636/722–7111 collect from abroad ⊕www.mastercard.com). **Visa** (☎800/847–2911 in the U.S. or 410/581–9994 collect from abroad ⊕www.visa.com).

CURRENCY & EXCHANGE

Because the U.S. dollar is gladly accepted everywhere, there's little need to exchange it. When paying in U.S. dollars, you may get change in Belize or U.S. currency, or in both.

The Belizean dollar (BZ$) is pegged to the U.S. dollar at a rate of BZ$2 per US$1. Note, however, that money changers at Belize's Mexico and Guatemala borders operate on a free-market system and pay a rate depending on the demand for U.S. dollars, sometimes as high as BZ$2.15 to US$1. Banks generally exchange at BZ$1.98 or less.

The best place to exchange Belize dollars for Mexican pesos is in Corozal, where the exchange rate is quite good. At the Guatemala border near Benque Viejo del Carmen, you can exchange Belizean or U.S. dollars for quetzales—money changers will approach you on the Belize side and also on the Guatemala side.

When leaving Belize, you can exchange Belizean currency back to U.S. dollars (up to US$100) at Belize Bank at the international airport. The Belize dollar is difficult if not impossible to exchange outside of Belize.

Most hotel prices are quoted in U.S. dollars, while most restaurant prices are in Belize dollars. In this guide, all Belize prices are quoted in Belize dollars. Because misunderstandings can happen, if it's not clear, always ask which currency is being used.

TRAVELER'S CHECKS

Traveler's checks should be in U.S. dollars, and the American Express brand is preferred. Most hotels and travel operators accept traveler's checks, and some restaurants and gift shops do. However, even in Belize City and popular tourist areas such as San Pedro, clerks at groceries and other shops may be reluctant to accept traveler's checks or will have to get a supervisor's approval to accept it. Some places charge a small fee, around 1% or 2%, if you pay with a traveler's check. Most banks will cash them for a fee of 1% to 2%, but it may require a long wait in line. In all cases, you will need your passport in order to use or cash a traveler's check.

Contacts American Express (☎888/412–6945 in the U.S., 801/945–9450 collect ⊕www.americanexpress.com).

▌PACKING

Pack light. Baggage carts are scarce at Central American airports, and international luggage limits are increasingly tight. Tropic Air and Maya Island Air officially have 70-pound (32-kilogram) weight limits for checked baggage. However, in practice the airlines rarely weigh luggage, and if you're a little over it's usually no problem. Occasionally, if the flight on the small Cessna or other airplane is full and there's a lot of luggage, some bags may be sent on the next flight, usually no more than an hour or two later.

Bring casual, comfortable, hand-washable clothing. T-shirts and shorts are acceptable near the beach and in tourist areas; more modest attire is appropriate in smaller towns and the same long sleeves and pants will protect your skin from the ferocious sun and mosquitoes. Bring a hat to block the sun from your face and neck.

If you're heading into the Cayo, the mountains, or the highlands, especially during the winter months, bring a light sweater, a jacket, and something warm to sleep in, as nights and early mornings can be chilly. Sturdy sneakers or hiking shoes or boots with rubber soles for rocky underwater surfaces are essential. A pair of sandals (preferably ones that can be worn in the water) are good, too.

Be sure to bring insect repellent, sunscreen, sunglasses, and an umbrella. Other handy items include tissues, a plastic water bottle, and a flashlight (for occasional power outages or use in areas without street lights). A mosquito net for those roughing it is essential, but people staying in hotels or lodges—even budget-level ones—don't need one. Snorkelers should consider bringing their own equipment, especially mask and snorkel, if there's room in the suitcase. Sand and high humidity are enemies of your camera equipment. To protect it, consider packing your gear in plastic ziplock bags.

Also bring your own condoms and tampons. You won't find either easily or in familiar brands.

▌PASSPORTS & VISAS

To enter Belize, only a valid passport is necessary for citizens of the United States, Australia, Canada, CARICOM member states, Great Britain, Hong Kong, European Union countries, Mexico, New Zealand, Norway, and Venezuela; no visa is required. Nationals of other countries require a visa and/or clearance by the immigration office. Check the Belize Tourist Board Web site for updates on visas. You can also check with the Belize Immigration and Nationality Department.

If, upon arrival, the customs official asks how long you expect to stay in Belize, give the longest period you might stay—you may legally stay for up to 30 days on the tourist card you'll receive on entry—otherwise, the official may endorse your passport with a shorter period.

You can renew your entry permit at immigration offices for a fee of BZ$50 per month for the first six months; after six months, it costs BZ$100 a month for up to six more months, at which time you must leave the country for 72 hours to start the process over. (Note that renewals aren't guaranteed.)

If you're young and entering Belize by land from Mexico or Guatemala, you may be asked to prove you have enough money to cover your stay. You're supposed to have US$50 a day, though this requirement is rarely enforced.

Citizens of the United States, Canada, and most other Western countries do not need a visa when entering Guatemala from Belize.

Info in Belize **Belize Immigration and Nationality Department** (☎501/822-2423 ⊕www.governmentofbelize.gov.bz). **Belize Tourism Board** (☎800/624-0686 ⊕www.travelbelize.org).

U.S. Passport Information **U.S. Department of State** (☎877/487–2778 ⊕http://travel. state.gov/passport).

GENERAL REQUIREMENTS FOR BELIZE	
Passport	Must be valid for 6 months after date of arrival.
Visa	Not required for Americans, Canadians, and European Union citizens, among others; a tourist card good for up to 30 days is issued upon arrival
Vaccinations	Yellow fever only if coming from an infected area such as parts of Africa
Driving	Valid driver's license from your home country
Departure Tax	By international air: US$36.25, usually included in the cost of your airline ticket; if not, it must be paid in U.S. dollars or by credit card. By land border into Mexico or Guatemala: US$18.75, payable in U.S. or Belize dollars. By water taxi or boat: US$3.75, payable in U.S. or Belize dollars.

▌ RESTROOMS

You won't find many public restrooms in Belize, but hotels and restaurants usually have clean, modern facilities with American-style—indeed American-made—toilets. Hot-water showers in Belize often are the on-demand type, powered by butane gas.

Restrooms in Guatemala use Western-style toilets, although bathroom tissue generally shouldn't be flushed but discarded in a basket beside the toilet.

Find a Loo **The Bathroom Diaries** (⊕www. thebathroomdiaries.com) is flush with unsanitized info on restrooms the world over—each one located, reviewed, and rated.

▌ SAFETY

CRIME

There's considerable crime in Belize City, but it rarely involves visitors. When it does, Belize has a particularly rapid justice system: the offender often gets a trial within hours and, if convicted, can be sent to prison ("the Hattieville Ramada") the same day. Tourist police patrol Fort George and other areas of Belize City where visitors convene. Police are particularly in evidence when cruise ships are in port. If you avoid walking around at night (except in well-lighted parts of the Fort George area), you should have no problems in Belize City.

Outside of Belize City, and possibly the rougher parts of Dangriga and Orange Walk Town, you'll find Belize to be safe and friendly. Petty theft, however, is common all over, so don't leave cameras, cell phones, and other valuables unguarded.

Thefts from hotel rooms, especially in Placencia Village, occur occasionally. Given the hundreds of thousands of visitors to Belize, however, these incidents are isolated, and the vast majority of travelers never experience any crime in Belize.

In 2005 and 2006 there were sporadic incidents at Belize–Guatemala border areas. In two or three cases, masked men believed to be from Guatemala held up tourist vehicles in the Mountain Pine Ridge in western Belize. The alleged ringleaders of the bandit gang have been arrested and remanded to jail, and as of this writing there have been no further incidents. Other incidents in recent years include robberies and carjackings on the Hummingbird Highway and near El Pilar Mayan ruins in El Cayo, and the murder of a young tourist in Stann Creek District in 2005.

The road from the Belize border toward Tikal has long been an area where armed robbers stopped buses and cars, and there also have been incidents at Tikal Park itself. The number of incidents has declined, due to increased patrols by the Guatemalan military, but you should ask locally about crime conditions before traveling to Tikal.

CONCERNS FOR WOMEN

Many women travel alone or in small groups in Belize without any problems. Machismo is not as much a factor in the former British Honduras as it is in Latin countries in the region. Unfortunately in the past, Guatemala has been the site of some disturbing assaults on women. These have occurred on buses, usually late at night in remote areas. Women should avoid making such trips alone. A more common complaint is catcalling, which is typically more of an annoyance than a legitimate threat. Most women, locals and foreigners alike, try to brush it off. That said, however, women make up a large percentage of the travelers in Guatemala, and the vast majority have positive experiences.

SCAMS

Most Belizeans and Guatemalans are extremely honest and trustworthy. It's not uncommon for a vendor to chase you down if you accidentally leave without your change. That said, most organized scams arise with tours and packages, in which you're sold a ticket that turns out to be bogus. Arrange all travel through a legitimate agency, and always get a receipt. If a problem does arise, the Belize Tourist Board or INGUAT may be able to help mediate the conflict.

Advisories & Other Information Transportation Security Administration (TSA) (⊕www.tsa.gov).**U.S. Department of State** (⊕www.travel.state.gov)

▌TAXES

The hotel tax in Belize is 9%, and 10% tax is charged on meals, tours, and other purchases at the hotel. The 10% Goods and Services Tax (GST), is supposed to be included in the cost of meals, goods, and services, but some businesses add the tax on instead.

When departing the country by international air, even on a short hop to Flores, Guatemala, you'll pay US$36.25 departure tax and fees. This must be paid in U.S. dollars. However, many airlines include the departure tax in the airline ticket price. Don't pay twice—check your airline to see if the tax is included.

When leaving Belize by land to either Guatemala or Mexico, there's a border exit fee of BZ$30, plus a conservation fee of BZ$7.50. This may be paid in either U.S. dollars or Belize dollars. For departures by boat to Guatemala or Honduras, you pay only the BZ$7.50 conservation fee.

Most Guatemalan hotels and some tourist restaurants charge an additional 10% to 20% tourist tax. The airport-departure tax is US$30. Guatemalan customs officials at the border will often ask for a 10 quetzal fee when you enter at Melchor de Mencos. There's no such official fee, but to avoid delays, it's probably best to pay.

▌TIME

Belize and Guatemala time is the same as U.S. Central Standard Time. Daylight Savings Time is not observed.

Time Zones Timeanddate.com (⊕www. timeanddate.com/worldclock)

▌TIPPING

Belize restaurants rarely add a service charge, so in better restaurants, tip 10%–15% of the total bill. At inexpensive places, leave small change or tip 10%. Many hotels and resorts add a service charge, usually 10%, to bills, so at these places additional tipping isn't necessary. In general, Belizeans tend not to look for tips, though with increasing tourism this is changing. It's not customary to tip taxi drivers.

In Guatemala, restaurant bills do not typically include gratuities; 10% is customary. Bellhops and maids expect tips only in the expensive hotels. Guards who show you around ruins and locals who help you find hotels or give you little tours should also be tipped. Children will often charge a quetzal to let you take their photo.

TIPPING GUIDELINES FOR BELIZE	
Bartender	BZ$1–BZ$5 per round of drinks, or 10% of the cost of the drinks
Bellhop	BZ$1–BZ$4 per bag, depending on the level of the hotel
Hotel Doorman	BZ$2–BZ$4 if he helps you get a cab
Hotel Maid	BZ$2–BZ$5 a day (either daily or at the end of your stay, in cash); nothing additional if a service charge is added to your bill
Hotel Room-Service Waiter	BZ$2–BZ$4 per delivery, even if a service charge has been added
Porter at Airport	BZ$2 per bag
Taxi Driver	Not usually tipped, unless he or she carries your luggage or performs other extra services
Tour Guide	10% of the cost of the tour
Waiter	10%–15%, with 15% being the norm at high-end restaurants; nothing additional if a service charge is added to the bill
Fishing Guides	BZ$40–BZ$50 a day

▌ VISITOR INFORMATION

ONLINE RESOURCES

For information on Belize, visit the official site of the Belize Tourism Board or the ToucanTrail.com site, which was developed by the tourist board and focuses on budget accommodations. Both sites have excellent general information on Belize.

BelizeForum.com is an active online community of Belize visitors and residents; many regulars are happy to answer questions, though occasionally discussions become heated. Belize.com is a little commercial, but it has a lot of insight. Also, Lan Sluder, the author of this guide and six other books on Belize, has his own site called BelizeFirst.com.

For destination-specific information, check out Ambergriscaye.com for San Pedro; GoCayeCaulker.com, CayeCaulkerBelize.net, and CayeCaulker.org for Caye Caulker; Belizex.com for the Cayo district and elsewhere; Placencia.com and DestinationsBelize.com for Placencia; SouthernBelize.com

INDEX

NOTES

NOTES

NOTES

ABOUT OUR WRITER

Belize First magazine founder Lan Sluder has been banging around Belize since 1991. In addition to authoring *Living Abroad in Belize, San Pedro Cool*, and other books on the country, he's written about it for *Caribbean Travel & Life*, the *Bangkok Post*, and Canada's *Globe & Mail*, among other publications. His favorite parts of Belize? Sarteneja and Punta Gorda. His children, though, prefer San Pedro and El Cayo.